WE STAND ON GUARD

AN ILLUSTRATED HISTORY OF THE CANADIAN ARMY

©1992 Ovale Publications
    A division of
    Tormont Publications Inc.
    338 Saint Antoine St. East
    Montreal, Canada   H2Y 1A3
    Tel. (514) 945-1441
    Fax (514) 945-1443

Graphic Design and Layout: Zapp

Canadian Cataloguing in Publication Data
Marteinson, J. K. (John Kristjan), 1939-
    We stand on guard

Includes index.
ISBN 2-89429-043-8
1. Canada.   Canadian Army—History.   I. Title.

UA600.M315 1992   355.3'1'0971   C92-090127-1

Printed in Canada

WE STAND ON GUARD

AN ILLUSTRATED HISTORY OF THE CANADIAN ARMY

by
John Marteinson

with
Brereton Greenhous
Stephen J. Harris
Norman Hillmer
William Johnston
and
William Rawling

Picture Research by Brian McCormack

CONTENTS

FOREWORD

Some years ago the noted military historian Colonel the Honourable George Stanley characterized Canadians as being 'unmilitary people'. That is no doubt true in the sense that Canadians have never been preoccupied with military force except in those few times when we have been threatened or have felt compelled to fight in defence of our own sovereignty and freedom, or that of others. But it is also true that the military has always played a significant part in the life of the country. Among the first inhabitants of this land, the Indian warriors were formidable fighters in defence of their homelands, and later as stalwart allies of the European colonists in defence of their settlements. French and British soldiers were among those early colonists, and many were instrumental in building the infrastructure of the settlements that enabled expansion and development. And from those early times there has always been a devoted cadre of men and women who have served the nation in uniform, preserving essential military skills and knowledge until those times that they have been needed. Perhaps we need to be reminded that in the course of the history of Canada our citizen soldiers have defended our democratic ideals in overseas wars when that has been necessary. They have been called upon countless times for help in fighting natural disasters, both at home and abroad. In recent years they have served with particular distinction in restoring and maintaining peace in far-flung corners of the globe. And in all those endeavours our soldiers have been at the forefront in creating a sense of national identity, in building national unity.

It is also true that whenever our 'unmilitary people' have entered military service — in war and in peace — they have proven consistently to be among the very best soldiers there are. That began to be evident in South Africa at the turn of the last century. It was demonstrated beyond any doubt during the First World War, when the Canadian Corps came to be known by friend and foe as the elite troops that never failed. That same high standard was displayed in the Second World War. More recently, in our overseas commitments with NATO in Europe and in the many peacekeeping missions undertaken in the last 40 years, Canadian servicemen and servicewomen have consistently set standards of excellence that few others have been able to match. Indeed, we Canadians have a rich and very proud military heritage, of which all Canadians ought to be aware. That heritage was bought at great price on the battlefields of Paardeberg, Ypres, Vimy Ridge, Passchendaele, Dieppe, Ortona, Normandy, the Scheldt and Kap'yong — to name just some of the significant Canadian victories and tragedies. And while we may all fervently hope for a truly peaceful future, members of our Forces — Regular and Reserve — will continue to 'stand on guard', ready as in the past for the time the nation may need to call upon their service once again.

This book depicts an important part of that distinguished military heritage — the development and glorious deeds of the Canadian Army and of the Land Force component of the Canadian Forces. This is a heritage that belongs to all Canadians, and it is presented here in a way that will appeal to more than just military 'buffs' or members of the Forces. It is my hope that it will enable many Canadians to become aware of the part played by our soldiers in the making of our great country.

A.J.G.D. de Chastelain
General
Chief of the Defence Staff

ACKNOWLEDGEMENTS

A book of this kind cannot be produced without the advice, assistance and cooperation of a great many people, and, on behalf of my collaborators, I would like to give grateful acknowledgement to all those who helped in the preparation of this tribute to the Canadian Army.

Very special thanks are owed to Rikki Cameron, former Curator of the War Art Collection at the Canadian War Museum, for her generous access to that superb collection, for her assistance in the selection of the paintings and drawings that add so much to this book, and for permission to reproduce them. Our thanks also go to William Kent who photographed those paintings.

I am deeply grateful to Cathy Murphy, Chief Librarian at the Canadian Forces Command and Staff College, for preparing the Index and for her constant help in the course of research and fact-checking, and to Dace Sefers, the Assistant Librarian at the College. I am also most appreciative of the cooperation extended by Ann Melvin, Librarian of the Royal Canadian Military Institute.

Assistance in the selection and acquisition of illustrations was provided by many institutions and individuals, and I would like to thank them all: Peter Robinson, Diane Martineau and Sharon Uno of the National Archives of Canada; René Chartrand and André Gousse of Parks Canada; Owen Cooke and Isabell Campbell of the Directorate of History Archival Collection; the Canadian Forces Photo Unit; the National Gallery of Canada; Captain Andrew Coxhead of The Royal Canadian Dragoons; Lieutenant-Colonel G. Dorfman of the Governor General's Horse Guards; Lieutenant-Colonel Bissonette of the Fusiliers Mont-Royal Museum; Major Giraud of the Royal 22e Régiment Museum; the Archives of Ontario; Le Château de Ramezay; Barry Agnew and Chris Jackson of the Glenbow Museum; the Museum of the Regiments in Calgary; Dr. Bernard Ransom of the Newfoundland Museum; Margaret Campbell of the Public Archives of Nova Scotia; Captain Toal and the Royal Canadian Regiment Museum; Captain Bennett of the Royal Regiment of Canada; Major Paul Lansey of the Toronto Scottish. I am also grateful to those who loaned photographs from their personal collections: Captain Chris Almey, Captain M.G. Murgoci, Lieutenant-General René Gutknecht, Dr. Jean Pariseau, Colonel G. Scott Morrison, Colonel John Beveridge and Lieutenant-Colonel T.J. Kaulbach. Special thanks are due to Gregory Loughton, Curator of the Royal Canadian Military Institute Museum, who gave many hours of his time to photograph the First and Second World War badges.

The majority of the maps in Chapters 1 to 12 are reproduced from the Official Histories of the Canadian Army or other Department of National Defence publications. They are reproduced with permission of the Minister of Supply and Services Canada, and courtesy of the Director of History, National Defence Headquarters. We are grateful to Fred Gaffen for permission to reproduce the maps in Chapter 15 — United Nations Peacekeeping Operations — from his book *In the Eye of the Storm*, and to William Constable, who drew those maps.

We would like to extend thanks to Pauline Dumont-Bayliss for assistance with research, and to Professor J.L. Granatstein for helpful comment on parts of the manuscript.

I am particularly appreciative of the support and encouragement given me throughout this project by Dr. Norman Hillmer, Dr. Alec Douglas, William and Edith Baxter, and Gwen Calhoun.

This book has been a labour of love for those of us who worked together to bring it into being, and I thank them all. Special mention must be made of the contributions of Brereton Greenhous and Stephen Harris, who wrote much of the text and whose constructive criticism made it a much better book. Brian McCormack, who did the picture research, deserves great credit for his selection of the illustrations. It is our hope that our work will serve to make Canadians more aware of the rich heritage of the Canadian Army, and of the many contributions to the nation by the men and women who over the years have served 'on guard'.

John Marteinson

CHAPTER 1

MILITIA ROOTS
1627-1867

by
Brereton Greenhous

The Canadian Army — styled at first the Canadian Militia and still wrapped in the various uniforms of the Volunteer militias of Nova Scotia, New Brunswick and Canada — was created in 1868: but behind it lay traditions of military service stretching back to the earliest days of European settlement in North America.

THE FRENCH AND INDIAN WARS

The first French settlers of Canada (more generally called Quebec) and Acadia had brought from their homeland the concept of a *levée en masse* which, at the call of the Crown, compelled every fit male between sixteen and sixty to muster for war or defence when required. The first occasion when the *levée* was called out seems to have been in 1627, at Port Royal (now Annapolis Royal in present-day Nova Scotia) when the *habitants* were unable to hold it against seventy would-be English colonists.

French colonists defending their settlement against 'roquois raiders. Drawing by C.W. Jefferys. NAC

Two years later Quebec fell, too, but the French got both colonies back in the Treaty of St. Germain, and in 1636 a Jesuit missionary, Father Le Jeune, was happy to see the meagre Quebec militia "engage in their warlike exercises."

The Diane [reveille] wakens us every morning; we see the sentinels resting on their arms. The guard is always well armed; each squad has its day of sentry duty. In a word our fortress at Kebec is guarded in time of peace as is an important place in the midst of war.

In New France, however, peace was a rare commodity and war was commonplace. Almost from the time of their arrival, the French Colonists in Quebec had to defend themselves against ambush and raids on their settlements by the Iroquois. The young men in the colony grew up learning the necessary soldierly skills for survival. And a great many ex-soldiers were sent from France as settlers: it has been said that of the first 10,000 colonists, fully one third had served in the French Army or Navy. A solid military foundation was thus established in New France. From 1689, as the French began to extend their reach into the interior, they increasingly came into conflict with the British Colonists to the south.

A Canadian Militiaman, ca 1690. CWM

The *habitants* and their English opponents (whom the French, derisively relating to their legitimacy and their Boston base, liked to call *les bastonnais*) combined with their respective Indian allies in an apparently endless succession of wars. The New Englanders, essentially sea-faring men, had their own militia traditions which reached down through the mists of history into the Anglo-Saxon concept of the *fyrd*. Most often this fighting followed a native pattern, — of ambush, skirmish, raid and counter-raid — that relied greatly on those wilderness skills at which the *coureurs des bois* excelled. The latter won many of the battles but few of the wars.

In 1690, for example, war parties of *Québécois* and their Algonquin allies struck south, ruthlessly and bloodily, as far as Salmon Falls in Massachussetts, and Schenectady, New York. From Massachussetts they were chased home by New England militiamen and Indians of the Iroquois confederacy. Those who had gone to Schenectady were pursued by New Yorkers and Mohawks who caught them napping "within a day's march of Montreal" and killed nineteen of them.

In the fighting for Acadia — which, piece by piece, fell permanently into English and New English hands between 1713 and 1755 — Louis Liénard de Beaujeu, a French officer, had "twenty Canadians" with him at Grand Pré in 1747 when he "attacked a house where there were twenty-five English, all armed to the teeth," he boasted to his father (in French, of course):

Rushing to the door, I came suddenly upon a sentry and I killed him. I entered the house and they fired three or four shots at me which only passed through my greatcoat. I fired my pistols at the captain, whom I killed, then gave the sergeant a bayonet thrust in the belly…. He fell, his intestines protruding from his abdomen, and I withdrew my gun which was all broken. I snatched the gun from another Englishman who had caught me by the neck; happily, I was the stronger and I killed him. I clubbed another one to death; and outside I fired on a fleeing Englishman and broke his arm….

It was all to no purpose in the end. Numbers, economics and the Royal Navy's maritime supremacy were ranged against them, especially along the Atlantic coasts. Wherever the English and New English ships could reach, slowly, inexorably, the *habitants* were driven in upon themselves.

In Nova Scotia, captains of militia were appointed at Canso as early as 1720, when the French still held Cape Breton Island. Discharged sailors and soldiers who were the first settlers of Halifax in 1749 were mustered as militia in December of that year as a result of ill-founded rumours of French and Indian preparations to attack the colony. That Nova Scotia militia was formalized in 1753 by a proclamation requiring "all Planters, Inhabitants and their Servants between the ages of Sixteen and Sixty" residing in the Halifax area to appear with a musket and ammunition whenever ordered to do so. Five years later the first elected Assembly

Militia in Halifax, ca 1749.

approved "an Act for establishing and regulating a Militia." There were, however, no uniforms and little organization. The rolls were to be updated at musters held twice a year — a procedure which was often neglected — and each militiaman was obliged to provide himself with a musket "not less than three feet long in barrel."

A soldier of the *Compagnies franches de la marine*, the first truly regular Canadian soldiers. While the men were recruited in France, the officers often were Canadian-born.
Painting by Eugene Lelievre; Parks Canada X 73.427.2

For the defence of Quebec in 1759, some 3,000 militiamen turned out to serve alongside the French regulars — but the pitched battles of the Plains of Abraham and St. Foy, in which stationary, upright men, standing shoulder to shoulder, fired and took the enemy's fire at a range of fifty yards, was not the kind of fighting the *habitants* preferred, or even understood. After the Conquest, British governors made widespread use of the respected *capitaines de milice* in the local administration of their new subjects and took the militia organization under their own wings. In 1767, Sir Guy Carleton reported that "the King's old subjects in this Province [i.e. those of British stock who had arrived after the Conquest] supposing them all willing, might furnish about five hundred men able to carry arms…". However:

The new Subjects could send into the Field about eighteen thousand men, well able to carry arms; of which number, above one-half have already served with as much valor, with more zeal, and more military knowledge for America, than the Regular Troops of France that were joined with them.

The French Canadians, however, were suspicious of the voluntary aspect of militia service which the English normally relied upon. Their tradition was one of mandatory universal service or selection by ballot.

THE AMERICAN REVOLUTION

Eight years later, in the American Revolutionary War, Canadians of both French and English origin fought Americans in the streets of Quebec's Lower Town when rebel general Richard Montgomery and some two thousand men attacked the city. Montgomery was killed, and the attack repulsed (in a New Year's Eve snowstorm) by a garrison which included nearly nine hundred militiamen. More often, however, the militia was called to transport and guard stores.

Learning that Montgomery had invaded Canada, the Nova Scotia legislature passed a highly-unpopular Militia Act authorizing the call out of one-fifth of the militia, to be selected by ballot wherever there should be insufficient volunteers. The plaintive response from Truro was a petition pointing out that:

…should a number of our Industrious Inhabitants, who have large families to support, be called away into any other part of the Province, their Lands would lie uncultivated and neglected, and perhaps their property may be Carried away or Destroyed in their absence to the ruin of Private families, the distress of Society, and hurtful to the Province in general.

The Fight at the Sault-au-Matelot Barricade, 1775 by C.W. Jefferys. French and British fought side by side to repulse American invaders in Quebec's Lower Town on 31 December 1775. NAC

Many militia companies indeed refused to muster and there were several local disturbances. At Liverpool, the leading citizens decided that "ye Fort aught to be dismantled, and that we keep up a Guard of two or three men, to give notice of the approach of any [American] Privateers, in which case we might Treat with them and let them know we would not Molest them if they did not attempt landing, etc."

The fort was not dismantled, and fifty-five British regulars were sent from Halifax to hold it; but in September 1780, the crews of two American privateers did indeed land, and promptly captured the fort. Militia officer Simeon Perkins and his men subsequently managed to take the American commander prisoner as he was wandering about the town alone, which led to an exchange of prisoners and an American withdrawal.

PEACETIME SERVICE

American independence brought thousands of embittered Loyalist refugees to barely-loyal Nova Scotia — soon spawning the ultra-loyalist colony of New Brunswick — and to Quebec, which, in order to accommodate two widely differing cultures, was divided into Upper and Lower Canada in 1791. Two years later, Britain went to war with revolutionary France, raising the spectre of attempts by either American or French democrats — or even both together — to invade British North America while the 'exigencies of the service' compelled the British Army to weaken its North American garrisons in order to strengthen its forces in other theatres.

Few of the colonists in the British North American provinces showed much enthusiasm for militia service, however. In Lower Canada, Militia Acts were passed in 1793 and 1796, but they did nothing of moment to alter the *status quo*. The legislature of New Brunswick created a militia in 1787, but even there, in the heart of Loyalist settlement, the organization laid out in the Act had little credibility. Many New Brunswickers had served the Crown in loyalist American regiments raised during the Revolution, and they had been permitted to retain their muskets when their regiments were disbanded in 1783, but many had since sold them in order to buy farm implements — muskets into scythes and pitchforks instead of swords into ploughshares. While the trained and experienced men were available, the arms needed by a citizen militia simply were not.

Lower Canada
Select Embodied Militia.
Painting by G. Embleton; Parks Canada

Periodic — and increasingly irregular — musters were held in all of the colonies, but they were usually poorly attended except for the odd volunteer companies of enthusiasts who chose to invest their own time and money in some very amateur soldiering. However, in an age before social security there were always poor young men seeking regular employment, and the need for local troops was filled by enlisting them into full-time paid service as 'fencibles'.

Fencibles wore British uniforms and were subject to the same harsh discipline as British regulars, with the singular and important exception that they could not be required to serve outside their own colony or province — although they might volunteer to do so. There would be many fencible regiments raised in the years between the end of the American Revolution and the end of the War of 1812 — among them the Newfoundland Regiment, the Royal Nova Scotia Regiment and the King's New Brunswick Regiment — but they were really more a part of the British Army than forerunners of a Canadian one.

Nelson's victory over the Spanish and French fleets at Trafalgar, in 1805, removed the French threat to North America forever: but there were soon new tensions with the Americans, brought about directly (historians differ over the more remote causes) by British interference with American vessels at sea. In 1812 they spilled over into war.

**Glengarry Light
Infantry Fencible.**
Parks Canada

**Royal Newfoundland
Fencible.**
Painting by Barry Rich; Parks Canada

For geographic, demographic and economic reasons beyond the scope of this book, the threat to Upper Canada loomed largest and, as tensions rose, the British commander-in-chief there, Major-General Sir Isaac Brock, struggled to make the best of a poor situation. In the spring of 1812 as Acting Governor he pushed through a Militia Act which created 'flank' companies of militiamen. (In the British Army, the two flank companies, one on the right and one on the left as they paraded, one of grenadiers and the other of light infantry, were considered the elite of each infantry regiment). They were to consist of "not more than one-third of the strength of such Regiment or Battalion, to be selected and formed from among such Militia-men as shall…volunteer for that Purpose, and who shall not be above the age of fifty nor less than eighteen." If there were not enough volunteers, then men between eighteen and forty-five could be conscripted.

The captains of these flank companies — soon designated as Active Militia — were to call out their men "for the purpose of being trained, exercised and instructed in military discipline" at least six times a month, until they were adequate soldiers, when the frequency of parades might decline to once a month. In time of war, they would be uniformed and 'embodied' into the service of the Crown. The remaining companies, rudely categorized as Sedentary Militia, were to be called out four times a year during peacetime, and at least once a month during war. Each man had to find for himself "a good and sufficient musket, fusil, rifle or gun, with at least six rounds of powder and ball."

As it is not ascertained whether Government will provide clothing for the Militia, …[General Brock] recommends in the event of any portion of them being in the meantime called out into the field, that for their own convenience, as well as for the benefit of the service, each man as far as circumstances and situations allow, provide himself with a short coat of some dark-colored cloth, made to button well around the body, pantaloons suited to the season, with the addition of a round hat. It is also recommended to the officers, on every occasion when in the field, to dress in conformity to the men in order to avoid the bad consequences of a conspicuous dress.

Canadien Voltigeur, 1812.
Parks Canada

Lower Canada Sedentary Militia, 1812.
Parks Canada

THE WAR OF 1812

Nineteenth-century historians, bent on creating a Canadian identity through the construction of a national myth, attributed too much to parts played by militiamen in the War of 1812. They certainly participated in all the campaigns of the war, but rarely played a key role. Mostly, they mounted guards, covered closed flanks, guarded prisoners or moved supplies, and the bulk of the fighting, appropriately enough, was left to British regulars and Canadian fencibles. After all, it was a British war. The Militia did play a significant part in the earliest phases of the war, however.

The British General Service Medal, with CHRYSTLER'S FARM bar, issued to survivors who applied in 1847. Bars for service at Fort Detroit and Chateauguay were also issued.

The fortified post of Michilimackinac, on Mackinac Island at the mouth of Lake Michigan, had been ceded to the Americans by the Treaty of Paris. It controlled the western fur trade from the Upper Mississippi and beyond, and consequently was vital to the economic well-being of both the western Indians and the great North-West Company of Montreal. Given a free hand by Brock to act as he thought fit as soon as he received notification that war had broken out, the officer commanding the tiny garrison of British veterans at nearby St. Joseph's Island, enrolled in the Militia every fur trader and *coureur des bois* he could lay his hands on, and set off with his regulars, thirty-odd militiamen, and some four hundred Indians, to capture the American post.

Its commander was taken by surprise — he did not even know that war had broken out — and quickly capitulated without a fight on 17 July 1812. The effects of Michilimackinac's fall were far greater than warranted by its immediate importance — which was substantial — for it confirmed the adherence of the western Indians to the British cause. That among other things, helped to ensure the fall of Detroit a month later.

Major-General Sir Isaac Brock
by J.W.L. Foster. NAC

Sir Isaac Brock was one of Canada's earliest war heroes. He came to Canada in 1802 in command of the 49th Regiment of Foot, which was stationed in York (Toronto) and in Niagara.

In 1810 he was sent to take charge of the Army in Upper Canada. The next year he was promoted Major-General, and because of the lengthy absence of the lieutenant-governor, Brock became both administrator of the Provincial government and military commander. As the threat of war with Americans loomed, General Brock organized the first all-volunteer militia in the province.

When war broke out, Brock reinforced the Niagara frontier, and proved to be a bold and skillful commander. His victory over the Americans at Detroit served to convince Canadians that the country could be defended. When the Americans attacked across the Niagara River at Queenston, Brock rode from Fort George to take personal command. He found the enemy force already on the heights, and hastily collected nearby troops and led them up the slope on foot. General Brock was killed by a single bullet during this gallant charge, and it was left to his deputy General Sheaffe to destroy the invaders later in the day. But Brock's spirit, and the memory of his successes in the first months of the war, continued to inspire the people of Canada until the war ended in 1814.

The timorous American Major-General William Hull, with some 2,500 men, had crossed the Detroit river into Upper Canada on 11 July. But having once settled on Canadian soil, he stopped in his tracks, and when Brock's Indian allies began to harass his men he retreated back across the river, into the stockaded walls of Fort Detroit. There he wrote to his government that he "had every reason to expect in a very short time a large Body of Savages from the North whose operations will be directed against this Army." His letter, aboard a sloop captured on Lake Erie, was passed to General Brock, who had heard "also of the sentiments which hundreds of his army uttered to their friends. Confidence in the General was gone, and evident despondency prevailed throughout."

Bolstered by that knowledge, Brock crossed the river and besieged Detroit with three hundred British regulars, four hundred militiamen, including "all the detachments of militia from York, Lincoln, Oxford and Norfolk" counties, and six hundred Indians. Fearing the threat of an Indian massacre if the fort should be carried by assault, Hull promptly surrendered up his whole force, including "thirty-five artillery pieces and a great quantity of stores."

QUEENSTON HEIGHTS AND CHATEAUGUAY

Two months later the Americans initiated another invasion, crossing the Niagara river below Queenston Heights on 13 October. Major-General Brock rallied a small contingent of militiamen and British regulars and charged up the face of the Heights. Brock was killed by a sharpshooter's bullet, and the Canadian defenders reeled. That morning, "an express arrived [at Niagara] from Queenston with an order for a reinforcement of 130 men of the Militia" and James Crooks set off along the Queenston road with his company.

On reaching Brown's Point I met on the road the officer in command of the Company of Militia stationed there, who inquired where I was going. On my answering, 'to Queenston' he said I was mad, and that if I proceeded we would all be taken prisoners, as our people there had been completely routed, the General killed and his Aide de Camp mortally wounded, besides that, 400 Yankees were on our flank in the edge of the woods, marching to attack Niagara. I replied that I was ordered to go to Queenston and would do so if I could, ordering my men at the same time to load with ball cartridge.

Tecumseh, the great war leader of the Shawnee. NAC/C-7042

When Crooks and his men arrived on the Heights, where the battle still raged though Brock was indeed dead, they waited for orders, until "General Sheaffe, with the remainder of the 41st Regiment, and Holcroft with a few artillery men and a six pounder, made their appearance." They were then employed to shore up Sheaffe's badly battered line and eventually "an order came for the Regular troops to front and attack, but no orders for the Militia to do so were received." So Crooks started his men forward himself, "in double quick time."

While pressing forward into the thick of the battle I espied an Indian giving the coup de grace to a Militia man whom he mistook for a Yankee, none of us being in uniform, but who turned out to be a man from Toronto named Smith. The poor fellow put his hand to his head and it was all over with him. The battle, though not of long continuance, was a very warm and close one.... The lines were very near each other, and every foot of ground the enemy gave way gave us an advantage.... After about half an hour's close engagement they disappeared in the smoke, throwing down their arms, and ran down the heights to the water's edge in the vain hope of reaching their own side....

The Battle of Queenston Heights, 13 October 1812, by J.D. Kelly.
Despite Brock's death early in the battle, reinforcements of British regulars, local Militia and braves from the Six Nations overwhelmed the invaders. It marked the end of American attempts to seize Upper Canada in 1812. NAC/C-273

The weight of the fighting (and the casualties) had certainly been borne by the British regulars, but Crooks' militiamen, together with the hundred or so others who had been on the scene before he arrived, helped to turn a finely-balanced scale. In his report on the battle, Major-General Sheaffe expressed his "very great satisfaction in assuring Your Excellency that the spirit and good conduct of His Majesty's troops of the militia and of the other provincial corps were eminently conspicuous on this occasion..." As for Crooks, "I have often since reflected how fortunate it was that I did not take that advice [which he was given at Brown's Point] and return to Niagara."

...had I done so, in all probability General Sheaffe would have retired to the head of the Lake with what force — mostly regulars — had been left in Fort George, the later action at Queenston would not have been fought, the 3,000 or 4,000 Americans at Lewiston would have crossed the river when they found the country abandoned, and the loss of Canada to Great Britain would have been sealed.

The colony's fate was still very uncertain in the spring of 1813, with the outnumbered British forces in Upper Canada strained and stretched to the limit in their efforts to stem the American tide. One desperate solution was an Incorporated, or Embodied, Militia for full-time voluntary service with the regulars. Bounties of eighteen dollars — a substantial sum at the time — were given to men who enlisted for the duration of the war, and they were promised grants of land when the war was won.

Subsequently, Embodied militiamen were to be found playing a supporting role on a number of battlefields — Chrystler's Farm, Chippewa, Lundy's Lane and Fort Erie: but no British troops were present to take the credit at Chateauguay on 26 October 1813, when French Canadian militiamen, under the command of Lieutenant-Colonel Charles de Salaberry, repulsed an ill-led American force which outnumbered them by five or six to one.

Lieutenant-Colonel Charles de Salaberry. At the outbreak of war in 1812, de Salaberry, who had served as an officer in the British Army, raised a regiment of Fencibles — the Voltigeurs Canadiens. NAC/C-9226

The Battle of Chateauguay, 26 October 1813, by H. de Holmfeld. Courtesy Chateau de Ramezay, Montreal

At Chateauguay the axe was as important as the musket. First on the scene, de Salaberry razed all the bridges in front of him, thus preventing the advance of the American artillery, then felled trees to construct four successive lines of *abattis*, or breastworks, in the enemy's path. He only needed one of them. When the Americans stumbled forward through the thick bush, "The action lasted about four hours," de Salaberry told his father:

...and it ended in the Enemy being obliged to return to his former position five miles back, leaving many of his dead & Wounded behind and a great number of his scattered men in the woods, also many drums, 150 Firelock[s] & Baggage etc. — The number of my men engaged did not exceed three hundred — The rest were in reserve in the lines I had constructed. Our killed and wounded are only 24 including officers. — There were none but Canadians among us.... Without arrogating to myself too much credit, I am proud to think that this defence on our part has at least prevented the American Army from penetrating to La Prairie — we are here situated about 35 miles from Montreal.

All this was in great contrast to what was happening in the Maritimes, where the Lieutenant-Governor of Nova Scotia, Sir John Sherbrooke, set the tone in a proclamation of 3 July 1812.

Whereas every species of predatory warfare carried on against Defenceless Inhabitants living on the shores of the United States contiguous to this Province and New Brunswick, can answer no good purpose, and will greatly distress Individuals: I have therefore thought it proper ...to abstain from molesting [them] and on no account to molest the Goods, or unarmed Coasting Vessels belonging to [them], so long as they shall abstain on their parts from any acts of Hostility and Molestation towards the inhabitants of this Province and New Brunswick, who are in a similar situation...

Belt plate of the 1st Battalion, Embodied Militia.

The New Englanders were no supporters of the war, either, and 'live and let live' became the unofficial watchword along the Atlantic seaboard as far as the locals were concerned, leaving the regulars and fencibles of both sides to skirmish among themselves.

Even in Upper and Lower Canada, as the war dragged on through 1814 there was less need for the militia to get involved in any serious fighting. The Americans were beset not only by military incompetence but, more importantly, political dissension. And with Wellington's Peninsular campaign concluded and Napoleon incarcerated on Elba, more and more British regulars were crossing the Atlantic.

On Christmas Eve 1814, the Treaty of Ghent brought the American war to a conclusion, and North America was restored to its pre-war political state. Nothing was gained by either side, and nothing was lost. The fencible regiments were disbanded, the Embodied Militia disembodied, and the Militia went home, all no doubt heaving great sighs of relief. Those who applied were awarded land grants in accordance with government promises, and much new territory was settled in this fashion.

As a result of the grants, including those to both regulars and militiamen, 200 new names made their appearance in the county [of Peel, in Upper Canada]. About 36 already resident in Peel, mostly pioneers or sons of pioneers in Toronto township, were given further lands within the county.

ORGANIZATION AND TRAINING

In Upper and Lower Canada, during the next fifteen years, the Militia was organized on a county basis, in regiments or battalions depending upon the population. The former consisted of from eight to ten companies, the latter of from five to eight: until 1823 a company numbered from twenty to fifty men, and after that date from thirty to eighty, but "owing to the wide unpopularity of military service...many were inclined to disregard even the very slight demands on the militiaman's time and energy." Nine years later, in New Brunswick, a young British officer reported that:

The militia were called out for three days' training, and the battalion which assembled at Fredericton 1,000 strong was composed of fine athletic men. Only 200 of them were armed, and about the same number had [uniform] clothing and accoutrements. There was also an African company, who had decked themselves [out] very gaily, and carried the only drum and fife in the field. They appeared quite proud of their occupation, not being exempted, as in the United States, from the performance of military duty. The province could, in case of emergency, furnish 20,000 men (but unfortunately there are neither arms nor clothing for one-tenth of that number) and six troops of yeomanry.

The sad state of the Militia in all of the provinces came about because the colonial governments all believed that the defence of British North America was Britain's responsibility. And they spent as little as was possible on the Militias, except in time of crises.

'Gentlemen with the umbrellas take ground to the right! Gentlemen with the walking sticks take ground to the left!'
An annual Militia parade, 1837. Drawing by C.W. Jefferys. NAC/C-73697

The annual musters of the county battalions in Upper Canada over time became major social events more than periods of serious military training.

In 1837, on the eve of the Canadian Rebellions, British-born Anna Jamieson, wrote somewhat critically of an Upper Canadian muster held at Erindale, outside Toronto.

A few men, well mounted, and dressed as lancers in uniforms which were, however, anything but uniform, flourished backwards on the green sward...; themselves and their horses equally wild, disorderly, spirited, undisciplined: but this was perfection compared to the infantry. Here there was no uniformity attempted of dress, of appearance, of movement; a few had coats, others jackets; a greater number had neither coats nor jackets, but appeared in their shirt sleeves, white or checked, clean or dirty, in edifying variety! Some

wore hats, others caps, others their own shaggy heads of hair. Some had firelocks, some had old swords suspended in their belts or stuck in waistbands; but a greater number shouldered sticks or umbrellas.... Now they ran after each other, elbowed and kicked each other, straddled, stooped and chattered; and if the commanding officer turned his back for a moment, very coolly sat down on the bank to rest.... The parade day ended in a drunken bout and a riot, in which, as I was afterwards informed, the colonel had been knocked down...; but it was all taken so very lightly...that I soon ceased to think about the matter.

THE CANADIAN REBELLIONS

Towards the end of that year the followers of Louis Joseph Papineau in Lower Canada and William Lyon Mackenzie in Upper Canada, each for their own reasons which need not concern us here, raised the banners of rebellion.

The first risings came in Lower Canada. British troops were relatively plentiful in the province, and the rebels were promptly put down in skirmishes at St. Charles and at St. Eustache with only marginal assistance from the English-speaking militia.

In Upper Canada, however, since the lieutenant-governor, Sir Francis Bond Head, had sent all his British regulars to help suppress the *patriotes*, the rebels were met by the Militia alone.

The battle between the *patriotes* and British regulars at St. Eustache, north of Montreal, on 14 December 1837. From a sketch by Lord Charles Beauclerk.
NAC/C-396

It was never much of a rebellion, anyway, going off 'half-cocked' in a reflex response to events in the lower province. Mackenzie had appointed Samuel Lount and Anthony Van Egmond — a Dutch officer who had seen service under Napoleon — as his military commanders and their forces gathered at Montgomery's Tavern, on Yonge Street, about eight miles north of Toronto.

Next day [wrote Mackenzie] we increased in number to 800, of whom very many had no arms, others had rifles, old fowling pieces, Indian guns, pikes, etc. Vast numbers came and went off again, when they found they had neither musquets or bayonets. Had they possessed my feelings in favour of freedom, they would have stood by us even if armed but with pitchforks and broom handles.

That night the rebels — without Mackenzie, who was no soldier despite his fiery language — started down Yonge Street to take the city. Somewhere in the vicinity of Yonge and Dundas, their advance guard met a twenty-strong militia picket and "what ensued was pure comedy: each side discharged their muskets and turned and fled in great precipitation in opposite directions."

Back at City Hall, according to the obsequious *Upper Canada Herald*:

The whole of Wednesday was spent in arming and organizing the men who flocked around the Town-Hall, and who now, strengthened by the loyalists from Niagara, Hamilton, Oakville and Port Credit, brought to this city by steamers and schooners, formed a very effective and zealous force; indeed the city seemed as if by magic transformed into a vast barrack or camp, and militia-men, 'pride in their port, defiance in their eye', assumed the attitude of disciplined soldiers and marched almost with as great steadiness and order.

Arrival of Loyalist Volunteers at the Parliament Buildings, Toronto, 7 December 1837. Drawing by C.W. Jefferys. NAC

Spurred on by the martial music of two bands, they reached Montgomery's at noon on the 8th. The firefight which followed was short and sharp. A dozen rebels were killed, two dozen more wounded, and the remainder fled. A great manhunt followed as loyalists hunted down rebels across the province. Lount and Van Egmond, among others, were captured: the former was hanged and the latter died in prison while awaiting execution. Lesser men were transported to Australia.

Mackenzie got away to the United States, however, where republican sympathizers rallied to his cause and began cross-border raiding, mostly into Upper Canada. Without exception these raids, planned and mounted by eccentric idealists, were badly planned and ill-led. Some petered out of their own volition, some were defeated by combinations of local militia and British regulars, some by Militia alone.

The stiffest fighting came in November 1838 when more than two hundred Americans landed at Prescott, on the St. Lawrence River, and established themselves in a stone windmill and several nearby stone houses which made excellent strong points. A small British force of soldiers and sailors was sent from Kingston, and the Militia of Glengarry, Dundas and Grenville counties were turned out as well. Between them, seventy regulars and seven hundred militiamen pinned the Americans down until more regulars arrived from Montreal, bringing a detachment of artillery with them. The guns finally pounded the enemy into submission after forty-five of them had been killed or wounded. Even then, they had inflicted eighty casualties, including twenty dead, upon the British and Canadians.

LACK OF ENTHUSIASM

These incidents did little to stimulate long-term interest in the Militia, however. Governments were little inclined to spend money on it, and hard-working farmers and artisans were unwilling to serve. In 1846, six years after the two provinces of Upper and Lower Canada had been united, a new Militia Act which simply harmonized the militia laws of the two old provinces made no significant improvements.

In Nova Scotia, the militia tradition had virtually disappeared, as the lieutenant-governor lamely explained.

It was perhaps natural that a disinclination should exist on the part of the Rural population to abandon, in a time of profound peace, their ordinary avocations, for the number of days necessary to keep the different Corps in a high state of discipline; and this feeling having been participated in, or yielded to, by the members of the Local Legislature, the periods for exercise were by degrees diminished or curtailed, until they became so infrequent as to be ineffectual for the purpose for which they were established, and were in 1844 altogether abolished.

In typical Canadian fashion, musters had to be hurriedly re-established in the face of American belligerence over the Oregon boundary in 1846. Two years later, another lieutenant-governor optimistically reported that:

The defence of Nova Scotia is provided for, ordinarily, by the presence of two or three Regiments of British Troops in its Garrisons, and the visits of the [Royal Navy] squadron in summer. An organized militia consisting of 26 Regiments including a force of 44,248 men...is provided for by Statute.... In peace they are rarely called out, except for inspection, but as every man in the province has the right to carry a gun and few grow up within it unpracticed in the use of firearms, they could soon be molded for self-defence, into valuable auxiliaries to any troops which in case of danger, the Imperial Government could spare.

Similar problems beset New Brunswick, where service was down to one ill-attended muster a year by 1850 and the Assembly wanted to abolish even that. The lieutenant-governor, Sir Edmund Head, objected vehemently, although he admitted that "no Militia organized against the wishes of people themselves can be of value." Four years later a new Militia Act suspended most of the duties outlined in earlier Acts and left the Militia totally moribund.

In these lean years, the only military activity in the province was in the New Brunswick Yeomanry Cavalry (later the 8th Canadian Hussars), an unpaid volunteer force that had been formed in 1848.

Quebec Volunteer Cavalry, ca 1840.

By 1855, when there were less than 2,000 British troops left in the Canadas (Upper and Lower Canada had been re-united in 1840) the government of the province, which could not rely upon the Royal Navy for its security as the Maritime provinces could to a great extent, felt compelled to re-vitalize its Militia. A new Act expressly retained the *principle* of universal military service — it lingered on in legal theory until 1950! — but recognized and allowed for its neglect in practice. Instead, there would be an Active, or Volunteer, Militia, not to exceed 5,000 men, who would be equipped and trained for ten days a year — twenty in the case of artillerymen — and be paid for their services. If they were to wear uniforms, however, militiamen had to supply their own.

VOLUNTEER MILITIA

By 1855 the British Empire was rapidly becoming one on which 'the sun never sets', and since many more people could read, many more people knew more about it. These were the days in which the myth of the Militia's part in thwarting the Americans of 1812 took root. And in the towns and cities of prospering Upper Canada there was a growing, if naïve, enthusiasm for all things military. The hectoring tones of American expansionism gave it a focus, and circumstances were ripe for a Militia revival. The new establishment in the Canadas was doubled through an amendment authorizing Volunteer units which would be equipped — but not paid! Still men rushed to join, and Volunteer units soon achieved considerable social status as exclusive male clubs, competing with each other in drill and shooting competitions.

Prince Edward Island militiamen of the Prince of Wales Volunteer Rifles, 1860, the first volunteer company to be raised in the province.
Prince Edward Island Museum

In Nova Scotia, provision for Volunteer units had existed in earlier Militia Acts, but officially nothing had been done to provide them. The impetus now came from Canada, however, and 1859 saw a Volunteer company being formed at Sydney Mines, in Cape Breton. The next year there was a battalion at Halifax (later known as the Halifax Rifles), and a year after that there were 1,500 Volunteers serving in thirty companies throughout the province, all willingly spending considerable sums of their own money to clothe and equip themselves. "The Province has so long existed without cause for alarm," wrote Lord Mulgrave, "that it is very difficult to persuade the people of the necessity of making an extra exertion in time of peace for the purchase of arms which they believe will probably never be required." It was a cry that would ring down the years again and again, from Confederation to the present day.

In 1862, a revised Act expanded the Volunteer concept in New Brunswick, so that there were soon 18,000 of them happily parading in their spare time in towns and cities all across British North America. Officers were business or professional men; other ranks were clerks, farmers or artisans. The early 1860s was a period of great expansion for the Militias in all of the British North American provinces. Many of the most famous of Canadian regiments were formed at this time, among them The Canadian Grenadier Guards, The Queen's Own Rifles, The Royal Rifles of Canada, Les Voltigeurs de Québec, The Royal Regiment of Canada, The Royal Hamilton Light Infantry, The Hastings and Prince Edward Regiment, and The Governor General's Horse Guards (unit names are those in current use). The enthusiasm was certainly there, even if the equipment was not always provided.

Men of the 13th Battalion Volunteer Militia (from Hamilton), assigned to guard the border at Prescott, Ontario against a possible American incursion, May 1865. NAC/PA-89325

FENIAN RAIDS

The price for this curious combination of romance and neglect was paid in 1866, when British North America was subjected to a number of Fenian Raids by Irishmen and Irish sympathizers from south of the border. Many of them were unemployed veterans of the American Civil War. Seeking Irish independence by attacking British colonies, the Fenians struck at New Brunswick's Campobello Island, into Quebec's Missisquoi county at Pigeon Hill, and across the Niagara frontier. The first two of these attacks came to nothing — the Fenians withdrew without fighting — but the third culminated in the disastrous Battle of Ridgeway.

Elora Volunteer Militia Rifle Company, one of the many small units raised against the Fenian threat in 1866. Archives of Ontario 3932 S-2573

The Canadian General Service Medal, with bars FENIAN RAID 1866, FENIAN RAID 1870 and RED RIVER 1870.

Six hundred Fenians crossed the Niagara River from Buffalo during the night of 31 May/1 June 1866 and occupied Fort Erie. They moved north along the river road to bivouac east of Stevensville the next night, hoping all the while that Irish-Canadians would rally to their flag. Meanwhile, four hundred British regulars and Toronto's 10th Volunteer Battalion were sent to Chippewa, in order to block two lines of advance towards the Welland Canal, while two other Volunteer units, Hamilton's 13th Battalion and Toronto's Queen's Own Rifles, were ordered to Port Colborne to protect the entrance to the canal from Lake Erie. Among the Hamilton men, Private George MacKenzie recalled:

About 9 a.m. we formed fours and our march to the front began. In the meantime, an excited crowd had assembled outside of the Drill Shed and the band of the 16th Regiment, British regulars, had come to play us down to the station. As we emerged upon the street the band struck up a lively air and a vast shout arose from the crowd. It was immensely thrilling. I felt as if I had risen to twice my ordinary stature.

They arrived at Port Colborne late that night — having picked up the York and Caledonia rifle companies of the Haldimand county militia and a Volunteer artillery battery from Welland, bearing only small arms, *en route*. The Queen's Own Rifles were already there, the Militia force now numbering some nine hundred, and, as senior officer present, Hamilton businessman Lieutenant-Colonel George Booker of the 13th, found himself in command.

During his whole military career he had never commanded a Brigade of Infantry, even at a review.... Chance threw him into the position of a Brigadier-General on the morning of a battle without any staff, without any mounted orderlies, without artillery or cavalry, and without a mounted officer in the field but himself.

Booker was told that the Fenians numbered no more than seven hundred and many of them were drunk. Actually, there were now no more than four or five hundred of them still under arms, the rest having abandoned themselves to drunken stupors or wandered off about their own uncertain business.

The next morning Booker set off to attack them, de-training his brigade at Ridgeway. They were now "a hungry, thirsty and depressed lot" according to MacKenzie, and "we trudged along the road in silence for about an hour." Suddenly their advance guard came under a scattered fire.

THE CRY OF 'CAVALRY!'

At the Fenians' first shots the column came to a halt and the Queen's Own deployed into line. Firing became heavier, and in fifteen or twenty minutes the Toronto men began to run short of ammunition. Booker called for his own battalion to advance through the Queens' Own, and they promptly did so. Everything seemed to be going nicely.

The Battle of Ridgeway, a more imaginative than accurate American depiction of the engagement. AO/9929

Then came that ridiculous and forever inexplicable alarm which turned our expected victory into defeat — the cry of 'Cavalry!'. It is said to have originated with the shouts of some excited skirmishers; it appears to me that it was conveyed to us by a bugle call. Whatever the origin, we were soon scampering back to our former position on the road, with the idea that we could form a square.

There was no cavalry, but panic spread very quickly. On the Fenian side:

We ran [forward] fast, many of us being barefoot after the march of the night before, but they ran faster, a confused crowd of red and dark green, throwing away their muskets, knapsacks and overcoats. We pursued them for three miles, into the town of Ridgeway, and found the place deserted by all except one man. Their dead and wounded lay along the road and in the fields.

The Fenians were not able to enjoy many of the fruits of victory, however. Already their scouts were bringing news of an impressive force of regulars on its way from Chippewa. Leaving nine dead and six seriously wounded behind them (and sixty-three others who were foolish or drunk enough to be taken prisoner), they retreated to Fort Erie and skirmished with a company of Welland militia there as they re-occupied the old fort. Their commander subsequently claimed that:

Many of my men had not a mouthful to eat since Friday morning; and none of them had eaten anything since the night before, and all, after marching nearly forty miles and fighting two battles — though the last could only, properly, be called a skirmish — they were completely worn out with hunger and fatigue.

On that basis they re-crossed the river, only to be arrested by the American authorities and then quietly released when the British government took no steps to extradite them. The Canadian Volunteers had lost nine dead and thirty-one wounded, and three others later died of exhaustion or sunstroke.

Armies — even militia armies — learn more from defeats than from victories. So do governments. Militia appropriations were increased, new equipment was provided, and summer camps were established so that Volunteers could be given more and better training. Mixed field brigades, each comprised of about five hundred British regulars and a thousand Volunteers (including cavalry and artillery) were introduced; together with brigade staffs, surgical and medical teams, and skeletal supply columns.

They would be needed if war should ever come against the now awesome power of the United States, as many feared it might. Indeed, such fears, together with the desire of the British government to have its North American subjects play a greater part in their own defence, were prime factors in the political process which culminated in Confederation. And the Militia in the provinces which were to form the Dominion of Canada constituted an excellent base from which the *Canadian* Army would grow and be responsible, finally, for the defence of the country.

The 46th Battalion (East Durham) in camp in June 1867, just prior to Confederation. AO/11747-E2-23

CHAPTER 2

CONFEDERATION TO THE BOER WAR

by
Stephen J. Harris

THE NEW NATION

1 July 1867 was a day for exuberant celebration. After sometimes difficult and frustrating negotiations, the Confederation process had borne fruit in the shape of a new country — the Dominion of Canada. In cities, towns, and villages across the land (if perhaps less so in Nova Scotia and New Brunswick) the official proclamation of the British North America Act was heralded in fine style. There were picnics, speeches, and, of course, parades and military displays.

The grandest spectacle was probably in Toronto. There, the Queen's Own Rifles and 10th Royal Grenadiers, already rivals for pride of place in the Ontario capital, joined with Colonel Denison's cavalry and two British regiments, the 13th Hussars and 17th Foot (the Leicestershire Regiment) on Denison's Common. Young boys waved Union flags as the troops went through their drill, and winced with surprise and glee when the Militia gunners fired their salute. The young women in attendance eyed (and were probably eyed by) subalterns resplendent in well-cut tunics and close-fitting overalls. Indeed, the Common was a riot of colour as the regiments marched past in their distinctive dress: scarlet for the Royals and 17th, catching and reflecting all the sunlight; blue, with white facings, for the cavalry; and dark, rifle green for the Queen's Own.

Canadian Militia parade on the Champs de Mars, Montreal. NAC/C-653

All in all it was an imposing display. The infantry were carrying modern Spencer repeating rifles, which had replaced the old muzzle-loading Enfields; the cavalry (who supplied their own horses, often hiring out from local stables) had just been issued with carbines; and the field battery had impressive-looking 6-pounder field guns and 12-pounder howitzers. The crowd probably never noticed that the drill was at times a little sloppy, or that the men's boots — the one item of dress the government did not provide — were not all of the same pattern. If they did happen to see these flaws, it is unlikely that they cared very much. After all, these were Canadian soldiers, heirs to a proud tradition as successors to the militiamen who (it was widely believed) had played the crucial role in driving away the Americans fifty-five years before. The events of the previous June, when some of these same soldiers had left the battlefield at Ridgeway, were best forgotten.

The Queen's Own Rifles parading on Denison's Common. Toronto. QOR Museum

CANADA'S FIRST MILITIA ACT

During the debates leading up to Confederation, much was made of the need for military reform in Britain's North American colonies, and political union was widely touted as one way of providing them with what John A. Macdonald described as a "concerted and uniform system of defence." This did not mean that the Militia of the new Dominion would stand alone — it was assumed that British troops would remain in the country — but that it would be made more efficient. Furthermore, when introducing the Dominion's first Militia Bill in 1868, George Etienne Cartier squarely linked the acquisition of political autonomy with the responsibility to defend it. "The crown of the edifice [of Confederation]," he declared proudly, "is military force."

There was, however, a considerable difference between Cartier's rhetoric and the realities of his bill. No provision was made to create even a small Canadian standing army, considered superfluous so long as the British garrison remained. And rather than adopt the twenty-eight day training year recently introduced for some units in the Maritimes, Cartier settled for the lower Ontario and Quebec standard. Accordingly, up to 40,000 men would be paid to train (at fifty cents a day) between eight and sixteen days a year, either at local headquarters or in summer camps. A major problem identified even before Ridgeway — the appalling lack of knowledge and practical field skills displayed by many Volunteer officers — was neatly side-stepped. Although they were welcome at the schools of military instruction run for the Militia by the British garrison, officers did not have to attend them in order to qualify for their appointments.

The Canadian government, in short, continued the pre-Confederation policy of buying defence on the cheap and, to an even greater extent, promoting style over substance. It had good reason for trying to do so, and for believing that Canadians would not object. For one thing, the country needed canals and railways, and these were expensive enough. For another, the simple fact that Canada was not fully independent and that Britain would decide whether the Empire was at war, was ample justification for asking the British Treasury to shoulder most of the Dominion's military burden and to keep their garrison in North America.

Private of the 10th Royal Regiment of Volunteer Militia, 1867.
Painting by R. Marrion. CWM

The New Brunswick Regiment of Yeomanry Cavalry, now the 8th Canadian Hussars, on parade in Fredericton in 1871. NAC/C-56415

Finally, Cartier did not want to upset the status quo with which so many were comfortable by imposing additional obligations on the Volunteers. Despite Ridgeway, Canadian militiamen were supremely confident in their military prowess. Many would have agreed with Colonel Denison when he remarked that British officers could not be considered "as even equals to the majority of ... Volunteer officers ... in intellect, education, military capacity, talent, or military knowledge." Beyond that, reform aimed at genuine efficiency might very well have threatened the social fabric of the Volunteer force, and chased its natural leaders away. The wealthy and influential men who formed the bulk of the officer corps did not want 'social inferiors' in their messes.

The Adjutant-General of Militia, a British officer, got it right in 1870. He admitted, on the one hand, that:

... if required for the defence of the country, the commander-in-chief has but to give the order, and in a very few hours more than 40,000 men of the active militia would stand forth to form the first line of defence, animated with as much courage and determination to defend their Queen and country as has ever been exhibited by any nation.

Observing, however, that manpower and morale were not good enough against a first-class enemy, he also lamented the Militia's woefully inadequate training, the shortage of rifles and ammunition, the utter lack of supply and service departments, and the absence of competent staff officers. But that kind of substance did not impress as much as a regiment parading on Denison's Common or Fletcher's Field, and as a result Colonel Robertson-Ross's comments fell largely on deaf ears.

The Queen's Own Rifles, forming a square. NAC/PA-51530

THE 1870 FENIAN RAIDS

Despite all its deficiencies, Cartier's Militia organization actually 'saved' Canada twice in 1870. When small bands of Fenians crossed over the border in May and June, the Quebec Volunteers responded quickly, eagerly, and in large numbers. The enemy was turned back after a brief skirmish at Eccles Hill without requiring the assistance of the British battalion watching the New York-Quebec frontier. Canada, it seemed, could handle minor crises quite well on its own. More significantly, even before the 'battle' of Eccles Hill, a combined Anglo-Canadian force of over a thousand men was on its way to Fort Garry. There it would throw out Louis Riel's provisional Métis government, secure Manitoba's entry into Confederation as Canada's fifth province, and send a message to Washington that Rupert's Land — the former Hudson's Bay Company territory ceded to Canada — would not be allowed to fall into American hands.

Men of the 60th (Missisquoi) Battalion skirmishing with a band of Fenians near Eccles Hill, Quebec, 25 May 1870. NAC/C-48837

THE RED RIVER EXPEDITION

In military terms, the Red River expedition was all anticlimax. Never having wanted to fight, Riel bolted from Fort Garry just as the troops arrived, three months after their departure from the east. Still, it was the very model of what Canada's immediate post-Confederation military policy was all about. Although it took some persuasion, the British agreed to organize the force, look after matters of supply, and contribute over a third of its strength, providing small contingents from the Royal Engineers, Army Service Corps, and Royal Artillery, and 350 officers and men from the 60th Rifles. Command was also given to a British officer, Colonel Garnet Wolseley, but he was selected mainly because the Canadian government was particularly happy with his work in training the Militia over the previous two years. The Canadian contribution consisted of two battalions, each about 380-strong, raised specially for the occasion from existing Militia units in Ontario and Quebec. The Militia battalions were given rigorous training at Toronto before they set off by rail and steamer to the Lakehead. As a local newspaper reported, much had been done in great haste:

Louis Riel.
NAC/C-52177

The bare and not over clean floor with the row of badly stuffed straw beds placed along the walls, and the general idea of untidiness, conveyed by the variety of garments, arms, accoutrements and other paraphernalia of a military life, strewed about in what appears to be an inextricable confusion, is not at all calculated to impress one with a desire for military honours, leaving out the question altogether of the monotony of the nearly constant drill to which the men were subjected, and which has already considerably dampened the ardour of several who volunteered without the remotest idea of what they would have to go through.

Although they did not have to fight, the Red River contingents were nevertheless severely tested. Compelled to take an all-Canadian route to the west, the troops had to cross the rugged Rainy Lake to Lake-of-the-Woods country by foot and shallow-draft boat. During this arduous trek they endured forty-five days of rain. Subsisting on salt pork, hard tack and

Expedition to the Red River by Francis A. Hopkins.
After reaching Thunder Bay, forty-seven arduous overland 'portages' were necessary to bring the men and
the supplies of the Red River Expedition to Fort Garry. This painting shows one such portage at Kabeka Falls.
NAC/C-2275

unsweetened tea, they had a terrible time, yet discipline appears to have broken down only once. In the second week of August, men from the 1st (Ontario) Rifles, trying desperately to reduce the load they were carrying, dumped the brine from a number of their pork barrels, ensuring that the meat would soon become inedible.

Once in Red River, after settling in and building temporary hutments, the Canadian battalions spent the winter showing the flag. When the initial body of volunteers took their discharge in the spring, replacements newly enlisted for the task were sent west to keep the two units of the Manitoba Force up to strength. Their establishments were gradually reduced as the threat of Riel's return (and Fenian raids) diminished, but the Ontario and Quebec Rifles remained in garrison in the west until 1877, when they were finally disbanded. The 60th Rifles, however, had left Fort Garry within days of their arrival, and were back in Montreal by early fall 1870. Just over a year later, in November 1871, they marched out of the gates of the Citadel at Quebec, boarded ship, and set sail for Halifax. There they manned the Imperial fortress as part of the only British garrison left in North America until Royal Marine Artillery gunners arrived at Esquimalt in the 1890s.

BIRTH OF A CANADIAN REGULAR ARMY

The withdrawal of the British regulars, decided upon before Wolseley had even left for the Red River, was a watershed in Canadian military history. Although Cartier had always linked political autonomy with the responsibility to defend it, he had so far been able to avoid much of the latter because of the British presence. Things were different now.

The British knew precisely what Canada should do: it was time for the Dominion to establish a small permanent force. To make this as easy as possible, London went so far as to offer to transfer the Royal Canadian Rifles, a regular battalion raised in Canada primarily from British veterans, to the Canadian establishment en masse. The Imperial authorities also pressed Ottawa to appoint a competent British officer (preferably their general at Halifax) to command the Militia. Both suggestions were politely rejected. Mindful of local feeling, the Canadian government was not yet ready to pay for a standing, regular army. And the right man, flexible enough to appease Dominion concerns and competent enough to satisfy the War Office, could not be found to take up the appointment of General Officer Commanding.

A detachment of Royal Engineers constructing a gun pit at Fort Clarence, part of the Imperial fortress at Halifax.
Public Archives of Nova Scotia/N-6014

'B' Battery, School of Artillery exercising on the St. Charles River, near Quebec in 1873. NAC/C-59098

34

Indeed, progress was made on only one front. Despite its hope that relations with the United States would improve to the point where fortifications were unnecessary, the Canadian government also knew that the former Imperial facilities at Kingston and Quebec could not be left unattended. Accordingly, on 20 October 1871 the formation of two batteries of garrison artillery was authorized to take over the fortresses, and to act as schools of instruction for the Militia. Each would be

Lieutenant-Colonel (later Major-General) Thomas Bland Strange, commandant of the Artillery School at Quebec. NAC

commanded by a British lieutenant-colonel, but the other eight officers were to be Canadian. The men, who signed on for periods varying between three and twelve months, were drawn from the Militia and the now disbanded Royal Canadian Rifles.

The two batteries flourished, both as gunnery schools and as the professional home of the Canadian artillery, and by 1874 their status had been significantly modified. Permanent commissions became available, offering a handful of Canadians the opportunity to pursue a military career, while the men signed on for a minimum of three years. Although the two fortresses never fired their guns in anger, the gunners were soon involved in maintaining peace and order and providing "Aid to the Civil Power." In August 1872, 'B' Battery at Quebec was ordered to intervene in a dispute between the local French and Irish populations, but its real test came in March 1873, when a mob threatened the Quebec legislature. Lieutenant-Colonel Thomas Bland Strange quickly sized up the situation, and directed Captain Short:

... to clear the street with the mounted men. He did so with his usual impetuosity. A passing street-car divided him from his detachment, and he was furiously assailed, receiving a deep cut in his forehead. The horse of a trooper slipping on the car-rails put another man at the mercy of the mob. The infantry portion of the Battery was advanced to the rescue. It was my habit when ordered on civil disturbance to fix bayonets before leaving barracks, with the ... object of keeping the fire low from the weight on the muzzle, producing the salutary effect on the mob which steel always does.... Bayonets being fixed, the advance of the men by sections with trailed arms had all the effect of a charge.... The men, who had long been exposed to the taunts and assaults of the mob, broke into a double and the rioters fled before them, seeking refuge down lanes and in doorways, whence they emerged as soon as the 'retire' was sounded. [I] was afraid of getting [my] men out of hand and had hitherto refrained from opening fire for fear of injuring foolish spectators who were not actually assaulting the troops. Now was [my] opportunity. [I] had long noticed the ringleader, a man in a blue blouse.... This Communist was followed by only a few of the most determined. I halted the rear section of eight men and opened fire. Half-a-dozen men and a cab horse dropped. Also the 'blue blouse'. Most of the others rose and limped off, but the 'blue blouse' remained on the pavement, and a little red stream trickled into the gutter, a suitable receptacle.

By today's standards this was rough treatment — and an excessive use of force — but things were different in Victorian times. The Army, both regular and reserve, was expected to maintain law and order, and the death of the odd rioter was not considered a matter of great consequence. Indeed, Strange boasted that "from that day to this [1896] no shot has been fired in the streets of Quebec." Assisting civilian authorities did not come without its risks, however. Strange's battery was also something of an emergency fire brigade, and not long after he had helped disperse the Quebec mob, Captain Short and one of his sergeants died helping to extinguish a blaze "in the stove-heated wooden houses of the suburb of St. Roch's."

The Craig Street Drill Shed in Montreal, 1872.
Chateau de Ramezay

A rural Militia battalion at annual camp. NAC/C-8338

The Militia also flourished in the years immediately following Confederation and the British withdrawal. Forty-four new regiments were formed between 1868 and 1875 (bringing the total to just over seventy), reflecting the threat of renewed Fenian activity, the new country's patriotic zeal, and — in their names — the very close bonds between Militia units and their community.

REGIMENTS OF CAVALRY AND INFANTRY FORMED 1868-1875

CAVALRY

	CURRENT NAME
1872	
1st Hussars, London, Ont	1st Hussars
2nd Cavalry (Dragoons), St Catharines, Ont	
Ottawa Troop of Cavalry, Ottawa, Ont	
1874	
King's Canadian Hussars, Kentville, NS	
1875	
3rd Cavalry (Dragoons), Peterborough, Ont	
4th Cavalry (Hussars), Prescott, Ont	

INFANTRY

1868	
59th Stormont and Glengarry Battalion, Cornwall, Ont	Stormont, Dundas, and Glengarry Highlanders
1869	
23rd Beauce Battalion, Ste Marie, Que	Le Régiment de la Chaudière
60th Mississquoi Infantry, Dunham, Que	
61st Montmagny and L'Islet Battalion, Montmagny, Que	Les Fusiliers du St-Laurent
62nd St John Fusiliers, St John, NB	
64th Voltigeurs de Beauharnois, Beauharnois, Que	4 Royal 22e Régiment
65th Mount Royal Rifles, Montreal, Que	Fusiliers Mont-Royal
66th Halifax Battalion, Halifax, NS	Princess Louise Fusiliers
67th Carleton Light Infantry, Woodstock, NB	1 Royal New Brunswick Regiment
68th King's County Battalion, Kentville, NS	
69th 1st Annapolis Battalion, Paradise, NS	West Nova Scotia Regiment
70th Champlain Battalion, Ste Genevieve de Batiscan, Que	
71st York Battalion, Fredericton, NB	1 Royal New Brunswick Regiment
81st Portneuf Battalion, Pointe aux Trembles, Que	
Kamouraska Provisional Battalion, Kamouraska, Que	
Dorchester Provisional Battalion, St Anselme, Que	Le Régiment de la Chaudière
Quebec Provisional Battalion, Ancienne Lorette, Que	Les Voltigeurs de Québec
Rimouski Provisional Battalion, Rimouski, Que	Les Fusiliers du St-Laurent
Timiscouata Provisional Battalion, Rivière du Loup, Que	Les Fusiliers du St-Laurent
1870	
72nd 2nd Annapolis Battalion, Wilmot, NS	West Nova Scotia Regiment
73rd Northumberland (NB) Regiment, Chatham, NB	2 Royal New Brunswick Regiment
74th Battalion (Rangers), Sussex, NB	1 Royal New Brunswick Regiment
75th Lunenburg Battalion, Lunenburg, NS	West Nova Scotia Regiment
Charlevoix Battalion of Infantry, Baie St Paul, Que	
1871	
78th Colchester and Hants Highlanders, Truro, NS	1 Nova Scotia Highlanders
93rd Cumberland Battalion, Amherst, NS	1 Nova Scotia Highlanders
94th Victoria Argyle Highlanders, Baddeck, NS	2 Nova Scotia Highlanders
Joliette Provisional Battalion, Joliette, Que	
Three Rivers Provisional Battalion, Three Rivers, Que	12e Régiment Blindé
St Hyacinthe Provisional Battalion, St Hyacinthe, Que	6 Royal 22e Régiment
1872	
Governor General's Foot Guards, Ottawa, Ont	Governor General's Foot Guards
62nd St John Battalion, St John, NB	1 Royal New Brunswick Regiment
76th Voltigeurs de Chateauguay, St Martine, Que	4 Royal 22e Régiment
77th Wentworth Battalion, Dundas, Ont	Royal Hamilton Light Infantry
79th Shefford Highlanders, Waterloo, Que	
1875	
80th Nicolet Battalion, Nicolet, Que	
Charlottetown Provisional Battalion, Charlottetown, PEI	Prince Edward Island Regiment
King's County Provisional Battalion, Georgetown, PEI	
Prince County Provisional Battalion, Summerside, PEI	
Queen's County Provisional Battalion, Charlottetown, PEI	Prince Edward Island Regiment

The Victoria Volunteer Rifles in camp at Beacon Hill, July 1880. British Columbia Provincial Archives 8673

Just as important, the government was also generous in its support to the citizen soldiers. Many units were able to train, with pay, for the full sixteen days provided for in the Militia Act, and those which attended the divisional camps established in 1872 found themselves part of formations 6000-men strong. These numbers gave a credibility to their efforts which financial restraint might have belied. At Niagara, in 1871, for example, the district staff noted that

... four Battalions were in rifle [green], the rest in scarlet, uniform clothing; the arms, generally speaking, were in good order, and the accoutrements, although of various kinds and some of obsolete pattern, were yet serviceable; many articles, however, were wanting, which had been originally issued by the Department but subsequently lost.

The most glaring and serious defect in the equipment of the infantry was the want of a suitable description of boot for marching. The majority of men wearing high heeled, narrow soled boots ... which are quite unsuitable for marching in. Many of the men too appeared in white summer boots, such as are used by women. In this respect the infantry corps were lamentably deficient.

Another commentator, a Militia colonel desperate to see military reform, was less positive:

Under present conditions, the camps are a mere sham. The men are blarneyed or bribed for the occasion only. Half-grown boys or decrepit old men, if they can only hold a rifle, are accepted with thanks, and when the camp is over, the whole thing vanishes like snow off a ditch.... There was not an ambulance at the camp I was at, nor a stretcher, not even transport for small arms ammunition. There was no medicine provided for the sick.... Not a Regiment in the Division would average half-a-dozen non-commissioned officers thoroughly conversant with their duties, nor three buglers who could perfectly sound a call. There wasn't an Armourer Sergeant in either of the Brigades, while there should be one in every Battalion.

There was a good deal of truth in what Colonel Davis, of the Haldimand Rifles, had to say. Although there was great eagerness to form new cavalry and infantry regiments, and batteries of field and garrison artillery, there was a complete lack of service support units. Not only were these un-glamorous, but the Militia Department itself saw no need for them. Thus, when men went to camp, with only a greatcoat and two blankets to keep them warm, and were issued the standard fare of beef and bread, they depended almost entirely on the concern their own commanding officers had for their well-being to supplement these staples by purchasing tea, sugar, salt, and vegetables.

A sham battle at a Militia Camp in New Brunswick, ca 1872. New Brunswick Provincial Archives

Despite the obvious discomforts, especially those caused by unsuitable footwear, the regiments nevertheless did their best while they were at camp. They spent most of their time on drill, route marches, target practice, and mounting guards. In 1872 the 6000 men at Niagara participated in their first large-scale sham battle. About two thousand men were stationed along the Niagara River in front of Fort George to repel an attack by the rest from Queenston Heights, site of Brock's victory sixty years before.

In New Brunswick, the tactical exercise that year involved the defence of Woodstock from an attack along the Medocnuakeag [Meduxnekeag] River:

On reaching the open, hilly, undulating country, the advanced guard became a line of skirmishers, and it was reinforced by the reserve deployed, all taking advantage of the nature of the ground to obtain cover. The detachment of cavalry sent forward ... brought intelligence of the whereabouts of the enemy, and fire was opened by our skirmishers, hitherto concealed, and a rapid advance was made by the reserve to gain the crest of a neighbouring hill commanding the position of the enemy. This effected, such an accurate fire was opened by the brigade that the enemy was compelled to retreat, but not without an attempt to turn our flank. However, a corresponding change of front on our part secured our holding the strong position and completed the rout of the enemy. It was subsequently ascertained that we had confronted but a portion of the enemy's force.... The cavalry, therefore, was at once sent in that direction for intelligence, and the brigade followed as quickly as possible.

In the ensuing fight, over "rough and broken ground ... interspersed with greenwood trees," there was some difficulty "in keeping the necessary communication by connecting links between skirmishers, supports, and reserve." But once the skirmishers opened fire, "all speedily regained their places, and the advance was steady."

This was all very well, but the Militia bloom began to fade as early as 1873. The novelty of military service was wearing off for those who had joined in 1868. And it began to matter that shabby uniforms were being worn because they were replaced only every five years — and that carelessly stored rifles were fast deteriorating. The sense of urgency which had propelled men to join only four or five years before had also diminished. At mid-decade the Fenians were by and large a spent force, while the Treaty of Washington signed in 1871 had settled many of the issues complicating Anglo-American relations. War with the United States was increasingly unlikely, and men returning home from parades or camp were often ridiculed by neighbours, being told, as one officer complained, that "they are fools for their pains, in going to drill." It was "better to remain at home, and work on their farms, as others do, and it will pay them better."

But it was the deepening economic crisis that did the most damage. Forced to reduce spending, the Liberal government elected in 1873 decided that the defence budget, and particularly the Militia training vote, could be cut back without increasing the risks to national security. For two years Militia units were offered a choice between eight days training at camp, or sixteen at local headquarters. In 1876, however, when the Militia budget stood at only one-third of what it had been in 1871, summer camps were abolished altogether. City units were authorized to spend eight days a year at their local drill sheds, but rural units could expect to train only every two years.

**Lieutenant-Colonel
George Taylor Denison**

Colonel George Denison was one of the most capable and colourful of the Militia officers of his day. A highly successful Toronto lawyer who in his later years was the city's senior police magistrate, Denison was also an active citizen-soldier for 59 years. He joined a family-raised and supported volunteer cavalry unit, Denison's Horse, when he was 16 years old, and was in command of the unit, then called the Governor General's Body Guard, during the 1866 Fenian Raids. Later he served as commanding officer of the Body Guard for 22 years between 1876 and 1898, during which time he led the regiment in the North West Rebellion in 1885. Denison was an avid student of military history and tactics. He wrote a number of books, among them *Modern Cavalry* (1868), *Soldiering in Canada* (1870), and *A History of Cavalry* (1877). This last book won first prize in a competition sponsored by the Russian Czar in 1877, and for many years was recognized as being the best cavalry history that had been written. It was translated into both German and Russian. In his writing he argued the tactical advantages of rapidly deployed mounted infantry in modern war, and undoubtedly had an influence on Canadian emphasis on mounted rifles instead of 'pure' cavalry in both the South African and the First World Wars.

The rural Militia, trying to live off its own resources, was soon in a state of decay. Despite attempts by many units to conduct informal training in off-years, at no expense to the public purse, turn-over was extremely high, and very few men attended more than one authorized training season. Those who did received even shabbier clothing, and rifles so poorly maintained that they were scarcely better than muskets. In the 73rd Northumberland (NB) Battalion, for example, it was quite acceptable for soldiers to wear civilian clothing once their issue uniform had been reduced to rags. City units were somewhat better off. In many regiments men could be persuaded to turn out voluntarily during the fall and winter, in part because of the social activities, sporting events, and other entertainments that became an increasingly important part of regimental life.

Wealthier units were also able to sponsor their own training. The officers of New Brunswick's 8th Regiment of Cavalry paid for annual camps throughout this period at Fox Hill, the estate of the unit's commanding officer, while Hamilton's 13th Battalion took up shooting with a vengeance, and was soon known for its marksmanship. The Queen's Own Rifles held field days in and around Toronto every year, and offered courses in signalling, military sketching, and first aid. Still, Montreal's 5th Fusiliers were probably the most innovative. Having decided, one year, to hold a regimental camp on St Helen's Island, they trained only in the evenings so that the men could work during the day.

Units of the New Brunswick Militia on parade at a Military Review in Fredericton, 1 July 1881, inspected by the Governor-General, The Marquis of Lorne. 8CH Museum

From time to time there was the added excitement of — and extra pay from — operations in aid of the civil power. The 73rd Northumberland Battalion and Newcastle Field Battery were called out in 1875 to guard rioters confined in the local jail, for example. Toronto and Montreal units were regularly asked to protect Orangemen and Catholics from each other or to put down illegal strikes. But relying on the Militia to maintain law and order had its drawbacks. When workers from the Grand Trunk Railway in Belleville, Ontario, went on strike, the local infantry battalion, the 15th Argyle Light Infantry, could not be called out because so many of its members either worked for the railway, and were already participants in the strike, or sympathized with it. Eventually a Toronto unit, the Queen's Own, was sent for. But they too had problems — of a different sort. The town of Belleville refused to pay the battalion for its work, and it took a lengthy court case before the men received their $3.00.

For the wealthiest units, however, the 1870s meant social activities, sporting events, and excursions. By the end of the decade the Foot Guards, the Victoria Rifles, the Prince of Wales Regiment, and the Queen's Own regularly exchanged visits on public holidays, and the military tournaments, sham battles, and concerts such events entailed became the highlights of the regimental year. Bands in particular took on a new importance, as they became the show-pieces of the Militia's public image. And, of course, wherever social status was important — which was almost everywhere in Victorian Canada — a Militia commission was a great badge of place. "An officer is useful to his regiment because he has the means to spend and the will to spend it," a Montreal newspaper explained; "the regiment is useful to him because the paths toward social distinction are smoothed for the Militia officer."

The first class at Royal Military College of Canada, Kingston, 1876. NAC/C-81401

41

Still, from a military perspective the decade of the 1870s was not entirely wasted. In April 1874 Major-General Sir Edward Selby Smyth was selected as the first General Officer Commanding (GOC) the Militia. A month later the government appropriated $50,000 to begin work on what, in 1876, would become the Royal Military College of Canada in Kingston, Ontario. To Prime Minister Alexander Mackenzie, these represented the first steps in a slow process that would lay "the foundation of a future national military system." The appointment of a GOC gave Canada a command structure of its own, completely independent from the British headquarters in Halifax. The Royal Military College, meanwhile, would turn out graduates who, after a suitable period of Militia service, would eventually fill senior staff and command appointments and bring about further reforms compatible with Canadian sensibilities and economy.

Following a brief but intense period of tension in 1878, when war with Russia seemed imminent, Mackenzie finally admitted privately that Canada should have its own small regular army, but concerned about the 'impatience' of Canadians regarding standing armies, he thought it best to wait a year or two until the economy had improved (and the Militia training budget could be increased) before embarking upon the project. He never got the chance. The Liberals lost the general election of 1878, and John A. Macdonald's Conservatives, no friends of a permanent force, returned to power. If they thought at all seriously about military affairs in their first few years back in office, it was only as a way of rewarding friends and associates with political appointments, and gaining some favour by reinstituting summer camps.

GROWTH OF THE PERMANENT FORCE

The government's announcement in the summer of 1883 that it would create a 750-man Permanent Force seemed, therefore, to be completely out of character. There was no new threat to Canadian security requiring these troops, and the money that would have to be spent on them was sure to anger the Militia, whose training budget had increased only marginally since the mid-1870s. Once it was seen, however, that all twenty-one officers appointed to the Infantry School Corps (forerunner of The Royal Canadian Regiment) and the Cavalry School Corps (Royal Canadian Dragoons) were loyal Conservatives, nine of whom had no previous military experience whatsoever, the government's purpose was clearer. So long as the Militia could be appeased with ringing declarations that the job of the regulars was to teach, not fight, and so long as Canada was essentially safe from attack, what harm was there in making even better use of the military establishment for patronage purposes? And if Imperial authorities were happy now that Canada had its regulars, so much the better.

'A' Company, School of Infantry on parade at Hermitage Creek, New Brunswick in 1884.
RCR Museum

'A' Battery, School of Artillery training on snow-shoes near Kingston, in the winter of 1885. NAC/PA-173003

Stamps issued to commemorate the centenary of the formation of Militia and Permanent Force regiments in 1883.

THE NORTH WEST REBELLION

The easy peace of Canadian life was shattered early in 1885. Louis Riel had returned to the North West, and was again leading the Métis and Indians as they made known their grievances to a federal government generally unsympathetic with their complaints about lost lands and lifestyles. When the North West Mounted Police tried to maintain order, they were beaten back at Duck Lake on 26 March. Six days later, nine people were killed at Frog Lake. On 15 April the Hudson's Bay Company post at Fort Pitt, which had a twenty-five man garrison of Mounted Police, was abandoned. To the politicians in Ottawa, the early victory at Duck Lake seemed likely to bring all the Indians of the region to Riel's side, and it was decided that action had to be taken quickly, and in strength.

The GOC, Major-General Sir Frederick Middleton, agreed. Sent west at the first hint of trouble, this veteran of New Zealand's Maori wars and the Indian Mutiny of 1857 saw at once that the crucial thing was to beat Riel and his one thousand fighting men immediately — before they could be reinforced by other Indians drawn into the struggle. He therefore asked the government to mobilize at least 2000 men, including the Permanent Force and the best city units.

Major-General Sir Frederick Middleton, General Officer Commanding the Canadian Militia, 1884-1890, who commanded the campaign against the rebels in the Northwest Territories in 1885.
NAC/C-86535

In fact, the Conservatives had killed just a few birds with many stones. Militia officers were not at all happy at the prospect of being taught by 'influential incompetents' whom they did not respect, while the regulars themselves were frustrated when their own training was circumscribed so as not to offend the Militia. British observers were not fooled. Yet as absurd as this situation appears from today's vantage point, these were only minor irritants in 1883 and 1884. The west was being opened, the transcontinental railway had to be completed; and there was money to be made. Despite their grousing, city units could still parade and conduct sham battles that made them look good. And for anyone who was interested in real soldiering, the British Army was the place to be.

All the faults of Canada's truncated military system were once again readily apparent. There was no trouble finding men — there never had been — and they were being kitted out at their headquarters as early as 28 March, the day after the mobilization telegrams were dispatched. But since there were no military supply and medical branches, these services had to be contracted out; and given the practices of the day, the demands of patronage had to be met, even in time of crisis. Ammunition, at least, would be in plentiful supply, thanks to the government's decision to set up its own cartridge factory at Quebec. But years of neglect had taken their toll on the Militia's Snider rifles; so many were found to be useless that an emergency order was placed in England for 10,000 Martini-Henry rifles.

The 10th Battalion (Royal Grenadiers) at rest in 'Camp Desolation' after a 42-mile march through snow from the rail-head at Dog Lake. NAC/C-6748

As had been the case in 1870, the troops would follow an all-Canadian route to the front. This time the railway could take them as far as Dog Lake, north of Lake Superior, but from there on they faced a much tougher ordeal than Wolseley's men. It was still winter, with temperatures well below freezing and deep snow on the ground, and they would have to walk a good part of the way where there were still gaps in the line. The distance from Dog Lake to Camp Desolation, where the railway began again, was forty-two miles, all difficult going. The ride on to Port Munro was ninety miles, but the hours on the train may have been as miserable as the Dog Lake trek: the men were on open flat cars, in sub-zero weather, "piled on top of each other." From Port Munro it was a twenty-mile hike across the windswept waste of Lake Superior to the next stretch of railway, where they again boarded flat cars for a short journey. Then it was back on foot for a further twenty miles across the lake. Another fifty miles by flat car brought them to Nipigon, where they again detrained, crossed another lake, and then made Red Rock, where the railway took them up again, all the way to Winnipeg.

By 22 April, before the railroad was finished, 3000 men had passed over this route, which would have tested the mettle of the most seasoned of troops. (One thousand more came west after the gaps in the line had been filled.) For militiamen who trained only in summer, had sedentary jobs, and were given the familiar pork, beans, hard tack, and unsweetened tea for nourishment, it was unimaginably miserable. Chilled to the bone, and exhausted from manhandling their guns and horses, the artillery probably had it the worst.

Winnipeg brought warmth, better food, and some drill and field training. Here, troops who had never been away from local headquarters were taught the rudiments of battle manoeuvre. Many, including those who had joined the 90th Winnipeg Rifles formed in 1883 (the first Western unit) and the 91st Winnipeg Light Infantry, formed in April 1885, fired a military pattern rifle for the first time. But they did not stay long.

The Governor General's Body Guard Crossing Lake Superior on the Ice by A.H. Hider.
Several gaps in the rail line had to be crossed by marching over the frozen surface of Lake Superior. Here, Lieutenant-Colonel George Denison is shown leading his regiment across Jackfish Bay on 11 April 1885.

By permission of the Commanding Officer, the Governor General's Horse Guards

45

The Halifax Provisional Battalion crossing a stream near Swift Current. NAC/C-5826

Middleton had worked out a simple strategy to beat Riel. "As he explained it to me," Major Charles Boulton, who led a locally-raised section of scouts, recalled:

General Middleton's original plan of campaign was to march his column from Fort Qu'Appelle to Clarke's Crossing. The second column, under Otter, was to march from Swift Current to meet him at the Crossing; and from that point the two columns were to move down the river to attack Batoche. There he proposed to join the two columns, and march to relieve Prince Albert, then to relieve Battleford, and after punishing Poundmaker to proceed with a portion of his force to Fort Pitt ... to attack Big Bear and release his prisoners.

They had to move quickly. With the spring run-off from the Rocky Mountains expected at any moment, Middleton wanted to take advantage of the fact that paddle steamers, laden with supplies, could move on the South Saskatchewan River all the way from Swift Current to the rebel capital at Batoche. Accordingly, he set out with 800 men through the Touchwood Hills, while Colonel Otter, who commanded the Infantry School at Toronto, covered the left flank with his 400 men. Far to the west, meanwhile, Major-General Thomas Bland Strange, now retired, would lead a small force along the North Saskatchewan, to Fort Pitt.

Middleton's planning was upset even before he began. Hearing of the Frog Lake massacre, he ordered Otter to forget about joining him at Batoche and to move to Battleford instead, which now seemed totally vulnerable. Although his own strength at the decisive point would be much reduced, Middleton still chose to push on, and (to the horror of his staff) to advance up both sides of the river — a division of his force which contradicted all that was known about principles of war.

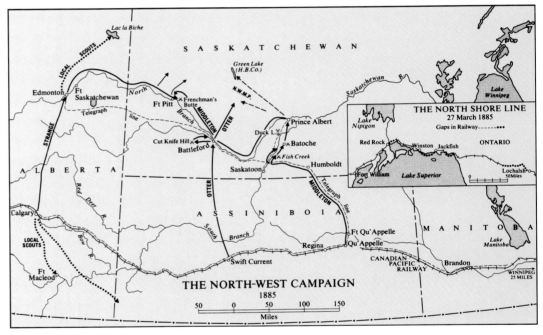

It was now that the Métis made their great mistake. A master of irregular warfare, Gabriel Dumont, Riel's chief lieutenant, begged his leader to authorize harassing operations against Middleton all along his approach march, but Riel vetoed the idea, preferring to fortify his capital. Dumont was almost certainly right. Hit and run raids might very well have spooked the untrained Militia, who were at their worst when unsettled. Beyond that, gambling everything on the defence of Batoche played into Middleton's hands. If he won, everything would be over.

THE BATTLE OF FISH CREEK

As it was, the Métis did sally forth on 24 April, aiming to ambush Middleton's column from the coulee of Fish Creek, which ran into the South Saskatchewan at right angles a few miles south of Batoche. But good work by Boulton's Scouts, Manitoba horsemen chosen in preference to eastern cavalry, prevented Dumont from achieving the surprise he needed. Boulton again:

We had hardly left this house to proceed on our way, when Captain Johnston, commanding the advanced scouts, reported to me that he had struck thirteen camp fires still warm, and a heavy trail leading away from them. I reported the circumstance to the General, who told me to obtain further information. I then ordered Captain Johnston to take the leading section, follow up the trail, and report to me.

They had not been gone many minutes when I heard bang! bang! and immediately after, a volley was fired at us.... I gave the command 'Left wheel, gallop!' and we charged down upon thirty or forty mounted men who were standing in the shelter of a bluff. When we came upon them they at once turned their horses and bolted for a ravine, or gully, about a hundred and fifty yards distant.

The skirmishing that ensued was uncomfortable for Middleton and his men. To bring effective fire to bear on the Métis they had to expose themselves on the skyline, where they were good targets for Dumont's men, who were cleverly concealed in good firing positions in the creek bed. After a few impetuous rushes by some of the Militia, all of which ended in failure, a stalemate set in, with sporadic firing when the enemy showed himself. As the day wore on, however, the advantage passed to Middleton. The Métis had engaged only half his force (the rest, including the 10th Royals, on the other side of the South Saskatchewan were working manfully to cross over and march to the sound of his guns), and he had a better supply of ammunition. The Métis, moreover, were generally unsuited to, and unhappy with, this kind of fighting. By early afternoon they began to drift away, one by one, so that as the sun began to sink, and the 10th Royals and Winnipeg artillery battery finally arrived on the field, Dumont had no more than fifty men left. Although the newly arrived units wanted desperately to attack, Middleton had seen enough: ten men were dead or dying, forty-five were wounded, and the confidence of his troops had been shaken. He called it a day. Dumont, despite receiving last minute reinforcements, also broke off the engagement.

The North West Rebellion Medal, awarded to all participants.

The Battle of Fish Creek, 24 April 1885. Middleton's force is shown engaging the rebel position in the gully. NAC/C-14220

'A' Battery firing at the rebels at Fish Creek. This photo by Captain James Peters is one of the first taken of Canadian troops in action. Peters Collection. NAC/C-3461

The Militia in fact had won, but Middleton's men had no sense of victory. Expecting Dumont to return that night, they spent a freezing night peering into the dark, waiting for an assault that never came. Lord Melgund, Middleton's military secretary (later, as Lord Minto, to become Governor General) caught the mood perfectly: "raw troops, totally unaccustomed to night work ... had come out for a picnic, and it was impossible to help feeling that war's hardships are doubly cruel to the civilian soldier."

Middleton had also lost his confidence. Worried that even a minor withdrawal could result in a rout (as had happened at Ridgeway), he decided not to move forward to Batoche until he had superior numbers and stable supplies — which, at this distance from Winnipeg and Swift Current, meant their coming by river. When the paddle wheeler *Northcote* finally arrived, a few days after Fish Creek, it was quickly incorporated into the GOC's battle plan. Fortified with wood and sacks of grain, and manned by the regular infantry, it was to steam through the rebel stronghold, creating a diversion.

BATOCHE

The column left Fish Creek on 7 May, two weeks after their first engagement, and arrived in front of Batoche the next day. The attack, scheduled to start on the 9th, went wrong from the beginning. The *Northcote* started early, and then went right through the town, ruining the effect Middleton wanted. Furthermore, the GOC soon found that his tactical situation was much like that at Fish Creek. He occupied the high ground, while the enemy was dug in below, with good fields of fire. Wanting no more wasteful and inconclusive fire fights, nor a blind frontal assault, and knowing that he could not withdraw, Middleton chose to build shelters and wait.

The Capture of Batoche. On 12 May, frustrated by two days of indecisive skirmishing, the Militia battalions stormed the Métis position without orders. This brought the rebellion to an end. CWM

In fact, this proved to be little better. There was nothing he could do, yet he could not do nothing. On 12 May, disgusted by the delay and by two days of futile demonstrations just out of enemy range, Middleton's Militia colonels relieved him of his burden. Whether by accident or design, the Royals and the Midland Battalion charged down the slope in front of them.

"The rebels immediately fell back," one eyewitness reported;

They could not stand a charge, the first charge made by a handful of the men. They got out of the pits and fell back. The advantage was quickly followed up. The Gatling gun and the 90th were ordered out and 'A' Battery and the guns. By this time the rebels were in full retreat. They were panic-stricken and it was a sharp running fight.... Cheer and cheer went up as the rebels got out of their entrenchments and rifle-pits and fled before the advancing column. They ran like deer, every now and then turning to fire. The troops advanced on the dead run, loading and firing without stopping, our men in a tremendous state of excitement and bent on paying off old scores with interest.... Close to Batoche, there was a slight check and the rebels poured in the lead to a pretty considerable tune. This is where they inflicted the most damage on us, but a volley, a ringing cheer, and a rush sent them flying again. They never stopped till they got into Batoche, where they made another stand, but the column, never weakening its pace, dashed on and drove them off again like so much chaff....

By early evening the town had been taken at a cost of five dead and twenty-five wounded. The Métis had lost fifty. Three days later, Riel surrendered.

'A' Battery, School of Artillery, with infantry at Batoche. James Peters Collection. NAC/C-3457

49

THE END OF CANADA'S FIRST WAR

The fall of Batoche broke the back of the Métis rebellion. Poundmaker's and Big Bear's Crees were still at large, however, farther to the west, where Otter had been sent. He had reached Battleford without a fight on 24 April, the day of Fish Creek, and had been ordered to remain there. But manufacturing an excuse to punish Poundmaker, he eventually set out for the Sand Hills, where the Crees had camped, and reached Cut Knife Hill (about twenty miles away) on 2 May. Otter occupied the hill, and then found himself under attack — and in the same tactical situation that had plagued Middleton at Fish Creek and Batoche. "Evidently we were in a trap," Lieutenant R.S. Cassels of the Queen's Own Rifles recorded in his diary:

The Battle of Cut Knife Creek. Colonel Otter's column was soundly thrashed by the Cree chief Poundmaker at Cut Knife Hill on 2 May 1885, but when Poundmaker heard of the Métis defeat at Batoche he gave up the struggle. CWM

Roughly speaking we occupied a triangular inclined plane — the apex resting on the creek and the base running along the crest of the hill. In front of the hill and parallel to the crest was a ravine, about two hundred yards distant, and running down from this ravine on each side of us ... was another ravine.... For half an hour we had quite hot enough work and the bullets came flying about us in a not over-pleasant manner. We were exposed to fire from three sides and had to grin and bear it.

After a sharp fight, and in danger of being surrounded, Otter eventually gave the order to withdraw to Battleford, and this, Cassels recalled, was "the most trying part of the day."

We had got about three hundred yards from the crest of the hill before the Indians knew what was up and appeared on it, but then a heavy fire opened on us and mighty hard work it was to walk quietly down with the bullets whistling by. The men behaved however with great coolness and steadiness and the artillery and ourselves retired alternately fifty yards or so at a time, then halted and kept up a steady fire. The Gatling was now near the creek and opened on the Indians and Captain Rutherford sent some shells among them from the far side and they evidently felt they had had enough. They did not attempt to follow....

Otter was fortunate that Poundmaker made for Batoche instead of pursuing. With Riel's surrender, however, the Indian leader gave up. Farther to the west, Strange's force reached Frog Lake and Fort Pitt, fought a brief skirmish against the forces of Big Bear, and then withdrew.

Once Poundmaker and Big Bear had surrendered, the North West Rebellion was over. It cost twenty-three soldiers killed, and 103 wounded. This was not very many, but it was enough to sow the seeds of discontent. Otter was criticized for his foolish and unnecessary independent action at Cut Knife Hill as well as for his heavy-handed discipline at Battleford; two Quebec battalions (but more particularly their commanding officers) were said to have lacked the will to fight; and Middleton himself was challenged because of his slow progress after Fish Creek. But the biggest scandals involved allegations of graft and corruption in the ordering, pricing and distribution of supplies through civilian contractors who secured government patronage. The web of suspicion eventually caught even Middleton, who had taken some furs as bounty. Perhaps the only participants to emerge with their reputations intact were the Militia who had assaulted at Batoche.

The Governor General's Body Guard in camp at Well's Hill. Gilinsky Collection

The Welland Canal Field Battery at summer camp in Niagara in 1890. NAC/C-5508

THE NEED FOR REFORM IN A MATURING ARMY

The lessons from the North West Rebellion were clear enough. Militia training was inadequate, and so was the department's supply, transport, and stores system. But few changes were forthcoming in the years immediately following the campaign. Although the defence budget rose gradually to $1.4 million in the late 1880s, the amount provided for Militia training remained small. Rural units still drilled only every second year, while city units continued to conduct sham battles on public holidays. Their value can be judged from the fact that the umpires invariably ruled the annual Thanksgiving contest between two Toronto units a draw. Scarcely any equipment was being purchased, and the Snider rifles with which most units were still equipped (the Martini Henry's had been put in storage) were now by and large only suitable for arms drill.

In some respects the regulars were even worse off. Although now solidly entrenched in the country's military organization, and with an increased establishment of 1,000 (to make room for an artillery battery at Victoria, mounted rifles at Winnipeg, and another infantry company), they were no better liked than before. The *Canadian Military Gazette* complained loudly at their pretensions, and promised its readers that it would never cease exposing those "who, like jackdaws in peacocks' plumes,

The School of Mounted Infantry, Winnipeg, 1891. Note the insulated stirrups to cope with the cold prairie winters.
NAC/PA-16007

want to be something they are not, and never cease bewailing the fact which makes officers nothing but merely school masters."

The regulars were certainly not treated like peacocks. Their pay rates compared unfavourably with Mounted Police salaries and there was no living-out allowance, so that officers with families (and no independent income) usually had to live in the single room allocated to them in barracks. The barracks themselves were usually inadequate. The hutments in Winnipeg, for example, had been built as temporary quarters for Wolseley's 1870 field force. In Toronto, Colonel Otter's wife found it necessary to ask the Minister of Militia to postpone improvements to the men's living areas so that she and her husband could have a furnace.

Perhaps even worse, nothing was done to shake the regulars out of the indolent (if not entirely comfortable) life it was all too easy for them to lead. Promotions came, if at all, as the result of seniority and patronage; and there was no sense that officers or men needed to study their profession. By the early 1890s the desertion rate in the Permanent Force was a staggering seventeen per cent per year, while those who left by purchasing their discharge or through having completed their engagement accounted for another thirty-nine per cent of the total establishment. That gave an annual turn-over rate of over fifty per cent among the other ranks. With the Volunteer Militia experiencing even higher attrition rates, the Canadian Army simply had no corpus of knowledge and experience.

Gunners of 'A' Battery, Royal Canadian Artillery, in winter uniform, ca 1896. Gilinsky Collection

Things began to change in 1890 when Major-General Ivor Caradoc Herbert arrived in Ottawa as GOC. He knew precisely what he was up against. The Militia would amount to nothing, he explained, until the regulars improved, and they would not get better until they were instilled with a sense of professional identity and obligation and were made to understand the importance of merit. To this end he persuaded the government to make regiments out of the dispersed artillery batteries and schools of infantry and cavalry — thus bringing about the formation of the Royal Canadian Horse Artillery, the Royal Canadian Dragoons, and The Royal Canadian Regiment. He also convinced the government to require senior Permanent Force officers to pass British Army courses to qualify for their appointments. Junior officers were to be sent to the British battalion at Halifax "to go through the mill of regimental life." At Militia Headquarters, meanwhile, he engineered the appointment of a Staff College-trained British officer, Colonel Percy Lake, as the country's first Quartermaster General, and gave him responsibility for mobilization planning and the creation of military supply and service departments.

The Militia had little use for the new regular regiments, considering them to have been "born in sin and conceived in iniquity." However, the citizen soldiers were not entirely ignored during Herbert's tenure. He released the Martini Henry rifles (kept in storage since 1885) to them in greater numbers, and in 1894 organized a large summer camp at Lévis, the first such event in years.

Priorities shifted dramatically in 1896. Herbert's successor was not nearly so preoccupied with the need to bring the regulars along, while Frederick Borden, Militia Minister in the new Liberal government, was a firm advocate of the citizen army. "Let the regular force understand," he declared, "that their office is to teach.... We have no standing army and do not need to have one." Major-General E.T.H. Hutton, appointed GOC in 1898, agreed wholeheartedly. A citizen's Militia, he wrote, "was the true form for an army for an Anglo-Saxon state to possess."

Whether Canadians, or indeed Sir Wilfrid Laurier's cabinet, would have responded to Borden's and Hutton's initiatives to improve the Militia on their own merits is a good question. What is clear, however, is that three crises between 1895 and 1898 rekindled Canadian interest in defence, and accelerated the pace of reform. In 1895 an Anglo-American dispute over the Venezuelan boundary threatened to result in war between the two that would necessarily have involved Canada. The government reacted quickly, sending Colonel Lake to England to purchase 42,000 Lee-Enfield rifles and carbines, new 12-pounder guns, and a few Maxim machine guns. At one swoop, the Militia would have modern weapons. Beyond that, Lake's small staff at headquarters began to work on a mobilization plan, the first to be drafted in almost thirty years, and when it exposed all the deficiencies in Canada's military organization used this information to convince Laurier that a comprehensive review of the Dominion's defences should be undertaken. Major-General E.P. Leach of the British Army would head the Committee.

Troopers of the Royal Canadian Dragoons in Toronto, 1896. Gilinsky Collection

Men of the 3rd Prince of Wales' Dragoon Guards strike threatening poses for the photographer during a brigade camp, June 1897. Gilinsky Collection

THE YUKON FIELD FORCE

Then, in 1898, there was the chance of trouble in the Yukon. The gold rush there had attracted prospectors from all over the United States, and the population of the territory was estimated to be eighty per cent American. Fearing a breakdown in law and order, and responding to the local commissioner's fear that a few unruly men might even take possession of the territory for the United States, the government decided to send a force of 200 well-armed regulars to the region. Authorized on 21 March 1898, the Yukon Field Force, under command of Lieutenant-Colonel T.D.B. Evans of the RCD, did not leave Ottawa until 6 May — it took that long to gather together the winter uniforms, rations, and other equipment required. Travelling by train to Vancouver, and then by ship to Wrangell (embarrassingly in US waters), the Field Force moved 300 kilometres overland over steep mountain trails, through mosquito-infested swamps, and dense forest and bush to Fort Selkirk and finally to Dawson, which they reached in mid-September. When they arrived they found that there was no need for military action to preserve civil order, so the troops took up garrison duty to assert the continuing authority of the Crown. Half the force returned home in July 1899, but for the better part of two years the remainder stood guard, acted as customs agents and police,

did drill, and attended church parades. This was a potentially demoralizing routine, particularly in the wide open society of the North, and the opportunities for disciplinary problems were many. But Evans seems to have maintained sufficient authority and control that such incidents were kept to a minimum. Indeed, when the Yukon Field Force was disbanded, its performance had given a much needed lustre to the reputation of the Permanent Force.

Far more would be gained thousands of miles away, in South Africa.

Men of the Yukon Field Force with their commanding officer, Lieutenant-Colonel T.D.B. Evans (front center, seated) outside their barracks. DND/RE686192

CHAPTER 3

THE SOUTH AFRICAN WAR

by
Brereton Greenhous

CAUSES OF THE WAR

The root causes of the second Anglo-Boer war in South Africa (there had been a first one in 1880-81, which the British lost) lay in the quarrel which has always existed between human rights and human greed.

Simply put, the Boer republics of the Orange Free State and the Transvaal, founded by puritanical, Bible-loving farmers of Dutch descent, disapproved severely of the boisterous, bacchanalian miners and freewheeling businessmen, mostly British, who had flocked there after the discovery of gold on the Witwatersrand in 1886. Fearful of being overwhelmed at the voting booths and thus losing control of their own countries, the Boers resolutely refused to give the vote to these *Uitlanders*, or Outsiders. Moreover, the *Uitlanders* were treated harshly in civil law and taxed much more heavily than the Boers taxed themselves. The Britons among them complained continually to the British government.

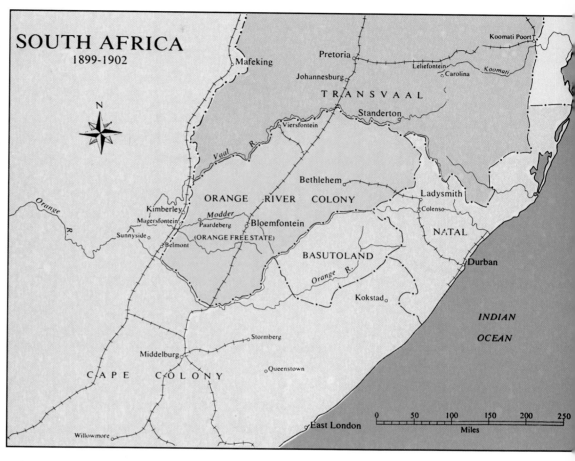

Because they did have influence at home, because there was untold wealth in the gold fields and diamond mines which were being developed with British money, in 1899 Britain uncompromisingly demanded that the republics enfranchise the British residents.

The Boers declined to be bullied, and Britain began to concentrate substantial forces along the borders between its South African colonies — the Cape Colony and Natal — and the two republics. That proved to be a gross miscalculation; the Boers were not a diplomatic people, nor one easily intimidated.

Believing that a British army was about to fall upon them, the Boers, with a citizen's militia very like that of Canada in form but quite different in content, struck first in October 1899. Trained from childhood to take advantage of cover and terrain while chasing big game or fighting Bantu tribesmen, thoroughly inured to hardship, hunger and thirst, consummate horsemasters, well-armed hunters and marksmen, they could move far and fast, and from well-concealed positions decimate the ranks of any enemy who moved and fought in more conventional ways.

Groups of mounted Boer militia, loosely organized in formations they called commandos, crossed into Cape Colony and Natal on 12 October 1899, whipped the British in several small skirmishes over the next few weeks, and were soon besieging the border towns of Mafeking (where future Boy Scout founder Robert Baden-Powell was in command) and Kimberley in the Cape Colony, and Ladysmith in Natal. However, the Boers, fighting only for what they saw as their natural rights, had no desire to go further. Nor, despite their small, well-equipped force of professional artillery, were they inclined to engage in costly frontal assaults against the besieged garrisons. Instead, they maintained desultory bombardments and waited for the British to make the next move, naively believing that they could now negotiate an amicable settlement from a position of strength.

THE CALL FOR CANADIAN PARTICIPATION

In Canada, long before the fighting broke out English and French had seen the South African dispute differently, in ways which cut across party lines. Generally speaking, romantic Anglo-Canadians viewed British policy as an imperial crusade to protect and advance the democratic rights of individuals; cynical French-Canadians, however, tended to look upon it simply as British imperialism, initiated to further the selfish concerns of British business at the expense of another non-English-speaking society. The first group felt that Canadians should wholeheartedly support the Mother Country, while the second held that Canada had no business getting involved in one of Britain's more dubious imperial ventures.

The Queen's South Africa Medal, awarded with appropriate campaign bars to all Canadians who served in South Africa. Members of Lord Strathcona's Horse were the first to be awarded the medal, and theirs bore the dates 1899-1900 on the reverse. When the war lasted beyond 1900, subsequent issues of the medal showed no dates.

Caught in the middle, the Laurier administration tried desperately to avoid committing itself to any coherent position, a traditional Canadian recipe for solving political problems made somewhat easier on this occasion by the fact that Parliament was not in session when the Boers made their move. Suddenly events overtook the government. The *Canadian Military Gazette*, a Militia mouthpiece, tried to force the government's hand by publishing details of the secret scheme for a Canadian contingent to South Africa which the General Officer Commanding the Militia, British regular Major-General E.T.H. Hutton, had prepared back in July at the instigation of Joseph Chamberlain, the British Colonial Secretary. Hutton's plan called for a mere five hundred Canadians to be placed directly under British command. There was no guarantee that they would even serve together. The War Office had no great confidence in the fighting potential of its untried, relatively undisciplined

'colonial' forces, and wanted Canadians more for their symbolic value — as an expression of imperial unity — than for any military virtues they might possess. Arrogant British officers feared that wild colonial boys might lack the harsh, unquestioning discipline which had always distinguished "the thin red line".

On the same day a telegram from Chamberlain reached Ottawa (where it was immediately leaked to the Press) thanking Canada for the offer of troops and noting that "infantry most, cavalry least, serviceable." No such offer had been made. Canada's inclusion in a circular telegram, sent to the other Dominions which certainly had made offers, was subsequently described as an error. Laurier might have thought it a carefully calculated one, for it served Chamberlain's purposes admirably. Pro-British Canadians now claimed

The King's South Africa Medal. After Queen Victoria's death, a second medal was struck for award to all who were serving in South Africa after 1 January 1902. Only 160 Canadians received this medal, mainly men who transferred to the Canadian Scouts of the South African Constabulary.

emotionally that the nation's honour was at stake. Sir Wilfrid, unable to respond to Whitehall as undiplomatically as he would have liked, told a friend that:

I have no sympathy for that mad, noisy, dull-witted and short-sighted throng who clamour for war.... War is the greatest calamity that can befall a nation....

Whilst I cannot admit that Canada should take part in all the wars of Great Britain, neither am I prepared to say that she should not take part in any war at all.... I claim for Canada this, that in future she shall be at liberty to act or not act, to interfere or not interfere, to do just as she pleases.

CANADA'S FIRST OVERSEAS EXPEDITIONARY FORCE

Nevertheless, on 13 October, the day after Boer commandos crossed into British South Africa, Laurier was driven to announce a contribution of one thousand men to the Imperial cause. One thousand — twice the number of Hutton's little scheme — would constitute an infantry battalion, a force large enough to justify keeping them together and one which warranted appointing a Canadian commander. Reluctantly the British agreed. Infantry the Canadians would be, recruited largely from the ranks of the Non-Permanent Active Militia (NPAM), but with a cadre of Permanent Force regulars and commanded by the country's senior soldier, Lieutenant-Colonel W.D. Otter, who had started his military career as a Volunteer private in the ranks of the Queen's Own Rifles. He had first come under fire at

Ridgeway, during the Fenian Raid of 1866, and had commanded a column in the North West Rebellion of 1885, though neither experience would be of much help to him in South Africa.

Eight companies, each 125 strong, were recruited on a regional basis, one from the west, three from Ontario, two from Quebec, and two from the Maritimes. Men were enrolled for a minimum of six months and a maximum of one year, and the ranks were quickly filled. Some NPAM officers relinquished their commissions to enlist as non-commissioned officers, with NCOs joining as privates, such was the enthusiasm to see active service. Otter's blunt (but private, to his wife) assessment of his new command was that "I have a splendid regiment as far as the men [are concerned] and fair officers."

Lieutenant-Colonel Otter (centre row, facing camera) and the officers of the 2nd (Special Service) Battalion of the Royal Canadian Regiment, shortly after arriving in South Africa. RCR Museum

Whether the Canadians could fight remained to be seen, but there was no doubt about their ability to organize. The 2nd (Special Service) Battalion, Royal Canadian Regiment, was concentrated at Quebec only sixteen days after Laurier's announcement, and fully equipped before the month was out. On 30 October the battalion sailed for South Africa, the first-ever Canadian overseas expeditionary force. The voyage took exactly a month. Drill was difficult on the crowded decks but there was much physical training and sports such as wrestling and boxing, while a small-bore rifle range was set up on the foredeck. Nevertheless, the Canadians were still far from being trained soldiers when they landed at Capetown.

Men of the Royal Canadian Regiment doing rifle drill aboard the SS *Sardinian* while en route to South Africa. NAC/PA-173032

THE CANADIANS ARRIVE

The Royal Canadian Regiment arrived at Belmont, on the railway line about 80 kilometres south of Kimberley, on 9 December 1899, the first day of what the British quickly came to call 'Black Week'. Anxious to relieve the besieged towns and restore his prestige, the British commander-in-chief in South Africa, General Sir Redvers Buller, VC — who would soon be better known as 'Reverse' Buller — had foolishly divided his forces and was trying to relieve all three places at once. More used to meeting opponents armed with flintlock muskets or spears rather than high-velocity magazine rifles, and unaccustomed to the sophistication of Boer tactics, each of the columns was driven back with heavy casualties by riflemen whom few of his soldiers ever saw, at Stormberg, Magersfontein and Colenso. That sent tremors of dismay throughout the Empire. British troops thrashed three times by an unruly mob of farmers! Had their officers learned nothing from the humiliation of defeat on Majuba Hill in 1881? Buller was relegated to a subordinate command in Natal and replaced by Britain's greatest military hero, 67-year-old Field Marshal Lord Roberts of Kandahar, whose only son had been killed at Colenso.

The Royal Canadian Regiment in Belmont in January 1900, awaiting orders to march against the Boers. NAC/PA-173035

It took a month for Roberts (and massive reinforcements) to reach South Africa, another month to plan and organize his campaign, valuable time which the Canadians, with the exception of one company and the Maxim machine-gun section, spent training — and guarding the vital railway, over which all Roberts' supplies must pass, against marauding Boers. 'C' Company and the machine-gunners, however, participated with British and Australian troops in a minor foray against Boer farmers settled in British territory who had raised a rebel flag. Catching them by surprise, Canadians came under fire on a foreign field for the first time since 1814 but suffered no casualties. A number of Boers were killed and wounded, 42 were taken prisoner, and the remainder fled.

Lord Roberts eventually started north along the railway line to Kimberley and Mafeking with 35,000 men, apparently intent upon ending those two sieges. But Roberts was a clever general, a master of the calculated risk. He surprised everybody, the Boers most of all, by leaving the railway and starting a cross-country flank march aimed at the Orange Free State capital of Bloemfontein, 180 kilometres to the east. It lay on another rail line which ran from Port Elizabeth on the Cape coast to Pretoria, the capital of the Transvaal. Only two weak brigades of cavalry continued north to relieve Kimberley. (Mafeking was eventually relieved by another force which included 'C' Battery, RCFA, a story which will be told a little later in this chapter.)

It was a bold move which caught the Boers off-balance. They had come to believe that no large British force would go far from a railway line on the arid, intractable wilderness of the high *veldt*. Away from the railway there was only animal transport — horses, mules and oxen — and men's own two feet to carry them forward. There was little water and less food and fodder. Small groups of hardy, knowledgeable men might traverse the *veldt* on horseback with only mild discomfort; larger forces, unused to such conditions and mostly on foot, would suffer great hardship at best, while any failure or interruption of a strained supply service could leave them to die of thirst or hunger.

A halt during the Royal Canadian Regiment's march to Paardeberg. In the foreground, left to right, are Lieutenant Blanchard, Lieutenant Hodgins, Captain Arnold and Lieutenant Ross. NAC/PA-173037

THE BATTLE OF PAARDEBERG

The Royal Canadian Regiment left Belmont by train on 12 February. At Gras Pan, sixteen kilometres up the line, they took to their feet and marched eastward for five days, about 120 kilometres, to the vicinity of Paardeberg Drift, or ford, on the Modder River. Here a Boer general, Piet Cronjé, was encamped with 4,000 men and as many more women and children. While they marched, two hundred supply wagons were captured in a Boer raid on a camp which the Canadians had just left, and food and water were soon in desperately short supply. When the battalion came across a filthy little stream, "everyone immediately made for it.... One man assured me he had just drunk five bottles' full," recorded Sergeant Hart-McHarg. "Hundreds of animals being watered and churning it up, men bathing, and others filling their waterbottles out of the same pond — it was a novel sight." One of the rank and file wrote home from Paardeberg to report that "the march there was simply terrible. Colonel Otter... need not be so hard on his men in the field. In camp he is all right, but when we got started he almost killed his men on the march and we had hardly anything to eat all that time."

Roberts had fallen sick and temporarily handed over command to his chief of staff, Lord Kitchener, a general in the traditional British mould. On 18 February Kitchener launched a piecemeal frontal attack on the Boer camp and was repulsed with the loss of 320 killed and 942 wounded. The Canadians, in the centre, made good use of what little cover

Men of the Royal Canadian Regiment fording the Modder River during the difficult cross-country march toward Paardeberg, 13 February 1900. RCR Museum

was available to establish a firing line within five hundred metres of the Boer trenches. Then:

the charge came, and the fire was awful. I can't see how so few were hit. It is simply a wonder to me that the regiment wasn't wiped out to a man. I wasn't in the charging line, and I am very thankful I wasn't. The men dropped right and left, and the [British] regiment on our right lost men in bunches. Darkness came on and how thankful we were for it — tired, hungry and thirsty, only the excitement keeping many of us up. Then came the wounded — it was awful. The dead were left on the field and buried the next day, Monday.

Another view of the crossing of the Modder River on 13 February 1900. The mounted men in the foreground are British troops from a supporting artillery battery.
RCR Museum

Eighteen of the Canadians were killed, three more would die of their wounds, and another sixty were wounded. One of the wounded, a Private Bradshaw who was shot through the neck and had his jugular vein smashed, owed his life to a fellow soldier, medical orderly R.R. Thompson, who crawled out to him despite "concentrated enemy fire" and lay there in the open for more than half a day, pressing a bandage to Bradshaw's neck until darkness made it possible for a stretcher party to bring him in. Writing to his brother, Thompson reported, "it was marvellous how I escaped, as my helmet was shot off my head by the enemy." He was recommended for a Victoria Cross by Colonel Otter, but the citation was not approved.

Cronjé could probably have escaped that night, but only by abandoning his sick and wounded which he chose not to do, hoping that other Boers would cut Roberts' supplies off and force him to retreat. Meanwhile, Lord Roberts had resumed command on the 19th and begun a systematic encirclement and bombardment of the enemy lines while the Boers slowly starved. By the early morning of the 27th, the anniversary of Majuba, Roberts was ready to finish them off.

'C' Company of the Royal Canadian Regiment climbing a *kopje* facing the Boer camp at Paardeberg on 18 February 1900. This was the first fighting in which Canadians took part. Twenty-one died and another sixty were wounded. RCR Museum

The Dawn of Majuba Day
by R. Caton Woodville.
On the morning of 27 February 1900, the anniversary of the battle of Majuba in the first Anglo-Boer War, the Royal Canadian Regiment participated in the hard-fought final attack on the Boer positions at Paardeberg. This painting shows the jubilation in the ranks on hearing the news of the Boer surrender.
By permission of the Royal Canadian Military Institute, Toronto

the left of the Canadian line heard and obeyed. In fact, some of them came back in such a hurry that one unfortunate fellow was bayoneted by a sentry of the Gordon Highlanders who thought that he was being charged by desperate Boers! The two right-hand companies never heard it, however, and by dawn were well dug in only a hundred metres or so from Cronjé's forward trenches.

As the sun rose the desperate Boers began their usual sniping, firing over the bodies of men hit during the earlier assault and now lying between the lines. "Woe to the man who was indiscreet enough to show his head and shoulders above the earthworks," wrote one of the Gordons' officers who apparently had a good view of the battlefield.

About 5.30 a.m. a wounded man, about 500 yards away, was seen to be making for our trenches under a heavy fire, but was at last observed to fall. Now and then between the volleys he was seen to wave his hands as if for assistance. Suddenly, from the left of our trenches, a form was seen to climb the earthworks in front of our trenches, and, jumping down, to make straight for the place where the wounded [man] lay, about ninety yards from the Boer trenches. Utterly regardless of the scathing fire which hissed around him, he ran on and at last reached the wounded man and tried to lift him, but it was too late, for the poor fellow had breathed his last. Seeing it was no avail, his would-be rescuer walked back over the ground he had covered, and although bullets whistled around him and tore up the ground in every direction, he coolly regained his trenches with a pipe stuck between his teeth. I have since ascertained his name was Private Thompson, of the Royal Canadians... it seems marvellous that he ever lived to get within four hundred yards of him [the dying man], not to mention getting back without a scratch.

At 2.15 a.m., in clear starlight, the Canadians started forward in two ranks, moving silently in extended order, with British battalions on both flanks. The front rank had its rifles and bayonets at the ready, the second carried picks and shovels. They advanced nearly four hundred metres before a sentinel's single shot was followed by a hail of fire. Everybody dropped to the ground and the front rank then returned the fire, keeping the Boers' heads down, while the rear rank dug like fiends, preparing a shallow trench to provide shelter during the day. Suddenly they were ordered to "Retire, and bring back your wounded with you." The source of this unfortunate order was never established (Was it a Boer trick? There were a few Canadians in the enemy ranks.) but

Once again he was recommended for the VC, and once again the citation was rejected. No medal for Private Thompson. In due course, however, he was to be rewarded with a decoration far more rare than the Victoria Cross. Learning that it could be cold on the high *veldt* at night, the 82-year-old Queen Victoria had knitted four or five woollen scarves, each of which bore the royal cipher, VRI, embroidered in silk. The Queen had intended to present them personally to deserving soldiers who had been recommended for, but not received, the VC, and who were subsequently elected to receive them by their comrades. The old lady died in January 1901, before she could do that, but at least four of the scarves did eventually reach qualified recipients, one of them being Robert Rowland Thompson. For half a century it rested in an Irish farmhouse — Thompson was Irish-born — but it is now carefully preserved by the Canadian War Museum.

The Queen's Scarf awarded to Private Robert Thompson of the Royal Canadian Regiment. This is the rarest of all gallantry decorations ever awarded to a Canadian. CWM

Meanwhile, one more short charge was likely to carry the day at Paardeberg, and the Boers were not keen on close-quarter fighting, with its inevitable heavy casualties. Surrounded, their situation was quite hopeless, and there were the women and children to consider. By 6 a.m. some of them had begun to raise the white flag and an hour later Cronjé finally surrendered. Thirteen more Canadians had been killed, another thirty-six wounded. That afternoon Lord Roberts told the survivors that, "we had done noble work, and were as good a lot of men as were in the British army." Watching the ragged Boers as they tramped off into captivity, Sergeant Hart-McHarg concluded that "the thought uppermost in my mind was, what a power the modern rifle is in the hands of a man who knows how to use it, acting on the defensive."

THE SECOND CANADIAN CONTINGENT

Hard-pressed by public opinion, even before the disasters of Black Week, Laurier had offered more men to the cause. But at that time the British had still only wanted nominal contingents of colonial troops as an expression of imperial solidarity, and his offer had been politely declined. Black Week — "the gloomiest week in our history for close upon a hundred years," according to one newspaper correspondent — changed all that, and the realistic and perspicacious Roberts (like most of Britain's best generals, he was from the Indian Army) asked for mounted men this time. Ottawa responded with two battalions of mounted rifles and three batteries of artillery. The 1st Canadian Mounted Rifles, under the command of Lieutenant-Colonel F.L. Lessard of the Permanent Force, formed around a cadre of Royal Canadian Dragoons, and were made up to strength by militiamen and volunteers mostly from eastern Canada. The nucleus of the 2nd CMR, under former NWMP Commissioner — now Lieutenant-Colonel — L.W. Herchmer, was composed of North West Mounted Policemen and completed by western Canadians, many of them Mounties or ex-Mounties. (The 1st would be rebadged as the Royal Canadian Dragoons in August 1900, after arriving in South Africa, while the 2nd would become simply the Canadian Mounted Rifles: and for the sake of clarity they will be identified by those titles during the remainder of this chapter.) Mounted infantry battalions were much smaller in numbers than regular infantry ones. Each battalion was organized in two squadrons, with four troops in each squadron and a battalion headquarters staff of fifty-three, for a total of 371 all ranks. The men were equipped with modern Lee-Enfield rifles and each mounted infantry battalion included two Colt machine-guns on galloping carriages.

Lieutenant-Colonel François Lessard, commanding officer of the Royal Canadian Dragoons, with Lieutenants Young and Van Straubenzee. RCD Archives

The three batteries of Royal Canadian Field Artillery, designated 'C', 'D' and 'E', were under the overall command of the Permanent Force's Lieutenant-Colonel C.W. Drury and were based on Permanent Force gunners supplemented by militiamen from Ontario and Manitoba in 'C', Ontario alone in 'D', and Quebec in 'E'. The two latter batteries, together with a small detachment of the CMR, sailed on 20 January 1900, to be followed a week later by the main body of the CMR. Finally, on 20 February, as the men of the original contingent lay under fire at Paardeberg, the Dragoons and 'C' Battery left Halifax aboard the S.S. *Milwaukee*. Each artillery battery had six 12-pounder field guns. These were relatively modern breech-loaders, capable of firing over distances up to 4700 metres, but they would be no match for the high-velocity Krupp field guns of the Transvaal artillery.

One of the bugbears with which the gunners had always had to contend was the recoil of the gun carriage.... Among various attempts which were made to check the recoil, a spade device fastened to the trail to act as a brake promised the best results at this time. But this improvement was slow in reaching Canada, and as late as 1900, when Canadian batteries fought in South Africa, the Commanding Officer had to report that "the guns were lacking many modern attachments, such as the 'recoil spade', the South African brake, etc."

Meanwhile, Parliament had resumed sitting in Ottawa. Laurier, who had initially argued that his administration had no constitutional authority to act, had subsequently dispatched troops by Order-in-Council and now had to defend his sudden change of front. One of his former supporters, Henri Bourassa, had already resigned his seat over the issue — and been promptly re-elected by acclamation in his Quebec constituency. On 13 March he put forward a motion which denied the government's right to behave as it had. Laurier's position was weak but although the House may have felt that he was wrong in principle it was equally certain that he was right in practice. Only ten French-Canadian members supported Bourassa.

There were yet more Canadians bound for South Africa. Railway tycoon Lord Strathcona had responded to the Imperial call with the offer of a privately raised cavalry regiment. Six hundred strong and organized in three squadrons, Lord Strathcona's Horse was recruited largely in western Canada from Mounties and ex-Mounties. Command went to Superintendent — now suddenly Lieutenant-Colonel — Sam Steele, a Mountie whose ego seems to have been as big as his physique. Money was no object to Strathcona, and "on March 15, this body of luxuriously equipped troops rolled into Halifax on beautifully appointed Pullmans and first-class coaches." They sailed the next day, together with "100 brave fellows who had gallantly come forward... to fill the gaps made in the First Contingent by Mauser bullets and enteric." Less prospect of glory but a better life expectancy was the lot of the 3rd (Special Service) Battalion, Royal Canadian Regiment, recruited for garrison duty at Halifax in March 1900 in order to release an Imperial battalion for service in South Africa.

The field hospital at Paardeberg Drift, where Canadian casualties were treated after the battle. RCR Museum

Lord Strathcona's Horse en route to South Africa aboard the S.S. *Monterey*.
NAC/C-171

THE RELIEF OF MAFEKING

'C' Battery, with the RCD the last to arrive in South Africa, was the first of the three RCFA units to get into action. Thirteen hundred kilometres north of Capetown, in the northern tip of Cape Colony, the garrison of Mafeking which had come under attack in the early days of the war was still holding out against a half-hearted siege. The commander, Baden-Powell, had signalled that he could not continue to do so past the end of May, when there would be neither food nor ammunition. A mounted column under Colonel Bernard Mahon, composed mostly of British South Africans, was pushing slowly north along the railway, intending to break the siege, while another force of Rhodesian mounted infantry under Colonel Herbert Plumer was advancing from the north, having started from Bulawayo, in southern Rhodesia (now Zimbabwe).

Mahon had a battery of artillery in support but Plumer did not, so 'C' Battery was dispatched to join him, via Beira in Portuguese East Africa. A ramshackle train carried the Canadians from Beira to the 'end of steel' at Marandellas, where there was a 500-kilometre gap to be crossed to reach Bulawayo, the northern terminus of the Capetown line on which Mafeking lay. The battery's horses, after four days in poorly ventilated boxcars, were in no condition to pull the guns so the normal, mule-drawn stage service between Mirandellas and Bulawayo was suspended, and the men travelled by stagecoach. Four of the battery's six guns went with them, pulled by stage line mules, leaving the other two guns and the horses to follow on as best they could.

On 9 May, the leading gunners under their French-Canadian CO, Major J.A.G. Hudon, railed south from Bulawayo. They detrained at Ootsi and marched the last forty kilometres to Plumer's camp at Sefeteli on 13 May. Here they found that three hundred of eight hundred men were on the sick list. On the morning of the 15th Plumer and Mahon joined forces east of Mafeking, and the next day they attacked the Boers. Fired on by enemy artillery at 4500 metres, Hudon pushed forward his four guns another thousand metres and started counter-battery fire.

We opened fire on a stone laager at 3,700 yards against artillery; and finding the range to be 3,350 yards, at once changed to time shrapnel with fuse 15½ [seconds]. The enemy's position appeared to be well protected by trees; and in elevation was about on a level with our own. We, however, silenced the Boer guns after a few rounds, driving the enemy from his position and following him with our shells, which were effective.

'C' Battery, Royal Canadian Field Artillery under fire from Boer guns, 16 May 1900, near Mafeking. RCA Museum

At four in the morning on 17 May 1900, the relieving troops marched into Mafeking, concluding a siege which had lasted seven months.

After Paardeberg, Roberts had resumed his march on Bloemfontein, capital of the Orange Free State, reached on 13 March. Although he was now back on a railway line, the Boers had blown most of the bridges to the south as they fell back, and it would be many months before the line would be in full operation again. Adequate food and clothing for the troops were still sadly lacking, and rigorous march and camp discipline were essential if men were to stay healthy. But the Canadians were mostly not regular soldiers and unwilling to adopt such drastic disciplinary measures as were required. Although their independent ways may have made them better fighters in the field, their hygiene standards left much to be desired (as Sergeant Hart-Mcharg had noted on the road from Gras Pan to Paardeberg). Dysentery and enteric fever now ravaged their ranks as they waited for their next assignment.

The Royal Canadian Regiment takes time out from campaigning for the rare luxury of a bath. Note the typical military tans — from the neck up. NAC/PA-173036

THE MODDER RIVER

Thus on 25 April it was a badly understrength battalion of the Royal Canadian Regiment which found itself the advance guard of a column under Brigadier-General Horace Smith-Dorrien ordered to clear the right flank of Roberts' proposed line of advance. In the vicinity of a village named Israel's Poort, about fifty kilometres northeast of Bloemfontein, where the Boers held a series of *kopjes* or small hills along the north bank of the Modder, the Canadians deployed for their next action. Ordered to advance, they came under a galling Boer fire and, in accordance with Smith-Dorrien's plan, took what cover they could find and returned the fire while waiting for other components of the column to outflank the enemy from the left.

At this stage of the operation, Lieut.-Col. Otter, cool and at his best when under fire, found it necessary to stand for a moment to view the enemy position. Probably his doing so attracted some crack shot in the Boer force, for a bullet tore through his chin and neck and another penetrated the badge on his right shoulder. Though painfully wounded, Lieut.-Col. Otter was not disabled and continued in command of the Battalion…. After three-quarters of an hour, the enemy fire slackened and Lieut.-Col. Otter, judging correctly that this indicated an intention to withdraw, ordered his Battalion forward…. Reaching their final objective, the Canadians occupied the Boer position and there bivouacked for the night.

Canadians in South Africa soon found that they did not fight alone. Picking lice or 'chatting' became an unending leisure activity. CDQ Archives

One Canadian had been killed and three, including Otter, wounded. Otter went to hospital (he would be away a month), and command of the battalion was assumed by the second-in-command, Major Laurence Buchan, an officer who seems to have been much more popular with the rank and file than Otter ever was.

A week later the column was in action again at Thaba Mountain, another thirty kilometres to the east and better understood, in defiance of its name, as a plateau standing about a hundred metres above the surrounding *veldt*. There the Boer position was bolstered by artillery and a unit of German volunteers fighting under Boer colours. This time British troops led the assault, taking a foothold on the high ground, and the Canadians, following up, spent an uncomfortable night lying out in the biting wind ready to repel any counterattack. The next morning they and the Gordon Highlanders swept the plateau clear of the enemy, at a cost to the Canadians of six more wounded.

It may not be out of place here to comment on the casualty figures, which no doubt seem very small to readers familiar with those rates which would often be incurred in two World Wars. They were certainly seen as significant at the time by the men involved. It should be remembered that the British Army had not been involved in a major war since the Crimea, nearly half a century before. With one exception, the first Anglo-Boer War, its experience since then had been pretty well limited to punitive campaigns against brave but unsophisticated and ill-armed tribesmen. In that kind of fighting, except for the disasters of Isandhlwana in 1879 and Maiwand in 1880, battle casualties had usually been light. Sickness and disease took the greater toll, just as it did in civilian life.

As for the Dominion troops, only those few Canadians who had campaigned in the North West Rebellion of 1885 had any practical knowledge of war, and that experience, too, had not been harsh in terms of casualties. Like most Britons, Australians and New Zealanders, their comprehension of warfare was a thoroughly romantic one. Medicine being what it was in the last quarter of the nineteenth century, they were much more accustomed to sudden death from natural causes than we are. Deliberate killing of one man by another, however, was still something of a shock to them and its effect should not be underestimated. Soldiers, even experienced British regulars, whose battalions had been under sporadic fire for two or three hours and who had seen perhaps half a dozen of their comrades killed or wounded in that time, could genuinely speak or write of a "terrific fire", and mean it just as much as those who, sixteen or seventeen years later, would recollect the horrendous casualties of the Somme and Passchendaele.

The 2nd Canadian Mounted Rifles chasing down small bands of elusive Boer guerillas in the Transvaal. NAC/PA-173029

The CMR, together with 'D' and 'E' Batteries — the initial shipload of the Second Contingent, who had landed in Capetown on 25 February 1900 — were first incorporated into a column which included West Australian and New Zealand mounted rifles and sent to suppress a minor Boer rising in the northwest corner of the Cape Colony. This rising was a worry to Roberts because, if it spread, it might well threaten his main line of communications. It was a task which involved no fighting but led the newly arrived Canadians to cover seven hundred kilometres of the semi-arid Karroo in a month of strenuous marching and counter-marching. Then the artillery batteries, their horses worn down badly, were left to support British soldiers guarding a stretch of the railway from Cape Town against the ever-present threat of marauding Boers. At this time the CMR rode north and east to join Roberts' main force at Bloemfontein, a force which already included both the RCR and the RCD.

The gunners soon concluded that the rail junction at De Aar "is not a joyous place to put in the time."

The water is bad, and it is very unhealthy. The hospital is full and the patients are dying at a rate of twelve or fourteen a week. The doctors and the parson are the only people who are busy. We drill in a desultory way, and supply gun carriages and occasional firing parties for funerals. The rest of the time we sit about in the microbe-infected dust and wonder if we left our 'appy 'omes for this.

THE ADVANCE TO PRETORIA

At the beginning of May the great advance on Pretoria began. There were now, in round numbers, 200,000 Imperial troops in South Africa facing perhaps 10,000 Boers. Roberts' strategy was appropriately simple. On an arc of more than 600 kilometres, 100,000 fighting men and 350 guns would converge on the Transvaal capital of Pretoria. From the west, General Sir Archibald Hunter with 10,000 men would drive from Kimberley through the western Transvaal. On the other flank, Buller with 45,000 men would march from Ladysmith through the southeastern Transvaal. And in the centre Roberts himself, with another 45,000 men, including the RCR, the RCD and the CMR, would follow the line of the railway north from Bloemfontein.

As usual, more casualties were caused by disease and hardship than by battle. The material demands of Roberts' troops were grossly overstressing the one uncertain railway line which ran back six hundred kilometres from Bloemfontein to East London, on the coast. But 'Bobs' continued to drive his men hard, rightly endeavouring to keep the enemy off-balance. Private W.A. Griesbach of the CMR (who would finish his military career as a major-general in the Second World War) like Colonel Otter, was not too impressed by the calibre of his officers. "We had, by this time, taken the measure of all our officers in our squadron. A few were good and the rest were not."

It was early spring in the southern hemisphere, sometimes raining and always cold at night.

… we slept in the two blankets carried under the saddle, our greatcoats and an oil sheet…. We would sometimes arrive in the bivouac in the pouring rain. We unsaddled cautiously and made a pile of our saddle, blankets and greatcoat and put the oil sheet over the top to keep the rain off. Before dossing down one had to defeat the wet ground. This was done by getting a spade from the ammunition cart and digging up a patch which looked something like the beginning of a grave, digging sufficiently deep to turn up the dry soil underneath…. Having turned up the dry soil one spread one's blankets over it and made a bed putting the oil sheet over the top…. We stood our saddles on end as windbreaks and slept soundly until reveille, only removing our boots.

An ambulance belonging to the Royal Canadian Regiment marching with the regimental column.
NAC/PA-173033

Lord Strathcona's horsemen were faring better. Because it was privately raised, with a great deal of newspaper hoopla, and commanded by Sam Steele — whose cultivated reputation for derring-do in the Canadian west preceded him wherever he went — public opinion had already established the Strathconas as something of an elite force. Thus, when an unusually daring plan was formulated to cut the one Boer line of communications with the outside world — the railway line running from Pretoria to Delagoa Bay, in Portuguese East Africa — the newly-arrived Strathconas were chosen to carry it out.

make an attempt from there to reach the Komati [river with his whole regiment] and destroy the bridge." But on reaching Eshowe, no more than a quarter of the distance they had to cover, the orders were countermanded and the regiment was ordered back to Durban. "I was sorry that the attempt was abandoned, for it would have been successful."

Instead, the Strathconas were ordered to join Buller's army, marching on Pretoria from Ladysmith in Natal. Buller had approximately the same number of men under him as Roberts had in the centre column, and a secure and complete

Men of 'C' Squadron, Lord Strathcona's Horse preparing for operations on the *veldt*. LdSH Museum

The regiment was shipped from Capetown to Durban, the capital of Natal, where two squadrons were disembarked and entrained for the Tugela River, the closest rail point to their objective then in British hands. Steele took the third squadron further along the coast, to Kosi Bay in Tongaland, where it was to be landed and ride north, across the Lebomba mountains, to blow a key bridge at Komati Poort, near the Transvaal-Portuguese East African border. Once the bridge was blown and the railway blocked, the other two squadrons would ride from the Tugela, and the whole regiment would try to hold the block against any Boer attempt to restore communications. Before Steele and the third squadron could be disembarked at Kosi Bay, however, a message from Durban reported (wrongly) that the Boers had got wind of the plan and were prepared to thwart it.

"On receipt of this intelligence, which the admiral had good reason to believe, and as there was no sign of the appearance of the guide who was to have met us at the bay, he called off the expedition and we sailed for Durban the same afternoon," wrote Steele. "I next received orders to proceed to Eshowe, in Zululand, as soon as possible and

railway line only half as long as Roberts' running back to Durban. But he did not press his advance, preferring to skirmish leisurely, eat well and sleep warmly as he fell far behind Roberts' pace. (An approach to war which earned him the alternative nickname of 'Sitting Bull'!). The Natal Field Force never did reach Pretoria: the two armies first linked up at Vlakfontein, in the southwestern Transvaal, on 5 July, a month after Roberts had occupied the second Boer capital. A month after that, as Buller's troops tried to clear the southeastern Transvaal of recalcitrant Boers, Sergeant A.H.L. Richardson won the first Victoria Cross ever awarded to a soldier of a Canadian regiment. When a patrol of thirty-eight Strathconas were surprised by double their number of Boers at Wolve Spruit, near Standerton, the Canadians galloped off in a hurry. Richardson, seeing one of his comrades down and wounded, "rode back under a heavy cross fire to within 300 yards of the enemy and rescued a trooper who had been twice wounded and whose horse had been shot."

Sergeant A.H.L. Richardson of Lord Strathcona's Horse rescues a wounded trooper whose horse had been shot when their patrol was ambushed by a large party of Boers at Wolve Spruit on 5 July 1900. Richardson, who was under heavy fire during this action, was awarded the Victoria Cross for his bravery. His was the first VC ever awarded to a member of a Canadian unit. LdSH Museum

The Victoria Cross. Founded by Queen Victoria in 1856, this is the highest award given to British and Commonwealth troops for gallantry in the face of the enemy. The four VCs awarded to Canadians in South Africa were the first to members of Canadian units, although four Canadians had received the decoration earlier while serving with British units.

That same evening, Steele (who never mentioned Richardson or his medal in his memoir of the campaign written many years later) tells us "I dined with Sir Redvers Buller and his staff.... He was possessed of the dry humour of a Mark Twain, keeping the table merry during the meal and drawing everyone else out. It was evident to me that he was held in great esteem and was a favourite with everyone." Most of the time, life was good in Buller's army. Gentlemen soldiers, out on the spree! Indeed, when a part of it finally caught up with Roberts' Canadians at Wonderfontein, a Dragoon, looking at the excellent condition of their horses, would comment that "they must have had an easy march up through Natal and the Transvaal to Belfast." Roberts' Canadians were in tatters.

Army rations were never popular with the troops, and they supplemented them whenever they could. Here, men of the Royal Canadian Regiment are shown buying chickens from a native family. NAC/PA-173038

There were minor engagements and skirmishes for all three armies as they closed on Pretoria, but with the main force, at least, "the pattern of the advance rarely faltered. The enemy was the veldt, not the Boers: a sun to fry you, and a frost to freeze you… too little trek ox to eat, too few biscuits — when there were rations at all." Looting was forbidden but hungry, threadbare Canadians were not enamoured of regulations. "As fast as we come up country, the farmers skip and we loot the farms," recorded one Dragoon with commendable honesty. "We've had chicken soup every night for the past week."

Occasionally we were issued composite wax candles. The wax we used to advantage for frying our hard tack [biscuits]. We would soak the hard tack in water and then cook them in the melted wax… not so bad when washed down with hot coffee! We often dried the tea leaves and coffee grounds and carried them separately, to be

used again. We rarely had any butter and the only fat we had was when, by good luck, we managed to get hold of a pig. Then we fared well for a few days.

The Royal Canadian Regiment had remained with what was now known as the Winburg column, marching on the right flank of Roberts' main force, while the Royal Canadian Dragoons and the Canadian Mounted Rifles rode with that body, taking turns to serve as scouts and advance guard with a British mounted infantry battalion. Typically on the Boer side, as reported by young Denys Reitz who rode as one of their rearguard:

As soon as it grew light we were astir, anxiously scanning the ground before us, and soon we made out dense masses of English [sic] infantry on the plain. First came a screen of horsemen, and behind a multitude of infantry, guns and wagons throwing up huge clouds of dust.

We looked in dismay at the advancing host, for there were thirty thousand men approaching, whilst on our meagre front there may have been between three and four thousand Boer horsemen, strung out in a ragged line on the rising ground to right and left of us.

It was plain from the very way in which the men sat their horses that they would not stand, and indeed, on this bare veldt and against such heavy odds, the task was manifestly beyond them. The enemy forces came on steadily until their scouts were close to us. When we fired on these they fell back upon their regiments; the batteries unlimbered and in a few seconds shrapnel was bursting over us.

Our line gave way almost at once…. The English troops being mainly infantry, their progress was slow, and, although they were quickly at us once more, we were able to retire before them with very little loss for the rest of the day…. We were in the saddle until sunset, for we had to exercise ceaseless vigilance to keep the English horses from the wagons that were struggling to get away.

There must have been over a thousand of these, for, in addition to General de la Rey's transport, there were a great many vehicles belonging to the civilian population fleeing before the oncoming invasion.

On the whole the men thought that he was a pretty good man. He knew all about horses and tried to look after them. He looked after his men in much the same way and for the same reasons. When he had occasion to reprimand his transport officer or quartermaster he did it in a loud voice within the hearing of everybody. When an officer failed in any job that had been given him the Colonel certainly let him know about it. At Kroonstadt, the officers, in a sort of 'round robin', complained to higher authority that Herchmer was medically unfit; secondly, that he was a lunatic and thirdly, that he was so unpopular with his men that some of them might shoot him. The latter allegation was distinctly untrue. The 'round robiners' were in much more danger of being shot by their men than Herchmer was…. At Kroonstadt higher authority relieved Herchmer of his command and when we rode away from that place he was left in a tent without a horse, or without a servant, which by common consent was a pretty shabby thing to do.

He was succeeded by Lieutenant-Colonel T.D.B. Evans, the talented and capable former commander of the Yukon Field Force, who Griesbach felt "had not a great deal of iron in his soul." At the end of the war Major-General Hutton,

A Colt machine gun and galloping carriage of the 2nd Canadian Mounted Rifles. Mounted units each had two of these weapons.
NAC/PA-173030

In the midst of this great advance came the dismissal of Lieutenant-Colonel Herchmer from command of the CMR. In his NWMP days he had been formally accused of poor man-management, and Griesbach (whose father was a Mountie) assessed him as "a man of intense energy, a bit tyrannical and sometimes abusive," but his tyranny seems to have been directed at his officers, not his other ranks.

(who had become the 'higher authority' of Griesbach's account after being sacked from his appointment as GOC in Canada for publicly criticizing political interference in the Militia) assessed him "as by far the best officer among the Mounted Troops." (Evans would survive the war, only to die suddenly in 1908, at the age of 48.)

Conditions were hard out on the *veldt* while pursuing the Boers, both for the men and for their horses. Here, a party of Dragoons pause at the base of a *kopje* for a lunch of hard-tack biscuits and tea. RCD Archives

Gradually the Canadians were making a name for themselves through their combination of initiative, fieldcraft and hard fighting. "So far, all the British soldier has learned in this war is to keep under cover when he is being fired at…," wrote Lieutenant E.W.B. Morrison, a Canadian journalist-turned-gunner with 'D' Battery who would command the Canadian Corps artillery in the First World War. "When not being fired at he chooses for preference a conspicuous position on the skyline or a hill top…. The Canadians keep under cover all the time… and the Boers never know when they will stumble on them, or how many will be there." It was an approach which led the Irish critic, Erskine Childers, to write after the war that "in sheer fighting efficiency the best of the seasoned Colonials, South Africans, Australians and Canadians, had undoubtedly excelled all other troops."

Roberts reached Pretoria on 5 June 1900, and the war should have been over. After all, both Boer capitals had now fallen. But the enemy promptly established an interim capital at Machadodorp, 280 kilometres east of Pretoria, on the Delagoa Bay railway. Roberts wheeled his army eastward and started along the railway, fighting two brisker-than-usual actions at Diamond Hill and Witpoort on 11 July and 16 July, the latter being where Lieutenant Harold Borden of the RCD, the

son of the Minister of Militia, Dr. F.W. Borden, was killed. The army pressed on towards Machadodorp, linking up with some of Buller's men approaching from the south, and routed the Boers again at Belfast. Believing that the war was over, Roberts jauntily annexed the Transvaal, handed over command to Kitchener, and left for Capetown, en route for England, home, and glory.

GUERILLA WARFARE

Annoyingly, the stubborn Boers refused to recognize defeat and turned to guerrilla warfare. The Canadians joined in the fatiguing, mostly fruitless, work of chasing small bands of sharp-shooting, *veldt*-wise guerillas in every direction across the endless expanses of southern Africa, burning Boer farms as they went. Alternatively, they endured the excruciating monotony of railway guard duties on key bridges and manning dusty, isolated blockhouses.

The Boers knew their country like the backs of their own hands. They moved about in small parties and apparently had the means of calling considerable forces together for a big job. They excelled in this sort of fighting and distinctly outpointed us at every move. They raided the railway, captured and destroyed convoys, surprised and cut up substantial parties of our people up to the strength of a regiment. They had begun to wear our uniform for lack of clothing and as their Mauser rifles wore out they used our rifles and ammunition.

All the Canadians had enlisted for a maximum of one year, and the year of the original volunteers was fast expiring. Asked to sign on again, most of the RCR who were still in the field (a considerable number were sick in British hospitals) preferred to take their release. They sailed from Capetown on 1 October, leaving 262 of their comrades together with the men of the RCFA, the RCDs and Lord Strathcona's Horse, to carry the Canadian colours. But a quarter-battalion of foot soldiers was of little use to the authorities now, and their services were soon dispensed with. At the end of the month Colonel Otter led the remainder of his battalion back to Capetown. They came home via the United Kingdom, where they were reviewed by the aged Queen Victoria, glorified by the Press, and lionized by the public.

After the fall of Pretoria, the Boers refused to surrender as the British had expected, but instead adopted irregular, 'guerilla' tactics. Their highly mobile 'commandos' excelled at hit and run engagements, such as destroying trains.
NAC/PA-173034

LILIEFONTEIN

Before that happened, the Royal Canadian Dragoons had won a peculiar distinction for themselves while serving with a 'search and destroy' column operating in the Komati river basin, in the northeastern Transvaal. The column, 1200 strong under a British officer, Brigadier-General Horace Smith-Dorrien, included British infantry and artillery as well as the CMR and 'D' Battery, RCFA. It moved in the traditional British fashion, with a slow and stately baggage train of ox wagons that stretched over some eight kilometres of *veldt*. On 7 November 1900, near a farm called Liliefontein, the column came under heavy fire from some three hundred angry Boers bent on driving it back and saving what farms they could from the torch. More commandos were seen arriving all the time, until they numbered perhaps five or six hundred, and Smith-Dorrien decided that on this occasion discretion was the better part of valour. He ordered a general withdrawal, to be covered by the Dragoons and a section (two guns) of 'D' Battery, with the CMR and a section of British guns on the exposed flank.

Because the baggage train moved so slowly, protecting it was a difficult chore. The *veldt* was treeless, with long rolling ridges, two or three kilometres from crest to crest, and the Canadians' tactics called for one field gun to limber up and withdraw to the next ridge back, while the other gun and the Dragoons held off the angry Boers. Then the other gun would withdraw, leaving just the Dragoons — who had one of the Colt machine guns on a galloping carriage with them — to hold off the enemy. The resumption of fire by the second field gun was the signal for the Dragoons to follow the gunners, and then the whole process would be repeated. But the pace of withdrawal was in reality dictated by the measured tread of the oxen.

Soon the Boers were buzzing around both flanks, compelling the Dragoons, less than a hundred strong, to form a deeper and deeper arc and further stretching Colonel Lessard's meagre resources. "I turned in my saddle and saw a sight the like of which had not been seen before in this war," wrote Lieutenant Morrison.

Square across our rear a line of Boers a mile long was coming on at a gallop over the plain, firing from their horses. It looked like the spectacular finale in a wild west show. They were about 1,500 yards away, but coming on rapidly and shooting at our gun, most of them, to try and stop it. I looked up the plain to the ridge we had to reach and I thought indeed we saw our finish.

A Royal Canadian Dragoon patrol on the *veldt*, October 1900. RCD Archives

Sergeant E. Holland of the Royal Canadian Dragoons manning a Colt machine gun at Liliefontein, 7 November 1900. Covering the retreat of a British column while under attack by Boer guerillas, Sergeant Holland, Lieutenant R.E.W. Turner and Lieutenant H.Z.C. Cockburn distinguished themselves, and all three were awarded the Victoria Cross.

Courtesy of the Commanding Officer, The Royal Canadian Dragoons

At that range, from the back of a galloping horse, even a Boer would only hit anything by accident, but the screen of Dragoons was much closer to the Boers than the guns were. The two troops under most pressure were those of Lieutenants R.E.W. Turner and H.Z.C. Cockburn, all of whom had wisely dismounted to fire. The machine gun was with them and a Boer participant in the charge remembered how, "as we came over the ridge bullets were flying and the Maxims [sic] were firing furiously 250 yards in front of us. As we dismounted we found ourselves among the nearest group of Englishmen [all their enemies were Englishmen to the Boers] and the riders following us rode right past us and stormed towards the Maxim."

Sergeant E. Holland, in charge of the machine gun which our Boer wrongly identified as a Maxim:

... looked for the limber horse but she was further away than the Boers. A trooper with four horses was nearby and I got one from him. I grabbed the gun — which was so hot that it burned my hands.... It was some trouble to get mounted but I managed it and started for the main body. The Boers followed me for 700 yards shooting at me, but he [sic] missed.

Lieutenant R.E.W. Turner, VC. During the First World War, Turner commanded both the 3rd Brigade and the 2nd Canadian Division in action, and later commanded all Canadians in England. RCD Archives

Smith-Dorrien had recognized what was happening and started his British infantry back towards the rear of the column. Their arrival, together with the intervention of the CMR, finally thwarted the Boers. The Dragoons had lost three killed and eleven wounded, among the latter both Turner and Cockburn, as the crestfallen column scurried back towards Belfast.

It has often been British policy to try and mitigate failure with a liberal distribution of decorations, and this time the Canadians were the beneficiaries. Turner, Cockburn and Holland were each awarded a Victoria Cross and Trooper W.A. Knisley, who was also recommended for a VC for rescuing a wounded comrade during the engagement, received the Distinguished Service Medal; Lieutenant Morrison became a member of the Distinguished Service Order for his efforts, and General Smith-Dorrien issued a special Order of the Day in which he proclaimed that he "would choose no other mounted troops in the world before them if he had his choice, and he sincerely hopes that the day may come when he may have them again under his command."

Whether the Canadians reciprocated his feelings is uncertain. Although the First Contingent had received one draft from Canada while in the field, and Lord Strathcona had taken care to see that his regiment had started the campaign with some replacements in hand to meet foreseeable needs, Ottawa had apparently overlooked the possibility that the Second Contingent might need some too. Since arriving in South Africa seven months earlier, the drain on their ranks from battle, disease and plain hard living had reduced the strengths of both the RCD and the CMR to less than a third of their establishments.

Colonel Lessard went to Pretoria to discuss the future of his men with the British authorities there. Three days later he was back, to tell them that each man had the choice of returning to Canada or re-enlisting in an irregular corps of Canadian Scouts which was being formed. The same choice was offered to the CMR and the RCFA, for men who could ride and look after themselves in the field were more in demand than ever now that the war had become nothing more than a counter-insurgency campaign. A few men volunteered, but the vast majority chose to go home, having learned that there was little romance and much hardship associated with real soldiering.

'... the best of the seasoned colonials... excelled all other troops.' After the departure of the official Canadian Contingents, the British sought to make good use of those who chose to remain. These are scouts from 'C' Company (Canadian) of the South African Constabulary, Transvaal, May 1902. NAC/C-7987

THE SECOND CONTINGENT GOES HOME

The remnants of the Second Contingent left South Africa on 12 December 1900, sailing directly to Canada, while the Strathconas left on 12 January, bound for England, where they marched through the streets of London to Buckingham Palace and heard King Edward VII tell them to "be assured that neither I nor the British nation will ever forget the valuable service you have rendered in South Africa." Their week in London was one long succession of parties and receptions, and when the regiment finally embarked for Canada on 22 February 1901, even its redoubtable commanding officer was feeling the strain. "This was the first time for years that I felt the need of a rest, and I took full advantage of it."

In South Africa the fighting dragged on. Mounted infantry scoured the *veldt*, foot soldiers manned blockhouses, while Boer women and children were herded into the original concentration camps where numbers of them died from disease and administrative incompetence. As a variety of Dominion and colonial contingents wound up their engagements with the Crown there was a demand for yet more hard-riding men to hunt down the diminishing bands of ragged, desolate Boers still in the field. The Dominions made fine recruiting grounds. A *second* 2nd Battalion, Canadian Mounted Rifles, this time paid for and equipped by the British government, arrived in South Africa in January 1902, but they saw little active service. The 3rd, 4th, 5th and 6th Battalions of Mounted Rifles reached the Cape only days before the exhausted Boers finally resigned themselves to foreign rule in the Treaty of Vereeniging, signed on 31 May 1902.

The Strathconas stopped off in London, England on their way home to receive their South African medals. Here Lord Strathcona is shown with his regiment. LdSH Museum

Altogether, 89 Canadians serving in Canadian units (there were a number of Canadians with other forces — even a few in the Boer ranks) were killed in action or died of wounds, and 252 were wounded. Another 135 died in accidents or by disease out of the 7368 who served in South Africa.

For their grieving families the price may have been high, but in terms of the national interest it was low. Canadians had established themselves as hardy, reliable, fighting men in the eyes of both Briton and Boer, a reputation bolstered by the four Victoria Crosses they had won — three in one day by the Royal Canadian Dragoons, one by the Strathconas — together with nineteen Distinguished Service Orders (for officers) and fifteen Distinguished Conduct Medals (for other ranks). Let us not forget Robert Thompson's Queen's Scarf. And the Militia establishment had learned some valuable lessons about the demands of modern war which would shortly be put into practice at home.

The Royal Canadian Regiment parades through London after returning from South Africa, December 1900. Glenbow Museum NA-3052-9

CHAPTER 4

SOUTH AFRICA TO THE GREAT WAR

by
Stephen J. Harris

THE DEPARTURE OF HUTTON

By the time Canadian troops returned from South Africa, General Hutton and his reforming zeal had gone. Although he and Militia Minister Fred Borden agreed in general on the kinds of changes that should be made, Hutton wanted to move too far, too fast to get rid of political influence in military (and particularly Militia) affairs. He had also severely compromised his position by appearing to have worked behind the scenes, in collusion with the Colonial Office, to secure Canadian participation in the Boer War. Incensed at the general's apparently higher loyalty to British interests, the Canadian government demanded that he be recalled, and with very little opposition from Britain, he was.

FREDERICK BORDEN AND ARMY REFORM

It was indicative of Borden's desire for reform, however, that significant changes were made to Canada's military organization between 1900 and 1903 despite the absence of a strong British General Officer Commanding. Moreover, many were aimed at the Permanent Force, both to make it more efficient and to improve the conditions of service for Canada's regular soldiers. A pension scheme, denied for two decades, was introduced in 1901. Pay rates were increased in 1902. And living-out allowances were made available to most officers in 1903, giving them an alternative to living in small rooms in cramped, old, and uncomfortable military barracks.

Senior officers of the Militia gathered after a 'Staff Ride' — discussion of theoretical tactical problems — at Niagara Camp in the summer of 1898. NAC/C-31361

The 3rd Battalion of the Royal Canadian Regiment changing the guard at Wellington Barracks in the Halifax Citadel, 1900.
PANS/N-6015

In the past, improvements along these lines would have been heavily criticized as unnecessary extravagances. But when Borden placed these measures before Parliament even such strong and vocal opponents of the Permanent Force as Sam Hughes held their tongues. Very likely the casualty lists from South Africa and the performance of the Royal Canadian Regiment at Paardeberg had something to do with this. In Borden's own case, it seems quite certain that the death of his son on active service had made him understand the 'unlimited liability' involved in a military career, a realization which made him better disposed towards the regular force.

These reforms were welcome enough, but there was more. Between 1903 and 1906 the size of the Permanent Force was doubled to 2000 officers and men to accommodate the formation of regular companies of Royal Canadian Engineers, Army Service Corps, Canadian Ordnance Corps, Canadian Army Medical Corps, Canadian Corps of Signals, staff clerks, an intelligence branch, and pay staffs. At the same time, authority over the engineering and stores branches was transferred from the Deputy Minister of the Militia Department to the General Officer Commanding, bringing them into the military chain of command.

For the first time, then, Canada's Permanent Force began to resemble a small standing army, complete in every way. Moreover, this army would have the opportunity to train for war even while continuing to fulfil its primary role of instructing the Militia. A large parcel of land was acquired for this purpose on the Ottawa River at Petawawa, and by 1905 the camp had already proved its value. The Royal Canadian Horse Artillery and Royal Canadian Garrison Artillery were both able to train at the new facility, and it was felt that they had "learnt far more of what they would have to do on [active] service than at any previous camps."

Some of these reforms also touched the citizen force. Militia counterparts of the regular force Engineers, Signallers, Ordnance Corps, and Service Corps were authorized, and the latter in particular soon made an impact. In 1905 the *Canadian Military Gazette* observed that the quality of food at summer camps had improved greatly because Service Corps units would not accept the inferior goods contractors had been accustomed to supplying in the past.

Regimental tent lines of the 8th New Brunswick Hussars at Camp Sussex in the summer of 1900. New Brunswick Provincial Archives

In 1907 the *Gazette* was even more lavish in its praise. "Why is it," the editor asked

... that ... with the soldier's wage as inferior to the labor wage ... we find our regiments going out in even better strength than formerly and with decidedly a better lot of men.... It is because the C.A.S.C. has so improved the comforts and conveniences of the men that the last hardship has been removed and only the real pleasures and advantages remain.

Not everyone went to camp, however. City regiments were still limited to training at their armoury, and although (the GOC reported)

... the Officers and men ... put in many more hours ... than the [Militia] Act requires...in the limited space of a drill hall it is impossible to impart anything beyond theoretical instruction on scouting, outpost duties, hasty entrenchments, the attack and defence of positions, tactical marches, etc., which are the more important portions of a soldier's training.

NCOs and troopers of the 8th Hussars attending a course at the Cavalry Corps school in Toronto in the winter of 1901. 8CH Archives

Musketry, the essential military skill of the time, was promoted by competitions such as the Dominion of Canada Rifle Association shoot at the Connaught range in Ottawa, September 1900. NAC/PA-16978

The city men were also unused to the rigours of outdoor life, something which became very clear at the grand military review held for the Duke and Duchess of Cornwall and York held in Toronto in the fall of 1901. Almost 11,000 militiamen from all over Southern Ontario were involved in the spectacle, which turned out, as one historian has noted, to be

> *... an unexpected triumph for the rural battalions. Not only had they marched far better than anyone had expected, proof of the value of annual camps and of the increasing competence of their officers, but they had also managed to look after themselves in camp while men from the arrogant city battalions had been unable even to erect their own tents. It was the city men, too, who had depended on civilian caterers for their meals, leading to scenes of disorder and much complaint, while the rural troops had fared much better with their own cooks and rations.*

In short, the Militia had much to learn before it became the efficient National Army — able to withstand the first few weeks of campaigning — called for by the Leach Committee, the body which had examined the state of Canadian defences following the 1895-1896 Venezuelan crisis.

Local militiamen parade near Calgary, 1901.
Glenbow Museum NA-1075-18

THE LAST GOC

It fell to Lord Dundonald, appointed GOC in 1902, to persuade the Dominion government to create this army. Dundonald was a terrible choice for such a delicate task. Like Herbert, he believed that nothing could be done to help the Militia until the regulars were thoroughly efficient, a view which, despite the recent softening of feelings, was still contrary to the mainstream of Canadian opinion. Moreover, he was also convinced that Canada must make itself ready to fight the United States, a scenario with which the government did not agree and did not want to accept. Finally, the GOC argued that as Canada's senior soldier he had a right to be heard by the Canadian public, whether the politicians liked what he was saying or not.

The 44th Battalion guarding a road during manoeuvres at Queenston, Ontario in June 1906. NAC/PA-16662

Dundonald was soon in trouble. When parts of his initial (and highly critical) annual report were suppressed by the Minister, the GOC not only let it be known that he had been muzzled, but also disclosed what had been kept from public view. The Governor General, Lord Minto, reported grimly that he doubted whether Dundonald would last out the spring, at which time the Canadians were sure to appoint one of their own as GOC. But he did survive, at least for a while, and was able to begin working towards his own plan of reform. For one thing, he secured a promise from the Minister that future vacancies in the Permanent Force officer corps would be filled in the first instance by graduates of RMC, next by graduates of Canadian civilian universities, and only then by Militia officers, who would be given probationary appointments until they had qualified. And when, in 1904, he learned that the defence budget would be cut for the next fiscal year, Dundonald persuaded Borden that Militia training should be sacrificed until the job of rejuvenating the regulars was complete.

But Dundonald's personality eventually got the better of him. When the government chose not to accept one of his nominees for a Militia appointment — a man who happened to be a well-known Conservative — the GOC complained publicly. He also gave the foremost Conservative defence critic, Sam Hughes, complete details of the alleged interference to be used against the government in the House of Commons. When this was discovered, he was promptly dismissed.

Members of the 31st (Grey) Battalion preparing to leave for home at the end of the summer camp at Niagara, 23 June 1906. NAC/PA-166653

THE BORDEN-LAKE PARTNERSHIP

Dundonald's departure gave Frederick Borden the opportunity to introduce sweeping changes at Militia Headquarters. The appointment of GOC was done away with, and replaced by a Militia Council and general staff system in which control, management, and direction of the Army would be shared by the Minister, a Chief of the General Staff, and the Adjutant General, Quartermaster General, and Master General of the Ordnance. This paralleled recent developments in Britain, where the old office of Commander-in-Chief of the Army had also been done away with.

Military efficiency was cited as the reason for this reorganization in both Britain and Canada. The creation of a separate general staff was intended to allow the CGS to concentrate on mobilization planning and operational doctrine and would in time, it was thought, provide the benefits of the Prussian military system within the British constitutional framework. However, in both countries the new structure was also intended to ease civil-military tensions. No longer would a single soldier be able to speak for the Army, claiming that he had independent authority over areas of purely military concern.

The guard at the entrance to the Halifax Citadel, 1902.

Critics of the new organization argued, however, that civilian power and influence over the Army had grown significantly and that the "doors of political interference" had been thrown wide open. Moreover, the provision in Borden's Militia Bill allowing a Canadian to be appointed Chief of the General Staff suggested, to some, that Imperial military solidarity was breaking down. This fear was reinforced, to a limited extent, when Canada formally took over responsibility for the fortresses at Halifax and Esquimalt in 1905-1906 — a move which brought, incidentally, a further increase in Permanent Force strength to 4000 officers and men.

General Sir William Dillon Otter

General Otter's life story reads like a history of the Canadian Army through the late 19th and early 20th centuries. He joined the Queen's Own Rifles in 1861 at the age of 18. He was with the Queen's Own at the Battle of Ridgeway in 1866, and rose to command that regiment in 1874. He joined the Permanent Force when it was formed, and was the first commanding officer of the Royal Canadian Regiment when the companies of the School of Infantry were united. He commanded a column under General Middleton during the North West Rebellion in 1885, and he took the Royal Canadian Regiment to South Africa in 1899. He was the first Canadian Chief of the General Staff 1908-1910, and was Inspector General 1910-1912. During the First War he was Director of Internment Operations. He retired in 1920 after 59 years of service, in the rank of General.

As it happened, however, Borden's organizational reforms did not slow the pace of the Canadian military renaissance. He was not about to sacrifice military efficiency at the altar of ministerial power, and a Canadian was *not* named as the first CGS. Instead, that appointment went to Major-General Sir Percy Lake, who had been Quartermaster General in the 1890s.

Lake and Borden worked well together, and together they oversaw the modernization of the higher organization of the Canadian Army. Officers from the Permanent Force were routinely sent to Britain to attend the Staff College at Camberley and various senior officers' courses. Meanwhile, until a sufficient number of Canadians had been staff trained, British officers were appointed to senior staff positions at Militia Headquarters to bring the country's mobilization planning up to date.

Major-General W.D. Otter, the Canadian commander in South Africa, replaced Lake as CGS in 1908, but this made little difference to the reform programme that was, by now, well under way. The opportunities for the Permanent Force to train were expanded, and mobilization planning continued. Indeed, partly at Otter's initiative, a mobilization planning committee was established at Headquarters to consider not only problems of home defence, but also what Canada might do to help Britain and the Empire overseas. Militia war establishments were revised to correspond to those drafted for the British Territorial Army, the whole of the force was organized into six divisions, and by October 1911 a revised mobilization scheme noted, for the first time, that a Canadian infantry division and a cavalry brigade might one day be called upon to serve abroad, alongside the British Army, against "a civilized country in a temperate climate."

This represented a revolution in the ordering and management of defence policy in Canada. In the past, Dominion governments had regularly rejected the notion that potential crises needed to be prepared for in advance; and no prime minister had ever been willing to suggest, ahead of time, that Canadian troops would leave North America to assist the Empire. Now, however, not only was contingency planning considered a normal and accepted function for the general staff, but overseas contingents were also being talked about.

A Militia camp in Eastern Ontario in the summer of 1907.
NAC/PA-31383

THE MILITIA RENAISSANCE

Major-General William Otter inspecting the 16th Light Horse at Fort Qu'appelle, Saskatchewan during Militia manoeuvres in June 1909. NAC/PA-31346

The Militia, too, benefitted from the Borden-Lake-Otter reforms. The number of days of paid drill was increased from sixteen to thirty; pay rates climbed; and bonuses were given to both good shots and those who returned for their second, third, and fourth camps. Regiments were authorized to take qualified musketry instructors on strength, the building of rifle ranges was accelerated, and the supply of ammunition to Militia units was significantly increased. Brigade and divisional camps were revived, so that in 1906 the number of men who drilled for at least twelve days rose to 40,000, a far cry from the ten thousand or so of the late 1870s. Khaki uniforms began to be issued to the Militia, replacing the denims and straw hats (or shabby, worn-out full dress) that had been the norm for many years. The Canadian-made Ross Rifle was distributed to the infantry while the artillery received 12-pounder breech-loading guns and even more modern 18-pounder quick-firing guns. Finally, the training syllabus was simplified for both the infantry and cavalry, the latter being employed ever more frequently as mounted rifles.

Although city units were still confined to local training, they were also encouraged to attempt more complex tactical exercises near home. Over the 1906 Thanksgiving weekend, for example, 4000 officers and men from urban regiments in Southern Ontario joined the Toronto company of The Royal Canadian Regiment for manoeuvres along the Credit River. "The operation, divisional, and brigade orders were clear and concise," the Inspector General reported, and were

... carried out in an enthusiastic and soldierlike manner, except in a few instances when two detachments of the Permanent Force failed to turn up at their prescribed rendez-vous, and wandered off upon their own account without escort or support; and where men were unnecessarily exposed to a fire that, in actual service, would have caused them most serious loss.

The mistake that caused the defeat of one side was that the commander left one of his flanks open. He, no doubt, was imbued with the idea that his enemy would do a certain thing, when in fact the enemy did the very opposite. It is dangerous to conclude that an enemy has but one line of defence or attack.

Everyone knows that the permanent force and many city regiments are well trained, but their individual training is not sufficient unless their organization, mobilization, and efficient handling ... is assured in time of peace.

Within three years, city regiments were again authorized to attend summer camp. In 1910 about 16,000 city soldiers did so, and when they arrived they found a completely new system in effect. Practically all ceremonial drill had been eliminated from the training syllabus, priority being given instead to all-arms "tactical work in the field" with special emphasis on "attack and defence," "information and reconnaissance," and "orders, reports, and protection."

A grand military parade was a central feature of the Tercentenary Celebrations at Quebec City in July 1908. NAC/PA-24720

Some of the camps, this year, were inspected by Sir John French, who would command the BEF in 1914 and who pulled no punches. While applauding the recent change in emphasis from parade drill to manoeuvres in the field, he added that much more should be done. Additional camp sites large enough to permit realistic tactical schemes needed to be opened, and great care taken to ensure that officers and non-commissioned officers used their time to learn. The proof of this had come at Petawawa, where five brigades of artillery had carried out their training. "The Imperial Inspector-General has accorded high praise to the field brigades," it was recorded:

The large area of ground available, and the commencement of the instructional gun-practice on the fifth day of training, showed most striking results in efficiency as compared with the unsuitability of the training areas at local camps and the separation of camp training from service gun-practice, the ultimate objective of all training.... It is gratifying ... to be able to report that, while there are still too many officers who are not yet expert in the 'Application of Fire', and who imagine, mistakenly, that their own natural intelligence will, when combined with a casual study of Field Artillery

Training, be sufficient to produce satisfactory results in battle ... yet there is evident a decided improvement in Artillery knowledge.... As regards Heavy Artillery, decided progress has been made this year in manoeuvre; officers are now realizing its necessity.

In asking units to spend more of their time in the field, and to spend more time doing tactical training rather than drill, the authorities were not ignoring the fact that full dress uniforms and military pageants and tournaments were every bit as important to city units as they had been thirty and forty years before. Recruits had to be attracted to the Militia somehow, and it was not because they had good reputations for field soldiering that the Queen's Own Rifles and Royal Highlanders (Black Watch) were able to raise second battalions. What Toronto lad who was not Scottish — Scots joined the 48th Highlanders — would have wanted to serve elsewhere when it was learned that in 1910 Sir Henry Pellatt, commanding officer and chief benefactor of the Queen's Own, would take six hundred officers and men to attend the British Army's autumn manoeuvres at Aldershot — at his own expense.

Lord Strathcona inspecting his regiment, September 1909.
LdSH Archives

In rural areas, meanwhile, summer training was increasingly scheduled so as not to conflict with the demands of farm life. In 1911, when New Brunswick's 8th Hussars took close to 350 officers and men to their annual exercise:

Summer camp fell just between planting time and haying time, so it was great for the farmers. There'd be notices posted about the dates, but you always knew it would come around that time.... First thing you'd do, you'd look around for a horse. A lot of boys got them at home. Others got them from relations or a neighbour for $1 a day. A few days before it was time to go you'd take your horse ... and have a veterinary look her over.... The horses had to be just right.... [Then] you'd draw your saddle ... and your uniform and you'd head for home and try them on for size.

Like all Dominion cavalry, the 8th Hussars were told to train exclusively as mounted infantry, something which had not gone down well among many of the country's horse soldiers. Indeed, to traditionalists it was impossible, if not entirely wrongheaded, to teach true cavalrymen to be a mounted rifleman at the same time. But Lieutenant-Colonel W.A. Griesbach, commanding Edmonton's 19th Alberta Dragoons and convinced that Canadian Volunteers were "of a superior intellectual type," thought otherwise and therefore asked his men to be both. Whenever possible, they were

... to seek for the opportunity of a cavalry charge [so that], such an opportunity presenting itself, the men slung their rifles, drew their swords and rode at a top speed to strike the enemy when he was shocked by artillery fire or surprised by our action, and when he presented to us a favourable target. On the other hand, we [also] endeavoured to train our men for mounted rifle action and practised, in particular, rapid changes of position to enable us to escape shell-fire and to confuse the enemy as to where we were or what we were going to do next.... Thus, one of our frequent practices was to seek first a covered position for our horsemen and then a rapid advance over open ground, usually at a gallop towards a good firing position or a position from which we could deliver an infantry assault....

The intensified (and more interesting) training paid off. Recruits were easier to find, and with the addition of new units like Griesbach's, the Militia establishment soon reached 75,000.

Militia cavalrymen from Carleton County during the summer camp at Petawawa, June 1910. The straw camp hats were known as 'cows breakfasts'. Ontario Archives

A Squadron of the 8th Hussars on parade during the summer camp, 1911.
8CH Archives

NEW REGIMENTS OF INFANTRY AND CAVALRY FORMED 1905-1910

CURRENT DESIGNATION

1905	
15th Canadian Light Horse, Calgary, Alta	South Alberta Light Horse
16th Canadian Light Horse, Yorkton, Sask	North Saskatchewan Regiment
95th Regiment, Regina, Sask	Royal Regina Rifles
96th Lake Superior Regiment, Port Arthur, Ont	Lake Superior Scottish
1907	
18th Manitoba Mounted Rifles, Winnipeg, Man	
1908	
Alberta Mounted Rifles, Vegreville, Alta	
19th (Alberta) Mounted Rifles, Edmonton, Alta	
20th Mounted Rifles, Pipestone, Man	
9th Grey's Horse, Wingham, Ont	
Saskatchewan Light Horse, Lloydminster, Sask	North Saskatchewan Regiment
98th Regiment, Kenora, Ont	
99th Manitoba Rangers, Brandon, Man	
100th Winnipeg Grenadiers, Winnipeg, Man	
101st Regiment, Edmonton, Alta	Loyal Edmonton Regiment
102nd Rocky Mountain Rangers, Kamloops, BC	Rocky Mountain Rangers
1909	
25th Brant Dragoons, Brantford, Ont	
1910	
26th Stanstead Dragoons, Coaticook, Que	
27th Light Horse, Swift Current, Sask	
Earl Grey's Own Rifles, Prince Rupert, BC	
70th Colchester and Hants, Truro, NS	1 North Nova Scotia Highlanders
72nd Highlanders, Vancouver, BC	Seaforth Highlanders of Canada
79th Highlanders, Winnipeg, Man	Queen's Own Cameron Highlanders of Canada
103rd Calgary Regiment, Calgary, Alta	Calgary Highlanders
104th Regiment, New Westminster, BC	British Columbia Regiment

Moreover, most Militia officers had finally realized that they shouldered more than just social responsibilities when they accepted their commissions. It was taken for granted that they should qualify for their appointments, and growing numbers were attending the Militia Staff Course, patterned after the syllabus at the British Army Staff College at Camberley, to prepare themselves for staff and command appointments.

SAM HUGHES AND THE GLORIES OF AMATEUR SOLDIERING

Calgary Militia parade on the Coronation Day of King George V, 1911. Glenbow Museum NA-4277-9

The Canadian military renaissance of the early 1900s was partly the product of the Borden-Lake-Otter reforms. But it also reflected a brief period when Canadian society itself was militarized. The years around the turn of the century saw the birth and burgeoning of the cadet movement in Canadian schools, of pseudo-military organizations like the Boy Scouts, and of William Hamilton Merritt's campaign to introduce national military service into the Canadian way of life. Although such sentiments of imperialism and nationalism could support the creation of a modern, professional Canadian Army, they were also in harmony with beliefs grounded in an earlier age — in the Canadian Militia myth and its glorification of the citizen soldier — and in their own way they validated the quintessential amateurism of the Victorian Militia. Little wonder, then, that during the period the 8th Hussars were at camp in 1911, hardly touching their sabres as they learned to be mounted riflemen, time was found for a mid-Victorian style parade:

On the first of July there would be a great day of military pomp and athletic endeavour, parades, racing, wrestling on horseback, tent-pegging, tugs of war. By then the horses and men were usually sufficiently schooled to make a reasonably good appearance. People would come in from all over the countryside and the camp would *swarm with their carriages and with themselves, hundreds, sometimes thousands of them. They would sit and picnic beneath the great elm trees as the sun grew hotter. At night the officers would hold a dance in the Bungalow and the soldiers would steal their ice cream and even their whiskey if a close eye wasn't kept.*

Such mid-Victorian-style soldiering soon had a strong and powerful advocate in the Conservative Militia Minister who took office in 1911. Imperialist and nationalist, soldier and politician, proponent of scouting, cadet corps, and rifle clubs, Sam Hughes was the amateur warrior *par excellence* — and a man who had pilloried the Canadian regulars of the 1890s for their efforts to copy a British Army which, he declared mischievously (but truthfully enough), had been trounced by the Boers at the battle of Majuba Hill in 1881. And when he was refused an appointment on the front-line in South Africa in 1899, something he desperately wanted, he chortled that the reason had nothing to do with his lack of experience, but rather that unlike British and Canadian regulars, he was not ready to run away at the first sight of the enemy.

Bands were an important aspect of the pomp and ceremony that was expected of Militia units in their home communities. Shown here is the mounted band of the 2nd Dragoons at Petawawa in the summer of 1912. Ontario Archives

Despite his genuine and vigorous hostility to the Permanent Force, Hughes sat quietly in the House of Commons when Borden introduced his initial reforms in 1901 and 1902. But by 1911 he was angry again, convinced that the balance had shifted too much in favour of the regulars, and as Minister of Militia he set out to change things. "The days of standing armies are gone," he declared; "The old Saxon days have returned, when the whole nation must be armed." As a result, the Permanent Force establishment was allowed to fall; the regulars were told to stop training for war, and to concentrate instead on their instructional duties; and British officers serving at Headquarters were insulted, so much so that some left for home.

For the Militia, however, these were glorious times. Drill halls were built across the country; city units flocked to summer camps; and, to help out friends and satisfy specific parochial interests, Hughes not only reduced the standards for commissioning into in the Militia but also approved the formation of a number of smaller city regiments to represent (in particular) the country's Scottish and Irish heritage and to make room for associates eager to join up now that it was easier to become an officer.

The Inspector General complained loud and long about the inefficiencies and expense involved in forming these smaller units, and he worried about "the number of totally unqualified officers" posted to them. He also objected to the picnic-like atmosphere prevailing in so many of the camps attended by city units. Yet despite these flaws, and General Otter's concern about "the want of discipline and qualification" in the Army, Hughes had somehow touched a nerve, and was managing to rekindle the country's military ardour in a way not seen since 1868-1869. Units found it easier to recruit, and attendance at summer camps increased enormously. 55,000 men took summer training in 1913, and 64,000 were expected in 1914. New regiments were swelling the Militia establishment, and sites for two new camps were acquired: one, north of Toronto, to be called Borden (after Sir Frederick) and the other at Valcartier, outside Quebec City.

Headquarters of the 6th Mounted Brigade during exercises at Camp Sewell, Manitoba in July 1914. This was the largest peacetime concentration of cavalry ever held in Canada: 5400 officers and men and 3400 horses were on strength. NAC/PA-22692

NEW REGIMENTS OF MILITIA CAVALRY AND INFANTRY FORMED 1911-1914

	CURRENT DESIGNATION
1911	
1st Regiment, BC Horse, Vernon, BC	British Columbia Dragoons
2nd Regiment, BC Horse, Merrit, BC	
18th Canadian Light Horse, Rosetown, Sask	
28th New Brunswick Dragoons, St John, NB	1 Royal New Brunswick Regiment
1912	
32nd Manitoba Horse, Robin, Man	Fort Garry Horse
33rd Vaudreuil and Soulanges Hussars, Rigaud, Que	
34th Cavalry, Winnipeg, Man	Fort Garry Horse
88th Victoria Fusiliers, Victoria, BC	Canadian Scottish Regiment
105th Fusiliers, Saskatoon, Sask	North Saskatchewan Regiment
100th Winnipeg Light Infantry, Winnipeg, Man	Royal Winnipeg Rifles
1913	
11th Irish Fusiliers, Victoria, BC	
50th Regiment, Victoria, BC	Canadian Scottish Regiment
51st Regiment, Sault Ste Marie, Ont	49th Field Artillery Regiment
60th Rifles, Moose Jaw, Sask	Saskatchewan Dragoons
Prince Albert Volunteers, Prince Albert, Sask	North Saskatchewan Regiment
1914	
55th Regiment, Montreal, Que	
70th Regiment, Hull, Que	Le Régiment de Hull
81st Hants Regiment, Windsor, NS	1 Nova Scotia Highlanders
107th East Kootenay Regiment, Cranbrook, BC	
108th Regiment, Kitchener, Ont	Highland Fusiliers of Canada
109th Regiment, Toronto, Ont	

In the summer of 1914, the Militia was very much supported by the community, especially in rural areas. NAC/PA-16351

Very soon, both the new camps would be occupied by many more men than Hughes had ever imagined — many of them coming from these new regiments.

Europe in the summer of 1914 was divided into two armed camps. Britain, France, and Russia (with sundry allies in the Balkans) stood on one side; Germany, Turkey, and the Austro-Hungarian Empire on the other. This division of Europe had resulted from many things: France's desire to avenge her defeat by Germany in 1870-1871 and to recover the provinces she lost then, Austrian fear of pan-Slavic nationalism, German concern that it was being encircled and denied a rightful 'place in the sun', and Britain's feeling that Germany was simply becoming too strong for Europe. The idea behind these alliances, it was said, was to so balance the power that no one country could gain a decisive advantage that might lead it to attack another. But with all of their complex military obligations, and the belief that with modern weapons victory could be achieved through a sudden, overwhelming offensive, these alliance also made it very easy for a small, minor irritation to become a big war.

When the Austrian Crown Prince was assassinated in Bosnia (now part of Yugoslavia) by a fanatic Serb nationalist, and the Habsburg Empire made demands for unacceptable concessions from Serbia, Russia jumped to Serbia's aid. Russian mobilization triggered a response in Germany, and Germany's mobilization accomplished the same reaction in France and Britain. A process of inexorable march toward war was thus begun; a process which no one was able to control.

Infantrymen take cover behind stooks of grain during summer exercises in Ontario in July 1914. NAC/PA-16392

CHAPTER 5

ENTRY INTO THE GREAT WAR
1914-1915

by
John Marteinson

The early summer of 1914 had been one of the best in years, and Canadians were little concerned with crises brewing in the most distant corner of Europe. There had always been problems in the Balkans, it seemed, and no one appreciated or even sensed that the nations of Europe had embarked on an uncontrollable march toward one of the most terrible of wars in the history of mankind.

It had been a particularly good summer for the Militia, which had grown to its greatest strength ever. In early July, over 60,000 men had concentrated at training camps across the country for two weeks of musketry, drill and tactical manoeuvres. As the militiamen returned to their homes at the end of the training, none had any inkling that thousands of them would soon be called on to fight for four long years in what would come to be known as the Great War for Civilization. And, despite their recent training, none of them were prepared for what they would encounter.

The mobilization of massive armies that had begun in Europe took its inevitable course toward war. Because of the German Army's inflexible strategy — the Schlieffen Plan — Germany was committed to seeking victory over France first, despite the fact that it was in large part reacting to Russian threats in the East. Accordingly, on 3 August the German Army moved en masse against France, through neutral Belgium. Britain, which had treaty obligations to protect Belgian neutrality, delivered an ultimatum to Germany to withdraw immediately. When the ultimatum expired at midnight on 4 August, Britain was at war with Germany.

Canada had no say in any of this. When Britain declared war, she did so for the whole Empire. Canada was also at war.

In fact, precautions had begun to be taken on 29 July, when Britain warned Ottawa of the deteriorating situation in Europe. The Royal Canadian Regiment was readied for a move to Halifax, and the port defences there, at Quebec, and at Esquimalt were fully manned. In Ottawa, at Militia Headquarters, it was time to dust off the mobilization plans. Two were on file. One, drafted in 1911 by then Lieutenant-Colonel, now Major General (and CGS) Sir Willoughby Gwatkin, called for an expeditionary force of one division and a cavalry brigade to be made up of composite units drawn from the various regions of the country according to their population. The other, drafted in the spring of 1914 by Lieutenant-Colonel G.C. Gordon-Hall, another British officer serving as Director of Military Operations, recommended that the division be formed by the best dozen or so Militia regiments.

Canadian patriotic symbols were widely used to stimulate recruiting in 1914.

From Canada in Khaki

A recruiting rally in Toronto in early August 1914. NAC/C-19200

Each plan was entirely hypothetical, of course — it was up to the government to decide what Canada's contribution would be — and each had its advantages and disadvantages. The formation of composite units, as recommended by Gwatkin, would probably have sacrificed some degree of *esprit de corps*, but it was one way around the fact that not all good units were up to strength, and that all good units had bad officers and men. Moreover, it would be easier to ensure that no region was asked to contribute more men than it could replace once there were casualties. Gordon-Hall, on the other hand, believed in the moral power of *esprit de corps*, and he worried about the reaction of the Militia when they discovered that, with the formation of composite units, already well-established units were being ignored as the country went to war.

However, both Gwatkin and Gordon-Hall agreed that the final selection of regimental officers should be left to the local divisional commanders, who knew them best, while the Chief of the General Staff should nominate brigade commanders and their senior staff officers. To avoid congestion, both plans called for units to be issued with their equipment and to do basic training at their local headquarters or, perhaps, camps organized in their home districts. Only when this was complete, and a final roster of officers and men had been determined, would the whole of the expeditionary force be brought together at Camp Petawawa, where it would receive the arms and equipment that had been purchased since the war began. Further training would take place there, so that when the division sailed for overseas it would require only some fine-tuning before it was ready to be sent into action. Gwatkin was quite prepared for this process to take weeks, or even months.

Klondike volunteers about to leave for Vancouver, late August 1914.
NAC/PA-4984

96

The Canadian government had actually offered a considerable force for overseas service on 2 August, but it was not until 6 August that Britain made known its eagerness to accept an infantry division. In the interim, sixty-two Militia units were placed on active service to guard vulnerable points such as harbours, dry docks, bridges, locks and canals, and electric power stations. On the evening of 6 August, the Minister of Militia, Sam Hughes, sent a night lettergram to the 226 Militia commanding officers across the nation announcing the formation of the Canadian Expeditionary Force, and inviting them to recruit volunteers for it. "The intention is to mobilize a contingent at Val Cartier, P.Q., where to secure the selection of the fittest more men will be assembled than in the first instance will be required."

Hughes, in other words, ignored both of the General Staff's plans and completely by-passed the normal military chain of command. Mobilization would he highly centralized — under the Minister's personal control — and all kitting-out and training would be done at the Expeditionary Force concentration point, the as yet unbuilt camp outside Quebec City. Sam Hughes would also be personally involved in all of the administrative and logistics preparations needed to assemble and send the contingent overseas. That there was a whole lot of confusion is an understatement, and for several days conflicting orders and counterorders produced something close to chaos. But men flocked to the Colours amidst great patriotic fervour.

While the recruiting of volunteers was being improvised in armouries and drill halls across the country, frantic efforts were begun to make a camp out of the scrub land at Valcartier. Roads and rifle ranges had to be built, water and sewage systems dug out (including twelve miles of water mains and sixteen of drains), the railway lines completed, and electricity and telephones installed. While most of this work was put in the hands of civil contractors, many of them political cronies of the Minister, the Permanent Force units not intended to be

Colonel Sam Hughes, Minister of Militia and Defence, 1911-1916. CDQ Archives

part of the CEF — the Dragoons, the Strathconas and A and B Batteries — were hastily sent to Valcartier to prepare for the arrival of the thousands of volunteers and to organize a program of training.

Since the Militia had never been permitted to maintain large stocks of uniforms or other equipment that might be needed for such an emergency expansion, there was an urgent need for just about every sort of thing that an army must have — weapons, uniforms, tents, blankets, wagons, vehicles, horses, medical supplies, rations and sundry other supplies and paraphernalia. And Canada's manufacturers were soon mobilized to the task. On 10 August, for example, contracts were placed for the manufacture of 65,000 pairs of boots, 35,000 caps, 15,000 greatcoats, 40,000 jackets, 33,000 pairs of puttees and 150,000 pairs of socks. Orders for all manner of needed equipment and supplies went out, with one proviso — that everything be delivered to Valcartier as soon as possible, but no later than 21 September.

Permanent Force units organized the training for the Canadian Expeditionary Force and administered the camp at Valcartier. RCD Archives

In the midst of the mobilization turmoil, one Canadian unit was raised in a very different manner. Even before the declaration of war, Captain Andrew Hamilton Gault, a veteran of the South African war, had offered to raise and equip a unit at his own expense. The offer, relayed through Ottawa, was quickly accepted by the British government, and the Princess Patricia's Canadian Light Infantry, named after the daughter of the Governor-General, the Duke of Connaught, was officially formed in Ottawa on 10 August. The Patricias recruited men from across the Dominion who had already seen military service, and by 19 August the battalion was at full strength. It was ready to sail for England by 28 August, but because of a shortage of shipping it joined the ever-growing ranks in Valcartier, and moved to Britain with the remainder of the Canadian Contingent.

Trainloads of men began to arrive in Valcartier camp on 19 August, well before its makeshift facilities were ready. The 20 thousand-man quota for a single division was greatly oversubscribed. On 22 August, Hughes told the House of Commons that 100 thousand men had volunteered, and that 27 thousand had got on the trains: "They simply climbed on and we couldn't keep them off." The desire for adventure no doubt appealed to many, but in areas like Ottawa, where the unemployment rate among tradesmen and unskilled workers was well above 50 percent, a purely economic motivation unquestionably played its part. For the British-born, who made up some two-thirds of the volunteers, duty to King and Empire was also a prime consideration. On 4 September, just a month after the declaration of war, 32,000 men and 8000 horses were at Valcartier.

Sam Hughes' initial plan was to organize the 1st Canadian Division on the basis of three brigades, each consisting of four 'numbered' infantry battalions, together with the usual mix of other arms and services — three field artillery brigades (equivalent to modern regiments), with 18-pounder guns, a heavy battery (60-pounder guns), three engineer companies, a signals company and the necessary Army Service Corps

support units. As they arrived, volunteers were assigned to provisional battalions according to where they had joined. By 1 September, however, so many more men had arrived than had been expected that the Division organization was restructured into four brigades — sixteen battalions.

As a result of the rather open invitation to serve, there was a very wide diversity in the military experience of the volunteers. Some had served in the Militia or the British Territorial Army, a few were Boer War veterans, while others had never before put on a uniform. Rudimentary training, therefore, took much of the available time. Drill, route marches and some elementary rifle shooting were about the only activities that most units were able to undertake. But the troops also had to be given medical examinations and inoculations, and issued with their uniforms and equipment. All this took even more time.

Royal Rifles of Canada volunteers, carrying Mark II Ross rifles, strike a 'soldierly' pose for the photographer. R22eR Museum

A group of very youthful First Contingent volunteers in typical living conditions at Valcartier.
R22eR Museum

In terms of equipment, 1st Division's troops would use the Canadian-designed Ross rifle, a wonderfully accurate weapon in target shooting, which was manufactured just outside Quebec. About half the contingent was issued current British-pattern web equipment; the rest had to make do with an older South-African war pattern which had no place for their packs and which cut the wearer severely under the arms. Each man was also to be issued with a 'MacAdam' shovel, a strange combination of shield and entrenching tool (with two holes in the shovel blade for sighting and shooting through) that had been patented by Sam Hughes' private secretary. The Expeditionary Force's transport was mainly horse-drawn, and 900 farm wagons and over 8000 horses were hastily purchased. Divisional ammunition columns were, however, slated to be motorized, and Canada's automobile manufacturers, eager for government contracts, responded with enthusiasm. Five different kinds of trucks were delivered to Valcartier, and all five were taken overseas. Vehicles for the motorized machine gun brigade formed under the command of Major R. Brutinel, a Frenchman resident in Canada, were purchased in the United States.

One of the five varieties of trucks hastily acquired for the Canadian Expeditionary Force. R22eR Museum

With so much going on at Valcartier, conditions were unavoidably chaotic. And continual interference by Hughes made things worse. Determined from the outset that the Expeditionary Force should bear his mark, he was preoccupied with who would serve in its officer corps. The divisional commander would be a 54-year-old British officer, Major-General E.A.H. Alderson, who had had Canadians under command in South Africa. As to the rest, Hughes was determined that they should share his values and his approach to soldiering. This meant, in the first instance, that many regular officers were not considered, certainly not for senior command, and also that many Liberals were ignored, or even dismissed. Command of the brigades, for example, went to Colonel R.E.W. Turner, who had won a VC while serving with the RCD in South Africa, and to Lieutenant-Colonels A.W. Currie and M.S. Mercer, all militiamen. The artillery was to be led by a regular, Lieutenant-Colonel H.E. Burstall, because of the technical complexities of that arm. In the battalions, meanwhile, at least one-third of the officers selected by Hughes had not met the minimum Militia qualifications for their rank. At times, Hughes made and unmade platoon, company, and battalion commanders on the spot. "Pipe up you little bastard," he yelled at one startled captain, "or get out of the service." Another captain, whom Hughes addressed by mistake as major immediately became one.

Some were overjoyed at what Hughes was doing. The old restraining hand of the Permanent Force, they said, was nowhere to be seen. Others were less impressed. Arthur Currie reported how everyone was at everyone's throat, with "every squirt of a politician" trying to win Hughes's favour. Major James Sutherland Brown, a regular just returned from the British Army Staff College, was disgusted by the antics of the "foolish and irritable minister [and] his crowd of sycophants."

One of the 16 battalions organized at Valcartier parades in front of a sea of bell tents.
NAC/C-36116

It had always been the government's intention to get the Expeditionary Force overseas as quickly as possible, and by the third week of September shipping agents had assembled a flotilla of 31 ships of sundry sizes and registry. One by one they docked in the harbour at Quebec, and loading began on 26 September. But the chaos continued. Far too little planning and preparatory work had been done for embarkation. No one seemed to know what was to be loaded when, or in which ships. Troops were all too often sent aboard only to find that there was no room for them, ordered to disembark, only to repeat the process again. Guns were put on without having their wheels removed, taking up unnecessary space. And horses, vehicles and baggage belonging to one unit were often loaded on ships carrying others. For lack of room a good deal of camp equipment that would have been most useful in England in the next months had to be left behind.

The grand convoy — the largest ever to sail from Canada — assembled in Gaspé Basin and sailed for England on 3 October, guarded by cruisers and battleships of the Royal Navy. On 6 October the convoy was joined at sea by a ship carrying the Newfoundland Regiment. The vaunted German submarine threat did not materialize, and the eleven-day crossing was comfortable and uneventful.

Troops board a train for the short journey to Quebec where they embarked for the voyage to England. R22eR Museum

Canada's Answer by Norman Wilkinson.
On 3 October 1914 the largest convoy ever to sail from Canada started out for England with the more than 30 thousand men of the Canadian Expeditionary Force and the many tons of equipment for the 1st Canadian Division. CWM 8934

1st CANADIAN DIVISION IN ENGLAND

The ships carrying the Canadian Contingent arrived in Plymouth and Devonport harbours on 14 October. The Division Commander, newly-promoted Lieutenant-General Alderson was at the dock to greet the first arrivals. Again inadequate planning was very much evident: unloading of the troop stores and equipment took nine days, and everything was piled indiscriminately on the docks and roadways. As the troops were disembarked, trains carried the men to hastily set-up tented camps on the edges of the British Army's training area at Salisbury Plain. Here, the units of the Division were meant to hone their fighting skills before joining the British Expeditionary Force in France.

By the time the 1st Division had sorted out their stores and had settled in, the war across the English Channel had taken a very different turn. The German advance had been stopped at the Battle of the Marne on 10 September, but repeated efforts by the French and British to push them back or to outflank them had failed. By mid-October the opposing armies had dug continuous lines of trenches that extended from the North Sea coast of Belgium all the way to the Swiss border. And these lines of trenches — dug ever deeper, expanded by the addition of successive lines of entrenchments, and increasingly protected by thick entanglements of barbed wire — remained the front line for much of the next four years. And on 12 October the first battle had begun at Ypres — a name that would become all too familiar to Canadians over the next three years.

Lieutenant-General Sir E.A.H. Alderson, first commander of the 1st Canadian Division, and commander of the Canadian Corps September 1915 to May 1916. CDQ Archives

The fourteen weeks that the units of 1st Division spent in England proved to be a miserable foretaste of the severe conditions they were to experience later at the front. Heavy rains began only a week after arrival, and it continued to rain for 89 of the next 123 days, turning the rolling countryside around Salisbury into a quagmire of mud. In addition, gale-force winds regularly blew down the tents. There was little fuel for heating, so uniforms, kit and blankets could never be dried out. With little hot water for baths or shaving or washing clothes, everyone felt dirty, and there was never enough food. "All was wetness, mud and misery," according to the Army's 'official' history of the war.

Wet and cold troops 'mudlarking' on Salisbury Plain, November 1914.
NAC/PA-22705

In these appalling conditions it was not surprising that some of the 'wild colonial boys' occasionally got themselves into a bit of trouble. Until General Alderson allowed 'wet' canteens to be set up, there were many incidents of rowdy drunkenness and brawling in the pubs in neighbouring villages.

The all-pervasive mud and rain also interfered seriously with training programs. Long route marches, drill, and digging trenches were possible, but the weather limited the amount of range practise, and many company and battalion field exercises had to be cancelled.

In mid-November, the Princess Patricia's Canadian Light Infantry, already well trained, were detached to the 80th Brigade of the British 27th Division, with whom they were to serve for the next seven months. The Patricias crossed to France on 21 December, and by the end of the first week of January 1915 they were in the line at St. Eloi. The unit thus became the first Canadians committed to battle in the First World War.

It was now that the poor quality of much of the Canadian equipment became all too apparent: boots disintegrated in the mud, wagons collapsed, and the Ross rifle gave unmistakable evidence of its tendency to jam under harsh field conditions. Nevertheless, by late January the Division was considered to be ready to go into action. On 4 February 1915, King George V came to Salisbury Plain for a Royal Review, and between 7 and 16 February the 1st, 2nd and 3rd Brigades were moved to France. The 4th Brigade was left behind in England as a training and reinforcement base.

At this same time the only Permanent Force units to go overseas with the First Contingent — The Royal Canadian Dragoons, Lord Strathcona's Horse and the two Royal Canadian Horse Artillery batteries — were brigaded with a British territorial cavalry unit, the 2nd King Edward's Horse, to form the Canadian Cavalry Brigade. The 6th Battalion was given back its original name, The Fort Garry Horse, and reorganized as the Cavalry Depot regiment. Command of the Cavalry Brigade was given to a high-spirited and innovative British officer, Brigadier-General the Right Honourable Jack Seely, who until shortly before the war had been Secretary of State for War in the British cabinet. Other than for a period in 1915, the Canadian cavalry served apart from the other Canadians, and they added their own laurels to the Canadian military heritage.

Back in Canada, a Second Contingent was already being prepared to move to Europe. Mobilization of this Contingent — intended to become the 2nd Canadian Division, as well as to supply reinforcements for both divisions — had begun even as the 1st Division was leaving Valcartier. Because Sam Hughes had gone to England in early October, this mobilization was carried out in accordance with General Gwatkin's 1911 plan, and things went very smoothly. Fifteen additional numbered battalions — the 18th to the 32nd — were authorized in early November, as well as four regiments of Mounted Rifles, additional artillery and sundry other logistics and service units. A further nineteen infantry battalions were approved in early December — the 33rd to 51st — and by the end of 1914 over 50 thousand troops were training in Canada.

The 10th Battalion pass Stonehenge on a route march during a brief period of dry weather in December 1914. NAC/PA-117875

INTO THE TRENCHES

A severe winter storm made the 1st Division's crossing to France long and rough and thoroughly unpleasant. And because of a submarine scare some of the ships had to remain at sea for nearly five days before arriving in port at St. Nazaire. The troops were thus greatly relieved to get ashore, and battalion after battalion formed up at dockside for a two-kilometre march to the railway station. Here the men were loaded into unheated boxcars which bore a label they would see many more times in the next three years — "men 40, horses 8". An extraordinarily circuitous rail journey took a long 43 hours to reach Hazebrouck in northern France. The Division had finally reached the front.

For the latter part of February each of the Canadian units spent a week in the trenches near Armentières with experienced British units, where they were given as good an indoctrination as was possible in that short time in fighting and living in the trenches.

On 3 March, 1st Canadian Division was made responsible for a 6000-metre sector of the front at Fleurbaix, some 5 kilometres south of Armentières. Two brigades were deployed in the trench lines, with the third held in the rear area in reserve. Actually, it is somewhat misleading to speak of 'trenches' in this sector, as the water table limited digging to about a half metre at best. The 'trench' lines therefore consisted largely of earth and sandbag walls built up roughly a metre and a half above the ground. To make these trench walls relatively solid — and thus bulletproof — the sandbag filling wherever possible consisted mainly of broken brick. Duckboards were laid on the trench floors in an effort, mostly wasted, to keep soldiers' feet out of the foul-smelling water in the trench bottoms.

Landing of the First Canadian Division at Saint Nazaire by Edgar Bundy.
Led by the pipes of the 13th Battalion, 18,500 officers and men came ashore in France on 15 February 1915. CWM 8121

The Fleurbaix sector was, generally, considered to be 'quiet' during the 21 days the Division spent there, although the Germans regularly shelled the trenches and the rear area. There was a brief flurry of excitement on 10 March when neighbouring British divisions launched an attack on the village of Neuve Chapelle, the first stage of what was intended to be a major offensive to break through the German lines toward Aubers Ridge. During the attack, the 1st Division was tasked to create a 'diversion' by pouring a heavy weight of fire onto the German line, thus pinning them down on their front. The attack was successful, but further advance was halted by a serious shortage of artillery ammunition, and by the arrival of German reinforcements. It was, nonetheless, a salutary lesson in the realities of warfare for the inexperienced Canadians: for the gain of only a few square kilometres the British suffered nearly 12 thousand casualties! Other lessons were also learned. There were many reports of the Ross rifle jamming during the rapid fire put in during the diversionary operation. And 'trench foot' — a breakdown of the skin of the feet caused by a combination of blood circulation being constricted by tight puttees and of feet being constantly wet and cold — was widely reported. The Division was relieved on 25 March. Even in this 'quiet' sector where there had been no real fighting, the Canadians had been bloodied: 68 men were killed and 210 wounded.

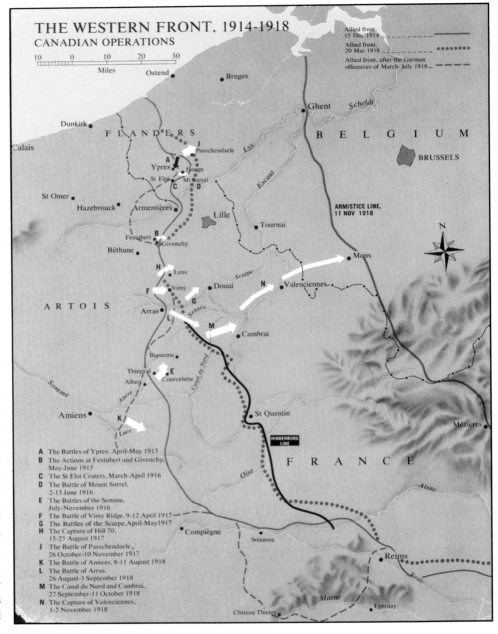

THE WESTERN FRONT, 1914-1918
CANADIAN OPERATIONS

Allied front, 15 Dec 1914
Allied front, 20 Mar 1918
Allied front, after the German offensives of March-July 1918

A   The Battles of Ypres, April-May 1915
B   The Actions at Festubert and Givenchy, May-June 1915
C   The St Eloi Craters, March-April 1916
D   The Battle of Mount Sorrel, 2-13 June 1916
E   The Battles of the Somme, July-November 1916
F   The Battle of Vimy Ridge, 9-12 April 1917
G   The Battles of the Scarpe, April-May 1917
H   The Capture of Hill 70, 15-25 August 1917
J   The Battle of Passchendaele, 26 October-10 November 1917
K   The Battle of Amiens, 8-11 August 1918
L   The Battle of Arras, 26 August-3 September 1918
M   The Canal du Nord and Cambrai, 27 September-11 October 1918
N   The Capture of Valenciennes, 1-2 November 1918

In the trenches south of Armentières. Official war photographers were not employed until the summer of 1916, so there are few photos of Canadians in action in 1915. Many periodicals, however, used illustrators to reconstruct battle scenes, and a number of these drawings were used by the Canadian War Records Office to illustrate the first volume of *Canada in Flanders*. The artists had no real knowledge of what happened in the field, so while the drawings are dramatic they were also generally inaccurate.

From *The Times History of the War*

THE SECOND BATTLE OF YPRES

On 1 April, 1st Canadian Division was ordered northward to join the 5th British Corps in defending what was known as the Ypres Salient. Here, the British had agreed to take over a sector of the line that had been held by the French Army.

Ypres, a large, ancient town in Belgian Flanders — more properly known as Yper, its Flemish name — had been the centre of hard-fought battles in October 1914 during the 'Race to the Sea' when the opposing armies tried, repeatedly, to outflank each other. Here, a leftover from the First Battle of Ypres, the Allied line 'bulged' in an 8-kilometre semi-circle (Salient) into German-held territory on the east and north of the town, and the ground rose gently towards the east to a series of 'ridges' that barely deserved the name. But in this generally flat countryside, those heights did give the Germans a major advantage: they could see much of what was happening between the Allied line and the town itself.

1st Canadian Division was assigned to defend a 4000-metre frontage in the northeast corner of the Salient, along with a narrow slice of ground that ran back to the northern outskirts of Ypres. The 28th British Division took over the sector on the right, while the French 45th Algerian Division retained the northern face of the Salient on the Canadian Division's left.

Between 14 and 17 April the Canadians gradually took over the sector. The 'defensive positions' left by the French barely existed. A forward 'line' consisted only of unconnected lengths of shallow trenches with frail breastworks to the front, most with no rear 'wall' or parados. Major Ormond, the Adjutant of the 10th (Calgary Highlanders) Battalion was clearly not impressed with what he found:

When the 1st Division moved into the Ypres Salient in April 1915, trenches, where they existed at all, were shallow and unconnected, and sandbag 'parapets' were haphazardly constructed.

From *Canada's Sons and Great Britain in the World War*

The trenches were extraordinarily filthy ... paved with dead Germans. When you'd move, bubbles would come up from the dead men. And it was very smelly. There was one place in the trench where there was a hand dangling through the parapet.... The wire in front was useless, very little of any kind and a lot of that simply smooth trip wire. It was so meagre that one of the machine gun sections ... walked through the wire and was on his way to the German lines when halted by a German sentry.

While a secondary line of trenches was shown on battle maps, it simply was not there, and a third line, some 4000 metres in the rear (later known as the GHQ line), consisted of no more than a 6-metre-wide belt of barbed wire and a string of strong points about 500 metres apart. The prospects of defending the sector against a concerted German attack were dismal, but that was precisely what was expected to happen, and soon.

Despite a ban on cameras at the front, a few private photos have survived. This shows Canadian troops in a reserve line.
NAC/PA-5723

General Alderson deployed the Division with two brigades at the front — 3rd Brigade, under Turner on the left, next to the Algerian Division, and 2nd Brigade, under Currie, on the right, bordering on the 28th British Division — each of which put two of its three battalions in the trenches. The others were kept behind the front both to develop a secondary line and to act as Division reserves. The 1st Brigade, commanded by General Mercer, was meanwhile assigned to the Second Army reserve for possible reinforcement of a 2nd Corps attack on the highest feature in the Salient, Hill 60, southeast of Ypres.

The Canadian front line for the most part ran in the shallow valley of a sluggish stream, the Stroombeek, with most of the trench line about 250 metres beyond the far bank. Some 1500 metres to the rear was the main height of ground in the Division's sector — Gravenstafel Ridge — which both brigades planned to use as a secondary defensive line. In the 3rd Brigade sector, a further 1000 metres in rear of Gravenstafel Ridge, the small village of St. Julien had been partially prepared as a strong point.

Intelligence reports were predicting a German offensive against the Salient any time after mid-April, and captured prisoners had even spoken of the planned use of 'poison gas'. Within the Canadian Division the construction of a defensible front line thus became an urgent priority. Thousands of sandbags were sent forward, and every available man was put to digging a continuous front line, as well as communications and support trenches, building up bullet-proof parapets and splinter-proof rear parados, and constructing barbed-wire obstacles in front of the trench lines. Some units were assigned to strengthen the defences at St. Julien and on Gravenstafel Ridge. All of this work had to be done at night to avoid being seen by the Germans, who were quick to call down artillery fire on any daylight activity they observed, as well as to avoid deadly accurate fire from German snipers. The increased intensity of the German bombardment after 18 April seemed to confirm that an attack was imminent, and work on improving the defences became even more urgent.

In a trench at Ypres. From *With the First Canadian Contingent*

Bruce Bairnsfather's cartoons, which captured the essence of life in the trenches, were popular with Canadian soldiers. 'Well, if you knows of a better 'ole, go to it', is one of the better known.

On the morning of 22 April troops in the forward area 'stood-to' an hour before dawn, as was usual routine. The German artillery resumed its heavy bombardment at daybreak, but as there was no other indication of an impending attack the units then went on with their now normal daylight routine — eating, shaving, cleaning their kit and rifles, and most important, getting some sleep after a long night of hard work. The troops could not know it, of course, but the Germans had indeed planned an attack for dawn that day, but had decided to postpone the assault because there was not enough wind for their experimental use of chlorine gas.

Late in the afternoon — just after 1600 hours — the German artillery concentrated its fire in a violent bombardment of the front line on the Canadians' left, and then gradually switched to the Canadian positions. An hour later the Germans opened the valves on 5700 cylinders of chlorine gas opposite the French positions. Even from within the Canadian area the resulting greenish-yellow cloud could be seen as it moved slowly through the French sector to a depth of nearly 2000 metres. Many of the French troops choked to death, writhing in their trenches. Others, overcome with panic at this pungent horror, fled in terror to the rear. The three German divisions that followed up advanced rapidly against almost non-existent defences. In fact, as the French divisions simply vanished, a gap nearly 4000 metres wide soon existed in the Allied line. And the whole of the Canadian Division's left flank was exposed!

Standing-to in the front line.
From *With the First Canadian Contingent*

What has been called the 'fog of war' quickly descended on 1st Canadian Division, and remained a problem for many hours. Telephone lines to many of the forward units were cut in the heavy bombardment, and those reports which were getting through to the various headquarters as to what was happening were often conflicting. For some time few knew that after advancing about 3000 metres into the French sector and reaching their assigned objectives, the Germans had halted for the night at about 1830 hours.

In the early hours of the battle, much of the action in the Canadian sector centred on the 13th (Royal Highlanders) Battalion — the left flank unit in the Division. As soon as Lieutenant-Colonel F.O.W. Loomis, the battalion commander, realized that the French were in trouble, he sent two platoons to reinforce his neighbour and strengthened the positions around St. Julien, where his headquarters was located. Loomis also did as much as was possible to prepare to defend the threatened left flank with the few troops at his disposal. To the southwest of the 13th Battalion in St. Julien, a battery of British 4.7-inch guns in Kitchener's Wood were the only troops between the former French lines and 3rd Brigade Headquarters at Mouse Trap Farm.

A field battery at the front. From *Canada's Sons*

At about 1900 hours, the 10th Field Battery, located about one kilometre north of St. Julien, was confronted by a large body of Germans marching southward. The Canadian gunners engaged the Germans over open sights at a range of under 300 metres, and sent an urgent appeal for help to Colonel Loomis at St. Julien. A mixed group of about 60 men from the 14th and 15th Battalions, and a machine-gun detachment from the 13th, were hastily sent forward. They became engaged in a fierce fight, but were ultimately successful in extricating the guns mainly because of the actions of one man, Lance-Corporal Frederick Fisher, who led the machine-gun detachment. At great personal risk, Fisher manoeuvred his machine gun forward several times into exposed positions from which he could bring effective fire onto the Germans, and they were ultimately forced to retreat. Fisher was killed in action the next day, but his valiant act did not go unnoticed: he was awarded the Victoria Cross posthumously. His was the first VC awarded to a Canadian during the First World War.

Lance Corporal Frederick Fisher, 13th Battalion, awarded the first Canadian Victoria Cross of the war at St. Julien, 22 April 1915.

As the evening wore on, the situation on 3rd Brigade's left remained very uncertain. Little of the flank was defended at all, and General Turner understood full well that the security of the whole of the Ypres Salient rested on his ability to improvise a coherent line of defence there. Aware that an undetermined number of the enemy had penetrated to the south edge of Kitchener's Wood, and believing that the best way to stabilize things was to drive them back, Turner asked for reinforcements from Division and from 2nd Brigade. At about 2000 hours, General Turner was informed that he had been given the 10th and the 16th (Canadian Scottish) Battalions for a counterattack on the wood. And at 2140 hours Brigade Headquarters issued orders for an attack to be launched less than two hours later.

The 10th and the 16th Battalions were finally assembled, although the 16th didn't arrive until 2345 hours. 'Zero' hour was set for midnight. The 10th Battalion was tasked to lead the attack, with the 16th following close behind. It was to prove to be an extremely difficult and costly operation. None of the officers or soldiers had any experience or training in night attacks, they did not know the ground or where the enemy was located, and no attempt was made to coordinate what each of the units would do once they got into the woods.

At midnight the 10th Battalion set off with two companies marching shoulder to shoulder in the front rank, the other two companies in two ranks 30 metres behind. The 16th followed another 30 metres in rear, in the same formation. About half the distance to the wood had been covered in relative silence when the leading line of the 10th came upon an unexpected hedgerow in which a wire fence had been erected.

Gaps were quickly cut in the wire, but the noise alerted the Germans, and flares and machine-gun fire met the battalions as they broke through. They charged the woods at a run, but large numbers were cut down in the withering fire. The covering artillery fire provided by the 9th and 12th Batteries was directed mainly at the far edge of the wood, so was not of much help in the assault. Many men did, however, get into the trees, but in both battalions most of the senior officers had been killed or wounded, and while many short and violent engagements took place, the soldiers quickly became confused and disoriented.

Eventually those troops that remained were rallied by the commanding officer of the 16th Battalion, and both units withdrew into a trench just beyond the south edge of the woods.

When a roll call was taken at dawn only 5 officers and 188 men answered in the 10th Battalion, while the 16th Battalion counted only 5 officers and 263 men. Well over a thousand men died or were wounded in the attack on Kitchener's Wood, and nearly a hundred were taken prisoner. The attack was no doubt a serious tactical failure, but that was certainly not for want of courage or enthusiasm on the part of the soldiers. They had done as much as could have been asked of them. They failed because the attack was poorly planned and badly coordinated, and because it was really beyond the capabilities of the still very inexperienced Canadian troops. Nonetheless, their effort may well have produced the desired strategic effect: the German high command paused and did not take advantage of the confusion or of the gap that still existed in the Allied line the next day.

Reinforcements continued to arrive in the 3rd Brigade area throughout the night. The 2nd (Eastern Ontario) and 3rd (Toronto) Battalions and part of the 7th (British Columbia) were put into the line to shore up the shaky defence north of St. Julien, five British battalions were sent to set up a hasty line southwest of St. Julien, and yet another counterattack was improvised for just before dawn. The 1st (Western Ontario) and 4th (Central Ontario) Battalions were given orders to support a French counterattack by striking toward Mauser Ridge, to the west of Kitchener's Wood. The French attack never developed, but the commanding officer of the 4th Battalion decided to carry out his order in any case, and at 0525 hours he began an advance. As soon as they got into the open, however, both battalions came under heavy artillery and machine-gun fire and took extremely large numbers of casualties. Once again the supporting artillery simply could not provide anything near the needed weight of suppressive fire.

The night attack on Kitchener's Wood by the 10th and 16th Battalions, 22 April 1915. From *Canada in Flanders*

The attack by the 4th Battalion on Mauser Ridge on the morning of 23 April. From *Canada in Flanders*

The 1st and 4th Battalions valiantly kept up their repeated attempts to advance, but the German resistance proved too strong. At 0830 hours General Mercer sent orders to dig in where they stood.

The Military Cross, instituted at the end of 1914 as a bravery decoration for junior officers. The first Canadian winner of an MC was Lieutenant W.D. Spinks of the 4th Battalion, for bravery during the attack on Mauser Ridge.

On the morning of 23 April the Canadians, who had shown superb fighting spirit in their first major engagement, still held firm. The original front line trenches were intact, and a thin but nearly continuous line of defence had been improvised on the Division's now open left flank.

For much of the remainder of the day, the main activity consisted of trying to improve the often precarious positions they had been forced to take up during the night and early morning. Some of the units were dangerously exposed to German sniper and machine-gun fire, most particularly the 10th and 16th Battalions in front of Kitchener's Wood, and the 1st and 4th Battalions in the open in front of Mauser Ridge. In these areas it was impossible even to get out of their hastily dug holes in the ground to rescue the large number of wounded, many calling repeatedly for help, who lay out in the open. And German artillery fire continued throughout the day against the Canadian 'front', adding to the already large number of dead and wounded. At brigade and Division headquarters one of the major problems was simply sorting out which units — or bits of them — were where, and in what strength.

British reinforcements began to arrive, and, complying with an order from 2nd Corps, General Alderson launched six British battalions in a further, and equally futile, counterattack against the German positions on Mauser Ridge. While some initial progress was made, extremely heavy casualties soon brought it to a halt. The 1st and 4th Battalions, who had dug in below Mauser Ridge after their failed attack earlier in the morning, joined the British units in the final stages of this effort, only to have even more of their men cut down. By nightfall, both units were at less than half strength.

During the course of the day, aerial reconnaissance had brought back reports of greatly increased enemy activity and of attack preparations opposite the original Canadian front, and it became obvious that a further German attack could be expected in the morning. Units holding the left end of the original Canadian line, now a narrow apex, were at greatest risk, and a decision was made to pull them back after dark. The 13th Battalion, and a British company of the 2nd East Kents that had reinforced them, were thus withdrawn to new positions near the western edge of Gravenstafel Ridge.

Darkness brought some measure of relief. The German bombardment let up, and the wounded could be recovered from the open fields and evacuated. Food was brought forward to the men, who had not eaten all day, and the much depleted stock of ammunition was resupplied. All through the night the Canadian units prepared themselves for the inevitable onslaught. And cotton-gauze masks were issued to some of the troops in the forward line in the hope they might provide some protection if the Germans again used gas.

Advanced dressing stations were the first stop for casualties evacuated by unit stretcher bearers. They were located as close to the front as was possible, and they were often shelled.

From *The Times History of the War*

THE BATTLE OF ST. JULIEN, 24 APRIL

While the German artillery kept up a bombardment much further north, nothing unusual took place opposite the Canadian lines during the night. Everyone, however, stood-to at 0300 hours. An hour later, sentries saw three red flares fired from a balloon tethered behind the German lines, and at once a ferocious bombardment hit all along the Canadian forward trenches. At the same time chlorine gas was released into No-Man's-Land opposite the 15th (48th Highlanders) and 8th (Winnipeg Rifles) Battalions. Ten minutes later wave after wave of German infantrymen climbed out from their trenches to follow the gas cloud, and an SOS was sent from both battalions for artillery fire. The response was immediate in the 8th Battalion sector, and the shrapnel barrage noticeably thinned the German assault. But there was no barrage for the 15th Battalion: the supporting battery had moved out of range during the night!

Gas Attack, Flanders, 1915 by Alfred Bastien. CWM 8086

As soon as the gas had begun to dissipate, the stricken left company was reinforced by a platoon from the rear, and every thrust by the Germans was thrown back, though at ever-increasing cost. Scores of acts of great personal bravery were recorded. One of the most notable of these was performed by Company Sergeant-Major Frederick Hall, who made a gallant attempt to rescue a badly wounded man who lay amidst heavy enemy fire forward of a trench. In his second attempt to reach the man, CSM Hall was killed just as he lifted the man to carry him to relative safety. He was awarded a posthumous Victoria Cross, the second of the war.

Company Sergeant-Major Frederick Hall, VC, 8th Battalion.

The 15th Battalion had an even more difficult time, in part because of the lack of artillery support, but also because of a slight rise in the ground in the centre of their sector. Here only one platoon of the centre company could give any fire support to the men on their right, who had borne the full effects of the gas. A stubborn resistance was put up, but eventually the survivors in the right company were forced to pull back. They attempted to make a stand 200 metres back, on the line of the Stroombeek River, but by 0600 hours they were so reduced that the Germans were able to penetrate to a depth of 700 metres — to the base of Gravenstafel Ridge — before they could be stopped. With the Germans now threatening their rear, the centre company was also forced to withdraw. The left company of the 15th, in what had been the tip of the apex, continued to fight, surrounded, until about 0830 hours when their ammunition was exhausted, and they were forced to surrender. By this time only a small remnant of

Gas attack on the 15th Battalion, 24 April 1915.

From Canada in Flanders

The deadly yellow-green cloud, 700 metres wide, was thickest along the inter-battalion boundary, and the men of the right company of the 15th and the left company of the 8th Battalion suffered its effects most severely. The wetted cotton-gauze masks gave little protection, nor did urine-soaked handkerchiefs which some men tried in desperation. Many fell in those two inner companies, and many more were blinded and near suffocation as the gas seared their eyes and lungs. Still, some struggled to man the parapets, while others, too overcome to stand, loaded rifles for their comrades as they lay at the bottom of the trench.

The gas cloud had missed the right-hand company of the 8th Battalion, and they raked the advancing German infantry with intense rifle and machine-gun fire. But the gas wasn't the only serious problem. In describing the fighting here, the official historian wrote:

The men of the centre and left companies who were still able to fight manned the parapet and emptied their Ross rifles into the advancing enemy, desperately jarring loose, with boot heel or entrenching-tool handle, stubborn rifle bolts that repeatedly jammed with the rapid fire.

At this first real test, the Ross rifle proved its complete inadequacy as a service rifle, no doubt at the cost of many Canadian lives.

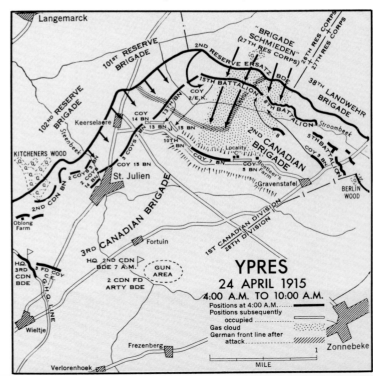

YPRES
24 APRIL 1915
4:00 A.M. TO 10:00 A.M.

Positions at 4:00 A.M. ——
Positions subsequently
occupied ....
Gas cloud
German front line after
attack ....

the 15th Battalion survived: their 647 casualties were the highest number suffered by any Canadian unit in a single action during the whole of the war.

On the northwest face of the apex, the Canadian front was heavily shelled along the whole length back as far as St. Julien, and there were many casualties. The 13th Battalion, which held the extreme end of the northwest face of the Canadian line, beat back an initial attack at 0400. A second, even heavier thrust came at 0830 hours, and this time the Germans could not be held. The battalion was forced to withdraw in full view of the enemy, and many more men were killed in the process.

Units that had not been engaged in this fight were hastily moved to bolster the now seriously endangered line. What was left of the 10th Battalion was deployed to Gravenstafel Ridge, and the beleaguered 8th Battalion got companies of the 5th (Western Cavalry) and 7th Battalions. The 16th was pulled back from Kitchener's Wood to strengthen a new line being created by 3rd Brigade, and the 2nd were sent to replace them. Companies and even platoons were thrown into the fighting with little regard to where their parent unit was located, and for many hours 'battalions' were simply ad hoc groups of men in the same general location.

The 13th Battalion (Black Watch) beat off a strong German attack before dawn on 24 April. Later attacks could not be held, and the unit took very heavy casualties as it was forced to pull back. *From Canada in Flanders*

The Second Battle of Ypres by Richard Jack.
Richard Jack's monumental work, which hangs in the Senate Chamber in Ottawa, was the first painting commissioned by the Canadian War Memorials Fund, set up by Lord Beaverbrook in November 1916. Many of the details are wrong, but it was the beginning of what would become the finest collection of war art in the world, now held by the Canadian War Museum. CWM

After five hours of intense fighting the Germans had succeeded in capturing the apex of the Salient, but nowhere had the Canadians been pushed back more than about 1000 metres. The day was far from over, however, and the Germans continued to attack repeatedly, with fresh battalions and in great numerical superiority.

In mid-morning the Germans mounted another major push against the 3rd Brigade units in the line northeast of St. Julien. Among the hardest hit of the units was the 7th Battalion. Its right-hand company had been all but destroyed in six hours of shelling, and the remainder were barely able to hold against the ever-increasing weight of the German effort. In this action yet another Victoria Cross was won. When every man in his crews had been killed or wounded, Lieutenant Edward Bellew, the Battalion Machine Gun Officer, manned one of the guns himself, pouring fire onto the advancing Germans until he was out of ammunition. He then destroyed the gun, and fought the enemy with pistol and then bayonet until he was overpowered and taken prisoner. His heroism was credited with having checked the German attack on his battalion.

On the Way to Roolers and Captivity by Arthur Nantel. Nantel was serving with the 14th Battalion (Royal Montreal Regiment) when he was taken prisoner during the fighting at St. Julien on 24 April. Here, Canadian and British prisoners are being escorted to the rear by German cavalry. CWM 8620

The Distinguished Service Order. Usually awarded to senior officers for commendable wartime service, it was sometimes awarded to junior officers as a gallantry decoration.

The situation continued to deteriorate northeast of St. Julien. All contact with Brigade Headquarters had been lost, so the commanding officers of the 7th, 14th and 15th Battalions decided amongst themselves to withdraw to a new line 300 metres to the rear. The 14th (Royal Montreal) and 15th were able to pull back, but the 7th Battalion was so closely pursued by the Germans that most of the men fell during the fighting withdrawal. "At the finish there was no ammunition and almost every rifle bolt had stuck."

By early afternoon enemy pressure forced a further withdrawal of 1000 metres. By this time the 3rd Brigade's very tenuous front beyond St. Julien consisted only of "survivors of fourteen companies belonging to five different battalions." In this confusion and disorder, the integrity of the defence of the whole Division was now threatened. 2nd Brigade, meanwhile, was still holding firm along its original front line as well as on Gravenstafel Ridge, but its left flank was now completely ex-

posed. And the small garrison on the Ridge was exposed to direct fire from the positions the Germans had just taken.

Without authority from Division headquarters, indeed without even informing either Division or 2nd Brigade, General Turner issued orders at 1340 hours for the whole of his Brigade to withdraw to what was called the 'GHQ Line' — 1500 metres southwest of St. Julien, and over 3500 metres in rear of Gravenstafel Ridge. At this very time, however, three fresh British battalions had begun to reinforce the 3rd Brigade. They had been sent forward by the Commander of 27th Division (who had been placed in charge of Corps reserves) to occupy positions some 500 metres south of St. Julien. Also at this time, General Currie personally went to the rear to look for units, British or Canadian, to shore up his left flank. Fortunately, the German division threatening Currie's brigade paused in their advance, and over the next several hours 2nd Brigade was able to begin the reorientation of its defences.

The Germans now focused their attention on St. Julien. The 2nd Battalion, acting on General Turner's order to withdraw to the GHQ Line, had literally crawled to the rear from their trench facing Kitchener's Wood. Part of its right-hand company and all that remained of the 3rd Battalion immediately to the west of St. Julien were, however, so heavily involved in close-in fighting that they could not pull back. This small group fought valiantly until about 1500 hours when, all ammunition gone and most of the men wounded, they were overrun. The last Canadians in the area, the small 13th Battalion garrison in St. Julien, put up a tenacious fight, but they too were overcome shortly after 1500 hours. Only an hour later, however, two additional British battalions joined the three already in position south of St. Julien. These five battalions halted another major German push southwards, and in a daring counterattack drove the Germans back beyond St. Julien.

The German offensive had been blocked, in large measure by the raw but tenacious troops of 1st Canadian Division.

That evening General Alderson was ordered by 5th Corps headquarters to launch a counterattack to retake St. Julien as soon as possible. He was given the 10th and 150th Brigades and five other British battalions for this operation, but not all arrived in time. The attack, carried out entirely by British troops, went in early on 25 April. The British could not, however, overcome the machine guns and the entrenched positions the Germans had established, and by 0915 hours it was over. The Germans inflicted more than 2400 casualties in these few hours, showing all too clearly the high cost of offensive operations in the type of warfare that had emerged on the Western Front.

Fighting continued in the Ypres Salient until the end of May, but most Canadian involvement ended on 25 April. The 1st and 3rd Brigades were sent to the rear for rest and reinforcement the next morning, while 2nd Brigade continued to hold a section of the line until the evening of 27 April, when it too was relieved. Division headquarters continued to be responsible for a much reduced sector until 3 May, but after 26 April, other than the Division artillery, its troops were all British.

Captain F.A. Scrimger, Medical Officer of the 14th Battalion, was awarded the Victoria Cross for 'greatest devotion to duty' on 25 April 1915.

One of the rare contemporary photos of the Ypres battlefield, showing a German casualty amidst the debris of battle.
RCD Archives

One Canadian unit — the Princess Patricia's Canadian Light Infantry — did remain. The Patricias, still with the British 80th Brigade, had served in the St. Eloi sector from 7 January to 23 March, during which time their commanding officer, Colonel Farquhar, was killed in the first major action in which Canadian troops played an important role. They came into the Ypres Salient on 9 April, and remained there until the end of May. The Regiment's action at Frezenberg Ridge on 8 May, when the Germans attacked in great strength, is particularly noteworthy. Early that morning much of the Patricias' front trench was blown away in a particularly violent bombardment, and most of the officers were killed or wounded. Lieutenant Niven, a platoon leader, took command of the battalion, and over the next nine hours the unit beat back repeated enemy attempts to advance. When the Patricias were relieved just before midnight, only 150 men remained. This gallant defence brought enduring honour to the unit and to Canada.

The Princess Patricias at Frezenberg by W.B. Wollen.
On 8 May, when all other officers had been killed or wounded, Lieutenant Hugh Niven took command; the remnants of the battalion beat back every German attack, but at the end of the day only 150 men remained. RCMI Museum

The Second Battle of Ypres was the 1st Canadian Division's baptism of fire. It is very much one of the 'great' battles in the history of the Canadian Army, perhaps even as much as Vimy Ridge and Amiens, or Dieppe, Ortona or Normandy in the Second World War. It was fought by young men who had only just become soldiers, young men who were totally unprepared for the horrendous sort of warfare in which gas, machine guns and massed artillery could kill and maim hundreds, even thousands in only a few short minutes. It was fought by men who were hindered at every step by rifles that failed them at the most critical moments. It was led by officers who, with rare exception, had little understanding of tactics or of operational planning, and even by some whose sole qualification for their rank was belonging to the right political party. But, all that said, it was fought by very brave men, men who never shrank from duty or great personal danger, men who showed remarkable initiative when it was most needed, and men who cared about their regimental brothers. They set an example for Canadians throughout the remainder of this hard-fought war, but the cost to the country was very high. 1st Canadian Division and the Princess Patricias took more than 6700 casualties in this battle, over 60 percent of the total strength of the infantry. And 1800 of those men were killed, while hundreds spent the remainder of the war years in German prisoner-of-war camps.

The battle-weary and much depleted units of 1st Division marched westward through the ruins of Ypres on 26 and 27 April for a period of much needed rest and recuperation. They were "a tough looking lot," wrote Private Wally Bennett of the 10th Battalion. "I hardly knew my own face: I hadn't seen a razor for seven or eight days, and my clothes were ragged and torn and still caked with mud." What the men wanted most was sleep, some food, a hot bath, and clean underwear and socks.

Reinforcements from England began to arrive in the Division's billeting area as early as 28 April, and over the next week the battalions were rebuilt as much as possible. No one had foreseen the possibility of so many casualties in so short a time, and even by stripping the 4th Brigade and sending all the 'spare' men who had been brought to England with the First Contingent, there were not enough to bring all battalions back up to full strength. General Alderson knew that it would not be long before the Division would be sent back into battle, and the new men were given a hasty indoctrination in the realities of trench warfare. The Division in fact had only two weeks to recuperate and prepare for the next series of bloody battles, this time in the No-Man's-Land at Festubert.

3rd Brigade troops together with French soldiers immediately after the battle.
DND/PMR-86-188

Canadians in a reserve line.
NAC/PA-5326

THE BATTLE OF FESTUBERT

At this early stage in the war, British and French leaders believed that the German Armies could still be forced into a major retreat if only the Allies could break through the enemy lines on a large enough scale. While even now it was recognized that the ever-more-strongly fortified trenches made the initial breakthrough exceedingly difficult, the generals were firmly of the opinion that persistence would win out, particularly if massive artillery bombardments preceded the infantry assault so that the enemy was "gradually and relentlessly worn down" beforehand.

In keeping with this theory, a major Allied offensive was planned for early May. The main effort was to be made by the French, just south of the junction with the British on the La Bassée Canal. The British part in this offensive was to be a two-division diversionary attack on Aubers Ridge. This grand Allied offensive began on 9 May, but the British attacks ended disastrously within twelve hours. Because he was still obligated to support the French, however, Sir Douglas Haig, the British commander-in-chief, decided to concentrate the British efforts on a narrow front between Neuve Chapelle and Festubert, just to the north of the Canal.

The first British attack at Festubert was launched at midnight on 15-16 May, after a 60-hour bombardment of the German lines. It was partially successful, and on a 3000-metre front the enemy withdrew to new positions in what had been one of their secondary lines. Interpreting this withdrawal as a sign that German resolve was weakening, rather than as the tactical move it actually was, General Haig ordered the attacks intensified. While few recognized it, a deadly war of attrition had begun. At this time 3rd Brigade was placed under command of 7th British Division to participate in an assault on 18 May. The remainder of 1st Canadian Division meanwhile was moved forward to prepare to relieve the 7th Division.

Over the next eight days, units of the 1st Division were to launch no less than five separate attacks in which they would be asked to accomplish impossible missions. No-Man's-Land between the Canadian and German trenches was waterlogged and completely flat and open, save for innumerable water-filled shell craters and remnants of drainage ditches, some as much as three metres wide. The German lines, situated on higher ground, dominated the whole of No-Man's-Land, and had been constructed so that a series of inter-linked, shell-proof machine gun emplacements could fire on much of this morass. And grossly inaccurate trench-maps that had been produced by the British compounded the planning and execution of every one of the attacks.

The first of the Canadian attacks at Festubert was put in by the 14th and 16th Battalions of 3rd Brigade at 1725 hours on 18 May. A British brigade had attacked an hour earlier immediately to the north, so the Germans were thoroughly

This highly stylized artist's reconstruction of 1st Division attacks during the Battle of Festubert gives some indication of the intensity of the fighting. From *The Times History of the War*

alerted when the Canadians set out. Both battalions came under heavy machine-gun fire as soon as they got into No-Man's-Land, and a severe shrapnel barrage brought all forward movement to a halt after the units had advanced only about 400 metres. Both battalions dug in during the night, while 2nd Brigade took over the line on 3rd Brigade's right.

The second attack took place in the early evening on 20 May, with 3rd Brigade tasked to take a 1000-metre section of the enemy's new line, along with a small orchard that came to be known as Canadian Orchard. 2nd Brigade was ordered to capture a strong point on the German front (designated 'K.5' on the trench map) which jutted into No-Man's-Land. "It was the same story of men advancing magnificently against a hail of machine-gun bullets," is how the official history describes the 3rd Brigade assault. On the left the 16th Battalion, showing great determination, captured the orchard and got to within a hundred metres of the German line. The 15th Battalion, on the right, took large numbers of casualties, but they advanced as far as an old section of the German trench before being forced to halt and dig in. It was a very different story in the 2nd Brigade sector where — only 100 metres into No-Man's-Land — every man in the forwardmost group was killed, and the 'suicidal advance' was called off by the commander.

In all of the attacks on German trenches at Festubert, 'bombs' — early varieties of hand grenades — proved to be among the most useful weapons. Each unit formed separate sections of 'bombers' from among the men who could throw accurately.

From *The Times History of the War*

The next evening yet another assault was made toward 'K.5' by the 10th Battalion. A three-and-a-half-hour bombardment had little effect on the German machine gunners, and the left company was cut to pieces. The other company, however, had remarkable success, and captured nearly 400 metres of the enemy line. They were quickly reinforced by a company of the 5th Battalion, and during the night they managed to beat off several counterattacks. But at daybreak the Germans began to shell the trenches with their heavy guns, and by noon casualties were so heavy that all but 100 metres of the captured trench had to be abandoned. General Haig personally berated General Alderson and his senior staff for the Canadians' repeated failure, and he ordered yet another attack for the next day.

The fourth of the attacks was put in at 0230 hours on 24 May. On the right the 5th Battalion took a novel approach, using twelve-foot-long bridges to cross a deep, water-filled ditch. Within a half hour of starting out, the 5th had captured the strong point at 'K.5' and over 100 metres of adjacent trench. But even that 'easy' operation cost the battalion 268 men. On the Division's left, a company of 3rd Battalion attempted to attack from the Canadian Orchard, but four German machine guns caught the men in the open, at a range of less than 100 metres, and all were killed.

A captured German trench at Festubert.
NAC/PA-5760

The 'Canadian Orchard' at Festubert, captured by the 16th Battalion on 16 May 1915.
NAC/PA-4447

Still one more attempt was made on the evening of 25 May, this time by the Canadian Cavalry Brigade (then called Seely's Detachment) who, to a man, had volunteered to serve as infantry because of the shortage of reinforcements. Seely's 1500 cavalrymen, none of whom had any experience in the trenches, had relieved the 2nd Brigade the previous evening. Their task was to clear another section of the German front trenches, from 'K.5', taken the previous night, to a strong point 300 metres to the northeast, designed 'L.8'. For this operation the Strathconas carried 200 chlorine gas 'bombs' — the first time that the use of gas had been authorized on the British front. The cavalrymen eventually, but wrongly, reported success. Being completely unfamiliar with the ground, and having totally inaccurate maps, they had lost their way and had actually worked their way along the wrong trench!

An artist's reconstruction of the attack by the Canadian Cavalry Brigade (then called Seely's Detachment) on the German strongpoint known as 'L.8'.
From *Canada in Flanders*

Members of
B Squadron of the
Royal Canadian
Dragoons in the
trenches at Festubert.
RCD Archives

The Canadians moved out of the trenches at Festubert on 31 May to take over the Givenchy sector, some three kilometres to the south. As they pulled out they left behind hundreds upon hundreds of dead Canadians to rot in No-Man's-Land; there had simply been no way to bring them out. The futile attacks at Festubert had cost Canada 2468 casualties for the gain of perhaps a thousand square metres of mud. No one, no force, could have done what had been asked of Canadian troops at Festubert. The German defences — the combined effect of reinforced strong points, machine guns in large numbers, thick barbed-wire barricades and plentiful artillery — had simply become too strong to be carried by men armed with rifles and bayonets. Unfortunately, it would take some time yet before that lesson would be understood by British generals.

GIVENCHY

The move to Givenchy gave the Canadians a two-week break from the intense fighting they had endured at Festubert. Here the Division was responsible for only 1000 metres of front, which required only one brigade in the line. Many of the men could thus enjoy some of the small pleasures still available behind the lines.

A section of the Canadian line at Givenchy. NAC/PA-5585

Estaminets, the village pubs, offered chips and eggs, and rough *vin ordinaire* was plentiful. Being able to keep clean was also a welcome novelty, and because the early June weather was unusually hot, many of the men took to swimming naked in the La Bassée Canal. Some officious staff officer is reported to have taken exception to this gross breach of decorum, and an order was duly passed down to the units forbidding swimming unless the men were clothed in "an adequate bathing costume". Quite obviously, none of the men kept bathing suits in their small packs at the front, but Canadian ingenuity saved the day: sandbags with two leg holes cut out provided an acceptable, if not very comfortable, solution.

The move to Givenchy also brought two other 'improvements' in the soldiers' lot. The disastrous Ross rifle was withdrawn, and all 1st Division troops were issued with the short Lee Enfield rifle, which was standard in the British Army. And the trenches in this sector were dry, a blessing in itself, but the dry ground enabled trenches to be dug deeper, giving far better protection in the front line, and making it possible to dig adequate communications trenches leading up to the front.

Soon after arriving in this sector, 1st Division was ordered to support a renewed Anglo-French offensive which was to begin on 15 June. This relatively long period of warning gave time for thorough reconnaissance and detailed planning at every level. The Division task was to capture two German strong points, one designated 'H.2', opposite the Division's northern boundary, the other 'H.3', 150 metres further north. The German front line in this area was very heavily fortified, and well protected throughout its length by a thick belt of barbed-wire entanglement. General Alderson and the Division staff knew, if the attacks on the strong points were to have any chance of success, that there had to be a lengthy and effective artillery bombardment, that adequate gaps had to be cut in the enemy's wire barrier, and that the German machine guns had to be knocked out before the assaulting troops got into No-Man's-Land.

By mid-1915, thick belts of barbed wire, such as shown here, had become a common feature of the battlefield landscape. Gaps had to be cut through the wire entanglements by artillery prior to any attack, or advancing troops got 'hung-up' and became easy targets for enemy machine guns.
NAC/C-30372

All of these considerations were included in the Division plan. There would be a 60-hour bombardment, the Division Artillery's 18-pounders were given the specific task of cutting the German wire, while three 18-pounder guns were specially fitted with armoured shields so they could be brought into the forward trench to fire over open sights at the German machine-gun emplacements just before Zero Hour. And to ensure that every man knew exactly what he was to do, the assaulting troops were put through detailed rehearsals in the rear area. It was a model of planning that would later be taken as an example for the whole of the Canadian Corps.

One further innovation was to be tried: British engineers were digging a tunnel under No-Man's-Land so as to be able to place an enormous mine as close to the 'H.2' strong point as was possible. This mine was to be exploded at Zero Hour to destroy the redoubt.

Zero Hour was set for 1800 hours on 15 June. Fifteen minutes before Zero the 18-pounder guns that had been hauled forward into the trench opposite 'H.2' opened fire on the German parapet, and at 1758 hours the mine was exploded. The 1st Battalion were ready to dash forward. But the explosion of the mine also blew back along the tunnel and killed a large number of the bombing party who were to lead the assault. The Germans, who had anticipated an attack, responded immediately to the explosion of the mine with a ferocious artillery barrage on the Canadian front. Consequently the 1st Battalion took a large number of casualties from the shelling even before getting into No-Man's-Land, and the 18-pounders in the front trench were both knocked out. (The third gun, further to the north, had not come into action, so that the machine guns at 'H.3' had not been dealt with.)

The two leading companies of the 1st Battalion, even though they had been hit by the German barrage as they went through the gaps in the wire, quickly got into the enemy's front trench. They were then able to 'lean-on' the covering barrage into the German second line. Here bombing parties set to work clearing the German trenches to left and right, but they were soon limited in what they could do because so many of the unit's bombs had been destroyed in the explosion of the mine. As the Germans recovered from the initial assault and bombardment, they began to mount increasingly strong counterattacks to regain the lost trenches.

During the 1st Battalion attack on 15 June, Private William Smith time and again carried bombs across No-Man's-Land to his comrades who were fighting in the German trench.

From Canada in Flanders

Artist's reconstruction of the action of Lieutenant Frederick Campbell of the 1st Battalion in stopping a German counterattack by firing a machine gun set up on Private Vincent's back. Campbell received the Victoria Cross for this act of gallantry; Vincent got a Distinguished Conduct Medal.

From *The Times History of the War*

The 1st Battalion's third and fourth companies were sent across to reinforce the companies already in the German line. Both companies, however, took heavy casualties while crossing No-Man's-Land from machine guns that had come back into action, particularly from those at the 'H.3' strong point.

Relentless German counterattacks soon created a critical situation for the Canadians in the enemy's second line. In this violent trench battle, one act of gallantry was particularly notable.

Lieutenant Frederick Campbell took two machine guns over the parapet, arrived at the German first line with one gun, and maintained his position there under very heavy rifle, machine-gun and bomb fire, notwithstanding the fact that almost the whole of his detachment had then been killed or wounded.

When our supply of bombs had become exhausted, this officer advanced his gun still further to an exposed position, and, by firing about 1000 rounds, succeeded in holding back the enemy's counterattack. This very gallant officer was subsequently wounded, and has since died.

The battlefield at Givenchy, photographed in 1919. NAC/PA-4451

Lieutenant Campbell was awarded the Victoria Cross, and the only other surviving member of detachment, Private H. Vincent, who supported the weapon on his back while Campbell fired, was awarded the Distinguished Conduct Medal.

German efforts to regain their lost front grew in ferocity during the waning hours of daylight. The 2nd and 3rd Battalions had both tried to send reinforcements, but because of intense machine-gun fire all had been stopped as soon as they stepped into No-Man's-Land. With reinforcement impossible, and with ammunition nearly exhausted, the 1st Battalion was forced to withdraw back to the Canadian line. The 3rd Battalion made another attempt late the next afternoon, but German machine-gun and artillery fire was so intense that the unit could not even cross No-Man's-Land and the attack was called off.

By 19 June the French offensive in Artois had ended in failure, so the British attacks were also called off. And on 24 June 1st Canadian Division was redeployed to a quiet sector of the front at Ploegsteert, some five kilometres north of Armentières and the Belgian border.

After three days of marching northward, the Division arrived at Ploegsteert, quickly dubbed 'Plugstreet' by the men, and on 27 June took over a 4000-metre line. 1st Division was to remain here for the next nine months, although the sector was substantially expanded later as the strength of the Canadian field army grew to Corps size.

A relief party marching through Ploogsteert Wood to the front line. From *The Times History of the War*

The warm summer months were a time of relative inactivity here. A 'live and let live' attitude seemed to prevail on both sides. There was an occasional exchange of light shelling and the odd sniper, but action directed at the Germans involved primarily night patrolling in No-Man's-Land and the experimental explosion of three mines in front of the Canadian trenches. A 1st Battalion soldier described this period as "life as good as it could be in the trenches."

The troops were in fact kept very busy. It had by now been recognized that trench warfare was likely to be a permanent feature of this war, and the near impenetrability of the elaborate system of trenches, bunkers and strong points developed by the Germans had been evident at Festubert and Givenchy. General Alderson thus decided to construct a strong complex of defensive works in the new Division sector, and there was a lot of work to be done, mainly at night.

Canadian defences at Ploogsteert. This is one of the early 'official' photos arranged by Lord Beaverbrook's Canadian War Records Office. *From Canada in Flanders*

The front line was strengthened in many ways: the forward trench was dug deeper so that men could walk upright, parapets were reinforced with additional layers of sandbags, and 'fire steps' were constructed along the front wall of the trench to enable men to get into position to fire over the now higher parapet. Wherever possible the trenches were zigzagged so as to create 'bays' for four or five men, both to limit the effects from shells bursting over the trench, and to prevent anyone firing down the whole length of it from a flank. Barbed-wire entanglements forward of the trenches were thickened, and concealed listening posts were dug forward in No-Man's-Land. And, to make themselves as comfortable as possible, the men were allowed to dig 'hoochies' into the rear walls of the trenches so that they could get under cover to sleep and eat. One innovation was the digging of deep, narrow 'safety' trenches just behind the forward line, where troops could go when the front line came under bombardment.

A second line of trenches — the support line — was dug some 50 to 60 metres in rear of the forward line. And a few hundred metres further back a series of sandbagged strong points were constructed to contain the guns of the Motor Machine Gun Brigade, which had arrived from England in late June. Covering the strong points was a subsidiary trench line about two kilometres in rear. All of these fortified lines were connected by communication trenches so men could move from one to the other under cover. It was a formidable defensive zone. And, as similar fortifications were built by both sides, the probability of assaulting infantry ever breaking through them became increasingly remote. The stage was being set for the horrible battles of attrition that would dominate warfare on the Western Front for the next two years.

FORMATION OF THE CANADIAN CORPS

The strength of the Canadian Expeditionary Force in Europe had by this time grown substantially. The 2nd Canadian Division had been formed in Canada on 25 May, under Major-General Sam Steele, and had moved to England in May and June. It was made up of 4th Brigade, under Lord Brooke (with the 18th, 19th, 20th and 21st Battalions); 5th Brigade, commanded by Brigadier-General David Watson (ex-2nd Battalion) (with the 22nd, 24th, 25th and 26th Battalions); and 6th Brigade, under Brigadier-General H.D.B. Ketchen (with the 27th, 28th, 29th and 31st Battalions). 2nd Division trained at Shorncliffe, in southern England, during the summer, and during one of Sam Hughes' periodic visits to England in August (during which he arranged to have himself Knighted), plans were agreed to move the Division to France in September, under the command of Richard Turner, who until then had commanded 3rd Brigade.

By mid-month 2nd Division was in France, ready to move into positions at the front. The commitment of two divisions to operations allowed for the formation of a Canadian Corps, and preparations for its establishment had been begun some time earlier.

The matter of command appointments had caused a degree of political fuss. At one time Sir Sam (as he now was) had considered having himself appointed as Corps Commander, while still carrying on as Minister of Militia, but reason prevailed and General Alderson, the only logical choice, was selected. General Arthur Currie was appointed to succeed Alderson in command of 1st Division. General Mercer was given command of Corps Troops and his replacement in 1st Brigade was Brigadier-General Louis Lipsett, who had done a sterling job as commanding officer of the 8th Battalion. Turner's successor in 3rd Brigade was Brigadier-General R.G.E. Leckie. The most controversial of all of these new appointments was in 2nd Brigade, where Sam Hughes' son, Garnet, was given command at his father's insistence. The younger Hughes had performed badly while Brigade Major of 3rd Brigade, and was roundly distrusted by the battalion commanders, one of whom even wrote a letter to a newspaper in Canada expressing his deep concern for the lives of young Canadians who would have to serve under Hughes' command.

The whole array of Corps Troops was brought into being under General Mercer — additional artillery, engineers, medical and logistics units — and a number of battalions which would later become part of 3rd Division were temporarily grouped here, including the PPCLI, the Royal Canadian Regiment, fresh from nearly a year of duty in Bermuda, and the (now dismounted) 1st and 2nd Canadian Mounted Rifle Brigades.

Canadian Corps headquarters opened on 13 September, taking over the sector held by 1st Division. Its front was extended five kilometres northward between 19 and 23 September, when 2nd Division occupied that part of the line. The Canadian Corps was now a substantial fighting force, with a strength of 1354 officers and 36,522 men. And in the next month its size would increase even more.

Canadian medical facilities grew along with the rapid expansion of the Canadian Expeditionary Force, and many nursing sisters were sent overseas. Shown here is Lieutenant Blanche Lavallée, en route to No. 4 Stationary Hospital in France. DND/PMR-86-344

WINTER IN THE TRENCHES

Stalemate descended over much of the Western Front just as the newly formed Canadian Corps consolidated its enlarged sector of the line. His Majesty the King visited the Corps on 27 October, and the next day the winter rain began. It came down in torrents day after day, and for much of the next four months the weather was as much of an enemy as were the Germans.

There was no escape from [the rain]. The trenches ... simply dissolved. The earth within the sandbags liquefied and oozed out. Everything collapsed. Every indentation of the ground filled with water.

Men at the front had to spend days on end in thigh-deep water. The lucky ones had waist-high rubber trench waders, but there were never enough of them to go around. And there was simply no shelter to go to: the dug-outs that had been so carefully prepared during the dry weather were either flooded or had collapsed.

The intensity of the rain let up somewhat in late November, and hand-operated pumps were able to keep down the level of the water in the forward trenches. But ankle-deep, slimy mud was everywhere and on everything. The men had only one uniform, and usually only two pair of socks, so there was no possibility of drying out clothing or boots. And, as there was no way to keep clean in these appalling conditions, everyone soon had a healthy crop of lice. As the temperature fell to near freezing for much of the next two months, it was sustained, bleak misery. The only brief respite from being cold, wet and dirty came once every ten days or so when units were marched through the divisional baths. Here, besides a luxuriously hot shower, the men got a clean pair of underwear, while their shirts and uniform were disinfected to kill the lice. The daily issue of a large tot of service rum, supposedly to ward off the cold, was just about the only pleasure the men had to look forward to.

There was always a lot of work to be done during the winter months in draining and repairing the continually eroding trenches. The Germans opposite obviously had similar problems, and they rarely created difficulties at the front. General Alderson, however, was insistent that if morale was to be maintained, the 'offensive spirit' had to be reinforced.

During the winter of 1915-16, the trenches that had been so carefully constructed during the summer filled with water, and the defensive works simply dissolved. From *With the First Canadian Contingent*

Keeping sandbags filled during the continual rain was a never-ending task: the contents all too quickly liquefied and oozed out. From *With The First Canadian Contingent*

The units, therefore, were pressured into keeping up a programme of night patrolling in No-Man's-Land as well as a full training schedule whenever they were out of the line. Several large-scale trench raids were carried out in November and December, and the first of these, put in on the night of 16-17 November, served as a model for similar raids in the future. Ninety volunteers from each of the 5th and 7th Battalions rehearsed day and night for ten days on ground similar to the objectives, until every man knew precisely what his role would be. While the 5th Battalion raid ran into problems, that of the 7th was a great success, and Canadian intelligence officers were particularly pleased to be able to examine the rubber gas masks carried by the twelve prisoners brought back.

On Christmas Day 1915 the formation of the 3rd Canadian Division was authorized under Major-General M.S. Mercer, who since September had been commanding the Corps Troops. 7th Brigade, commanded by ex-Strathcona Brigadier-General Archie Macdonell, consisted of the Patricias, the RCR, and the 42nd and 49th Battalions. 8th Brigade, commanded by Brigadier-General V.A.S. Williams, former Adjutant-General of Militia, was made up of the 1st, 2nd, 4th and 5th Battalions of the Canadian Mounted Rifles. The 9th Brigade was not formed until late February 1916, but the first two brigades began their operational indoctrination before the end of the year. At the beginning of 1916 the Canadian Corps had grown to close to 50 thousand men, and more were on the way.

Captains Alexander and Nunn of the Newfoundland Regiment
in the front line at Suvla Bay in Gallipoli, November 1915.

Provincial Archives of Newfoundland and Labrador, VA 37-113

The Newfoundland Regiment, which had moved to Britain in October 1914 with the convoy carrying the First Canadian Contingent, spent the winter of 1914 in training camps in Scotland. In early 1915 the Regiment was moved south to the large British camp at Aldershot, and in September was sent to Egypt en route to its first operational commitment — the Gallipoli peninsula in Turkey.

An Allied force of British, Australian, New Zealand and French divisions had landed in Gallipoli in late April 1915 in hopes of opening the Dardanelles to supplies to Russia, and of drawing several of the Balkan nations to the Allied side in the war. Lethargic generalship, however, had led to near disaster, condemning the Allied forces to shallow beach-heads, where, as on the Western Front, both sides dug in and

bitter trench warfare ensued. The Newfoundlanders were among the many reinforcements sent in to bolster the hard-pressed British.

The Newfoundlanders were put ashore at Suvla Bay, on the western side of the peninsula, on the night of 19 September to reinforce the beleaguered 29th Division. From the very beginning the Regiment had a difficult time. The Turks, on commanding heights of ground, poured artillery, machine-gun and sniper fire onto the unit line, and casualties grew day by day. Even resupply by night was a serious problem, and there was often a severe shortage of food and water. The unit played an important part in advancing the Division line on 4 November, and in hard fighting at Caribou Hill two Distinguished Conduct Medals and a Military Cross were awarded.

In late November the weather became the principal enemy, as it was in Flanders. A severe winter storm struck on 26 November, and three days of torrential rain and sleet created flash floods that washed away entire trenches and much of the unit's equipment. The temperature fell rapidly to well below zero, and the sleet became an intense blizzard. Water bottles froze solid, and, with no shelter and no food, the men suffered severely. A number even died from exposure. By 10 December the Regiment was down to quarter strength.

The hopelessness of the Gallipoli campaign had by then been recognized, and British authorities decided to withdraw. On 20 December the Newfoundlanders were evacuated from Suvla, pressed by the Turks even as the last man pulled out. They served until 12 January at Cape Helles, the southern tip of the peninsula, assisting in the final evacuation of the force. By then only 170 men were left.

The Newfoundland Regiment was moved to France on 22 March 1916, where the small remnant of the unit was built up once again into a well-trained fighting unit, and prepared for their next engagement — on the Somme.

The 1914-15 Star, awarded to Canadian and British soldiers who served in a theatre of war prior to 31 December 1915.

'Dugouts' of the Newfoundland Regiment at Cape Helles, at the tip of the Gallipoli peninsula, January 1916.
Provincial Archives of Newfoundland, VA 37-311

CHAPTER 6

IN THE MUD OF FLANDERS AND FRANCE
1916-1917

by
John Marteinson

Throughout the early winter months of 1916 the Canadian Corps held the muddy front from Ploegsteert to just north of Kemmel. The cold, damp weather continued to cause enormous misery to the troops until well into March, when the rain let up somewhat. Casualties — mainly from German shelling — continued to mount, even though there was no major action. Over the first three months of 1916, 546 men were killed, and 1543 were wounded. Morale, however, remained remarkably high despite the relative inactivity, the constant discomfort and the steady losses. Some escape was occasionally possible, as the troops were now permitted short periods of leave in the towns in the rear area where they could drink plentiful quantities of rough *vin rouge*. But one of the new amenities most welcomed by the troops were the improvised laundry facilities now being set up alongside the Divisional baths. When they did get the rare luxury of having a shower, the men no longer had to put on damp and filthy uniforms.

A Night Raid by H.J. Mowat
Canadians became the acknowledged experts among the Allies in the art of mounting trench raids to harass the enemy and to gain information. CWM 8559

Early in January the Corps said farewell to a group that had served with 1st Division since late June of 1915. While the place of horsed cavalry was no doubt questionable in a war dominated by machine guns and massed artillery, 'Seely's Detachment' was reconstituted as the Canadian Cavalry Brigade. The Fort Garry Horse, mobilized as the 6th Battalion, was brought from England to replace a British unit, the 2nd King Edward's Horse, and a Machine Gun Squadron was formed to give the brigade that bit of extra 'punch'. The Canadian cavalrymen were grouped with the British 5th Cavalry Division to train for the major Franco-British offensive of the year — a great push to be launched in July astride the River Somme. The hope still existed that a massive infantry assault could break the German line, and that cavalry, in great numbers, would be needed to "gallop through the 'G' in Gap", and roll up the German defences. For the remainder of the war, the Canadian Cavalry Brigade served apart from the Canadian Corps.

While the Corps sector was indeed 'quiet' in this period, the Germans were never quite allowed to let down their guard. Night patrols and ambushes in No-Man's-Land were routine operations, and trench raids were mounted periodically as a means of keeping pressure on the enemy. The main value of the raids, however, was probably in allowing some scope for the innate ingenuity and cunning of Canadian soldiers.

Cold and extremely wet weather caused enormous misery throughout the winter of 1915-16. This cartoon from *Canada in Khaki* was not much of an exaggeration.

3rd Canadian Division, meanwhile, was brought to full operational status. Its battalions, and later entire brigades, were put into the line with 1st and 2nd Divisions between mid-January and mid-March for periods of intense training in the methods of fighting and surviving in the trenches. Indeed, so many infantry battalions were now being raised and sent to England that the government at this time offered to form a 4th Division. The Canadian Corps was thus being built into a fighting force that few would have thought possible a year earlier.

A trench on the Canadian front. NAC/PA-1326

THE ST. ELOI CRATERS

By the end of February 1916, the commander of the British Second Army had concluded that the Canadian Corps was now ready to take over a more active sector of the front. Plans were thus made for the Corps to exchange sectors with its northern neighbour, V British Corps, in the southeast part of the Ypres Salient.

Prior to this exchange of sectors, however, the British had been told to straighten a 500-metre section of the front at St. Eloi, where the Germans held a slightly elevated feature which projected uncomfortably into the British line.

Two hours before dawn on 27 March the British artillery began an intense barrage over the whole depth of the German position, and six large mines were blown. The effects of the massive explosions were far greater than had been expected. "The eruption blotted out old landmarks and collapsed trenches on both sides like packs of cards," reads the official history. What was dubbed Crater 3, in the centre, was 15 metres deep and more than 55 metres across. Craters 2, 4 and 5 were only slightly smaller. And each was surrounded by a 50-metre-wide lip of muddy earth that rose as much as six metres above ground level. These four craters were so close together that they formed a virtually impassable barrier, and the mounds of debris blocked all view forward from the old British front line.

Manning the front line in the Ypres Salient, April 1916. This was one of the first photos showing Canadian troops wearing steel helmets, which were issued in March 1916. NAC/C-6984

135

During the early hours of 4 April units of Brigadier-General Ketchen's 6th Brigade relieved the then exhausted British in front of St. Eloi. There they encountered conditions that could not have been worse. In most places the forward 'trench' was little more than a shallow indentation in the mud, and in daylight it proved to be in full view of enemy artillery observers. The reserve line, behind the craters, was little better, except that the Germans now were not able to see it because of the crater lips. Here the explosion of the mines had obliterated long sections of what had been the British front trench, and what remained of this line was nearly a metre deep in water.

On 4 and 5 April the Germans shelled the St. Eloi front with greater intensity than had ever been experienced in the Salient. By noon on the 4th, over half of the men in the forward companies of the 27th Battalion had been killed or wounded, and the unit was forced to pull back, leaving only small detachments with machine guns forward of the craters. Heroic efforts were made by large working parties from 4th and 5th Brigades during the next two nights to dig forward and support trenches, and to dig a communications trench from the forward line to the rear, but their work was only a rough beginning of what was needed.

The 29th Battalion began to relieve the much depleted forward companies of the 27th Battalion after dark on 5 April. The relief was not yet completed when, at 0330 hours, the Germans attacked. It was impossible to put up much resistance in these circumstances, and within three hours the Germans had seized the four large craters in the centre. A number of counterattacks were attempted during the next week, but they accomplished little. The 31st Battalion reported that they had retaken Craters 4 and 5, but they had in fact occupied the smaller Craters 6 and 7, on the left. The mistake was not identified for more than a week, and some of the misdirected efforts to dislodge the Germans may have occurred because of confusion as to locations. On 13 April General Turner, the Division Commander, cancelled any further attempts to regain the craters, and both sides consolidated positions where they stood.

The fighting at St. Eloi was a most unsatisfactory introduction to battle for 2nd Division. In nine days of frustrating effort, in the very worst of conditions, it had taken 1373 casualties, and to no purpose. The sodden condition of the ground, together with the difficulty in determining locations caused by the greatly altered lay of the terrain, were among the reasons for the failure to dislodge the Germans from the craters at St. Eloi. But the real responsibility rested with leaders who, once again, simply had asked the soldiers to do the impossible.

The Military Medal, instituted in March 1916 for award to non-commissioned officers and men for acts of bravery in the field. The MM ranks just below the Distinguished Conduct Medal.

Blame, of course, had to be placed somewhere. The Army Commander and General Alderson wanted to remove both Generals Turner and Ketchen, but in the end — in the interest of not offending Canadian sensibilities — it was General Alderson who would go. On 28 May, he was relieved on orders from Ottawa, supposedly because the government lacked confidence in his ability to hold the Canadian divisions together. There is no doubt that he was badly treated. His competence in the field, first as Division and then as Corps Commander, could not be questioned, and it is to him that credit is due for building Canada's field army from a mob of rank amateurs to one that was skilled and well-trained. The new Corps Commander, fortunately, was perhaps even more competent, and grew to be greatly respected by all Canadians. Lieutenant-General the Honourable Sir Julian Byng, who had commanded the Cavalry Corps, IX Corps at Gallipoli, and XVII Corps in France, arrived to take command of the Canadians on 29 May.

Lieutenant-General Sir Julian Byng, commander of the Canadian Corps from May 1916 until after the great triumph at Vimy Ridge in April 1917. After the war, as Lord Byng of Vimy, he served as Canada's Governor General.

NAC/C-21572

THE BATTLE OF MOUNT SORREL

While the Corps sector of the Ypres Salient had been quiet since the fighting at St. Eloi, for some time the Germans had been preparing an attack into the 3rd Division area, on the Corps' left, aimed at seizing the higher ground between features known as Mount Sorrel and Hill 61, and particularly a ridge, aptly named Observatory Ridge, which jutted into the Salient for 500 metres. Some warning signs of a possible attack had been detected, but as no additional German troops had been reported moving into the region, no unusual precautions were taken.

Early on the bright, sunny morning of 2 June 1916, the Commander of 3rd Division, Major-General Mercer, and the Commander of 8th Brigade, Brigadier-General Williams went forward to inspect the positions held by the 4th Canadian Mounted Rifles at Mount Sorrel. They had just reached the 4th CMR's front trench when a vicious artillery bombardment came down at precisely 0600 hours. General Mercer was killed by a shrapnel burst, and General Williams was seriously wounded. "For forty hours a veritable tornado of fire ravaged the Canadian positions from half a mile west of Mount Sorrel to the northern edge of Sanctuary Wood," states the official history. The 4th CMR line was literally blown out of existence; only 76 out of 702 officers and men survived the shelling. When the German infantry came forward after the explosion of four mines at 1300 hours, they met very little resistance from what had been the Canadian front. In a very short time, Mount Sorrel and Hills 61 and 62 were in German hands.

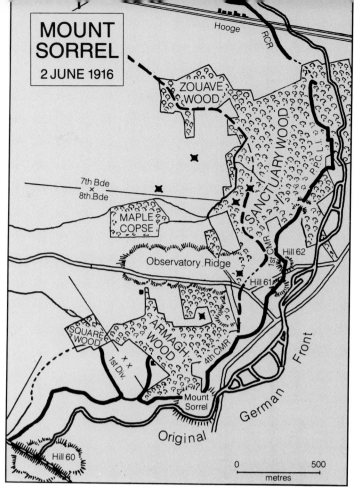

The advancing Germans were stopped an hour later only because of a resolute and truly heroic stand put up by the PPCLI in Sanctuary Wood and by the 5th CMR in Maple Copse.

The Defence of Sanctuary Wood by Kenneth Forbes.

This painting shows the gallant defence of the wood by the Princess Patricia's Canadian Light Infantry on 2 June 1916, during which over 400 casualties were suffered.
CWM 8157

General Byng was determined to recapture all of the ground lost and he tasked Currie's 1st Division to plan and carry out a deliberate counterattack. When Second Army agreed to provide every piece of artillery in the Salient in support of the operation — 218 guns — General Currie was able to adopt the same tactics used so successfully by the Germans: destroy the enemy with massive artillery fire *before* the infantry assault. The planning was extremely thorough. Reconnaissance of the enemy positions was carried out every day and compared with aerial photographs taken of the new German trenches. And the artillery carefully registered every target that would be fired upon in the short time immediately before the attack. When the plans were made, units were able to rehearse their attacks in great detail.

On 12 June the whole of the German line between Sanctuary Wood and Hill 60 in the south was bombarded for ten hours. Then for forty-five minutes before Zero Hour another vicious barrage struck the Germans. At 0130 hours on 13 June, in heavy rain and under the cover of a thick smoke screen, the attack went in. There was only slight, isolated resistance, and within an hour the attacking battalions had regained the original Canadian line, or what remained of it in the wake of the shelling. General Currie's set-piece counterattack was a total success. But again, the cost of the fighting in the first half of June had been high: the Corps lost nearly 8000 men in this battle, including a Division Commander.

A section of the original Canadian front line after it had been recaptured by the 1st Division on 13 June 1916. NAC/PA-811

Men of the 22nd Battalion in the line, July 1916. NAC/PA-262

The Canadians remained in the Ypres Salient into August, and while there was no serious action, many changes took place. Major-General Lipsett was named to replace General Mercer in command of 3rd Division, and the Ross rifle was replaced by Lee Enfields in both 2nd and 3rd Divisions. Perhaps the most important event of the summer was the arrival of 4th Division in mid-August. The Corps was now complete, with a strength of nearly 100 thousand. While 4th Division would still need some time to train and develop cohesion before it was ready for operations, it had arrived just in time to begin preparations for what would be one of the most difficult battles of the war.

THE BATTLE OF THE SOMME

A grand Allied offensive for 1916 had been in the making since early December 1915, when the French and British high commands had agreed on a major joint offensive along the inter-Army boundary in the Somme Valley. Despite the repeated failure of Allied offensives in 1915, the generals still remained confident that a massive attack on a sufficiently broad front — supported with enormous quantities of artillery — could break the German line and possibly even bring the war to an end. The 'Big Push' was scheduled to begin on 1 July 1916. And as early as February the planning and logistics preparations were begun — particularly the production and stocking of tons of artillery ammunition.

The Germans, however, beat the Allies to the punch and launched their own massive offensive in late February, at Verdun in eastern France. The German high command had concluded that the only way to win the war was to 'bleed' the French until they were exhausted. Attrition was now their strategic goal, not the capture of ground or a breakthrough. And they nearly succeeded. The French clung to Verdun, and poured hundreds of thousands of men into the cauldron there. By mid-summer they had lost nearly 300 thousand men, a third of them dead. With such enormous casualties, the French had to reduce their contribution to the Somme offensive. But they still insisted that the offensive had to go ahead, if only to relieve pressure at Verdun.

The ground over which the advance was to take place in the British sector on the Somme was far from ideal. As was so often the case on the Western Front, the Germans held the commanding heights — here a substantial chalk ridge which rose as much as 100 metres above the surrounding ground. The Germans had occupied the same positions since October 1914, and the many defensive lines built up over 18 months were among the most highly developed on the whole of the front. Many of the trenches contained deep underground bunkers where the German troops lived, and where they could go for shelter from artillery bombardment. To protect the forward lines, two broad belts of thick wire entanglement had been laid along the whole front, and everywhere machine guns were sited to cover the wire. And, as the Germans could observe well beyond the British front, they were fully aware of the extensive preparations for the coming offensive. There was no surprise at all at the Somme.

Canadian Artillery in Action by Kenneth Forbes.
While the Canadian Corps was not involved in the Battle of the Somme until September, the Canadian field artillery was there from the outset. This painting shows a 6-inch howitzer firing during the attack on Thiepval on 16 July 1916. CWM 8158

At 0730 hours on 1 July, after seven days of devastatingly heavy bombardment from 1537 guns, the artillery lifted onto the German second line. And on a 32-kilometre front, eleven British and six French divisions started forward from their trenches into No-Man's-Land. In the British sector they marched forward in eight waves, with about 100 metres between each of the long rows of men. These soldiers were so weighted down with extra ammunition, rations and sundry entrenching equipment that they simply couldn't move beyond a slow walking pace. And all along the front the German defenders scrambled up out of their underground shelters, ready with their rifles and machine guns as soon as the first wave of the British approached their wire obstacle belt. Then the German artillery joined the fray, covering No-Man's-Land with a rain of shrapnel.

Wave after wave came forward, bayonets fixed, and wave after wave were cut down as they clambered over the dead and wounded of the previous assaults. Except on the right, where an advance of about 1000 metres was made, very little if any ground was gained. And at the end of the day, over 57 thousand men had been killed or wounded, the largest number in a single day in British history. It was a catastrophe.

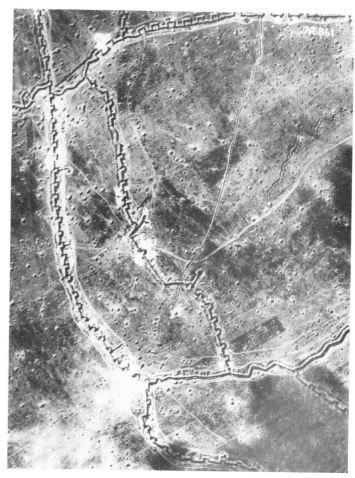

An aerial view of part of the shell-torn Somme battlefield.
CDQ Archives

Men of the Newfoundland Regiment at Beaumont Hamel on 1 July 1916, shortly before the attack in which the battalion suffered so heavily.
Imperial War Museum Q-62

The Newfoundland Regiment, part of the 29th Division, suffered very heavily in this assault. When the first two waves of the division had failed to reach the German line just south of Beaumont Hamel, the Newfoundlanders were ordered forward on their own. They, however, encountered serious difficulty in getting through the gaps in their own wire: the Germans had every one covered by machine-gun fire, and many of the men were killed or wounded. Those who did make it continued toward the German line, some 600 metres away. Many more were cut down in No-Man's-Land, and only a resolute few got to the German wire. But by 1000 hours it was over: 310 men had been killed and 374 wounded. The Newfoundlanders had given everything they had. At the end of the day only 68 men were left.

General Haig continued to press the attack without let-up for the next twelve days, and little by little, but at ever increasing cost in lives, the Germans were pushed back. By the end of July a footing had been gained on Thiepval Ridge, and by early September most of the German Second Position had been taken. The Allied line had been advanced by at most 6000 metres in over two months of very hard fighting. But

200 thousand British, and 70 thousand French soldiers had been lost in the process. General Haig needed fresh troops to be able to continue, and the Canadian Corps was to furnish some of them.

In mid-August the Canadians began to pull out of the Ypres Salient to a training ground at St. Omer, near the English Channel, where they were to be put through advanced training in the conduct of the attack. There was even some optimism amongst the troops about going to a new battlefield. The ground at Ypres already bore too heavily the reminders of constant death and destruction. The Regimental History of the 2nd Battalion vividly described what the Canadians were leaving:

... the soft breezes wafted over Hill 60 carried a distillation of nauseating stenches from the decomposing bodies littering No-Man's-Land, and myriads of disease-laden blow-flies which hatched in them.

On 27 August the Corps marched southeastward toward the Somme, and on 3 September began to take over a 3000-metre section of the front along Pozières Ridge from the Australians.

Death Valley from Windy Corner by W.T. Topham.
Topham's watercolour depicts a sector of the Somme battlefield. CWM 8885

1st Division's horse-drawn transport shown at a rail siding to pick up fodder, July 1916. NAC/PA-225

The first week in the trenches at Pozières proved to be a small foretaste of the intense fighting the Corps would see on this new front over the next three months. 1st and 3rd Brigades were under heavy shelling for much of the time, and repelled frequent small attacks. The first Canadian Victoria Cross of 1916 was won by a 2nd Battalion junior NCO on 9 September. Corporal Leo Clarke was in charge of a small group constructing a barrier in a newly captured section of trench, when twenty Germans counterattacked down the trench. All of his party were killed, and Clarke took on the enemy by himself, despite having been wounded by a German bayonet. He advanced against the Germans, and beat them off with his pistol and with rifles he took from men he had shot. Corporal Clarke never knew about his award; he was killed in action three weeks later, before it had been announced.

Corporal Leo Clarke, VC,
2nd Battalion CEF.

THE BATTLE OF COURCELETTE

The first of the major attacks on the Somme in which the Canadian Corps would play a part took place on 15 September. This action was notable for two concepts that were tested in battle for the first time; the use of tanks to support the infantry in penetrating enemy trenches, and the use of the 'rolling barrage' which enabled the infantry to keep close behind the advancing artillery fire. Here was the beginning of the reintroduction of the tactical principle of fire *and* movement, which appeared to have been forgotten since the trench lines appeared two years before.

In the first of two attacks that the Canadians put in on 15 September, 2nd Division, on the right, had the main part. Beginning at 0620 hours, 4th and 6th Brigades, each with three tanks in support, attacked toward the village of Courcelette. Their objective was the capture of two adjoining German lines known as Sugar and Candy Trenches, which ran in an irregular pattern roughly 800 metres short of the village.

Private Donald Fraser of the 31st Battalion described the attack in his diary.

The air was seething with shells. Immediately above, the atmosphere was cracking with a myriad of machine gun bullets, startling and disconcerting in the extreme. Bullets from the enemy rifles were whistling and swishing around my ears in hundreds, that to this day I cannot understand how anyone could have crossed that inferno alive.... All around our men were falling, their rifles loosening from their grasp. The wounded, writhing in their agonies, struggled and toppled into shell holes for safety.... On my front and flanks, soldier after soldier was tumbling to disablement or death, and I expected my turn every moment. The transition from life to death was terribly swift.

A Tank at Montauban by W.T. Topham.
The 2nd Division attack on Courcelette on 15 September was supported by six tanks, which were used for the first time at the Somme, somewhat unsuccessfully. CWM 8891

This drawing by F. Matania depicts the 21st Battalion's intense fight to capture the Sugar Factory just south of the village of Courcelette on 15 September 1916. CWM 87063

The rolling barrage — where the artillery fire advanced by 100 metres every four minutes — nonetheless proved to be relatively effective, but the tanks for the most part got stuck or broke down so were of little real value. 4th Brigade, on the right, reached Candy Trench by 0700 hours. The 21st Battalion here became engaged in a stiff fight in the ruins of a sugar factory, but the resolute boys from Eastern Ontario soon managed to overpower the Germans. By 0730, 6th Brigade reported that they were firm in Sugar Trench. 2nd Division had a resounding success in its first big offensive action.

General Byng ordered a continuation of the attack to begin at 1800 hours, the earliest that artillery support could be arranged. The 22nd and 25th Battalions (5th Brigade), after taking out a line of German outposts in particularly vicious hand-to-hand fighting, were able to advance rapidly to the far edge of Courcelette. But once there, they came under repeated, violent counterattacks. The 22nd Battalion beat off no less than seven attacks during the night, and the Germans continued to try to regain the village for much of the next day.

3rd Division had an even more difficult fight on the Corps' left, where 7th and 8th Brigades attempted to capture the Fabeck Graben trench line. The assaulting battalions were under heavy artillery and machine-gun fire the whole way across No-Man's-Land, and they had to struggle forward from one shell hole to the next. The Patricias eventually got into the eastern end of Fabeck Graben and made contact with the 5th Brigade units on the far edge of Courcelette. They then fought westward along the trench until they linked up with the 42nd Battalion. In the meantime, the 4th CMR, on the left, had captured a part of the trench line in their sector, and established blocks on the flanks still held by the Germans. By dark 3rd Division had control of all but a 250-metre length of the Fabeck Graben trench.

The next line of German defences, known as Zollern Graben, ran roughly 1000 metres north of the Fabeck Graben line, the two coming together just to the west of Courcelette. This line, and in particular a strong point on the left known as Zollern Redoubt, was the Corps' next objective. 3rd Division mounted a hasty attack toward Zollern Graben on the evening of 16 September, but the troops were all pinned down by machine-gun fire, and it was unsuccessful.

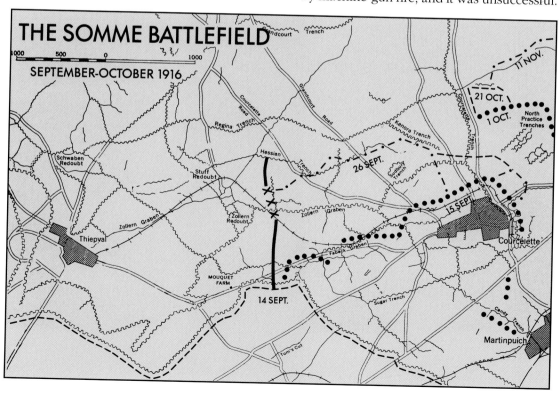

THE SOMME BATTLEFIELD

SEPTEMBER-OCTOBER 1916

Meanwhile, two of 7th Brigade's battalions captured the section of Fabeck Graben which the Germans had thus far managed to hold. During this action a VC was won by Private John Chipman Kerr of the 49th Battalion. Kerr, despite being wounded, "ran along the parados under heavy fire until he was in close contact with the enemy, when he opened fire on them at point-blank range, and inflicted heavy loss. The enemy, thinking they were surrounded, surrendered. Sixty-two prisoners were taken and 250 yards of trench captured."

Several further attempts were made over the next several days to advance on Zollern Graben, but the enemy by then had reinforced his positions, and all failed. German resistance along the whole line had stiffened considerably, and, after 22 September, repeated attacks would measure 'progress' in gains of a few metres at a time. In its first major operation on the Somme, Canadian soldiers had proven that they were at least the equal of their British counterparts. While not much ground had in fact been taken, the men showed innate tactical skill, determination and courage. All of these qualities would be sorely needed in the next battles.

Private John Kerr, VC, 49th Battalion CEF.

Shrapnel bursting over the Canadian line, September 1916. NAC/PA-733

THIEPVAL RIDGE

The next stage in the bloody fighting on the Somme is known officially as the Battle of Thiepval Ridge. In reality it was simply a continuation of the general attack northward to one more of the seemingly endless lines of German trenches. The Corps objective for this operation was Hessian Trench in the left of the sector, and a spur of that line running to the right in the direction of Courcelette, known as Kenora Trench. Both were about 1000 metres from the Canadian front line.

As had become routine procedure, the attack was preceded by three days of artillery bombardment. Zero Hour was set for 1235 hours on 26 September, a warm pleasant autumn day. As the first wave of men began their march across the shell-scarred No-Man's-Land, they were hit by heavy shrapnel and by devastating fire from 'nests' of machine guns which the Germans had cleverly positioned well forward of their trench line to avoid the Canadian's barrage. It seemed that men fell with every step, and enemy machine guns cut down the second wave just as they climbed onto the parapet.

1st Division's assault battalions nonetheless struggled forward despite growing numbers of casualties. 2nd Brigade, on the left, fought its way through the Zollern Graben trench, and, even with constant fire directed at them from German machine guns in the Zollern Redoubt less than 1000 metres to their left and rear, they inched their way forward until just short of Hessian Trench. Some elements of 5th Battalion in fact managed to penetrate beyond Hessian Trench — almost to the next line, Regina Trench. At this point, however, the Germans launched strong counterattacks against both battalions, and 2nd Brigade was forced gradually to give way, although a foothold was maintained by 5th Battalion in a section of Hessian Trench. In the 3rd Brigade sector on the right, both 14th and 15th Battalions resolutely battled their way to their objectives. 14th Battalion got into Kenora Trench by mid-afternoon. The Germans counterattacked repeatedly, but the 14th held out until the following evening. By that time, however, they were down to 75 men, too weak to withstand yet another German assault, and they had no choice but to withdraw. By nightfall on the 26th only two short segments of the Hessian-Kenora Trench objective had been taken, and they were far from securely held.

A Canadian heavy howitzer in action at the Somme. NAC/PA-800

This famous photograph of men of the 78th Battalion scaling the parapet has become symbolic of Canadian sacrifice in the bloody fighting on the Somme. It was in reality staged for the photographer in training trenches well behind the lines.

NAC/PA-648T

In this, as indeed in all of the attacks on the Somme, the intense shrapnel and machine-gun fire took a very heavy toll. In the first two weeks of fighting there were nearly 15 thousand casualties, two thirds of whom were wounded and evacuated to medical facilities for treatment. That so many of the wounded survived is itself an indication of the high quality of care provided by the Medical Corps in Advanced Dressing Stations near the front, and at field and general hospitals further to the rear. Evacuation of the wounded from the battlefield was always the biggest problem. Stretcher bearers went in immediately to the rear of assaulting companies, and they routinely acted with great bravery in giving first aid and in carrying men to the rear. But at the Somme they were often simply overwhelmed by the sheer number of men who needed help. Corporal Charles Brown of the 4th Battalion remembered his unusual experience.

My first dressing was put on by a German Sergeant, a German Army Medical Corps Sergeant. He tied my arm up, put a tourniquet on, and he says, 'There you are, Canada,' in very good English. 'That'll do until they find you. I've got to hurry up and get out of here,' he said, 'I'll be caught myself.' I remember him saying that to me, and you'd think that he was one of your own friends.

Even when prisoners of war were enlisted to carry stretchers, as they often were, it was generally many hours, sometimes even days, before a thorough search could be made of the battlefield for wounded who had taken cover in shell holes or craters. At the Advanced Dressing Stations, unit medical officers gave sustaining care to the seriously wounded, and they were then evacuated — often on light railway trolleys — to field hospitals equipped to do emergency surgery. Ultimately the seriously wounded ended up at general hospitals or convalescent units in England (in soldiers' slang, Blighty), and men generally came to refer to being wounded as "getting a Blighty".

There was only sporadic fighting over the next three days. 2nd Division attempted to advance on Regina Trench on 28 September, but the assaulting units were stopped by uncut wire entanglements, and many men of the 24th and 25th Battalions were mowed down by machine-gun fire. On 29 September, the 2nd CMR, which already held a short sector taken over from the 7th Battalion, cleared the whole length of Hessian Trench as far as the Corps' left boundary. The next day British units took the remaining section of Hessian Trench on the Canadian left. The battle for Thiepval Ridge thus simply dwindled away. In places, the Corps had advanced the Canadian line by about 1000 metres, and part of the objective had been taken. But it was no victory.

Grisly scene in a trench
near Courcelette,
September 1916.
NAC/PA-639

On sentry duty in a
front line trench,
September 1916.
NAC/PA-568

THE BATTLES FOR REGINA TRENCH

The Commander-in-Chief, General Haig, decided to renew the Somme offensive on an increased scale in October, despite the several hundred thousands of dead and wounded in the three months since the battle had begun.

For the Canadian Corps, the final stage of the Battle of the Somme entailed a series of attacks on the next of the German trenches — this one known as Regina Trench. These attacks were among the most costly of all of the futile battles of attrition in which the Corps had participated since the Canadians arrived on the Somme in early September.

The first attack on Regina Trench was put in on the afternoon of 1 October by the 5th and 8th Brigades, only two days after the weak and exhausted units had finally secured Hessian Trench. It was a disaster even before it began. Many of the assaulting troops were hit in the jumping-off positions by our own artillery falling short. Inadequate artillery support was in fact the main cause of the most serious problems: in many areas Regina Trench had not been hit at all by the preparatory barrage, and perhaps even more serious, the German wire had in most places *not* been cut. Entire companies were wiped out crossing No-Man's-Land, others were slaughtered by torrents of machine-gun fire when they came upon the uncut barbed-wire belts. A few greatly reduced companies did get into Regina Trench, only to be driven off or in some cases overpowered by incessant German counterattacks. The day ended with over half of the attacking force dead or wounded, and with no gain at all.

The second attack was launched before dawn on 8 October by two brigades from each of 1st and 3rd Divisions, this time on a slightly reduced frontage. It was, unfortunately, much the same story as on 1 October. In the 3rd Division sector, only the Royal Canadian Regiment got into Regina Trench in strength, but alone, and after fighting off three counterattacks, they were eventually forced to abandon it. In the 1st Division, a number of severely weakened companies, sometimes only platoons, also succeeded in getting into the German trench, but they too were all forced to withdraw when they ran out of ammunition and bombs. In all of these engagements, large and small, the soldiers showed remarkable determination and great personal bravery, most unreported and unrewarded, but one instance in this battle does stand out. When the 16th Battalion found that the wire to their front had not been cut and came under a hail of rifle and machine-gun fire, Piper James Richardson "strode up and down outside the wire, playing his pipes with the greatest coolness. The effect was instantaneous. Inspired by his splendid example, the company rushed the wire with such fury and determination that the obstacle was overcome and the position captured." Piper Richardson was killed shortly afterwards; he was awarded a posthumous Victoria Cross. But the bravery of Richardson and countless others was to no avail: the day ended with the Corps holding only its original positions, and with a further 1364 casualties.

A man wounded in the fighting is helped to an aid station by a Medical Officer. NAC/PA-642

This was the last of the Canadian Corps' attacks on the Somme. On 17 October the 1st, 2nd and 3rd Divisions began to move northward to a sector of the front between Arras and Lens. 4th Division, which had only arrived on the Somme early that month, and the whole of the Corps artillery would,

however, remain for another month and a half in an environment well-described by Colonel Goodspeed in *The Armed Forces of Canada 1867-1967*:

The weather had deteriorated, and the chalk, pulverized by the guns and drenched with rain, assumed a mortar-like consistency. It packed and balled on the foot like slushy snow, and there was no telling where this yellowish mud was merely inches deep or where it had filled shell-holes and even trenches in the folds of the stripped and wasted ground. Soldiers wept with frustration as they floundered forward. When they fell — and they fell often — clothing and equipment, plastered with mud, grew incredibly heavy.

4th Division participated in three further attacks on Regina Trench as part of II British Corps. In the first, the division's baptism of fire on 21 October, the earlier difficulties with artillery support had apparently been completely overcome, and the assaulting battalions — the 87th and 102nd — were able to follow the creeping barrage right into a 600-metre section of Regina Trench. A second, minor attack on 25 October, when the 44th Battalion was sent forward alone against a part of the German line further to the east, was a disastrous failure, partly because of woefully inadequate artillery fire. But Captain Ed Russenholt remembered mainly the mud:

We went in on the night of the 23rd. We were to attack on the morning of the 24th, and the mud was so terrible that about every other step you know you had to take hold of your rubber boot to pull your foot out and you were carrying on your back all the things that you would need, extra bombs and all this sort of stuff.

Mud-spattered men of the 4th Division coming out of the line, October 1916. NAC/PA-832

German dead after the capture of Regina Trench by the 4th Division. NAC/PA-868

A third, and final attack was put in shortly after midnight on 11 November, against the only section of Regina Trench still in German hands. This time every aspect of the operation went exactly as planned, and 4th Division consolidated its positions in the whole of Regina Trench in just over two hours. This once formidable line, for which so much blood had been spilled, was by then "a mere depression in the chalk, in many places blown twenty feet wide, and for long stretches almost filled with debris and dead bodies."

When the fighting stopped, there was no victory to celebrate. Never had the hoped-for breakthrough come even close to being achieved, and the end of the war was still nowhere in sight. The Battle of the Somme instead is remembered for the wasteful slaughter of hundreds of thousands of young men, and to no purpose. If anything was accomplished, it was to force the Germans to call off their offensive at Verdun. There were 29,029 casualties in the Canadian Corps, nearly the total strength of two divisions. And nearly 8000 of those men — or half of one division — were killed. It was a very high price to pay for six kilometres of badly torn-up ground.

The Somme had been a battle of artillery bombardments more intense than had ever been experienced anywhere, of devastating machine-gun fire, and of barbed wire "so dense that daylight could barely be seen through it." It had also been a battle of hundreds upon hundreds of heavily-laden infantrymen marching slowly across No-Man's-Land in long orderly lines into the enemy artillery and machine guns and barbed wire. And doing it over and over again. The fundamental tactical principle of fire *and* manoeuvre — which was already well understood before the war — had been forgotten or ignored. Fire then manoeuvre was what had been attempted on the battlefield, but all too often the shelling churned up the ground so badly that manoeuvre in fact became impossible. The lessons were slow to be learned, but there were signs, finally, that new ways of thinking, and tactics, were being adopted. The introduction of the tank — a mobile gun that was proof against shrapnel and machine-gun bullets — was one of those innovative adaptations, even though the experiment with them at the Somme had not shown their real potential. The creeping barrage was another important adaptation. And some, at least on the German side, had begun to think about infantry attacking in small groups, advancing in short rushes from one fold in the ground to the next. Fortunately there were leaders in the Canadian Corps, particularly General Currie, who knew that better methods still had to be found.

Canadian soldiers buried where they fell in the barbed wire of the bloody Somme battlefield. NAC/PA-967

A ward in a Canadian Field Ambulance. NAC/PA-29

Lieutenant F.M.W. Harvey, VC,
Lord Strathcona's Horse.

Even as the fighting on the Somme was in its last throes, the Allied commanders-in-chief were making plans for another grand offensive in the spring of 1917. The French were to make the main effort between Reims and Soissons, but first the British were to launch a subsidiary offensive in April to draw off the German reserves. In that offensive, the Canadian Corps was to anchor the British north flank by seizing Vimy Ridge, which by then the Germans had turned into a near-impregnable fortress. Preparations for that attack began in early January 1917.

At this same time, the Germans were completing preparations for a great strategic withdrawal on nearly 100 kilometres of their front between Arras and Soissons. Here, some thirty kilometres behind the existing front, they had constructed what the Allies came to call the Hindenburg Line, where they could implement a new defensive concept based on strong points and depth.

The Germans began the withdrawal to the Hindenburg Line on 4 February 1917. By 19 March only rear guards remained, but they had been tasked to resist stubbornly the

inevitable Allied move forward. The job of pushing back the German rear guards fell in large part to the cavalry. And the Canadian Cavalry Brigade, who had spent much of the last year serving in an infantry role in quiet sectors of the front, got their first opportunity for mounted operations.

For four days, between 24 and 28 March, the Canadian Cavalry advanced on a 20-kilometre front east of Peronne. The Germans were pursued relentlessly. The Dragoons, Strathconas and Fort Garrys liberated one village after the other, some in sword-drawn mounted charges, others in dismounted assaults, particularly when held up by machine guns. In one of these actions, in front of the village of Guyencourt, Lieutenant F.M.W. Harvey of Lord Strathcona's Horse won a Victoria Cross when he charged forward on foot, alone, to take out a machine gun that had caused heavy casualties in his troop. In these few days of mounted action, the Canadian Cavalry Brigade showed the same resolute determination, the same spark that had already brought such high regard for the Canadian Corps by friend and foe alike.

Canadian cavalry in action during the advance to the Hindenburg Line, March 1917. NAC

THE BATTLE OF VIMY RIDGE

The battle of Vimy Ridge has assumed a special place in Canadian history, and indeed in the history of the Canadian Army. It was the first time that a large-scale operation had been carried out by the whole Corps of four divisions. It was also the first truly successful offensive carried out by any of the Allies since the war began. But perhaps most significant, it marked a turning point in Canadian history, for it brought a sense of national identity that simply never before had existed. Some have said, perhaps with some justification, that Canadian independence was bought at Vimy Ridge.

The Canadian Corps had been sitting in 6500 metres of trench in front of Vimy Ridge since late October 1916. The men in the Corps already knew the features of the Ridge well by the time planning for the offensive began. It was a formidable objective, which the French had tried twice before to capture — unsuccessfully — at the cost of 130,000 dead and wounded. Rising to a height of 147 metres, the chalk ridge completely dominated the British-Canadian front and served as a natural bulwark for German retention of the important mining and industrial area at Lens. The ground was riddled with caves and tunnels, both natural and manmade, and combined the advantages of observation and concealment. The western slope rose gradually over open ground, with excellent fields of fire for machine guns and artillery. The steep, heavily wooded eastern slope gave almost complete cover to the enemy's depth positions, but the slope was really too steep to permit the Germans to hold substantial forces there, so that their reserves were actually several kilometres back on the Douai plain. The southern portion of the Corps sector was essentially flat, open farmland for nearly 3500 metres before the end of the ridge was encountered.

The Germans had exercised considerable skill and ingenuity in locating and constructing fortifications which added

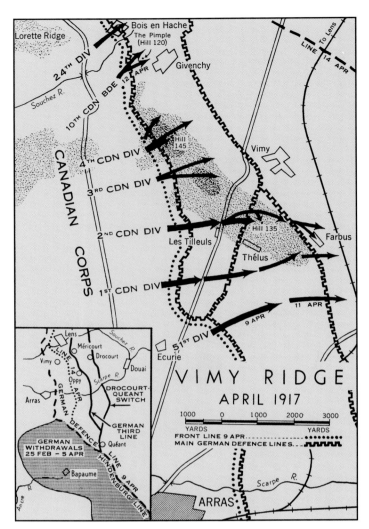

immensely to the natural strength of the Ridge. There were three main defensive lines opposite the Canadian Corps. The first line followed the forward slope and consisted of at least three (in some places four) trench systems, all connected by a maze of communication trenches. The second line, between 600 to 1000 metres to the rear, lay mostly behind the forward crest, linking up with the northern extremity of the Hindenburg Line on the right (southern) flank just beyond Arras. Still further back — too far to affect a limited assault on the Ridge — the Oppy-Méricourt Line extended north to Lens, with a branch line running south to Vimy. In between were many heavily fortified positions, such as those at Farbus, Thélus, and La Folie Farm. The sector was at this time held by three German divisions, of which ten battalions were forward in the line.

An aerial view of the trenches on Vimy Ridge.
NAC/PA-2366

From the outset, General Byng knew that thorough planning and preparation would be the keynotes of success for his attack. The first stage of the preparations entailed the gathering of detailed intelligence on the German defensive layout, much of which came from the Royal Flying Corps, and precise analysis of what needed to be done in each location to overcome the defenders and the terrain. Only then were the plans made. Because of the location of the German positions, and because of the lay of the ground, the Corps plan called for the attack to be carried out in four phases. The objective for each phase was indicated by a coloured line. The first objective for all four divisions, labelled the Black Line, took in the enemy's most forward defences at the foot of the ridge. The second objective, the Red Line, ran along the crest of the northern part of the Ridge, and included the highest feature, Hill 145, but on the southern flank, where the distance to be covered was greater, the Red Line lay well short of the higher ground. In the two southern division sectors, two more bounds would be required to reach the rear crest of the Ridge, these objectives being labelled the Blue and Brown lines. Each division was to assault with two brigades up and a third in reserve, but in the south the reserve brigade of the 1st and 2nd Divisions would leapfrog through the initial assault brigades to carry both the Blue and Brown Line objectives. The achievement of each phase line was to be marked by a pause for reorganization before the rolling barrage resumed.

Behind the line, a mock-up of the German defences was reproduced in great detail from aerial photographs. Tapes showed the location of trenches, and flags indicated strong points. On this model every unit down to platoon level was able to rehearse every step in the attack until each man knew exactly what he was to do and where he was to go. General Byng injected great enthusiasm into these training schemes, "patiently accompanying battalions 'over the tapes' and explaining details to all and sundry." To help in ensuring that every soldier knew what his role was in the greater scheme, over 40 thousand maps of the terrain were distributed within the Corps.

A cook with his helper at work in a reserve trench at Vimy.
NAC/PA-834

To rehearse every step in the coming attack, a detailed mock-up of the German defences on Vimy Ridge was set up behind the lines. NAC/PA-3666

The great tactical change, brought about by General Currie, was the emphasis on manoeuvre by platoons and sections: they were to use their own firepower to manoeuvre around enemy strong points. Platoons were taught that German defenders were to be pinned down by section Lewis light machine guns, then outflanked by riflemen and 'bombers' throwing grenades.

Nothing like this had ever been done by the British, and the Canadian soldiers loved it. Morale soared because the troops understood what they were being asked to do, and how it all was to fit together. Even more important, in this instance they knew that every effort was being made to reduce the risks to them.

Bringing forward the hundreds of tons of ammunition needed for the intense bombardment was not without its difficulties. NAC

Meanwhile, the Engineers were extending the roads and light railways so that the necessary stores and ammunition could be brought forward. Hundreds of kilometres of telephone and telegraph cable were buried deeply to ensure that communications could not be knocked out by German artillery, and arrangements were completed for water supply, casualty evacuation and other services. An important aspect of these preparations was the construction of numerous deep subways and tunnels to move the assaulting troops to the front lines under cover.

The artillery barrage was also very carefully planned, taking into account the state of the ground and the number of trenches to be crossed. The general principle adopted was to have a standing barrage in front of the creeping barrage that supported the infantry. The moving belt of fire, which was twice rehearsed, would advance at a rate of about 100 metres every four minutes, and salvos of shrapnel were to be fired to mark the beginning of each new stage of the assault. For this battle, there were enough artillery field guns to allocate one for every 20 metres of the front in the attack. The heavier guns were tasked to search and sweep areas beyond objectives from which enemy small arms fire might be employed against our troops. And, immediately prior to the assault a bombardment with gas shells was to be brought down on all German batteries, on command posts and on headquarters. For the 2817 guns of all calibres, over 40 thousand tons of ammunition had been stockpiled for the day of the attack.

As the date set for the operation grew nearer, the artillery methodically destroyed the essence of the German defences. To help in overcoming the great tactical problem of the war — infantrymen closing with the enemy in the face of that deadly combination of machine guns and barbed wire — all known enemy machine-gun emplacements were to be subjected to a virtually continuous bombardment. And the enemy wire was to be deluged with shells employing a new type of super-sensitive fuze, designed to explode on contact with even the sloppiest, most liquid kind of mud. All shrapnel splinters would thus have the effect wanted against the enemy wire.

Canadian railway construction workers preparing the ground for a new line to carry stores and ammunition forward.
NAC/PA-1663

As darkness fell on Easter Sunday the infantry battalions began moving forward to their assembly areas, guided by luminous painted stakes and in many cases completing their journey through specially constructed tunnels cut in the chalk. The enemy's forward wire had already been cut by artillery fire, and patrols now cut lanes through the Canadian wire so that forward companies could file through to occupy the shallow ditches in No-Man's-Land from which they would assault. By 0400 hours on Easter Monday, 9 April, the troops were in position, without alarming the German outposts sometimes a bare 100 metres away. At 0530 hours every British and Canadian gun began to fire and, simultaneously, two great mines exploded under the German front line. An awed observer described "a clamour such as had probably never been heard in the world since mountains were raised from its molten surface." Heavy guns deluged German batteries and ammunition dumps with high explosive and gas shells. Artillery observation posts were either destroyed or were clouded by smoke and their telephone communications disrupted.

The weather was miserable on the morning of the attack, but this was not altogether a disadvantage for the Canadians. A driving wind from the northwest made the infantry shiver as they followed the barrage closely across the cratered and soggy ground; but it blew the falling snow and sleet into the defenders' faces. Coming after a comparatively quiet night, the first hurricane of the bombardment had taken the Germans by surprise, and many failed even to get out of their deep dugouts before the Canadians were at the entrances. There was some hand-to-hand fighting, but the assault was a rapid and unqualified success. Within thirty minutes the six assaulting battalions of the 1st Canadian Division had cleared all three trenches of the German forward defences. After the planned pause, during which the objective was consolidated under cover of a standing barrage, the rear companies continued the advance behind the creeping barrage to capture the Red Line.

The Taking of Vimy Ridge, Easter Monday, 1917 by Richard Jack. CWM 8178

Advancing through the German wire entanglements during the attack on Vimy Ridge. NAC/PA-1087

A regimental history contributes a graphic description of the scene:

Preceding the lines of attacking troops, the three waves which advanced steadily as if on parade, were the smoke and dirt of shells. The shrapnel burst in white puff-balls, mingling the metallic crash with the high explosive that erupted miniature volcanoes of earth in black, gaseous clouds. Among the lines and in the rear laboured devoted stretcher parties, themselves subjected to the same dangers as the wounded men to whom they brought succour. Groups of prisoners, mud-stained and dejected, marched back across the battlefield that had lately been their own terrain; curious small columns followed the advance stolidly, carrying Stokes mortars, heavy Vickers machine-guns, stretchers, picks, shovels, ammunition, water and bombs. Fleet and lightly equipped Battalion and Company runners darted through the mass with messages of great moment.

The Division pressed forward to Farbus Wood, sending patrols onto the railway. The Corps Cavalry, the Canadian Light Horse, then launched patrols against the nearby village of Willerval, but this attempt at exploitation was easily defeated by German machine guns. At the end of the day 1st Division, on the extreme right of the Corps, had advanced four kilometres across a strong system of trenches and had captured about 1300 prisoners. General Currie wrote of "a wonderful success — every line captured on time, every battalion doing equally well."

The experience of the 2nd Canadian Division, advancing on a frontage of 1300 metres, was very similar. Its leading brigades were disposed with two battalions forward, one in support and one subdivided into carrying parties. So effective was the counterbattery fire that for seven vital minutes there was no reply from the German gunners and the initial advance went like clockwork.

The 29th Battalion (2nd Division) in the assault on Vimy Ridge. NAC/PA-1020

Across No Man's Land, walking, running and jumping, we followed the whitish-grey puffs, which lifted every four minutes as we advanced; we passed through the enemy's wire and jumped into his trenches, pulled ourselves out of these and went on, the attacking waves continuing to follow the barrage while we, the 'moppers', broke off at prearranged points to search the trenches and dug-outs.

The tanks assigned to them proved quite useless. The condition of the pulverised ground was so bad (there were several feet of loam overlying the chalk of the Ridge) that all were out of action at an early stage of the battle. Nevertheless, by 0605 hours the four assaulting battalions had reached the Red Line.

As the 2nd Division ascended the slopes of the Ridge the frontage of the attack widened, as planned, to about 2100 metres. To meet this situation the 13th Brigade of the 5th British Division was introduced on the Canadians' left flank. The British troops cooperated with the 6th Canadian Brigade in the division's principal task of the day — the capture of Thélus and Hill 135. At 0935 hours five battalions of the two brigades moved forward behind a barrage. Bomb, bayonet and Lewis gun were employed methodically to crush stubborn resistance in the village. After taking Hill 135 the British cleared the Bois du Goulot, capturing numerous guns and much ammunition. The net result of these operations on the Canadian southern flank was that both the 1st and 2nd Divisions had captured all of their assigned objectives according to plan.

In the centre of the Corps sector, the 3rd Canadian Division was no less successful, though experiencing some trouble on its northern flank. The movement of the troops into their assault positions was facilitated by two of the longest subways on the entire front (one over 1700 metres long), which brought the men directly in to the foremost trenches. The initial phase of the attack was hampered by a profusion of mine craters occupied by the enemy, and to add to the difficulty the divisional frontage of 1300 metres increased to 1850 metres in the central portion of the Ridge at La Folie Farm and Wood. However, since the Division had only two lines of objective to take, it was able to perform the task with two brigades, keeping the third in reserve. Both brigades advanced with three battalions in the van, the fourth battalion in each instance having a support and 'mopping up' role.

Capture of a German Trench at Vimy by W.B. Wollen.
Courtesy the Royal Canadian Military Institute, Toronto

Machine gunners consolidating captured positions on Vimy Ridge.
NAC/PA-1017

159

The leading companies were upon the enemy before his machine guns could get into action, one Canadian unit capturing more than 150 Germans (many only half-dressed) in a tunnel connected with their second trench. After the severe bombardment the enemy's resistance was very weak. Trenches had been obliterated, and even the strong second line was so battered that only its deep dug-outs remained. Many Canadian soldiers actually failed to recognize the third trench system and pressed forward into the halted barrage. La Folie Farm, believed to be a nest of machine guns, had been thoroughly demolished; it was quickly overrun without resistance. By 0730 hours, only two hours after the attack began, the troops were in the western edge of the Bois de la Folie, on the reverse slope of the Ridge. The only serious difficulty in this sector occurred on the left flank, where the 7th Canadian Brigade was exposed to heavy fire by the 4th Division's delayed advance against formidable Hill 145. The situation remained critical for some hours while the 42nd Battalion (Royal Highlanders of Canada) formed a long defensive flank and consolidated their position. Finally, at 1330 hours the Brigade Commander was able to report that his entire command was "dug in, traversed and wired."

On the left, the 4th Division had the two most difficult assignments of the battle: to capture Hill 145, the highest point on Vimy Ridge, and to form a defensive flank for the entire Canadian assault. Because of the hill's commanding position, its tactical importance was keenly appreciated by both sides. Whoever held it could enfilade the crest of the Ridge. As might be expected, the enemy's defences on Hill 145 were particularly strong. Two lines of trenches surrounded the summit and, although these had suffered severely from preliminary bombardment, the defenders were able to obtain comparative immunity in nearby mine workings.

The difficulty of the Zouave Valley was overcome by tunnelling six subways into its eastern slopes and constructing deep communication trenches. For the actual assault the Canadians relied on surprise to cover the few hundred metres separating them from the German first and second trenches. In later stages of the operation it was hoped that artillery and machine-gun barrages would forestall any counterattack from dug-outs on the reverse slope or from Givenchy until defensive positions had been established.

Having successfully crossed the Zouave Valley, the 4th Division attacked simultaneously with its sister formations, having the 11th and 12th Brigades on the right and left, respectively. An infantry account described the first phase:

As the barrage advanced ... Infantry, now thoroughly aroused with the enthusiasm of battle, rushed forth from their jumping off lines on the instant, where they had been assembled from the tunnels, dug-outs and all their places of concealment. They were irresistible and what Boche survived that terrible barrage and hail of machine-gun bullets were soon despatched with the bayonet if they lost a moment in throwing up their hands and shouting 'Kamarad'. On our infantry went until they reached the forward guns of the enemy yet in action. The crews were promptly taken care of and their own guns quickly turned on the fleeing enemy and he was treated to his own shells at point blank range. The first objective was reached and consolidated and victory seemed complete although it was only early morning.

Sappers at Work: A Canadian Tunneling Company
by D. Bomberg.
Extensive tunneling was done at Vimy, particularly in the 4th Division sector, to bring troops under cover to within a short distance of the German trenches.
National Gallery of Canada 8108

Craters such as this, the Grange Crater, added to the difficulties of the assaulting troops in the 3rd and 4th Division sectors. NAC

Unfortunately, however, the 11th Brigade ran into heavy opposition in the centre of its front. This resistance not only dislocated the formation's advance to its second (and final) objective, but also exposed flanking units to enfilading fire. It was necessary to organize a further attack during the afternoon without artillery support, since the opposing troops were hopelessly entangled in the target area. Then the 85th Battalion (Nova Scotia Highlanders) swept forward. "They put on their own barrage with Lewis guns fired from the hip, crossing that desperate zone of fire with as much steadiness as if on parade.... The very audacity of their demeanour was one of the greatest factors of their success." Contact was restored with the 12th Brigade and, although fighting continued throughout the night, the Division succeeded in capturing the summit of Hill 145. The 10th Brigade completed this part of the operation in a night attack which drove the Germans to the bottom of the reverse slope in the early hours of 10 April.

The difficulties of the 11th Brigade seriously hampered its flanking formation, the 12th Brigade, on the extreme left of the Canadian Corps. As elsewhere along the front, the first objectives were speedily secured. But later advances were exposed to enfilading fire from both flanks: on the right, due to the 11th Brigade's inability to advance, and on the left, because of German occupation of Hill 120 (the Pimple) at the northern end of Vimy Ridge. Adding to the Canadians' difficulties was the terrible state of the ground, a maze of water-filled shell-holes and craters. The Brigade suffered severe casualties in this morass. At the end of the day the 72nd Battalion (Seaforth Highlanders of Canada) had only 62 all ranks who were not casualties out of the 400 who entered the battle; 11 out of 13 participating officers were killed or wounded. Eventually the Brigade was forced to consolidate about halfway to the 'Red Line' (its second and final objective); but the Canadians then held the northern slopes of the Ridge.

Empty shell cases line a road in rear of Vimy Ridge after the attack.
NAC/PA-1349

The Pimple, Evening by A.Y. Jackson. CWM 8216

Although the Canadians had thus performed their main task in the battle, there remained the necessity of eliminating the resistance on the northern flank by taking the Pimple. An interval of three days occurred before this was completed. Patrols had established that the enemy was holding his last positions in strength, and he was now fully alert. Moreover, bad weather prevented renewal of the attack. In the meantime trenches were dug, machine-gun emplacements were constructed and barbed wire strung as the Corps consolidated its objectives.

In the early hours of 12 April, the 10th Brigade of the 4th Canadian Division took up its position for the decisive operation against the Pimple. So frequently had every detail of the impending assault been rehearsed over the taped battlefield at Château de la Haie that the ground was well known to all. In the darkness before the attack, snow began to fall — but once again a westerly wind helped to blind the enemy. After a short bombardment by heavy and medium howitzers, 96 18-pounders brought down a barrage of shrapnel, behind which the well-practised infantry began their advance. The deep mud and slippery going would have made progress slow without any opposition from the enemy, however, and the infantry were quite unable to keep up with the barrage, which moved forward at the same rate which had proven so satisfactory three days earlier — 100 metres every four minutes. Moreover, during the lull of the preceding two days, the enemy had replaced the Bavarian garrison of the Pimple with the 5th Prussian Guard Grenadiers and these elite troops fought fiercely. But the German trenches were already broken, with the enemy mainly occupying shell-holes and dug-outs, and once the Canadians got up to them they infiltrated their positions with quick results. Lewis guns and bayonets were used at close quarters with devastating effect.

A participating battalion recorded the scene:

Immediately the attack is over, the snow stops and the sun shines out brightly. The men enjoy a wonderful panorama of the country beyond Vimy. This view is made even more exciting by the sight of German limbers galloping to the rear, down the Lens-Arras road.

Meanwhile the 24th British Division, on the Canadians' left, captured Bois en Hache, the last German position on the neighbouring Lorette Ridge. These achievements permitted British and Canadian observers to overlook the enemy's trenches behind the northern tip of Vimy Ridge, between Givenchy and Angrès, and the Germans had no option but to withdraw still farther east.

But in spite of the great victory on Vimy Ridge there were powerful factors limiting the possibility of immediate pursuit. The main problem was the terrible condition of the shell-torn ground, making the forward movement of artillery and ammunition an exceedingly difficult and tedious business. Nevertheless, preparations were made for a new attack, to gain Givenchy and the line of the railway between Bailleul and Vimy.

On 13 April the Canadian Corps advanced all along the front. By the end of the next day the Corps had reached the outworks of the Oppy-Méricourt Line and the situation began to stabilize. By the evening of 14 April it was apparent that this phase of the struggle was over: the battle for Vimy Ridge had been fought and won. In five days the Corps had made an unprecedented advance on a front of 6 kilometres, capturing more than 4000 prisoners and 54 guns at a cost of over 11,000 casualties.

One of the temporary cemeteries established near the front line. This one, near Vimy, was the burial ground of some of those who died in the battle. NAC/PA-1372

On the Allied side there would be no greater success until the Battle of Amiens in August 1918. Vimy Ridge also established the Canadians' reputation as 'storm troops', a reputation they would continue to enhance until the end of the war.

Shortly after the battle, General Sir Julian Byng was promoted to command the Third Army, and a Canadian, Arthur Currie, was promoted Lieutenant-General, knighted, and given command of the Canadian Corps on 9 June 1917. He retained that command until the end of the war.

General Sir Arthur Currie
by Sir William Orpen. CWM

Sir Arthur Currie is unquestionably Canada's most distinguished field commander. Prior to the First World War he was a Militia artillery officer, and in 1914 took command of the 50th Gordon Highlanders. In October 1914, at Valcartier, he was appointed to command the 2nd Brigade. In recognition of his very skillful leadership at the Battle of Ypres, when the Canadian Corps was formed, he was promoted Major-General and appointed to command 1st Canadian Division. After the Battle of Vimy Ridge he was promoted Lieutenant-General, knighted, and appointed to succeed Sir Julian Byng in command of the Canadian Corps. Under his leadership the Canadian Corps gained the reputation of never failing, of being the elite force on the Allied side. British Prime Minister Lloyd George said that he had considered making Currie commander-in-chief of the entire British Army had the war continued. Currie was never popular with the troops, but he was a man of great integrity and he always insisted on meticulous planning so as to keep casualties among his men to the absolute minimum. At the end of the war he was promoted to the rank of full General and appointed Inspector-General of the Militia, but his accomplishments and service to the country were never adequately recognized. Unsatisfied with the limitations of peacetime soldiering, he soon left the Army. From 1920 until his death in 1933 he was Principal and Vice Chancellor of McGill University.

A recruiting poster directed at French-Canadians. By early 1917 the number of volunteers was nowhere near the number of casualties that had to be replaced. CWM

Even as the Canadian Corps was consolidating and slightly extending its gains after the great victory at Vimy Ridge, the effects of nearly three years of carnage were beginning to find expression. A pervasive sense of hopelessness that the war would ever be brought to an end seemed to grip the populations of the Allied countries. By early spring the Russian Army simply began to disintegrate as soldiers, in ever-growing numbers, just quit fighting and walked rearward to their homes. In early May, the French Army also began to show the effects of exhaustion and of rage at the senseless slaughter that had accompanied the spring offensive. At first only isolated units refused to obey orders to attack, but by late June, troops in all but two of the 56 French divisions had joined in the mutiny. The French Army was in fact temporarily only willing to stand on the defensive. The only glimmer of hope on the Allied side was the American entry into the war. In the meantime, the burden of carrying the Allied banner, of preventing an Allied defeat, fell to the British.

Disillusionment and war-weariness were also being felt in Canada. After the long lists of casualties that had come out following the battles at Ypres and the Somme, the number of men volunteering for service overseas dropped sharply. By early 1917 the number of volunteers was simply nowhere near the number of casualties that had to be replaced. While the relatively large number of troops held in Britain still enabled the units of the Canadian Corps to be kept up to strength, it was already apparent that this would not long continue. After attending the first Imperial War Conference and visiting the Corps in France, Prime Minister Sir Robert Borden returned to Canada convinced that selective conscription would have to be introduced if the country was to continue to meet its obligations for the duration of the war. Even though he knew that it would split his party, and possibly even the nation, Borden introduced a Military Service Bill in the House of Commons on 11 June. Conscription became law in Canada on 29 August 1917. It was no doubt a neces- sary measure, but its consequences would be felt by the nation for many years into the future. In the meanwhile, the Canadian Corps was shouldering its share of the British obligation to keep pressure off the demoralized French.

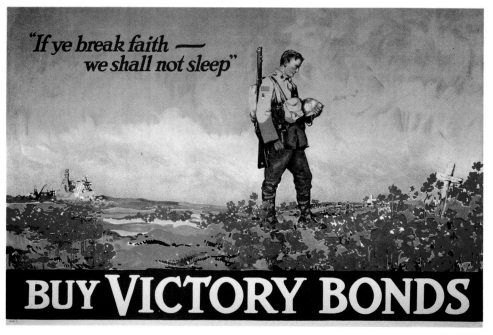

Patriotic themes, this one capitalizing on John McCrae's poem *In Flanders' Fields*, were used both to stimulate recruiting and to sell war bonds.
CWM 56-05-11-022

THE BATTLE OF HILL 70

While the French Army was forced to pause to rebuild the shattered morale of its units, General Haig had decided that the British would launch a major offensive in Flanders beginning in late July. Haig had several objectives for this offensive. He knew that the British simply had to attack to focus German attention away from the French sector, but he also believed that the liberation of ports on the Belgian coast would eliminate German submarine activity in the Channel, and in the process he just might be able to outflank the German Army and bring about a general withdrawal.

Armourers at work repairing Lewis guns. NAC/PA-1272

The Canadian Corps were to play a supporting role in this grand scheme. General Currie's first major task as Corps Commander was to launch an attack on the town of Lens, some six kilometres north of the Canadian positions at Vimy Ridge. The purpose of this attack was to divert the enemy's attention from Flanders, and to prevent the movement of German reserves northward.

General Currie, always thorough in his preparations for every attack, made a personal reconnaissance of the area into which the attack was to go. He was not pleased with what he saw. The town and its industrial suburbs were heaps of stone and brick, rubble and ruins, through which wound mazes of trenches connecting hundreds of machine-gun nests. And this once thickly built-up area was completely overlooked by two dominating features — Hill 70 some 2000 metres to the north, and Sallaumines Hill to the east — both in German hands. Lens offered only the sure prospect of slow and costly defeat.

General Currie managed to persuade the Army commander that Hill 70, on the north side of the town, would be a far more tactically feasible objective than attempting an extremely costly and slow struggle into the ruins of Lens. "If we have to fight at all, let us fight for something worth having," Currie said.

The planning and preparations for the attack on Hill 70 were carried out in the same meticulous detail as had been done prior to the assault on Vimy. Once again, artillery would be used to paralyze the German machine guns and trench lines before and during the infantry assault; counterbombardment would put the German artillery batteries out of action; and, to achieve the attrition of German reserves — which is essentially what the battle was intended to accomplish — massive artillery fires would be used to defeat the inevitable German counterattacks. Again, as at Vimy, the troops were briefed in great detail on their tasks in the assault, and careful rehearsals were held for all units on replicas of the battlefield set up behind the lines.

Much of the transport within the Canadian Corps was still horse-drawn in 1917. Keeping the horses properly shoed was thus an essential task. NAC/PA-1563

A light railway bringing ammunition forward for the Battle of Hill 70.
NAC/PA-1757

The attack on Hill 70 began at 0425 hours, just before dawn, on 15 August. Ten battalions of the 1st and 2nd Divisions went forward behind a rolling barrage on a 4000-metre front, while heavy guns pounded the German trench lines and known strong points. And to contribute to the enemy's confusion, 500 drums of burning oil were fired by means of a large mortar-type projector to create a thick smoke screen between the built-up area and the intermediate and final objectives.

Private Arthur Lapointe of the 22nd Battalion recorded the attack in his diary.

Zero hour! A roll as of heavy thunder sounds and the sky is split by great sheets of flame. Our guns have given the signal. 'Forward!' our captain shouts, but his voice is lost in the cannonade. Shells pass in salvos over our heads and through the deep roaring of the guns I can hear the staccato rat-a-tat of machine guns. I scramble over the parapet and, with Michaud, am one of the first in No Man's Land. Our company is forming up and the moments of delay seem endless. A few hundred yards in front of us, red, yellow, and green rockets rise from the German lines, as the enemy tells his artillery, supports, and reserves that we are attacking.... The noise of the barrage fills our ears; the air pulsates, and the earth rocks under our feet....

We reach the enemy's front line, which has been blown to pieces. Dead bodies lie half buried under the fallen parapet and wounded are writhing in convulsions of pain. A ghastly business! We keep on. The barrage rolls ponderously forward, sowing death and destruction. Through clouds of smoke, I catch sight of German soldiers running away.

Within twenty minutes the leading wave of infantry had reached the first objective, the Blue Line, at the crest of the hill, and in most sectors the final objective — the base of the hill on the enemy side — had been taken by 0600 hours. Only in the 2nd Brigade sector, on the far side of Hill 70, did the Germans put up a determined resistance. Here, in a well-fortified chalk quarry, the 7th and 8th Battalions had a desperate fight which carried on for more than 36 hours before the last of the German defenders were overcome.

The really intense fighting at Hill 70 came with the ferocious and repeated German counterattacks. Over the next three days, no less than twenty-one attacks were mounted by the Germans against the Canadians' newly won positions. Just as General Currie had intended, each time the Germans came forward their ranks were severely depleted by carefully directed artillery concentrations. The forward observation officers made good use of the newly introduced wireless (radio) sets to bring down deadly accurate fire. Still, many of the assaulting Germans got through to the Canadian lines, and throughout the three days and nights of fighting there were many instances of violent hand-to-hand battles with grenades, bayonets and rifle butts. Four Victoria Crosses were awarded for gallantry during this fighting, three of them to men who died during the battle: to Private M.J. O'Rourke, a stretcher-bearer with the 7th Battalion; to Private Harry Brown, a 10th Battalion runner; to Sergeant Frederick Hobson, a section commander with the 20th Battalion; and to Major O.M. Learmonth, a company commander in the 2nd Battalion. It was also during this vicious battle that the Germans first used mustard gas against Canadians. 1st and 2nd Field Artillery Brigades both suffered heavily when this ugly blister gas was fired on their gun positions.

A trench amidst the ruins of a suburb of Lens. NAC

The chalk quarry on Hill 70, in which the 7th and 8th Battalions fought a costly battle to overcome the German defenders. NAC

By 18 August, after taking nearly 20 thousand casualties, the Germans gave up their attempts to retake Hill 70. General Currie recorded that "it was altogether the hardest battle in which the Corps has participated." There had been nearly 6000 Canadian casualties, but the Corps had clearly won yet another victory.

Canadians occupying the German trenches on Hill 70 after the battle. NAC/PA-1717

The fighting continued on the outskirts of Lens until 25 August. Another two Victoria Crosses were won during this period — by Sergeant-Major Robert Hanna of the 29th Battalion and by Corporal Filip Konowal of the 47th — and another 3000 casualties were taken. The Canadian Corps was firmly in control of all but the centre of the town. One might question whether the ground taken was worth the effort, or the lives lost, but the strategic objective of preventing the movement of German reserves to Ypres was certainly achieved.

PASSCHENDAELE

The focus of the Canadian Corps was now to turn northward, back to Ypres where the Canadians had begun the war two and a half years earlier.

The Third Battle of Ypres, more usually known as the battle of Passchendaele for the infamous attacks that ended the campaign, began at the end of July 1917. This was to have been the first stage in Field Marshal Haig's grand offensive in Flanders, during which he hoped to break out of the Ypres Salient and then clear the whole coast of Belgium. The initial battle, however, lasted only four days before it ground to a standstill in the pernicious mire that was to be the dominant feature of all operations in the Salient for the next four months. The name Passchendaele indeed became synonymous with unending fields of mud. A second assault launched in a heavy mid-August downpour was even less successful, and after the first few weeks the British had lost over 68 thousand men for a gain of little over 4000 metres. The obvious futility of the fighting caused morale in the British Army to plummet so severely that, for the first time in the whole of the war, there was serious concern about the possibility of widespread mutiny. All thought of a major breakout was abandoned, but the obstinate Haig, seemingly oblivious to the waste of so many men's lives, insisted on pressing forward to achieve some sort of 'victory' to end the year. The offensive was renewed with slightly more success in dry weather in late September. British and Australian divisions pushed forward just beyond Gravenstafel Ridge. But the final objective, the 'victory' symbol Haig so much wanted — Passchendaele Ridge — was still 2500 metres across an appalling morass when he decided to bring in the Canadian Corps, which now had the reputation of never failing.

The desolate fields of stinking mud and water-filled craters that awaited the Canadians at Passchendaele. NAC/PA-2195

In mid-October the Canadians moved into the Ypres Salient for their third tour of battle there. Although the sector taken over from the Australians was almost precisely that held by 1st Division prior to the gas attack in April 1915, there was little there that any of the veterans would have recognized. Three years of intense shelling had reduced the countryside to a desolate wilderness of scummy water-filled craters, ragged tree stumps and deep glutinous mud. Roads had virtually disappeared, so guns and other heavy equipment simply could not be moved without enormous effort. Even infantrymen took over eight hours to trudge the six kilometres from Ypres to the front through often knee-deep mud. Bodies and other gruesome debris of the many earlier battles lay half-buried everywhere, and the whole area was engulfed in the putrid stench of decaying flesh. Of all of the battlefields in which Canadians fought during this war, Passchendaele was by far the worst.

When General Currie first visited the battlefield he was appalled at even the thought of sending men to fight in these dreadful conditions, and he made the strongest possible protests to the Army commander and to Haig. He estimated that the advance of 2500 metres would cost 16 thousand casualties, and he asked if it were worth that high price. In fact Currie wrote in his diary, "Passchendaele is not worth one drop of blood." But he was overruled, and ordered to attack on 26 October.

Having no option, General Currie, as always, was determined that preparations for an attack must be as thorough as possible, and that the artillery — as at Vimy and Hill 70 — must effectively neutralize the enemy before the infantry assault. That was a tall order here; on taking over the sector, the Corps had only nine days until their first attack was scheduled to go in. And the difficulties that had to be overcome in that short time were daunting.

The 8th Battalion moving to the front, just prior to the Canadian Corps being sent into the Passchendaele mud. NAC/PA-1994

Among the top priority tasks was a detailed study of the enemy positions. Opposite the Canadians, as on much of the front except at Vimy, the Germans had implemented a new defensive doctrine. Their front 'line' now consisted primarily of a checkerboard of reinforced concrete 'pillboxes', sited to provide interlocking arcs of machine-gun fire, along with machine-gun positions in fortified shell craters. The pillboxes had walls nearly two metres thick, so were proof against all but a direct hit from heavy artillery. The main line of resistance, where the bulk of the German infantry were held, was a thousand metres or so to the rear of this 'forefield' of machine-gun nests. The Canadians had never before encountered this type of defence, and it required some alteration to tactical concepts and to the supporting artillery plan.

A German pillbox on Bellevue Spur.

The most serious of the problems, however, concerned the artillery. Many of the guns taken over from the Australians had been found to be unserviceable, and many others had simply disappeared in the sea of mud. The rest were dangerously bunched together on the few patches of firm ground that remained, making them easy targets for enemy counterbombardment. Currie succeeded in getting more guns allocated to the Corps, but only after he appeared at a meeting with Haig completely covered in mud, fresh from making a personal count of every one of the guns in the field.

But the big problem was mobility. The deep mud and the lack of roads meant that guns could not be moved forward (so they would always be in range of the enemy) except with enormous difficulty. It also meant that the thousands of tons of ammunition needed to support the assault would have to be brought up to gun positions on mules, a slow and uncertain means of supply. Manhandling the guns had been attempted. Private Gordon Smith of the 46th (South Saskatchewan) Battalion told of the experience when his battalion was detailed to help the Gunners:

We had ropes tied onto the wheels and they had these big wooden cleats fastened on to stop them from sinking. I'd venture to say there was two hundred and fifty, maybe three hundred men on one gun trying to pull it up. We might get a hundred yards or so.

Such hopeless immobility would doom the Corps attack to failure. But Canadian ingenuity came to the fore. The solution was to build roads, plank roads, just like the 'corduroy' roads used in early Canada, and lay them over the mud. The problem of guns sinking into the mud when they fired would be solved in the same way: build platforms to give the guns relatively firm firing positions as they were moved forward. Over the next week thousands of men — engineers, pioneers and infantrymen — were employed in the Herculean task of cutting and sawing timber, and in laying roadways as far forward as possible. Gun platforms were put together and, closer to the front, plank footpaths were laid over the worst of the mud to enable the movement of the infantry to the front and to ease the rearward movement of the inevitable casualties.

Canadian Gunners in the Mud, Passchendaele, 1917
by Alfred Bastien. CWM 8095

Pioneers creating a path through the mud with 'duckboards'. NAC

Currie knew that forward movement would be very slow because of the thick mud, so his plan called for a three-stage attack, each with limited objectives, and with pauses of several days between the phases to allow for redeployment and replacement of units.

The first phase, scheduled for the early morning of 26 October, was expected to be the most difficult because the ground that had to be crossed was the most severely waterlogged. In the centre of the Corps sector was a flooded area nearly 500 metres wide which ran at right angles to the front much of the way to Passchendaele village. This limited the attack frontage in the 4th Division to a single battalion, and, by separating the divisions, meant that there could be little mutual support.

The men of the assault battalions were brought forward several days beforehand so they wouldn't be totally exhausted when they started out. Plank mule tracks and narrow pathways called 'duckwalks', which weaved between the shell holes, were the only way to get forward over the last 3 kilometres to the front. Private Percy Hellings of the 46th Battalion described this harrowing journey:

If you stepped off the duckwalk you were in trouble. There'd be a piece blown out.... If one or two could get across, maybe they could push the duckwalks back a bit, but it was all in the dark.... I didn't step far enough. I went up to my waist.... They pulled me out, but the first thing you know there's another guy in there. It was pretty slow progress.

171

At Zero Hour on 26 October, to lighten their load, the troops abandoned their mud-laden greatcoats in the cold slime of the shell craters where they had spent the night. Step by difficult step they plodded forward behind the covering barrage, which inched toward the enemy much more slowly than usual to allow the infantry to keep up.

On the left, the 3rd Division objective was a line 1200 metres away. The area to be taken included a vital piece of higher ground in the centre, known as Bellevue Spur, which was dotted with pillboxes. Despite the exhausting effort of wading through the mud, and an ever-growing toll of dead and wounded from enemy machine guns that raked the featureless ground, the attack initially made remarkably good progress. Within an hour both the 4th CMR and the 43rd (Cameron Highlanders of Canada) Battalion had begun clearance of the forwardmost pillboxes. At one point in this operation two companies of the 4th CMR were forced to halt by deadly bursts of fire from one of these strong points. Nineteen-year-old Private Thomas Holmes, who had only just joined the unit as a reinforcement, without orders dashed forward from shell hole to shell hole and put the machine guns out of action with a single bomb. He then ran back to his section, got another bomb, and again rushed to throw his bomb into the pillbox entrance. This valiant act forced the enemy garrison to surrender, and won for Private Holmes the Victoria Cross.

The intensity of the German artillery fire increased very greatly about this time, and little by little the ranks of the forward companies were decimated. By mid-morning the 9th Brigade had begun to fall back. The situation was stabilized temporarily on Bellevue Spur, however, because of the superb leadership shown by Lieutenant Robert Shankland of the 43rd Battalion. In the midst of what was becoming a full-scale retreat, Shankland rallied the survivors of several companies, and established a tenuous defence which held out against several violent counterattacks until the 9th Brigade was able to mount a relief attack shortly after noon. For his efforts he was awarded the VC. In the afternoon, the 52nd Battalion worked its way forward, crater to crater, until it was well beyond Shankland's position. Then, moving against the strong points from the rear, the men of the 52nd attacked and captured one pillbox after another and secured much of Bellevue Spur. Captain Christopher O'Kelly, who led his company in the taking of six of the pillboxes, won the third Victoria Cross of the day.

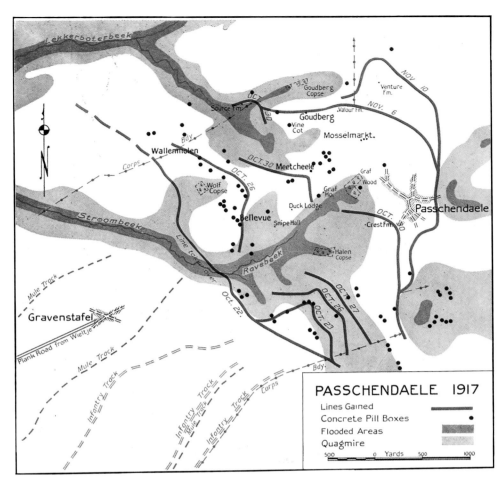

By late afternoon both sides gave in to their exhaustion, and the battle simply ground down. Both 3rd Division brigades were well short of their objectives, but they consolidated their gains as best they could on the lips of water-filled shell craters and in the captured pillboxes.

Duckboards being carried past a pillbox on Bellevue Spur. NAC

Two wounded men, a German and a Canadian, share a light in the mud.
NAC/PA-3683

On the 4th CMR front, one incident was particularly noteworthy. The Battalion chaplain, Captain W.H. Davis, made his way forward of the Canadian positions, carrying a cane with a white handkerchief tied to the top, and began to search for wounded men. The Germans, only a few hundred metres away, held their fire and he was soon joined by a number of unit stretcher-bearers. Seeing what was happening, a few Germans cautiously came out to do the same thing, and a temporary truce developed. Before long many Canadian and German stretcher-bearers were working together, carrying the wounded of both sides to a central pillbox that for a time became a centre for the exchange of the wounded. This unofficial armistice lasted for nearly two hours before some Canadian gunner called for fire on the troops in the open, and sent everyone scurrying for their holes. It was significant, however, as one of those fleeting moments in this appalling war when compassion and the lack of animosity between the soldiers of both sides had an opportunity to be shown.

In the 4th Division sector on the right, the 46th (South Saskatchewan) Battalion had a difficult time from the moment they left the start line.

Our own guns were in this sloppy murk and they couldn't keep the range [as they sank in the mud as a result of recoil] and they dropped short. The Germans were using overhead stuff. We were right in the middle of it — getting shelled from both sides.... They were coming down just like rain.

As the battalion advanced it was subjected to steady and deadly fire from the flanks and from pillboxes to its front. The unit history tells of repeated bursts of fire which picked off a man each time until very few were left in the leading platoons. The remnants of the battalion succeeded in fighting their way onto the line of their objective, but they were soon forced to withdraw by scores of Germans sweeping forward in counterattacks. A handful of officers, however, rallied nearby companies of the 47th and 50th Battalions, together with the survivors of the 46th, and this group again advanced and re-took much of the ground that had just been lost.

The gains in this first phase were indeed small, but they were significant in light of the terrible conditions of the battlefield. And the Canadians did take higher and somewhat drier ground which gave them a much better base for the opening of the next stage four days later.

In the worst of the mud, it took six or even eight men to carry a stretcher. Many of the wounded simply were never recovered. NAC/PA-2140

Meanwhile the heavy task of collecting and getting the many wounded to Advanced Dressing Stations in the rear continued throughout the night and well into the next day. All too many of the walking wounded never made it that far; many stumbled or slid off the duckwalks and drowned in the liquid mud of the shell holes, others drowned trying to cross the flooded Stroombeek, and some simply died of exhaustion on the way. The battalions who had carried the assault had all lost more than half their men.

The second attack went in just before dawn on 30 October, with fresh battalions that had been brought up to the front two days earlier. It was a cold, windy morning as the troops started forward from their shallow, wet holes to follow the covering barrage toward the German positions. But, as on the 26th, they were soon met by heavy shrapnel and by machine-gun fire that seemed to rake every part of the naked ground. But everywhere the determined Canadians pressed on.

On the far left, the 5th CMR had the most difficult ground to cross — a low lying swamp that had once been a wood — but they nonetheless achieved the most notable advance of the day. Their success was in large part due to the gallant leadership of Major George Pearkes. Pearkes, who had taken a piece of shrapnel in his left thigh just as the attack began, led his troops forward through deep mud and bog and drove the enemy out of the swamp. His men, however, were being cut down by machine guns in two strong points beyond a flooded area on the Corps left boundary. He detailed the remnants of a platoon to attack one of these, and he personally led a bayonet charge on the other, known as Vapour Farm. The Germans tried repeatedly to dislodge the 5th CMR from these positions, but even though most of the men were

wounded and their ammunition nearly all gone, Pearkes and his depleted companies held out until a relief party from 2nd CMR reached them after dark. Major Pearkes, in later life to become a Major-General and then Minister of National Defence, was awarded the Victoria Cross.

Prisoners-of-war were routinely used to help the wounded get to medical care in the rear, often without guards. NAC/PA-2060

In the centre, the 49th (Edmonton) Battalion and the Princess Patricia's Canadian Light Infantry encountered a storm of fire as they started out, and very large numbers were killed or wounded in both units in the first few minutes as they struggled forward. The 49th Battalion lost nearly 75 percent of their men in an advance of just over 500 metres, and their colonel ordered the few that were left to dig in. But there were great acts of heroism in the maelstrom. When his company was held up by a machine gun soon after starting out, Private Cecil Kinross dashed forward alone over the open ground, and destroyed the gun and its crew. This act of great personal bravery enabled the unit to continue the advance, and he too was awarded the Victoria Cross.

The Patricias were having an equally difficult battle to the right of the 49th. Most of their officers had been lost within the first hour, but, with the lead companies commanded by their sergeant-majors, they pressed forward until the unit became pinned down by savage machine-gun fire from a pillbox on the edge of the ruins of the village of Meetcheele. At this point Lieutenant Hugh MacKenzie of the 7th Machine Gun Company came forward to take charge. He led a diversionary frontal attack on the pillbox, while Sergeant George Mullin worked his way up to the strong point. Here Mullin took out a sniper post in front of the concrete emplacement and then climbed on top of it, all the while under heavy fire, where he shot the machine gunners with his revolver. He then rushed the entrance of the pillbox, and a frightened enemy garrison surrendered to him. Meetcheele was thus taken by shortly after 0800 hours, and both Lieutenant MacKenzie and Sergeant Mullin were rewarded with the Victoria Cross. By then, however, the Patricias were too weakened to go further, and they established a precarious defensive line which held firm against several counterattacks until they were reinforced in mid-afternoon by fresh companies from the Royal Canadian Regiment. In these few hours of fighting the Patricias were reduced to less than 200 men.

Across the broad swamp that separated the divisions, 4th Division had a much more successful battle, although casualties there were almost as severe as in the 3rd Division units. The 72nd (Seaforth Highlanders of Canada) Battalion reached its objective on the Blue Line by 0930 hours, and even sent a patrol forward into the village of Passchendaele. The 78th (Winnipeg Grenadiers) Battalion, while faltering because of heavy casualties just as they left their jumping-off point, were rallied by the battalion second-in-command, Major John McEwan. McEwan led the unit forward at a mad pace over the 800 metres to their final objective; he was given the Distinguished Service Order for his inspiring leadership. The 85th (Nova Scotia Highlanders) Battalion, on the Corps right, (whose commanding officer, Lieutenant-Colonel Ralston, would become Minister of National Defence during the Second World War) also suffered many casualties in the early stage of the attack, but they fought doggedly, shell hole to shell hole, and the Germans opposing them broke and fled. Just three-quarters of an hour after Zero Hour they too were on their objective.

Once again the Canadian Corps had shown that it could accomplish the near impossible. The Australian and British Corps to their right and left had both failed to make any appreciable gains. The fighting on 30 October left the Canadians poised to take Passchendaele in the next phase of the offensive, but the limited advance of some 1000 metres had cost a further 2321 casualties, 884 of them killed in action.

Digging trenches in the mud at Passchendaele was simply impossible. To get some protection from shell bursts and machine-gun fire, shell craters generally had to suffice. Rubberized ground sheets were often laid over the mud in a generally vain attempt to keep relatively dry, as in this photo of a detachment of the Canadian Machine Gun Corps.
NAC/PA-2162

One notable action occurred on 31 October. The (42nd Royal Highlanders) Battalion, which had relieved the Patricias, made a valiant attempt to clear a strong point known as Graf House, on the edge of the swamp south of Meetcheele. This group of pillboxes continued to cause serious problems for units in both divisions, and had repelled several earlier attempts to capture it. Lieutenant Meyer Cohen led his platoon in a daring night attack, and forced the Germans to abandon the pillboxes. The enemy, however, quickly mounted a strong counterattack. Cohen was killed, and his men, fighting until they were out of ammunition, had no choice but to pull back. This small action is illustrative of the many personal feats of bravery that went unrewarded, officially unnoticed, except in the annals of unit histories.

The week-long 'pause' before the next attack brought a flurry of activity in the Corps. The 3rd and 4th Divisions were relieved by 1st and 2nd Divisions in early November. And feverish preparations for the upcoming battle were everywhere evident. Guns of all calibres were laboriously moved forward, the plank roadways and light railways were extended to carry ammunition and supplies closer to the front, and the plank mule tracks and duckwalks were repaired and brought much nearer to the forward positions. The Germans harassed these preparations as best they could with their artillery, and they moved fresh forces onto Passchendaele Ridge to strengthen their defences.

WINNERS OF THE VICTORIA CROSS AT PASSCHENDAELE

Private Thomas Holmes,
4th Canadian Mounted Rifles

Captain Christopher O'Kelly,
52nd Battalion

Private Cecil Kinross,
49th Battalion

Sergeant George Mullin,
Princess Patricia's Canadian
Light Infantry

Corporal Colin Barron,
3rd Battalion

Major George Pearkes,
5th Canadian Mounted Rifles

The third attack was made on 6 November. At 0600 hours every gun within range in the whole of the Salient opened up on the German positions, and two minutes later the six assault battalions charged forward. The Germans seemed to have been taken by surprise, and their retaliatory bombardment was relatively ineffective. While all of the Canadian battalions still suffered many casualties during their advance, Passchendaele and the whole of the Green Line objective had been taken by 0745. In this overwhelming success, two more Victoria Crosses were won. Corporal Colin Barron of the 3rd (Toronto) Battalion took out a machine-gun post which had halted his unit by crawling forward over completely open ground and, at pointblank range, destroying the gun and crew. In the 27th (Winnipeg) Battalion, Private James Robertson, also by himself, took out a machine-gun emplacement by hurdling over a barbed-wire entanglement and destroying the crew with his bayonet. Robertson was killed later that same day helping to rescue wounded comrades who were exposed to enemy fire. From the wilderness of mud and destruction on top of Passchendaele Ridge, the victorious Canadians looked out onto deep green pastoral fields untouched by the war.

One further attack was made on 10 November to take the part of the ridge which was still in German hands. It took place in a driving rainstorm that made forward movement nearly as difficult as heavy enemy fire. The Germans put up strong resistance, but within just over an hour most objectives had been taken, except where the British, on the left, failed, once again, to do their part.

The Battle of Passchendaele was over. The Canadian Corps had succeeded — in the most appalling of conditions — where everyone else had failed. The victory had been hard won, but it was hollow nonetheless. The capture of Passchendaele Ridge served no tactical or strategic purpose, nor did it bring the war any closer to an end. But it cost Canada 15,654 casualties. Over 2600 men died in the taking of 3000 metres of putrid mud, and well over 1000 of these were never recovered from the mud. Passchendaele will forever live in Canadian military heritage as a symbol of the useless waste of young men's lives.

There is a story that is repeated in nearly every recounting of this battle. On 17 November, Lieutenant-General Sir Launcelot Kiggel, Haig's Chief of Staff, came to visit Passchendaele.

As his staff car lurched through the swampland and neared the battleground he became more and more agitated. Finally he burst into tears and muttered, 'Good God, did we really send men to fight in that?'

The Canadian Corps began to pull out of the Ypres Salient on 14 November. They were sent back to the familiar and more welcome Vimy Ridge front, where they spent the winter. Passchendaele was their last encounter with attrition warfare. Despite the fortified trenches and the wire and the machine guns, some degree of mobility was about to be restored on the Western Front. The first demonstration of that would occur just as the Canadians Corps was arriving in the lines forward of Vimy and Lens.

The desolation of the Passchendaele battlefield. NAC/PA-40139

THE CANADIAN CAVALRY AT CAMBRAI

For some time both the British and the Germans had been working on operational concepts that might offer some hope of breaking the hopeless stalemate that had set in on the Western Front. While the Germans developed a new type of 'infiltration' tactics, the British pinned their focus on tanks.

Tanks had, of course, already failed to perform according to expectations when first used at the Somme in October 1916 and again in the early stage of the Passchendaele offensive: they simply could not move across ground that had been badly torn up by shelling. But proponents of the tank convinced Field Marshal Haig that they should be tried on a 'fresh' battleground, and the front at Cambrai was chosen for the test. What had been intended simply as a large-scale raid, however, gradually became transformed at Byng's Third Army headquarters into a full-blown offensive. Three hundred tanks and five infantry divisions would smash through the formidable Hindenburg Line, and when the gap had been secured, the five divisions of the Cavalry Corps would sweep through and capture a large area behind Cambrai.

The Battle of Cambrai began at daybreak on 20 November 1917. The Germans were taken by surprise, and the tanks quickly rumbled over the Hindenburg defences. Once the Germans had recovered from the initial shock, however, their resistance stiffened, and the pace of the tank advance slowed significantly.

That morning the Canadian Cavalry had moved forward into the outskirts of the village of Masnières, to await orders to gallop forward to capture a German corps headquarters on the northeast side of Cambrai. Opposite Masnières the British advance, without tanks, had, however, been halted in front of strong German positions, but the Canadian cavalrymen were not aware of that development. Shortly before noon the only bridge in Masnières over the St. Quentin Canal had collapsed under a tank that had tried to cross, and elements of the brigade were put to work improvising a crossing at a canal lock 300 metres east of the village.

Fort Garry Horse on the March (II) by Alfred Munnings. CWM 8585

At 1400 hours, believing that the British had opened the way, Brigadier-General Seely ordered the Fort Garry Horse to proceed across the canal. B Squadron of the Garrys had just crossed when Seely received orders to call off the cavalry advance.

Not yet aware that they were heading off behind the German lines on their own, B Squadron rode forward, destroying an entire German battery at swordpoint, and charging several parties of enemy infantry. They took a growing number of casualties in this advance, but the Garrys found that the German defences beyond the canal were light and disorganized. Toward dusk, Lieutenant Harcus Strachan, who had taken over when the squadron leader was killed soon after clearing the canal, realized that the remainder of the brigade was not in fact following behind. German reinforcements had by now begun to arrive in large numbers from the direction of Cambrai, so Strachan decided that the best chance of getting his men back to the British line would be to go on foot after dark. On their way back they bluffed their

way through some enemy positions, but had to fight, hand-to-hand, through others, taking sixteen prisoners in the process before arriving at the collapsed bridge where their story began. Strachan's squadron was the only cavalry to have got behind and engaged the enemy that day, and he was awarded a Victoria Cross for his gallant leadership. Given the relative ease with which that one squadron advanced well into enemy territory, the question has remained, "Would it have made a difference if large numbers of cavalry had gone through?"

At Masnières, the Newfoundland Regiment, still with the British 29th Division, took very heavy casualties in the attack on the Masnières-Beaurevoir Line, and it held out resolutely against repeated German counterattacks over an eleven-day period until withdrawn on 4 December. The Newfoundlanders' stand here was of such heroic quality than an unprecedented honour was bestowed by the King: the Regiment was granted the title "Royal", the only time this distinction was given to any unit in the whole of the war.

Lieutenant Harcus Strachan, who won a VC at Cambrai, leads his squadron of Fort Garrys through a village near the battlefield, early December 1917. NAC/PA-2215

The now *Royal* Newfoundland Regiment, the only unit granted that distinction during the First World War, marching through a French town in late 1917.

Provincial Archives of Newfoundland and Labrador B9-5

The offensive at Cambrai came to a halt on 22 November. It failed more because it was too ambitious, with too few reserves, than because the tanks did not measure up. Indeed the tanks were not as mechanically reliable as they might have been, but with some modifications they would more than prove their worth in the Allied offensives later in 1918. A new era of mechanized warfare had in fact seen its birth.

But the overall situation for the Allies was not particularly favourable. The Czarist government in Russia was overthrown by the Bolsheviks in early November, and just as the battle of Cambrai was being fought the Russians took themselves out of the war. The Germans were thus able to begin to move their entire army to the Western Front. They even now were preparing for a grand spring offensive to win the war before the Americans could arrive in strength. And their success in a counterattack at Cambrai in early December proved the soundness of their new infiltration (Hutier) tactics; they too had found a way out of the stalemate of trench warfare and attrition.

CHAPTER 7

THE ROAD TO VICTORY
1918-1919

by
John Marteinson

As 1918 dawned there was no question that the character of the three-and-a-half-year-old war had begun to change — and change significantly. Russia was now out of the war, and the Germans had begun to transfer 44 divisions to the Western Front. Italy had suffered a major defeat at Caporetto late in the autumn, and was able to re-establish its defences only with the injection of French and British divisions taken from the few precious reserves remaining on the Western Front. The British and French were now stretched very thinly indeed, and maintaining the fighting strength of the field armies was becoming increasingly more difficult. Disillusioned by the huge number of casualties at Passchendaele, the British government, moreover, had begun withholding all but a trickle of reinforcements, and there was talk of simply 'holding out' for a year until a great push could be mounted in 1919. And that would depend on the arrival of enough Americans to tip the strategic balance. While five US divisions would land in France by the end of January, it would still be many months before a strong American army could take to the field in an offensive. So, while methods of breaking loose from the fruitless battles of attrition may well have been discovered, for the Allies there was still no prospect in sight of a satisfactory conclusion to the war.

The Germans were, of course, very much aware of their temporary strategic advantage, but equally aware of their inevitable end once the Americans could deploy in force. Already they were planning an offensive aimed at driving the British 'into the sea', and bringing the war to a decisive conclusion before the Americans arrived in strength. Thus, as the Allies hunkered down to await the Americans and as the Germans prepared for their upcoming offensive, the whole of the Western Front remained relatively quiet. The Canadians Corps continued to occupy the Lens-Vimy sector of the line, while the Canadian Cavalry Brigade, still dismounted, held a sector of the line near the Omignon River.

Canada meanwhile, was having its own manpower crisis. Prime Minister Robert Borden's Unionists had won a majority in the federal general election in November, in part because of the soldiers' vote, and in January 1918 conscription was

Canadian Sentry in the Moonlight by Alfred Bastien. CWM 8060

finally brought into force. The government, however, experienced many difficulties in implementing compulsory service. Widespread claims for exemptions had to be dealt with, and there were even riots. It would be late summer before the first of the conscripts would reach the Corps in France, and in the intervening period the number of replacements available to be sent from Canada fell far short of the number required.

With nearly 20 thousand men serving in a home defence role in England as part of 5th Canadian Division, the shortage of replacements for the Corps was, however, largely a book-keeping contrivance. This division, commanded by Major-General Garnet Hughes, Sir Sam's son, had been formed in February 1917, but had not been sent to the front because of concern over maintaining the strength of an additional three brigades in combat. Early in 1918, however, Hughes and a number of surplus officers, who had gone to England with reinforcement battalions, used their political influence to bring pressure on the Overseas Ministry to 'increase' the size of the Canadian field force to six divisions. Pointing out that the British had 'solved' their manpower shortage by reducing the number of battalions in each brigade from four to three, these men suggested that if the Canadians were to follow suit, the men surplus to the smaller brigades in the five existing divisions could be used to form a sixth. That would allow the formation of a second Canadian corps, and consequently a field army headquarters to command the two corps. And an enormous number of officers would be needed to man the many new headquarters, even though less than 4000 front-line troops would be added to already existing strength.

If ever proof were needed of General Currie's integrity, it was in his opposition to this scam. Had he simply gone along with the plan, he would no doubt have been promoted to the rank of full General in command of a Canadian field army, but he opposed the scheme most vehemently. He argued that the Corps was then the most effective fighting force on the Allied side, and that adding a plethora of inexperienced head-quarters staffs for so small an increase in fighting strength would only serve to reduce the effectiveness of Canadian troops. Currie won that battle, and was also able to engineer the disbandment of Hughes' 5th Division. The infantrymen thus made available provided the reinforcements needed to keep the units of the Corps up to strength until into the final stages of the war.

A soldier's life in the front line, February 1918. NAC/PA-2468

Trying to dry socks over an improvised heater. NAC/PA-1571

THE GERMAN MARCH OFFENSIVE

The relative quiet of the winter was suddenly shattered at 0430 hours on 21 March 1918, when the fire of 6000 guns drenched the southernmost 65 kilometres of the British line. This bombardment has been described as the most ferocious thus far experienced during the whole of the war; the ground shook as far as 30 kilometres from the Fifth Army sector. For five hours this rain of shrapnel and gas shells struck at British gun lines, at company, battalion and brigade headquarters, at support positions and at every defended locality at the front. When the German storm troopers swarmed forward through the heavy fog that blanketed the entire battlefield, there was little resistance. Whole companies had been wiped out, and the few positions that were still manned were soon bypassed and surrounded. Thirty-seven German infantry divisions followed on, and within a matter of hours the enemy had penetrated to the rear of the Fifth Army's forward defensive zone.

On the British side it was pandemonium. With forward units completely overrun, and with rearward communications lines almost non-existent, division, corps and army headquarters had little understanding of the extent of the disaster. It was only later in the afternoon, after the fog had lifted and reconnaissance aircraft had returned, that the British high command could piece together a picture of their perilous situation.

The German drive toward Amiens carried on for nine days before it was halted, and in the confused and fragmented battles during that time, two Canadian brigades played important roles — the Canadian Cavalry Brigade and the 1st Canadian Motor Machine Gun Brigade. Both were hastily deployed southward on 22 March.

Major-General Frank Worthington later recalled his experience with the Machine Gun Brigade.

The situation was very confused and very fluid ... you'd find a Brigadier fighting a platoon mixed with Highlanders and riflemen and all sorts of things.... The methods used by the Motor Machine Guns was very simple. We would take the four or eight guns of a battery and open fire as the enemy would be advancing and bring them to a halt. Then the enemy would get ready to shell us out and the thing to do was to move your guns back to a rear position — maybe a thousand yards back, maybe five hundred — and as the enemy started to move forward again, then you'd give it to them again. Day after day it was the same sort of thing. If things were quiet on one front, you'd get into your vehicles and move someplace else.

As most of the British units had lost their own machine guns in the opening hours of the battle, the Canadian machine gunners played a vital role in delaying the almost unopposed German advance. And, being motorized, they were able to move quickly from place to place to fill critical gaps as temporary defensive positions were improvised.

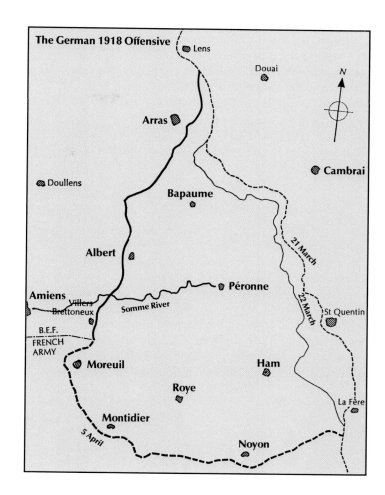

Armoured cars of the 1st Motor Machine Gun Brigade. NAC

183

The Canadian Cavalry Brigade arrived in the southern part of the Fifth Army sector just as the last remnants of the British defences were collapsing. Initially they assisted in covering the withdrawal of the British 18th Division across the Crozat Canal, and became involved in intense, close-quarter fighting to prevent the British being cut off. Later, as the Germans pushed forward relentlessly, the Brigade was split into three ad hoc elements — a dismounted force and two mounted detachments. Over the next three days these three groups, together with similar bodies from other brigades of the 2nd Cavalry Division, fought many widely separated actions, sometimes under French command, helping to re-establish defensive lines that had broken and putting in counterattacks on forward German positions. Their great advantage was mobility. They could rush from one position to another to fill a critical gap, fighting mounted or dismounted as the situation required, bolstering beleaguered British infantrymen for a time, disengaging, and going to the next threatened point. Lieutenant-Colonel W.H. Elkins, Commanding Officer of the Royal Canadian Horse Artillery recalled that "... we had a very great advantage in that show because we'd been trained in open warfare."

We had these light guns and very well-trained men in mobile warfare, and we were able to stay up some time after the field guns had to retire, and then get away, so we were very useful.

The Germans, however, just couldn't be stopped, even though their advance had been resisted as fiercely as was possible by the survivors of the Fifth Army units. Amiens was now seriously threatened, and it appeared that the Germans were about to drive a wedge between the British and the French armies.

The Cavalry Brigade was reunited late on the 27th, and after a day of providing support to the French near Montdidier, withdrew into a bivouac well behind the line of action for the first rest in four days.

Brigadier-General
the Right Honourable
J.E.B. Seely,
Commander of the
Canadian Cavalry Brigade.
IWM

The Canadian Cavalry Brigade during the German offensive. Sketch by Sir Alfred Munnings. CDQ Archives

By 29 March German troops were also exhausted, and their supply lines long and unreliable. Their great offensive was all but spent. But Amiens was in sight, and the attack was renewed. British and French resistance had begun to stiffen but a gap several kilometres wide still existed at the junction of the French and British armies. It was at this point that the Canadian Cavalry Brigade was called upon to play out its most significant role of the whole of the war.

By the morning of 30 March German advanced guards had firmly established themselves on Moreuil Ridge, between the British and French, and it was apparent that they had to be stopped. General Pitman, commander of the 2nd Cavalry Division, ordered General Seely to race to the area and restore the situation.

Seely gave orders for the Brigade to move quickly to Castel, on the Avre River, and he and Major Connolly, his Brigade Major, galloped off to make a reconnaissance. On the way forward, he encountered the commander of a French division, who explained that he was about to withdraw his troops. Seely got him to agree, however, that if the Canadians could take the ridge, the French would continue to hold in the village of Moreuil. Seely soon found that the Germans had occupied the triangular wood on the ridge in considerable strength, and he came up with a hasty plan. He would use the Dragoons, who would be the first to arrive, to occupy the southern and eastern corners of the wood. He would send one Strathcona squadron around the northeast corner to disperse any enemy who might be attempting to move into the wood, and then occupy the eastern face. The remaining two Strathcona squadrons would attack dismounted through the wood from the west, and the Fort Garrys would be kept in reserve. It was a plan that emphasized rapid reaction by individual squadrons rather than coordinated action by the brigade as a whole, but Seely clearly believed that risks had to be taken.

When the regiments arrived at the base of the ridge, squadrons deployed much as Seely had envisioned, although C Squadron of the Dragoons never quite made it to the southern tip. The Dragoons were met with a hail of machine-gun fire as they entered the wood, and for the next hour, five squadrons, some remaining mounted, engaged several hundred Germans in a confused melee.

C Squadron of the Strathconas, commanded by Lieutenant Gordon Flowerdew, was ordered to make for the northeast corner of the wood, to support the Dragoon squadron then fighting its way southward from that point. As Flowerdew's squadron rode up a steep embankment just after rounding the corner, they came upon a group of several hundred German infantrymen who were deploying in the open. Flowerdew wheeled his men into line and shouted, "It's a charge, boys, it's a charge." One troop was given hasty instructions to dismount on reaching the enemy to seize their machine guns.

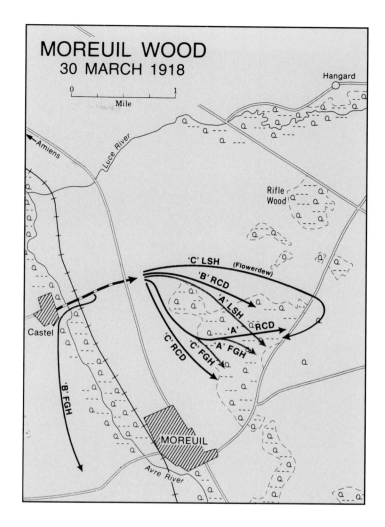

The Germans took a dreadful toll of men and horses as the Strathconas rode onto them. Flowerdew himself was hit at least four times, but still he led his men over one line of the enemy and then the other. Many Germans were killed with the sword, and still others by the troop that had dismounted and captured several machine guns. But over 70 percent of Flowerdew's troopers had fallen during the charge, and the survivors wheeled into the woods midway down the southeast face. The enemy infantry, however, broke and retreated. Lieutenant Gordon Flowerdew died the next day of his wounds, but his gallantry was rewarded with a posthumous Victoria Cross.

Intense fighting with sword, pistol, bayonet and rifle meanwhile continued in the wood. Seely sent two squadrons of the Fort Garrys into the fray as reinforcements, and little by little the Canadian cavalrymen cleared all but the southern end. Toward noon the 3rd Cavalry Brigade arrived to bolster the position, and the two brigades held out against several determined counterattacks until well into the night when the British 8th Division arrived to relieve them.

The Charge of Flowerdew's Squadron by Sir Alfred Munnings. CWM 8571

The Germans counterattacked in strength the next day, and succeeded in re-taking Moreuil Wood and Rifle Wood, to the north, from the 8th Division. Once again the cavalry were ordered to restore the line. On 1 April the Canadian Cavalry Brigade attacked Rifle Wood, dismounted, with the Fort Garry Horse leading. Once again the cavalrymen showed their prowess in dismounted operations; although taking heavy casualties, Rifle Wood was cleared of the enemy within two hours.

Operation *Michael*, the German advance in the direction of Amiens, came to a halt where the Canadian Cavalry stood at Moreuil Wood. The effort to split the British and French armies, and to end the war by driving the British into the sea, had failed. But it was a near run thing. Over the course of the next two months the Germans would undertake several more offensives, and each indeed made notable advances. But their strength was spent, and their best chance for a decisive victory had been thwarted.

Canadian Cavalry after the action at Rifle Wood. NAC

At the time, the Canadian Cavalry Brigade was given much of the credit for single-handedly stopping the German offensive at the very point when the threat was at its most intense. That, we now know, was not entirely accurate; the Germans just did not have the reserves — or the physical strength — to carry on much further. But no one can deny that our cavalry played a very important part in maintaining the link between the British and French armies at the very moment that the French were almost at the point of withdrawing to concentrate on the defence of Paris. Marshal Foch, who on 3 April was appointed Commander-in-Chief of the Allied Armies to coordinate all future operations on the Western front, wrote to General Seely after the war:

I will never forget the heroism of the valiant Canadian Cavalry Brigade. In the month of March 1918, the battle was at the gates of Amiens. It was essential, at any cost, to ensure that the two armies were not separated. On 30 March at Moreuil, and on 1 April at Hangard, your Brigade succeeded, because of its superb ability and its offensive spirit, in checking the enemy and in breaking its will. In large part thanks to your brigade, the situation — hopeless at the beginning of the battle — was restored.

The urgent need for reserves to assist in checking the German advance meanwhile brought about a temporary splintering of the Canadian Corps. Between 23 and 27 March the divisions, one by one, were stripped away to bolster more threatened sectors. The British high command had routinely done this with the Australians, and there had indeed been a few occasions when Canadian formations had served for brief periods under British command. But Canadian troops never liked that, and General Currie had successfully resisted a British move to use Canadian divisions piecemeal at Passchendaele. In this instance, however, Currie understood the strategic crisis facing the high command, and he seems to have accepted the detachment of two divisions to help stem the German onslaught. But when all four divisions were taken from him he protested vehemently, and even raised the issue with the Canadian Overseas Minister in London. He argued pointedly that the relationships between the different levels of headquarters — and the trust that the soldiers had in the staffs — were very different (read better) in the Canadian Corps, and that Canadians were most effective when employed together, under Canadian control. The highly nationalistic nature of Currie's objections very much annoyed the British military hierarchy, but he got his way. In a matter of days, 3rd and 4th Divisions were restored to his command, and a week later the Corps was made responsible for an adjacent sector into which 1st Division had been deployed. 2nd Division, however, did not return until 1 July.

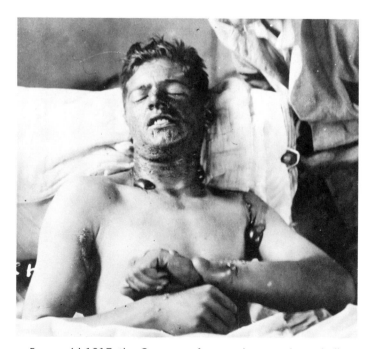

From mid-1917, the Germans often used mustard gas shells during artillery bombardments. This photo shows the terrible blistering caused by mustard gas. NAC/C-80027

General Currie's efforts to hold the Corps together as a fighting entity were fully supported by Prime Minister Borden, and an important precedent was firmly established. In all future operations, Canadian units and formations were not to be broken up!

Even after abandoning their thrust towards Amiens, the Germans continued to press subsidiary attacks throughout the spring and early summer. In mid-April they struck in Flanders, regaining much of the ground the British and Canadians had taken at such great cost in the Passchendaele offensive. In late May the French were attacked on the Chemin des Dames, and the Germans penetrated nearly 50 kilometres toward Paris before they were stopped on the Marne. But, even though the initiative seemed to be held firmly by the Germans, the Allied leaders were also beginning, secretly, to make plans for their riposte — one in which the Canadians would play a leading role.

The Corps was taken out of the line in early May, and the next two and a half months were spent in preparation for the upcoming offensive, even though no one knew when or where it might be. A number of organizational changes were implemented to improve the Corps' overall capability in the attack. Each division received an additional machine-gun company, an engineer brigade (to eliminate the need to use infantrymen for construction and maintenance tasks), and a mechanized transport company (for the rapid forward movement of ammunition and supplies). But perhaps most important was the intense training given to the soldiers in the tactical skills needed in 'open warfare': the use of cover and concealment in advancing rapidly over open ground, manoeuvring within platoons, (i.e., the movement of 10-man sections against enemy positions while being 'covered' by fire from other sections), infiltration around enemy strong points, the use of smoke to conceal movement, and cooperation with tanks. And there was arduous physical conditioning through 50-kilometre-long route marches. When the Corps once again took over a section of the front in mid-July, Currie had seen to it that his men were mentally and physically prepared for offensive operations, and morale could hardly have been higher!

A Sniper in the Cemetery, Neuville-Vitasse by Alfred Bastien. CWM 8070

THE BATTLE OF AMIENS

The front forward of Amiens had been selected as early as May by General Foch and Field Marshal Haig as the location for limited Allied offensive intended to relieve the threat to the vital railway line running from Paris to the north of France. While the French and British would both play a part, Foch and Haig had agreed that it would be the 'colonial storm troops' — the Canadians and Australians — who would have the principal roles. While the attack was initially planned for June, the German offensive on the Marne forced postponement until early August.

Lice were always a problem for soldiers in the trenches. These men are hunting for what they called 'seam squirrels'. NAC/PA-1400

As the Germans had overrun the sector only in late March, it was still relatively weakly defended. There were no extensive trench complexes, no concrete pillboxes, and no deep belts of barbed wire. If surprise could be achieved — and its importance had been seen in every Allied and German offensive since Cambrai — these light defences offered the prospect of quick success. Secrecy, therefore, became the guiding principle in all of the preparations for the battle. General Currie was not informed that the Canadians would be involved until 16 July — just over three weeks before it was to begin — and he was asked to keep information about the operation from all but key staff planners until the last minute. Battalion, brigade and even division commanders were not briefed until 29 July, one day before the move south to Amiens was to begin!

Since the arrival of the Canadians on a new front, particularly if adjacent to the Australians, would give a clear signal to the Germans that an attack was imminent, an elaborate deception plan was devised. The Australian Corps, already holding a section of the Amiens front, took over what was to be the Canadian start line from the French, giving the impression to the enemy that the Allied defences there were

The 75th Battalion at rest during the Canadian Corps' period of intense training in 'open warfare'. NAC/PA-1543

in fact being *thinned*. And when a few Canadian officers were allowed to go forward to see the ground over which they were to attack, they were dressed in Australian uniforms. The most complex aspect of the deception measures, however, involved sending a large group north, to Kemmel Hill in Flanders. Here, two units — the 4th CMR and 27th (Winnipeg) Battalion — were sent in on a trench raid, during which they were careful to leave behind enough equipment and insignia that the Germans would easily recognize as being Canadian. In addition, the Corps wireless (radio) section began transmitting bogus messages with the intention of convincing the enemy that Canadian Corps headquarters was being set up in the north, and two casualty clearing stations were established near the front, always a sure sign of an impending assault. As the Germans already suspected that the Canadians might be preparing an attack in Flanders, these efforts served brilliantly as confirmation of their (faulty) intelligence.

The movement of over 100 thousand Canadian troops to a concentration area south of Amiens was done under the same cloak of secrecy. The troops were told nothing, and it was all done at night between 30 July and 3 August. In the concentration area everything was hidden in large woods and in farm buildings — the many thousands of men, 20 thousand horses, over 1000 guns and hundreds of tanks. Most of three divisions were in fact crowded into a single 2 x 3-kilometre wood well within range of enemy artillery. While everyone was kept under cover during daylight, there was grave concern that the Germans would still somehow discover their presence. Corporal R.H. Camp of the 18th Battalion remarked, "If the Germans ever got wise, oh it would have been a terrible slaughter, because we were packed in there so tight...."

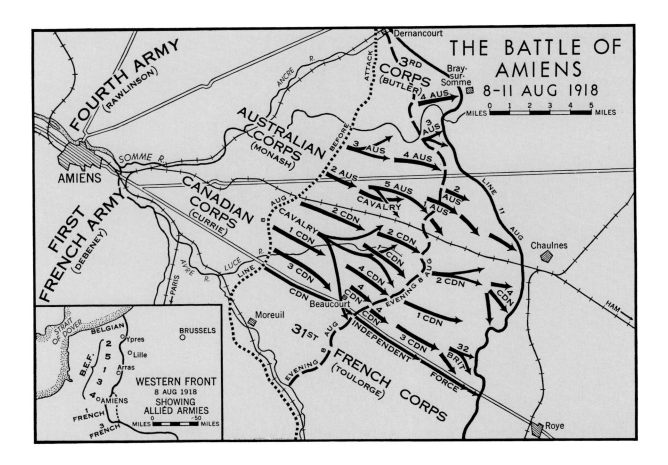

The need for secrecy in fact created a logistics nightmare. Because the Corps was not permitted to establish its own ammunition and supply dumps, there were very serious problems in moving the seven thousand tons of artillery shells and nearly 10 million rounds of small-arms ammunition from British dumps miles behind the front. And there were only two roads, and not nearly enough trucks. The Canadian Army Service Corps, however, performed a near miracle, but it was a close-run thing; the last load of ammunition for the guns was delivered only hours before the attack began. Many of the units still, however, had to scrounge grenades and rifle ammunition from neighbouring French units.

The plan for the attack was very simple. There would be no preliminary bombardment, except on the French front. A rolling barrage would begin at Zero Hour, and tanks would lead the infantry through the enemy's forward defences, as at Cambrai. The main effort would be made in the centre, by the five Australian and four Canadian divisions, against three objective lines — the forward German defences, the reserve localities and gun lines, and then a final line well into the enemy's depth. An elaborate counterbombardment plan would ensure that the enemy's artillery could not disrupt the advance.

On the 7500-metre front, the initial break in would be made by the 1st, 2nd and 3rd Divisions, each with one brigade up. A second brigade would come into line as the frontage widened, the third brigade in each division remaining in reserve. The 4th Division formed the Corps reserve, destined — together with the cavalry — to take the lead south of the River Luce when the 1st and 3rd Divisions reached the intermediate objective line.

Each of the assaulting divisions would have a battalion of 42 heavy (Mark V) tanks under command, while 4th Division was allotted 36. Also available were two battalions of *Whippet* light tanks, armed with machine guns, which would accompany the cavalry. And, more than any other battle yet fought, Amiens involved air power. Each of the corps had a squadron of two-seaters allocated to it for reconnaissance patrols and artillery observation duties. These corps squadrons were protected by eight single-seater fighter squadrons, some of which would engage in close ground support when circumstances permitted.

On the morning of 8 August surprise was retained until the very last minute. Soon after midnight, two Handley-Page bombers, flown by Canadian pilots, began to patrol the front at low level, the noise of their engines attempting to drown out that of the tanks moving up to the line.

The regimental history of the 48th Highlanders describes these tense moments. At 0408 hours,

A strange, wild thrumming filled the air and merged with the hammering roar of low aircraft. And from their hiding places in the shadows, beginning to lift with dawn, charged the tanks. At full speed they came, lurching, wobbling, waddling to battle. They had 800 yards to go before the barrage commenced and they were covering it as fast as their rocking, swaying awkwardness would let them....

Canadians moving past dug-in French troops forward of Amiens on 8 August 1918. NAC/PA-2925

The first gun fired at 0420 hours, as the first infantryman and the first tank went 'over the top'. There was little opposition as battalion after battalion swarmed forward into a heavy mist that limited visibility to a few metres and made direction-keeping very difficult. Isolated pockets of the enemy were simply bypassed and left to be dealt with by units coming up behind. Private Bill Macklin of the 19th Battalion recalled his experience on the Canadian left flank.

... the shells came over our heads with an appalling shriek in the fog ahead and we simply lit cigarettes, shouldered our rifles, and walked off after the shells. This is what we did until we reached the (first) objective....

Private S.J. Carr, a Lewis gunner with the 10th Battalion, remembered, "In no time at all we were right out in nice, pleasant open countryside. That was the best executed and the best picked out plan that was ever pulled off."

As was so often the case during the war, the tanks proved to be somewhat of a disappointment. Many got lost in the fog, others broke down, and in the south of the Corps sector a number bogged down while trying to cross the Luce. But this seemed to have made little difference; by 0820 the first objective — the Green Line — had been taken, and fresh brigades were well on their way to the next.

Troops dig in on the intermediate objective, while a *Whippet* tank passes through, late morning on 8 August.
NAC/PA-2926

By mid-morning the fog began to lift and the pace of the advance slowed, mainly because of resistance from nests of enemy machine guns, whose crews could now see their targets. Four Victoria Crosses were won on 8 August — all for gallantry in taking out machine-gun posts. The first went to Corporal Harry Miner of the 58th Battalion, who was killed as he made his *third* single-handed charge of the morning. Two VCs were awarded to members of the 13th Battalion; to Private John Croak, and to Corporal Herman Good, who later in the day also personally captured a German field artillery battery. Yet another was awarded to Lieutenant James Tait of the 78th Battalion, who "dashed forward alone" and killed the crew of a concealed machine gun, enabling his men to capture a further twelve machine guns.

Captain James Tait, VC, 78th Battalion

The 3rd Division, in the south, reached the intermediate objective — the Red Line — just before 1000 hours. At this point the Canadian Cavalry Brigade, the vanguard of the 3rd Cavalry Division, passed through with a battalion of 32 *Whippet* tanks. The intention was that the cavalry, with light tanks to deal with machine-gun emplacements, would be able to exploit rapidly across what was now 'open' country. Unhappily, this intended cooperation did not work out. The *Whippets* were too slow to keep up with cavalry galloping cross-country, but they outpaced the horsemen whenever machine guns were encountered. Private N.R. Nagle of the 78th Battalion remembered the cavalry going forward.

... A whole brigade of cavalry came down the one bank of this ravine and passed through our lines and went into action. The part that remains in my memory was the wonderful sight of these, oh maybe a thousand or so horsemen, just going down one side of the valley and into action. Within an hour they had so many casualties.

The Royal Canadian Dragoons and Strathconas charged forward with true cavalry elan. Along the Corps' right boundary they advanced nearly four kilometres and captured several hundred prisoners, but enemy machine-gun fire killed hundreds of their horses, and the cavalry thrust was soon blunted. They had been committed too early — before a real gap in the enemy defences had been torn open.

Canadian Cavalry going into action at Amiens.
NAC/PA-1797

4th Division passed through both the 3rd Division and the Cavalry Brigade just before 1300 hours, but the leading battalions got ahead by only about 2000 metres before being halted by the same machine-gun fire that had stopped the cavalry. Elsewhere, however, the Canadians pushed on. What little enemy resistance was offered in the 1st Division sector in the centre was quickly overcome, and the final objective was reached by 1330, well ahead of schedule. Colonel Dan Ormond, who commanded the 10th Battalion which had led the division's advance, recalled:

We had some difficult fighting as we approached the final objective, which was a line of old British trenches. But we were there ahead of time so we could have gone on for I've no idea how much longer. It wasn't the opposition from the Boche that stopped us at all, it was a matter of having to wait for the artillery to be leap-frogged forward.

2nd Division, bordering the Australians on the left, faced a much more resolute and better-led enemy, but even there the advancing Canadians could not be stopped, and they were firm on the final line by early evening.

In just over fourteen hours the Canadian Corps had thrust forward by twelve kilometres, and the Australians by nearly as much. In the process nearly two German divisions had been obliterated. The Canadians alone took over 5000 prisoners-of-war in that brief time. General Ludendorf later called this the "black day of the German Army in the history of this war." And while the German Army was still far from being defeated in the field, the morale of its high command had suffered an irreparable blow; *they* were now convinced that they would lose the war!

Cavalrymen with drawn sabres escort German prisoners to the rear. NAC/PA-2853

The British high command were almost as taken aback as their German counterparts. General Currie later wrote:

… Senior staff officers hurried up from GHQ to see me and ask what I thought should be done. They indicated quite plainly that the success had gone far beyond expectation and that no one seemed to know just what to do. I replied in the Canadian vernacular: 'The going seems good: let's go on!'

German Prisoners
by F.H. Varley. CWM 8961

Lieutenant Jean Brillant,
VC, 22nd Battalion.

Motor Machine Gun Brigade cars going into action at
Amiens. NAC/PA-3015

The Germans rushed up reserve divisions on the afternoon and evening of 8 August, and when the offensive was renewed on the next afternoon a much more determined enemy resistance was met across the whole front. As on the first day, enemy machine guns caused the biggest problems. Another four Victoria Crosses were awarded on 9 August for extraordinary valour in silencing guns that were holding up the advance: to Sergeant Raphael Zengel of the 5th Battalion, and to Corporal Alexander Brereton and Corporal Frederick Coppins, both of the 8th Battalion. Even among these feats of heroism, the award to Lieutenant Jean Brillant of the 22nd Battalion was particularly notable. On two separate occasions Brillant charged and captured enemy machine-gun nests. Both times he was wounded, but he still refused to leave his company. Subsequently, when a field gun fired on his men over open sights he led a charge against it, and even when wounded a third time he carried on until he fell unconscious from loss of blood. His gallant leadership and superb example were in part responsible for the 22nd Battalion making the greatest gains of the day.

The Canadians had hammered forward for five kilometres on the 9th, and took three more on the 10th, but the enemy brought up another eight fresh divisions before nightfall of the second day. As always during the First World War, railways permitted the defender to reinforce his failing front much faster than the attacker could widen and deepen any gap that he might create. Another ten divisions would arrive by midnight on the 11th, despite efforts by the RAF to destroy the Somme bridges and thus isolate the battlefield. Then too, the advance had reached the edge of the 1916 Somme battlefield, with mazes of old trenches and barbed wire. Colonel A.G.L. McNaughton, commander of the Corps Artillery and in later years Chief of the General Staff, remembered that stage in the battle.

... We were coming up against the Roye wire, the strongest wire I've ever seen in my life ... uncut, far worse than new wire because it ran through the hay fields and you couldn't see the damn stuff. I remember going around with General Currie and saying that what we needed was a new break where we could get our legs under us and start again.

The prospects of any further success were very slight, and casualty figures were rising. Currie, recognizing the impracticable and, as ever, anxious to avoid it, recommended that the attack be broken off. Haig agreed.

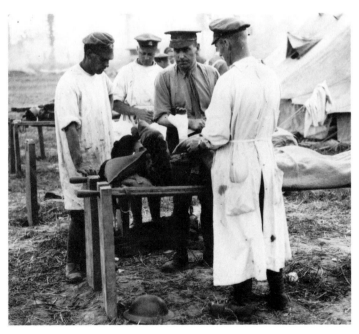

Medical Officers at a Canadian Field Ambulance treating a
wounded officer in the open during the Amiens offensive.
NAC/PA-2890

The fighting continued until 19 August, but after the 10th it involved mainly small, albeit often sharp and bitter actions to straighten the line and to clear some of the old trenches that the Germans had fortified and were attempting to hold.

Amiens was a great tactical victory. The Canadian Corps had advanced 22 kilometres on a front of 10 thousand metres, and had captured nearly 9000 prisoners. These gains had cost nearly 12 thousand casualties, but this time at least there had been real purpose, and very substantial results. This battle changed the course of the war; it brought the end in sight! And, as the London *Times* wrote in August 1918, "… it was chiefly a Canadian battle."

As the Canadian Corps began to leave the Amiens battlefield on 19 August for Arras, where they would soon begin the next advance of the last 'Hundred Days', the Germans had already decided to open negotiations for an armistice. But there was still hard fighting to be done, and Marshal Foch had again picked the Canadians to lead the way through one of the most difficult battles of the last phase of the war.

Sir Douglas Haig reviews a Canadian battalion after the victory at Amiens. NAC/PA-2900

BREAKING THE HINDENBURG LINE

After the highly successful offensive at Amiens was broken off, Marshals Foch and Haig agreed that the Allies would then press the Germans relentlessly in a series of successive attacks at different points along the front. The Canadians had only just begun to arrive back in their familiar positions east of Arras when General Currie was told that the Corps was to begin an offensive on 26 August aimed at breaking through the formidable Drocourt-Queant Line, which formed the northern hinge of the Hindenburg Line. It was a daunting task. The area forward of the Canadians was a thick web of trenches and fortifications, some among the most highly developed on the whole of the Western Front. And the Germans were determined to hold the Hindenburg Line firmly; it was their last real bastion in the west.

What came to be known as the Battle of the Scarpe began at 0300 hours — two hours before dawn — on 26 August. Behind the usual thick barrage, three divisions burst forward into the darkness, the British 51st Highland Division on the left, 3rd Canadian Division in the centre, and 2nd Canadian Division on the right. Two strongly held hill features were both taken in flanking attacks, and for much of the day only isolated pockets of stiff resistance were encountered. Lieutenant Charles Rutherford of the 5th Canadian Mounted Rifles won a Victoria Cross in a hard fight for the village of Monchy-le-Proux, but the enemy for the most part seemed unwilling to make strong stands against the reckless Canadians until late in the afternoon. By nightfall, as the forward troops began to approach a trench system known as the Fresnes-Rouvroy Line, German resistance grew more resolute. Throughout the night the enemy put in one counterattack after another, but the Corps retained its gain of nearly 6000 metres, and with relatively light casualties.

Over the Top by Alfred Bastien.
This painting depicts the Royal 22e Regiment assault on the Fresnes-Rouvroy Line on 28 August 1918. CWM 8058

It was, however, quite a different story over the next two days. The Germans brought in fresh divisions and many additional machine guns. As they renewed their attack, the Canadians confronted line after line of trenches and, all too often, thick uncut barbed wire, and the fighting reverted to the metre-by-metre slogging of earlier trench battles. While advances of up to 3000 metres were made in some places, casualties were extremely heavy; some units lost over half of their men. Major Georges Vanier, in later years a Major-General, a distinguished diplomat and Governor-General of Canada, was brought forward late on the 27th to take command of the remnants of the 22nd Battalion after their commanding officer had been wounded.

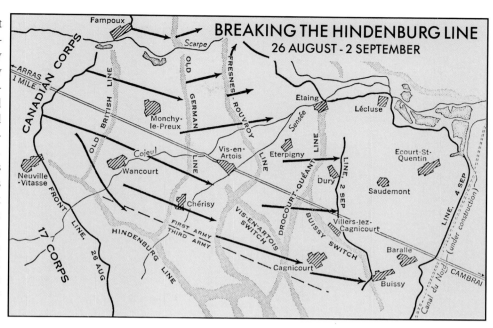

I reached the Battalion at dusk. The troops were scattered in shell holes without any definite trench line. I got in touch with Lieutenant-Colonel Clark-Kennedy, in command of the 24th Battalion, which had attacked next to the 22nd. Our staffs at the headquarters and in the companies were so depleted that we decided to spend the night together in one headquarters....

At about 9:30 the next morning, the 28th August, a staff officer ... arrived with the news that our two battalions would be attacking again at 12:30 that day. Clark-Kennedy, a most gallant officer, and I looked at each other but didn't say much. But each knew what the other was thinking, knowing how depleted our battalions were....

I called a meeting in a large shell hole of the few officers who were left. I told them about the attack and, in the circumstances, there was only one thing to do. When the barrage fell the officers were to rise and call on the men to follow.

Major Vanier was hit in the chest soon after the attack went in, and while his wound was being dressed a shell shattered his right knee. All of the officers in the Van Doos were killed or wounded during the day, and at one point the unit Medical Officer found himself having to take command. Colonel Clark-Kennedy, who valiantly led his 24th Battalion in repeated charges against enemy positions, was later awarded the Victoria Cross.

First aid being given to one of the Canadian casualties. NAC/PA-3231

The only significant gain on 28 August was further to the north, where 9th Brigade, attacking on a narrow front, penetrated through the Fresnes-Rouvroy Line defences. By evening both 2nd and 3rd Divisions were thoroughly exhausted, and General Currie brought in the 1st Canadian and 4th British Divisions to take over.

Vicious fighting continued periodically over the last three days of August as Canadian units gradually completed the capture of the Fresnes-Rouvroy defences. But just 2000 metres beyond stretched the even more formidable Drocourt-Queant Line, which the Germans called the *Wotan Stellung*, the Odin Line.

The Drocourt-Queant Line was the northernmost extension of the great Hindenburg Line fortifications, and its capture would put the entire German defence line at risk. It consisted of a front line sited on the forward slope of a long, bald ridge, and a support line roughly a thousand metres in back, at the base of the rearward slope. Deep concrete shelters protected its occupants, and hundreds of reinforced concrete machine-gun posts provided inter-locking fire over a dense mass of barbed wire that extended the whole length of the position. Currie knew that this could be the most difficult task ever undertaken by the Corps, and he called a pause until the artillery could be re-positioned and thorough preparations completed.

As the sun rose on the morning of 2 September, a barrage of unprecedented weight fell on the enemy, and the 1st and 4th Divisions, along with a British brigade on the left flank, rushed forward. Two companies of Mark V tanks (16) with each division flattened lanes through the maze of wire, and the leading waves of infantrymen swarmed into the German front trench. In most places enemy resistance was far lighter than had been expected, although there were many fierce fights. The first of seven Victoria Crosses to be awarded for action on this day was won by Lance Corporal William Metcalf of the 16th Battalion. When his unit was pinned down by fire, the official citation states that he

... rushed forward under intense machine gun fire to a passing tank. With his signal flag he walked in front of the tank, directing it along the trench in a perfect hail of bullets and bombs. The machine gun strong points were overcome, very heavy casualties were inflicted on the enemy, and a very critical situation was relieved.

Much of the forwardmost defence line was taken by 0800, and the Germans surrendered in droves.

Canadian troops and German prisoners take cover in a trench, while an artillery observer watches the fall of shells, early September 1918. NAC/PA-3127

However, as units pressed forward to the crest of the ridge, beyond the first trench line, the intensity of enemy artillery and machine-gun fire grew tremendously. Lance Corporal George Black of the 72nd Battalion remembered his company's efforts to advance onto the enemy support line.

The ground on the far side of that ridge — Mount Dury they called it — was absolutely open, nothing whatsoever to give a person any kind of cover. So as soon as anyone made any move to get over the top there'd be this hail of bullets from I don't know how many machine guns, and they'd be cut down in a minute. A lot of men went down there trying.

By mid-afternoon, however, the whole of the Drocourt-Queant Line was in Canadian hands, and in the evening the 1st Division pressed forward to take a subsidiary trench line three kilometres beyond. But the fighting had been heavy and very costly. And six more VCs were won: by Private Walter Rayfield of the 7th Battalion, by Sergeant Arthur Knight of the 10th Battalion, by Lieutenant-Colonel Cyrus Peck, commanding officer of the 16th Battalion, by Private Claude Nunney of the 38th Battalion, who already was the recipient of both the Distinguished Conduct and the Military Medal, by Captain Seymour Hutcheson, the Medical Officer of the 75th Battalion, and by Private John Young, a stretcher bearer with the 87th Battalion.

Currie called a halt in late evening, and issued orders that the advance was to resume the next day. But during the night the enemy withdrew behind the Canal du Nord, more than six kilometres further on, and the Corps was able to sweep forward to the west bank of the canal without opposition. And, as important, the Germans had also begun to withdraw all along the British front!

It was yet another victory laurel for the Canadian Corps, one that General Currie thought was perhaps even greater than that won at Amiens. And it was a major contribution to the ever-nearer defeat of the German Army.

The French, Americans and British continued the process of attacking successively at key points along the whole of the front, and while these were carried out, the Canadians had a well-deserved three weeks of rest while plans were made for the next stage in their relentless advance of the last 'Hundred Days'.

Victoria Cross Winners

Lieutenant Charles Rutherford,
VC, MC, MM,
5th Canadian Mounted Rifles

Private Claude Nunney,
VC, DCM, MM, 38th Battalion

Lieutenant-Colonel W.H. Clark-Kennedy,
VC, CMG, DSO,
24th Battalion

Private Walter Rayfield,
VC, 7th Battalion

Sergeant Arthur Knight,
VC, 10th Battalion

Lance-Corporal William Metcalf,
VC, MM, 16th Battalion

THE CANAL DU NORD TO CAMBRAI

As part of the continuing series of Allied thrusts, the next task for the Canadians was to cross the Canal du Nord, to their front, and take the city of Cambrai nine kilometres beyond.

The dry section of the Canal du Nord where the Canadians crossed on 27 September 1918. NAC

Currie made a detailed reconnaissance of the canal forward of the Corps position, and determined that a frontal assault offered little but the prospect of disaster. The canal itself was nearly 100 metres wide, and on each side a further 400 metres was flooded swampland. Moreover, the ground for several thousand metres on both banks was completely open and dominated by strong German positions on the heights on the far side. Slightly to the south, however, was a 4000-metre section of the canal that was not yet complete; the bed was dry, and the surrounding ground was firm. Currie asked that the Corps boundary be shifted southward, so that the crossing could be made there. Once firmly established on the far bank, he planned to have the divisions fan out laterally before thrusting eastward toward Cambrai. This plan entailed considerable risk, for the whole of the Corps would have to be bunched in a small area near the crossing sites — dangerously so if discovered by the Germans — and it was a very complex manoeuvre to have to execute under fire. But, it did at least offer some prospect of achieving surprise, and that always appealed to Currie.

After dark on 26 September, the 1st and 4th Divisions assembled their men in rear of their positions in the Drocourt-Quéant Line, and silently moved to crowded assembly points near the canal. At 0520 hours on the 27th, the opening barrage crashed over the enemy defences and his gun positions, and four battalions of the 1st and 10th Brigades dashed across the dry canal bed. Light opposition on the east bank was rapidly overcome, and within an hour a 2000-metre-deep bridgehead was firmly held. Follow-on units then took the lead. On the right, heavy opposition was soon encountered by 4th Division just west of Bourlon Wood, and the advance there was also hindered by heavy fire coming from the flank because a British attack had not kept pace. However, little by little units of the 11th and 12th Brigades fought their way forward against an enemy force twice their size, and by 2000 hours the vital heights of Bourlon Wood had been cleared. On the left, 1st Division had an easier time. In that sector a final bridgehead objective, 5000 metres from the canal, was reached by 1400 hours, and the 11th British Division, attached for the assault, passed through to fan out on the far left. By nightfall, units of 2nd Brigade had pushed onward another 5000 metres until they were stopped by thick wire barricades in front of the last remaining trench line in the area, the Marcoing Line. The day had brought another tremendous success for the Corps!

Three more Victoria Crosses were awarded for gallant leadership that day in taking out enemy strong points: to Lieutenant Graham Lyall of the 102nd Battalion, to Lieutenant Samuel Honey of the 78th Battalion, and to Lieutenant George Kerr of the 3rd Battalion.

The Germans this time were determined to stop the Canadians, and in short order seven additional divisions were thrust into battle forward of Cambrai.

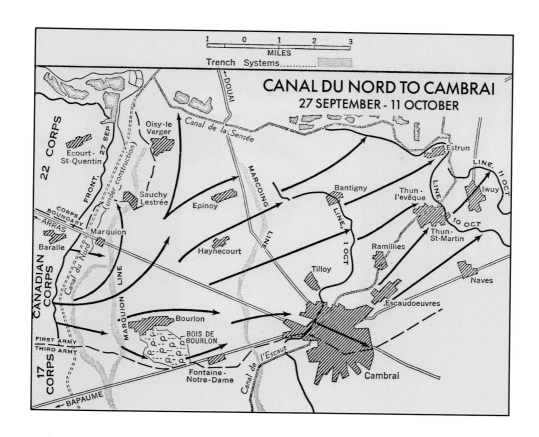

CANAL DU NORD TO CAMBRAI
27 SEPTEMBER - 11 OCTOBER

Advancing beyond the Canal du Nord. IWM

Lieutenant George Kerr,
VC, MC, MM, 3rd Battalion

Captain John MacGregor,
VC, MC, DCM,
2nd Canadian Mounted Rifles

Lieutenant Milton Gregg,
VC, MC,
Royal Canadian Regiment

Sergeant William Merrifield,
VC, MM, 4th Battalion

Sergeant Hugh Cairns,
VC, DCM, 46th Battalion

The Marcoing Line was the principal preoccupation of both Canadian divisions on the 28th. It was very hard fighting throughout the day, and casualties increased with every hour. Small gains, however, continued to be made, mainly because of innumerable, mostly unnoticed acts of bravery. One of the most notable of these took place in the Royal Canadian Regiment. When the battalion was held up by uncut wire, Lieutenant Milton Gregg crawled forward during a severe artillery bombardment to find a passage through the entanglement. When he did find a narrow gap, Gregg went back to his company, picked a few men, and led them into the enemy trench. There they fought with bayonet, bomb and rifle butt, and destroyed several machine-gun nests. Gregg and his men held off a strong counterattack, and when they began to run out of bombs, even though seriously wounded, Lieutenant Gregg crawled back to his own lines to get more. Having beaten off the enemy, this small party proceeded to capture the whole of the trench in front of the company. For his extraordinary valour, Milton Gregg, in later life a Brigadier and a minister in the Federal Cabinet, was decorated with the Victoria Cross.

The whole of the Marcoing Line was eventually taken on 28 September. Over the next three days, however, only some small gains were made on the north side of Cambrai, and they proved to be extremely costly in the face of very determined German defenders. With the troops now very tired, and with casualties nearly as high as in the worst of the battles at Ypres, General Currie broke off the attack on the night of 1 October.

Canadian Highlanders moving forward into the battle for Cambrai. NAC

Despite the bitter resistance, the Germans were in reality on the verge of defeat. At General Ludendorf's insistence, the German chancellor made an approach to the American president on 4 October to ask for armistice negotiations. The German nation was in fact close to collapse, but the Army leadership believed that it had to hold on so that ground could be traded for better armistice terms.

While the Canadians paused at Cambrai, the British, French, Belgians and Americans continued to press forward all across the Western Front. When the Canadian attack was resumed shortly after midnight on 9 October, the Germans were caught preparing to withdraw to a new defensive line — the Hermann Line — which they were trying desperately to establish well to the northeast, near Valenciennes. Over the next hours, Canadian units entered the suburbs of Cambrai, even while German rearguards were making last ditch attempts to destroy key installations. At this juncture saving the few remaining bridges over the Canal de l'Escaut became an important priority. Captain Norman Mitchell of the Canadian Engineers led a small party of sappers ahead of the infantry into the northern suburb of Escaudoeuvres. He found the main bridge there prepared for demolition, and he began to cut wires leading to the explosive charges. When an enemy platoon attempted to charge the bridge, Mitchell and his sergeant held them off, and he continued the task of removing the explosives even though he knew that the Germans might blow the demolitions at any moment. For his bravery and devotion to duty, Captain Mitchell was awarded the Victoria Cross. Later that same morning, General Loomis, commander of the 3rd Division entered Cambrai formally to mark its liberation. The division battle flag which was then presented to the mayor still has a place of honour in the city council chamber.

A Canadian soldier takes cover to avoid sniper fire during the fighting at Cambrai, early October 1918.
NAC/PA-3266

A Canadian patrol in the rubble-strewn city of Cambrai, 9 October 1918. NAC

The Canadian Corps, which had been in action nearly continually since 22 August, was relieved on 11 October and the Arras-Cambrai battle came to an end. In those 47 days the Corps had advanced over 37 kilometres, and had, for varying periods, encountered nearly one-quarter of the German divisions in France. The Canadians once again had been the spearhead of the Allied offensive. Nearly 31 thousand casualties were suffered in that six-week period, two-thirds in the costly fighting for Cambrai. But the troops now knew that there was purpose to their sacrifice: the end of this long and bloody war was finally in sight. Armistice negotiations were taking place, but the Allied push was to continue for another month until the enemy surrendered.

THE LAST CAVALRY CHARGE

At the very time that Cambrai was being liberated by the Corps, the Canadian Cavalry Brigade, which was part of the 3rd Cavalry Division some 20 kilometres southeast of Cambrai, was itself liberating a whole series of French villages.

Early on the morning of 9 October British infantry were halted at Maretz by machine-gun fire from strong German rearguards that were attempting to protect the enemy retreat to the Hermann Line. 3rd Cavalry Division was called forward to break the impasse, and the task of attacking the rearguards was given to the Canadians. Brigadier-General R.W. Paterson, who had taken command of the Canadian cavalry after their battle at Moreuil, sent in the Strathconas and the Fort Garry Horse. Lieutenant James Dunwoody, a troop leader with the Garrys, led what was to be the last cavalry charge of the war against enemy machine gunners in the Bois de Gattigny.

We clattered over the heads of the amazed South Africans, and the Germans were so surprised to find horsed cavalry coming at them that I think they must have lost their nerve. They were firing high, firing low, but there was a distinct flavour of hail stones coming at us all the time and horses and men were dropping rapidly. We got to the edge of the wood, which was a high embankment, (afterward we found there were 62 machine guns in it) and just as we reached there my horse was shot and killed and I was wounded in the thigh. However, about a third of our men got through, and we scrambled up the bank and started to work with our rifles and revolvers.

The gallant charge of the Fort Garrys forced the Germans to pull back, and Lieutenant Dunwoody, recommended for a VC, was awarded the Distinguished Service Order. For the remainder of the day the three regiments of the brigade galloped forward time and again, outflanking the German rearguards, attacking dismounted when necessary, and took one village after another. By nightfall they had advanced more than 14 kilometres, and had taken over 400 prisoners.

Cavalry and Tanks Advance at Arras by Alfred Bastien. CWM 8092

This proved to be the last action of the war for the Canadian Cavalry Brigade. There had been little opportunity for mounted action in this war of trenches and machine guns, and the cavalrymen had spent most of the war serving as infantry in the trenches, but it was a fitting and gallant last engagement. In future, the cavalry would trade their horses for more potent steeds; tanks were to be the rebirth of cavalry mobility in the wars to come.

On another more distant sector of the front, the Royal Newfoundland Regiment, serving with the 9th British Division, was making a notable contribution to the success of the British advance in Flanders. The battalion was particularly heavily involved on 14 October, during which time 94 machine guns and eight field artillery pieces were captured. Here, the heroic deed of one young soldier stands out. At one point the battalion's attack was held up by the fire of an enemy battery firing at point blank range. Seventeen-year-old Private Thomas Ricketts

Private Thomas Ricketts, VC,
Royal Newfoundland Regiment

... at once volunteered to go forward with his section commander and a Lewis gun to attempt to outflank the battery. Advancing by short rushes under heavy fire from enemy machine guns with the hostile battery, their ammunition was exhausted when still 300 yards from the battery. The enemy, seeing an opportunity to get their field guns away, began to bring up their gun teams. Pte. Ricketts, at once realizing the situation, doubled back 100 yards under the heaviest machine gun fire, procured further ammunition, and by very accurate fire drove the enemy into a farm. His platoon then advanced without casualties, and captured the four field guns ...

Ricketts was awarded the Victoria Cross. He was the youngest of Canada's VCs.

A German machine gunner who died in the battle for Cambrai.
NAC/PA-3441

THE PURSUIT TO MONS

On 16 October the Germans resumed their withdrawal to the new Hermann Line, which was anchored on the city of Valenciennes, some 25 kilometres to the northeast of the Canadian Corps positions. Patrols confirmed that the enemy had left behind only rearguard troops, and the next morning the Canadians began a somewhat cautious pursuit. Everyone sensed that the war could not continue much longer, and, to keep casualties to a minimum, Currie gave orders that decisive engagements were to be avoided.

The Victory Medal. All Allied nations issued a medal with a similar design and ribbon.

The British War Medal 1914-1918.

For the next week the Corps pressed forward slowly against only sporadic opposition. The going was difficult, nonetheless, mainly because the retreating Germans were systematically demolishing bridges and extensively cratering the roads. Serious problems were thus encountered in moving guns and ammunition, and in bringing forward the whole range of supplies, including food, water and fuel, needed by a large army on the move. But there was an enormous spirit of optimism among the troops, and they were warmly welcomed by the people in the many villages that were liberated. At times almost a carnival-like atmosphere prevailed.

Every house you go near, you are hauled in and made to drink black coffee till you can hardly see. For the last three nights I have slept in a feather bed.... The troops coming out of the line are absolutely bedecked with flowers, and the horses carry so many that the poor beasts don't know what to make of it.

wrote Lieutenant Brookes Gossage of the 66th Field Battery.

By the evening of 23 October the lead elements of the Corps had closed to within a few kilometres of Valenciennes and to the banks of the Escaut Canal to the north of the city. But the British who were advancing on both flanks were still some distance back, so General Currie called a halt until they caught up.

It soon became apparent that the Germans were preparing to make a determined stand at Valenciennes. Because of extensive flooding to the west and north, the only approach onto the city was from the south, where the enemy had positioned five divisions in defences centred on a prominent wooded feature named Mont Houy. On 28 October, a British attack captured the hill, but strong counterattacks pushed them off. Once again the unbeatable Canadian Corps was called in.

Currie was more determined than ever, at this late stage in the war, "to pay the price of victory in shells and not in the lives of men." Brigadier-General Andy McNaughton, one of the most capable of all artillery commanders on the Allied side, once again produced a brilliant bombardment plan. At 0515 hours on 1 November 10th Brigade attacked, covered by the "heaviest weight of fire ever to support a single infantry brigade in the whole war." Three hours later the 44th, 46th and 47th Battalions had completed the capture of Mount Houy and had advanced 4000 metres into the southern outskirts of Valenciennes. Reconnaissance patrols went forward into the city in the afternoon, and during one of these Sergeant Hugh Cairns of the 46th Battalion won the last Victoria Cross of the war when he killed a large party of enemy who were preparing an ambush.

A patrol moves cautiously into the outskirts of Valenciennes, 1 November 1918. NAC/PA-3379

Valenciennes was occupied the next morning. The Canadian Corps had fought its last major battle of the war.

The Germans were now reeling back all along the front, but everywhere they left behind a screen of snipers and machine guns who periodically still put up a stiff fight. It rained continually as the Canadians pressed forward cautiously into Belgium, still well in advance of the British, and by 10 November the Corps reached the outskirts of Mons. Here there were a number of heavy skirmishes, but by daybreak Mons had been secured without a single Canadian casualty. The streets of the city were soon filled with jubilant citizens celebrating their liberation when word was received that an armistice would come into effect at 1100 hours. The war was over!

Not everyone got the word in time. Private George Pria of the 28th Battalion was leading a patrol north of the city when he was killed by a sniper at two minutes to 11. Elsewhere Canadian troops greeted the peace with quiet uncertainty. "What a strange and peaceful calm followed. Not a cheer went up from anyone," wrote Private Patrick Gleason of the 46th Battalion.

THE AFTERMATH

The euphoria following the armistice soon gave way to practical considerations. While everyone, understandably, wanted to go home to their families as soon as possible, the disbandment of the Corps and repatriation of more than 120,000 men had to be done in an orderly way, and that would take some time.

In the meanwhile, two divisions of the Corps were selected to be part of the Allied occupation force in the Rhineland. This was appropriate recognition of Canada's part in winning the war, and General Currie stood with great pride on the bridge at Bonn on 13 December taking the salute as the 1st and 2nd Divisions formally crossed the Rhine.

Little by little the enormous mass of the Army's equipment was turned in for disposal, and the men sent to England to await their turn to sail home. Most were back in Canada by the end of May. General Currie, one of the last to return, arrived in Halifax almost without official recognition in late August. It was hardly the reception deserved by the best general Canada had ever produced, and one of the finest and most competent of any of the Allied commanders during the whole of the war.

The Canadian Army built a reputation during these four years of war as one of the finest fighting forces ever to be sent into battle, of always succeeding where others had failed. Sir Arthur Currie wrote:

In no battle did the Corps ever fail to take its objective; nor did it lose an inch of ground, once that ground was consolidated; and in the 51 months that it had been in the field the Canadian Corps has never lost a single gun. I think one cannot be accused of immodesty in claiming that the record is somewhat unique in the history of the world's campaigns.

Pipers of the 42nd Battalion lead a victory parade through the streets of Mons after the Armistice on 11 November 1918.

NAC/PA-3523

**Canadians
Outside
the Depot,
Siberia, Russia**
by Louis Keene.
CWM 8334

And the bravery and sacrifice of the men who were responsible for the Army's accomplishments nurtured a sense of national pride that Canadians ever after would acknowledge. But the cost was very high. Of the 619,636 men and women whom served in the Army, 233,494 were casualties — 59,544 of whom died for their country.

Canadians were extremely weary of war, just as the people in all of the countries that had participated, and there was great hope that this really had been "the war to end all wars". The Army that had given Canada such cause for pride was rapidly demobilized. The last remnant of the wartime Army — a 5000-man brigade that served briefly in Siberia during the waning days of the Russian revolution — was home by late June. But the seeds of the next European war had already been planted in the harsh terms of the armistice that the Allies imposed, and the next twenty years would in fact be only a long truce.

General Currie takes the salute
on the bridge at Bonn, Germany
as the 22nd Battalion crosses the Rhine,
13 December 1918.
NAC/PA-3778

In Flanders Fields

—

In Flanders fields the poppies blow
Between the crosses, row on row,
That mark our place; and in the sky
The larks, still bravely singing, fly
Scarce heard amid the guns below.

We are the Dead. Short days ago
We lived, felt dawn, saw sunset glow,
Loved, and were loved, and now we lie
        In Flanders fields.

Take up our quarrel with the foe:
To you from failing hands we throw
The torch; be yours to hold it high.
If ye break faith with us who die
We shall not sleep, though poppies grow
        In Flanders fields

John McCrae
—

Punch
Dec 8·1915

CHAPTER 8

BETWEEN THE WARS
1919-1939

by
Stephen J. Harris

RE-ESTABLISHING THE REGULAR ARMY

Planning for the post-war reorganization of the Canadian Militia began a good year before the Armistice of 11 November 1918. Eager to capitalize on the existence of the large wartime Army, and hoping that all Canadians would gradually learn to accept the idea of conscription if compulsory military service became a routine fact of peacetime Canadian life, the Chief of the General Staff devised a scheme which would require all fit young men to undergo four months of military training when they reached eighteen years of age, to be followed by two years' service in the Militia. Major-General Willoughby Gwatkin also anticipated that the Permanent Force would grow to at least 20,000 men, both to supervise the training of these conscripts and to allow it to undertake the division-sized manoeuvres necessary for the Army to maintain the expertise learned at such cost on the Western Front.

Gwatkin was dreaming. The Great War was not known as "the war to end all wars" for nothing, and by the time the Expeditionary Force came home in 1919, Canadians had had enough of conflict. The last thing they wanted to do was to think about (much less pay for) preparing for the next war. "The people of this country do not propose to submit to the God of militarism," *The Farmer's Son* declared in 1921, and most nodded in agreement. Moreover, with Germany defeated, the Soviets absorbed in consolidating their revo-

Canadian 'spies'. Lieutenant Colonels Hodgins and Prower, with Colonel James Brown, scout potential invasion routes into Vermont and New York in the summer of 1922. DND/PMR-87-516

lution in Russia, and Japan and the United States both Allies, the Dominion had no obvious enemies. "Whom shall we fight?" Liberal leader Mackenzie King asked in the House of Commons. What was the Army for? Finally, the First World War had not only sapped the country's finances, leading the government to impose, as a temporary measure only, the first tax on income, but there was also a big job of social and economic reconstruction to pay for.

The Royal Canadian Regiment marching to the Peel Street Barracks, October 1919. RCR Museum

Accordingly, although the Army brought back five divisions' worth of equipment from Europe (less all trucks and armoured fighting vehicles), the government was not prepared to spend more for the moment: a large, well-equipped Army was simply too expensive for the country's Treasury. And as much as Gwatkin hoped that adopting a policy of peacetime conscription would eventually salve the wounds of the wartime manpower crisis and eventually bring the country together through a commonly shared sense of civic responsibility, no government was about to risk its political future by testing the theory.

As a result, when reconstituted, the post-war Regular Army remained pitifully small, totalling no more than 5000 all ranks despite an authorized establishment twice that size. Its regiments, too, were understrength, numbering no more than 250 to 300 instead of the war establishment of about 1000, and as before they were scattered about the country in company stations so as to be accessible to the part-time Militia.

A few things had changed, however. With the tremendous development of communications technology since 1914, the Royal Canadian Corps of Signals had much greater prominence, and signallers were soon involved in building and manning radio networks for the Air Force, Mounted Police, and other government departments, particularly in the far north. In the infantry, meanwhile, two new regiments were created to reflect their special status in the Great War: Princess Patricia's Canadian Light Infantry, which would serve in the west, and the Royal Vingt-Deuxième Régiment. With the formation of the latter, French-speaking Canadians at last could pursue a professional military career during which they could speak their own language.

The Royal Canadian Corps of Signals exercising with flags at Camp Borden in 1922. NAC/PA-92384

REORGANIZING THE MILITIA

The transition to peace was somewhat more difficult for the part-time Militia. At the end of the war, Canada actually had two armies — the pre-war Militia on the one hand, and the Canadian Expeditionary Force on the other — each of which had its own regimental identities, traditions, uniforms, and claims to battle honours. The question was which to keep on the order of battle. To Major-General A.C. Macdonnell, beloved commander of the 1st Division, the answer was clear: "Better that a dozen peace [Militia] regiments should go to the wall," he declared, "than the CEF units be lost." The Chief of the General Staff thought otherwise, however, and in the end convinced the government that the credibility of the existing Militia must be protected. Thus, although a few CEF units like the Royal Montreal Regiment, the Toronto Regiment, and the Toronto Scottish Regiment, all of which had overpowering political support, were added to post-war establishment, it was decided that the history and record of the Canadian Expeditionary Force would be preserved in, by, and through regiments of the pre-war Militia.

The generals were confident that veterans would ignore this slight to their accomplishments in France and Flanders and that they would eventually transfer their allegiance to the Militia unit which Ottawa decreed now perpetuated their wartime battalion. They were wrong. Most veterans had better things to do than put on a uniform again, even on a part-time basis. Most of the young men who came of age in the early 1920s, meanwhile, knew enough about war to understand that there was nothing at all romantic about it — or joining the citizen Army.

Despite their lack of interest — and, in some cases, outright hostility — the Militia would nevertheless survive. There was always a minority willing to sacrifice its spare time for the country, and in urban areas where wealthy benefactors could still be found, some units did relatively well in attracting recruits. But when summer camps were reinstituted in 1924, the overall turnout was much as it had been in the 1880s. In some respects, then, it seemed that things had not changed much since Victorian times — except at Militia Headquarters.

The Royal Canadian Dragoons performing their musical ride, 1923.
RCD Archives

The Fort Garry Horse at Camp Hughes, Manitoba in June 1924. FGH Museum

THE ARMY AND ITS PLANS

When General Gwatkin left the Army to take up the appointment of Inspector General of the fledgling Air Force, he became the last British officer to serve as Canadian CGS. Indeed, with the end of the war the top echelon of the Army was entirely Canadian, and most of the officers serving in Ottawa had held senior staff or command appointments in France. Their battlefield experience had taught them a good deal, but one of their lasting memories was of the unhappy consequences resulting from working for a minister like Sam Hughes who had been free to treat the Army as his personal fiefdom, and whose amateur enthusiasm had eventually cost lives.

Convinced, then, of their professional competence to manage the country's military affairs, they believed that they must insinuate themselves formally into the defence policy-making process so that the advice they were now well qualified to give would not be ignored as it had been in August 1914. Once this had been accomplished, they were sure the Army would be in good shape.

Two things had to happen. First, it was hoped that the existence of a comprehensive set of mobilization plans and defence schemes would not only deter future ministers from imposing foolish programmes on the Army, but also establish the minimum levels of spending required to ensure that it had adequate training and equipment. Second, the general staff set out to involve other government departments — to co-opt them, really — in the process of military planning so that they would be forced to share responsibility for the country's state of military preparedness — or the blame for its unpreparedness.

Despite sometimes desperate manoeuvring, the soldiers never quite succeeded in achieving their objectives. To be sure, mobilization plans were drafted — four of them, to be exact, beginning with Defence Scheme No. 1, Colonel James Sutherland Brown's worst-case scenario for a war between Britain and the United States in which Canada would be the main battleground. And by 1938 the government had approved a reorganization of the Militia to produce the six-division field army (including six armoured regiments) that was called for by Defence Scheme No. 3, the plan to send a second expeditionary force to Europe.

Major Milton Gregg, VC, carries the RCR Colour on a regimental parade, 1927. RCR Museum

HRH The Prince of Wales inspects a Royal 22e Régiment Guard of Honour in Quebec City, 1927. R22eR Museum

Calgary Highlanders are issued Lee Enfield rifles at the summer camp at Sarcee, June 1927. Glenbow Museum PA-1091-201

But all attempts to co-opt other government departments foundered when the Department of External Affairs — headed by officials who had no great respect for soldiers, and who believed that the Army wanted to create a 'war psychology'— neatly evaded every offer to become involved in defence planning. For their part, the Conservative and Liberal governments of the inter-war period were equally adept at sidestepping opportunities to declare that they even had defence policies. Indeed, nothing of substance was said between 1920 and February 1937, when a modest rearmament programme for home defence was finally announced, and it was only in 1938 that the Defence Minister agreed (informally and in private) that the general staff should even consider the possibility of Canadian involvement in another world war.

There was certainly no leadership from the Prime Minister. Although he had told both Adolf Hitler and the British government in 1937 that Canada would stand by the Mother Country in the event of war, Mackenzie King dared not risk the same announcement at home. And when, following the German absorption of all of Czechoslovakia in March 1939, he carelessly hinted that Britain could count on Canadian support if war broke out, he felt it necessary to back-track just a few days later:

The idea that every twenty years this country should automatically and as a matter of course take part in a war overseas for democracy or self-determination of other small nations ... to save, periodically, a continent that cannot run itself and to these ends risk the lives of its people ... bankruptcy and political disunion, seems to many a nightmare and sheer madness.

As might be expected, governmental indifference to the Army meant that very little equipment was purchased to replace the materiel brought back from France in 1919. When he retired as CGS in 1935, for example, General McNaughton reported that the Army had no modern anti-aircraft artillery, that its field guns were outranged by at least 3000 yards, and that the stocks of ammunition were sufficient only for ninety minutes' firing at Great War rates. There were also no mortars, tanks, or antitank guns. Moreover, despite the rearmament programme adopted in 1937 things had not improved much by September 1939, when the entire Canadian Army boasted sixteen Vickers light tanks (equipped with light and medium machine guns), twelve Carden-Lloyd tankettes (nothing more than small, tracked carriers), 29 Bren light machine guns, four two-pounder antitank guns, and two experimental armoured cars. There were also a few trucks and, of course, a few thousand rifles.

General A.G.L. McNaughton

General Andrew McNaughton ranks among Canada's most distinguished soldiers. He was commissioned in the Montreal Field Battery in 1910 while still a student at McGill University. In 1914 he went overseas with the Canadian Field Artillery. His competence was quickly recognized, and he was in command of an artillery regiment on the Somme. In late 1916 he was made Counter-Bombardment Officer for the Canadian Corps. While in that position he perfected the new science of locating enemy artillery by means of sound-ranging and aerial observation, and he organized a highly effective means of collecting and processing artillery intelligence. The Canadian Corps' great success at Vimy and in all subsequent battles of the Great War were in large measure due to his 'scientific' gunnery innovations. By war's end he was a Brigadier-General in command of the Corps' heavy artillery. His extraordinary talent was seen, and he was asked to stay on in the Regular Army. In 1929 McNaughton was promoted Major-General and appointed Chief of the General Staff. The depression years were frustrating times for the CGS as little was spent on defence, and in 1935 he accepted the appointment as president of the National Research Council. Shortly after the outbreak of war in 1939 he was recalled to the Army to command 1st Canadian Division. He was promoted Lieutenant-General and given command of the Canadian Corps in December 1940, and when a second corps was formed in 1942 he became commander of the First Canadian Army. When senior British officers questioned his capability as a field commander, he returned to Canada and on retirement was promoted full General. In November 1944 he became Minister of National Defence. At the end of the war he was appointed chairman of the Canadian section of the Permanent Joint Board on Defence, and in 1948-49 served as Canadian ambassador at the United Nations.

ARMY TRAINING

Needless to say, the Army was not equipped for modern war in 1939. It was not trained for it either. Things had not been intended to work out that way. When General Currie returned to Canada to take over the Army in 1919 he looked forward to carrying out divisional manoeuvres each year, and with the five divisions' worth of equipment brought back from France, he believed that the Army should be able to build upon the knowledge and experience acquired during the Great War.

But when the strength of the Permanent Force was only 5000 all ranks, and many of the best officers and men from the Canadian Corps chose not to join the puny post-war Army, all these hopes melted away. Scattered about the country so that they could instruct the Militia, the under-manned and undernourished companies and squadrons of the Permanent Force had little opportunity to train beyond the platoon or troop level, and when they were able to get into the field they often reverted to tactics and ideas which pre-dated the Great War. In the Royal Canadian Dragoons, for example, "the cavalry charge was once more the approved method of attack" despite their experience of machine guns "which in ninety minutes at Moreuil Wood had cost the [Canadian] Cavalry Brigade three hundred men and eight hundred horses."

The problem was not that Regular Force officers were entirely unaware of modern developments. They had to study for, and pass, British Army promotion examinations for each step in rank. At least two were sent each year to the British and Indian Army staff colleges, and those destined for senior rank attended the Imperial Defence College. But until 1927 they had few occasions to practice what they had learned, and more often than not, the only time they saw more than two hundred regular soldiers under arms was during aid to the civil power operations — and particularly during what became an annual tour of duty in Cape Breton Island, when the miners and steel workers went on strike. Thankfully, there was very little violence: "the duties of the troops were more boring than arduous ... with nothing to relieve the monotony but the strikers' epithets, which grew rather wearisome after awhile..."

Intervening in labour disputes may have tested discipline, but it did nothing to improve the Army's proficiency at tactics. Junior officers had so little practical experience that by the late 1920s they were failing their promotion examinations at alarming rates. Indeed, things were so bad that the field exercises scheduled for 1927 were abandoned because it was felt so little would be accomplished; and when the regulars assembled again at Petawawa in 1928 there was little or no improvement. One British officer observing the exercise commented that every unit was "quite unfitted" for the schemes they attempted, and much less ready for actual operations. Indeed, Major Eady wondered whether the Permanent Force regiments could ever be relied upon to provide "complete units for war."

The Lord Strathcona's Horse parade at full peace strength, August 1930. LdSH Museum

The staff of Vernon Camp, many from the British Columbia Dragoons, May 1930. LdSH Museum

The first course on the Carden-Lloyd universal carrier, London, Ontario, 1935. RCD Archives

By 1930 Canada was in the midst of the depression, and almost no collective training took place. While the engineers eventually found work supervising the construction of unemployment relief camps and the signallers were still busy in the north, where they built navigation aids for the government's fledgling air mail service, the infantry, cavalry, and artillery were limited to repetitive individual training, and they gradually began "to moulder away quietly in disuse." They also suffered horrendous problems of retention, losing as many as twenty percent of their men annually to civilian life despite the stagnant economy.

The situation began to improve in 1936. The first Carden-Lloyd tankettes were issued to The Royal Canadian Regiment, which was authorized to undertake three weeks' training at Camp Niagara, and an Armoured Fighting Vehicles Training Centre was established, first at London and then at Camp Borden. It received its first Vickers tank in 1938. Although two future generals recalled that, by this time, they were studying "General J.F.C. Fuller and other up-to-the-minute experts, fire and movement, and other modern ... tactics," just how much they were learning could be questioned. During the 1938 Permanent Force manoeuvres at Niagara and Petawawa (the last dry runs before war broke out) it was obvious that some very fundamental things had been ignored. At one point, "field guns at a road piquet were sited so as to face each other, threatening each other."

At another:

When an enemy AFV sited well to a flank and behind a reservoir opened fire on the cavalry there was considerable delay in getting under cover or taking action ... The simplest method, viz, to obtain support from the 18 pr gun from the piquet immediately in the rear was not tried, and it was not until the cavalry had worked around the flank ... and dismounted, that the AFV was compelled to withdraw

— but not before it had seriously delayed the advance. In the infantry, meanwhile, one officer recalled, "We were sadly lacking in field experience as a battalion.... We had become hopelessly bureaucratic and it was deemed impossible for a battalion to perform even the simplest procedure without issuing a four-page written order to at least forty addresses."

The commandant of the exercise knew exactly what he had seen. "Full value for the funds expended," he concluded, "cannot be obtained so long as the present limited establishments are imposed and modern equipment is lacking." Colonel W.H.P. Elkins was, of course, talking about the Permanent Force, which would make up no more than one-third of the first of the six divisions the general staff believed should be committed to a major war. In the Militia, which would complete the rest of the overseas Army — five and two-thirds divisions — the situation was worse, much worse.

MILITIA TRAINING

Training in the Militia did not begin until 1922, when the post-war reorganization of the force was more or less complete. But with Army's budget hovering at about $12 million, that portion allocated to the part-time force allowed, on average, no more than half of the Militia to be trained each year, for a period seldom exceeding nine days. Moreover, priority was given to training officers, non-commissioned officers, and technical specialists, with the result that there was usually no money left over to pay the other ranks, particularly in infantry and cavalry regiments. Until 1925 most units drilled only at their local drill halls and armouries, never venturing into the field, and they considered themselves fortunate if they got to the rifle ranges for four days a year. In most cavalry units, two men had to share one horse when the regiment went out for its weekend rides.

These hard financial times and the general anti-military feeling of the early 1920s caused the Militia's effective strength to fall drastically. By 1924 a number of battalions mustered fewer than a hundred all ranks, a good number of whom were overage men who had had to remain at home during the Great War. Regiments therefore had to be creative in order to attract recruits. Some spent a good deal of time and effort finding jobs for prospective members; others turned to sports and field days; and some, like the Royal Hamilton Regiment, rekindled their pre-war enthusiasm for shooting. Wealthier city regiments, particularly those in central Canada, once again relied upon ceremonial displays and excursions to New York, Boston, Buffalo, and Rochester to boost morale, but these trips were expensive, and their cost had to be underwritten by the officers' mess or rich honourary colonels.

Moreover, now that the Militia department supplied only khaki service dress, the colourful full dress uniforms which had attracted recruits a half century before also had to be purchased at regimental expense. Even the Foot Guards in Ottawa, who put so much store in drill, dress and deportment, did not have a complete and proper set of scarlet tunics and bearskin caps.

The situation became even more desperate after 1929. The Great Depression forced the Army's budget below $10 million, and the Militia's share fell to less than $2 million. Except for specialists there were no more camps; in many units all members turned over their annual allocation of four days' pay to regimental funds; and training was generally restricted to low-level drill and sand-table tactical exercises. Courses on map reading, signalling, military law, and minor tactics taught by Permanent Force sergeants at the Royal Schools and local armouries were the closest most Militiamen approached to modern soldiering. But in years when polio was rampant, even these sessions had to be curtailed.

Officers of the Fort Garry Horse pose for a formal group photo. FGH Museum

It was probably the fact that Militia regiments were also social organizations that kept most of them going in these lean years. Although there was next to no training — and few excursions to Buffalo, Seattle, Chicago, and New York — regimental messes remained open, and some sense of fellowship and belonging to the regimental family could be maintained. That was one reason why the wholesale reorganization of the Militia proposed in 1936 was opposed so strongly at the local level. Intended to modernize the Army,

it also demanded that a number of units disappear. But when the government seemed to treat its citizen soldiers with careless disregard, there was no compelling reason why members of the Toronto Regiment should feel obliged to amalgamate with the Royal Grenadiers, why the Wentworths would want to join the Royal Hamilton Light Infantry, why members of the Lunenburg Regiment would want to put up Annapolis flashes, or why the Vancouver Regiment should wish to combine with the Irish Fusiliers.

A Ford armoured car during trials in the spring of 1938. RCD Archives

The Royal Canadian Dragoons on a patrol exercise, Camp Borden, 1938. RCD Archives

A panoramic view of the unveiling ceremonies at the magnificent Canadian War Memorial atop Vimy Ridge, 26 July 1936. Over 6000 veterans returned to France for the dedication by His Majesty King Edward VIII.

NAC/PA-803934

THE VIMY MEMORIAL

If the reorganization of 1936 was, in a sense, the low point for many Militia units between the wars, one of the highlights was the dedication on 26 July that same year of the superb monument to the valour of the Canadian Corps constructed atop Vimy Ridge, on 250 acres of land ceded permanently by France to Canada. Although the pilgrimage of veterans to the ceremony was sponsored by the Legion rather than by the Department of Militia and Defence, this was the first occasion between the wars when the Dominion government pulled out all the stops to pay homage to its soldiers. Over 6000 war veterans returned to France on the Vimy Pilgrimage, on ships escorted by the Royal Canadian Navy, where they watched King Edward VIII unveil the imposing monument, attended by former Prime Minister Sir Robert Borden, Lady Currie (Sir Arthur's widow), and the President of France, among others. Perhaps the diary of one veteran, written in a kind of off-hand fashion reflecting the fact that he was one of those being honoured, puts things best:

A vast throng of people here. In addition to Canadians there are streams of natives coming to Vimy from all directions and in addition there are some 2000 pilgrims from England.... Thousands of French war veterans are here also. Airplanes make a spectacular flight over the crowd and over the monument, flying in formation .... Speeches well heard through the amplifiers. Unveiling by King well done.

HM The King is accompanied by representatives of the Canadian and French governments and Canadian veterans at the conclusion of the dedication ceremony. NAC/PA-803936

TOWARDS ANOTHER WAR

The Vimy Memorial was dedicated to men who fought and died in "the war to end all wars". By the summer of 1936, however, the seeds of the next conflict were already being laid. Adolf Hitler had reclaimed the Rhineland, and Mussolini had just annexed Ethiopia, and no one had lifted a finger to stop them. As we have seen, the Canadian government never truly reconciled itself to the need for rearmament before war finally broke out, but as the Depression waned, and international tensions grew, a little more money was made available for training. The Regulars probably benefitted most, but even if they had to simulate most of the accoutrements of modern war, Militia units were also able to take some advantage of the situation. In 1937, for example, the 8th Hussars stimulated the local economy by renting privately owned cars at $10 a day to help them undertake 'mechanized' operations. The next year, many regiments spent a full week at camp — the Black Watch arrived at Valcartier 500 strong — where they studied "the defence" in what all agreed was the most comprehensive training since the war. The most fortunate units — primarily those in southern Ontario — were able to participate in the Permanent Force's manoeuvres, and thus became familiar with the Carden-Lloyds, the experimental armoured cars, and the new Bren light machine gun.

In 1939, over 47,000 Militiamen were scheduled to undergo training in 'the attack' following a night approach march. However, before this cycle could be completed in late August, a number of regiments had already been called out on active service to protect vital points. On 10 September, war was declared, and mobilization of the Canadian Active Service Force, the overseas Army, began at once.

The Canadian War Memorial in Confederation Square in Ottawa, unveiled by His Majesty King George VI during the Royal Tour of Canada, May 1939. DND Photo

The 8th New Brunswick Hussars on a 'mechanized' exercise with automobiles in the summer of 1938. 8CH Museum

CHAPTER 9

EXPANSION AND MISFORTUNE 1939-1943

by
Brereton Greenhous

In 1914 a British declaration of war had automatically meant that Canada was also at war, although even then the essential nature of their contribution was a matter for Canadians alone to decide. On 3 September 1939, however, when the Second World War began, the Imperial relationship had advanced to the stage where Canada as a self-governing member of the British Commonwealth was no longer legally committed by British decisions.

Thus Canada did not formally join the Allied ranks until Parliament spoke, on 10 September: but that decision was more a matter of form than substance. A week earlier, Colonel Maurice Pope, the Army's Director of Military Operations, had been instructed by Ian Mackenzie, Minister of National Defence, "to convey to the Chiefs of Staff that they were to give effect to all the defence measures which would be required in a state of war and to fire on any blinking German who came within range of our guns — but that we were not at war." Mackenzie may well have used a coarser adjective than Pope cared to put into print but that hardly affected the intent of his order. Whatever the legal niceties, to all intents and purposes Canada was at war as soon as Britain was.

Mobilization of an Active Service Force had already begun and recruiting was in full swing but had some "blinking" German come within range of Canadian guns he might not have been in any great danger. In addition to an appropriate number of outdated rifles, light machine guns and field artillery pieces for its 4500 regular soldiers and 50,000 militiamen, Canada had only sixteen light tanks (feeble machines, hardly worthy of the name), four 2-pounder anti-tank guns and four 3.7-inch anti-aircraft guns, twenty-three rather pitiful Boyes anti-tank rifles (which could only hope to penetrate even the lightest armour), and twenty-nine of the new Bren light machine guns.

As in the First World War, patriotic posters were used to spur recruiting in 1939. CWM

First World War Renault tanks purchased from the United States as scrap metal by the 'Camp Borden Iron Foundry' to train Canada's armoured corps.
RCD Archives

Nor was there much of a romantic rush to the Colours, as there had been in 1899 and 1914. Among more educated Canadians, there may have been a sense that this was a war of ideology — democracy versus totalitarianism — in which Canada stood on the side of democracy by choice as well as tradition. Among others the motive was often economic: although the worst of the Great Depression was over, its fetid essence lingered on.

Me? I didn't know what the war was about. All those names didn't mean a thing to me.... Quite honestly, I didn't know anything and I don't think anybody else did either. Who read the newspapers, anyway?

I joined up because I was making three and a half bucks a week pumping gas in a station on the main drag of Kelowna.... I was twenty, I didn't have a bean, no hopes, nothing, ... so I joined up. Went down to Vancouver in a freight car in October and joined up. As simple as that. No patriotism. No saving my country from the Nazi hordes. Just simply, I joined up....

Prime Minister Mackenzie King was particularly anxious to ensure that there would be no need for conscription, and consequently no politically disastrous, disunifying, man-power crisis like that of 1917. Canada *must* avoid any repetition of the horrendous casualty rates which had marked the First World War, an aim which might best be achieved, it seemed to him, by putting the weight of national effort into the air arm — and especially into the training of that arm.

For political reasons, there would have to be a Canadian contribution to the British Expeditionary Force (BEF) in France but it could be kept to a minimum. Terminology was more important than numbers. Twenty-two years earlier, Canada had mustered a corps of four divisions, and now she could hardly seem to do less — but a corps of two divisions would still be a corps! The Cabinet decided upon the mobilization of two divisions for overseas service. Militia regiments were called out by units and brought up to strength by voluntary enlistment, nearly 60,000 joining in September alone.

Members of Princess Patricia's Canadian Light Infantry set out for England, December 1939.
NAC/PA-163406

224

McNAUGHTON TAKES COMMAND

That same month the Cabinet decided to send one division overseas as soon as possible, and four days later the Chief of the General Staff, Major-General T.V. Anderson, recommended that it be the 1st Division. There was never much doubt in anyone's mind about who would command it, or — when the time came — the new Canadian Corps.

Major-General A.G.L. McNaughton had been chairman of the National Research Council since 1936 but he was still technically a soldier, 'on secondment', as army jargon had it. Putting his academic robes and business suits back in the closet, McNaughton donned his old uniform and toured the country, inspecting his embryonic corps. Years of political neglect had taken their toll in terms of initiative and vigour, as well as in kit and equipment. At Bridgewater, NS, he found that the West Nova Scotia Regiment:

... was accommodated in an old curling rink. The ice had been scooped out and straw thrown down for these recruits to sleep on. They had no blankets, and nobody had bought blankets for them. There were no palliasses [long linen sacks like mattress covers which could be filled with straw]. They had no underwear and their boots were poor. Two hundred men were without caps. Most of these things were procurable on the public market but there was an unawareness on the part of the staff down there what their responsibilities were.

All across Canada it was not much different, but somnolent staff officers had a much better idea of exactly what their responsibilities were once McNaughton had passed by. Lethargy was replaced by frenetic activity, much of it to good purpose, but (to take just one example) no amount of zeal could make boots without leather. In Toronto, the Royal Regiment of Canada was able to accept the offer of a public-spirited citizen to purchase 130 pairs of boots from local shoe stores; in Moncton, NB, however, where the Carleton and Yorks, like the West Novas, were sleeping on loose straw, "only 66 pairs of boots could be secured. Many men who were reporting in with inferior footwear and light clothing had to be excused from training parades. There was a great deal of suffering from colds and sore feet."

Major-General A.G.L. McNaughton, appointed commander of 1st Canadian Division in September 1939. NAC/PA-132648

Private Jack Bernard
of the British
Columbia Regiment
says farewell to his
young son, New
Westminster 1940.
NAC/C-0038723

In Poland, using armoured formations and aircraft as spearheads for the mass of foot soldiers and horse-drawn supplies which still comprised the bulk of their army, the Germans were practising a new kind of fast-moving, three-dimensional warfare which *Time* magazine promptly christened *Blitzkrieg*, or Lightning War. Time and space took on a new meaning in the path of the onrushing *Wehrmacht* and manoeuvre was suddenly more important than firepower. Raw courage, conventional wisdom and stubborn determination, which the Poles had in abundance, were not enough to stop the *Panzers*.

Neither Britain nor France had any direct access to the Polish fronts, and both were unwilling to divert the Germans by attacking in the west. Nor were they aware that the Non-Aggression Pact which the Soviet Union and Germany had signed in August included a secret clause dividing Poland between them. As soon as it was clear that the Allies would do — *could do!* — nothing meaningful, Josef Stalin unleashed his own armies. By 5 October 1939, all resistance was at an end in the east and the so-called 'Phoney War', or 'sitzkrieg', was firmly established in the west.

WINTER IN ENGLAND

Nevertheless, McNaughton was anxious to get his men overseas as soon as possible. Winter was at hand, and:

... we didn't want to have to try and train troops in a very cold climate, scattered in different locations and without proper facilities, when in England we would have training areas and ranges available to us in a much more moderate climate. I wanted to get these people together in a climate I could do something with, for although the British climate is raw and damp it's no worse than what we would encounter on the other side of the Channel and the environmental similarity would be useful in acclimatizing our people.

In London the Chief of the Imperial General Staff welcomed the idea, and the Canadian liaison officer attached to the War Office wrote home to report that "the reputation Canadians earned in the last war has not been forgotten...." All 16,000 men of the division, and an administrative 'tail' identified as Canadian Military Headquarters, were in England by the turn of the year. McNaughton held the appointment of senior Canadian officer overseas as well as divisional commander, with his First World War subordinate and long-time protégé, Brigadier H.D.G. Crerar, in charge of CMHQ.

The 1st Division was quartered in damp Victorian barracks at Aldershot (each large barrack room heated only by one small coal stove, for which there was not nearly enough coal) just in time to endure the coldest winter in Britain for half a century. There was much to be done. Initially, emphasis was on drill, musketry and — shades of 1918! — trench warfare. Writing the history of the Hastings and Prince Edward Regiment, Farley Mowat has recorded how:

Training progressed from the basic squad drills to field training. Each day the companies marched out to the broad plains beyond Aldershot where they learned about war — as it had been.... Miles of trenches grew and spread across Salisbury Plain and the pathetic futility of it went quite unnoticed. No voice cried out against that monumental folly.

So it went, through the winter months of the 'phoney war'. Then, on 9 April 1940, the *Blitzkrieg* was turned against Scandinavia. Denmark fell in a day and Oslo, the Norwegian capital, twenty-four hours later; but mountains and poor lines of communication made the capture of much of Norway a more difficult proposition, even for the *Wehrmacht*. The British and French each put small expeditionary forces together and began to land them at key points along the coast — at Namsos and Andalsnes in an effort to pinch out a German parachute landing at Trondheim, and at Narvik in an attempt to hold the north of the country and thus, at the very least, interdict the shipping of high-grade Swedish iron ore — important in the manufacture of armour plate — down the Norwegian coast to the factories of the Ruhr.

Tween Decks
by
George Pepper.

Canadian troops making the Atlantic crossing aboard the liner *Queen Mary*, which could carry 5000 men.
CWM 13807

A CLASH OF COMMAND

Because most trained British soldiers were already in France or Norway, the War Office turned to McNaughton when they decided that more men were required to re-take Trondheim. Another thirteen hundred men would be enough, they felt, and McNaughton concluded that the Princess Patricias and the Edmonton Regiment — one regular battalion and one militia, both with substantial numbers of men of Scandinavian descent in their ranks — should form the Canadian contribution.

The two battalions left Aldershot for Scotland on the evening of 18 April 1940, expecting to embark for Trondheim very shortly. In the words of McNaughton's biographer, however, in the end "the only battle to come out of this ... was a paper one between Ottawa and McNaughton." Mackenzie King was, at that moment, in the United States, and in his absence J.L. Ralston, the Minister of Finance, was acting as prime minister. Nor was the Minister of National Defence in Ottawa, for Norman Rogers, who now held that post, was en route to London. Ralston appointed himself to act in Rogers' place as well as the prime minister's, and set about asserting his 'little brief authority'.

Ralston was a corporation lawyer and a nitpicker, obsessed with legal detail and often unable or unwilling to delegate; he and McNaughton had clashed more than once when he had been Minister of Militia and Defence, back in the 1920s. Now, fastening on technicalities in the midst of an emergency, he upbraided the general for involving his troops "without prior reference to National Defence and approval of Canadian Government."

Rogers, arriving in London, sided with McNaughton, pointing out that "there are dynamic features in present military situation which argue against too rigid limitations upon actions taken to meet possible emergencies." But no conclusions had been reached when the Norwegian commitment was cancelled as suddenly as it had been requested. The British now thought that they could take Trondheim unassisted. Of course, they couldn't! Indeed, they only managed to hold Narvik briefly; the last Allied forces in Norway were evacuated on 7 June.

The most significant aspect of this brief alarum was that it re-kindled the old animosity between Ralston and McNaughton. That might not have mattered if Norman Rogers had not died in an air crash six weeks later, or if the Prime Minister had not appointed Ralston to take his place. As things turned out, however, it eventually played a part, for better or worse, in the Army Overseas being split in two against McNaughton's advice, in his subsequent resignation, and in General Crerar's accession to the post of senior officer overseas and the command of First Canadian Army.

1st Division troops on a route march in southern England.
NAC/PA-177678

Newfoundland gunners in England.
Provincial Archives of Newfoundland and Labrador B5-129

THE FALL OF FRANCE

When the last Allied troops left Narvik, their departure was hardly noticed by anyone except the Norwegians. While the world's attention was focused on events unfolding there, on 10 May 1940 a German attack through Luxembourg, out-flanking the fortifications of the Maginot Line which guarded the Franco-German border, had chopped a great hole in the French defences. That night Winston Churchill became British prime minister, but willpower and words were not enough to stem the German tide. The *Panzers* struck straight for the coast, driving a wedge between two French armies, the Belgians and the BEF to the north, and the great bulk of the French forces to the south. Allied strategists were out-thought, Allied staffs were out-manoeuvred and, to put it bluntly, Allied forces (including the British — the French and Belgians were not the only ones at fault) were generally out-fought. France would fall in three more weeks, and disaster loomed ominously over Britain as the Belgians surrendered — they could do little else — and the BEF and more than a hundred thousand Frenchmen were trapped against the Channel shore.

Communications were breaking down and General Sir Edmund Ironside, the Chief of the Imperial General Staff, ordered McNaughton to Calais and Dunkirk, where he was to examine the situation and then advise the War Office whether moving the 1st Division to France, in order to cover the evacuation of the BEF, was a realistic option. Meanwhile, his men were to embark at Dover and be ready to sail at a moment's notice.

Men of the Fusiliers Mont-Royal take a break during training in England. NAC/PA-177580

The next few hours were marked by the passage of a series of often conflicting messages between McNaughton and the War Office as the possibilities of holding Calais and/or Dunkirk were assessed, approved, re-assessed and discarded. The first Canadians to embark, disembarked, and then re-embarked only to disembark again before returning to Aldershot. Twenty-four hours later, "as we were going to bed that night," recalled Captain George Kitching of the Royal Canadian Regiment:

... we were again ordered to reload and head for Dover.... We reloaded all our equipment on the train and stood by for immediate take-off. The next day we were ordered to 'stand down' but to leave the trains loaded. After another alarm to be ready to move we were advised that the whole operation was cancelled.

On 26 May the British Cabinet authorized the evacuation of the BEF and as many of the French troops as wished to come with them and could be taken off. Operation *Dynamo*, a now legendary event in British history, began the next day and 338,000 soldiers (including 110,000 French) were lifted from the Dunkirk beaches before it ended on 4 June. The garrison of Calais was not so lucky and it was compelled to surrender just as *Dynamo* began.

Nissen Huts by George Pepper.

These cheap, quickly-built but cold and uncomfortable corrugated iron huts were home to thousands of Canadian servicemen in England. CWM 13738

1st BRIGADE IN FRANCE

Most of the BEF's equipment had been abandoned, and Britain was now left isolated and almost disarmed as far as ground forces were concerned. The *Panzers* turned west and south against the demoralized remnants of the French armies, while Mussolini's Italians, taking advantage of the resounding German victory, crossed the French border on 10 June. There arose, however, in some optimistic minds, a forlorn hope that the Brittany peninsula, in the northwest corner of France, might still be held if a defensive line could be established across its base.

The only formation in Britain fit to fight besides the Canadians was the 52nd (Lowland) Division, and both were placed under the command of Lieutenant-General Sir Alan Brooke, who had commanded II Corps of the original BEF before returning to England. Brooke, like McNaughton, was a gunner, intelligent, strong-willed, and sometimes acerbic, and their disagreements dated back to an earlier war when they were both artillery staff officers in the Canadian Corps.

The Lowlanders began the move on 7 June, and the Canadians started to follow them on the 8th — just two days before Norman Rogers' untimely death. Ottawa had been kept fully informed, however, and Rogers had already authorized McNaughton to do as he thought fit. A concentration area just outside the port of Brest had been agreed upon, and the 1st Brigade led off; but when its motor transport arrived at Brest, the vehicles were immediately despatched inland in small 'packets'. Route cards were handed out and, in warm summer weather, one by one, small convoys of trucks, many commanded by sergeants or corporals, drove off into the interior of wine-rich France! As might have been predicted, "The arrival of some of them [at Rennes], untrammelled by discipline, was rollicking; there were 'some reports of drunkenness and reckless driving'."

The three troop trains which carried the bulk of the brigade fared rather better from the disciplinary point of view but, after a day of stops and starts, George Kitching found:

It was becoming increasingly difficult to handle some of our own soldiers at this time and I think that the NCOs and young officers were getting a little concerned. After all, they had been on the train for about eight hours, the available food was limited and we were not able to tell them just what was going to happen. In addition, a few of them had obviously had too much to drink. At this difficult period the decision was made to return to Brest. Apparently the French Government and Army had both given up. General Alan Brooke gave orders for us to re-embark in Brest and return to England.

Portrait of a Canadian Soldier by Lilias Torrance Newton.
CWM 14250

The train in front of them was misrouted on the return trip. It was soon:

... on the way not to Brest but to St. Malo. By great good fortune at that port there was a British steamer, the Biarritz. British troops of many regiments were already on board, but room was made for the Canadians. The overloaded vessel left harbour on the morning of the 16th and reached Southampton that afternoon.

"At the moment of reversal," said McNaughton, acidly, "the Division was some six hundred miles from head to rear in a great big U, which is quite a substantial length of column for a division, to say the least." Moreover, the re-embarkation at Brest was something of a panicky, ill-directed business. The Royal Canadian Horse Artillery (horses lingered on only in the name) was twice instructed to destroy its guns, and twice the order was countermanded. Eventually Lieutenant-Colonel J.H. Roberts was permitted to load as many guns as he could in an hour and three-quarters, and he embarked not only all twenty-four of his own regiment but, in addition, a dozen Bofors anti-aircraft guns, seven predictors, three light armoured carriers, and 'several technical vehicles' belonging to British units.

LICK THEM over there!

COME ON CANADA!

In the chaos of embarkation, however, nearly all the 1st Brigade's transport — more than two hundred vehicles — was left on French shores. Through no choice of Roberts, the RCHA's tractors and ammunition limbers had to be abandoned even though, when their ship sailed, the nearest Germans were still many kilometres away, and there was "still room enough to take everything that was on the docks." Yet by 'saving the guns', Roberts, an otherwise undistinguished officer, had made himself a marked man who would soon be promoted beyond the level which his moderate abilities warranted.

Fortunately, only six men were left behind. One of them had been mortally injured in a motorcycle accident and could not be evacuated. Corporal R.J. Creighton of the Hastings and Prince Edward Regiment fell into German hands and had the unwelcome distinction of becoming Canada's longest serving prisoner-of-war; and the other four subsequently succeeded in making their way back to England, Sapper F.P. Hutchinson of the Royal Canadian Engineers being awarded the Military Medal for his escape — the first Canadian Army gallantry award of the war.

A last look at the French coast at the end of the foray into France in June 1940.
IWM F-4869

A group of the Fusiliers Mont-Royal near Reykjavik, Iceland in July 1940.
FMR Museum

The tented camp of the Royal Regiment of Canada, Iceland, July 1940.
RRC Museum

Even before the German attack on France, the *Blitzkrieg* against Scandinavia had brought Allied fears of enemy expansion into the Atlantic, fears which had been exacerbated by the attack on France. Iceland, until 1918 a Danish colony, had retained its ties to the Danish monarchy after independence. What would happen there, now that the Germans were in Copenhagen? The Icelanders had no army and the British government had promptly sent an infantry brigade to the island. Then it had requested Ottawa to reinforce it, and the fall of France had made the need more urgent than ever in Whitehall's eyes. Where once they had asked for a Canadian battalion, now they wanted the whole of the 2nd Division — at least until an astonished Winston Churchill learned of the request and minuted his Foreign Secretary, Anthony Eden,

that "it would surely be a very great mistake to allow these fine troops to be employed in so distant a theatre.... We require two Canadian divisions [in England] to work as a corps as soon as possible."

The Royal Regiment of Canada had reached Reykjavik on 16 June 1940, and the Cameron Highlanders of Ottawa (a machine-gun battalion) and Les Fusiliers Mont-Royal arrived on 9 July, just two days after Churchill had penned his minute. The Camerons, who had been assigned to the 3rd Division but sent to Iceland because their training was relatively advanced, spent the winter on the island, but the other two battalions sailed for England on 31 October to join their comrades of the 2nd Division.

DEFENDING BRITISH SHORES

Turning back to a broader picture of the war, Adolf Hitler admired the British Empire and believed that it gave an essential degree of stability to regions of the globe in which he was not directly interested; for the moment, at least, he only sought German hegemony over Europe and *Lebensraum* — living space — in the east. He hoped, therefore, to negotiate a settlement with the British, but Churchill would have none of it, and he half-heartedly concluded that he must now invade England. He ordered the *Luftwaffe* forward to airfields in Norway, Holland and northern France, the *Kriegsmarine* (German Navy) to

Maintenance on a 5.5 by W.A. Ogilvie. CWM 13438

gather ships and barges in the Channel ports, and the *Reichsheer* (German Army) to make ready to storm the Kent and Sussex beaches.

Defending England posed almost as many problems as attacking it, given the dire straits in which the British now found themselves. The BEF had lost or left nine-tenths of its armour and artillery on the roads leading back to Dunkirk, and it would take time to re-build and re-equip the army. On 1 July 1940 the Canadians, now the only fully trained and equipped division in the country, became one half of VII Corps, Britain's pitifully small strategic reserve south of the Thames — the other half of it consisting of a British armoured brigade and two brigades of New Zealand infantrymen! McNaughton was appointed to command, while a First World War VC winner, now Major-General George Pearkes, took over the 1st Division.

All southern and eastern England was consumed with activity. "Gone were the days of fantasy," wrote Farley Mowat, recording the history of the Hastings and Prince Edward Regiment.

The tactics of the old war went back into their coffins. The phrase 'static defence' became anathema, and the new slogans were 'flexible defence' and 'counter-attack'. The countryside erupted in a rash of tank-traps, road blocks, machine gun nests, pillboxes and barbed wire obstacles. The whole shape of infantry training changed with the new emphasis on air defence, dispersal and the use of one-man slit-trenches instead of elaborate trench systems.

It was a time of improvisation. Molotov cocktails — beer bottles filled with gasoline and fitted with a wick — were devised to deal with German tanks.... Working parties slaved at digging defence works. Companies stood-to at dawn, for weeks on end, to be ready to repel the anticipated paratroop invasions. Twenty civilian buses from the streets of London, painted khaki now, were attached to the Regiment so that it could move quickly to any threatened point.

Even small arms were in short supply, so short in fact that the British, in an ironic twist of fate, welcomed the arrival of 75,000 Ross rifles from Canada. More useful reinforcements were on their way. On 17 May, Ottawa, shocked out of its political and economic reservations by the dramatic turn of events in Europe, had authorized the formation of the 3rd Division, "to be available for such service as may be required in Canada or overseas," together with the despatch overseas of the 2nd Division (under Major-General V.W. Odlum) and a cadre of corps troops.

Ten days later — on the day that the evacuation of Dunkirk began — the government decided to recruit a 4th Division; and three weeks after that, Parliament passed the National Resources Mobilization Act, which provided for compulsory mobilization of men and resources "as may be deemed necessary or expedient ... for the efficient prosecution of the war.... " The only reservation was that the powers it conferred on the Cabinet might not be exercised "for the purpose of requiring persons to serve in the military, naval or air forces outside of Canada and the territorial waters thereof."

Corporals Johnson and
Gordon of the
Canadian Scottish
pause during a house
clearing exercise in
southern England.
NAC/PA-162246

Tank gunners of the
Governor General's Horse
Guards score hits on the tank
range at Niagara, June 1941.
GGHG Museum

It was well understood in Ottawa, if not formally proclaimed as yet, that the 3rd and 4th Divisions would inevitably be going overseas as well, now that the war had become so critical. In July, the mobilization of eight additional infantry battalions for internal security duties — one more would be enough for another division — was authorized. And in August, bowing to the irrefutable evidence of the *Blitzkrieg*, National Defence Headquarters announced the creation of a Canadian Armoured Corps.

(For some curious bureaucratic reason each of the armoured regiments were given a number rather than a name, and they were usually designated thus in official correspondence throughout the war. Informally, however, they all retained their former titles — which were eventually bracketed behind their numbers — and that is the way that they will be identified in this book.)

During October, the first five battalions of the 2nd Division arrived in England to replace the New Zealanders in VII Corps. The British armoured brigade left, too, when the balance of the 2nd Division — including the two battalions from Iceland — arrived, and at the turn of the year a re-born Canadian Corps inherited the VIIth's commander and its GHQ Reserve role. Alan Brooke, now commander-in-chief of Home Forces, watched a Canadian Corps exercise and thought it "a great pity to see such excellent material as the Canadian men controlled by such indifferent commanders."

A Canadian-built *Ram* tank, used by Canadian armoured regiments in England for training, shown on a stamp issued in 1942.

In Canada, NRMA men — contemptuously called 'zombies' by the Active Service soldiers and the latter's friends and relatives — were now being conscripted in ever-growing numbers, at first for three weeks' training but soon for longer periods. The 1st Canadian Army Tank Brigade, composed of the Ontario, Calgary and Three Rivers Regiments and commanded by Brigadier F.F. Worthington, went to England in June 1941, and the 3rd Infantry Division, under Major-General C.B. Price, would follow it in August and early September.

2nd Division Bren-gun carriers during an exercise in England, June 1941. NAC/PA-177144

ENGINEERS AT GIBRALTAR

The entry of Italy into the war and the possibility that Spain might join the Axis powers at any moment had greatly increased the importance of Gibraltar, that tiny peninsula appended to Spain which commanded the entrance to the Mediterranean and had housed a British garrison since 1713. Its most conspicuous feature was the massive Rock, net-worked with tunnels and caverns that provided protection against any amount of bombing or artillery fire. More caverns were needed as "a matter of urgency", and the Royal Canadian Engineers in Britain had no shortage of hardrock miners in their ranks. One tunnelling company was sent out in November 1940, and then a second in March 1941, to excavate a hospital and a command centre in the heart of the Rock, and use the excavated material to extend an airfield runway out into the Bay of Algeciras.

The last of them returned to England late in 1942, nearly eighteen months after Hitler turned on his Soviet ally in June 1941. Suddenly and unexpectedly, the Commonwealth had another ally, albeit a morally questionable one. Churchill, however, proclaimed his willingness to make an alliance with the devil himself in order to beat the Germans.

RCE Officer; Levelling with Bulldozer by Charles Comfort. CWM 12359

THE SPITZBERGEN EXPEDITION

The remote and forbidding Spitzbergen archipelago, a thousand kilometres from the geographic pole, eight hundred from Norway's North Cape, suddenly assumed some importance. About two-thirds of the 2800 residents were Russian coal miners and their families, and there were local radio stations broadcasting weather reports which were surely useful to the enemy and could sometimes be picked up in Norway. Whitehall decided that the mine machinery and radio stations must be destroyed, coal stocks burned, and the population evacuated — the Russians to Russia and the Norwegians to Britain.

A reinforced company of the Edmonton Regiment, a company of the Saskatoon Light Infantry (who, despite their title, were actually machine-gunners), and the 3rd Field Company, RCE, together with small detachments of Norwegian infantry and British engineers, the whole under the command of Canada's Brigadier A.E. Potts, were sent to do the job, codenamed Operation *Gauntlet*. They were carried there by the Royal Navy, did it, and were back in England three weeks later.

On 27 September 1940, the Germans and Italians had signed a ten-year military and economic pact with the Japanese, in which each of the signatories promised the others mutual assistance in the event that any one of them became involved in war with a power not then a belligerent. When Germany attacked the Soviet Union in June 1941 the Japanese had not responded, however. On the other hand, when the Japanese attacked the United States' Pacific fleet at Pearl Harbor on 7 December 1941, Hitler kept his bond — and, in the long term, unwittingly sealed his own fate! Never having travelled outside western Europe, and perhaps aware how poorly American industry had met the challenge of war twenty-three years earlier, he had no conception of America's now awesome industrial organization and military potential.

An aerial view of burning coal stocks on Spitzbergen. CDQ Archives

HONG KONG CATASTROPHE

At the same time as they bombed Pearl Harbor, the Japanese also attacked British and French colonies within their reach — one of them being the British Crown Colony of Hong Kong where the garrison, from 16 November, had included the Royal Rifles of Canada and the Winnipeg Grenadiers. What were Canadian soldiers doing there? After all, the entire population, including the garrison, were simply hostages to fortune in the eyes of almost everyone except the General Officer Commanding there from November 1938 to July 1941. The GOC in question was a Canadian in British service, Major-General A.E. Grasett, who (without any first-hand experience to base his belief on) firmly despised the fighting qualities of the Japanese soldier.

When his term of command ended, in July 1941, Grasett had returned to England via Canada. In Ottawa he met with his old RMC classmate, Harry Crerar, who had been brought back from Britain to preside over the expansion of the Army as Chief of the General Staff. Crerar subsequently reported that Grasett had told him that "the addition of two or more battalions to the forces then at Hong Kong would render the garrison strong enough to withstand for an extensive period of siege an attack by such forces as the Japanese could bring to bear against it." However, the possibility of obtaining these units from Canadian resources was not discussed, or even mentioned.

Given the fact that the British Chiefs of Staff had repeatedly decided not to commit more of their own troops, that may seem unlikely; but since there were no witnesses to their conversation and Grasett never put his version on record, it is impossible to refute Crerar's account. Nevertheless, once Grasett arrived in England he put his case for increasing the garrison to the Chiefs of Staff, suggesting that Canada might supply the troops. A formal request to Ottawa soon followed, and Crerar recommended that "the Canadian Army should take this on."

It could be done, he explained, "without reducing the strength of our Coast Defence garrisons and without further mobilization," so the Cabinet approved. Thus two battalions and a brigade staff, short of vehicles, machine guns, mortars and ammunition, reached Hong Kong on 16 November 1941 — less than a month before the Japanese would attack.

The Royal Rifles of Canada disembarking at Hong Kong, 16 November 1941.
CDQ Archives

It has frequently been pointed out that the two battalions chosen — designated as 'C' Force and brigaded under Brigadier J.K. Lawson — were neither trained nor equipped to expeditionary force standards. That is quite true, but irrelevant. Two battalions of the best-trained and equipped troops in the world could only have prolonged the agony for a few more hours or days, and two divisions would have done little better. The fundamental and overwhelming mistake, from a Canadian perspective, was to have sent 'C' Force there at all.

The Winnipeg Grenadiers and the Royal Rifles march to Sham Shui Po Barracks in Hong Kong, 16 November 1941.
NAC/PA-49746

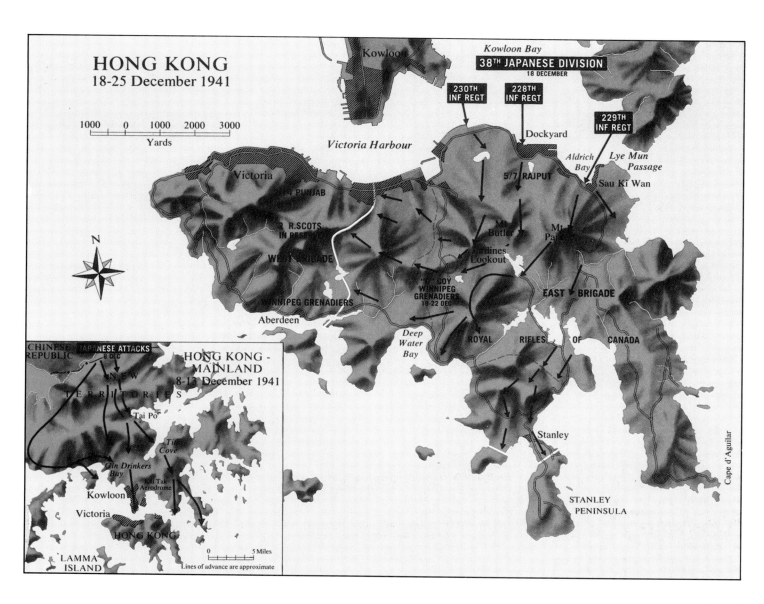

Trench Mortar by Charles Scott.
Glenbow Museum, Calgary, 62.70.4

Grasett's successor, Major-General C.M. Maltby, had about 11,000 fighting men under his command, including British, Indian, Canadian and local Volunteers. The ground to be defended came in two parts, the New Territories on the mainland and the island of Hong Kong itself, separated from the Territories by a narrow channel between two and five kilometres wide. Maltby chose to try and defend the mainland, where the first attack came on 8 December, with some of his British and Indian troops.

The Japanese advanced with a numerical superiority of about three to one, and in five days the Territories were lost, the bulk of their defenders being successfully evacuated to the island. The garrison was then reorganized into two brigades, one, with the Royal Rifles in its ranks, commanded by an Indian Army officer, and the other, including the Winnipeg Grenadiers, by Brigadier Lawson. The two Canadian battalions, viewed by Maltby as not yet fit to fight, were initially assigned to hold the seaward side of the island.

The Pacific Star, awarded to Canadians who served in Hong Kong.

On 18 December Japanese infantry stormed the mainland shore, overrunning one of the Indian battalions, and the Canadians turned about and "marched to the sound of the guns". Among those killed the next day were Brigadier Lawson (who told General Maltby by telephone that the Japanese were firing on his headquarters at close range and he was "going outside to fight it out") and Company Sergeant-Major J.R. Osborn of the Winnipeg Grenadiers who was posthumously awarded the Victoria Cross for throwing himself upon a Japanese grenade, smothering the explosion with his body in order to save a group of his men.

In his careful study of the Hong Kong tragedy, *No Reason Why*, Carl Vincent concluded that:

Company Sergeant-Major
John Osborn, VC

The two Canadian battalions performed the bulk of the fighting for the Island, particularly during the first five days....

... The Royal Rifles executed more counter-attacks at company level or above than the British and Indian battalions combined, and the Winnipeg Grenadiers had the next greatest number....

... There was a great deal of muddle and confusion (much at levels beyond the control of the battalion), the troops were often slow in moving, lack of weapon and tactical training cost them lives, but they only halted or withdrew under the most grave circumstances. It is a fact, moreover, that whenever the Japanese ran into problems it was usually the Canadians who were responsible. When the Japanese regimental commanders, whose standards were extremely high, recorded 'strong opposition', 'fierce fighting', and 'heavy casualties' they were almost always referring to fighting against the Canadians. It is a very conservative estimate to say that at least half the Japanese casualties [a total of 675 killed and 2079 wounded] were incurred in battles against Canadian troops.

It was all to little purpose. During the afternoon of Christmas Day, General Maltby advised the governor that "no further effective military resistance is possible," and Hong Kong was then surrendered to the enemy. The Canadians had lost approximately 300 killed and 500 wounded out of a garrison total of 3500 killed, wounded and missing. Another 250 were destined to die in captivity, four of them being shot without trial for trying to escape: of the 1973 men who sailed from Vancouver in October 1941, there were 557 who never returned.

There was, of course, a great outcry in Canada, for it was obvious to anyone with the faintest understanding of military matters that their soldiers should never have been sent to Hong Kong. Regrettably, however, the issue became confused with party politics over the need for universal conscription. When the government was compelled to appoint a Royal Commission to investigate the circumstances surrounding the unfortunate affair, the Prime Minister's old friend and Chief Justice of the Supreme Court, Sir Lyman Duff, was the commissioner. Taken all in all, the Commission, like so many of its ilk, was a whitewash. Only the Quartermaster-General's department of the General Staff was blamed, for not outfitting the contingent as well as it should have done.

Of the nearly 1700 Canadians taken prisoner at Hong Kong, 250 died in captivity. This photo shows some of the Canadian prisoners-of-war shortly after their liberation in August 1945.
NAC/PA-151738

CONSCRIPTION

The threat posed by initial Japanese successes was worrying the Canadian public — and therefore Mackenzie King — and the General Staff (although it discounted any direct threat) was happy to take advantage of the situation. The Army was still expanding and there might — just might! — be a need for conscripts to be sent overseas if Canadians became involved in heavy fighting on a large scale. It was best to be prepared, they persuaded the Cabinet. Accordingly, in January 1942 the government went to the country on the conscription issue and, overall, the electorate answered with a resounding 'Yes' although Quebec took an exactly opposite stance. With conscription for overseas service now on the books, however, Crerar wrote to McNaughton, telling him that:

... our departmental appreciation indicates that manpower is available to maintain a Canadian Army of eight Divisions, of which two will be in Canada, for a war period of over six years from now....

... we should be able to reinforce the Corps [in England] during 1942 with not only the 4th Division but another Armoured Division as well. This would result in too large a Corps, but have you ever considered the pros and cons of a Canadian Army comprising 2 Corps each of 2 Divisions and an Armoured Division?

The 5th Armoured Division, under Major-General E.W. Sansom — created in part by taking units from the 4th Infantry Division and leaving only a cadre of the latter in existence for the time being — had joined its brethren overseas by the end of the year. So had General Crerar, succeeding Victor Odlum in command of the 2nd Division and acting as corps commander when McNaughton took sick leave in November 1941. Promoted to lieutenant-general, he would become GOC I Canadian Corps in April 1942, when the formation of First Canadian Army lifted McNaughton another step in the military hierarchy. His place in Ottawa was taken by the Vice-Chief, Lieutenant-General Ken Stuart.

Returning from Night Duty
by J.L. Shadbolt
The Veterans' Guard, made up of older men who had served in the First World War, acted as guards at prisoner-of-war camps in Canada. CWM 14284

TRAINING IN ENGLAND

Meanwhile, the Cabinet, heavily influenced by the Japanese scare, rejected the idea of a sixth division overseas. Three divisions, composed largely of conscripts, would be kept in Canada, although the 4th, now to be converted into a second armoured division, would go to England during the second half of 1942. Training intensified, both in Canada and England, and battle drills were introduced. Recruits were practiced in moving under live fire (directed well to the side or overhead) and put to "crawling elbow deep in stale animal intestines, getting doused with pig's blood...."

Unfortunately, such useful, realistic approaches to the training of junior officers and other ranks only addressed part of the problem, ignoring the equally important issue of battle doctrine and its application by commanders at battalion level and above. British (and therefore Canadian) doctrine was far too ponderous by German standards. Built on First World War experience, even if foxholes and slit trenches had replaced the old continuous trench systems, it stuck firmly to the principle that "artillery conquers, infantry occupies" disputed ground. But no matter how well it was handled, the logistics of artillery slowed the pace of battle; if the enemy was defeated in a set-piece fight he could never be kept on the run, for time was always needed to 'bring up the guns' — and even more to bring up ammunition — before another move forward could be made.

A Cameron Highlanders of Ottawa machine-gun section navigates a stream during an exercise in June 1942. NAC/PA-177140

Sappers of 9th Field Squadron, Royal Canadian Engineers practice bridge building.
NAC/PA-177143

Troopers of the 4th Princess Louise Dragoon Guards during a 1st Division exercise near Hastings. NAC/PA-177142

In the Canadian case these problems were compounded by the number of higher commanders and senior staff officers who were gunners by trade. A fine example of what could result from their prejudices is noted by Major-General George Kitching in his memoir, *Mud And Green Fields*.

Guy Simonds also ran a couple of Tactical Exercises Without Troops, in one of which the commander of our armoured brigade, Brigadier Bradbrooke, ran afoul of Simonds.... The situation in the TEWT was that the armoured brigade had reached its objective and was anxious to push ahead whilst the enemy was disorganized. Simonds laid it down that the armour should pause, reorganize on its objective and then wait until the artillery had caught up with them before advancing any further. Brad disagreed strongly with this policy and went on to commit 'hara kiri' by saying, "Why should I wait for another 24 guns when I've got over 150 of them in my tanks? I don't need the artillery to shoot me on to anything and I can get there quite well by myself."

... the atmosphere became instantly electric. Guy Simonds was an artillery man and to a gunner this was heresy of the worst kind.... Brad remained unconvinced and lost his command.

Poor Bradbrooke, with his *Panzer* way of thinking, never did get to command a formation in the field.

THE DIEPPE RAID

It was, then, ironic that the raid on Dieppe should have failed in part because of a dire lack of fire support, particularly so since, in this case, it could not have delayed the raiders in any way, nor caused any logistics problems, for there would have been no need to put artillery ashore.

During the spring and early summer of 1942 the war was still not going well for the Allies. In the Pacific, the Japanese advance had been stopped at Midway, but in southeast Asia they had taken Malaya, Borneo, the Dutch East Indies and Burma, and were hammering at the gates of India. In North Africa, the bastion of Tobruk had fallen and the *Afrika Korps* seemed poised to take Alexandria and the Suez Canal. On the Eastern Front, Russian counterattacks had expired with the coming of spring and, in the south, the Germans had begun a drive into the Caucasus: it even seemed possible that the Germans might close a gigantic pair of armoured pincers around the whole of the Near East. Nevertheless, and despite American pressure, the British Chiefs of Staff were determined not to open a Second Front as Stalin was demanding. Brooke, for one, was (probably rightly) convinced that a 'Second Front Now' (as the slogan of the time demanded) would fail. Perhaps a bigger-than-usual raid, something on an entirely new scale, would satisfy Britain's allies.

Lord Louis Mountbatten's Combined Operations HQ had cooked up a plan to raid Dieppe — code-named Operation *Rutter* — which, in true commando style, relied heavily upon surprise. But this would be too big a raid for his men to handle by themselves, and the Canadians — increasingly frustrated by the lack of action — were offered the leading role. McNaughton accepted and nominated the 2nd Division, now commanded by Major-General J.H. Roberts, which Crerar considered the best trained division in the corps — perhaps because he had just relinquished command of it himself!

Despite a guarantee of strong fighter cover — Dieppe was selected largely because it was within fighter range — the Royal Navy was not prepared to risk heavy ships in the Channel: and, at the last moment, it was decided that a heavy air bombardment planned to immediately precede the landings on the main beach might hamper the advance of the tanks through the town. Fire support would therefore be limited to that available from the 4-inch guns of eight destroyers and some thirty squadrons of fighter-bombers and light bombers.

Hindsight confirms that the element of surprise was absolutely vital, but once again the Navy upset the applecart by arguing that the concentration of shipping offshore, if all the landings were carried out simultaneously, would be too congested to control. Consequently, the commando assaults, and those at Puys and Pourville, were timed for 0450 hours — "the beginning of nautical twilight" — and those on the main

beaches for half an hour later. Although these unwise arrangements were concocted by essentially British staffs, the Canadians accepted them without demur. McNaughton had no complaint. Crerar expressed himself "satisfied that the revisions ... add rather than detract to the soundness of the plan as a whole" and thought that "given an even break in luck and good navigation, the demonstration should prove successful." "A piece of cake" was how General Roberts described it to his men.

Men of the Fusiliers Mont-Royal during an exercise on 9 August 1942, ten days before the raid. NAC/PA-177146

Platoons of the Royal Regiment of Canada board landing craft in England on 18 August 1942. CDQ Archives

Practices on the Isle of Wight had not gone well, however. Timings were often off and the Navy had trouble landing the troops at the right places. *Rutter*, first scheduled for 5 July and then postponed until the 8th because of bad weather, was finally cancelled on that date. Mountbatten, however, anxious to further his own interests, re-mounted it a month later as Operation *Jubilee*, apparently without mentioning the matter to either Churchill or the Chiefs of Staff.

On 18 August 1942, 237 ships and landing craft left five British ports before nightfall, bound for Dieppe. At first everything went extraordinarily well, but then the flotilla on the eastern flank, carrying No.3 Commando towards Berneval, ran afoul of a German coastal convoy. In the ensuing fire-fight the landing craft were "completely scattered, some of them being damaged." Only seven landed their troops, and the occupants of six met with such resolute resistance from an aroused enemy that they could do nothing. The men in the seventh, landing in front of a narrow gully half a kilometre down the coast, scrambled up it, got behind the battery which was their objective, and suppressed its fire for an hour and a half by accurate sniping. On the other flank, at Vasterival, No.4 Commando achieved total surprise and destroyed its target in a model operation of its kind.

The heavy firing which marked the battle with the German convoy did not disturb the enemy unduly. His convoys were often attacked by roving motor gun boats or bombers, and the sound of gunfire offshore at night was not uncommon. But, having been raided before and expecting to be raided again, his coastal garrisons were always in a fairly high state of readiness whenever conditions of moon, tide and weather suggested that a raid might be in the cards. So it was on 19 August 1942, except that an enthusiastic young commander of the under-strength company at Puys had decided on his own to have *all* his men actually manning their posts an hour before dawn on this particular day.

The sky was lightening noticeably when the first wave of the Royal Regiment of Canada approached the beach at Puys, twenty minutes late. "Then in a moment a thundering over our heads, and in its wake a rushing shuffling sound, like wild geese flying in the darkness," remembered one young soldier lucky enough to survive (although he spent the rest of the war in a prison camp) whose reaction was probably typical of men coming under hostile fire for the first time. "We began to hear small arms fire. I did not understand. What was happening?"

Troops of the Cameron Highlanders of Canada climb aboard a landing craft for the run into Dieppe, 19 August 1942. NAC/PA-113245

Soldiers of the Essex Scottish peer over the bow of a landing craft as they approach Red Beach for the frontal assault on Dieppe. Over 30 percent of the unit were killed or wounded within the first twenty minutes.

CDQ Archives

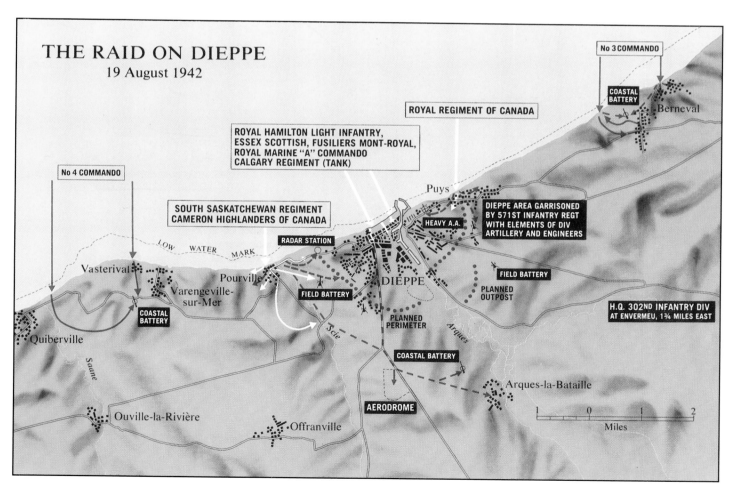

THE RAID ON DIEPPE
19 August 1942

No 3 COMMANDO

COASTAL BATTERY

Berneval

ROYAL REGIMENT OF CANADA

ROYAL HAMILTON LIGHT INFANTRY,
ESSEX SCOTTISH, FUSILIERS MONT-ROYAL,
ROYAL MARINE "A" COMMANDO
CALGARY REGIMENT (TANK)

No 4 COMMANDO

Puys

DIEPPE AREA GARRISONED
BY 571ST INFANTRY REGT
WITH ELEMENTS OF DIV
ARTILLERY AND ENGINEERS

SOUTH SASKATCHEWAN REGIMENT
CAMERON HIGHLANDERS OF CANADA

HEAVY A.A.

LOW WATER MARK

RADAR STATION

FIELD BATTERY

Vasterival

DIEPPE

Pourville

FIELD BATTERY

PLANNED OUTPOST

Varengeville-sur-Mer

COASTAL BATTERY

PLANNED PERIMETER

H.Q. 302ND INFANTRY DIV
AT ENVERMEU, 1¾ MILES EAST

Quiberville

Scie

Arques

COASTAL BATTERY

Saane

Arques-la-Bataille

Ouville-la-Rivière

AERODROME

Offranville

1   0   1   2
Miles

One of his fellow foot soldiers, Private Steve Mitchell, who was also lucky enough to end up in a prison camp, could have given him the answer. On the beach beyond the sea wall:

There's a scraping underneath [the landing craft]; now the seamen drop the ramp and we brace ourselves, ready to go when our turn comes. The right-hand section moves out and we follow suit, trying not to step on the bodies of comrades in the middle row ....What a carnage! Get off this hulk fast, Mitch, before that bullet with your name gets here! Good; I've made it. But there is a buddy we call Smiler lying on the beach trying to shove his intestines back into the gaping hole in his stomach, and he is still smiling....

Our beach is about three hundred yards long by about seventy yards wide. At either end are what seems to be natural rock promontories going away out into the water. On these rock buttresses the Nazis have built concrete pillboxes from which they can cover us with withering fire. Far back from the top of the cliff they have batteries of their new six-barrelled mortars, all pre-set to cover every square inch of the beach.

We shoot, but there is nothing to shoot at; our enemies are all unseen....

The Distinguished Conduct Medal. Twenty DCMs were awarded for gallantry at Dieppe.

A dwindling band of survivors on the beach endured the German fire for about three hours before raising the white flag. Only two officers and 65 men — mostly those whose landing craft had pulled back off the beach before they could set foot on it — returned to England out of the 554 who had embarked; and two-thirds of the three platoons of the Black Watch which were with them were also lost.

Lieutenant-Colonel C.C. Merritt, VC

On the other flank, at Pourville, the South Saskatchewan Regiment got ashore only two minutes late, "without a shot being fired" at them, thus demonstrating the inestimable virtue of surprise. Lacking adequate fire support, however, they could not take the headland on their left which lay between them and Dieppe and not only dominated the main beaches but also housed a German radar station that 'boffins' in England had hoped might be looted with advantage. They had been landed astride the River Scie, and the one bridge across it was under constant fire. Striding about on the bridge and its approaches while encouraging his men to dash across, Lieutenant-Colonel C.C. Merritt won the VC.

The Queen's Own Cameron Highlanders, following them ashore a half-hour later, were met by heavy fire from the headland — their colonel was killed instantly — and most of them were soon either casualties or pinned down close to the beach. Those who got clear, under the second-in-command, moved cautiously inland for about three kilometres, then saw German bicycle troops approaching in the distance. There was still no sign of the tanks they had expected to meet and they were now under fire from three directions, so they wisely began to withdraw towards the Saskatchewans' bridgehead perimeter.

The Dieppe Raid by Charles Comfort.
The Royal Hamilton Light Infantry and tanks of the Calgary Regiment assaulting the Casino on White Beach. CWM 12276

In front of Dieppe itself, the Essex Scottish, the Royal Hamilton Light Infantry and the Calgary Regiment tanks were supposed to touch down at 0520 hours and so they did, more or less. But warned by the garrison of Pourville and the sounds of battle less than three kilometres distant, the garrison of the town had now had the best part of half an hour to man their defences. Five squadrons of RAF fighter-bombers scourged the cliffs of the two headlands and the buildings fronting on the pebbly beach as the Canadians landed. The attack was momentarily terrifying, no doubt, but far too brief in duration to suppress the enemy for long.

As at Puys, most of the attackers were trapped beyond the seawall and pinned to the beach, vainly seeking cover from the mortar fire to their front and machine-gun fire from the headlands on both sides. Company Sergeant-Major Cornelius Stapleton of the Essex Scottish, among the very first to land, immediately led a dozen men in a seventy-metre dash over the wall and across the Esplanade without anybody being hit. For two hours, he and his men roamed the town, shooting up Germans whenever they came across them but too few in number to make a major impact on the course of the raid. Getting back to the beach was harder but they accomplished that, too, in due course. (When the time came to evacuate the beach, Stapleton — who was later awarded the Distinguished Conduct Medal, was told by his CO to stay with the wounded: good soldier Stapleton obeyed and was taken prisoner.) The RHLI were to the right of the Essex, some of them opposite the Casino which extended across the Esplanade to a point right above the sea wall. It offered cover from fire once the strong point constructed in its seaward side had been neutralized — something easier said than done — and some of the 'Rileys' fought their way through the building, room by room, and got into the town, but again there were too few of them to do much good and, like Stapleton, they eventually came back.

Most of the men in both battalions were still trapped on the beach.

I threw my body on to the coarse gravel beach and squirmed my way towards the concrete sea wall. I had to get through a mess of barbed wire already strewn with bodies and finally pulled myself up to the wall where a soldier lay dead, draped over the barbed wire that ran along the top. Carefully I raised my head to see what was happening on the other side of the wall, but quickly withdrew it for it seemed that the whole German army was shooting at me personally.

I could see that some of the tanks had made it to shore and were churning up the gravel. They would turn and fire, then head up the beach a few yards and repeat the procedure.

249

Several of the Calgary Regiment's *Churchill* tanks are shown in this captured German photograph taken after the battle on 19 August. In the distance, partly obscured by smoke from the burning landing craft, is the West Headland from which the beach was raked by machine-gun fire. NAC

This was the *Churchill* tank's introduction to battle, and it was soon obvious to their crews how much better off they were than the unprotected infantry. Their armour was proof against any of the German anti-tank guns, from any angle, and no tanker was injured while inside his tank. Nevertheless, they met with little success. Half of them failed to get off the beach, either bottoming out on the shingle or having the pebbles jam or break their tracks.

The fifteen (or seventeen — accounts differ) which succeeded in crossing the sea wall found it impossible to enter the town, for all the exits from the Esplanade had been blocked by concrete barricades and the engineers who were assigned to blow the blocks away with explosive charges were all either dead, wounded, or pinned down on the beach. Frustrated, the tanks rumbled aimlessly to and fro, shooting at the more obvious targets. One flushed some German infantry and "made a dash for them.... Both gunners opened up and we got plenty of them. Even had the pleasure of running down one who tried to dodge us."

On board the command ship, HMS *Calpe*, General Roberts received a signal reporting the "Essex Scot across the beaches and in houses" — a message which may have referred to Stapleton and his men. It seemed an opportunity for exploitation, and he ordered the Fusiliers Mont-Royal to land behind the Essex. By that time, however, the beaches were shrouded in smoke, the coxswains of the boats could not see the shore clearly, and an unexpectedly strong tide was running. The main body of the Fusiliers were landed under the cliffs of the West Headland. One of their warrant officers remembered afterwards:

... the wounded and dead who [soon] lie scattered on the beach. Some of the wounded were trying to swim out to the boats [and] many were bleeding heavily, reddening the water around them. [Once ashore,] mortar bombs are bursting on the shingle and making little clouds which seem to punctuate the deafening din.... The wounded scream ... the blood flows from their wounds in a viscous, blackish tide....

Roberts launched his last reserve, the Royal Marine Commando, but as it approached the shore under a hail of fire its commanding officer realized that a landing could only be fruitless and costly. He stood up in the bows of his boat and signalled the others to retire before falling mortally wounded.

Mopping Up After the Battle by Franz Martin Luenstroth. CWM 14422

At 0900 hours the order was given to begin evacuating the beaches two hours later — the delay being necessary in order to organize the naval aspects and to make sure that everybody got the word. Even leaving Dieppe was not easy. Wallace Reyburn, a Canadian war correspondent, had earlier gone ashore at Pourville, where now:

... the beach was dotted with prone figures on the sand and men running out to the boats.... From each end there was the raking fire of machine guns.... Mortar shells exploded on the beach and sent cascades of sand and pebbles far and wide. Snipers picked off men as they ran. Focke-Wulfes [fighters] came roaring down low and spat their cannon fire and machine guns at us. I watched a Junkers 88 [bomber] that had managed to slip through our fighters come trundling (it seemed so slow and laborious compared with the Focke-Wulfes) along about a hundred feet above the beach and drop its bombs as it got over the boats.

Among those left behind was one who stayed voluntarily. Captain John Foote, the padre of the RHLI, chose to stay and succour the wounded. He, too, was subsequently awarded a VC.

The greatest single disaster in Canadian military history was now complete. Out of the 5000 Canadians embarked, only 2210 returned to England and more than 600 of

Captain the Reverend
John Foote, VC

those were wounded: 900 had been killed and over 1900 had been taken prisoner, nearly 600 of them being wounded as well. In Canada, families were left to mourn their dead, or worry over sons and brothers in prison camps, as the full casualty figures were released over the better part of a week.

251

No amount of training can duplicate the harsh realities of war and the men who went to Dieppe were still neophytes at their trade. The shock of battle — intense battle — was too sudden, the phenomenon too violent, to be handled without at least a leavening of men accustomed to combat. In the aftermath of Dieppe that was recognized, and soon arrangements would be made for selected officers to be attached to British units fighting in North Africa and so gain some practical experience.

Senior officers had accepted British planning uncritically, it was argued, and that was certainly true, but it would have been professionally fatal for any of them to have rejected the opportunity for action when their men were growing increasingly impatient and the Canadian public had been pressing to hear of them in action. McNaughton and Crerar escaped virtually unscathed. General Roberts, however, was quietly relieved of his command a few months after the raid, and never again held an operational appointment.

Some 1200 men were evacuated from the beaches at Dieppe and Pourville, none from Puys, between 1100 and about 1220 hours. Those who remained behind, 1946 officers and men, surrendered and spent the rest of the war in German POW camps. FMR Museum

EXERCISE *SPARTAN*

First Canadian Army — still, in McNaughton's words, "a dagger pointed at the heart of Berlin," but just a little blunted for the moment — resumed 'training and duties'. The first of some 350 officers and NCOs left for Tunisia, where they were to hone their knowledge of war and their combat skills while serving with British units actually fighting the enemy. The 4th Armoured Division, given to General Worthington when Brigadier R.A. Wyman took over the 1st Army Tank Brigade, arrived in England and a second Canadian corps was formed, General Sansom stepping up a rank to command it, with his 5th Armoured Division going to Major-General C.R.S. Stein. Both the Canadian corps headquarters were under the control of McNaughton in Exercise *Spartan*, which took place in March 1943 under the overall direction of General Sir Bernard Paget, now GOC-in-C British Home Forces. McNaughton's six divisions — two armoured and four infantry, three of them British — were assumed to be breaking out of a bridgehead established on the Continent. The Canadian divisions involved were the 2nd and 3rd Infantry and the 5th Armoured.

Spartan proved to be something of a fiasco. II Corps headquarters had not yet 'shaken down' properly, vital signal equipment of various types (much of it on loan from British formations) only arriving "a couple of days" before the exercise began, and this was the first occasion on which the whole of the 5th Armoured Division would exercise together. Hoping for the best — he was ever the optimist — McNaughton felt, nevertheless, that more would be gained than lost by having both II Corps HQ and the 5th Division participate; and he pressed that view on Paget.

Canadian Tanks Manoeuvring by Will Ogilvie. CWM 13268

Men of the Régiment de Maisonneuve taking part in Exercise *Spartan*, March 1943. NAC/PA-177138

The Canadian Voluntary Service Medal, authorized in 1943 for award to all volunteers for 18 months wartime service. The bar denotes overseas service.

KISKA AND THE ALEUTIAN ISLANDS

Across the globe, on 11 May 1943 American troops invaded Attu, one of two remote Aleutian islands occupied by the Japanese in June 1942. The Japanese garrison died hard, all 3000 of them — there were only three badly wounded survivors — and their deaths cost the Americans nearly 4000 casualties, including 550 dead. As soon as the attack on Attu was reported, however, the Canadian CGS, General Stuart, was inquiring whether it was "too late to consider some form of [Canadian] army participation."

Men of the Régiment de Hull waiting to board ships for Kiska.
NAC/PA-168356

He may have been right, but the inevitable foul-ups in communications and inadequate staff work led to enormous frustration and some magnificent Canadian cursing on the congested highways and byways of southern England. Convoys going one way down narrow country lanes met other convoys coming the other, and the resultant traffic tangles took hours to sort out. Messages were sent and never received; whole units went astray or, if they did not, then their rations did. And all this confusion put another black mark against McNaughton's name at the War Office.

It was not, and the Cabinet eventually decided to commit a reinforced brigade group to the re-occupation of the other island, Kiska. Brigadier H.W. Foster was brought back from England to command the Canadian Fusiliers, the Winnipeg Grenadiers (reformed since the destruction of the original battalion at Hong Kong), the Rocky Mountain Rangers and the Régiment de Hull, together with the appropriate complement of supporting arms and services.

Probably a majority of the soldiers assigned to the invasion of Kiska were NMRA conscripts, and an Order-in-Council of 18 June 1943 authorized their employment in Alaska. A significant number of them deserted during their training, but they were replaced and training went on. For logistics reasons, American weapons were substituted for some of the Canadian ones, but not all. Maintaining the 13th Brigade Group was going to be complicated, to say the least, if there was serious fighting to be done.

There was also the 1st Special Service Force, a unique, commando-type organization formed in the early summer of 1942. It was composed of two over-strength battalions of American volunteers and one of Canadians, equipped and trained to American standards and commanded by an American. It, too, would go to Kiska.

Americans and Canadians stormed ashore, through the usual thick Aleutian fog, in two landings on 15 and 16 August 1943, only to find that the Japanese had all left by submarine three weeks earlier. Despite the lack of opposition, that pleasant realization came to the attackers only gradually, however. There were cases of mistaken identity in the fog and "The Canadians had one soldier wounded by unidentified machine-gun fire on 16 August, and one officer killed by a mine the following day," according to Colonel Stacey. "Later three other fatal casualties were caused by enemy booby-traps or accidents with ammunition."

Had the war ended in May 1943 instead of May 1945, those words might have provided a fitting epitaph for the Canadian Army, at home and overseas. Despite the occasional forays into actual operations outlined in this chapter — the two which had involved hard fighting, Hong Kong and Dieppe, had both been disasters through no fault of the regimental soldiers concerned — by far the larger part of an ever-growing Army had spent most of the war in camp or barracks. That, however, was about to change.

Signallers play cards while awaiting transport to Kiska.

NAC/PA-177681

Canadian troops go ashore on Kiska. The joint Canadian-American force found that the Japanese had already withdrawn. 16 August 1943.

NAC/PA-163408

CHAPTER 10

ITALIAN ODYSSEY
1943-1945

by
Brereton Greenhous

A NEED FOR ACTION

A hockey team which is always practising but never plays a game is sure to be plagued by low morale. Players become bored, and some — often the better ones on ice — begin to miss practices, quarrel with their coaches and, eventually, quit the team. As for their disillusioned supporters, there will soon be booing in the stands and many demanding more action or their money back.

So it is with armies and wars. In the spring of 1943, as Exercise *Spartan* concluded, there was still no sign of First Canadian Army — McNaughton's "dagger pointed at Berlin" — actually being stuck between Hitlerian ribs! Problems of morale and discipline were becoming endemic among over-trained and under-motivated soldiers — too much drinking, too many brawls, and too many men going 'Absent Without Leave'. Major-General H.L.N. Salmon who now commanded the 1st Division (which had been overseas for two-and-a-half years, mostly without any prospect of action) had been promoted to his present post, in part at least, because he was a motivator and a disciplinarian. The same personal qualities

were also prominent in the make-up of Brigadier R.A. Wyman, who had taken over the 1st Army Tank Brigade. In their respective spheres, these two formations had endured more tedium than any others, and in them the frustrations were greatest.

At home, too, there was disgruntlement with the Army's apparently passive stance. The Navy was convoying essential war supplies to Britain and Russia, the Air Force was carrying fire and high explosives into 'Fortress Europe', but the Army was only occupying itself in 'training and duties'. In Parliament, an Opposition speaker regretted that, "while Australia and New Zealand are fighting gallantly on the sands of Africa, personnel of the Canadian Army are not there." And the Ottawa *Journal*, quietly overlooking the catastrophes of Hong Kong and Dieppe, editorialized that "All other Empire troops have had battle experience…. Only Canadians … have not been tried. This, we confess, seems strange. To a great many it is disturbing."

Prelude to Invasion
by Will Ogilvie.

A Seaforth Highlanders platoon is briefed on its tasks in the invasion of Sicily while en route to the Mediterranean.
CWM 13505

Anything which disturbed 'a great many' voters also disturbed Mackenzie King. At his behest, Defence Minister J.L. Ralston had asked Winston Churchill (in October 1942) if he could arrange for Canadian troops to get into action "at the first opportunity." Three months later, President Franklin Roosevelt, Prime Minister Churchill, and their respective Chiefs of Staff, met at Casablanca, in Morocco, to determine upon a joint strategy for the coming year. The Americans favoured a 'Second Front Now' in northwest Europe but the British felt that was still too risky a prospect. A compromise was reached in the decision to attack what Churchill mistakenly called "the soft underbelly of Europe". Sicily or Sardinia were the likeliest targets. Sicily was within fighter range of Malta and thus the Allies could be sure of air superiority over any beachhead. Sicily it would be.

When King's request was put to Churchill again — with rather more urgency this time — in mid-March 1943, General Crerar quickly canvassed his friends in Whitehall. "Harry Crerar to dinner," wrote British General Sir Alan Brooke, the Chief of the Imperial General Staff, in his diary:

... and a long harangue from him as to the necessity of getting some Canadians fighting soon for Imperial and political reasons.... I had to remind him that the main factor that had, up to date, militated against their use in Africa was the stipulation made by the Canadian Government that the Canadian Army must not be split up and must only be used as a whole — a conception that McNaughton had always held with the greatest of tenacity....

Seaforth Highlanders training with Vickers machine guns, December 1942.
NAC/PA-177137

Major-General E.W. Sansom inspects the British Columbia Dragoons in England.
NAC/PA-152487

Three things were certain: first, if Canadians were to see action in the near future it could only be in the Mediterranean theatre; second, given the semi-permanent shipping crisis that beset the Allies, no purely political motivation could justify moving any large body of troops to another theatre; and third, if the Canadian government's request was to be met, then its Army overseas would *have* to be splintered.

Fortuitous logistical problems gave Mackenzie King and his cohorts their desires. Allied planners had reluctantly concluded that since North African ports could only handle limited tonnages, the British force for the invasion of Sicily — the famous Eighth Army — would have to draw an infantry division and an armoured brigade directly from the United Kingdom. British formations had already been assigned, but that could easily be changed. The 1st Division and the Army Tank Brigade would fill the bill admirably, since "both political and military reasons make it essential that Canadian forces be brought into action this year."

RCD Armoured Cars Under Air Attack by E.J. Hughes. CWM

THE SICILIAN COMMITMENT

The Eighth Army commander, Sir Bernard Montgomery, asked that General Salmon and some of his senior staff officers fly out to Cairo in order to coordinate arrangements with the planners there. Salmon's aircraft unfortunately crashed with the loss of all on board, and McNaughton appointed, as his successor, Major-General G.G. Simonds, a dynamic, 34-year-old artillery careerist who had just taken command of the 2nd Division (in succession to the unfortunate Roberts) after completing a short tour as an 'observer' at Eighth Army headquarters.

Simonds flew out on 1 May, arriving in Cairo on the 4th. In the course of the next four days, the Canadian part in the invasion of Sicily — Operation *Husky* — was confirmed and instructions cabled back to England so that planning could start for ships to be 'combat loaded' — equipment being placed aboard in the reverse order to that in which it would subsequently be unloaded on the Sicilian beaches. On the 12th, Simonds was back in England to supervise the preparation of his new command. American-designed and built *Sherman* tanks were 'standard issue' in the Mediterranean theatre and the tankers had to swap their *Churchills* for *Shermans* and begin accustoming themselves to their livelier steeds. For both formations there were many changes in clothing and equipment in order to conform to Mediterranean practice;

and for the long-suffering infantry there was a renewed emphasis on training — this time in amphibious operations — which seemed bearable in the light of rumours that they would soon be in action.

Two 'assault' convoys, which joined forces off Algiers, carried the 1st Division and the Three Rivers Regiment — some 20,000 men — to battle. Two more, a week behind them, brought the balance of the Tank Brigade, together with a 1200-bed hospital and a reinforcement depot to be set up initially in Tunisia. Three ships of the first convoys were torpedoed en route, with the loss of fifty-eight men, forty guns, and some five hundred vehicles.

"The attack came in the evening, just as it turned dark," CBC war correspondent Matthew Halton, who was aboard one of the stricken ships, later told his listeners. "I was in the [officers] dining room at the time...."

It wasn't long before the guns of the convoy opened up and the Ju 88s made their first run over.... There was a terrific explosion which seemed to lift us out of our seats, and then the lights went out and the ship took a very sharp list to port. I was eating a piece of pie at the time, and seemed to have the impression that when I last saw it, it was floating in the air about on a level with my eyes.

... The planes were coming over at mast height, and as they came all the guns in the convoy opened up on them with coloured tracers, shells and bullets. As they passed over our masts the guns all converged in my direction, and all those coloured tracers gave the impression that it was me and not the planes they were shooting at.

Alpine training, British Columbia, July 1943. NAC/PA-177679

Headquarters of the Governor General's Horse Guards during an exercise in the summer of 1943 in Sussex.
NAC/PA-177094

THE INVASION OF SICILY

The vast majority of the quarter-million men garrisoning Sicily on the night of 9-10 July, were poorly-led Italians, with no great enthusiasm for fighting, who probably felt much as Halton had done a few nights earlier, when his ship was attacked. The Germans had only two divisions there, both held in reserve, well back from the beaches, ready to launch counterattacks once the point of Allied main effort could be discerned. There was no single landing, however; more or less simultaneously, over nearly two hundred kilometres of shoreline, the Americans landed in the southwest, at Gela and Licata, while on the east coast, south of Syracuse, the Anglo-Canadians made *five* separate landings. The 1st and 2nd Canadian Infantry Brigades straggled ashore on the southern-most tip of the island, near Pachino.

Opposition was light in some places, nonexistent in others; and that was probably just as well, since the landing process was complicated by unexpectedly deep water between an offshore sandbar and the beach. As the landing craft carrying Lieutenant Farley Mowat of the Hastings and Prince Edward Regiment — who, it must be admitted, was shorter than most — grounded on the sandbar:

A section of the Princess Patricias pass an Ontario Regiment *Sherman* tank during the advance into Sicily, 19 July 1943.
NAC/PA-166755

Revolver in hand, Tommy gun slung over my shoulder, web equipment bulging with grenades and ammo, tin hat pulled firmly down around my ears, I sprinted to the edge of the ramp shouting, 'Follow me, men!' — and leapt off into eight feet of water.

Weighted as I was, I went down like a stone, striking the bottom feet first. So astounded was I by this unexpected descent into the depths that I made no attempt to thrash my way back to the surface. I simply walked straight on until my head emerged.

A squadron of Three Rivers' tanks was ashore by noon and the infantry began to push inland, into the mountainous centre of the island, hampered more by lack of transport, dust and heat, than by the enemy. It was not until the fifth day, just outside Grammichele, that they first came under German fire, from artillery and tanks. The 'Hasty Pees', supported by Three Rivers' tanks, took the town by noon at a cost of twenty-five casualties. After that, in the words of the Canadian Official History of the campaign, "There were many sharp engagements with the Hermann Goering division, along tortuous rocky roads; and the Germans were experts in delaying tactics, with ambushes, demolitions, and minefields dominated by machine guns and [high-velocity anti-tank] 88s."

Landing in Sicily by Will Ogilvie.
The 1st Canadian Division comes ashore at Pachino, 10 July 1943. CWM 13420

Sometimes the enemy had decamped in haste, without taking time to bury his dead. Finding one of them was a sobering experience for a young officer of the Princess Patricias, Lieutenant Sydney Frost.

He had been caught in our barrage and his lower body was a horrible mess of bone, flesh, guts and torn uniform. I reached inside his camouflaged jacket and pulled out a wallet. Papers, postcards and pictures fell to the ground. I picked up a blood-stained postcard he had apparently written home but never posted. On the front was a picture of his idol — Adolf Hitler.

The poor misguided bastard, I mumbled to myself. Thousands of miles from home, his shattered body lies abandoned by his comrades on a barren Sicilian mountainside. Soon the peasants will steal his boots; the follow-up troops will take his watch and Iron Cross.

I was tempted to take them myself, but I had to move off quickly to keep up with the timing of the barrage ....

The Canadians trudged through the hills to the west of Mount Etna, bypassing Enna and fighting their way into Assoro and Leonforte, meeting their first reverse at Nissoria, and finally capturing Agira. For them the Sicilian campaign ended on 7 August when they were squeezed out of the contracting front as the Allies closed on Messina. The transformation from trained apprentices to journeymen warriors had cost them 2310 battle casualties — 562 killed, 1664 wounded, and 84 taken prisoner.

Montgomery was pleased with their performance, telling war correspondent Peter Stursberg that they "were terrific on the beaches and during the drive inland. Absolutely terrific." (An informal dresser himself, he did, however, once take some exception to a Canadian bulldozer driver wearing nothing but a looted top hat and his issue boots in the stifling July heat. The sapper, mindful of military protocol but apparently feeling a salute was hardly appropriate, doffed his hat and wished the army commander a cheerful "Good day, boss.") Montgomery thought well of Simonds, too, advising Lieutenant-General E.L.M. Burns, who would come to take over the Canadian Corps in January 1943, that he was 'first class'; but his relationship with another Canadian general was soon not nearly so sweet.

Generals McNaughton and Stuart had arrived in North Africa on 6 July, ostensibly to meet with the overall Allied Commander, American General Dwight D. Eisenhower, and discuss with him the "organization and preparation of Canadian forces in Canada for later use in war against Japan." That was probably an excuse. McNaughton ardently wanted to see and talk with his men in the field, and he sought to go to Sicily. Richard Malone, then brigade major of the 2nd Brigade and shortly to become Canadian liaison officer at Montgomery's Tactical HQ, has recorded what happened next.

Tank at Cross Roads
by Will Ogilvie.

A Three Rivers Regiment *Sherman* tank guards a Sicilian road junction.
CWM 13609

General McNaughton talks with Major Irvine of the Saskatoon Light Infantry during his visit to Sicily, 22 August 1943.
NAC/PA-136200

McNaughton was politely told by Alexander that he could not go to Sicily "owing to the shortage of transport." He promptly flew back to England, in order to explain to the Chief of the Imperial General Staff (his old enemy, Alan Brooke) that "representatives of Canada could visit Canadian troops at their discretion." He was in Sicily a month later, and in six crowded days visited every Canadian unit, querying and examining each aspect of their operational and administrative experiences under Montgomery. To one gunner officer, "he seemed quiet, diffidently kindly, and genuinely interested in us and how we were getting along." He also met Montgomery, noting that the latter had "acquired a peacock which had now been trained to sit on top of his caravan" and suffering through "a good deal of this personal and Eighth Army egotistical nonsense," although he claimed "to have listened with all courtesy and attention."

Mussolini had been deposed in late July. His successor, Marshal Pietro Badoglio, announced that Italy would stand by her Axis partner but Hitler was nobody's fool! He prudently began moving more German troops through the Alpine passes from Austria, establishing an occupation force in fact, if not in name. A formal Italian surrender was proclaimed on 8 September (they soon became identified as 'co-belligerents') but the change came too late for the Allies to derive much practical advantage from it. By then, northern and central Italy were firmly in German hands.

ACROSS THE STRAIT OF MESSINA

No one had conquered Italy from the south — 'from the bottom up', so to speak — since the Byzantine general, Belisarius, in the 6th Century AD. There was virtually nothing to be said for invading the mainland, other than that it might be presented as a substitute Second Front while avoiding for another year the much greater risks associated with a cross-Channel assault on France. But if the chance of failure was certain to be less, the gauge of victory would be uncertain — and expensive! An apparently endless series of steep-sided ridges ran off the central mountain 'spine' of the Appenines, at right-angles to the inevitable axes of advance; when the mountains petered out, the vast Lombard Plain, networked with embanked rivers and canals, began; and beyond that the land rose towards impregnable Alpine passes. Any idea of breaking through them into the Third Reich was no more than a pipedream. Nevertheless, the British chiefs of staff successfully pressed their strategy on the Americans. Italy it would be.

Again the Canadians participated in the Eighth Army landing at Reggio di Calabria, on the toe of the Italian boot, on 3 September 1943. Although ULTRA intercepts of top secret enemy signals had established that the Germans had withdrawn from the toe of the Italian boot, Montgomery had insisted on a massive preliminary barrage — an act of "absurd over-insurance" in the opinion of British historian, Sir Michael Howard. The initial Canadian landings were made by men of the 3rd Brigade and the 2nd was supposed to pass through the beachhead, fighting its way inland.

There would be much hard fighting before the Italian campaign was over, but there was none at all on that first day. As he crossed the Strait of Messina in a Royal Navy landing craft, infantry, (LCI) Major Strome Galloway of the RCR noted (in his quite illegal diary — soldiers were forbidden to keep diaries, in case they fell into enemy hands and revealed vital Allied secrets) that, "The sky is azure blue, the sea likewise. It is like a pleasure cruise."

The captain of this LCI ... has a small monkey as a pet and is feeding it lemonade out of a spoon. The captain, his No.2 and myself are drinking gin and lemon.... We are fast approaching the sandy shore just north of Reggio. Some naked troops are already in swimming! Twelve hours ago this area was under a terrific pre-invasion bombardment ....

... Apparently when Third Brigade landed the Italian soldiery surrendered in organized groups. Third Brigade therefore pushed on and have now seized First Brigade's objectives.

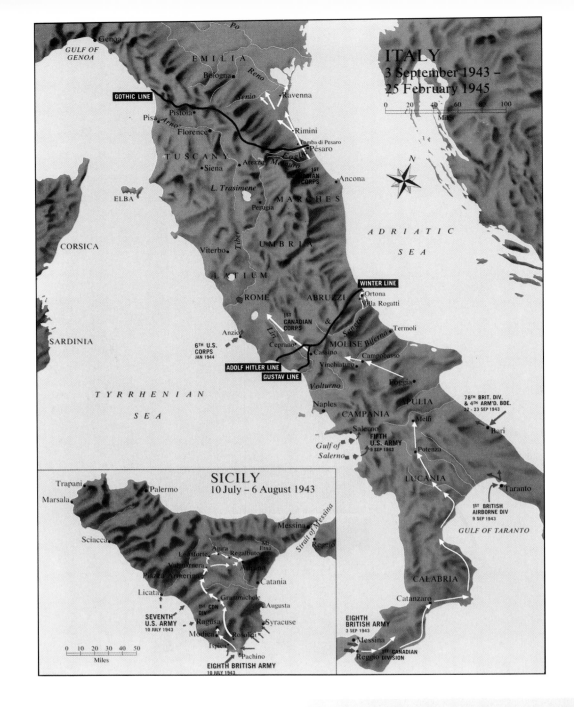

ITALY
3 September 1943 –
25 February 1945

0   20   40   60   80   100
Miles

GULF OF
GENOA

Genoa

EMILIA

Po

Reno

Bologna

GOTHIC LINE

Senio

Ravenna

Pistoia

Arno

Rimini

Pisa

Florence

Tomba di Pesaro

Pésaro

Coglia

TUSCANY

Arezzo

Metauro

1ST
CANADIAN
CORPS

Ancona

Siena

L. Trasimene

MARCHES

ELBA

Perugia

CORSICA

Viterbo

UMBRIA

Tiber

ADRIATIC

SEA

WINTER LINE

Ortona

Villa Rogatti

ROME

ABRUZZI

1ST
CANADIAN
CORPS

&

Sangro

Termoli

Biferno

SARDINIA

Anzio

6TH U.S.
CORPS
JAN 1944

Lir

Ceprano

Cassino

MOLISE

Campobasso

ADOLF HITLER LINE

Vinchiaturo

GUSTAV LINE

Volturno

Foggia

TYRRHENIAN

SEA

Naples

APULIA

Melfi

78TH BRIT. DIV.
& 4TH ARM'D. BDE.
22 - 23 SEP 1943

Bari

CAMPANIA

Salerno

FIFTH
U.S. ARMY
9 SEP 1943

Gulf of
Salerno

Potenza

LUCANIA

Taranto

1ST BRITISH
AIRBORNE DIV
9 SEP 1943

GULF OF TARANTO

SICILY
10 July – 6 August 1943

Trapani

Palermo

Messina

Marsala

Strait of Messina

Messina

Reggio

Sciacca

CALABRIA

Agira

Mt.
Etna

Regalbuto

Leonforte

Catanzaro

Valguarnera

Adrano

Piazza Armerina

Catania

EIGHTH
BRITISH ARMY
3 SEP 1943

Messina

Licata

1ST
CDN
DIV

Grammichele

Augusta

Reggio

1ST CANADIAN
DIVISION

SEVENTH
U.S. ARMY
10 JULY 1943

Ragusa

Syracuse

Modica

Rosolini

Ispica

Pachino

0   10   20   30   40   50
Miles

EIGHTH BRITISH ARMY
10 JULY 1943

The Royal 22e Régiment lands on the Italian mainland,
3 September 1943. NAC/PA-117114

There was no opposition; but there was a touch of what might be described as artificial excitement. "There is a zoo in town and our shelling broke open some cages," wrote Montgomery to his patron, Brooke. "A puma and a monkey

1st Field Company, Royal Canadian Engineers build a Bailey bridge over an ancient stone bridge, Straorini, 4 September 1943. NAC/PA-177088

escaped and attacked some men of the HQ, 3rd Canadian Infantry Brigade, and heavy firing was opened by the Canadians. It is a curious war...."

Pushing inland, the Canadians again encountered more difficulty with narrow, unsurfaced roads and blown culverts and bridges than with the enemy. However, when one American and one British corps, spearheads of the American Fifth Army, stormed ashore in the Gulf of Salerno (which was as far north as fighter cover from Sicily could range) six days later, they met stiff opposition. The success of the landing hung in the balance for ten days, before the cautious, ponderous advance of Montgomery's British infantry up the west coast (supported by the Canadian tank brigade which had had its designation changed to 1st Canadian Armoured Brigade in late August) persuaded the Germans to pull back and start their leisurely, calculated retreat to the Alpine redoubt. Then the Eighth Army formed on the right of the Allied line, reaching inland from the Adriatic shore, while the American Fifth kept to the Tyrrhenian, or west, side of the peninsula and the advance on Rome began.

The tactical concept which the Germans had employed so successfully in Sicily would be used again and again. Major-General Richard Heidrich, commander of the newly-arrived 1st Parachute Division, — which would spend much of its next two years opposing the Canadians — explained to his men exactly what was meant.

Moving inland from Reggio di Calabria, 3 September.
NAC/PA-177095

263

A Calgary Regiment *Sherman* tank overlooking the village of Potenza, 20 September.
NAC/PA-136197

A section of the West Nova Scotia Regiment hitch a ride on a Calgary tank during the advance toward Potenza, 18 September. NAC/PA-177155

Delaying actions will not be fought in a main defensive line, but on lines of resistance. The distance between such lines will be great enough to prevent the enemy from engaging two of them from the same artillery positions. He must be obliged to move up his artillery to each line....

It is best to site these lines of resistance along forward crests [of ridges], so that it is always possible to disengage and withdraw under cover.... The troops will not retire in the face of enemy patrols — the latter will be destroyed — but only when the enemy really mounts an attack. If it can be ascertained that the enemy is preparing for a major attack, the main consideration is to make a timely withdrawal....

Even without such tactics, Allied progress must have been slow. Usually, the only use for armour was as mobile fire support for the 'Poor Bloody Infantry', and before the end of September all three regiments of the Canadian Armoured Brigade were being shifted about between the two Eighth Army corps, as operational exigencies dictated, to do just that. (The Canadian infantry would remain with V Corps until I Canadian Corps was formed). Indeed, for much of its time in Italy, the armoured brigade would work with British infantry while Canadian infantrymen were being supported by British tanks — one of the many things that McNaughton had feared might happen and sought to prevent! The troops, however, didn't seem to care: all they asked for in their partners was military competence, a willingness to share the burden, and a sense of humour.

Skirmish followed skirmish as the Germans slipped back from ridge to ridge. "Everywhere we went," reported Lieutenant-Colonel C.B. Ware of the PPCLI, with only slight exaggeration, "we found that the enemy had left just about the day before." Of course, that was not always what happened, and men were killed and wounded in skirmishes when the Germans made a stand: however, casualties in September, October and November totalled only 1200, of whom just over 300 were killed. Such moderate losses, together with the enthusiastic reception that their soldiers' well-reported exploits were receiving at home, encouraged politicians in and out of uniform to follow the example of Oliver Twist and ask for more — a corps headquarters for General Crerar, so that he might acquire operational experience at a high level, and therefore a second division, which was the prerequisite for a corps HQ.

I CANADIAN CORPS IN ITALY

The British were not keen to see another corps established in their under-manned and over-headquartered army in Italy, but they were reluctantly willing to accept one provided that the division which came with it was *not* armoured. That posed a problem for the Canadians. The despatch to Italy of a second infantry division would have left the two Canadian armoured and one infantry divisions still in England forming a tactically most unbalanced corps. Therefore an armoured division it must be, explained Ottawa, and the 5th Division sailed for Naples (where General Simonds was given command in order that he might broaden his experience by handling armour), while Crerar and his corps HQ went to Sicily until room could be found for them on the mainland.

Unfortunately, somebody in the War Office had neglected to notify Sir Harold Alexander, the usually mild-mannered commander of Allied ground forces in Italy, of what was happening.

The proposed move of the Canadian Armoured Division has come as a complete surprise to me. We already have as much armour in the Mediterranean as we can usefully employ in Italy.... I do not want another Corps Headquarters at this stage. I shall be grateful if I can be consulted in future before matters of such importance are agreed upon. These decisions upset my order of battle which in turn affect my plans for battle.

Mountain Stronghold, Hill 736 by Will Ogilvie.
A Loyal Edmonton Regiment position in Southern Italy. CWM 13457

265

McNAUGHTON'S RESIGNATION

McNaughton, in England, was unhappy, too, left with an Army HQ but only one corps. After some huffing and puffing on the part of the British, it was agreed that the Army organization should be maintained even though, when it came time to invade France, First Canadian Army would have to take under command at least one non-Canadian corps. Then, of course, the British high command could certainly question his capacity to handle an army in battle; and, since British troops would likely be involved, they would have the right — even the duty, if they genuinely felt he was incapable — to veto his appointment as army commander.

In November, Defence Minister Ralston and General Stuart, the CGS, arrived in London and there were 'angry exchanges' between them and McNaughton over this splitting of the army. They then met with Sir Alan Brooke and General Paget, still the commander of Britain's Home Forces, who told them that McNaughton was not "physically equal" to the demands of command in the field — an assessment which they happily relayed back to Ottawa. McNaughton, when he heard what had happened, promptly submitted his resignation to the Prime Minister since he "could no longer remain ... responsible to any government of which he [Ralston] is a member."

King, typically, looked at the political implications rather than the morality of what was happening, and regretted the pace of events.

McNaughton has many more friends than Ralston in the Army and in the country. It may be that McNaughton is not physically equal to the task, but there can be no doubt that Ralston and General Stuart have been a little over-anxious to get a change made instead of allowing time to help bring this about. I have been afraid of this right along. I think they have been most anxious to get Crerar in McNaughton's place. One danger there is that Crerar may seek to bring about conscription. McNaughton would never admit it. However, I feel now the absence of any need of conscription can be made very apparent and will not be attempted at this stage.

The Van Doos make a night advance to Mount Gildone, south of Campobasso, 11 October 1943. NAC/PA-115072

Meanwhile, Paget had peremptorily told McNaughton that he and Brooke both believed that he "was not fit to command the Canadian Army in the field." Another resignation cable from McNaughton explained to King that "I have accepted these statements." In the circumstances, he had no other option. The man who had built First Canadian Army would never lead it into battle. Actually, for a brief moment it looked quite possible that it would never go into battle, as an army, under anybody at all. But, in the wings, General Crerar was awaiting his call to centre stage. Until he heard it, General Stuart, who had succeeded McNaughton as senior officer overseas and chief of staff in London, would 'babysit' the army.

Men of the Carleton and York Regiment come under fire during the clearing of Campochiaro, 23 October 1943.
NAC/PA-114482

A section of the Royal Canadian Regiment moving through Campobasso, October 1943.
NAC/PA-129776

THE WINTER LINES

In Italy the weather had broken, vastly exacerbating the engineering and logistics problems of any further Allied advance. A CBC war correspondent explained it to his listeners.

I wish you could see the approaches to our Italian battlefield. The whole army has only three narrow roads along which to get at the Germans. Imagine a great army trying to manoeuvre along three narrow roads. Scores of thousands of vehicles have to keep moving backward and forward all the time and this on these three roads, filing up and down the sides of deep gorges and over improvised bridges just wide enough to hold one vehicle, and probably under shell fire. There is one place where the engineers had to build five bridges over five demolitions in a space of four hundred yards; and there is the drenching rain and the deep quagmires of mud.

The Germans had sited the defences of their winter lines across the narrowest and highest part of the peninsula, in unfortunate proximity to one of the greatest of medieval treasures. Their Gustav Line had depth as well as breadth. The one corridor through it (leading to Rome) was that of the Liri valley, its entrance dominated by the great buttress of Monte Cassino capped by its thousand-year-old Benedictine abbey — which the Germans announced they would not fortify or use, in an eventually fruitless attempt to preserve it from the arbitrary violence of high-explosive. And, because the Liri valley was the key to Rome, the Germans had also constructed a second line of defences across it — known to the Allies as the Hitler Line — some twelve kilometres further back.

Major-General Chris Vokes (left), with Brigadiers Hoffmeister and Wyman, near the Moro River, 8 December 1943. NAC/PA-131064

268

ORTONA

Over on the Adriatic side of the peninsula, the Gustav Line lay beyond the River Sangro, where the Eighth Army was facing the little fishing port of Ortona and Montgomery was blithely calling on his men to take "a colossal crack" at the enemy. At the end of November, while the Canadians delivered a diversionary attack along the upper Sangro, British troops struggled across the lower reaches of the river — it was hardly a colossal crack which they delivered — and established themselves on the high ground to the north. Then the Canadians moved down to the coast to become the spear point of the attack. One more river — the Moro — and a tangled network of ravines and gullies frequently obscured by vines and olive trees lay between them and Ortona.

The Moro is in itself no infantry obstacle, but is soft-bottomed and in conjunction with the muddy condition of the whole valley is a complete tank obstacle.... The valley is about 500 yards across, and on the enemy side terminates in an abrupt cliff for most of its length. The enemy are well dug in and are supported by numerous heavy weapons. There is little wire but considerable mining has been done.

In three days of bitter fighting the Canadians — supported at first by British tanks, and then by those of the 1st Armoured Brigade (less the Three Rivers Regiment which was left with the British) — established themselves on the jumbled ground beyond the Moro. Their next objective was the ridge carrying a road from Ortona to the inland town of Orsogna, which lay athwart their front and was guarded by the 'abrupt cliff' soon to be known and remembered simply as The Gully. Only one narrow, well-defended, road snaked up that cliff-like bank and otherwise its steep, scrub-covered sides were virtually impassable to tanks.

The Canadians attacked — and the Germans counterattacked! Between 10 and 19 December, the 1st Division made eight attacks on The Gully. A Protestant chaplain with one of the armoured regiments described the infantry "going up into the line" through the mud and rain. "Single file, they trudged along, guns carried anyhow, ammo slung around them, trousers bagged, and down at heels." Many of them were trudging to their death. Major Charles Comfort, an official war artist with the division, used words as well as pictures to describe the fighting.

... edging forward in quick, staggering bounds, crawling breathlessly in the muck through writhing vineyards, dragging the mortars, the bombs, the Brens [light machine guns], the PIATs [Projectors, Infantry, Anti-Tank, in military jargon], the grenades ...; flanking the position under covering fire, rushing in the half-light through sheets of blinding flame, hurling the grenades and closing in ...; stumbling, cursing, tearing at the wire, alert with the horrible necessity of killing....

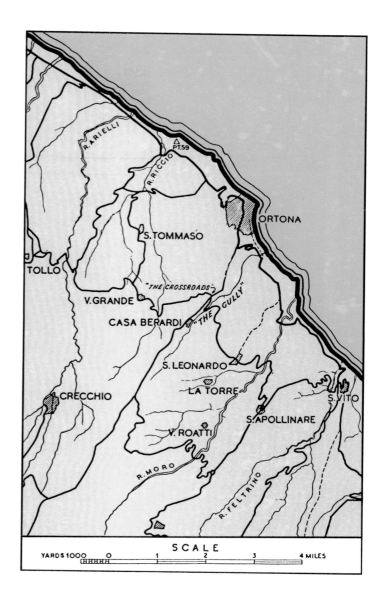

Counterattacks took a heavy toll of *Panzergrenadiers* and their commander was replaced by his superior, General Heinrich von Vietinghoff, who felt that he had not used them well. Paratroopers moved in to reinforce the battered survivors and more Canadian attacks were repulsed. Finally — it might well have been tried earlier — a probe around the head of The Gully, where it petered out on higher ground, opened a route to the ridge for the Royal 22e Régiment and a squadron of Ontario tanks, while the Carleton and Yorks and the West Nova Scotians pinned the enemy from the front.

Turning towards Ortona, the 'Van Doos' pushed down the highway and Captain Paul Triquet won a Victoria Cross at the Casa Berardi on 15 December. With only eleven of his men still fit to fight, and together with four Sherman tanks of the Ontario Regiment, he held the farm against repeated counter-attacks until reinforcements began to filter in at nightfall. More tanks also arrived during the night; and the next day the men of the 3rd Brigade continued to push their enemies back. Then it was the turn of the 2nd Brigade.

Major-General Christopher Vokes (who had succeeded Simonds in command of the division in November) thought the Germans were wilting now, and that "pressure from this flank and on his front would cause an early collapse." He could not have been more wrong.

The fight for Ortona was "a carnival of fury," according to Matthew Halton. "There was something different there, something heroic and almost super-human and, at the same time, dark as night."

The houses were stone, close-packed, with narrow alleys between them. Every so often, one or more houses on both sides of the streets had been fortified and these miniature fortresses, garrisoned by paratroopers, had to be blown apart by the fire of tank and antitank guns. Lieutenant K.M. McBride of the Seaforth Highlanders analyzed the fighting from an infantry subaltern's perspective.

Casa Berardi by Charles Comfort.
'C' Company of the Royal 22 Régiment took very heavy casualties in capturing the German strong point at Casa Berardi, three kilometres southwest of Ortona, and held it against repeated counterattacks. Captain Paul Triquet was awarded the first VC in the Italian Campaign for his gallant leadership. CWM 12255

The most satisfactory and safe method of operating was in small groups of three or four men.... Every time we located an enemy position we usually lost a man and, in most cases, our casualty received an entire burst of machine-gun fire. It was 'dirty' fighting because every man was well aware that before we found the next nest [of enemy] we would have another serious casualty.

Pummelled by mortars, dazed but determined, the enemy paras hunkered down in the ruins and the infantry had to winkle them out. Block by block, they were driven back, past the great church which "had been blown in half and stood out five storeys high, as though cut right through the dome with a giant cleaver," back into the warren of medieval buildings around the ancient castle, perched on a bluff overlooking the Adriatic. The principal problem for the Canadians was trying to coordinate properly the various arms — a most complex and difficult business in such obstacle-ridden, close-quarter fighting: "we became involved in a vicious circle," wrote the commanding officer of the Loyal Edmonton Regiment, Lieutenant-Colonel J.C. Jefferies.

Seaforth Highlanders approach
Ortona along a coastal path,
21 December 1943.
NAC/PA-152749

Loyal Eddies in the outskirts of
Ortona engaging dug-in
Germans, 21 December.
NAC/PA-163935

The infantry would be brought up to form a bridgehead over a rubble pile. It would be necessary for them to clear mines under cover of smoke, or else to extend the bridgehead further in to allow the sappers[field engineers] to work. Under such circumstances, the leading infantry got to a point where it [sic] needed tanks in support to shoot up the upper floors of buildings. If the infantry lost contact with the sappers, the tanks did not get up in time.

Tanks were invaluable where the streets were sufficiently open to allow them to pass. The Germans posted snipers on the roofs of buildings; and the tank gunners of the Three Rivers Regiment blew the top floors away with 75mm high-explosive shells.

Casualties were heavy on both sides and surgeons worked themselves to the point of exhaustion.

They had this field dressing station ... and they were bringing the wounded guys in ... and every once in a while, say every hour, one doctor would come out and look at the new guys they'd brought in.

He'd look closely, and if they were dead by then he'd just point and the stretcher guys would haul them out. But there were quite a few, more than just three or four, who were just fearfully smashed up, that the doctor would look at and he'd know the guy was going to last another hour or something like that. He'd point to them, too, and they would be loaded and taken out into the dark and laid down beside the dead to die.

On the German side, their Commander-in-Chief, Field Marshal Albert Kesselring, felt it necessary to commit his meagre Army Group reserve to what had become a battle of prestige as much as military advantage. He told von Vietinghoff that, "We do not want to defend Ortona decisively, but the English have made it as important as Rome.... You can do nothing when things develop in this manner; it is only too bad that ... the world press makes so much of it."

While the 2nd Brigade ploughed into Ortona, the 1st was attempting to bypass it. On Christmas Day, the Royal Canadian Regiment "advanced 800 yards through the tangled, rain-swept vineyards" along the hill roads to the west. Major Strome Galloway had just become acting CO of the battalion, his predecessor having gone down with a severe attack of jaundice and *his* predecessor having been wounded, in the course of a week.

At our Command Post the Christmas cheer was limited to Yuletide colours — we had a crock of red and green peppers soaked in olive oil! The peppers went down well with bully beef, some farmhouse bread we came upon and some homemade wine. The olive oil helped restore our weapons to working order after the mud and grit had been scraped out of the working parts.

A war film photo depicting the vicious house-to-house fighting that took place in the ruins of Ortona. National Film Board

A wounded man being brought to an aid post in Ortona.
NAC/PA-112944

Outside our building men were dying. In the muddy vineyards they found their peace on earth — the Christmas message through the ages. But they didn't hear any angels sing, only the stutter of machine-guns, the crack of rifles and the screaming, whining and thudding of the shells and mortar bombs. They were as far from Bethlehem as Man could ever get.

On the night of 27-28 December the enemy finally abandoned Ortona, to re-align his defences along the banks of the next rivers north, first the Riccio, and then the Arielli.

THE 5th DIVISION ON THE ARIELLI

By January 1944, the 5th Division's 11th Infantry Brigade was considered combat-ready (the division mustered only two brigades, one armoured and one infantry). Their armoured colleagues were not, however, since they were still having serious problems with the 'clapped-out' *Shermans* of the British 7th Armoured Division which the Canadians had taken over on their arrival in Italy; making those overworked tanks fit for battle was a battle in itself. Meanwhile, to give the infantry innocents a taste of battle (the need for it was obvious to Lieutenant-Colonel J.V. Allard of the Royal 22e, who "heard a few neophytes from the 11th grumble because they had to dig their own trenches") the 11th Brigade was attached to the 1st Division and took over a part of the static Arielli front.

They were content, if not happy, there, knowing that they were playing their part in the war at last. Nineteen-year-old Corporal Fred Cedarberg of the Cape Breton Highlanders took his turn on guard and brooded on 'sunny Italy'.

Only my eyes, the bridge of my nose and upper cheeks showed through a knitted balaclava that swathed my head under a steel helmet. I stared over the shell-shredded sea of mud and wet snow. Whistling tunelessly, I stamped my cold, wet feet and swore, and watched my breath exploding into instant puffballs of steam in the freezing air ....

... The burned-out Sherman tank, thirty yards off from the northwest corner of our position ... pointed its twisted 75-millimetre gun skyward. And the slit trenches guarding the defense perimeter were always half full of water — the damp snow that fell by night, and the cold rain by day.

But on the other side of the peninsula, the American Fifth Army was about to try outflanking the Gustav Line by a landing at Anzio, forty miles south of Rome, a landing which would cost the 11th Brigade dearly. Alexander and Sir Oliver Leese (a hearty Guardee in the Redvers Buller tradition who had succeeded Montgomery) wanted the Eighth Army to "keep the enemy from moving any of his divisions away from our front" while the Anzio bridgehead was established. The hapless 11th Brigade was about to become their chosen instrument.

The Canadian divisional and brigade commanders directly concerned, Vokes and Kitching, supinely accepted British arrangements for an assault by the *three* battalions of the brigade upon *two* battalions of German paratroops manning the Arielli defences. (A numerical superiority of three to one was generally considered to be the minimum required for a successful attack; two to one would have been unreasonable odds even for battle-hardened soldiers, and was outrageous for raw novices.) Moreover, their own detailed planning was poor and its execution a disaster.

The attack was poorly coordinated, with the Perth Regiment and the Cape Bretons advancing separately and the supporting artillery and tank fire going awry. Predictably, the paratroopers cut them to pieces. Fred Cedarberg watched in horror as:

The Irish [Regiment of Canada], the battalion in a holding position in case of enemy counter-attacks, accidentally shot up some bewildered, confused Highlanders, mistaking them for Jerries. All afternoon, unnerved and numbed, the remnants of the two assault companies clung to the soggy ground, pounded relentlessly by German mortars that churned the mud and water into great spouts. In the darkness, the living withdrew, shocked and tired.

Some of the Canadians simply dropped their rifles and ran. Who could blame them? This was not war as John Wayne fought it in the movies — this was something horribly different. The brigade was withdrawn for the moment, its morale at a low ebb, and the front settled down in mud and misery to wait for spring.

At the beginning of February the 11th Brigade returned to the line in the company of the 5th Armoured Brigade, and a week later the two Canadian divisions, 1st and 5th Armoured, together with a British armoured brigade, were placed under the command of General Crerar in the guise of I Canadian Corps. Crerar's tenure as corps commander would be brief, however. He would fly back to England in mid-March, and General E.L.M. Burns — who had come out to take command of the 5th Armoured Division in January, when Simonds was promoted to lieutenant-general and appointed to II Canadian Corps — would then be promoted and given I Corps. The 5th Armoured Division was handed over to Brigadier (promoted to Major-General) B.M. Hoffmeister, a militiaman from Vancouver and a mere battalion commander when the 1st Division had landed in Sicily. Before the war was over he would prove himself to be the best of Canada's generals.

Major-General B.M. Hoffmeister, commander of 5th Armoured Division. NAC/PA-132779

8th New Brunswick Hussars tanks lined up for an 'indirect' shoot onto the Tollo crossroad, February 1944. The Hussars fired over 700 rounds in 90 seconds.
8CH Archives

CASSINO AND THE LIRI VALLEY

At the other end of the Gustav Line, Monte Cassino still barred a Fifth Army advance on Rome, even though its VI (US) Corps, (with a British division and the American-Canadian 1st Special Service Force under command) had seized a bridgehead at Anzio in mid-January. Expanding the bridgehead seemed impossible and even supplying it was becoming a logistical nightmare, as ships and landing craft were withdrawn for the forthcoming assaults on France. "I had hoped that we were hurling a wildcat on to the shore," lamented Churchill, "but all we had got was a stranded whale."

Alexander and Clark puzzled over how to break the deadlock. Monte Cassino seemed to be the key. The Americans and the Free French had each tried to take it and failed. Elements of the Eighth Army had been brought across the Appenines to try their luck, and the New Zealanders had tried twice and failed — the second time after their commander, Sir Bernard Freyberg, convinced that the Germans were using the abbey as an observation post, had successfully demanded its destruction by Allied bombers!

Abandoning any direct attempt to carry it for the moment, Alexander now did what he probably should have done in the first place. He lined up American, French, British and Polish formations along the thirty-five-kilometre stretch of the Gari and Garigliano from Cassino to the sea. Assaults launched simultaneously all along the front must surely rupture over-stretched German defences at some point: and to that end the Americans would attack along the coast; the French through the Aurunci mountains, between the coast and the Liri valley; the British into the valley itself; and the Poles into the mountains just east of Cassino. And once the Germans were fully committed, the Anzio garrison would make another attempt to break out from its beachhead.

The British (and Indian) XIII Corps was to attack across the Gari, which became the Garigliano where the Liri joined it, just beyond the British front. If they were successful, they would then drive up the valley towards the Hitler Line and, if they could break through that second line as well, then I Canadian Corps, held in reserve, would pass through and exploit towards Rome. If, on the other hand, they were stopped before reaching the Hitler Line, the Canadians would move up alongside and both together would break through....

As might have been expected, given the stubbornness of German resistance to date, the first scenario was wildly optimistic. During the night of 13-14 May, an Indian infantry brigade, supported by tanks of the Ontario Regiment, crossed the Gari and, together with the 78th British Division, advanced about four kilometres. German officers on the upper slopes of Monte Cassino — there was now no reason not to use the ruins of the abbey — watched what was happening on the valley floor and organized their troops accordingly, so that the attackers were first slowed and then stopped in their tracks.

Route 6 at Cassino, Italy
by Charles Comfort. CWM 12369

Supplies were carried in 'jeep trains' on 'Inferno Track' at the Cassino front. NAC/PA-140132

Adhering to British doctrine, a complex and inflexible artillery fire plan had been devised, and each phase of the assault was carefully timetabled to the barrage — a rigidity which denied the attacking infantry any chance to seize fleeting opportunities.

The night before the attack, the chaplain of the Seaforth Highlanders noted in his diary that "my boys move in tonight …. New boys with fear and nerves and anxiety hidden under quick smiles and quick seriousness. Old campaigners with a faraway look. It is the hardest thing to watch without breaking into tears." One of his 'old campaigners' was Private Charles Johnson, an American who had been with the battalion since 1940 and would be wounded only moments after the events he describes. Johnson recalled, in later tranquillity, that:

My mind had but one thought; to get through the [German] barrage, get through the barrage…. No one except the wounded or the dead stopped…. Over to the left a German jumped up and seemed to be raising his hands when he was killed by one of our fellows. Directly ahead and about fifty yards away a Jerry stood up and held his machine-gun in his arms. A long burst tore into 8 Platoon to my right. I fired two rounds from the hip at the same time that others must have fired. The Jerry folded up and fell. I stepped on his bloody head as I passed over the position a few seconds later.

The Canadians moved in on the British left, General Burns assigning the 1st Division, supported by a British armoured brigade and the Three Rivers Regiment, to lead his attack on the Hitler Line, with only the 5th Division available to exploit any success. The enemy defences were formidable: wire and minefields were sited to funnel attackers into preselected killing grounds; concrete emplacements housing antitank and machine guns, and so sited as to provide interlocking fields of fire, were sprinkled plentifully across the axes of advance. For the first time there were *Panzerturm* — tank turrets sunk into concrete — and a deep, steep-sided ravine (reminiscent of Ortona's Gully) called the Forme d'Aquino angled across the axis of advance and multiplied the eternal problem of successfully coordinating infantry and armour.

Canadian infantrymen advance under mortar fire into Castrocielo, just to the south of the Melfa River, 23 May 1944. NAC/PA-177099

Three Rivers Regiment tanks support 3rd Brigade's advance to the Hitler Line, 17 May 1944. NAC/PA-177098

Thus the Hitler Line was breached, the Canadians incurring nearly a thousand casualties during the day, one-third of them dead and two-thirds wounded. The Germans, with a far smaller pool of men to draw from, lost nearly as many, the majority of their losses coming in the form of prisoners of war.

That, however, was suddenly the least of their problems. II (US) Corps had crossed the Garigliano and was now 'advancing rapidly' along the coast. In the mountains between the Americans and Canadians, agile, lightly equipped Goums (Moroccan tribesmen) of the French Expeditionary Corps were racing forward over ground which their enemies had assessed as more or less impenetrable. And only half an hour after the attack on the Hitler Line had begun, the "beached whale" at Anzio had launched its long-heralded breakout along a line which threatened to cut off all the Germans south of Valmontone. Monte Cassino, under attack by the Poles who had now almost surrounded it, was abandoned during the night of 17-18 May.

Nevertheless, there were very real difficulties in front of the 5th Armoured Division, about to go into battle as a division for the first time under a man who had never commanded a division in battle before! The valley was narrowing, and the British on Hoffmeister's right had been given the only highway in the valley as their axis of advance, the Canadians being left with secondary roads. Moreover, General Burns had chosen to put an ad hoc 1st Division brigade group into the line on his extreme left, hard against the Liri. Thus one armoured and better-than-two infantry brigades were being squeezed into a two-mile-wide corridor between the British and the river. But the ground was flat and firm, offering the chance to mass armour, if only on a small scale.

There was the usual intensive artillery 'stonk'. The ground ahead was 'close', which meant that visibility was limited and ranges would necessarily be short. The tanks set off in fine style, however. A troop leader in Lord Strathcona's Horse recollected how:

'Push on now' came the Colonel's voice over the wireless and sixty tanks began to roll forward, spreading out into formation ... a feeling of exhilaration began to take hold. Others had been hit but I was indestructible. Then it happened. One moment, the world around me was full of vivid colour ... and then suddenly, in the fraction of an instant, everything had turned to inky blackness.... At that same instant, from what seemed a long way off, there came a mighty metallic clang as though some great anvil had been struck by a giant sledgehammer.

Lieutenant John Windsor's tank was knocked out, one of seventeen the Strathconas lost that day in bitter duels with German Panther tanks before reaching the Melfa River, a tributary of the Liri that crossed the Canadian line of advance.

155mm Gun by Charles Comfort. CWM 12321

CROSSING THE MELFA

The British 78th Division, meanwhile, had again been stopped in its tracks over to the right, close under the frowning buttresses of Monte Cairo; and in order to bypass an enemy strong point it was ordered to swing over on to General Burns' constricted front, along a route still assigned to his 5th Armoured Brigade. The ensuing traffic foul-up was predictable, but the reconnaissance troop of the Strathconas, commanded by Lieutenant E.J. Perkins, reached the Melfa in mid-afternoon. They found a possible crossing point, did a little pick-and-shovel work, and got their three surviving *Honey* tanks across the river to seize a small bridgehead on the far bank.

Dashing for cover during the advance to the Hitler Line, 22 May. NAC/PA-136205

Just as infantry brigades needed armoured regiments to support them, armoured brigades needed infantry. The 5th Brigade had the motorized Westminster Regiment as its infantry component, and a company of the Westminsters under Major J.K. Mahony scrambled across the river (without their vehicles, of course) to reinforce Perkins' troop. The near bank was now littered with the wreckage of war.

Lieutenant-Colonel
J.K. Mahony, VC

Squadron-Sergeant-Major R.C. Cunniffe, of the Strathcona's 'A' Echelon, described the scene.

As far as one could see through the trees and hedges to the south of it, the eerie light from burning tanks blended grotesquely with the glow of the setting sun; smoke from burning oil and petrol mingled with the dust that hung over the valley to give the effect of a partial eclipse. Now and then, as the ammunition in the burning tanks caught fire, the sharp staccato crackling of the small arms and the loud reports of the 75mm shells seemed as an echo of the afternoon's tumult, punctuated by the steady whine and explosion of the 'Moaning Minnies' [German multiple mortar shells] landing in the river bed.... Hot and tired, and confessedly stunned by the ferocity of the battle through which they had come, the tank crews dug slit trenches, set out dismounted machine-guns in defensive positions, brewed tea and wondered 'What now?' as they listened to the fire-fight on the far bank of the Melfa.

Inspired by Mahony, who was twice wounded, the Westminsters held their little perimeter against repeated counterattacks until nightfall enabled another company to cross and artillery could be moved up close enough to support them. Mahony won the second Canadian VC of the campaign, Perkins — who may have deserved as much — the Distinguished Service Order, a decoration very rarely awarded to a subaltern and, when it was, often called the 'poor man's VC'.

The division pressed on for another four miles, until it became necessary to cross the Liri itself. As usual, all the bridges had been destroyed, but the infantry got across, as infantry almost always does. The engineers hastily began to build a Bailey bridge so that the armour might follow, but more haste resulted in less speed: the bridge was not put together properly and it promptly collapsed into the river, delaying any further advance for twelve valuable hours.

That was a setback which Hoffmeister's senior sapper admitted "has given us a bit of a black eye." There were other failures in command and control at corps and divisional level (Hoffmeister was a long-time infantryman with no prior experience in handling armour when he took over the division, but perhaps his greatest virtue was that he never made the same mistake twice) but in the end it made no great difference. War correspondent Stursberg, overflying the battlefield in an artillery observation aircraft, reported that "it's becoming a mad chase in blinding dust over bumpy mud roads to keep up with the Canadian advance now."

Lord Strathcona's Horse tanks in the Liri Valley, May 1944. NAC/PA-140208

The threat to the enemy from Anzio was developing apace, the French were still advancing on the left, and the Germans were withdrawing as fast as they could. They might still have been too late to get out, however, if the public relations-conscious American General Mark Clark had not been seduced by his ambition to go down in the history books as the man who took Rome, and turned his troops to that end rather than cutting across the German line of retreat. The Eternal City — which the enemy declared an 'open' city and made no attempt to defend — fell on 4 June 1944, its capture overshadowed to some extent by Operation *Overlord*, the cross-Channel invasion of France which took place just two days later.

Reinforcements Moving Up
by Lauren Harris. CWM 12712

REST AND REORGANIZATION

The Canadian Corps went into reserve to rest and refit, while the 1st Armoured Brigade supported British formations pursuing the enemy towards Florence. Sir Oliver Leese, dissatisfied with General Burns' performance in the Liri battles, requested his replacement, and the brouhaha which followed brought General Stuart from Canada to hear both sides of the case. He talked with Alexander and Leese, and then (with Burns' concurrence, if not his blessing) interviewed the two divisional commanders, Vokes and Hoffmeister, who gave their superior a grudging vote of confidence. Burns, his authority seriously weakened and his position far from secure, stayed on for the time being but his chief of staff had to go, together with his corps engineer. And, in the 5th Division, Hoffmeister sacked the commander of his infantry brigade.

Then he and Burns set about absorbing the lessons they had learned, the most essential and demanding being organizational. Another infantry brigade was necessary if maximum use was to be made of the armoured one — two to one was the appropriate ratio, in divisions or corps; and since Ottawa would not or could not provide it — a shortage of volunteers was already causing anxiety — they had to create one from their own resources. The 12th Infantry Brigade was cobbled together from the 5th Armoured Brigade's Westminster Regiment, parts of the corps' light anti-aircraft regiments (since the remnants of the *Luftwaffe* in Italy were no longer a significant threat) which were rebadged as the Lanark and Renfrew Scottish, and the Princess Louise Dragoon Guards, who were rudely dismounted from their tanks.

Its control and communications techniques honed to a finer edge, and its officers — especially those of the 5th Division — chivvied into improved performance, I Canadian Corps came back into the line in August 1944, just as the Americans invaded southern France through the Riviera (the 1st Special Service Force was with them) and the Eighth Army closed on the enemy's next major defensive position, north of Florence.

Captain J.A. Gardiner, Royal Canadian Army Medical Corps, examines a wounded prisoner, 24 May 1944. NAC/PA-144981

Canadian infantrymen advancing through an Italian village. NAC/PA-37627

INTO THE GOTHIC LINE

Sir Harold Alexander planned a joint Anglo-American attack against the centre of the Gothic Line, over the Florence-Bologna axis where the mountains were less rugged than usual in Italy. Neither Clark nor Leese liked that idea, however, both wanting as little as possible to do with each other and the latter being particularly vehement in his opposition to a combined assault. As usual, Alexander was unwilling to assert himself; and he agreed that the Eighth Army's attack should be shifted to the Adriatic coast while the Fifth would make the thrust towards Bologna unassisted, starting a few days later.

On the frontage now assigned to I Canadian Corps, the main German defences stretched along the far bank of the Foglia river which lay, in turn, some seven or eight miles from the start-line, beyond a jumble of precipitous hills. The 'old hands' of the 1st Division would lead the way and, if they could gain enough momentum, might surprise the enemy and 'bounce' right through the Line. In that case, the 5th Armoured Division would follow through, pushing on past Coriano and over the San Fortunato ridge, into the valley of the River Po which drained the vast Lombardy Plain. If, however, the 1st Division stumbled before crossing the Foglia and a set-piece attack became necessary, then the 5th would move up on the right and the two formations would attack abreast. Kesselring's meagre German resources were, as usual, carefully sited. He expected the main attack to come on the Florence-Bologna axis (where Alexander had first proposed it) and was reluctant to move men away from there,

at least until some other point of main effort became apparent. After all, the British or Canadians never did anything very fast. There would be time enough to reinforce any other sector once it was quite clear to him that a major attack was developing there.

Starting from behind the usual artillery barrage (which mostly fell on empty fields and vineyards since nearly all the enemy had already withdrawn to positions out of range), the 1st Division, supported by British tanks, attacked at midnight on 25-26 August. Almost inevitably, it did indeed stumble — over the complexity of the ground, demolished culverts and bridges, and two stubbornly-fought delaying actions — so that after forty-eight hours Burns ordered Hoffmeister to move up on Vokes' left. Kesselring was slow in moving his reserves, however, even though (in the transcript of an intercepted telephone conversation) a German staff officer pointed out to a colleague that "if they really are Canadians, Chief of Staff will have to adopt quite other measures. For then it will be a true major operation." As the two divisions closed on the Foglia, the Germans suddenly discovered that they were being out-generalled.

The Gothic Line was still not fully manned as the 5th Armoured — carefully arranged so that it could shift relatively easily from its narrow, winding axis of advance into a broad arrowhead assault formation — assembled in battle array behind the crests of those tangled hills. In the valley bottom beyond the crest, there were minefields and wire; and on the far slopes, bare rolling hillsides offered long fields of fire for "concrete-emplaced 88 and 75 mm high-velocity guns mounted in steel turrets [which] were all over the place. They covered every avenue of advance."

A platoon of the 48th Highlanders of Canada moving forward to the Gothic Line, near the River Foglia, 27 August 1944.
NAC/PA-177533

281

Bofors Light Anti-Aircraft Gun and Crew
by Lauren Harris. CWM 12661

The crew commander of one of the four tanks which comprised Vokes' regimental headquarters recorded how:

We advanced over quite rolling country.... An infantry officer ... asked where we were going. I advised [him that] I did not know but was following the colonel. He then stated there were no infantry beyond this point and told me to advise Col. Vokes [by radio]. This I did — however, we continued to advance ... and then turned right up [towards] a road on top of a hill. On our way up we lost the last tank in the line.... We now came under heavy fire from our right, however I was unable to spot the enemy guns. The remaining RHQ tanks were knocked out at this point and [my tank] received a direct hit on the gun mantle with what must have been an H[igh] E[xplosive] shell.

At the end of the day — 31 August 1944 — the British Columbia Dragoons had only eighteen 'runners' out of the 54 tanks they had started with, and 51 officers and men were casualties — including the fatally-wounded Vokes, who got no medal for his valour. Only the VC could be awarded posthumously and that decoration would have been an appropriate recognition, not only of his personal courage but also of the importance of his decision to 'go it alone'. And surely no Canadian ever deserved one more.

Behind Point 204 lay another hill, Point 253, which backstopped the relatively shallow Gothic Line. It was taken the next morning by the Princess Louise Dragoon Guards, fighting as infantry for the first time and losing almost a third of their strength in doing it. The 1st Division, on the right, which had efficiently widened the hole drilled by the 5th, now dropped briefly into reserve while Hoffmeister pressed on. A nighttime advance to the next river line, the Conca, kept the enemy on the run. Two nights later, it was the 1st Division's turn again as the two divisions leapfrogged forward. Strome Galloway noted in his diary that:

The whole countryside indicated the retreat of the enemy. For miles around burning homesteads and haystacks, glowing like hundreds of cigarette butts in a darkened room, illuminated the otherwise pitch-dark landscape. There was something more ominous in this than just what met the eye. The enemy was not merely being destructive. He was levelling haystacks and crops so as to deprive our advancing army of cover....

Thirty hours later, preceded by a short, sharp burst of artillery fire and some close support from the Desert Air Force, combined arms teams of infantry, armour and assault engineers swept across the valley into the heart of the Gothic Line. Three times the Cape Breton Highlanders, supported by a squadron of the 8th Hussars, attacked the village of Montecchio and three times the enemy, entrenched on a bluff just behind and overlooking the village, repulsed them. Finally, the Perth Regiment, hooking in from a flank, killed most of them and drove the others off.

Laying the blame on lesser mortals — as generals are apt to do — Kesselring has explained in his *Memoirs* that, "The 26th Panzers, moving in very late, got off to a very bad start which affected the whole front. In the night of 30-31 August the first Green Line — with no equivalent position behind it in the whole depth of the Adriatic sector — had to be surrendered." From the Canadian perspective, however, the moment of decision came on the 31st, when the tankers of the British Columbia Dragoons and the exhausted, decimated Perths were ordered to attack and take a key hill feature, Point 204. (The number relates to height above sea level in metres.)

The Perths, slow to rally after their earlier exertions, could not go on at once; but the Dragoons' CO, Lieutenant-Colonel Freddie Vokes, the younger brother of the 1st Division's commander, decided to attack anyway. His squadrons roared up an exposed hillside, running a gauntlet of interlocking fire from high-velocity 88mm guns and hand-held *Panzerschreckn* — antitank rocket missiles — from entrenched infantry.

The Signals
Centre
of Headquarters
5th Armoured
Division near
Castelnuovo.
NAC/PA-177103

**Shermans at
Ronta**
by
Campbell Tinning.
CWM 13998

CORIANO

The British on the left were also advancing, but through more difficult country, and in their haste to keep up with the Canadians they failed to secure the high ground and soon found themselves in all kinds of tactical trouble. The 5th Armoured, pushing past Monte Gallera and down the San Besanigo spur towards the Marano, were brought to a halt on 5 September by fire from the little town of Coriano, which lay on a parallel ridge over to their left, on the British side of the corps boundary. An offer by Hoffmeister, transmitted through Burns, to take it from the flank was politely declined by the British; they would do it themselves, thank you very much. But several British attempts stalled, and five valuable days elapsed before they could bring themselves to accept Canadian help.

Finally, after four days of waiting and two of preparation, British and Canadians attacked together on the night of 12-13 September 1944, the former along the ridge, the latter across the shallow valley which lay between them and Coriano. After a tremendous artillery barrage, the Cape Breton Highlanders assaulted the north end of the Coriano ridge, the Perths on their left, with the Irish Regiment of Canada passing through to 'mop-up' the town. Each infantry battalion had a squadron of the New Brunswick Hussars in support. An anonymous Hussar remembered it thus.

The dark autumn night leaped and vaulted with sights and sounds, flickered, jumped and rolled with the clash of heavy weapons and at times, in moments when they could be heard, with the human cries of wounded men. Tracers stitched across it. Explosions tore it apart. German Spandaus burped. The more deliberate Brens answered them. The infantry went on ahead of the tanks because the Besanigo stream was there as an anti-tank obstacle, and a man could get over it but armour couldn't.

It was the work of the engineers to bridge the stream and get the tanks across....

I saw one little engineer go down into the valley with nothing on his head at all. Just sitting there on his bulldozer. I said to myself, 'goodbye, young man.'

As the infantry reached the floor of the valley and crossed the ditch and went on, their wounded were taken back as they could be. The dead were left till a time of greater quiet....

Canadian tanks and infantry battered their way into Coriano from the north and west, driving a desperate enemy into the arms of the British 1st Armoured Division approaching along the ridge from the south. The Germans lost about twelve hundred men (including over eight hundred prisoners, most of whom fell into British hands) while Canadian losses totalled only a little more than two hundred, all killed and wounded.

Coriano Ridge Under Bombardment
by Campbell Tinning. CWM 13867

SAN FORTUNATO

Kesselring (who subsequently noted that "enemy armoured formations, particularly Canadian tanks, [are] no longer sensitive to artillery, but carry on even under heaviest fire concentrations") had used the time gained by British reluctance to accept Canadian help to strengthen the defences of his reserve position — the so-called Rimini Line — which ran along the San Fortunato ridge, ten or twelve kilometres further back. The 5th Division went into reserve and the 1st took its place, to take San Fortunato on 19 and 20 September, in yet another grisly struggle. Lieutenant Sydney Frost of the PPCLI, badly wounded in October 1943, hospitalized for eight months, and now just returned to his battalion, crested the ridge and found his way forward "blocked by a heap of German dead."

They had taken shelter from the bombardment in caves dug into the sides of the sunken road. When the barrage lifted, they came out of their holes to take up their battle positions on the crest of the hill. But the Edmontons were too quick for them. They got to the positions first and caught a whole company of the enemy. All were killed, wounded or taken prisoner.

Bodies, parts of bodies, helmets, gory uniforms, shattered weapons fill the roadway. Our blood-soaked boots crunch through this obscene mess.… I feel neither elation nor even satisfaction at this horrible scene — only relief that the corpses are the enemy and not our own.

From the top of the ridge, the victors looked out over the Lombard Plain. Flat land, at last!

Newfoundland gunners of the Royal Artillery test a communications line, Italy 1944.

Provincial Archives of Newfoundland and Labrador B5-95

Sergeant P.J. Ford
by Charles Comfort.

Sergeant Ford of the Patricias was one of the most widely experienced NCOs of the Canadian Army when this portrait was painted in July 1944.
CWM 12282

THE NEED FOR MORE MEN

Over the past three weeks I Canadian Corps, caught between the rock of operational necessity and the hard place of finding trained replacements, had incurred considerably more casualties than the reinforcement pool could provide. In one of the armoured regiments, "for the first time that fall we used four-man crews" instead of the usual five. "In a good number of cases it might even have been more advisable to go in with three-man crews than with some of the reinforcements they sent us." Generally speaking, the infantry were even worse off.

The Minister of National Defence, J.L. Ralston, who had been prominent in the decision to send a Canadian contingent to Italy, spent nine days with it at the beginning of October. According to the official history, "Everywhere he went he invited the men to discuss their problems with him" — and the problem he heard most about, the one presented most often and most angrily, was that of the growing shortage of replacements.

I'd just been shifted from the Princess Pats over to the Cape Breton Highlanders, over on the Fiumicino, and settling in I realized that things were worse than I thought. Men were short, and worn out, and there wasn't enough reinforcements coming up. The reinforcement pool was just about empty, and I guess north-west Europe was getting most of the new men....

What ground our asses down was these NRMAs in Canada. I don't know how many.... Twenty or thirty thousand, the ones they called Zombies. Fight for Canada but not for democracy, if you want to put it that way. They wouldn't sign for overseas.

The Italy Star, awarded to all who served in Sicily and Italy.

The story of the manpower crisis which had begun to haunt the Army Overseas, both in Italy and northwest Europe, will be recounted in more detail in the next chapter. But the long and short of it was that for the remainder of the war, both in Italy and northwest Europe, too few men would have to do too much fighting. In reserve for the moment, however, they "slept as exhausted kings might sleep" on an Adriatic beach.

You could lie out there in the water or on sands as lovely as those at Shediac, and a few miles on you could see the RAF bombing Rimini.... The easygoing way they did it made you think the war had been going on so long that even this had become routine; even the death of a city as big as Moncton.

INTO THE LOMBARD PLAIN

For the Eighth Army commanders and staff, the Lombard Plain had long been seen as 'the Land of Lost Content' — a great broad plain stretching to the horizon and beyond where armour could run riot, as it had in the Western Desert of blessed memory, driving the enemy before it like sheep to the slaughter. It was all a great self-inflicted delusion. The army went down into the Romagna, the southeast quadrant of the plain, and found it laced with rivers and canals, many of them channelled between steep embankments which inhibited tank movement as thoroughly as the southern hills and ridges had done, and made life inconceivably difficult for the decimated and embittered infantry.

I Corps inched forward from one river line to the next, across the Marecchia to the Fiumicino, from the Fiumicino to the Rubicone (Julius Caesar had crossed it, going the other way, two thousand years before), from the Rubicone to the Pisciatello, and from the Pisciatello to the Savio. There Private E.A. Smith of the Seaforth Highlanders won Canada's third VC in Italy on 22 October 1944. Playing their part in fighting off a counterattack on an insubstantial Seaforth bridgehead — insubstantial because the tanks could not get forward — Smith's two-man, PIAT tank-hunting team:

> ... came under fire by approaching enemy tanks, but making good use of cover got close enough to disable one Mark V tank. Ten Germans jumped off the back of this tank and charged Smith, but he shot down four of them with his tommy gun, and the others did not stay longer. A second tank opened fire from a greater distance, and more German infantrymen tried to close with the Seaforth man, but he fought them off with his sub-machine gun, protecting his wounded comrade in the ditch until they finally withdrew.

Private E.A. Smith,
VC

Countersigning the recommendation for "Smoky" Smith's medal was one of General Burns' last acts as corps commander. The Eighth Army was about to change hands, General Leese having been posted to the Far East, and his successor was Sir Richard McCreery who would shortly tell Burns "that he was not satisfied with me."

Lieutenant-General Charles Foulkes
by Charles Comfort.
General Foulkes took command of
I Canadian Corps in Italy in December
1944, and led it through the hard
fighting of Battle of the Rivers. He
remained in command of the Corps
when it was transferred to northwest
Europe.
CWM 12284

This time there was no reprieve and Major-General Charles Foulkes, who had been commanding the 2nd Infantry Division in northwest Europe, was promoted to command I Corps in Italy. Vokes, who acted as corps commander in the interval between Burns' departure and Foulkes' arrival, switched appointments with Major-General H.W. Foster, the commander of the 4th Armoured Division in northwest Europe.

For the tired, war-weary Canadians the sonorous sequence of river lines continued through October to late December, from the Savio to the Ronco, the Ronco to the Lamone, the Lamone to the Senio, the Senio to the Montone, the Montone to the Santerno. It meant nothing to most of them that they had, together with their Allies, throughout 1944 "pinned nearly forty German divisions in Italy and the Balkans, about a sixth of the total German ground forces."

Each line, in turn, meant hard fighting and more good men killed or wounded. Among the Canadians on the Lamone, a seriously understrength 'B' Company of the RCR:

... lost 41 out of its assault strength of 72.... 'C' Company fared worse.... Out of an assault strength of 69, the company lost 48. They fought well. When the bridgehead was finally ours, some days later, the bodies of the dead were found. Several lay beside heaps of empty cartridge cases showing they had fought to the bitter end....

Despite shocking losses the fighting continued all month. Reinforcements arrived in streams, often becoming casualties the same day, or dying before they knew even their corporal's name....

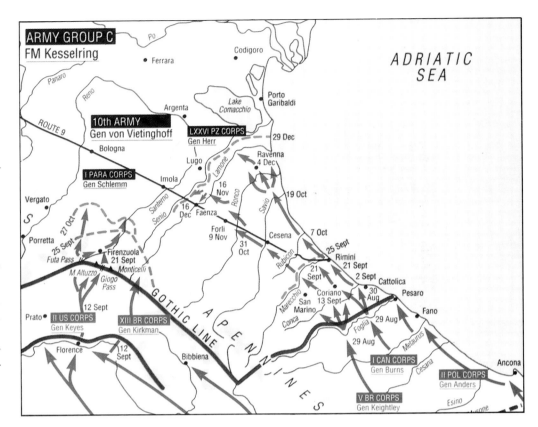

Canadian tanks cross one of the many muddy river lines encountered in the autumn of 1944. NAC/PA-173521

Paying such brutal prices, the infantry would secure a lodgement upon the far bank of each river in turn, but bridging it under fire in the mud and rain or snow was always an engineering dilemma, and there were endless problems in getting tanks and antitank guns forward. Lowering clouds usually closed off any possibility of close air support, so that the foot soldiers were always finding themselves pinned down in what the official history would one day call an "all too familiar pattern of infantry unsupported by armour engaged in costly effort against strong enemy positions." Losses continued to mount but, try as they might, the Canadians could not get beyond the Senio.

No one else could do better and some were doing much worse. "… by the end of the year, the situation was one of stalemate, the line having remained virtually static from the area around Spezia in the west to that near Ravenna in the east." On 30 December 1944, Alexander decided "to go on the defensive for the present and to concentrate on making a real success of our Spring offensive." On the Canadian front the enemy still held two bridgeheads to the east of the Senio which were eradicated in early January. Then the corps settled down to wait for spring.

Reinforcements march forward through the incessant winter rain, northern Italy, January 1945. NAC/PA-173549

FIRST CANADIAN ARMY

Ottawa, which had once been so anxious to split the Army Overseas, had been politicking to reunite it for the past six months. Neither the British nor the Americans had been anxious, however, to supply shipping just to oblige the Canadians and nothing had been done. Now the Combined Chiefs of Staff, had decided that their strategic aims might best be served by moving five divisions from the Mediterranean to northwest Europe, and that the Canadians might be among them. "I am very glad to learn from you," Mackenzie King told Churchill on 9 February 1945, "that operational considerations now make it possible for the Canadian Army to be united again."

There was no more serious fighting in Italy after I Canadian Corps sailed from Leghorn for southern France, en route to the Netherlands, a month later. Of the 92,757 Canadian soldiers who served in Italy, more than a quarter became casualties. Nearly 5500 were killed and almost 20,000 wounded, with another 1000 taken prisoner. During the whole campaign, Allied casualties totalled about 190,000 in the American Fifth Army and 123,000 in the Eighth Army (including the Canadians). Approximately 435,000 German soldiers were lost, including 214,000 officially recorded simply as "missing".

Winter quarters of the Ontario Regiment in the San Clemente mountains, near Bologna, 21 January 1945. NAC/PA-151745

CHAPTER 11

THE VICTORY CAMPAIGN
1944-1945

by
Brereton Greenhous

PREPARING FOR *OVERLORD*

Whatever the risks — and they were great, for no operation of war is as risky as landing on a strongly-defended shore — an invasion of occupied France, launched across the English Channel, offered the only practical prospect of the western Allies playing a crucial military role in defeating Hitler.

In the early spring of 1944 the Russians were doing rather more than their part on the Eastern Front, where the initiative had changed hands a year earlier and the Red Army was now marching inexorably towards Berlin. In southern Europe, however, progress was either slow or nonexistent and the ramparts of the Alps, still rising far behind the battlefront, made it virtually certain that the Anglo-American armies could not reach the German *Reich* by any Italian route in the foreseeable future.

At sea, the U-boat menace had been beaten and the western powers were now virtually supreme, but that supremacy did little in itself to weaken Germany's largely self-sustaining continental empire. And in the air, despite the vehement protestations of various 'bomber barons', the much-vaunted Combined Bomber Offensive was proving to be more of a running sore on German industry and morale than a fatal blow to Hitler's ambitions. Sooner or later, the Anglo-Americans and their allies — among which the Canadians were the most powerful — must venture ashore in north-west Europe.

Gunners Buckland and Campbell of the 5th Field Regiment, Royal Canadian Artillery clean their rifles after range practice, England. NAC/PA-177091

As the planning process for Operation *Overlord* matured, deception and concealment came to play a large part in achieving strategic and operational surprise. Sea and air superiority (both assured by 1943) were absolutely essential — and the narrower the sea crossing was, the easier they would be to maintain. Wherever the lodgement might be made, it had to be launched from the United Kingdom and it had to be within effective range of land-based fighter cover. The cliff-lined Pas-de-Calais, just across the Strait of Dover, was closest, but for that very reason it was also the most strongly fortified. Moreover, along those well-defended shores the narrowing English Channel meant high tides and unremitting exposure to storms blown in by the prevailing southwesterly winds.

A Canadian Women's Army Corps mechanic at work in England, summer 1944. NAC/PA-177084

The decision *not* to land there was made very early in the planning process, while every effort was made to convince the enemy to the contrary. A 'notional' army group was established in southeastern England and for many months radio messages were bandied about from one fictional formation to another, dummy tanks and vehicles were constructed for the benefit of *Luftwaffe* photo-reconnaissance machines, and false information was leaked to German agents in neutral countries. The *Wehrmacht*, already stretched by the demands of other fronts, braced its forces to meet invasion there and consequently prepared rather less in other places.

The genuine attack was planned for the Baie de la Seine, west of Le Havre, where the Cotentin peninsula would give some protection to the armada of shipping required. Only a thin crust of strong points, fronting on open sandy beaches suitable for amphibious tanks and a variety of landing craft, offered excellent terrain and ideal circumstances for the assault. Subsequently, the capture of Cherbourg, at the tip of the Cotentin, and prompt restoration of the harbour facilities there, would provide the major port essential for later operations.

American General Dwight D. Eisenhower, whose friendly grin masked a fairly gritty character and an unusual capacity to tolerate and manage vainglorious and imperious subordinates, would be the Supreme Allied Commander. That most conceited egotist, but proven master of the setpiece battle, General Sir Bernard Montgomery, had been brought back from Italy to command all Allied ground forces at least until such time as American troops in France distinctly outnumbered their Commonwealth counterparts. The American First Army, under General Omar Bradley, was to land on the right, its first task outside the bridgehead being to isolate the Cotentin peninsula. Second British Army, under Sir Miles Dempsey, would go ashore on the left, assigned to seize the town of Caen, a key transportation and communications link between central France and western Normandy, some twelve kilometres inland.

When the bridgehead had been secured, the Americans would add George Patton's Third Army to their order of battle and the British would be joined by First Canadian Army under General H.D.G. Crerar, a rather colourless Permanent Force gunner. Once it had seemed likely that the initial Anglo-Canadian assault would come under command of First Canadian Army and its first commander, A.G.L. McNaughton. Indeed, the Canadians in England had long trained under that assumption. But the despatch of a complete corps to the Mediterranean by October 1943, together with British doubts about the operational competence of McNaughton, his abrasive relationships with senior British officers, and the machiavellian politicking of Canadians who envied or disliked him, had forced McNaughton's resignation.

A mass para-drop by the 1st Canadian Parachute Battalion, Salisbury Plain, February 1944.
NAC/PA-177102

Troops go ashore from a landing craft during an exercise on the English coast in preparation for the invasion, May 1944.
NAC/PA-151749

A radical shift in planning had quickly followed and First Canadian Army had been shuffled aside. With Montgomery as ground force commander, that would have been inevitable in any case, given the strained relationship he had developed with McNaughton and the strength of their respective personalities. But it was easier with the crusty old Canadian out of the picture. Canadian soldiers would still play a part in the landings, but now Dempsey would have the 3rd Canadian Infantry Division and 2nd Canadian Armoured Brigade (and subsequently II Canadian Corps, until First Canadian Army came into the field) under his command.

Some senior Canadians with Italian experience were brought back to England for *Overlord*, promoted, and given new appointments. Lieutenant-General Guy Simonds took command of II Corps, the 4th Armoured Division going to his former chief of staff and brigade commander from Italy, George Kitching; and Brigadier R.A. Wyman, who had led the 1st Armoured Brigade through Sicily and southern Italy, was now asked to give a repeat performance with the 2nd. Major-General Rod Keller, who had commanded it for nearly two years in England, retained the 3rd Infantry Division which, with Wyman's tanks, would represent Canada in the initial seaborne assault.

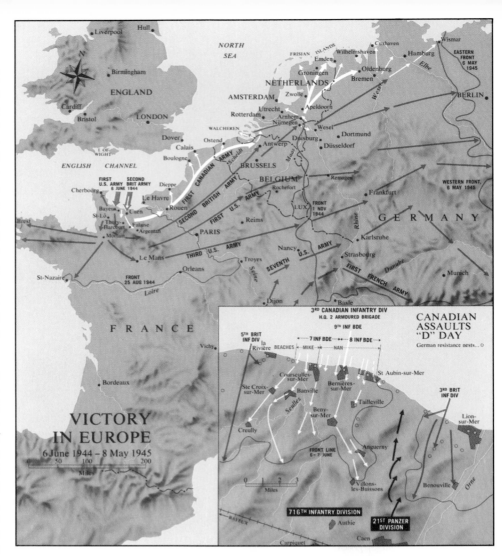

Chaudières Embarking for the Normandy Assault
by H. Beament.
CWM 10012

D-DAY FIGHTING

The first Canadians in France on 6 June 1944 were not from either of those formations, however. They were men of the 1st Canadian Parachute Battalion, serving with the British airborne division assigned to secure the partly-flooded, low-lying land east of the River Orne and the adjacent Caen canal, which formed the eastern edge of the beachhead. They dropped just after midnight with orders to demolish a bridge over the turgid Dives River, thus hampering any German advance from that flank, and then cover the backs of British paratroopers attacking a coastal artillery battery which seemed (wrongly, as it turned out, since the guns there lacked the necessary range) to threaten the invasion beaches.

They accomplished those tasks before withdrawing into a defensive perimeter around the Orne bridges with the loss of 113 — 19 killed, 10 wounded and 84 taken prisoner. The large proportion taken prisoner reflected landings which left many paratroopers isolated from their peers and far beyond the intended drop-zone.

Meanwhile the seaborne Canadians stormed ashore on *Juno* beach, which stretched some twelve kilometres from St-Aubin-sur-Mer to the hamlet of La Valette just beyond Courseulles-sur-Mer. Although the defences of western Normandy were not nearly as strong as those in the Pas-de-Calais, they were quite strong enough. There were iron stakes with explosive charges wired to their tops in the inter-tidal zone, minefields and barbed-wire blocking beach exits and funnelling attackers into pre-registered target zones, and anti-tank and machine guns arranged to provide interlocking fields of enfilade fire and mutual support. Beyond the beaches, but well able to put indirect fire down on them, were plenty of mortars, favourite German weapons — deadly, cheap, and easy to use.

Fortunately, perhaps, the enemy was short of good soldiers, given the vast numbers required to man the Eastern Front. The *Juno* defences were manned by five companies of the 736th Infantry Regiment — "in comparison with a first-class field regiment, its fighting value has been assessed as 40% in a static role and 15% in a counterattack," the Canadians were told in pre-invasion briefings — and behind them, in ready reserve, so to speak, were only two companies of *Panzergrenadiers* and two of an antitank battalion of the 21st *Panzer* Division.

D-Day
by Tom Wood.
CWM 10558

Further back, lay the rest of the 21st *Panzer*, and further back still, held in operational reserve, was the newly-created and still untried 12th *SS* Hitler Youth Division of fearsome potential — young Nazis of seventeen or eighteen under a cadre of older officers and NCOs who were veterans of the Eastern Front. It was this division, decimated and vastly out-numbered long before the end, but still fighting hard, which would bear the brunt of Canadian attacks in Normandy.

The *Juno* beaches were almost exactly the same length as those that the Canadians had faced at Dieppe, but not nearly as strongly held and much more heavily attacked. In simple terms, at Dieppe the Canadians had met two battalions of German infantry with six of their own and one armoured regiment: on *Juno* they would first encounter no more than one infantry battalion with six of their own and two armoured regiments. And this time they would have easier beaches to land on, amphibious DD [Duplex Drive] tanks to lead the way, AVREs [Armoured Vehicles, Royal Engineers] to blast beach exits through seawalls, and flail tanks to smash corridors through minefields. Behind them would come three more infantry battalions and another armoured regiment, artillery and signals and medical units; and then an ever-growing torrent of men, vehicles, food, fuel and ammunition, and all the complex paraphernalia of contemporary war.

A heavy air bombardment that preceded the assault did little harm, but there were naval guns of every calibre on call to pound strong points into rubble; fighter-bombers on call to blast targets indicated by forward air controllers on the ground; and such novelties as specially-fitted landing craft [LCT(R)s] which fired salvoes of *eleven hundred* 3-inch rockets (each one the equivalent of a 6-inch shell) to drench the beach defences moments before the soldiers landed.

Even so, the well-tested military maxim — that which can go wrong, will! — still applied. The Royal Winnipeg Rifles, assaulting at Courseulles-sur-Mer, on the extreme right of the Canadian front, landed minutes ahead of those 1st Hussars' tanks supposed to accompany them, and the 'Little Black Devils' took heavy punishment before the tanks' 75mm guns could blast out the last of several resolutely-held pillboxes.

Immediately to the left of the Winnipeggers, across the Seulles river, "we are getting close now and the bombardment stops," wrote a young officer of the Regina Rifles. "So far not a shot has been fired from the defenders on the beach. Will it be a pushover? We soon have the answer in the form of machine-gun fire and shells from pillboxes which are apparently still open for business despite the terrific pounding they have taken." The Reginas and their squadron of tanks landed together and cleared the streets of Courseulles only to find that the defenders had tunnelled between buildings in constructing their defences. They had to clear parts of the village more than once as determined enemies popped up behind them.

D-Day — The Assault
by Orville Fisher.

Fisher's painting depicts the
first moments of the Canadian
landing at Bernières-sur-Mer,
and the formidable beach
obstacles confronted by the
Queen's Own Rifles.
CWM 12469

Behind the Winnipegs, the Canadian Scottish were soon ashore but the advance of the 7th Infantry Brigade then went more slowly than had been hoped. Scottish spearheads and a third squadron of Hussars jabbed towards the brigade's objective, the Caen-Bayeux railway, but when their commanding officer "tried to get permission to push on, this was not granted and shortly afterwards we received preliminary orders to freeze — this meaning enemy tank counterattack possible." Possible, but not likely. No one on the Canadian front had yet seen an enemy tank, nor would they until the following day. But the fear of German armour was profound in the hearts and minds of Anglo-Canadian commanders.

A somewhat blurred photo of troops disembarking from a landing craft at Courseulles, taken by an Army cine-photographer accompanying the first wave.
National Film Board

On the extreme left of *Juno*, the 8th Brigade's North Shore Regiment found that the St-Aubin strong point "appeared not to have been touched" by the preparatory bombardment. The North Shores and C Squadron of the Fort Garry Horse spent much of the day securing the village and its immediate environs. Later, the battalion's chaplain, Father Hickey, remembered how:

... the beach was sprayed from all angles by the enemy machine-guns and now their mortars and heavy guns began hitting us. Crawling along in the sand, I just reached a group of three badly wounded men when a shell landed among us, killing the others outright. As we crawled we could hear the bullets and shrapnel cutting into the sand around us.... A ramp had been placed against the [sea] wall by now. Over it we went ... two stretcher-bearers ahead of us stepped on a mine ... half-dazed, we jumped down again behind the wall.

A 'Duplex-Drive' (amphibious) *Sherman* of the First Hussars in Courseulles, 6 June 1944. 1st Hussars Archives

The Queen's Own Rifles, facing the strongest defences, landed in the centre, at Bernières, some time before their squadron of Fort Garry tanks began to trundle up the beach, and before any of the Royal Engineers' AVREs reached the scene. Moreover, several of their landing craft blew up on mines as they approached the shore, disorganizing their assault. While their comrades tried to suppress German fire with fire of their own, riflemen rushed the strong points, hurling grenades though the fire ports. Their diarist later noted that "the support all around has been very disappointing — none of the beach defences have been touched and this caused very high casualties among the assault companies." How strange it was to find that, only forty minutes after the landing craft touched down, "a café just 100 yards off the beach is opened up and selling wine to all and sundry" on a day in which the battalion lost nearly one hundred and fifty men (sixty-three being killed), and won five awards for gallantry.

Once the Queen's Own were through the village and pushing inland, the Régiment de la Chaudière began to file ashore and the advance towards Bény-sur-Mer and Anisy began. But the 8th Brigade did no better than the 7th, getting no more than halfway towards its assigned objectives on D-Day. Behind it, the 9th Brigade, consisting of the North Nova Scotia Highlanders, the Highland Light Infantry of Canada, and the Stormont, Dundas and Glengarry Highlanders, together with the tanks of the Sherbrooke Fusiliers, prepared to resume the advance next morning.

Men of the Régiment de la Chaudière advancing through Bernières, 6 June. NAC/PA-131436

3rd Canadian Division's reserve, 9th Brigade, coming ashore at Bernières-sur-Mer on the afternoon of 6 June. NAC

Although none of the ultimate D-Day objectives had been reached anywhere along the Allied front — the Canadians came closer than anyone else — the initial phase of *Overlord* was nevertheless considered a notable success. Cold calculations had predicted that about one in seven of those who went ashore on the first day would be drowned, killed, wounded or taken prisoner. In fact, the figure turned out to be about one in fifteen (the Canadian casualties totalling slightly more than 1000, of whom 350 were killed or died of wounds, out of the approximately 15,000 who landed that day), such was the effect of careful preparation, deception, surprise, the weight of fire support from sea and air, and those elements of luck and courage which play their part in every battle.

FIGHTING FOR A FOOTHOLD

The first real setback came the very next day, however, when the 9th Brigade, with the North Novas and a squadron of Sherbrooke tanks in the lead, were counterattacked from a flank by the leading elements of 12th *SS Panzer* Division, under the redoubtable Brigadier-General Kurt Meyer who had reached the battlefield on a motorcycle — his favourite and frequent form of transport! — during the night. Communications with the ships and naval guns offshore could not be established, while the brigade's own field artillery regiment had been slow off the mark that morning and proved to be out of range when desperately needed. Not a fighter-bomber or rocket-firing fighter was to be seen, beneath the pervading cloud cover.

Caring for the wounded below the sea wall at Courseulles, 6 June.
NAC/PA-132384

Back in England the briefing had seemed very sound.... The artillery would land and the guns would support the advancing troops. On the right and left other divisions would keep abreast. The North Novas had only their own objective [Carpiquet airfield, just west of Caen] to consider. How differently things had turned out! The heavy artillery fire was coming from the very area the [British] division on the left was to have captured. And there was not a gun in range to support the Novas, though they were yet three miles short of their objective, and a day late getting where they were. Night was coming, and maybe would bring some change in their luck.

Only when they had fallen back some four kilometres and were, at last, within range of the guns, was Meyer's counterattack brought to a halt, with the loss of more than two hundred men killed, wounded and taken prisoner, and twenty tanks destroyed. Carpiquet airfield, which some of them had actually glimpsed that morning from the high ground south of Authie, would not be seen again by Canadian soldiers until 4 July.

With the 9th Brigade set back on its heels, Meyer then set off on his handy motorbike to stem the 7th Brigade's advance, six kilometres to the west; and he did so that night, recapturing Putot-en-Bessin from the Winnipegs. It was re-taken by the Canadian Scottish on the 8th, but the casualties were uncomfortably heavy — the Scots lost 125 men, 45 of them killed, and the Winnipegs 256, 105 being fatal. Deplorably, about 45 Canadians were murdered after being taken prisoner. Meyer's officers and NCOs, hardened on the Russian front, did not all fight by Geneva Convention rules. And although the Allies could bring an ever-growing superiority in men and guns and machines to bear, it was becoming more clear every minute that *Panzergrenadiers* were formidable opponents.

Despite three years or more of training, and just as in the Mediterranean, the Canadians had entered battle as ill-prepared apprentices. Mistakes made under an English heaven had been mere technicalities, easily forgotten or ignored: in the hell of Normandy, however, they cost lives and limbs, not to mention minds. Unlike Italy, here every metre of ground was vital to the Germans, for there was no great mountain range like the Alps to guard their western border. There was only the Rhine, and German generals (not to mention Adolf Hitler) had learned too much about war to delude themselves into believing that a river could be a major obstacle. Thus the battle for Normandy was just as hard-fought, just as intense, as those for Stalingrad or Kursk had been.

Carpiquet Airfield, Normandy
by Orville Fisher.
The airfield at Carpiquet, 5 kilometres west of Caen, was the scene of heavy fighting on
4 July 1944, when the Fort Garrys with the Queen's Own and the Chaudières attacked troops of the
12th SS Panzer Division. CWM 12439

EXPANDING THE BRIDGEHEAD

As the enemy recovered from his initial shock, resistance stiffened and the advance slowed. What followed, for all the fighting troops in the bridgehead and for none more than the Canadians, was two months of very bitter fighting. The eventual success of *Overlord* has tended to obscure the fact that it was a desperately close-run affair that may well have been decided by Allied air superiority and tactical airpower. Caen itself, initially an exclusively British objective to be attained on D-Day, did not fall (to an Anglo-Canadian assault) until 9 July, nearly five weeks later.

Under cover of darkness the Germans reinforced their hard-pressed lines as best they could. During daylight the Allies inched forward in battles increasingly reminiscent of the First World War. Indeed, before the northwest Europe campaign ended in May 1945, it had been established that it was more dangerous to be a Canadian rifleman there during the Second World War than it had been to be his father during any similar length of time on the Western Front a generation earlier.

The Allies poured resources ashore, at first over the beaches and then also through the artificial harbours established at Arromanches and St-Laurent. In the first week of *Overlord* 340,000 men, 55,000 vehicles, and over 100,000 tons

Clearing the Germans out of Caen, 10 July 1944.
NAC/PA-132727

of stores were landed — and before the end of the month more than a million men would be in France despite the destruction of the American port at St-Laurent in a storm which blew up on 19 June.

Among them were many more Canadians. The 2nd Infantry Division entered the line on 11 June, it and the 3rd then coming under Simonds' II Corps headquarters. The last Canadian formation, 4th Armoured, arrived during the second half of July, going into the line at the end of the month, bringing the strength of II Corps to nearly 80,000. General Crerar reached France on the 18th, although the terrible congestion in the beachhead (the *Luftwaffe* might have done decisive damage from the air, had it been able to achieve even a temporary air superiority) meant that his First Canadian Army HQ could not become operational until 23 July.

Stormont, Dundas and Glengarry Highlanders
by Orville Fisher.

Fisher's painting shows the SDG Highlanders fighting in the outskirts of Caen, July 1944.
CWM 12618

THE FALAISE POCKET

The deadlock finally began to break with Montgomery's poorly planned Operation *Goodwood* (18-19 July), a failed Anglo-Canadian gambit that Montgomery, unable ever to admit weakness, would later claim was only intended to 'fix' the weight of German armour on the eastern end of the bridgehead and draw reserves from the American front. It did those things, but he had certainly expected it to do much more. A week later, at the other end of the front, Bradley's Operation *Cobra* finally broke open the enemy ring, setting the scene for Patton's Third Army to hook south to the Loire, and then east toward Paris and the German frontier. American armour and motorized infantry raged across central France.

On that same day as *Cobra*, 25 July, in the abortive course of Operation *Spring*, just south of Caen, the Canadians of the 2nd Division lost nearly 500 killed and more than 1000 wounded or taken prisoner in a near-repetition of Dieppe. Indeed, it was, after Dieppe, the costliest day of the war for Canada. The Black Watch suffered most heavily, setting themselves — through no fault of their own — on a path which would make them the hardest-hit of all Canadian units in the course of the war. But while they were suffering, the Americans were moving.

Infantrymen of the 8th Brigade waiting to go into action near Caen, 18 July. NAC/PA-129128

Tanks Moving Up for the Breakthrough by George Pepper. CWM 13795

The Germans still in western Normandy were suddenly in danger of encirclement. Instead of authorizing a withdrawal when the threat became obvious and ominous, Hitler foolishly ordered a counterattack (which inevitably failed) and made a bad situation much worse. A whole army soon found itself trapped inside the aptly-named Falaise 'pocket', with the Americans at Argentan, twenty kilometres south of Falaise, facing north, and the Canadians pushing south from Caen, towards Falaise, in an effort to close it. Chance more than intent had put the Canadians at the centre of gravity — what the Germans would call the *schwerpunkt* — of a decisive battle.

Two attempts by Simonds to close the gap, Operations *Totalize* and *Tractable*, enjoyed only limited success, however, and progress was far too slow. Despite prodding by Montgomery, II Canadian Corps could only make slow progress against Meyer and his valiant defenders of the pocket's mouth. Even the CBC's Matthew Halton admitted as much, telling his audiences that:

There's still no swift rush southward. We're not yet in Falaise. The German Army is not disintegrating. Not yet. In fact, they're still putting up a bitter fight for every village. They know, as we know, that if we break through there, it's the beginning of the end of the German Army in the West. And slowly, we are breaking through. And we all know that history is alive right here among us. Men press forward saying: 'Perhaps this is the last great battle of the war.'

Of course, it was not: and to make it such would have required an adventurousness and flexibility quite alien to most Allied armies. Among the Canadians, generally speaking, the fault lay not with the regimental soldier or his officers, but in the slow, deliberate British doctrine, founded in First World War experience, to which commanders rigidly adhered. They had long over-emphasized firepower at the expense of manoeuvre, and under-emphasized the coordination of the three combat arms — infantry, armour and artillery — which was, and is to this day, the essence of mobile warfare.

In the tangled mountains of Italy, those ponderous tactics were sometimes appropriate, but even there they left much to be desired on other occasions. In Normandy, over the open, rolling fields between Caen and Falaise, they were simply inadequate. Progress was slow; and slowness, inevitably, led to hard fighting and heavy casualties. Formulas that had plagued Anglo-Canadian planning since D-Day were hardening into principle, with unfortunate results.

Tanks of the Fort Garry Horse massing near Bretteville le Rabet for Operation *Tractable*, 14 August 1944. In the foreground is a flail tank, used for clearing lanes through minefields.

NAC/PA-113659

Artillery and armour moving forward astride the Caen-Falaise road during Operation *Totalize* August 1944.

NAC/PA-116536

Tactical and operational weaknesses were compounded at the strategic level, where Montgomery still controlled the ground battle. Arbitrary boundaries, inflexible procedures, and monumental egos (of Bradley and Patton, as well as Montgomery) excused — or prevented — the Americans from pressing north to meet Crerar's men and close the pocket. Tens of thousands of Germans fled eastward, out of its slowly narrowing mouth, ravaged and decimated as they went by the awesome power of tactical air forces. A Canadian officer, taken prisoner, was among them.

All roads, and particularly the byways, were crowded with transport two abreast, grinding forward. Everywhere there were vehicle trains, tanks and vehicles towing what they could. And everywhere there was the menace of the air.... At the sound of a plane, every vehicle went into the side of the road and all personnel ran for their lives. The damage done was immense, and flaming transport and dead horses [much German transport was still horse-drawn] were left in the road while the occupants pressed on, afoot.

Finally, a frustrated Montgomery authorized the Americans to cross the previously sacrosanct army group boundary, and Polish troops under First Canadian Army command succeeded in meeting them at Chambois, southeast of Falaise, on the evening of 19 August. The Falaise pocket was thus closed, although many trapped Germans were still making desperate attempts to break out. The next day, Major David Currie of the 4th Armoured's South Alberta Regiment won a VC while plugging a hole at St-Lambert-sur-Dives and was actually photographed 'in the act', so to speak. The same picture also showed a young German officer in the act of surrendering to a sergeant-major of the Argyll and Sutherland Highlanders of Canada — a prisoner who was never seen again! Many years later, the officer's mother saw a print of this famous picture and wrote to the Department of National Defence enquiring what had happened to her son? No one could tell her.

Major David Currie of the South Albert Regiment (left, with pistol in hand) accepts the surrender of the German garrison in St-Lambert-sur-Dives, 19 August 1944. Currie was awarded the Victoria Cross for his gallant leadership during the attack of the village. NAC/PA-111565

The Germans had mustered about half a million men for the Normandy campaign, and of those roughly 200,000 were killed or wounded and 210,000 taken prisoner. The Allies now had two million men ashore, and had lost, in killed, wounded and prisoners, 200,000. The Canadian portion of the Allied total was 18,500 casualties (5000 of them fatal). It says much for Canadian courage, if not for Canadian generalship, that the 3rd Division had suffered more than any other division in Montgomery's armies and the 2nd Division was hurt nearly as badly. But their losses pale in comparison to those of the 12th *SS*, which had begun the campaign with over 20,000 men and 150 tanks; all that got away, across the River Seine, were some three hundred men and ten tanks.

Demolished Railway Bridge at Elbeuf
by Orville Fisher.

After the destruction of the bulk of their army in Normandy in the Falaise pocket, the Germans blocked a rapid Allied advance by destroying all bridges over the Seine River.
CWM 12470

MANPOWER SHORTAGES

For Canadians, those losses were a serious matter at a policy level as well as a personal one. The Army could ill-afford them, since it had been expanded to its present size without any serious consideration of what might happen once it went into battle. As early as November 1943, as casualties had begun to mount in Italy, the Director of Staff Duties had told the Chief of the General Staff, Lieutenant-General Ken Stuart, that "the question of our ability to maintain an Army formed within the present manpower base [i.e., volunteers] did not enter as a factor into the determination of the manpower ceiling."

Casualty rates in Normandy had proven to be much the same as in Italy. Thus, as early as 7 August (following on Operation *Spring*) the 2nd Division had found itself 1700 men under strength, and Simonds could see even greater shortages developing shortly.

No definite information is available to this Headquarters concerning further arrivals of infantry general duty reinforcements and it is felt that, for one reason or another, the system for the supply of reinforcements to this theatre is not functioning satisfactorily and that reinforcements in sufficient quantities to take care of actual and probable losses are not immediately available.

At Overseas Headquarters, in London, nothing much was done. General Stuart had become Chief of Staff there in January 1944 and he seems to have set about downplaying the crisis, absolutely forbidding any messages on the subject of manpower to be sent back to Ottawa without his personal approval of the text. Consequently, those which were transmitted did nothing to clarify a developing crisis. The British and Americans, involved in similar situations, were busily combing their supply and administrative services for former infantrymen, re-mustering gunners and tankers as infantry, and, as a last resource, reducing some units to 'nil strength' in order to reinforce others.

Stuart was not the only general at fault. Even allowing for economies of scale, it is hard to understand why, in the European theatre, less than 4 percent of American troops were assigned to headquarters' duties, compared to the Canadians' 13.6%. Patton, finding that he was short of 9000 infantry, lopped an arbitrary 5% off the establishment of all his headquarters' organizations, and later wrote that "even the 10% cut which we subsequently made had no adverse effect." Stuart, in England, and Crerar, in France, did nothing significant to ameliorate the Canadian crisis, however. There was also a crisis in field command. The 3rd Division's Rod Keller, stretched beyond his limits by the stresses of command, was wounded (by misplaced American bombs) on 8 August. His replacement was Brigadier — now to be Major-General — Dan Spry, brought back from Italy. Major-General Harry Foster, promoted from command of the 3rd Division's 7th Brigade, took over the 4th Armoured Division from George Kitching, who was blamed by Simonds for what were, in some part at least, the faults of others — not excluding Simonds himself.

Two brigadiers, seven regimental or battalion commanders, and similar proportions of subordinate ranks from majors to corporals, were also found wanting by their respective superiors, and replaced. There was no disgrace in that. Command in battle is possibly the most difficult and stressful job in the world and many fine men have failed at it, even when their side was winning. Moreover, there was then (and is now) no adequate selection procedure other than trial and error. Commanders at every level can only be tested in battle, and many are then found to have been promoted in error.

Advanced Dressing Station
by Will Ogilvie.

A Royal Canadian Army Medical Corps dressing station near Pont de l'Arche in northern France.
CWM 13216

FORWARD TO THE SCHELDT

After Falaise the Germans were in such disarray that the Allies might have driven straight through to Berlin if they had been able to focus even a third of their combined strength on a relatively narrow front and then put all their logistics effort into keeping it moving. But military alliances have their own agendas and their own political prices. Who would quarterback such a thrust? Who would carry the ball? Montgomery and Patton were the obvious choices but they could never have worked together.

Since British sensitivities had to be considered and it could not be an all-American backfield of Bradley and Patton, Eisenhower opted for a more deliberate advance along the whole offensive line, British and Canadians on the left, Americans and French on the right. And, since the Americans now greatly outnumbered their allies and were determined to exercise exclusive control of their own armies, Montgomery was required to relinquish his appointment as overall ground commander and revert to the more limited command of the Anglo-Canadian forces. No doubt it was some consolation to be promoted to the ultimate rank of field marshal.

Meanwhile, Hitler had labelled the various Channel ports 'fortresses', to be held "to the last bullet and the last man." Happily, their commanders generally took a more realistic view. First Canadian Army marched up the Channel coast in early September, taking Dieppe and then dropping off brigades from the 3rd Division to besiege and capture, one by one, Boulogne, Cap Gris Nez, Calais, (Dunkirk, invested in turn by Canadian, Czechoslovak and French formations, would hold out until the end of the war) and Ostend.

Second British Army, on the Canadians' right, aimed straight for Brussels and Antwerp. Taking the latter's docks and railway facilities more or less intact was important, for the length of supply and transportation routes from Cherbourg was beginning to slow the Allied advance more than the Germans could. Another great port, much closer to the front, would shorten those routes dramatically and simplify the logistics build-up needed to plough into Germany on a broad front.

A 4th Canadian Armoured Division tank during the advance along the Channel coast. NAC/PA-162667

The British liberated the docks at Antwerp, and the 2nd Canadian Division arrived to finish clearing the city in mid-September. But even when that was done, shipping could not reach the port until both banks of the West Scheldt estuary, leading up to Antwerp, had been swept clean of the enemy, and that requirement had been overlooked by a Montgomery busily politicking for command of a narrow thrust into the North German plain, aimed at Berlin. Soon a frustrated and impatient Eisenhower had to signal him that "unless we have Antwerp producing by the middle of November our entire operation will come to a standstill."

Infantrymen in Boulogne, France
by Orville Fisher.

Troops of the Highland Light Infantry advance against snipers in the ruins of Boulogne, September 1944. CWM 12529

THE BRESKENS POCKET

Montgomery assigned the task of clearing both banks of the Scheldt to an over-committed First Canadian Army; and General Crerar, in turn, ordered the 3rd Division (with only initial assistance from the 4th Armoured's infantry brigade, since the terrain was quite unsuited to tank forces) to clear the southern shore, the so-called 'Breskens pocket'; while the 2nd Division was to take the South Beveland peninsula and island of Walcheren on the northern side of the estuary.

It is a military 'rule of thumb' that an attack will normally require a superiority of numbers, on the part of the attackers, of three to one or better. The German defenders of the Breskens pocket numbered some 14,000, about three-quarters of them hastily pulled together after the Normandy debacle from men on leave from the Russian and Italian fronts. (In November, a First Canadian Army intelligence summary would assess them as "the best infantry division we have met.") Only a very small proportion of the Germans were support troops, and the numbers on each side were more or less the same.

It was unreasonable of Montgomery to ask — and of General Crerar to accept, for that matter — that the task be accomplished without additional forces. Perhaps both of them assumed that the enemy's isolation would weaken his morale and his willingness to fight. If so, it was a false assumption. The Germans were well equipped and had substantial stockpiles of food and ammunition. The landward side of the pocket, especially that part which fronted on the Leopold Canal where the ground had been deliberately flooded, was both strongly fortified and heavily manned.

Colonel C.P. Stacey, the official historian of the campaign, would subsequently call this front 'unpromising' — and surely that was the best that could be said for it. Perhaps it looked that way to General Crerar, too, for on 27 September he was evacuated to England suffering from a persistent intestinal ailment. He would be gone for a month and, in his absence, the authority of army commander was taken by Simonds, while the 2nd Division's Charles Foulkes became the acting corps commander.

In the Normandy campaign there had never been an open flank to attack. Here there was, and Simonds proposed the expected frontal attack across the canal (by the 7th Brigade), to engage enemy attention while the 9th Brigade made a simultaneous amphibious assault from the rear. Additionally, a small subsidiary attack on the landward side, some ten kilometres east of the 7th Brigade's assault, was to be staged by the 4th Armoured Division's Algonquin Regiment, and a fake assault — all noise and sparkle — mounted by the Argyll and Sutherland Highlanders at yet another point, in attempts to distract the enemy. The division's third brigade would be used to reinforce success at either point.

Such complex concepts are always easier to plan than implement, however. The distractions failed to distract and the attack across the Leopold Canal met fierce opposition, made all the worse by the fact that the amphibious landing had had to be postponed for forty-eight hours rather than being launched simultaneously. There was no good reason why the attacks over the canal could not have been postponed likewise — a few hours either way made no strategic difference — and synchronization restored, but that was not done.

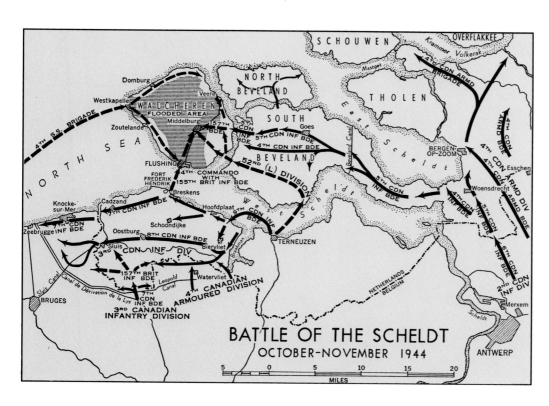

BATTLE OF THE SCHELDT
OCTOBER-NOVEMBER 1944

General H.D.G. Crerar
by T.R. MacDonald.
CWM 13151

General Harry Crerar graduated from Royal Military College and was commissioned in the Royal Canadian Artillery in 1910. He served throughout the First World War with the artillery, winning a DSO in 1917. After the war he remained with the Permanent Force, and attended both the British Army Staff College and the Imperial Defence College. He organized the 1936 reorganization of the Militia, and was Director of Military Operations 1935-38. He served as Commandant of Royal Military College 1938-39. Early in the Second World War he organized Canadian Military Headquarters in England, returning to Canada in 1940 to become Chief of the General Staff. In 1941 he returned to England to take command of I Canadian Corps, which he led in Britain and in Italy until February 1944, when he was appointed General Officer Commanding-in-Chief of First Canadian Army. Crerar commanded First Canadian Army throughout the campaign in northwest Europe. He was promoted full General in October 1944. He retired from the Army in 1946.

Crerar was an officer in the traditional gunner style — immaculate, punctual, precise, and punctilious. He had a reputation as being a superb staff officer, but was not known as an innovative or particularly inspiring field commander.

With German attention focused exclusively on their canal defences, "heavy casualties were suffered by both sides and the ground was littered with both German and Royal Winnipeg Rifle dead." In due course, the Reginas and Canadian Scottish crossed the canal, too, and on the brigade level that translated into 533 casualties in a week, 111 of them fatal. Moreover, it proved beyond the brigade's capabilities to expand a toehold into a foothold until the attack from the sea began to take effect.

One short stretch of coast, which lay immediately west of the shallow Braakman inlet, along the south shore of the estuary, was less well-defended than the rest. In Operation *Switchback* the 9th Brigade's three battalions, crowded into *Buffaloes* — amphibious, tracked troop carriers, capable of grinding their way over virtually any surface — were put ashore on the mud flats between the hamlet of Hoofdplaat and the Braakman at 0200 hours on 9 October.

The Germans were caught by surprise and off-balance, for once, just as they had been on D-Day. "There was no opposition, except for a few shots in the Highland Light Infantry area; and shelling from the German coastal batteries at Flushing, across the West Scheldt, did not begin till dawn." But the enemy reacted as quickly as ever, once he recognized what was happening, and the 9th Brigade — and the 8th, which was soon put ashore behind it — had hard fighting to come. Very soon, "you were right in the middle of it," recalled Captain Jock Anderson, the chaplain of the HLI. "The Germans were on the next dyke, a couple of hundred yards away at most. It was almost like standing at one edge of a square. There would be one lot of them on this side, one on that, and one ahead of you."

Infantry of the 3rd Division, who came to be known as the 'water rats', in the mud of the Breskens Pocket.
NAC/PA-131252

Tank Destroyers of the 5th Anti-Tank Regiment, RCA
by Bruno Bobak.
CWM 11994

"The land all through here is like a checkerboard, utterly flat between dozens of intersecting dykes," wrote the North Novas' Lieutenant Donald Pearce.

The dykes are about twenty feet high on the average, and maybe forty feet wide, with sloping grassy sides. We scramble over them, or drive on top of them; they are bad to fight over, but merciful to hide behind.

Attacks had to go in along dykes swept by enemy fire. To go through the polders meant wading, without possibility of concealment, in water that at times came up to the chest. Mortar fire, at which the Germans were masters, crashed into every rallying point. Spandaus sent their whining reverberations across the marshes. Our own artillery was deprived of much of its effectiveness because of the great difficulty in reaching an enemy dug in on the reverse slope of a dyke. Even that most potent weapon, the Wasp [armoured flamethrower], was denied both cover and room to manoeuvre.

There were other hazards, besides the Germans. In that "welter of mud and chill" platoon commanders of the North Shore Regiment found themselves ordered back to company headquarters, creeping, crawling and running under fire, to "receive information and forms for selling Canada Bonds to the troops."

Nevertheless, slowly, inexorably, the Germans were pressed back; and with that pressure came an inevitable weakening of resistance to the tenuous lodgement so expensively established and desperately held by the 7th Brigade.

Eventually, all three brigades found themselves fighting their way *west* as the Germans withdrew to their coastal defence stronghold at Knocke-sur-Mer, on the North Sea shore. But if the Canadians were clearly exhausted by then, and ravaged by battle, the Germans were in even worse shape as the inevitable conclusion approached. When Knocke finally surrendered without much of a fight, "the fort turned out to be bigger than we could possibly have guessed."

The whole thing was a good two miles in extent, interconnected below ground by dozens of deep brick and cement tunnels that branched hither and yon through the town at safe depths, connecting up with a maze of sub-tunnels that led to living quarters far below that again, perfectly immune to attack by air, sea or land.... They had built this fort for eternity. They had put four years into making it — it was, in fact, still being worked on when we took it. They surrendered it in fifteen minutes, and almost without firing a shot.

More than twelve thousand Germans were taken prisoner in the pocket, the cost of taking them and clearing the pocket being almost two thousand Canadian casualties, just over three hundred being fatal. The non-fatal casualty figure was bolstered by a high proportion of neuro-psychiatric (NP) cases — battle exhaustion — which accounted for over 16% of the infantry total. "Of the NP cases occurring during this battle, about 90% had three months or more of battle experience"; in other words, they were the ever-fewer veterans of Normandy. It seemed that even the bravest men could only stand so much.

SOUTH BEVELAND AND WALCHEREN

On the other side of the Scheldt, on 2 October the 2nd Division had begun to push towards the base of the South Beveland peninsula against most stubborn resistance and numerical odds no better than those endured by the 3rd Division on the south shore. As with the Breskens pocket, 'bouncing' the enemy right out of the peninsula might have been no great problem a month earlier, when the Germans had still been in total disarray from the debacle in France and British troops had sped through Antwerp almost unopposed. But Montgomery's mind had been fixed on more remote objectives at that time, and he and Dempsey (the commander of Second British Army) had failed to drive their exhausted armour across those few undefended kilometres to Woensdrecht, the little town which straddled the narrow base of South Beveland.

Now it fell to the 5th Brigade's Black Watch, not yet by any means fully recovered from the horrendous casualties it had suffered in Normandy, to try and reach it — by means of the usual frontal assault in daylight — "against an enemy of proven strength and resourcefulness" who knew very well how important it was to hold them off.

Since, as we have noted, the 2nd Division's Foulkes was acting as corps commander, his division was temporarily in the hands of Brigadier R.H. Keefler, a pre-war Militia artilleryman who had no experience in commanding a brigade (reflecting the biases of the old Permanent Force, most senior Canadian commanders were recruited from the supporting, rather than combat arms) while 5 Brigade, which would conduct the first assaults, was commanded by Brigadier W.J. Megill, a Permanent Force signaller who had started his military career in the ranks and commanded the brigade since February 1944.

Whoever devised it, the tactical plan handed down to him was "fundamentally cockeyed" in the opinion of the Black Watch's commanding officer, who may have complained but, in the end, did as he was told. The attack might have begun in the pre-dawn darkness, or even at sunset — as with the Leopold Canal, a few hours either way could have made little difference. Instead it was ordered for the cold flat light of early morning, on Friday the 13th of October! "By 1000 hours the leading company lay on the start line, their ranks cruelly decimated by the withering fire," wrote the historian of the Toronto Scottish, some of whose machine guns and mortars had been assigned to provide fire support for the Highlanders.

The next company lined up and began to pass through. For two hours they too tried vainly to advance and a very small gain was made. The remaining companies then took their turn, each advancing a short distance at alarming cost. The gruelling battle carried on throughout the day and as evening fell the reformed companies were still pushing on, yard by bloody yard. Every conceivable form of support was ordered up. Tanks were available but could not negotiate the flooded fields nor the narrow roads.... Shortly before midnight, the survivors reached their objective but were too few to hold it against a counter-attack.

This time there were 183 casualties, including all four company commanders. And nothing to show for them.

The Royal Hamilton Light Infantry was ordered up, Lieutenant-Colonel W.D. Whitaker insisting on planning his own attack. It went in, at 0330 hours on a dark October night, close behind a barrage laid down by a hundred and seventy guns, and by daylight his 'Rileys' held most of the town. They were counterattacked — standard German tactics — and the ensuing fight for Woensdrecht lasted for five days, until the thwarted Germans gave up and dourly began to back down the peninsula towards Walcheren.

The Fort Garry Horse advancing along the Beveland Canal, 29 October 1944.
NAC/PA-138429

Tanks of the South Alberta Regiment in Bergen op Zoom, October 1944. NAC

In due course the Canadians reached the causeway that linked Walcheren to the mainland. Every metre of it, 1200 of them, straight and flat, could be raked by fire from the far end. There was another way on to the island — a ford that reconnaissance parties of a British division would eventually find and use to put one of their infantry battalions across — but that was not for Foulkes or Megill. There was no time to waste searching for alternatives which might, or might not, be there. Their men would attack straight down the causeway!

It says much for the courage of Canadian soldiers and regimental officers, if not for the professional acumen of their commanders, that they not only did so but actually won a toehold on the island. Again, the assault was initiated in daylight — but fortunately also in a driving rain which significantly reduced visibility. Starting at 1000 hours, a half-strength company of the Black Watch got "to within 75 yards of the far bank" but could do no more, mortar and machine-gun fire pinning them to shallow holes clawed out of the mud. In mid-afternoon supporting tanks were

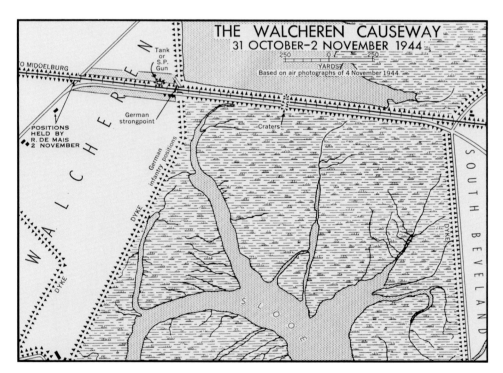

ordered up (virtually to certain death since the enemy had an 88mm high-velocity antitank gun sited to fire straight down the causeway) but fortunately for the tankers, artillery fire had cratered the road enough to make it quite impassable to armour.

Infantry Near Nijmegen, Holland by Alex Colville. CWM

There was one more battalion in the 5th Brigade, the Régiment de Maisonneuve, and it was now ordered forward in another night attack. Their D Company, in the lead, "started out with eight officers. In twenty minutes we had three," and soon the company was down to forty totally exhausted men, pinned in a bridgehead at the end of the causeway that was still under direct observation and fire from three directions.

The commander of a British division temporarily serving with II Canadian Corps was instructed to take up the burden. That realistic and competent officer objected vehemently to what he viewed as quite an unreasonable order.

I said that I did not consider an attack down the 1500 metres of straight causeway ... was a viable military operation, and that we would try and find another route. The Canadian Corps commander said there was no other route and that we had to go in at dawn the next morning. I again protested that it was not a viable military operation, that we would have very heavy casualties and achieve nothing.

Their attack was cancelled and the Black Watch told to withdraw (taking more casualties in the process). The Calgary Highlanders were sent up to mount a night attack, and that too was driven back. At dawn the Calgarys tried again, and this time they succeeded in putting the survivors of two companies on the far shore. They could get no further, however, and found themselves trapped between the water and the great dyke which encircled the island and held the North Sea at bay as tenaciously as the Germans were holding them. One of the Calgary companies — in numbers it was less than a half company — was commanded by Captain C.F. Clarke.

For manoeuvring, we had just the space between the top of the dyke and the water back of it. When the tide came in, it wasn't very much. The enemy were using 81mm mortars on us, at less than fifty yards range. They were dug in on the land side of the floodbank and we were on the water side....

... We were strung out in a long thin line, and couldn't do anything; we couldn't move one way or another. Each time we tried to go over the dyke we took a hell of a beating. About this time Jerry launched a counterattack at the end of the causeway, at our point of contact with D Company....

D Company was being forced back; that would leave us exposed at both ends — our rear was now in danger ... and eventually we moved back behind the crater in the middle of the causeway and held on.

The France and Germany Star, awarded for operational service in France, Belgium, Holland and Germany.

The 1939-45 Star, awarded for service in operations during the Second World War.

Foulkes, ambitious and determined to please his superiors, gave him forty-eight hours to find another route or lose his command! Whether he could have enforced that alternative is highly doubtful, but even as he spoke British engineers were discovering and exploring a narrow ford, only passable at low tide to men on foot, some three kilometres south of the causeway. The next night, Scottish infantry waded across and a battalion was soon established on the other side, pressing on the rear of the enemy's defensive perimeter at the end of the causeway. Their situation was still so constricted, however, and German defences so firm, that they found it as difficult to expand their position as the Canadians at the end of the causeway were finding it with theirs. Stalemate!

There was yet a third way on to Walcheren, encompassing an alternative that Simonds had proposed as a possible 'last resort' back on 21 September but which surely should have been a first resort rather than the last. While heavy bombers were employed to blow great holes in the encircling dyke and flood the centre of the island, thus constricting the movement of German reserves, British commandos launched two amphibious assaults essentially similar to that employed by the 3rd Division in Operation *Switchback*.

They landed at Flushing and Westkapelle just before dawn on 1 November, and a week later the island was in British hands, losses being little greater than those incurred by the Canadians and Scots in their fruitless essays from South Beveland. The channel was already being swept for mines and on 28 November the first convoy steamed into Antwerp. It was only fitting that the leading ship was one built in a Canadian shipyard and named *Fort Cataraqui*.

The Defence Medal, awarded to all with more than six months overseas service.

The War Medal, 1939-45, awarded to all servicemen with more than 28 days service during the war.

CONSCRIPTION

Infantry replacements were becoming ever more difficult to find, and those that were coming up to the line were — in the opinion of their veteran comrades and officers, both in Italy and northwest Europe — all too often ill-trained and unprepared. They had complained about that time and time again, only to have their claims refuted by Simonds and buried in headquarters' files. The issue only became a public one when a well-known Toronto sportsman and entrepreneur, Conn Smythe, who had been wounded in Normandy and evacuated to Canada, gave an interview to the *Globe and Mail* in September. He argued, quite rightly, that "large numbers of unnecessary casualties result from this greenness, both to the rookie and to the older soldiers who have the added task of trying to look after the newcomers as well as themselves," and thought that "the relatives of the lads in the fighting zone should ensure no further casualties are caused ... by the failure to send overseas reinforcements now available in large numbers in Canada."

The public uproar that followed sent J.L. Ralston, the Minister of National Defence, scuttling off to Europe to see for himself. The personnel records of individual reinforcements were interpreted to mean that their training was generally adequate — fighting soldiers knew better, and told him so — but the outright shortage of men was obvious and undeniable. Every infantry unit was badly under strength. Back in Canada in mid-October, he told the Cabinet that General Stuart "had painted too rosy a picture" and insisted that the government must now despatch conscripts overseas.

The Cabinet split on the issue. Prime Minister Mackenzie King consulted McNaughton, just retired from the Army, and (for the moment) his nominee to be the next governor-general of Canada! McNaughton, long out of touch with the home army and convinced of his own charisma, told him that enough volunteers for overseas service could still be found from among the ranks of NRMA conscripts; and the prime minister, who had been holding Ralston's written resignation in his hands since the conscription crisis of 1942, decided that this was the moment to produce it. His new Minister of National Defence was none other than McNaughton.

Yet another campaign was launched to convert conscripts into volunteers. It failed just as conclusively as its predecessors, however, despite the McNaughton charisma, and King was left with no alternative but to put through an Order in Council authorizing the army to ship overseas up to 16,000 conscripts (out of a possible 32,000) — a decision that resulted in a minor mutiny at Terrace, BC, and the desertion of a considerable number of the chosen but unhappy few.

The exact dates on which the first conscripts to serve overseas began to filter into the battle as reinforcements are difficult to specify, but the first draft to go overseas left England for the Continent on 23 February 1945 and it is likely that they were joining infantry battalions before the end of March. Before the war ended, in early May, 2500 would have been taken on the strength of field units and 69 of them would have been killed and 244 wounded.

Gas Drill
by Molly Bobak.

CWAC in training in Alberta, 1944.
CWM 12059

Nijmegen Salient, December 1944
by Alex Colville.

A soldier of the North Shore Regiment strips his Bren gun during a pause in the action.
CWM 12188

WINTER ON THE MAAS

The Ardennes offensive, Hitler's last great roll of the dice in the West, intended to hook north and re-take Antwerp and Brussels, cutting off the whole of 21 Army Group, was met and beaten back at the end of December. The Canadians played no significant part in the Battle of the Bulge (although the 2nd Infantry and 4th Armoured Divisions were prepared to help in holding the northern shoulder of the Allied line if the need had arisen).

Eisenhower's strategy called for clearing all of the Rhine's west bank before advancing into Germany on a broad front, with Bradley's Americans pushing up from the south and Montgomery's Anglo-Canadians squeezing down from the north. But on Montgomery's side, the infantry divisions of First Canadian Army had undergone a particularly hard time in clearing the Scheldt, and badly needed rest, re-training, and reinforcement. Perhaps that was why he had originally decided to use Second British Army's XXX Corps as his main instrument in the Rhineland, with II Canadian Corps filling only a supporting role.

That did not please Simonds, who now took advantage of the delay to press the case for his corps taking a leading part, arguing that "to leave the Canadians out of so important and decisive a battle would be a bitter disappointment to the troops." The troops, of course, might not have been as disappointed as he thought if the honour had fallen to someone else. Nevertheless, his wish was granted. XXX Corps was put under Crerar's First Canadian Army, which was assigned to conduct the operation even though more than two-thirds of the divisions involved would be British; and Simonds' II Canadian Corps was given a distinctly more prominent role than had originally been planned.

(In Simonds' favour, it should be noted that he would have radically altered Montgomery's plan if he could, believing that the Rhine could be 'bounced' by a surprise attack directly across it, a tactic which might well have worked. But that idea contradicted Eisenhower's basic Allied strategy, even though, in due course, George Patton was to do exactly that. Nor was it one likely to appeal to Montgomery after the Arnhem disaster of September — one "bridge too far" was quite enough for him.)

A Queen's Own Rifles patrol near Nijmegen, January 1945.
NAC/PA-177598

Gunners of the 5th Field Regiment in action near Malden, Holland, 1 February 1945. NAC/PA-177569

Meanwhile, the Canadians held the line of the Maas and young Donald Pearce of the North Novas kept up his diary (against all regulations at the time, but to the great joy of later military historians).

There is a telephone in my dug-out, in a niche I have cut with a bayonet into the solid dirt wall.... I often pick up the phone and listen in. The difference in voices! The people at HQ, relaxed, confident, unworried, loud (they shout over the phone), whistling, singing, joking, playing cards, and sounding as if they were in a news-room in Canada. The men at the observation post just overlooking the enemy positions whisper into the phone, and there is a catch in their voices; they are tense, worried, their hearts are sometimes beating hard enough to make their voices quiver a little. They try to end conversations with our headquarters as soon as possible, and seem to be talking with their heads pulled down between the lapels of their greatcoats....

... Back again in trenches, the December rain and hail, one day clear in four, two hours of windy sunshine per week, mud literally to the ankles. On some days, we lie in the mud and the warmth of our bodies keep it soft, while the wind thickens it or freezes it where we are not lying. I keep telling myself my father's generation of soldiers did this for four years and that I have it easy....

We eat twice a day, morning and night. Food is brought down a twisting, slippery path, mined along the fringes, under cover of darkness and between scattered bursts of enemy fire, for they know our prandial habits. Then we pass it from dug-out to dug-out, so much to this, so much to that, an extra portion to those who were out on patrol last night. We try to keep the rain out of the bread, and the dirt from the trench tunnels out of the mess-tins as they are passed back and forth in the slow rain, with sometimes grunts of gratitude, sometimes cursing, with ponderous oaths when the food is poor, dirty, cold or scanty. But, miraculously, the men are OK. What is called their 'morale' is, in fact, really quite high.

**Lieutenant-General
G.G. Simonds**
by Charles Comfort. CWM 12384

Lieutenant-General Guy Simonds graduated from Royal Military College and was commissioned in the Royal Canadian Artillery in 1925. He qualified as an Instructor in Gunnery in 1932 and attended the British Army Staff College. On mobilization of the 1st Canadian Division in 1939, he was selected as a member of the operations staff. In 1940 he was promoted Lieutenant-Colonel and given command of the 1st Regiment, Royal Canadian Horse Artillery. While in England, he conducted the first War Staff Course for the Canadian Army. Simonds was promoted Brigadier in 1941 and made Chief of Staff of I Canadian Corps. He commanded 1st Infantry Brigade 1942-43, after which he became Brigadier, General Staff of First Canadian Army. He was promoted Major-General in April 1943 (at age 39) and appointed to command 1st Canadian Division. He led the 1st Division during the invasion of Sicily and in Italy. In November 1943 he assumed command of 5th Canadian Armoured Division in Italy, and in January 1944 was promoted Lieutenant-General and placed in command of II Canadian Corps, then preparing for the invasion of northwest Europe. He led II Corps throughout the campaign in France, Belgium, Holland and Germany. After the German surrender, he became commander of all Canadian forces in Holland. He returned to Canada in 1949, after a tour of duty at the Imperial Defence College in Britain, to be commandant of the National Defence College and the Canadian Army Staff College. He served as Chief of the General Staff from February 1951 to August 1955, when he retired from the Army.

INTO THE RHINELAND

The singularly unpleasant process of clearing the west bank of the Rhine began on 8 February 1945. It involved an extremely complex battle plan encompassing ten divisions, and technically it was probably a more difficult battle than any other engagement of the northwest Europe campaign.

The only convenient thing about the battlefield was that it had fairly clear boundaries. It lay between the Maas and the Rhine, measuring some fifty kilometres by twenty to thirty, and broadening slightly as the two rivers diverged. After that, one complication lay piled on another. More than a third of the area — that third closest to the Rhine — was flooded and the other two-thirds were little more than a gigantic mud patch as a result of the winter rains. Much of the land was heavily wooded and there was little 'grain' to it, with few distinctive ridges or valleys.

In military parlance, it was all 'close' country — that is, fields of vision and of direct fire were usually short. Part of the old pre-war Siegfried defences (the German answer to France's Maginot Line) lay athwart it, albeit at a sharp angle to the intended axis of advance; and the enemy had now had four months to build additional strong points and adapt existing ones to 'all-round' defence. An amalgam of these factors made for a very complex battle, extremely difficult for higher headquarters to 'read' on an hour-by-hour basis, and the brunt of the decision-making seems to have fallen on the two corps commanders, Sir Brian Horrocks and Simonds.

The initial assault, labelled Operation *Veritable*, was carried out by three divisions of XXX Corps, together with the Canadian 3rd Division on that flooded left flank, hard against the Rhine, since by now no one knew more about fighting over flooded land than Spry's 'water rats'. It began with the destruction of the ancient city of Cleve, key to German reinforcement and supply, by three hundred heavy bombers, and was shortly followed by a preparatory artillery bombardment in which 1400 guns fired the heaviest barrage of the war, to date. "We had to have a thousand rounds of ammunition dumped at each gun position for the artillery bombardments." All that high explosive simply set the pattern for what was to follow.

The controlling feature and key objective of *Veritable* was the so-called 'Materborn gap', a three-kilometre stretch of open country between Cleve, on the edge of the flooded land, and the Reichswald to the south. The British burst through it on the 11th, having advanced twelve kilometres in three days of costly forest fighting. The 3rd Canadian Division, riding in *Buffaloes* once again, had a somewhat easier time since, as the Germans on the higher ground were driven back and British spearheads angled in towards the Rhine, those in front of the 3rd Division had little choice but to follow suit for fear of being cut off.

The Régiment de Maisonneuve at Den Heuval, Holland by George Pepper.
CWM 13764

A *Buffalo* amphibious personnel carrier passes men of the North Shore Regiment near Nijmegen, during the beginning of Operation 'Veritable', 8 February 1945.
NAC/PA-140424

As the advance continued, however, and the British weakened, the 3rd Division side-stepped right on to the higher ground in an effort to maintain momentum, and the 2nd Division (now commanded by a pre-war militia officer, Major-General Bruce Matthews, since Charles Foulkes had been promoted to take command of I Corps in Italy), came up on their right to take over from a hard-hit British 53rd Division.

The ultimate objective for both Canadian formations was now the Goch-Calcar road, the start line for the second phase of the Rhineland battle, Operation *Blockbuster*; and the spearhead of the attack was provided by the 2nd Division's 4 Brigade, with the Fort Garry Horse providing tank support.

Attack was followed by counterattack, and then by counter counterattack, as the Canadians struggled forward.

The Germans practised their traditional tactics of giving ground under pressure but then immediately launching counterattacks to recover the lost ground before the Canadians could consolidate their successes. When that happened, infantry companies which had been badly weakened in the initial assault were often cut off and assailed from all sides. The ultimate response was to call down artillery fire on their own positions, as the Royal Hamilton Light Infantry's Major J.M. Pigott did on the night of 19-20 February. The Canadians, in their slit trenches, were likely to suffer less than the Germans, caught in the open as they pressed in on their enemies.

Moving Up Through Wyler by Paul Goranson. CWM 11413

Men of the Regina Rifles near Calcar, Germany, 16 February 1945. NAC/PA-177577

The counterattack melted away and the advance resumed, but the end of Joe Pigott's war was only minutes away. As he recollected events himself:

At this moment, Sergeant-Major Stewart ('Pinky') Moffatt ... got hit by a sniper in the lower jaw, smashing it badly and knocking out his teeth. He was in agony.... I picked him up with the idea of putting him in the hallway of a farmhouse ... out of harm's way until he could be taken away to a hospital.

Upon opening the door, I found myself face-to-face with a young German soldier, about six-foot-four, with a grenade in his hand. We stared at each other for a few seconds, and then he threw it. It landed on the body of poor Moffatt, whom I immediately dropped, and it then exploded on my chest.

I was wearing a set of experimental infantry body armour. It saved my life. The grenade blew a great big dent in it — my chest was black and blue for about six weeks after that — but if I hadn't had it on, I would certainly have been killed. As it was, shrapnel from the grenade pierced my windpipe and I was severely wounded. I was blown back out into the farmyard. For me, that was the end of the war.

In the pages of a book, using only words and pictures, it is hard, if not impossible, to convey the sickening ferocity of warfare like this. When the 3rd Division's Queen's Own Rifles came to clear the hamlet of Mooshof, just beyond the Goch-Calcar road, in order to "capture ground which was considered essential for the development of future operations":

Sergeant Cosens' platoon, with two tanks in support, attacked enemy strong points in three farm buildings, but were twice beaten back ... and then fiercely counter-attacked, during which time the platoon suffered heavy casualties and the platoon commander was killed.

Sergeant Cosens at once assumed command of the only other four survivors of his platoon, whom he placed in a position to give him covering fire, while he himself ran across open ground under heavy mortar and shell fire to the one remaining tank, where, regardless of danger, he took up an exposed place in front of the turret and directed its fire.

After a further enemy counter-attack had been repulsed, Sergeant Cosens ordered the tank to attack the farm buildings, while the four survivors of his platoon followed in close support. After the tank had rammed the first building he entered it alone, killing several of the defenders and taking the rest prisoner.

Single-handed, he then entered the second and third buildings, and personally killed or captured all the occupants, although under intense machine-gun and small-arms fire.

Just after the reduction of these important enemy strong points, Sergeant Cosens was shot through the head by an enemy sniper and died almost instantly.

Aubrey Cosens was posthumously awarded the Victoria Cross.

Veritable was a cruelly expensive battle, costing the British nearly seven thousand casualties and the Canadians nearly two thousand — a ratio roughly proportionate to their respective commitments — while the Germans lost about twelve thousand killed, the same number taken prisoner, and perhaps another twenty thousand wounded. There was more to come, under the rubric of *Blockbuster*.

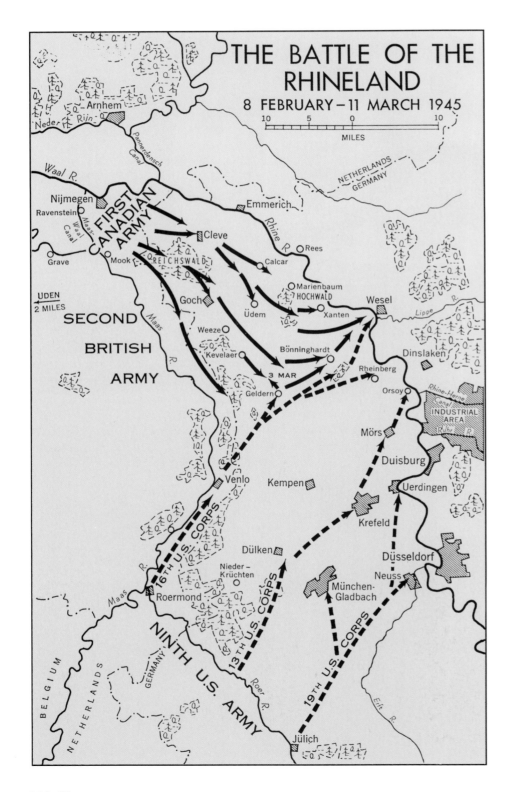

Sergeant Aubrey Cosens, VC

OPERATION *BLOCKBUSTER*

In the south an American advance down the Rhine, towards the Anglo-Canadians, required a crossing of the Roer river; but the enemy managed to blow two key dams which controlled its water levels, flooding its course and speeding up the current, so that the river became impassable until the flow subsided. That delayed the American offensive by two weeks. They did begin to move on 23 February, however, and once they were across the river they moved steadily north, since the Germans had turned the weight of their defences to face the British and Canadians. From a German perspective, it was vital to hold on to the west bank as long as they could. At Wesel, some fifteen kilometres southeast from where the Canadians now stood, and twenty north of the Americans, two bridges — one road and one rail — crossed the Rhine; and the remnants of seventeen or eighteen German divisions were slowly withdrawing towards those bridges.

With the Goch-Calcar road in Canadian hands, the 4th Armoured Division (Chris Vokes, who had been brought back from Italy after a year in command of the 1st Division, had exchanged places with Foster) was brought into the line in place of the badly battered 3rd; and the 2nd and 4th advanced more or less abreast into the next belt of forest, consisting of the Hochwald, Tüschenwald and Bambergerwald. The low ridge covered by these woods is about twelve kilometres long, rising in a convex arc no more than sixty metres above the farmland to the north and west — and the Germans had spent the last two weeks constructing what defences they could along the forward edge of the forest.

On the left, the 2nd Division would attack into the northern edge of the Hochwald, an assault "which might mislead the enemy into expecting a drive along the northern axis and conceivably cause him to draw his reserves in that direction...." The main attack would come on the right, into another narrow gap in the woods, this one no more than a kilometre wide between the Hochwald and Tüschenwald. It lay in front of the 4th Armoured Division, which had the British 11th Armoured Division on its left, and General Simonds believed that the armour might smash its way through the gap in a 'deliberate' attack, delivered with full artillery support.

However, rushing it with tanks was not a practicable operation of war against an enemy securely entrenched and adequately equipped with both antitank guns and *Panzerschrecken* (German 'bazookas', or hand-held, rocket-propelled, infantry weapons, deadly to armour at close range). There were limits to the effectiveness of artillery bombardments restricted in time. Nor did the division include enough infantry — only one brigade, consisting of three battalions — to lever open the German defences, whatever the corps commander might think and other gunners try to do, and Vokes should have demanded more resources before committing any. They tried, however, once before dawn and once in daylight, and were twice repulsed.

Wounded Canadians being loaded aboard a jeep ambulance near Udem, Germany, 27 February 1945.
NAC/PA-177595

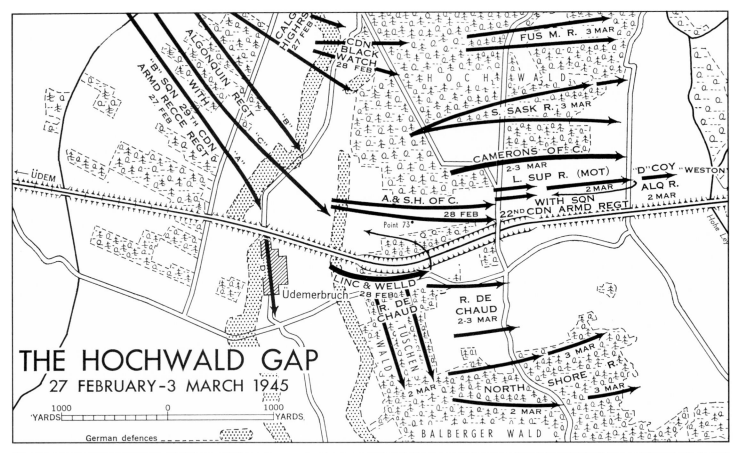

THE HOCHWALD GAP
27 FEBRUARY-3 MARCH 1945

ÜDEM

CALG HIGHRS 27 FEB

CDN BLACK WATCH 28 FEB

FUS M. R. 3 MAR

HOCHWALD

S. SASK R. 3 MAR

"B" SQN 29TH CDN ARMD RECCE REGT 27 FEB

ALGONQUIN REGT WITH "C"

"B"

CAMERONS OF C. 2-3 MAR

"D" COY "WESTON

L. SUP R. (MOT) 2 MAR

ALQ R.

A. & S.H. OF C. 28 FEB

WITH SQN 22ND CDN ARMD REGT 2 MAR

Point 73

Üdemerbruch

LINC & WELLD 28 FEB

R. DE CHAUD

R. DE CHAUD 2-3 MAR

TÜSCHEN WALD

NORTH SHORE R.

3 MAR

2 MAR

3 MAR

2 MAR

BALBERGER WALD

Hohe Ley

1000 YARDS 0 1000 YARDS

German defences _ _ _ _ _ _

Troops of the Argyll and Sutherland Highlanders south of the Hochwald, 6 March 1945. NAC/PA-138353

There was viciously bitter, close-quarter fighting in forest, muddy field and bomb-wracked town and village. Roads were few and poor, and mud was sometimes as much an enemy as the Germans. Trying to get to their start line, the tanks of the South Alberta Regiment, with riflemen of the Algonquin Regiment clinging to their hulls, "got stuck, were pulled out, and got stuck again." When they were finally in position, "it must be realized that owing to the bogged vehicles the squadrons and companies were now at half strength." In A Squadron:

All their tank troop leaders, with the solitary exception of Lt. R. Crawford, had become stuck and consequently Lt. Crawford was in the lead. In the darkness he was unable to see the tank ditch which was dug in a wide circle around [the town of] Udem and his tank fell into it.... The squadron strength was now 8 tanks with 4 carriers attached, the [latter] remnants of the Algonquin R carrier platoon under Capt. Sanstrom.... Fire came from the right and fire from the ridge to their left. Not one anti-tank gun could be pinpointed. The first three tanks were now immobilized with two burning and the last two tanks had been hit by bazookas. The three centre tanks were virtually pinned to their positions and ... after firing all their ammunition, all crews bailed out. Of the carriers, two had been hit and two were still all right. These last two were loaded with the wounded and found their way back on the same route they came.

... As they were leaving they saw some men being taken prisoner.

The Canadian Grenadier Guards, working with the motorized infantry of the Lake Superior Regiment, were also taking their lumps. By 1 March they were down to 21 tanks, only a quarter of their establishment strength, and composite squadrons were being formed in last-ditch attempts to create tactically effective sub-units. When one of those composite squadrons, thirteen tanks strong, accompanying the Lake Superiors, charged forward in the pre-dawn darkness of 2 March, "six tanks bogged down in the heavy mud," one was disabled by an 88mm antitank shell, and another "by a grenade thrown into the turret" — a testimony not only to the short-range nature of much of the fighting, but also to the pitching accuracy and courage of some anonymous (and probably soon deceased) German soldier.

All this before daybreak. Shortly afterwards, two more tanks "foundered in shell holes" and the attack lost all momentum "when four tanks of the Governor General's Foot Guards" (regimental tradition combined with inescapable operational realities occasionally resulted in bizarre contradictions of title and function which ought to have properly puzzled German intelligence officers) and a company of the Algonquins "joined in the fight, heading for the same objective as C Coy, LSR."

Tanks of the Governor General's Horse Guards advancing through Arnhem, 15 April 1945.
NAC/PA-130119

*Now the action was rapid: enemy machine guns opened up
and some were silenced, anti-tank fire knocked out three of the Foot
Guards tanks, an attack led by five [German] Tiger tanks was repulsed by our artillery and by the fire of our reserve tanks in the
Gap.... The movement ceased — pinned to the ground, our infantry
held on all day.*

The 4th Division was exhausted for the moment and
Simonds ordered the 3rd Division back into the line in the
4th's place, and the 2nd Division's 6 Brigade to help. Between
them, they drove home the wedge that the 4th Division had
hammered into the Hochwald-Tüschenwald gap and by the
morning of 3 March the enemy was in retreat once again. It
remains an incomprehensible enigma, however, how an
army composed of boys and (at best) middle-aged veterans,
as the German Army now was, ill-equipped, poorly-supplied,
and laced with only a few veterans, retained the cohesion and
fighting ability that it did in these desperate last days.

Major Fred Tilston, VC

It should not be assumed that all the hard fighting occurred in the gap. It was important to keep up the pressure all
along the German front, and meanwhile the 2nd Division had
been pushing into the Hochwald proper. Its 5 Brigade had
borne the brunt of the initial assault, the Black Watch being
particularly hard-hit once again and giving new meaning to
the traditionally sympathetic "poor bloody infantry" expression. With 6 Brigade despatched to the 4th Division's assistance, Matthews was left with only 4 Brigade to press his own
attack.

This time it was led by the Essex Scottish, and most particularly by Major Fred Tilston whose inspiring courage won him a Victoria Cross. In the words of his citation:

Though wounded in the head, he continued to lead his men forward, through a belt of [barbed] wire ten feet in depth.... When the platoon on the left came under heavy fire from an enemy machine gun post, he dashed forward and silenced it with a grenade; he was first to reach the enemy position and took the first prisoner ...

As he approached the woods he was severely wounded in the hip and fell to the ground. Shouting to his men to carry on without him and urging them to get into the wood, he struggled to his feet and rejoined them as they reached the trenches on their objective. Here an elaborate system of underground dug-outs and trenches was manned in considerable strength and vicious hand-to-hand fighting followed.

Such had been the grimness of the fighting, and so savage the enemy resistance, that the Company was now reduced to only 26 men, one quarter of its original strength. Before consolidation could be completed the enemy counter-attacked repeatedly, supported by a hail of mortar and machine gun fire from the open flank. Major Tilston moved in the open from platoon to platoon, quickly organizing their defence and directing fire against the advancing enemy....

When the supply of ammunition became a serious problem, he repeatedly crossed the bullet-swept ground to the Company on his right flank to carry grenades, rifle and Bren ammunition to his troops.... He made at least six of these hazardous trips....

On his last trip he was wounded for the third time, this time in the leg ... he fired his men with grim determination and their firm stand enabled the Regiment to accomplish its object of furnishing the Brigade with a solid base through which to launch further attacks to clear the forest, thus enabling the Division to accomplish its task.

The Essex Scottish took more than a hundred casualties, and Tilston lost both legs. He had been wounded before — in Normandy — and that earlier wound would eventually cost him the sight of one eye as well.

Troops of the Princess Patricia's Canadian Light Infantry cross the Ijssel River in *Buffaloes* during Operation 'Cannonshot', 11 April 1945.
NAC/PA-133333

ACROSS THE RHINE

Meanwhile, the Germans squeezed back across the river, blowing the bridges behind them at the last minute. They did that all along the Rhine except at Remagen, more than a hundred and twenty kilometres south of Wesel, where the American First Army captured a railway bridge still in good enough shape to move infantry over it. In twenty-four hours, half a division was on the other bank and pontoon bridges were being constructed to take armour across, but "Remagen was in near-impossible terrain for the massive armoured breakout that the Allies needed." It exited into a shallow saucer of farmland that merged into forested hills very similar to those which the Anglo-Canadians had just fought through in the Rhineland. And one Reichswald, one Hochwald, were enough. In any case, the American way of

war was not to plod forward, metre by painful metre, but wait until they could smash an armoured fist straight through.

Although the German forces in the west had now been reduced to a rump of some twenty-six grossly under-strength divisions, (in the east the Russians, now closing on Berlin, were facing the equally under-strength remnants of five times as many), finally Eisenhower, Bradley and Montgomery were in agreement. They all wanted to get their armour out on to the North German plain where it could run wild; and to that end there must be an amphibious crossing of the Rhine further downstream.

A 'Melville' bridge over the Rhine at Emmerich, 2 April 1945.
NAC/PA-177570

Infantry Advancing by Alex Colville.
The Highland Light Infantry of Canada advance toward Wessel, April 1945.
CWM 12171

The initial crossing, by the British 51st (Highland) and 15th Divisions and American 30th and 79th Divisions, was left to Montgomery, an admitted master (even by his American rivals) of the setpiece assault; and it came just after dark on 23 March, in the vicinity of Wesel. It was preceded by a massive artillery barrage — 2500 guns firing for twelve hours — and an equally massive air bombardment, and followed by the landing of two airborne divisions, one British, one American, on the east bank. With the British division went the 1st Canadian Parachute Battalion — the only Canadian troops to participate in the assault phase of the crossing — and paratrooper Corporal F.G. Topham won the fourth and last Canadian VC of the campaign (and last army VC of the war) while succouring the wounded.

Corporal Frederick Topham, VC

Although some groups of enemy would still fight well, Operation *Plunder* was a clear case of using a sledgehammer to crack a hazel nut. The six divisions of the first wave, four delivered by assault boat and two by parachute, probably outnumbered the entire total of organized German forces on the east bank, who could muster less than fifty tanks between them. And upstream, near Oppenheim, George Patton had already begun to sneak his Third Army across the river a day earlier, with the loss of only 34 men killed or wounded, in an obvious (and successful) attempt to embarrass Montgomery. Once across the Rhine, Patton's tanks would not stop until they reached the River Elbe and the Russians.

The first Canadians, the Highland Light Infantry of the 3rd Division's 9th Brigade, crossed the Rhine while Topham was bandaging wounds and carrying men to safety, and during the afternoon the rest of the brigade made their way across. The next day the American Ninth Army broke out of the Remagen bridgehead, moving so quickly that the harried Germans could never regain their balance. In a matter of days the Americans had surrounded the Ruhr, Germany's industrial heartland, and compelled the surrender of half the remaining enemy forces in the west.

The South Saskatchewan Regiment under fire near the Oranje Canal, Holland, 11 april 1945. NAC/PA-138284

THE END OF HITLER'S WAR

Although good men would still die, and others be wounded, the Anglo-Canadian effort was winding down as the opposition weakened, and the initiative was passing more and more to the Americans. The British, heading for Hamburg, hung on the flank of the US Ninth Army, and First Canadian Army turned left to clear northern Holland and the Dutch-German border as far as the Weser river. For the last few days of the war, all the Canadian troops in Europe would fight under Canadian command. I Canadian Corps, which had begun to arrive in Belgium at the end of February after its long trek from northern Italy, was re-united with its parent formation and now joined in the rout, slicing through the western Netherlands.

The war was virtually over. In his steel-and-concrete bunker, deep under the heart of Berlin, just before 1530 hours on the last day of April 1945, Adolf Hitler put a pistol barrel in his mouth and pulled the trigger. Five days later, at a few minutes to eight in the morning, a sharp-shooting rifleman of the Lake Superior Regiment, riding on a tank of the Canadian Grenadier Guards along a road just north of Oldenburg, "drilled the bicuspids of a German poised with a bazooka ready to fire." It was, so far as can be ascertained, the last Canadian bullet of the war against Germany, for at eight o'clock exactly the cease-fire sounded in Europe.

Lieutenant-General Charles Foulkes, commander of I Canadian Corps, accepting the surrender of German forces in the Netherlands, 5 May 1945.

NAC/PA-138588

Among the fighting troops, at least, "There were no cheers and few outward signs of emotion." Canadians killed and wounded in Italy had totalled nearly 25,000, and losses in northwest Europe amounted to 44,735. Perhaps the lucky ones were giving thanks for their own survival — perhaps they were remembering fallen comrades.

It is, of course, impossible to be precise about comparison of casualties between wars. They are calculated on very different bases, and there are many variables. Factors such as a smaller proportion of soldiers in combat formations, and the number of division/months spent in the field must be taken into account. But even taking account of these complications, battle casualties — killed and wounded — among front-line Canadian soldiers in the Second World War reached higher proportions than they had done in the Great War of awesome and terrible legend.

Fully-armed German troops march into captivity after the cease-fire, Aurich, Germany, 5 May 1945. NAC/PA-143950

Victory Parade
by Orville Fisher.
Canadian troops parade through liberated Rotterdam, 10 June 1945.
CWM 12651

WINDING DOWN THE WAR

There was still the war against Japan to be won. In early September 1944, the Chiefs of Staff had concluded that Canada should "be represented in the final assault on the Japanese homeland" by contingents of soldiers, sailors and airmen. The Canadian Army Pacific Force, of "one division with [the] necessary ancillary troops," should operate in the north or central Pacific theatres, they thought, and they accepted that this would mean operating under American command. The Cabinet approved those proposals on 22 March 1945 and the American Chiefs of Staff followed suit on 15 May, stipulating, however, that the Canadians adopt American staff organization, switch from British to American equipment (except for uniforms), and "be trained in the United States under the overall supervision of the United States Army Ground forces."

Command of this 6th Infantry Division was given to Major-General B.M. Hoffmeister, the pre-war part-timer who had commanded the 5th Armoured Division with such distinction in Italy and northwest Europe. Volunteers were called for and enough veterans — some 39,000 — came forward to meet initial requirements, although there remained some serious doubts about the long-term viability of the force should it become involved in heavy or prolonged fighting. Preliminary training began in Canada, prior to moving to Fort Breckinridge, Kentucky; but that move had not begun when, immediately after the dropping of two atomic bombs on Hiroshima and Nagasaki on 8 and 9 August 1945 respectively, the Japanese surrendered unconditionally. On 1 September orders were issued for the disbandment of the Pacific Force.

Men of the Fusiliers Mont-Royal pose below a battle-scarred statue in Berlin, 14 July 1945. NAC/PA-177593

The 8th Hussars parade past General Crerar during the 5th Division victory parade. NAC/PA-137891

In Europe, a Canadian Army Occupation Force, to be stationed in northwest Germany, was recruited from the ranks of those who did not wish to join the Pacific Force but were willing to forgo their priorities for demobilization. But the Canadian government soon proclaimed that "the serious administrative problems that are involved in maintaining comparatively small forces at so great a distance" made it an excessively expensive luxury. Withdrawn by stages, commencing in April 1946, the Occupation Force was officially disbanded on 20 June 1947, no one having the foresight to realize that the onset of the Cold War would bring another contingent, the 27th Canadian Infantry Brigade, back to Germany less than four years later.

Repatriating troops take a last look at England, 21 June 1945.
NAC/PA-177085

CHAPTER 12

THE POST-WAR ARMY AND THE WAR IN KOREA

by
William Johnston and Stephen J. Harris

TOWARDS A POST-WAR DEFENCE POLICY

When the Second World War finally came to a close, Canada was arguably the fifth military power in the world, trailing only the United States, the Soviet Union, Great Britain, and China. Just over one million men — two-fifths of the male population between the ages of eighteen and forty-five — had donned uniform, 708,500 of them in the Army. But the good hopes Canadians had about the future in August 1945 had very little to do with the their country's military might and the strength of its armed forces. It stemmed, rather, from the completeness of the Allied victory, and from the determination being shown by so many countries that they would not allow the events of 1939-1945 to be repeated.

Representatives of fifty nations signed the United Nations charter on 26 June 1945, and the wartime Big Four — Britain, America, Russia, and China — were among them. With all the major powers participating, and given its provisions for organizing multi-national forces under UN auspices and command, the United Nations Organization seemed to have corrected two of the fundamental flaws of the old League of Nations, and in the process to have given teeth to the principle of collective security.

An RCAF *Dakota* drops supplies to troops participating in Exercise *Musk Ox*, a test of the Army's ability to operate in the Arctic, 26 April 1946.
DND/ZK 1009-1

Supplies for Exercise *Musk Ox* being picked up at Cambridge Bay, NWT.
NAC/PA-134304

Both the will and the way to lasting peace appeared to exist, and because of that the Canadian government decided that there was no need for Canada to maintain large armed forces once Japan had been defeated. Its view changed scarcely at all even after Igor Gouzenko's revelations about Soviet espionage networks at work in the Dominion and Winston Churchill's warning that an Iron Curtain had descended from Stettin to Trieste. The general staff's call for a standing Army of 50,000 to 60,000, backed by compulsory service, was rejected out of hand, and by 1947 the Permanent Force comprised only two small armoured regiments, three understrength infantry battalions (still occupying company stations), and about eight batteries of artillery. "If — which may God forbid — we should get into a war in the next two or three years," Defence Minister Brooke Claxton admitted in a moment of rare candour, the Regulars "would be available to the extent of their numbers, but obviously a force of eight or nine thousand troops altogether with training cadres and administrative personnel would not have any perceptible effect in any war that we can contemplate."

The Militia was in no better shape. The general staff had wanted to maintain six divisions of well-trained reservists, but government policy dictated otherwise. The recruiting and training of the other ranks was actively discouraged; summer camps were reserved for officers, specialists, and NCO's; Highland units were told that kilts would no longer be issued; and low pay ceilings limited the number of week-night parades. Faced with the loss of these traditional stimuli to recruiting, attracting few veterans, and fighting against the widespread belief that a lasting peace had been won, Militia regiments did what they could to keep their numbers up, but few succeeded. In some proud, old units with enviable war records, effective strength dropped to as low as one hundred; in others, little more than a platoon or troop could be mustered.

A mid-day camp during *Musk Ox*, 3 May 1946. NAC/PA-167257

A TIME FOR FIRMER PLANS

The widening gulf between East and West soon threatened Canada's somewhat splendid isolation and the easy neglect of military preparedness which it had made possible. The United States was worried about the threat to North America posed by Soviet air power, and the Canada-US Basic Security Plan produced under the aegis of the Canada-US Permanent Joint Board on Defence and the bilateral Military Cooperation Committee outlined specific responsibilities for each of the two countries, particularly in the realm of air defence. As a result, a number of Militia infantry battalions on the approaches to major cities — including the Sault Ste. Marie and Sudbury Regiment, Prince of Wales's Rangers, Scots Fusiliers, Dufferin and Haldimand Rifles, Brockville Rifles, Irish Fusiliers, and 2nd Battalion, Canadian Scottish — and two armoured units — the 2nd/10th Dragoons and Manitoba Mounted Rifles — were converted to anti-aircraft artillery.

But the joint Basic Security Plan did not stop at air defence. Although the likelihood of a Russian attack in Europe was considered remote, at least in Ottawa, preparation for that contingency had to be included in the plan, and consequently the Militia (now the Reserve Force, later the Canadian Army (Reserve), and finally, again, the Militia) was given a new lease on life. Units were encouraged to begin recruiting, and training for all ranks was once again authorized. Two-week summer camps were reinstituted, and war surplus equipment began to find its way to the Reserve, so that by the end of 1948 the British Columbia Dragoons boasted twenty-seven vehicles on unit charge.

Recruiting was also accelerated in the Regular Force (later the Canadian Army (Regular), and by June 1948 its combat arms units averaged just over eighty per cent of their war establishment. Collective training at platoon and company levels resumed, and to find the 'educated' officers necessary for modern war, the Canadian Officers' Training Corps was established at civilian universities to supplement the output from RMC, which reopened as a cadet college in 1948. That year the National Defence College (for senior officers and civil servants) opened at Fort Frontenac, Kingston, where it was collocated with the Canadian Army Staff College.

The Governor General's Horse Guards during summer camp at Petawawa, 1949. GGHG Archives

THE MOBILE STRIKING FORCE AND THE DEFENCE OF THE NORTH

It was not just in Europe that the Army had to be prepared to fight, however. In a period of increasing tension, fear, and suspicion, it seemed to some that the Russians might attempt lodgements in the far north — either to divert attention from the moves they had planned in Europe, or to build weather stations, navigation facilities, and even airfields for the use of their strategic bombers in an air attack on the American heartland. The Canadian Army was therefore compelled to look at the region 'North of 60' not just as a laboratory for winter warfare, but as a potential theatre of operations in which control of the Alaska Highway would be vital. The road had to be defended, as did the airfields and radio stations built alongside it during the Second World War. The question was how.

Deciding very early on that permanent garrisons in the north would be an extravagant commitment against Soviet lodgements likely to number less than two hundred men, Army Headquarters devised a scheme to create an airborne/air transportable counterattack force (later called the Mobile Striking Force) within the Regular Army which would operate, depending on the nature of the threat, in units ranging from a single company to an all-arms brigade group whose objective was to eliminate lodgements within forty-eight hours of their being established. To begin with, an airborne company would be selected from each of the three regular infantry regiments, augmented by a few gunners, sappers, signallers, drivers, and mechanics.

8th New Brunswick Hussars refuelling during summer training at Camp Utopia in 1949.
8CH Archives

The creation of the Mobile Striking Force was announced with considerable fanfare, highlighting the rebirth of Canadian airborne forces and the support which would be provided by the RCAF's Air Transport and Tactical Air Commands. "In a country of Canada's large area and comparatively small population," the 1949 DND annual report declared, "it is essential to have in active service a highly trained and mobile force capable ... of defending our territory against any possible sudden attack." In August of that year the MSF took part in its first major exercise, when the airborne company of Princess Patricia's Canadian Light Infantry made a parachute assault on an 'enemy'-held Fort St. John.

Five months later, Exercise *Eagle* was followed by *Sweetbriar*. Involving 5000 service personnel from Canada and the United States, *Sweetbriar* was the largest and probably most famous of the MSF exercises. Once again, the PPCLI (supported by RCAF Mustangs and Mitchells) made an airborne assault, this time to disrupt enemy lines of communications, while the rest of the Mobile Striking Force acted as the vanguard for a combined Canadian-American force making a conventional road march up the Alaska Highway. When everyone had returned home, the Defence Minister announced proudly that *Sweetbriar* confirmed the Regular Army's readiness "to fulfil its functions of aiding in the defence of North America."

In fact, the exercise had done nothing of the sort. Lacking equipment, 3000 men understrength, and rarely training for its role, the Mobile Striking Force was always more chimera than real, and Army Headquarters decided that it had failed miserably. The MSF was not the dedicated, quick-reaction force that had been talked about the year before, but simply elements of the Regular Army — the same Regular Army that was hypothetically allocated to Europe — called by another name.

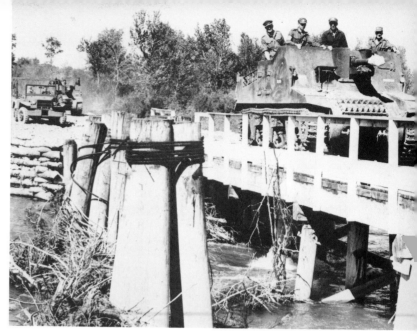

An 18th Field Regiment self-propelled 25-pounder gun during summer training at Wainwright, July 1951.
Glenbow Museum PA-1599-5547

Critics blamed the government for these deficiencies, but after *Sweetbriar* Army Headquarters very quickly lost faith in the MSF's original concept. For one thing, the exercise proved that the task of eliminating lodgements was well beyond its capabilities. For another, following the Soviet nuclear test of 29 August 1949 and the revelation that the Russians would soon have aircraft capable of delivering atomic bombs to targets in central North America, the whole idea of lodgements became ridiculous. Why would the Soviets risk their own highly trained airborne forces to fight for small bits of Arctic Canada when they could bomb Chicago? Accordingly, although the Mobile Striking Force continued to live on until the mid-1950s, and elements of it continued to train in the Arctic, the MSF gradually became a brigade-sized, general purpose home defence force to meet Canada's obligations to the Canada-US Basic Security Plan — in short, the forerunner of 1 Canadian Brigade Group — and by 1953, the only troops committed to Arctic defence were Militia units from Western Command.

Men of the Calgary Highlanders at Camp Wainwright during Exercise *Sweetbriar*, 13 January 1950.
Glenbow Museum PA-1599-6945

TOWARDS A EUROPEAN FOCUS

While the Mobile Striking Force slowly faded into oblivion, the eyes of Canadian soldiers and politicians turned increasingly to Europe. Following the Communist coup in Czechoslovakia in February 1948 and the Berlin blockade in June, it looked very much as if the Russians would begin their quest for world domination there. The countries of Western Europe responded quickly, forming a mutual defence union, but fearing that this was not enough, Canada led the way in giving this European effort a trans-Atlantic character, and in April 1949 was instrumental in the creation of the North Atlantic Treaty Organization. NATO was the country's first formal peacetime military alliance, and it was also the first time that a Canadian government admitted openly, and in advance of a crisis, that the best place to defend Canada was "as far away ... as possible" in combination "with other friendly powers." "The only war which would involve Canada," the 1949 White Paper announced, "would be a war in which communism was seeking to dominate the free nations." It would be a war "for survival".

The North Star symbol adopted by the North Atlantic Treaty Organization.

That year the strength of the Regular Army was increased to just over 20,000, while that of the Militia rose to 43,000 from 37,000 in 1948. Training in the Regular Force began to be conducted at the regiment and battalion level, and was to proceed to "the initial phases of formation training." In the Reserves, an additional fifteen days training was authorized for officers, NCOs, specialists, and tradesmen. But clinging to what was left of Canada's comfortable isolation, the government was not yet ready to commit Canadian troops to Europe, and it was not about to concede that membership in NATO required the acquisition of new equipment to provide the Armoured Corps, for example, with the 844 tanks it required to fill its war establishment. "The North Atlantic Treaty is a pact of peace," the DND report for 1949-1950 declared optimistically, and its final result "will not be to increase ... expenditures [but] by pooling resources ... to reduce expenditures which each of the countries would have found necessary ... had there been no pact." Something had to be done to help the Europeans, however, and to this end the government offered Italy, Holland, and Belgium a divisions' worth each of British-pattern kit — it had been decided that the Canadian Army would henceforth use American equipment — and additional 25-pounder guns to Italy.

General Eisenhower, NATO's Supreme Allied Commander Europe, inspects 27th Brigade on their arrival in Rotterdam, 25 November 1951.
NAC/PA-179034

The act of aggression that altered the thinking of Canada and the West, however, did not occur on the centre stage of Europe. It came instead on an unlikely peninsula in the Far East.

THE INVASION OF SOUTH KOREA

Until the North Korean invasion of the South in June 1950 thrust the backward Asian country to the forefront of world affairs, it had received little attention from western policy makers. In fact, many ordinary Canadians may not have known where it was, if they had ever heard of it at all. A Japanese protectorate since 1905, the Korean peninsula had been divided along the 38th parallel into Soviet and American zones of occupation at the end of the Second World War. Unhappily, in neither sector were conditions ideal.

As leader of the new southern republic, Washington placed its support behind Dr. Syngman Rhee, a seventy year-old, US-educated exile who had spent half his life living in the United States. Rhee assumed the presidency of the Republic of Korea (ROK) following the 1948 elections and quickly moved to consolidate his power base by eliminating all political opposition, including the persistent groups of Communist guerrillas active in the countryside. The Soviets, meanwhile, established a repressive Communist dictatorship in the northern half of the country under their protégé, Kim Il Sung. They also trained and equipped the 135,000-strong Korean Peoples Army, which contrasted sharply with the ill-equipped and poorly trained units of the south. This imbalance in forces did not concern Washington, which continued to rely on the ability of its military advisers to control the situation.

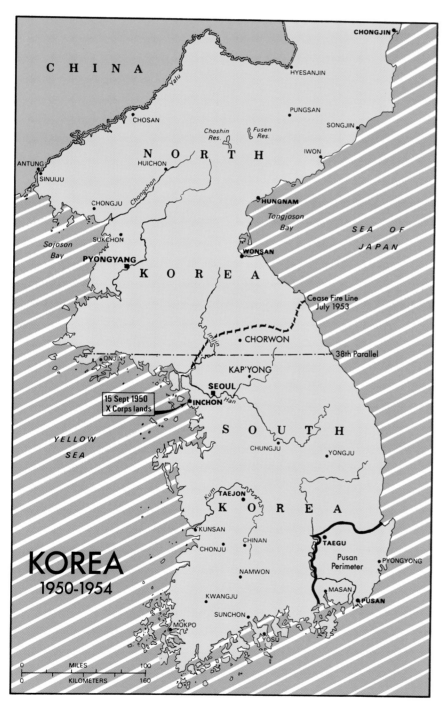

KOREA 1950-1954

The Canadian Korea Medal, awarded to all men with one or more days service on the posted strength of a unit in Korea.

The United Nations Service Medal — Korea, awarded to troops of all nations' forces under United Nations command in Korea or Japan. The inscription on medals issued to Canadians could be in English or French.

The United States was jolted out of its complacency in the early morning hours of 25 June 1950 when ten North Korean divisions, led by T-34 tanks and supported by over 1600 artillery pieces, brushed aside the ROK army and swept south. The attack seemed to confirm the views of hardline members of US President Harry Truman's administration. In the spring of 1950 a joint State and Defense Department study, NSC-68, had recommended a massive military buildup of American nuclear and conventional forces to deter Soviet aggression and contain any attempts at Communist expansion. The attack on South Korea convinced Truman that the 'Red menace' had to be met with military force wherever freedom was threatened.

As the South Korean capital of Seoul fell to the Communist invaders on 27 June, a US-sponsored resolution was presented to the United Nations Security Council recommending "that the members of the United Nations furnish such assistance to the Republic of Korea as may be necessary to repel the armed attack and to restore international peace and security in the area." A Soviet boycott of the council's proceedings prevented the USSR from exercising its veto. At his headquarters in Tokyo, General Douglas MacArthur, the Supreme Commander Allied Powers, was instructed to deploy the forces of his Far East Command in support of the ROK forces.

Washington's resolve to contain Communism was not matched by American military capabilities. The mighty war machine built up during the Second World War had been largely dismantled, while the buildup recommended in NSC-68 would take several years to implement. In the meantime, MacArthur's available ground force consisted of the four US divisions currently occupying Japan. These, however, were understrength and poorly trained for active operations. Indeed, the first of the divisions despatched to Korea, the 24th Infantry, was badly mauled in its initial encounters with the North Koreans in early July, and was scarcely battleworthy by month's end. It was soon joined on the peninsula by the 1st Cavalry and 25th Infantry Divisions which, together with the South Korean troops that remained, formed the US Eighth Army. By 1 August these forces had been driven into a defensive perimeter behind the Naktong River, in the southeast corner of the country, surrounding the city of Pusan.

New Year's Eve by Edward Zuber.

Zuber, who served in Korea with the Royal Canadian Regiment, produced the only first-hand Canadian artistic record of the war.
CWM 1986-158/7

Ottawa, meanwhile, was initially cautious in its response to the crisis. The Far East had never been an area of national interest, while Canada's most notable military involvement in Asia, the Hong Kong expedition of 1941, had ended in disaster. It was not an experience the Canadian government cared to repeat. Nevertheless, there was a growing feeling in the country that some sort of action had to be taken to support the United Nations and collective security. Responding to the pressure, Prime Minister Louis St. Laurent informed the House of Commons at the end of June that Canada would only participate as its "part in a collective police action under the control and authority of the United Nations." The government agreed to a United Nations' request to send two military observers — one army, one air force — to Korea to serve on a UN commission and announced that three RCN destroyers were to be despatched from Esquimalt to the Far East to cooperate with other UN naval forces. Three weeks later, it also agreed to allocate an RCAF transport squadron, No. 426, to operate its *North Star* aircraft between McCord Air Force Base, Washington and Japan.

RECRUITING THE SPECIAL FORCE

The Chief of the General Staff, Lieutenant-General Charles Foulkes, favoured a proposal to contribute an infantry brigade to a Commonwealth division, but recommended keeping the Mobile Striking Force intact for North American defence and recruiting a special force for service in Korea. With the UN forces hemmed in about Pusan, public and opposition pressure was mounting on the government to act. Finally, on 7 August, the Prime Minister announced to a nationwide radio audience that a Canadian Army Special Force would be recruited and "specially trained and equipped to be available for use in carrying out Canada's obligations under the United Nations charter or the North Atlantic pact." Fit young men would be required, preferably veterans of the Second World War. The decision to raise an entirely new force, however, meant that Canadian participation in the fighting would be delayed for many months. At least one officer, Lieutenant-Colonel F.E. White, who was witnessing the poor performance of the ROK and US forces in Korea as a member of the UN Commission, hoped "that our chaps don't arrive in time to participate in this shambles as it is without doubt the most... unfriendly little unpleasantness imaginable."

Recruiting offices across the country were swamped with applicants to join the Special Service Force as soon as the government announced that a brigade would be sent to Korea.
NAC

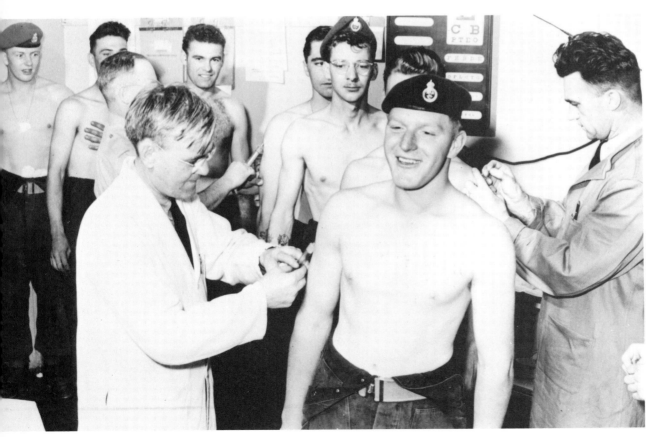

Recruits for the 2nd Battalion, Princess Patricia's Canadian Light Infantry lined up for a battery of immunization shots.
Glenbow Museum PA-1599-6128

Having finally taken the decision to send a brigade to Korea, the government succumbed to the public's desire to make a military contribution as quickly as possible and proceeded to fill the ranks of the Special Force with undue haste. The day after the Prime Minister's radio announcement, recruiting offices across the country were swamped with volunteers eager to sign up. In the words of the official history:

... the situation was one that generated legend. But among the anomalies of this unique method of recruiting, the enlistment of a man with an artificial leg and one who was 72 years old stand out as highlights. There is at least one recorded case of a civilian who on impulse got on board a troop train in Ottawa with a newly enlisted friend and was found weeks later in Calgary, drilling with the PPCLI.

Men enlisted in the Special Force were members of the Canadian Army Active Force but were limited to an eighteen-month term of service. Since "the Army would not wish to retain the "soldier of fortune type' of personnel on a long term basis," this allowed enlistment standards to be lowered without affecting the recruits joining the regular battalions. As part of the Active Force, the new infantry units were organized as second battalions of the three existing regiments — the Royal Canadian Regiment, the Princess Patricia's Canadian Light Infantry, and the Royal 22e Régiment. The enrollment procedures, however, had an inevitable effect on the number of useful soldiers actually produced. By the time recruiting into the Special Force ended in March 1951, 10,218 men had been enlisted, of which 2230 had been discharged and 1521 had deserted. Nevertheless, a solid core of more than 7000 fit and keen young soldiers was created to defend Canada's interests in the Far East.

Private Heath Mathews, 2nd Battalion, Royal Canadian Regiment. One of the most widely known photos of Canadians in Korea, it has become symbolic of the hard-slogging infantryman's war.

RCR Museum

To lead the men of the Special Force, the Minister of National Defence, Brooke Claxton, asked that a veteran from civilian life be selected so as to be on the same footing as his men. Foulkes recommended the former commander of the 9th Canadian Infantry Brigade in northwest Europe, Brigadier John M. Rockingham, for the appointment. Rockingham was working as the superintendent of a British Columbia bus company, and engaged in a frustrating negotiation with the drivers' union, when he received a phone call from the Minister offering him the command. After informing his wife what was happening, 'Rocky' flew to Ottawa to begin the work of organizing the brigade.

**Major-General
John M. Rockingham**

Major-General John M. Rockingham enlisted in the Canadian Scottish Regiment in 1933 at the age of 22. He went overseas in 1940 with that regiment as a Lieutenant. In 1942 he was posted in the rank of Major to the Royal Hamilton Light Infantry, and was in command of the RHLI (4th Brigade, 2nd Division) in Normandy in early July 1944. In August 1944 he was promoted to the rank of Brigadier and given command of the 9th Infantry Brigade, which he led with distinction until the end of the war in Belgium, Holland and Germany. After the war he returned to British Columbia, where he held a number of senior management positions with public utilities. Having left the Army with a reputation as one of the most effective brigade commanders, he was asked by the Chief of the General Staff to return to the Army to take command of 25th Brigade as soon as the government had decided to commit forces to the United Nations in Korea in August 1950. Rockingham led 25th Brigade in action in Korea until April 1952. He chose to remain in the Regular Army, and attended the Imperial Defence College in England until December 1953 when he was given command of a recreated 1st Canadian Infantry Division. In 1957 he was appointed General Officer Commanding, Quebec Command, and in 1961 he took over as GOC Western Command. He retired from the Army in 1966.

The Commonwealth Division Commander with commanding officers of 25th Brigade units. Front: Major-General Cassels, Mr. Menzies (Liaison Mission, Tokyo), Brigadier Rockingham. Rear: Major Rochester, 57 Field Squadron, Lieutenant-Colonel J.A. Dextraze, 2 R22eR, Lieutenant-Colonel R.A. Keane, 2 RCR, Lieutenant-Colonel J.R. Stone, 2 PPCLI. NAC

In selecting his battalion commanders, Rockingham gave preference to civilian veterans but chose only two from several score applicants. They were, however, two of the best fighting infantrymen that the Canadian Army had produced during the Second World War. Lieutenant-Colonel J.R. Stone was a legend in the Loyal Edmonton Regiment, where he had risen from private to commanding officer, earning not only two DSO's and an MC but the universal respect of his soldiers. His familiarity with the Italian Apennines proved useful in Korea while commanding 2 PPCLI. Lieutenant-Colonel J.A. Dextraze, who had also been commissioned from the ranks, won his first DSO while commanding an infantry company in Normandy and another as the twenty-four year old commanding officer of Les Fusiliers Mont-Royal in Germany. He took command of 2 R22eR. The command of 2 RCR went to a Permanent Force officer, Lieutenant-Colonel R.A. Keane, DSO, who had commanded the Lake Superior Regiment (Motor) of the 4th Canadian Armoured Division.

By the end of August, some 8000 men had enlisted in the Special Force. To reduce the time needed to prepare the troops for combat, the infantry, armour and artillery units of the Special Force were to train under the supervision of the corresponding 'parent' unit of the Active Force while engineer, signal and ordnance troops were sent to their respective corps schools. These arrangements allowed most units to begin functioning as separate entities by mid-October under the command of their own officers. As encouraging as this progress was, no specific date was assigned for the completion of training, in large part because of a determination by all concerned not to repeat the mistake made a decade earlier when two undertrained infantry battalions were sacrificed in Hong Kong. In the end, the decision as to when the Special Force would be ready for Korea was left to its commander.

Early on in the process, authorities in Ottawa recognized that a warmer location would have to be found to train the brigade during the winter months. After rejecting possible sites in Okinawa, California and Alabama, a US Army base near Seattle, Washington was agreed upon. The various units of the Special Force arrived at Fort Lewis throughout November to begin advanced training and brigade-level exercises. Once concentrated, they were officially designated as the 25th Canadian Infantry Brigade. Even as these arrangements were being made, however, events in Korea were altering Canadian plans.

Private Steven Towstego, 2 PPCLI, shares a drumstick with Korean children, Christmas 1950.

NAC/PA-151514

Royal Canadian Army Service Corps trucks taking supplies forward along a mountain road north of Pusan, January 1951.

NAC/PA-133339

THE PATRICIAS IN KOREA

While the US Eighth Army stabilized its defensive perimeter around Pusan in late August, General MacArthur had begun planning a daring amphibious assault on the port city of Inchon, twenty miles west of Seoul and more than two hundred miles away from the beleaguered UN forces to the southeast. Overcoming the scepticism of his military planners, MacArthur successfully landed X US Corps (consisting of the 7th Infantry and 1st Marine Divisions and an ROK Marine Regiment) at Inchon on 15 September. While the invasion forces advanced on the South Korea capital, the Eighth Army broke out from its lines and drove north. The two forces made contact on 27 September as the last Communist elements were forced out of Seoul.

The virtual collapse of North Korean resistance allowed the UN Command to mount a rapid pursuit towards the 38th parallel. On 28 September, ROK units began advancing into North Korea while American forces waited for the go-ahead from Washington. The American administration was convinced that Kim Il Sung's regime had to be destroyed, but were concerned about the impact that a UN invasion of the North would have on world opinion and the possibility that such a move would provoke the Chinese or Soviets to intervene. It was finally decided to give MacArthur the green light to proceed north of the parallel "provided that at the time of such operations there has been no entry in North Korea by major Soviet or Chinese Communist Forces."

The 1st US Cavalry Division began the advance north of the parallel on 10 October. Twelve days later, the Eighth Army had captured the capital of Pyongyang. North Korean resistance was now in total disarray and the victorious UN forces were able to continue their advance north towards the Yalu River and the border with China. The war seemed to be won.

2 PPCLI troops take up fire positions in a ditch near Pusan, 18 January 1951. NAC/PA-170785

These developments had an immediate impact on Canada's plans for the 25th Brigade. Following an interview with MacArthur, the head of the Canadian Military Mission, Far East, Brigadier F.J. Fleury, cabled Ottawa that the Supreme Commander now felt that the Canadian brigade would be of "no significance" in view of the current situation, but suggested that a "small token force" be sent to show the flag. The government agreed, and designated 2 PPCLI as the Canadian representative for what it now believed would be occupation duties only. Although the future employment of remaining units of the brigade was left up in the air, training was to continue unabated in the hope that firm discipline would counter any ill effects on morale.

The Patricias spent less than four days in Fort Lewis before embarking for Korea on 25 November. Lieutenant-Colonel Stone's unit was selected because its training schedule had been least disrupted by the railway strike, while Rockingham considered its commander to be "the most suitable CO to work in an independent role, far from Canada and subordinate to British and American formations." The battalion had yet to do any serious advanced training; that would have to await its arrival in the Far East. By the time the Patricias sailed into Pusan harbour one week before Christmas 1950, however, the conflict had become an entirely new war.

As MacArthur's forces advanced confidently towards the Yalu, the Communist Chinese government was preparing to take action. Undetected by US air reconnaissance, nearly 200,000 Chinese had moved across the Yalu and taken up positions half-way between Pyongyang and the Chinese border. On 25 October the ROK II Corps was attacked and routed by Chinese forces, while elements of the 1st Cavalry Division were similarly mauled on 1 November. Despite growing evidence that Peking was intervening in a massive way, McArthur did not believe that China posed a serious threat. A three-week lull in the fighting following the initial attacks led the Supreme Commander to suggest that the Chinese had shot their bolt. Announcing that the troops would be home by Christmas, a confident MacArthur launched a new offensive aimed at the Yalu on 24 November.

It proved to be a disastrous decision. Counterattacks by superior numbers of Communist troops soon forced the UN forces to retreat. As the Chinese, using infiltration tactics, surrounded units and interdicted the roads south, the retreat degenerated into a rout. In the east, the 1st Marine Division was almost encircled along the Chosin Reservoir and had to fight its way south to the port of Hungnam before being evacuated in late December. Pyongyang was soon abandoned as the Eighth Army continued its headlong retreat until the 16th, when defensive positions were finally established along the Imjin River north of Seoul.

Patricias on patrol, February 1951. NAC/PA-115034

Men of B Company, 2 PPCLI, moving
forward through a Korean village,
February 1951.
NAC/PA-115564

The crisis had an immediate impact on the 928 Patricias who disembarked at Pusan on 18 December 1950. Rather than remaining in the vicinity of the port to complete their training, the Eighth Army commander, General Walton Walker, ordered the Canadians to proceed to a training area near the city of Suwon, twenty miles south of Seoul, a move suggesting that the Americans were planning to commit the Patricias to combat before they were fully trained. With the Hong Kong disaster in mind, Stone's instructions from Ottawa had stipulated that he was "not to engage in such operations, except in self-defence, until you have completed the training of your command and are satisfied that your unit is fit for operations." Although Stone was most reluctant to begin his relationship with the Americans by refusing an operational commitment, he had little choice. After producing a copy of those instructions, Walker agreed to grant the eight week training period that Stone considered necessary.

The Patricias' initial impressions of Korea and its people differed little from those of most westerners. Immediately noticeable was the stench that hung over the countryside, a result of the centuries old practice of fertilizing rice paddies with human waste. Canadians were also struck by how little the Koreans seemed to value human life. Brigadier Rocking-ham remembered one incident when a Korean truck struck and killed a young child. "The driver got out of his cab and dragged the child by its foot to the side of the road and then headed back to his truck. The ROK truck was being followed by several Canadians who would not let the Korean just drive away. I intervened in the incident and made a report to the Korean army. They didn't actually say 'so what' but managed to convey that impression."

Private John Hoskins, 2 PPCLI, during the advance
on Hill 419, 24 February 1951.
PPCLI Museum

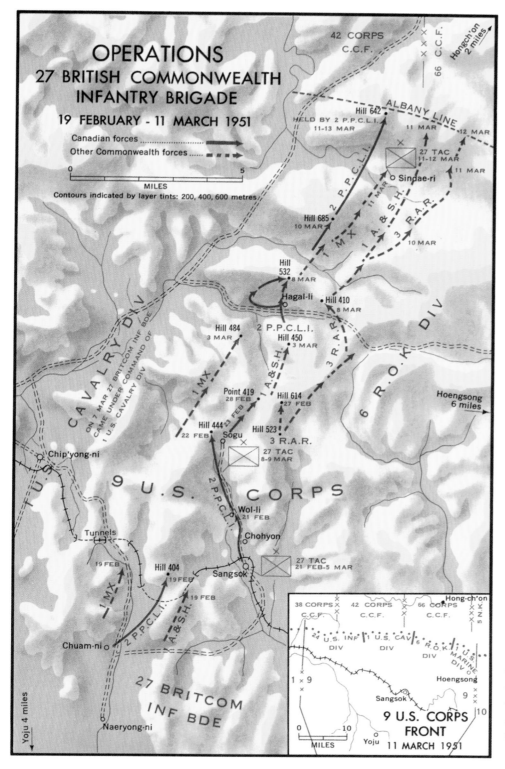

**OPERATIONS
27 BRITISH COMMONWEALTH
INFANTRY BRIGADE
19 FEBRUARY - 11 MARCH 1951**

Canadian forces ....
Other Commonwealth forces ....

0   MILES   5

Contours indicated by layer tints: 200, 400, 600 metres

42 CORPS
C.C.F.

Hongch'on 2 miles

66   C.C.F.

ALBANY LINE

Hill 642
HELD BY 2 P.P.C.L.I.
11-13 MAR   11 MAR   12 MAR

27 TAC
11-12 MAR

Sindae-ri   11 MAR

Hill 685
10 MAR

1 MX   1 A. & S.H.   3 R.A.R.

10 MAR

Hill 532
8 MAR

Hagal-li   Hill 410
8 MAR

Hill 484
3 MAR

2 P.P.C.L.I.
Hill 450
3 MAR

Point 419
28 FEB

Hill 614
27 FEB

Hill 444
22 FEB

Sogu

Hill 523

3 R.A.R.

27 TAC
8-9 MAR

Hoengsong
6 miles

Chip'yong-ni

9 U.S. CORPS

CAVALRY DIV
ON 7 MAR 27 BRITCOM INF BDE CAME UNDER COMMAND OF 1 U.S. CAVALRY DIV

1 MX

2 P.P.C.L.I.

Wol-li
21 FEB

Chohyon

6 R.O.K. DIV

Tunnels

19 FEB

Hill 404
19 FEB

Sangsok
19 FEB

27 TAC
21 FEB-5 MAR

1 MX

Chuam-ni

2 P.P.C.L.I.

A. & S.H.

**27 BRITCOM
INF BDE**

Naeryong-ni

Yoju 4 miles

38 CORPS   42 CORPS   66 CORPS   Hong-ch'on
C.C.F.   C.C.F.   C.C.F.   N.K.

24 U.S. INF   1 U.S. CAV   R.O.K.   U.S.
DIV   DIV   DIV   MARINE DIV

1 x 9

Sangsok   9

Hoengsong

0   10   10

MILES   Yoju

**9 U.S. CORPS
FRONT
11 MARCH 1951**

After spending Christmas in Pusan, the PPCLI spent six productive weeks training along the Miryang River. By mid-February Stone considered his men to be battle ready and the battalion was assigned to the 27th British Commonwealth Infantry Brigade, an experienced formation that had taken part in the breakout from Pusan in September. The brigade consisted of an Australian and two British battalions supported by a New Zealand artillery regiment, all under the command of a British general. The Patricias joined the brigade just as it was preparing to take part in the Eighth Army's counteroffensive to force the Communists back to the Han River. The Chinese drive south had been halted in mid-January, but not until Seoul had once again fallen into enemy hands. On 21 February the Eighth Army, now under the command of Lieutenant-General Matthew B. Ridgway, began its advance behind the firepower of massed artillery and air strikes.

The 27th Brigade moved northeast along a typical line of Korean hills some thirty miles west of Seoul. On the 22nd, the Patricias suffered their first casualties, four killed and one wounded, during a two-platoon attack on Hill 444, one of many numbered features for which Canadians would die in the ensuing twenty-nine months of combat. Over the next three weeks the brigade made a deliberate advance of eleven miles against the stubborn resistance of well dug-in Chinese soldiers. By 9 March, however, the enemy had broken contact and retreated, leaving the brigade free to advance to its objectives by the 13th. These initial battles cost the Canadians fifty-seven casualties, including fourteen dead, but left them in high spirits. They also outlined a number deficiencies. Stone cabled Ottawa that his troops:

...show lack of basic training, particularly in caring for weapons and equipment. Much 'scruff' that was hastily recruited has now been returned to Canada. Troops here are fit, morale high, show lots of guts in close contact.... Officers are generally good but junior ranks show need of a company commanders school.

Guns of the 2nd Regiment Royal Canadian Horse Artillery, providing fire support to 2 RCR, June 1951.

NAC/PA-128280

The 27th Commonwealth Brigade returned to the offensive at the end of March with a methodical advance up the valley of the Kap'yong River. The Patricias crossed the 38th parallel on 8 April, meeting only sporadic resistance in occupying their objective, a two mile-long ridge extending north from the *Kansas* line, on the 16th. Early in the operation, the battalion was visited by Brigadier Rockingham who was in Korea to gain a first-hand appreciation of the situation prior to the despatch of the rest of the Canadian brigade. An entire day spent scrambling up the rugged hillsides to visit each company position gave him some idea of the difficulties. Twenty-five days in the high hills of Korea also took its toll on the Patricias and, although no major actions took place, the troops were reported to be "in no condition to continue their advance without rest."

Their enemy, on the other hand, demonstrated considerable skill in fieldcraft — being for the most part battle-hardened veterans of the Chinese civil war — but lacked heavy weapons. Those they did have had either been captured from the Japanese or were American arms taken from the nationalist *Kuomintang*. In many respects the Chinese were still tied to a guerrilla style of warfare and lacked the communications to operate cohesively beyond the regimental level. The unsophisticated nature of their army did have some advantages, however. The Chinese soldier required only eight to ten pounds of supplies per day as opposed to the sixty pounds used by his UN counterpart, a matter of some significance given the fact that supplies could only be moved at night (to avoid air attack) and generally had to be carried south by tens of thousands of porters.

By mid-March, the Communist forces were in retreat all along the front. Seoul was liberated for a second time on the 15th as the enemy withdrew to fortified positions north of the 38th parallel. This retreat once again raised questions about the United Nations' war aims: whether to drive the Communists out of all Korea and risk a general war with China, or simply to contain the enemy north of the dividing line. While Washington and her allies opted for the safer course, MacArthur issued several inflammatory statements advocating all-out war. Truman reacted to this challenge by firing the controversial general on 11 April and replacing him with General Ridgway.

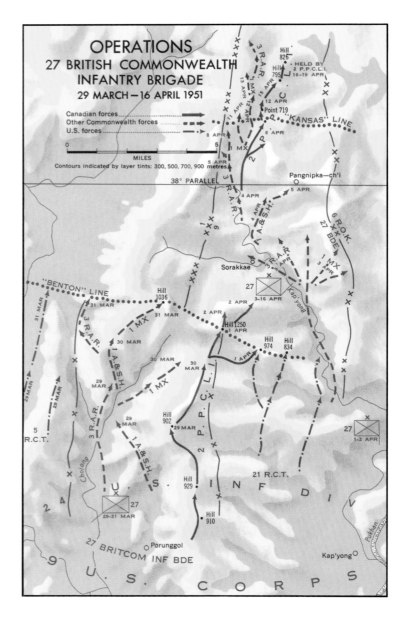

OPERATIONS
27 BRITISH COMMONWEALTH
INFANTRY BRIGADE
29 MARCH – 16 APRIL 1951

KAP'YONG

With the occupation of the *Kansas* line, the entire Eighth Army was now north of the 38th parallel except for a small portion on the Republic's west coast that lay north of the Imjin River. The light opposition encountered during their advance was due to the enemy's deliberate withdrawal to prepared positions. By 20 April battle-weary Chinese and North Korean formations had been replaced at the front by fresh troops from the 3rd Chinese Field Army. The 27th Brigade, meanwhile, had been relieved by the 6th ROK Division and placed in IX Corps reserve immediately north of the village of Kap'yong, some thirty miles behind the front line.

When a new Chinese offensive opened on 22 April 1951, it completely routed the South Koreans and sent them streaming south down the Kap'yong valley past the 27th Brigade. The positions held by the Commonwealth troops on Hills 677 and 504, astride the river, "effectively controlled all entrances to and exits from the valley" and "could not have been better chosen as a place to hold open an escape route." The Patricias held the higher of the two hills on the western side of the valley while the other was occupied by the Royal Australian Regiment and a company of US tanks. By nightfall on the 23rd, as the last remnants of the 6th ROK Division passed down the valley, the Australians were attacked by leading elements of the Chinese 118th Division. Dug in on their own hill, the Canadians could only watch and listen to the battle being waged across the valley. The Australians put up a hard fight, but by late afternoon of the 24th, with their company positions infiltrated and battalion headquarters under attack, 3 RAR was given permission to pull back, each company commander being ordered "to bring out their troops as best they could."

In the front line near the Han River, 20 May 1951.
NAC/PA-178946

Silent Night
by Edward Zuber.
CWM 1989-0328-009

The withdrawal left the Canadians on Hill 677 as the forward unit in the brigade's defences, with both of its flanks open to the enemy. Immediately south of 2 PPCLI was the 1st Battalion of the 5th US Cavalry Regiment. The remaining units of the brigade were held in reserve. The Patricias' company positions had been assigned by Stone after a careful reconnaissance of the feature. D Company was placed immediately west of the hill's summit, with B Company on the forward slope to the north, C Company to its right and A Company covering the northeastern flank.

In response to the withdrawal of the Australians on the evening of the 24th, Stone shifted B Company from the northern slope to the southeastern side nearest the river to cover the battalion's exposed flank. They did not have long to prepare their new positions. At 2200 hours mortar and machine-gun fire was opened on the company followed shortly after by a series of wave attacks against the forward platoon. When their position was overrun, the men were forced to fight their way back to the main company.

While B Company was heavily engaged, about one hundred Chinese infiltrated through to attack battalion headquarters, but were driven off by the concentrated fire of .50 calibre machine guns and 81-mm mortars. Shortly after 0100 hours, D Company, on the western side of the hill, was also attacked by successive waves of Chinese troops. The Chinese practice of using bugle calls to form up on the start line and commence an assault, together with the firing of tracer ammunition as a guide to the objective, usually gave a company commander sufficient warning to call in artillery and mortar fire and break up these formations. By sheer weight of numbers, however, the enemy succeeded in infiltrating D Company, completely overrunning one platoon and killing two machine-gun crews in their weapons pits. After assuring battalion headquarters that his own men were well dug-in, the company commander called in an artillery barrage on his own positions. The air bursts drove the enemy back down the hill. Although sporadic attacks continued until dawn on the 25th, the Chinese could not dislodge the Patricias.

The 2nd Battalion, Royal 22e Régiment prepare to board a train for Seoul and the front, Pusan, May 1951.

R22eR Museum

In daylight the Canadians found themselves completely isolated, as the Communists had cut the only road to the rear. Supplies had to be parachuted in to the battalion by four C-119 transports until the Chinese pulled back at 1400 hours and contact with the rest of the brigade was re-established. By late afternoon, most Chinese activity had ceased as they awaited developments on other sectors of the front. To the Canadians' great relief, casualties amounted to only ten killed and twenty-three wounded. Although the position had been skillfully organized and defended, Lieutenant-Colonel Stone offered the best explanation for the surprisingly low casualty total.

Kapyong was not a great battle as battles go; yet it was a good battle, well-planned and well-fought. In retrospect, however, it would appear that Kapyong was the intended limit of the Chinese offensive. Had that limit been eight kilometres further south, in all probability the 2 PPCLI would have been annihilated. The numbers that the Chinese were prepared to sacrifice against a position meant that eventually any unsupported battalion in defence must be overrun. The Chinese soldier is tough and brave. All that he lacked at Kapyong were communications and supply. The Patricias were fortunate that he did not persist in his attacks.

Further to the west, the other British brigade in Korea, the 29th, was not so fortunate. It was defending the direct road to Seoul along the south bank of the Imjin River when it was attacked by three Chinese divisions and suffered one thousand casualties, including one battalion of The Gloucester Regiment that was virtually eliminated, losing 670 of the 850 men it took into the fight. Their stand, however, together with that of the Australians and Canadians, helped to stem the Communist offensive. By 1 May, the Eighth Army had ended its retreat and was once again planning another advance to the 38th parallel.

For their part in the action at Kap'yong, 2 PPCLI was awarded the Distinguished Unit Citation by the United States government, the only unit in the Canadian Army ever to receive that honour. Following the battle the 27th Brigade was re-organized, with the two British battalions being replaced by others, and was renumbered as the 28th British Commonwealth Infantry Brigade. The Patricias remained with the new brigade, occupying a series of defensive positions until the end of May, at which time they were finally able to rejoin the formation they had originally left six months before.

Troops of A Company, 2 RCR moving forward to positions in the front line.
NAC/PA-129742

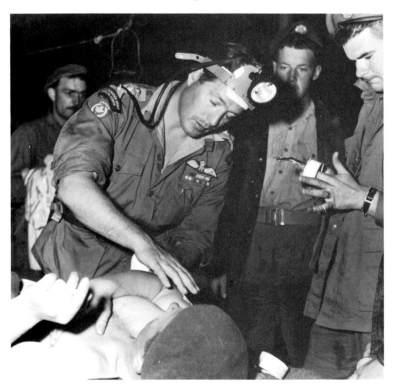

2RCR casualties being treated at 25 Canadian Field Hospital, 20 May 1951.
NAC/PA-178947

THE CANADIAN BRIGADE ARRIVES

The balance of the 25th Canadian Infantry Brigade Group, its training at Fort Lewis completed, arrived at Pusan on 4 May 1951 after a two-week voyage across the Pacific. After unpacking their equipment, the Canadians headed for the front to take part in the advance back to the *Kansas* line. As the two battalions arrived in their concentration area near Hwach'on in the early hours of 19 May, however, Rockingham was ordered to relieve an American unit holding positions on the Han River, east of Seoul, at 0900 hours that morning. Since most of the equipment for his infantry was still en route, the Canadian commander was unwilling to commit his troops to combat until they were completely ready. His instructions from Canada allowed for a direct reference to be made to the Chief of the General Staff "should orders be given to commit Canadian troops in an operation which, in his opinion, would involve unnecessarily large casualties." Rockingham protested the order to both Corps and Army headquarters, and was prepared to refer the matter to Ottawa when it was cancelled.

The Canadian brigade did not take an active part in the offensive until five days later when it was placed under the command of the 25th US Division during its advance north of Seoul. On 29 May the Canadians encountered only light resistance in crossing the 38th parallel. The brigade's first major action came on the 30th during an abortive attack by 2 RCR on the village of Chail-li. The battalion's attempt to capture the area's dominant feature, Hill 467, by a flanking movement was easily defeated by the enemy's infiltration tactics (which isolated companies from each other), and the Royals were forced to withdraw under heavy fire at a cost of six men killed and twenty-five wounded.

After this engagement the brigade was placed in reserve, together with the British 29th Independent Infantry Brigade and the 28th British Commonwealth Infantry Brigade, in anticipation of the formation of the 1st Commonwealth Division. Within the divisional setup, Rockingham was to retain administrative control of all the former units of the brigade group, but would have operational control only of the three infantry battalions and the armoured squadron. Other units, such as the 2nd Regiment, Royal Canadian Horse Artillery and the 57th Independent Field Squadron, Royal Canadian Engineers, were placed under divisional control, although for the most part they continued to be used in support of the 25th Brigade.

Patricias cross the Imjin River in assault boats, June 1951. NAC/PA-132638

Prior to the 1st Commonwealth Division becoming operational on 28 July, however, the Canadians carried out a number of tasks while attached to other formations. The Patricias returned briefly to the 28th Brigade from 6 to 11 June in order to establish a 'patrol base' across the Imjin River north of its junction with the Hantan. This base was used to launch reconnaissance patrols into a salient formed by the bend in the Imjin River where it turns from south to west and flows into the Yellow Sea. The salient was to feature prominently in the operations of the 25th Brigade over the next two years. The PPCLI were relieved in the bridgehead on 11 June by 2 R22eR. On 18 June the Canadians were placed under the operational control of the 1st US Cavalry Division and took over a section of the front southwest from the city of Ch'orwon. For the next month the brigade mounted a series of large patrols — usually consisting of at least one infantry company, a troop of tanks, an artillery battery and a troop of engineers — to probe the enemy's forward positions.

2 RCHA guns in action near Chorwon, 21 June 1951. NAC/PA-128867

355

ACROSS THE IMJIN

Following its formation at the end of July 1951, the 1st Commonwealth Division held a front that extended westward from the Imjin-Hantan river junction, with the 29th British and 28th Commonwealth Brigades in the line, and the 25th Brigade in reserve. The Chinese positions were five to six miles back from the Imjin, forming a large No-Man's-Land within the curve of the river. Throughout August the Canadians conducted several reconnaissances-in-force into the salient to establish the enemy's intentions and capabilities. They patrolled as far as Hills 187 and 208, some seven miles into the salient, without encountering any significant opposition.

The lack of enemy reaction undoubtedly influenced the subsequent decision to advance the divisional front and set up permanent positions north and west of the Imjin to eliminate the salient. Operation *Minden* commenced on 11 September and involved a modest three mile advance to the *Wyoming* line. Canadian casualties of only three killed and ten wounded attest to the absence of a determined enemy. There followed a two week period of consolidation, and the construction of supply roads running forward from the two high-level bridges constructed by US engineers over the Imjin.

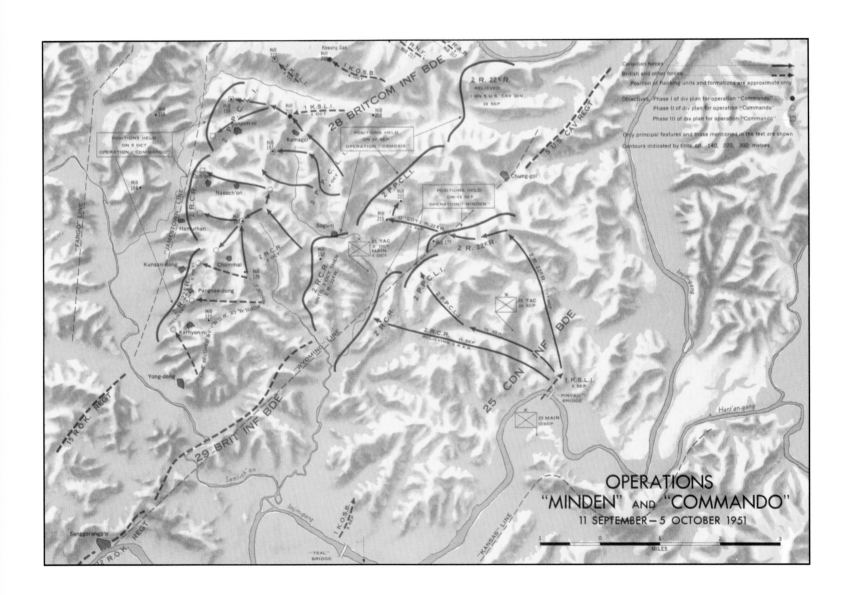

OPERATIONS
"MINDEN" AND "COMMANDO"
11 SEPTEMBER – 5 OCTOBER 1951

Brigadier Rockingham discusses operations with officers of the Patricias, 7 October 1951.
NAC/PA-128875

Even as *Minden* was completed, Eighth Army was planning a further advance of 6000 to 8000 yards to the *Jamestown* line, northwest of *Wyoming*, by all four divisions of I US Corps, of which lst Commonwealth Division was one, and the 25th Division of IX US Corps. The move was intended to drive the Communists off their winter line of defences and force them to dig in on less favourable ground. One of the Commonwealth Division's key objectives was Hill 355, the dominant feature within the salient, while the portion of *Jamestown* assigned to the Canadians ran along the valley of an un-named tributary of the Sami-ch'on River. At the northern end of the valley the line turned east past Hill 355 and on to the Imjin.

The operation, codenamed *Commando*, began on 3 October with an attack by the 28th British Commonwealth Brigade, on the division's right, aimed at Hills 227, 355 and 317. H-Hour for the 25th Brigade came at 1100 hours the following day, with 2 RCR advancing on the left and 2 PPCLI on the right, while 2 R22eR was held in reserve. The RCR encountered little serious opposition in reaching their objectives by 5 October, while the Patricias had a tougher fight capturing Hill 187 on the way to theirs. The 28th Brigade, meanwhile, had to overcome a more determined enemy in securing its key hills, a fact reflected in the casualty totals. The Canadians escaped with only four killed and twenty-eight wounded, while the division's totals were fifty-eight dead and 262 wounded.

STALEMATE

With the Hwachon reservoir that supplied both water and electric power for Seoul securely in UN hands by mid-October, Washington now felt that the territorial gains made during *Commando* formed an acceptable demarcation line for the two Koreas — provided that a suitable truce could be negotiated with the Communists. More importantly, the political will needed to launch a full-scale invasion of the North, with the enormous casualties that such an offensive would entail, no longer existed in the West. Truce talks that had broken off in August were resumed on 25 October in the village of Panmunjom located in the No-Man's-Land between the two armies. On 12 November the Eighth Army's commander, General James Van Fleet, was ordered to refrain from taking any major offensive action and restrict his forces to defending their existing front. Local attacks were still permitted, in order to sustain morale and demonstrate a continuing will to fight, but no operation larger than battalion strength could be mounted without Ridgeway's approval.

Sensing the growing war-weariness of Western public opinion, the governments in Peking and Pyongyang were willing to drag out the negotiations indefinitely to test the UN's resolve. While they did so, the Communist armies, free from the threat of a major UN offensive, tunnelled deep into the Korean hillsides to create defensive positions that were impregnable to artillery fire, and forming a barrier fifteen to twenty-five miles in depth along the entire 155 mile front. By the end of December the strength of their defences allowed the Communist negotiators to adopt an uncompromising stance at the peace talks. They were confident that their lines could not be easily broken, while their own armies mounted enough offensive operations to maintain a steady flow of UN casualties.

Van Doo soldiers use Strathcona tanks as taxis when moving out of the line. The trucks waiting for them are from 54 Company, RCASC.
NAC/PA-129108

Bowling Alley by Edward Zuber.
A typical mountainside defensive position in Korea.
CWM 1986-158/11

Along the Commonwealth Division front, the Chinese reacted to the *Commando* advance by mounting a series of probing attacks throughout late-October and November, aimed at retaking the more prominent hills. On 4 November a Chinese attack against the 28th Brigade succeeded in recapturing Hills 217 and 317 on the right flank nearest the Imjin River. A British counterattack failed to dislodge the enemy, and both features remained in Communist hands for the remainder of the war. The 25th Brigade held off repeated attacks from 2-6 November, most of which were largely broken up by artillery and mortar fire before they reached the forward positions. Those Chinese determined enough to continue the advance through the shelling were driven off by Bren-gun and rifle fire. A determined attack against Hill 355 later in the month was defeated by 2 R22eR and an American battalion of the 3rd Division. The loss of 'Little Gibraltar' would have necessitated a withdrawal from that section of the *Jamestown* line under its observation.

2 R22eR soldiers take cover when caught in the open by enemy fire, 23 October 1951.
R22eR Museum

Lieutenant-Colonel J.A. Dextraze (holding radio handset) controls the advance of 2 R22eR from his mobile headquarters, summer 1951.
R22eR Museum

For their part, the Canadians continued to mount several large patrols in order to inflict casualties and obtain information on the lay-out of enemy defences. One such raid was carried out at dawn on 23 October by one company from each of the three battalions. With the aid of supporting artillery and tank fire, two of the three companies reached their objectives on the main hilltops across the valley. The enemy's bunkers and trenches were then mined and booby-trapped before the Canadians withdrew in the early afternoon, having lost five killed and twenty-one wounded. While most of November was taken up in fending off Chinese attacks, another large raid was mounted on the night of 10-11 December by a company of Patricias and a 35-man fighting patrol from 2 RCR. As was often the case in these raids, the Canadians were unable to capture any prisoners. Since the raiders were loathe to follow the Chinese into their tunnels, they had to be satisfied with "testing and probing the enemy defences", a largely ineffective result for the effort expended.

A Canadian Engineer, with his Korean helper, prepares an explosive charge during road construction, February 1952.
NAC/PA-178895

Throughout this period the Commonwealth Division was under pressure from the American command to carry out more large raids "to show the enemy that we can still be offensive and to keep our soldiers sharp." This policy was resisted by General Cassels, however, who argued that "neither object was necessary so far as his troops were concerned." While patrolling remained a fact of life throughout the conflict, the Commonwealth division was never able — or willing — to match the expertise and daring exhibited by their Chinese opponents.

In mid-January 1952 the 25th Brigade was replaced in the line by the 28th Brigade and moved into divisional reserve. For the next seven weeks the Canadians prepared new positions along the *Wyoming* line astride the Sami-ch'on River, in anticipation of a possible withdrawal should an armistice be concluded at Panmunjom. Hopes that a quick end to hostilities could be arranged, however, foundered on the question of exchanging prisoners.

The war's longer than anticipated duration created a number of manpower problems for the authorities in Ottawa. Most of the Special Force had been recruited in August and September 1950 and the eighteen-month enlistment period was due to expire in the spring of 1952. Despite the terms of service that governed its individual soldiers, the units of the 25th Brigade were regarded as permanent elements of the Active Force. The need to provide sufficient soldiers to fill the ranks of both the Mobile Striking Force in Canada and the 27th Brigade in Europe only made the situation worse. The government hoped to ease the manpower shortage by re-enlisting the 'soldiers of fortune' of the Special Force under Active Force regulations, but their efforts met with only limited success as fewer than 2850 of the more than 10,000 Special Force volunteers chose to become regular soldiers.

A further complication resulted from the American and British policies that required soldiers to spend no more than one winter in Korea. Following suit, the CGS decided to replace entire units in Korea after one year's service. It was felt that this method of rotation would promote greater unit cohesion than the American practice of replacing soldiers on an individual basis. The first rotation began in October 1951 when two companies of 1 PPCLI arrived to take over from two companies of the 2nd Battalion. The entire 'handover' was completed by 10 November.

Brigadier M.P. Bogert is briefed on the Patricia defensive layout during the handover from Brigadier Rockingham. RCR Museum

A Company, 2 RCR preparing to move from a reserve position into the front line, March 1952. NAC/PA-129770

Men of 23 Transport Company, Royal Canadian Army Service Corps arrive in Korea to replace 54 Company, 10 April 1952. NAC/PA-178897

When the 25th Brigade returned to the front line on 9 March 1952, its other units had only a few weeks remaining of their service in Korea. Advance parties for 1 RCR and 1 R22eR flew to the peninsula later that month, while the main bodies followed by sea. The 1st battalions were sent to the Far East under strength, and were brought up to establishment by absorbing those men of the 2nd battalions who were not yet eligible for rotation. Two days after the 1st battalions took over their front line positions on 25 April, Rockingham handed over command of the brigade to Brigadier M.P. Bogert, a pre-1939 regular whose experience in Italy during the Second World War included command of The West Nova Scotia Regiment and the 2nd Infantry Brigade. In the next several weeks, the engineers of the 57th Field Squadron were relieved by those of the 23rd; No. 25 Canadian Field Ambulance was replaced by No. 37; the 2nd Regiment, RCHA by the 1st; and C Squadron, Lord Strathcona's Horse was rotated with B Squadron.

One of Bogert's first acts as brigade commander, however, created a political furor in Ottawa. In mid-May the UN Command had requested that the Commonwealth Division furnish two companies of infantry to guard prisoners-of-war on the Korean island of Koje-do. Complying with the order, Bogert assigned B Company 1 RCR to the job, and promptly informed Ottawa of the development. Events on Koje-do over the previous year gave any Canadian involvement on the island a far greater political than military implication. By the spring of 1952, some 70,000 North Korean and Chinese prisoners had been crowded into thirty-seven large, adjoining compounds on the island where, guarded by poorly disciplined US and South Korean servicemen, they were left to run their own affairs inside the wire. Throughout the winter of 1951-52, Communist fanatics within the camps had intimidated their fellow prisoners into staging large-scale riots to protest the American policy of screening out Korean prisoners who wished to remain in the south. As a propaganda tool designed to portray the United Nations as brutal murderers of unarmed prisoners, the Communists scored a major coup. Several guards and more than one hundred prisoners were killed in the disturbances which climaxed on 7 May with the seizure of the American camp commandant. Although he was released unharmed three days later, the entire unsavoury affair had received a bad press, not least of all in the Canadian media.

TACTICAL DIFFICULTIES

The American attempt to share the world's disapproval with their UN allies did not sit well with the Canadian government. As the official history candidly admits, Ottawa's "determination to follow a UN line, rather than a US one, did not extend to the assumption of a portion of the blame for what appeared to be a very lax and inefficient prisoner of war operation." While the Canadian government agonized over its response, the RCR company on Koje-do had a relatively uneventful two months of guard duty, despite continuing violence at other camps. Together with a British company, the Canadians restored order within their assigned compound and even managed a peaceful transfer of their prisoners to a new camp before returning to the 25th Brigade in mid-July.

By the time the regular soldiers of the 1st battalions had assumed their place in the line in May 1952, the stalemated pattern of the ground war was firmly established. Offensive operations, by both sides, were confined to company or platoon-sized raids, backed by artillery and mortar fire, of the other sides' defences. In organizing their defensive positions, the Commonwealth Division had relied on laying extensive minefields across their front to slow down an attack and provide time for artillery fire to defeat it. It was discovered, however, that Chinese skill in reconnaissance negated the effectiveness of the minefields, which soon proved to be as much a handicap to the defenders as they were to the enemy. To avoid their own mines, Commonwealth patrols had to enter No-Man's-Land through clearly marked gaps. However, when patrols moved out through a gap they inevitably found a party of Chinese waiting in ambush at the far end. Infantry also had to contend with enemy artillery targeted on the gaps through which they hoped to get back to their lines, often leaving as an unattractive alternative a return directly through one of the division's minefields.

B Squadron of the Strathconas at Teal Bridge on the Imjin River, just after taking over from C Squadron, June 1952. LdSH Museum

Since mines proved such a poor defence against the Chinese, reliance had to be placed on aggressive patrolling to keep the enemy on their own side of the valley. Unfortunately, the brigade's ability to patrol effectively left much to be desired. Although it was set up too late to have much effect, a brigade patrol school was opened on 25 May 1953 in an attempt to correct some of the faults. The officer in charge of the school, Major W. H. Pope, a soldier with considerable experience in Korea, held a dim view of the Canadians' performance, stating in June 1953 that:

... for the past year and more the enemy has held the tactical initiative in no-man's-land. He has raided our outposts and forward positions and ambushed our patrols at will. We, on the other hand, with only one or two exceptions, have not carried out any successful operations forward of our lines.

Part of the difficulty lay in the daily expectation that a cease-fire was about to be concluded at Panmunjom and the resulting "humane desire of commanders to avoid risking lives in the possible last days before an armistice [that] has led to a purely defensive patrolling policy of which more aggressive enemy commanders have taken full advantage." By employing specially trained troops on reconnaissance patrols, the Chinese had a detailed knowledge of Commonwealth forward positions and activities before launching a raid. The enemy also never sent "out more than one to three men recce [reconnaissance] patrols, unless he has sufficient men of a well-trained reserve or patrol company standing by to ensure his retaining control of the battlefield once contact has been made."

The Canadian brigade, on the other hand, employed outposts in No-Man's-Land to provide warning of an enemy attack. Each night three to four men would occupy the outpost positions which quickly:

... became well marked not only by the telephone lines leading to them but also by the quantity of empty tins of self-heating soup and the occasional beer bottle surrounding them... [so that] the enemy always knew where they were. They have therefore furnished a most convenient source of prisoners to the enemy. Certainly they provided early warning of the enemy's approach but when the approach was merely to the outpost position for the purpose of successfully raiding it, this early warning became a dubious advantage.

The Canadians' fighting patrols, those that were intended either to raid enemy positions or ambush his patrols, were equally unsuccessful. One of the brigade's few successful patrols was carried out by a six man RCR team led by Lieutenant H.R. Gardner. Setting out before dawn on 24 September 1952, Gardner led his men behind enemy lines along a path he had reconnoitred two weeks earlier during a forty-eight hour lay-up patrol. Positioning four of his men as a 'firm base' along his intended line of retreat, Gardner and Corporal K.E. Fowler, who had accompanied him on the earlier patrol, proceeded along a covered path to a field kitchen where they managed to subdue a Chinese prisoner and return safely to their own lines.

Troops of 1 R22eR march along a muddy path through rice paddies, April 1953.
R22eR Museum

The field defences originally constructed along the Jamestown line had, to a considerable extent, been determined by the relative absence of Chinese artillery. Open fire bays, light wiring and shallow trenches were all that were required to protect against Communist small-arms fire. When the Chinese settled in to their defensive positions during the winter of 1951-52, however, they were able to bring forward their artillery and mortars. As their volume of fire increased, the Canadian senior operations officer at Division Headquarters, Lieutenant-Colonel E.A.C. Amy, noted that "a certain uneasiness was apparent in the division." By the spring of 1952, the Chinese were able to "concentrate one hundred guns to blanket a single company position. The only defence of a company so bombarded is to crawl into the bunkers or crouch beneath the overhead cover of the fire bays and try to stay alive until the Chinese infantry are on the position. Then it becomes a matter of extremely close-range fighting, sometimes even hand-to-hand." Major W.H. Pope also felt their were serious problems, noting that "our 'counterattacks' always went in after the enemy had withdrawn.... Without doubt the enemy's ability to raid successfully our strongest platoon and even company positions adversely affected our morale."

Despite the rather sombre picture presented, it should be noted that the vast majority of Communist attacks were mere raids and were not meant to seize and hold ground. The *Jamestown* line itself was not seriously threatened by the enemy, while Commonwealth troops could take some satisfaction from the great many Chinese that were undoubtedly killed by artillery and mortar fire. Nevertheless, the division's shortcomings had an unsettling effect. In Colonel Amy's view, it was the attack against B Company 1 RCR, defending Hill 355 on 23-24 October 1952 that "supplied a clear warning. It was obvious then that the Chinaman could smash our defences almost any time he chose."

A Nursing Sister and medical orderlies in a field dressing station. CDQ

Incoming by Edward Zuber. Enemy artillery fire on the *Jamestown* line position of B Company, 1RCR, prior to the Chinese attack on Hill 355 on 23 October 1952.
CWM 1989-0328-008

The enemy's preparations for this attack began with a heavy bombardment of the position during the first three days of the month. As recorded in the official history, the artillery fire destroyed one of the forward company's outposts, which was then abandoned. This allowed Chinese patrols to move in close enough to the forward slopes "to throw stones into the perimeter wire, a device which was probably intended to draw the defenders' fire and determine the defensive arrangements." By the time B Company moved into the forward positions at last light on the 22nd, "it found the field defences very badly damaged." Enemy shelling increased during the night and continued through the next day as weapons pits were buried, bunkers caved in, and telephone lines were cut. Just after sunset on the 23rd the Chinese "suddenly put down a tremendous concentration which lasted for eight to ten minutes. Then it lifted to the positions on the left and right, where it held for some 45 minutes, effectively sealing B Company off from its neighbours."

As the artillery shifted, the Chinese infantry moved onto the position. Those men who were able withdrew to the neighbouring companies. By 1943 hours it was evident "that no friendly troops remained in action" in B Company and the Commonwealth artillery shifted its fire from the forward slopes to the company area itself. At 2100 hours enemy artillery fire suddenly increased on the neighbouring companies. This was interpreted by the Canadians as signalling yet another attack, but was in all probability made to cover the Chinese withdrawal. The RCR counterattack, however, did not 'go in' until 0110 hours on the 24th. "After a brisk fire-fight during the approach, the left platoon [of D Company] moved into the former positions of No. 4 Platoon without meeting further opposition and the right platoon occupied the No. 5 Platoon area in the same manner. By 3:30 am the platoons had linked up and the situation was restored." RCR casualties in the engagement, the majority of which were sustained by B Company, amounted to eighteen killed, thirty-five wounded and fourteen captured.

Although the Canadians could claim a victory for having turned back another Chinese attack, Division Headquarters 'took the warning to heart' and instituted a programme to improve the division's field defences. Trenches were deepened to a minimum of six feet, overhead cover was provided for fire trenches and bays, and prefabricated concrete bunkers were put in place. At the end of November the division also redeployed its brigades, placing all three in the line, each with two battalions forward and one in reserve. It was hoped that by giving each brigade a complete sector in depth greater attention would be paid to improving their defences. The need for improvement, however, appears to have been greatest in the 25th Brigade area. While headquarters explained the redeployment as being necessary to eliminate a three-battalion front, "which was proving too much for [brigade commanders] to control properly," it seems that the actual

'One bottle per man per day.' Troops of 3 R22eR line up for their beer ration. R22eR Museum

reason had more to do with the numerous complaints headquarters was receiving from the other brigades every time they took over positions previously occupied by the Canadians. As the Australian historian Jeffrey Grey explains:

Canadian units tended to dispose of rubbish by the simple expedient of throwing it out in front of the wire. Since much of this consisted of empty ration tins and the like, it meant that the positions were clearly outlined in bright, reflective material easily visible to the Chinese and giving a good indication of the strength in which the position was held.... The Canadian brigade also tended to keep to itself, and officers of other nationalities on the divisional headquarters soon came to leave liaison with the brigade to the Canadians among them.

Of equal seriousness were some of the Canadian attitudes to operations. Their defensive positions were generally inadequate, and prompted complaints from battalions of other brigades.

First Kill, The Hook by Edward Zuber.
The Hook was the key feature of the Canadian defensive position on the Sami-ch'on River during the winter of 1952-53. CWM 1986-158/9

Following the redeployment, the Canadians took over the left sector of the division's front astride the Sami-ch'on River. The high ground to the west of the river, known throughout the division as the 'Hook', was the key feature on the left flank since it afforded observation into the lower Sami-ch'on valley. Its importance gave it priority in the construction of better field defences. The engineers of the 23rd Field Squadron spent December and January digging extensive tunnels that ran into the hill from the forward fire bays in each of the 'Hook' and 'Right of Hook' company positions. These served as shelters during heavy bombardments or as a refuge if the enemy succeeded in getting on to the position, thus allowing friendly artillery fire to clear the area. Although the Chinese did not attack the feature during the time that the Canadians occupied it, these defences proved essential to its successful defence by a British battalion in late May 1953 when, prior to concluding an armistice, the Communists attempted to force the division back to the Imjin by capturing the entire 'Hook' position.

At the end of January 1953, the Commonwealth Division was placed in corps reserve for the first time since its formation in July 1951. By the time it returned to its old positions in early April 1953, the 25th Brigade had largely completed its second rotation, as 3 RCR and 3 R22eR arrived to replace the 1st battalions. The 3rd battalions had been formed in January 1951 to train replacements for Korea and had managed the difficult task of melding into cohesive units despite a high turnover in personnel. The only major action the brigade was to see, however, occurred on the night of 2-3 May 1953 when C Company 3 RCR was heavily attacked on Hill 97, just north of the village of Hamurhan. Once again, the Chinese overran the position, killing twenty-six Canadians, wounding twenty-seven and capturing a further seven.

The new brigade commander, Brigadier Jean-Victor Allard, clearly viewed the engagement as a Canadian defeat and took immediate action to improve the brigade's defences and tactics, including setting up the patrol school. He also began a programme of moving the brigade's tanks into the valley each night and engaging selected Chinese positions at dawn in "a highly successful destructive shoot.... This special effort, combined with vigorous and aggressive patrolling, kept the Chinese on the far side of the river. Brigadier Allard felt that he had discovered the key to successful defence in Korea." Whether the lack of enemy activity was due to the new tactics or resulted from the Communists' intention finally to conclude an armistice is not known. Unfortunately, a Canadian commander willing to recognize the brigade's faults and take corrective action had arrived too late to have much of an impact on operations. The final weeks of active hostilities passed quietly in the Canadian sector until, at 2200 hours on 27 July 1953, the guns fell silent for the first time in over three years.

WITHDRAWAL

Under the terms of the agreement concluded at Panmunjom, the *Jamestown* line became the demarcation line separating the two Koreas. Each side had seventy-two hours in which to withdraw 2000 metres from its defensive positions. As confidence in the cease-fire grew in coming months, the Canadian brigade settled in to a more peaceful routine. The third general rotation, completed in the spring of 1954, also brought new units to Korea: battalions of The Black Watch (Royal Highland Regiment) of Canada, The Queen's Own Rifles of Canada, and The Canadian Guards. By the fall of 1954, however, it was agreed that the Canadian contingent would be reduced to one infantry battalion, one field ambulance unit, and the necessary administrative support. The 25th Brigade Headquarters was transferred to Camp Borden at the end of the year, while the last Canadian infantry battalion in Korea, the Queen's Own Rifles, returned to Canada the following spring. Finally, in June 1957, the last remaining Canadian Army unit, the Canadian Medical Detachment, left the peninsula.

In all, 21,940 members of the Canadian Army served in Korea and Japan prior to the armistice. At its peak, in January 1952, Canadian Army strength in the Far East reached 8123 all ranks. The static nature of the war contributed to its low casualty total of only 309 men killed in action. As in previous wars the heaviest toll fell on the foot soldier; all but fifteen of the dead were infantry. A further 1202 men were wounded or injured in action while thirty-two became prisoners of war.

The low number of casualties allowed the conflict to fade gradually from the Canadian public's attention. The initial enthusiasm for supporting the United Nations did not survive the stalemate on the ground or the protracted and, at times, seemingly irrational peace talks. Canada's contribution to containing Communist expansion in Asia was, therefore, left to a relatively small number of professional soldiers for whom the war's indecisive conclusion denied a clear sense of victory. It was only years later, when returning veterans were able to see first hand the tremendous economic strides that the Republic of Korea had achieved, that a true sense of accomplishment was finally able to take hold.

Privates Vaillancourt and Petit watch over the cease-fire line, November 1953.

R22eR Museum

Men of the 2nd Battalion, Queen's Own Rifles of Canada arrive to oversee the cease-fire, March 1954. The dog is the battalion's mascot, in care of Lieutenant M.C. Vipond.

NAC/PA-178900

CHAPTER 13

THE POST-WAR ARMY
IN CANADA AND NATO

by
Stephen J. Harris

COMMITTING THE ARMY TO NATO

The Korean conflict propelled Canada and its Army into a new age. Fear that the war in Asia was only a prelude to some further Communist initiative in Europe invigorated the North Atlantic Treaty Organization, and suddenly it no longer seemed good enough for Canada simply to give surplus British-pattern equipment to the Italians, Dutch, Belgians and Danes. Indeed, pressure for Canada to commit armed forces to Europe mounted steadily over the summer of 1950, and both Washington and London made it abundantly clear that naval and air forces would not be sufficient, British Prime Minister Sir Winston Churchill's going so far as to ask for two to three divisions.

Ottawa declined for the moment, Lester B. Pearson complaining that Canada was "a small ... nation with local defence problems." But when Chinese troops crossed into Korea in November, giving credence to the view that this was no small local war but part of the Communists' drive for world domination, the government at least had to think seriously about the problem. Although it still took two months before a decision was announced, on 30 January 1951 Canadians learned that significant naval forces, eleven fighter squadrons, and a division would be assigned to or ear-marked for NATO. To finance this commitment, the defence budget would rise sharply from $403 million in 1950 (2.7 percent of gross national product) to $1,907 million by 1953 (7.6 percent of GNP), and the size of the regular Navy, Army, and Air Force would grow to about 105,000.

Exercise Quick Train — Fort Beauséjour by Charles G. Gosbee.
Centurion tanks in the armoured regiment's barracks in Iserlohn, Germany during a NATO alert exercise.
CWM 16738

This marked a revolution in Canadian foreign and defence policy. Canadian soldiers had been committed to a likely war zone before the fighting began only once before, at Hong Kong in 1941, and that had been a disastrous expedition. The new policy also brought a revolution in army organization. Since long before Confederation, Canada's first line of defence had been its Militia, and citizen soldiers had jealously guarded their pride of place in the country's military hierarchy. However, the establishment of a one-brigade European garrison backed by two more brigades at home meant that many more regular troops would be required, and before long the Permanent Force would eclipse the Militia in strength, status, and significance — something long-time citizen soldiers found increasingly difficult to accept when, in the course of things, some very proud old regiments were dropped from the reserve order of battle. But that part of the Army's story lay some time in the future when, in February 1951, Army Headquarters began to flesh out the details of how Canada's NATO contribution should be organized.

So far as Lieutenant-General Charles Foulkes, Chief of the General Staff until 30 January 1951, was concerned, the British and Americans would be well-satisfied if the brigade committed to Korea were transferred to Europe once the war in Korea was over. But it might be useful, he added, for the Army to establish a training division in Europe. That would not only close the gap between Canada's ultimate promise to the Alliance and the number of combat troops actually serving on NATO's front line, but it would also serve the interests of the Army at home and overseas if Canadian soldiers had the opportunity for first-class training amongst their Allies.

Foulkes also had firm views on how and where the Canadian contribution should be organized. He had been a major player in the 1947 decision to re-equip the Canadian Army with weapons and vehicles of US origin, and in the early stages of planning for NATO he had more or less assumed that the Canadian component would have American-pattern equipment and, organized as a US-style regimental combat team of all arms, serve in the American zone of Germany in a US division.

More by happenstance than design, however, the Korean War had delayed the 'Americanization' of the Canadian Army. Having to expand itself, both to fight in Asia and stand on guard in Europe, the US Army had very little kit to spare for its northern neighbour, while the traditional institutional ties between the Canadian and British Armies were prolonged and strengthened by virtue of 25 Brigade's association with the Commonwealth Division in Korea. Traditionalists, then, had good reason to ask why the same could not be done in Europe.

Lieutenant-General Guy Simonds succeeded Charles Foulkes as Chief of the General Staff on 1 February 1951. An anglophile, Simonds had spent most of his time since the war in Britain serving as Vice-Commandant at the Imperial Defence College, and the perception that "he hardly knew ... the Canadian point of view" was surely strengthened as a result. Although he dutifully accepted the possibility that Canada's NATO contribution might be organized along American lines and serve under US command, the new CGS firmly believed that Canadian troops would do better in a British formation if they were not to serve under Canadian command. Commonwealth soldiers all spoke the same language, militarily; they had similar and compatible customs and doctrine; they were used to serving together; and they usually did so very well.

Major Cyrille Falardeau of the Fusiliers Mont-Royal, a company commander in the 1st Canadian Infantry Battalion, gives directions to his platoon commanders during an exercise in Sennelager, Germany, August 1952.
NAC/PA-180055

Despite Simonds' appointment as CGS, however, and his lobbying of Defence Minister Brooke Claxton, the decision as to where the Canadians would go had yet to be made when the government announced on 4 May 1951 that Canadian troops would soon be proceeding to Europe. Indeed, the final decision was not made in Ottawa, but was left to the Supreme Allied Commander, General Dwight D. Eisenhower, who in the end fashioned a wonderfully Canadian compromise. 27 Infantry Brigade, it was announced, would go to Northern Germany, in the British sector, while the eleven RCAF fighter squadrons, flying US-designed F-86 *Sabres*, would serve in the south, with the Americans. The Army, it turned out, would use a mixture of British and American equipment (including the former's *Centurion* tank).

Simonds was perfectly satisfied with Eisenhower's choice; and so, in the end, was the government. Although accommodation in the north would be tight for the first year or two (and the Canadians would initially serve in Hannover where, it was alleged, relations between the local citizens and the British occupying forces were not the best), there were better training grounds there. More important, the politicians assumed that the separate, national identity of the Canadian contingent would be better respected by the British who, after many years, had finally learned to be sensitive about such issues — or at least more sensitive than the Americans were proving to be.

Men of the 2nd Independent Field Squadron, Royal Canadian Engineers, bridge a stream during an exercise near Soltau, Germany, May 1954.
NAC/PA-180059

79 Field Regiment fires a 21-gun salute in celebration of the coronation of Her Majesty Queen Elizabeth II, Hannover, Germany, June 1953.
NAC/PA-180053

THE FORMATION OF 27 BRIGADE

Finding troops for 27 Brigade was almost as difficult as deciding where it should serve. There were, in effect, two 'regular' armies on the Canadian establishment, the Permanent Force and the Korean Special Service Force, neither of which could be drawn on for the moment. The former — the mobile striking force/active force brigade group of 1 RCR, 1 PPCLI, and 1 R22eR — had to remain at home to fulfil Canada's commitment to provide a brigade for the defence of North America. And although some complained that these battalions were inadequately trained themselves, someone had to supervise the basic training of the replacement units (3 RCR, 3 PPCLI, and 3 R22eR) and reinforcements destined for Korea. So far as 25 Brigade was concerned, since the Chinese entry into the war it was clear that the Canadians could not be withdrawn from Korea in time for the government's self-imposed deadline for getting troops to Europe: 31 December 1951. Moreover there were legal ramifications involving 25 Brigade and its replacement battalions. Most of the men, and some of the officers, had signed on 'for the duration' only, and so were not available for general service.

In short, a new force would have to be raised for 27 Brigade, and neither Simonds nor former army commander General Harry Crerar had any doubt about how this should be done. Pointing out that, apart from Iceland, Canada was the only NATO member still fielding an all-volunteer army, they urged the minister to adopt some form of compulsory service to shoulder its new defence burden. But the experience of two world wars was such that conscription was never going to be easily sold to the politicians — especially when the country's security was not clearly at stake — and the generals' advice was rejected out of hand.

In that case, Simonds argued, the NATO brigade should be recruited out of the Militia. Knowing, however, that very few Militia units could raise a complete battalion, and wanting the broadest possible geographic distribution, the CGS proposed that six composite infantry, rifle, and highland battalions (called, simply enough, 1st and 2nd Canadian Infantry, Rifle, and Highland Battalions) should be created from fifteen Militia regiments, each of which would supply two companies. That would be enough to form two infantry brigades, one to serve in Europe and the other to be held back in Canada as its eventual replacement by rotation. Each would be supported by a composite armoured squadron and an artillery battery, which would also come from Militia units.

The PANDA battalions (as the NATO force was called) were kept purposely generic because their members would be organized in companies bearing the names (and wearing the uniforms) of their parent Militia units. This was designed to facilitate recruiting — Simonds was a great believer in the power of the Militia to find men if they could continue to be affiliated with their regiments. And it would allow relatively easy and painless expansion if war broke out. Each of the companies could become a battalion so that, together with the three existing Regular Force battalions in Canada, there would be a field force of two divisions.

Infantry and tanks of 27 Brigade during an exercise in Munsterlager, Germany, April 1952.
NAC/PA-180054

The Chief of the General Staff, Lieutenant-General Guy Simonds, and Brigadier W.A.B. Anderson observe a bridging exercise, Soltau, Germany, October 1953. NAC/PA-180061

Canadian troops serving in Europe have on many occasions given help during natural disasters. In February 1953, Canadians built dikes during flooding in the Netherlands. NAC/PA-180057

The PANDA companies were to be formed in their home towns, at local headquarters, where the volunteers would sign their attestation papers, be kitted out, and (with some help from the Regulars) undertake rudimentary basic training. They would sign on for three years, but married men had the option of requesting their discharge after one, and single men after two. (There was no thought, at this time, of allowing families to accompany the brigade to Europe.) All had to have a top-flight battle 'PULHELMS' profile — a medical, psychological, and intellectual fitness evaluation devised by the Canadian Army. The men would be engaged initially as privates, although they might carry acting rank, while officers could apply for short service or permanent commissions. It was hoped that units would concentrate their most experienced volunteers in their new 'E' company, which would move quickly to Valcartier where the composite battalions would be formed. The 'F' companies, on the other hand, would likely proceed to camps in Canada, return to their home station for the winter (should suitable other quarters not be found) and then await further developments in 1952.

Thus were born six strange hybrid infantry battalions: 1st and Second Canadian Infantry Battalions — formed from the Hastings and Prince Edward Regiment, Les Fusiliers de Montréal, the Carleton and York Regiment, Algonquin Regiment, and Loyal Edmonton Regiment; 1st and 2nd Canadian Rifle Battalions — formed from the Queen's Own Rifles of Canada, Victoria Rifles of Canada, Royal Hamilton Light Infantry, Royal Winnipeg Rifles, and Regina Rifles; and 1st and 2nd Highland Battalions — formed from the Black Watch (Royal Highland Regiment) of Canada, North Nova Scotia Highlanders, 48th Highlanders of Canada, Seaforth Highlanders of Canada, and the Canadian Scottish Regiment.

A Royal Canadian Dragoon *Centurion* is ferried across the Weser River during I British Corps' Exercise Spearhead II, August 1952.
NAC/PA-180056

A Royal Canadian Regiment parade, summer 1953.
RCR Museum

Towns and cities not represented by these units were taken care of in the selection of artillery, armoured, and combat service support sub-units. The gunners for the composite 79th Field Regiment, RCA, would come from the 6th, 11th, 14th, 29th, 34th, and 39th Field Regiments. The armour, though destined to serve in either the Royal Canadian Dragoons or Lord Strathcona's Horse, would be drawn from the Governor General's Horse Guards, Halifax Rifles, 8th New Brunswick Hussars, Three Rivers Regiment, Prince Edward Island Regiment, British Columbia Regiment, King's Own Calgary Regiment, British Columbia Dragoons, Fort Garry Horse, and Le Régiment de Hull. Engineers were to be raised by the 6th, 33rd, and 56th Field Companies/Parks; medical personnel came from the 7th Field Ambulance; and combat service support from the 17th and 32nd Transport Companies, Royal Canadian Army Service Corps, 7th Ordnance Company, Royal Canadian Ordnance Corps, and 127th and 227th Infantry Workshops, Royal Canadian Electrical and Mechanical Engineers. 27 Brigade would cost about $21 million, the total army NATO force over $35 million.

The Militia units selected for PANDA because of their geographic location, strength, recruiting potential, war record, and efficiency at recent summer camps set out immediately to raise their active force troops and companies, and most had little difficulty doing so. Despite the growing economy, there were enough Second World War veterans around who wanted to protect the peace they had won in Europe six years before, and enough newcomers who hoped that a show of resolve now might prevent war later. The fact that they could sign up for a limited engagement clearly helped many to make their decision, and by mid-summer, following the move to Valcartier, the various elements of 27 Brigade began to take shape.

Royal Canadian Horse Artillery gunners manhandle a 25-pounder gun into position during an exercise in Camp Gagetown.
DND/EC-7562

375

THE EARLY YEARS IN EUROPE

After a few months training, 27 Brigade set sail for Germany from Wolfe's Cove in November 1951, and under the command of Brigadier Geoffrey Walsh, went into quarters on the outskirts of Hannover in December, where it would remain for almost two years. At home, meanwhile, the companies allocated to the second battalions of infantry, highlanders, and riflemen trained at local headquarters until they were concentrated at Camp Borden in early summer 1952, and then Valcartier. In the fall they moved to Ipperwash, on the shores of Lake Huron, and then to Wainwright, Alberta — where they would remain until 1953.

Brigadier Geoffrey Walsh, Commander of 27 Brigade 1951-52.

As had been forecast, Hannover was not a particularly friendly or happy garrison for 27 Brigade, despite the considerable efforts made to provide recreational facilities for the troops. It was described as a stronghold of both Communism and neo-Nazism — an interesting, if incompatible mix — but the upshot of that city's extreme leftist and rightist political sentiments was that its attitude to the Canadians was at times "quite hostile and provocative." Because of this, General Simonds wanted the brigade relocated as quickly as possible, preferably to the area around Soest, where relations with the local population proved quite good whenever the Canadians were in training there.

The move was essential if morale in the force was to improve, but morale problems in 27 Brigade were not entirely the fault of the burghers of Hannover. Despite their best efforts, recruiters had found some very round pegs for perfectly square holes — though not nearly so many as had turned up in the Korean Special Service Force — and the overall level of experience was not quite so high as had been anticipated. Furthermore, the main weaknesses lay in the realm of administration and supply, two areas that could easily affect morale, and deficiencies ran from a lack of bedding and winter gloves to shortages of weapons and ammunition. In part, perhaps, because no families had come to Europe, the absent-without-leave rate was also high.

However, the most basic problem of all was that the composite battalion idea had not really worked. For one thing, there was great difficulty building up any institutional focus or loyalty to the generic battalions. For another, when the first of the married men took leave for home in early 1953, it was found that three or four of the contributing Militia regiments could not generate enough recruits to keep their companies up to strength. That cut to the heart of the whole philosophy of the composite regiments as they now existed. It made little sense to perpetuate the Algonquins, Regina Rifles, and Seaforths in the Regular Army, for example, if vacancies in these companies had to be filled from surplus volunteers provided by the Carleton and Yorks, Queen's Own, or Black Watch.

Private Wallace Todd, Royal Canadian Regiment, is introduced to the FN-C1 rifle by Lance Corporal Garnet Bliss, Germany, April 1955.
NAC/PA-180064

As it was, by late 1952 Army Headquarters, and the CGS in particular, were becoming increasingly alarmed by other aspects of the Army's disparate organization. Although the Permanent Force now numbered 49,000 — the strongest it had ever been in peacetime (Reserve strength, by comparison, stood at 47,000) — its battalions were not fully interchangeable, and its soldiers were not all subject to exactly the same rules and regulations or terms and conditions of service.

The units of 27 Brigade, with their short service commissions and provisions for the early release of married men, had no liability to serve in Korea, while the Korean Special Service Force (25 Brigade and its replacements in 3 RCR, 3 PPCLI, and 3 R22eR) had not signed on for service in Europe. Only the 'real' Permanent Force — 1 RCR, PPCLI, R22eR, RCHA, and the two armoured regiments — could be sent anywhere, and in fact they were sent to Korea beginning in the fall of 1951.

Private B. Anderson, a cook with 2 RCR, prepares a meal for the troops during the summer concentration at Camp Gagetown, June 1956.
DND/EC-7241

2 RCR bren gun carriers during Exercise Morning Star, Gagetown, July 1956.
DND/EC-7549

REORGANIZATION 1953

What was necessary, Simonds advised, was a consolidation and rationalization of the Army's organization so that there were just fifteen battalions of infantry (three for Europe, three for Korea, three for home, and six for rotation), two or three armoured regiments, and a like number of regiments of horse artillery that could be sent anywhere. To accomplish that, the CGS first considered retaining two battalions of the RCR, PPCLI, and Van Doos, and one each from the nine strongest Militia units contributing to PANDA. However, he soon changed his mind. If the regimental system was to function properly and according to traditional precepts, nine single-battalion units would not allow enough flexibility in appointments, promotions and transfers. Simonds therefore proposed to reorganize the Regular Army into six infantry regiments. The three pre-war units would remain on the order of battle, of course, the RCR and PPCLI having two battalions each, the Royal 22e three, but the composite rifle and highland battalions would be redesignated as regular battalions of the Queen's Own Rifles of Canada and The Black Watch (Royal Highland Regiment) of Canada, the senior Militia rifle and highland units.

What to do with the composite infantry battalion was more difficult. Not wanting to perpetuate a PANDA unit with a specific territorial identity (like the Loyal Edmonton Regiment, for example) he chose instead to create a new, four-battalion regiment of Canadian Guards, of which one battalion would be bilingual. Although a number of Canadians objected to what they considered to be an unnecessary and unwanted imposition of British forms and practices on the Canadian Regular Army, Simonds resolutely defended his decision. The Guards should be able to recruit nationally, he said, and there was nothing wrong with infusing the standards of the Household Brigade into the Canadian Army.

Badge of The Canadian
Guards, formed
16 October 1953.

Badge of the 8th Canadian
Hussars (Princess Louise's),
formed 29 January 1957.
8CH Archives

The Canadian Guards parade during the
Dominion Day ceremonies at
Gagetown, 1 July 1956.
DND/EC-7319

The new Permanent Force regiments were all formed on 16 October 1953, but the 3rd and 4th Battalions, Canadian Guards, survived less than four years, being disbanded on 31 March 1957. However, the Regular Force did not become demonstrably weaker with their disappearance. Consistent with the Army's need for more armour, regular components of the 8th Hussars and Fort Garry Horse were added to the establishment on 29 January 1957 and 11 October 1958.

Once the reorganization was complete, and it was clear that all elements of the Permanent Force held the same terms of reference, battalions of the Guards, Black Watch, and Queen's Own were sent to Korea, while 2 RCR, 2 PPCLI, and 2 R22eR, the original Korea battalions, moved to Europe in October and November 1953 to serve in the now renamed 1st Canadian Infantry Brigade. They were replaced by 2 Canadian Infantry Brigade two years later, comprising the first battalions of these three regiments, and then two years later by 4 CIB, made up of 2 QOR of C, 2 Canadian Guards, and 3 Royal 22e Régiment. When the armoured element was beefed-up from a squadron to a full regiment in the spring of 1958, 4 Canadian Infantry Brigade was renamed 4 Canadian Infantry Brigade Group.

Lieutenant-Colonel S.V. Radley-Walters, first commanding officer of the 8th Canadian Hussars.
8CH Archives

The Canadian Forces Decoration, instituted in June 1950 for award to all ranks for 12 years of service.

Lieutenant-Colonel J.C. Gardner and RSM E.J. Armer crew The Fort Garry Horse's first *Centurion* during ceremonies marking the formation of the regular regiment, Camp Petawawa, 11 October 1958. DND Photo

The NATO brigade also changed its location in 1953, leaving behind the much disliked town of Hannover and moving into campsites set up at Soest (Fort Henry, Fort York, and Fort Chambly), Werl (Fort St. Louis and Fort Victoria), and Hemer/Iserlohn (Fort Prince of Wales, Fort Macleod, Fort Beauséjour — the old German Seydlitz Barracks — and Fort Qu'Appelle.) With the completion of married quarters in 1957, it became possible for families to accompany the units serving in Europe, and the tour of duty was increased from two to three years. Not only was this cheaper, given the cost of rotation, but the number of minor offences fell significantly.

There was new construction in Canada as well. Work Point and Currie barracks in Victoria and Calgary were fitted out for their resident battalions, which would be found from the two designated 'Western' regiments — Princess Patricia's Canadian Light Infantry and the Queen's Own Rifles of Canada. The Canadian Guards would be accommodated at Camp Petawawa and at Picton, Ontario, while the Black Watch, designated an 'Eastern' (predominantly Maritime) unit would call Aldershot, Nova Scotia home. The biggest project of all, however, was to complete construction of the 440-square mile Camp Gagetown, which was to be built down river from Fredericton, New Brunswick, just outside the small community of Oromocto. Gagetown would eventually be home station for the Black Watch, and it would also be the main training ground for 1 Canadian Division, which was re-formed in 1953. Besides being the largest military camp in the British Commonwealth, Gagetown was also one place where, to the consternation of legions of military drivers, it was almost easier to bog down on the top of a hill than on bottom land.

Pilot's Wings, worn by Canadian Army glider, fixed-wing and helicopter pilots until unification of the Forces in 1968.

RE-EQUIPMENT

With expansion, of course, came a need for more, and more modern, kit and equipment of every kind. So far as uniforms were concerned, cotton drill bush dress emerged as the summer field uniform (complete with a curious, squared-off baseball-type cap which disintegrated when washed), while tropical worsteds ('T-dubs') became the summer service dress, much to the embarrassment of anyone who had to wear them for any length of time and, more particularly, had to sit down for even just a few seconds: wrinkles multiplied with every crossing of the leg and spread rapidly over the whole garment. Behind the scenes, instructions were issued to design a new combat dress that would be worn year 'round, replacing both battle and bush dress, and which (in its final form) would mark the end of puttees forever.

Although the idea of converting the Army to American-pattern equipment was still current in the mid-1950s, in fact procurement had taken a much different — and much more multi-faceted — direction. The Army's main battle tank, the *Centurion*, was British, as were the *Ferret* scout cars selected for the 'sneak and peak' activities of the reconnaissance squadrons. The artillery in Europe actually gave up their American 105 mm guns, returning to the old, reliable British 25-pounders, but these were eventually replaced by American 105s and 155 mm guns. American 2-1/2 ton trucks (the 'deuce and a half') replaced the old, square, universal pattern vehicle of Second World War fame, but when it came to finding fully tracked armoured personnel carriers for the infantry, the Canadian-designed *Bobcat* was the Army's first choice — as were the home-grown *Heller* antitank rocket and *Iroquois* flame thrower. But the *Bobcat* was never a viable proposition, economically, once other armies decided to use their own designs, and in the end the US M-113 became the Canadian choice for APC. In the antitank role, on the other hand, the Army used (at various times) the American 106 mm recoilless rifle, the French *Entac*, and the Swedish *Carl Gustav*, and in the 1970s replaced its *Centurions* with German *Leopard* tanks.

Members of the Canadian Guards during Exercise Morning Star, Camp Gagetown, June 1956.
DND/EC-7290

Tank-infantry cooperation training by members of 3 R22eR and the RCD, Sotau, Germany, September 1958.
DND/EF-7075

When it came to personal weapons, Canada very quickly jumped on the bandwagon of NATO standardization, viewing it as even more logical and rational than converting to American equipment. Accordingly, the infantry lost their tried and true Lee Enfield .303 rifles, and received instead the semi-automatic Belgian designed FN, firing the NATO standard 7.62 mm round. Old soldiers complained bitterly, as only old soldiers can, about the new weapon, but in time they learned to accept it — and the fact that they would never 'slope arms' again. Indeed, when the FN was itself replaced in the late 1980s, old soldiers complained again, observing that the new lightweight C7 was not a 'real' rifle like the FN. It took rather longer for the fully automatic FN C2 to replace the *Bren* light machine gun — perhaps the finest such weapon every produced — and even longer for the *Sterling* submachine gun to replace all the variants of the cheap (and not always reliable) *Sten*. Still, by the end of the 1950s the Regular Army was undoubtedly better off than it had ever been. Four regiments of horse artillery, four armoured regiments, and thirteen infantry battalions were all up to strength. All had been issued modern kit that could be used to good effect, and there was the promise of more and better to come.

THE ARMY AND NUCLEAR WEAPONS

Yet just as the Permanent Force found its feet, as it were, the ground beneath it began to shift. In Guy Simonds's day it was taken for granted that the brigade group in Germany was the advance guard for at least all of 1 Canadian Division, and perhaps also for a Canadian Corps of two or three divisions. It was also taken for granted that the next war would be fought like the last one — except that casualties would be heavier because of the increased firepower available to both sides — and that it would last a long time.

In January 1954, however, American Secretary of State John Foster Dulles had given US foreign and defence policy a new look with the pronouncement of the strategic doctrine of massive retaliation — which held that any Communist move, anywhere in the world, that could be construed as threatening the security of the 'Free World' would be met with an all-out nuclear attack on the Soviet homeland. At the same time, it was made clear that the East's numerical superiority in Europe could be offset by the use of low-yield tactical nuclear weapons there.

L-19 aircraft were used by the Royal Canadian Artillery for air observation between 1955 and 1968.
Here a group of Air OP pilots are briefed on a mission during Exercise Morning Star,
Gagetown, July 1956.

The movement of tanks to training areas by rail was a common occurrence in Germany, but the first time this had been done on a large scale in Canada was for 1st Division's Exercise Morning Star. Here RCD tanks are unloaded from flat-cars in Camp Gagetown.
DND/EC-7231

Dulles's strategy was meant to deter aggression, but if the deterrent failed it also meant that the next war would be very much unlike the last. Not only would Europe, the Soviet Union, and North America be subjected to atomic air attack, but the NATO battlefield on the inner German frontier would also see the detonation of hundreds of nuclear warheads. Under the circumstances, World War III was likely to be brutish, nasty, and short, offering little time for national mobilization, Second World War-style (and probably not even the 180 days required to get 1 Canadian Division into the field.) In short, NATO's war seemed increasingly likely to be a 'come-as-you-are' war, a fact that was formally recognized in December 1954 when the Alliance adopted both elements of Dulles's policy and halved its land forces requirement from the sixty-five divisions of the 1952 Lisbon meetings to a trip wire/shield of about thirty. Following from all this, 1 Canadian Division was disbanded *as a formation* in 1957-1958.

The Canadian government was not altogether happy with these changes, Lester B. Pearson explaining that the maxim

... that only a limited use of force, proportionate to the circumstances and strictly necessary to accomplish specific objectives can be justified as self defence is, I think, inherent in the principles of natural law.... If ... aggression on any lesser scale breaks out, it seem to me to be vitally important that the force — political and military — used against the aggressor should be for a limited and declared purpose.

But the principles of 'natural law' rarely govern international affairs; and as Pearson himself had warned as long ago as 1950, the very nature of the NATO alliance meant that it was possible for the US to lead its colleagues down paths they preferred not to follow. Thus, although Canada did not acquire nuclear weapons in 1954, the very fact that NATO had adopted a tactical nuclear doctrine for the European battlefield forced Canadian soldiers to think about the consequences of fighting in a nuclear environment, whether their government approved or not. And as O.D. Skelton had asked in the 1930s, how many hypotheses like this did it take before they became a commitment?

Not that many, perhaps. "The possible effects of nuclear weapons on the tactical handling, organization, and equipment of ground forces is under continuous study by the Canadian Army," the Department of National Defence *Annual Report* for 1954-1955 explained:

The work is not an isolated effort, but is in concert with the overall studies being conducted by the Allied nations. High priority is being given to a study now in progress ... bearing in mind the necessity of being able to fight efficiently in a conventional or an atomic war.

Paratroopers from the Royal 22e Régiment preparing for a jump from a 'Flying Boxcar' during Exercise Eastern Star, Gagetown, June 1957. DND/EC-8274

A Lord Strathcona's Horse tank crew prepares breakfast beside their improvised shelter, summer 1957. DND/EC-7520

1st Battalion, Black Watch of Canada parade through the city of Werl, Germany in the autumn of 1959.

Exercise *Morning Star*, conducted by 1 Canadian Division at Camp Gagetown in 1956, assumed that both sides had "approximately forty nuclear missiles of varying size for use during the first two weeks of any conflict." Although it is not clear whether the division actually 'owned' and controlled the atomic warheads 'available' to it, it did request at least eight nuclear strikes against bridges, troop concentrations, and in direct support of its attacks. During Exercise Eastern Star, held in 1957, the division clearly controlled its own nuclear weapons. Similarly, at the annual concentration of 1 Canadian Infantry Brigade — the 'Army of the West' — in Alberta, both the 'enemy' and 'our troops' were given nuclear weapons, and "all tactical thinking rotated around the problems imposed by the employment of these weapons."

The same sort of thing was happening in Europe. In 1952 and 1953 79th Field Regiment had fired only conventional rounds, figuratively and literally, but in 1954, during Exercise Battle Royal, 2 RCHA (in the words of the regimental history) "through the good fortune of having captured an 'enemy' officer carrying plans of a forthcoming attack ... were able to adjust their fire plan so as to score a bull's eye with the first atomic strike against the opposing forces." In 1958, after NATO decided to use tactical nuclear weapons "in response to any aggression that was not of a minor nature," they featured prominently in the Northern Army Group's exercises.

Men of the 2nd Battalion, The Black Watch board *HMCS Algonquin* for an amphibious exercise on the coast of Newfoundland, September 1959.

DND/EC-7315-2

An 8th Canadian Hussars tank clatters through a German village during NATO manoeuvres in the autumn of 1962.

8CH Archives

The Canadian formation gave a good account of itself.... In fact, in its flank protection role the Brigade Group moved too quickly for the planned progress of the advance, and the Exercise Director arranged for an enemy atomic missile to be exploded in the brigade area. It must be acknowledged that this action did slow down the pace of the Canadians....

but not before they launched their own atomic strikes in return.

General Simonds and Major General W.H. Macklin, formerly Adjutant General, both complained about the nuclear-based "strategic quackery" emanating from Washington. But so long as the NATO nations could (or would) not match Soviet conventional strength in Europe, tactical nuclear war seemed the only way to redress the balance. And in 1961, *The Canadian Army Journal* welcomed the arrival in the Canadian brigade of the first surface-to-surface missile able to fire nuclear warheads:

Until the 762 mm rocket equipment (nicknamed Honest John) became a Canadian artillery weapon in 1961, there was a gap in the fire-power available to Canadian ground forces .... The adoption of the Honest John ... has filled the gap and we now have a simple, medium-range, fast-moving, hard-hitting weapon capable of firing either nuclear or conventional types of warhead. The Honest John fits neatly into the present artillery family of weapons. Armed with a nuclear warhead it can provide at the target end the destructive effect of thousands of tons of TNT. Thus it provides the Artillery with a weapon capable of deep penetration and overwhelming fire-power.... The ever-changing threat and the intensity of the cold war will create demands on the Canadian Army which can only be met by the acquisition of improved items of equipment. The Royal Regiment of Canadian Artillery is confident that the Honest John gives them a greatly enhanced ability to carry out one aspect of their traditional role of giving fire support to the armour and infantry and of winning battles.

The launching of an *Honest John* rocket by 1 Surface-to-Surface Missile Battery, Germany, 1964.
DND Photo

C Squadron of the Fort Garry Horse and the 1st Battalion, Queen's Own Rifles practice tank-infantry cooperation, Fort Beauséjour, Germany, spring 1963.

NATO Photo

What the editors of the *Journal* did not mention was that in 1961 the Canadian government had not yet decided whether to equip the RCAF's *Bomarcs* and CF 104s or the Army's *Honest Johns* with the nuclear warheads they needed to be effective. Indeed, the Conservatives would never truly come to grips with the issue of whether the acquisition of nuclear warheads was the right thing to do.

Who should have been more afraid of the *Honest Johns* — the enemy or the troops who were to be supported by this "simple ... free flight rocket" with a maximum range of thirty-seven kilometres — was a question which few wanted to answer at the time. But the need to give the Canadian Brigade group more fire support had been evident since 1957 when, as a result of cutbacks in the British commitment to NATO following the demise of 'national service', the formation's role had changed from that of a Corps reserve counterattack force to one of the pillars of the main defensive line. As Major General George Kitching, then Vice Chief of the General Staff, had reported in 1961, this had forced the Canadian brigade to become involved with tactical nuclear weapons, unofficially, even before *Honest Johns* were obtained.

Sappers of 4 Field Squadron, Royal Canadian Engineers train with booby-traps at Sennelager, Germany, July 1962.

DND/EF-62-9459-28

[The Canadian Brigade] has an area of ground to defend and whether our government likes it or not, it has, on a loan basis, for operations, two eight-inch nuclear artillery pieces under its command — and in addition, is supported by the fire of other nuclear weapons from neighbouring divisions and brigade groups. Once the Brigade is in its positions, it is boxed in as part of the thin red line where little initiative or manoeuvre or decision is permitted to the Brigade Commander.

General Kitching did not much like this new role, believing that it did "not make the best use of a Canadian formation," but he and Brigadier M.R. Dare, commanding 4 CIBG, were determined that it would do its best to hold the main defensive line (alongside the British 5 Brigade Group and the Belgians) from Petze to Wenzen — although in a rather more mobile fashion than the NATO planners had originally intended. This was evident in the 1963 Exercise Keen Blade, which ended unhappily for the brigade commander:

The general theme of the exercise was as follows: firstly an 'Alert' move of all units to practise survival locations. This was followed by a night move of the complete brigade group ... to our exercise deployment area. After we had completed our deployment and the development of the defensive position, I was ordered to mount a battalion attack to challenge an enemy force which had moved to limited objectives across the frontier.... After this phase ... the enemy made his main crossing over the frontier and major assault against the Brigade. Our covering force, on the enemy side of the River Leine fought a delaying action through the night and up until mid-afternoon of the following day.... The next phase was the major battle of the main obstacle itself ... and the enemy was successful in establishing a major bridgehead on our right sector.... When the major enemy thrust on the right had been stabilized I launched a counterattack by the Fort Garry Horse with two companies of infantry in support of nuclear weapons.... My untimely demise occurred shortly before exercise 'cease fire' as the result of a very accurate enemy nuclear strike....

Ferret scout cars of the Fort Garry Horse Reconnaissance Squadron exercise with one of the Squadron's CH-112 helicopters near Soest, Germany, spring 1963.
NATO Photo

A tank of A Squadron, The Fort Garry Horse, commanded by Lieutenant C.W. Cathcart, passes through ruins of the German kaiser's hunting lodge in the training area at Sennelager, June 1963.

DND/EF-9532-51

The lessons learned in 1963 led to an 'argument', the Fort Garry Horse history notes, between Brigadier Dare "and a variety of senior British officers" who believed that the defensive screen on the enemy side of the obstacle should be able to hold out for thirty-six hours. Dare's view was that twelve hours was more likely, and to test his conclusion a major exercise was held in October 1964 in which the Canadians, having practised Soviet tactics at their annual Sennelager and Soltau concentrations, were to become the enemy force launched against this screen.

'War' began at midnight on 5 October. The night was a particularly black one and the approach marches to the 'Blueland' border were begun at 2200 hours. At H-hour, just after refuelling, the border barriers were crashed in seven places by our small battle groups. It was a night of mad dashes into enemy territory and of immense confusion on both sides. Some of the battle groups got badly lost, others hit minefields and had to find ways around them. A German Panzer Grenadier battalion headquarters was captured intact and a half-squadron of British armoured cars were taken, some twenty miles behind the frontier, the crews still in their sleeping bags. The Recce Squadron helicopter troop, because their aircraft had been grounded, were infiltrated with the PPCLI Battle Group through the British screen, across the river line and behind their main defensive positions, to play saboteur and report back the disposition of the British units. By 0530 hours the leading scout cars and tanks [of the Fort Garry Horse] had reached the obstacle — the Warburg River. The British were forced to withdraw what they could of their screening troops and blow the remaining bridges. Some of their troops remained trapped on the Canadian side of the river and quickly put in the bag. Five and one-half hours! Total success! The Canadian theories were totally substantiated and once again Canadian ability had been proven.

Moreover, "a strong British and German counterattack later in the day was beaten off," with B Squadron of the Fort Garrys, strategically located on a ridge line overlooking a valley, destroying "almost an entire regiment of British tanks."

It is probably no exaggeration to say that Exercise *Treble Chance* marked the apex of the postwar history of the Permanent Force. The winds of change were already blowing, and within four years the Canadian Army would no longer exist as such. Before taking account of these winds, however, it is time to look back and see how the Militia fared during these happy times for the regulars.

THE MILITIA IN THE 1950s

In fact the Militia (or Reserve Army, as it was still called) did relatively well in the mid-1950s. Intimately involved in the raising of both the Korean Special Service Force and 27 Brigade, most Militia units found it reasonably easy to recruit now that the Canadian public was more or less convinced that the Soviet threat was indeed real. Further laurels were won whenever reservists were called out to help civil authorities cope with national disasters. Like their colleagues in Vancouver in the late 1940s and in Winnipeg in 1950, regiments in Ontario's Golden Horseshoe were ordered out in the fall of 1954 to clean up after Hurricane Hazel, the grizzliest duty going to those who searched for bodies in the valley of Toronto's Humber River, where houses had been built along the flood plain. Recruiting was also helped as full ceremonial dress (and blue patrols) reappeared — not just in the bands — as new equipment (as well as bush dress and 'T-dubs') began to filter down as well. High School cadet corps, compulsory in many jurisdictions, also flourished during the 1950s, attracting many to their parent Militia units, and numbers of young men financed their way through university in the Canadian Officers Training Corps designed to find the next generation of officers for the Militia.

8th Hussars mascots on parade: Princess Louise, rescued by members of the regiment near Coriano, Italy in 1944, and her foal, Princess Louise II, held by Sergeant G.A. Bickerton at Camp Sussex, 1954.

8CH Archives

Training also improved. The number of days for which militiamen could be paid rose to sixty in 1951, and that year 12,000 officers and men attended summer or winter camps. The number grew to 14,000 in 1953, and 15,000 in 1954, and many commanding officers reported that they had never seen such enthusiasm among their men. There was a nice blending, too, of youth and experience. Second World War (and Korean) veterans could be found in all but the most junior ranks — although there were still some long-in-the-tooth lance corporals — but there was new blood as well.

Still, rearmament had been costly, and the Reserve Army establishment was somewhat unwieldly. It was to rationalize this structure (and to facilitate expansion of Canada's NATO commitment) that General Simonds asked a committee chaired by Major-General Howard Kennedy to find the organization best suited to allow the citizen army to meet the requirements of the post-war world. Reviving the term 'Militia' — so that the Reserve was now called 'The Canadian Army (Militia)' — and reaffirming its role as the mobilization base for any field army, the Kennedy Report released in 1954 called for even better training, but while it demanded a greater commitment in time and energy on the part of citizen soldiers, it also sought to make the reserve training syllabus more flexible, taking account of the fact that most Militiamen had both families and jobs and could not attend courses which involved blocks of more than two or three weeks at a time.

There were also changes in organization. Taking note of the increased importance of armour, and concluding that certain aspects of home defence (particularly coastal and anti-aircraft artillery) could be dispensed with, the Kennedy Report recommended a considerable increase in the number of Militia armoured units. On the other hand, to cut down on overhead thirty-five Militia brigade and other formation headquarters were consolidated in twenty-six Militia group headquarters.

The Militia battalion of the Queen's Own Rifles fires a 'feu-de-joie', summer 1957.
Toronto Scottish Museum

1st Battalion, Irish Regiment of Canada parade during Exercise Flourish at Niagara Camp, summer 1957.
Toronto Scottish Museum

Troopers of The Fort Garry Horse (Militia) load 76mm rounds into a *Sherman* tank during the regimental gun camp at Shilo, summer 1958.

FGH Archives

Generally, this was all to the good, but as is inevitable in any such reform someone had to suffer, and in this case fine old units and names were dropped from the order of battle. In Ontario, The Essex Scottish, who had taken part in the Dieppe raid, and the Kent Regiment amalgamated to form a two-battalion Essex and Kent Scottish, while the Argyle Light Infantry and Midland Regiment were folded into the Hastings and Prince Edward Regiment and the Canadian Fusiliers and Oxford Rifles became the London and Oxford Fusiliers, and the Highland Light Infantry and Perth Regiment were joined. In New Brunswick, The Carleton and York Regiment and North Shore (New Brunswick) Regiment, both with proud records from the Second World War, were joined together in a two-battalion Royal New Brunswick Regiment, while to the east the North Nova Scotia, Pictou, and Cape Breton Highlanders were amalgamated to form a two-battalion regiment of Nova Scotia Highlanders. In the west, The Winnipeg Light Infantry joined the Royal Winnipeg Rifles, while the Prince Albert and Battleford Volunteers and Saskatoon Light Infantry became the two-battalion North Saskatchewan Regiment.

Amongst armoured units, Montreal's 6th Duke of Connaught's and 17th Duke of York's joined to form the Royal Canadian Hussars, and the 15th Alberta Light Horse and South Alberta Regiment merged into the South Alberta Light Horse. In Quebec, Le Régiment de Lévis amalgamated with Le Régiment de la Chaudière, which had served proudly in Normandy, Le Régiment de Québec amalgamated with Les Voltigeurs du Québec, and Le Régiment de Montmagny was joined with Les Fusiliers du St-Laurent. The Elgin Regiment became part of the Royal Canadian Armoured Corps.

The Kennedy Report also observed that links should eventually be established between all Regular and Militia regiments. As a beginning, it recommended that the Governor General's Foot Guards and Canadian Grenadier Guards should become the 5th and 6th Battalions, The Canadian Guards; the London and Oxford Fusiliers the 3rd Battalion, Royal Canadian Regiment; and Le Régiment de Châteauguay and Les Fusiliers du St-Laurent the 4th and 5th Battalions, Royal 22e Régiment. This was done, but the Loyal Edmonton Regiment resisted its designation as a battalion of Princess Patricia's Canadian Light Infantry so firmly that the affiliation never really caught on.

The Militia continued to flourish following the implementation of the Kennedy Report. Armoured regiments trained on their *Shermans*, but were reasonably certain that they would see *Centurions* at Meaford or Sarcee. The infantry, meanwhile, were still walking into battle, but by now everyone had heard about the *Bobcat* armoured personnel carrier, and it seemed only a matter of time before mechanization was achieved. For the gunners, the future promised self-propelled guns.

By 1956, however, the foundation upon which the Kennedy Report had been based had crumbled away. Now that it was unlikely that 1 Canadian Division would ever be sent to Europe, what need was there for a Militia to serve as the mobilization base of a nonexistent field army? Could it not be put to better use at home, where there was a definite requirement for bodies of disciplined and trained troops to help Canadians recover from the horrors of nuclear war — to dig out from and survive the irradiated rubble created by the atomic and hydrogen bombs sure to fall on the country in the event of all-out war?

The Kennedy Commission had considered setting the Militia to this task, but it had been rejected for fear not only that the force would suffer as a result, but also (somewhat contradictorily) because it was possible that the Militia might come to be regarded as a safe haven for those who wanted to avoid active service. But with the growth of Soviet air (and missile) power, Canada's vulnerability to nuclear attack was obvious, and Army Headquarters turned decisively away from sending vast convoys across the Atlantic.

Mounted March-Past for His Excellency General Georges Vanier, the Governor-General, at Camp Gagetown, autumn 1961. RCD Archives

Members of the Canadian Postal Corps sort Christmas mail, Soest, Germany, December 1963.

The 2nd Battalion, Black Watch team during the General Crerar Marches, Hoogeveen, Holland, May 1963.
DND Photo

THE MILITIA AND NATIONAL SURVIVAL

Civil Defence, in short, could no longer be ignored. Accordingly, the training issued for 1957 spoke openly about the need to have a "nucleus in Militia units capable of assisting the Civil Defence Organizations in the event of national disaster or emergency" and a plan to create Mobile Support Groups (who would undertake search and rescue operations in bombed out localities) was put forward. The training directive issued for 1958 was even more straightforward. While the aim was still "to prepare the Militia for its role to assist in any future mobilization for Active Service and for defence," 'emphasis' would be given to civil defence.

To *The Globe and Mail*, it seemed that, "The first step in what may be eventual elimination of Canada's reserve forces was announced today. Army Headquarters said summer camp for the 42,000-man Militia will be cut out and more emphasis placed on civil-defence training." The number of training days was reduced to forty from sixty (with an addi-

tional ten available *if* they were used for civil defence training) and it was decided that all weapons except for rifles and light machine guns would be removed from reserve armouries — a terrible blow for artillery and armoured units.

Commanding officers who knew their men complained bitterly that Militia strength would soon dwindle to nothing — and they were almost proved right. Recruiting plummeted after 1959, and most units had great difficulty retaining those who had already joined. But before the rot got too far, however, the new CGS, Lieutenant-General Geoffrey Walsh, announced late in 1963 that having emphasized national survival for three years, it was "now ... time for the Militia to go back to their corps training." "I feel," he added, "that if they are well trained as militiamen, it is very easy for them in survival operations." But the winds of change were blowing at the Militia too; and although it would soon be freed of its heavy civil defence responsibilities, within five years nothing would be the same.

Simulated casualty evacuation from the National Survival training site in Camp Gagetown, during the 1963 summer concentration.
DND/ZK-1983-5

396

CHAPTER 14

THE POST-UNIFICATION LAND FORCE

by
Stephen J. Harris

INTEGRATION

Paul Hellyer was a man with a mission even before he was named Minister of National Defence following the Liberal victory in April 1963. Convinced several months before that John Diefenbaker's government had, indeed, abrogated firm commitments to acquire nuclear warheads for the Army's *Honest Johns* (and the *Bomarcs, Voodoos,* and *Starfighters* of the RCAF), and knowing that all these weapons systems would be of only marginal use without them, he led the fight within the Liberal Party to reverse itself and adopt a pro-nuclear defence platform for the forthcoming election. Canada should fulfill its nuclear obligations now, he told party leader Lester Pearson in December 1962, but it should then "negotiate new roles more compatible with our desires." Whether these would also require the Canadian forces to have a nuclear capability could be determined at the time.

Hellyer's advice came just under three months after the Cuban missile crisis when, for a period of about two weeks, the world hovered on the brink of all-out war because the Russians had had the temerity to place ballistic missiles in Cuba, only ninety miles from Florida. To some, the crisis was proof enough of the dangers of nuclear proliferation, and sufficient reason for Canada to say no, no matter how different the circumstances might be. To most, however, the missile crisis said something quite different despite their horror at the prospect of war. The government's lack of action — officially, Canada did nothing for at least two days; unofficially, at Defence Minister Douglas Harkness's insistence, alerts were called and naval forces were deployed — somehow melded with its confusion about the propriety of acquiring nuclear warheads, and anger about both swelled up. By November, opinion polls showed a growing majority in favour of Canada's joining the nuclear club, even if in a second-hand way.

Back to the Road by Charles Gosbee.
An M-109 self-propelled 155mm gun and tracked vehicles of A Battery, 1st Regiment Royal Canadian Horse Artillery during an exercise in Germany. CWM 16737

Regimental heritage was seen to play an important role in the Canadian Army in the 1960s. Shown here is the Guidon of the Fort Garry Horse, presented by Lord Alexander of Tunis in August 1964. It is typical of the colours carried by armoured regiments. FGH Photo

Hellyer's mission involved more than nuclear warheads, however. An ambitious man, he hoped to do something with the Defence portfolio that would enhance his own political future; yet he was also genuine in his desire to find new roles for the forces because by 1963 the old ones had become very expensive. An inkling of what he was considering had already been published in the Department of National Defence Report for 1956-1957, when he was Associate Minister of National Defence in the dying days of Louis St-Laurent's administration. "It has become increasingly evident," the report explained

... that a young and growing country as vast as Canada cannot possibly, by itself, maintain the whole range of military forces, equipped with all types of costly ... weapons systems, essential today for the various roles.

Instead, the Dominion should consider limiting itself to "those lines of cooperative endeavour which are within the means of the nation and which have the prospect of providing the most practical result in concert with Allied and friendly nations."

Although there was some risk in alienating extreme nationalists (particularly after US General Lauris Norstad, NATO's outgoing Supreme Allied Commander Europe, told an Ottawa press conference that, Diefenbaker's statements to the contrary, promises had not been kept), by early January 1963 it looked to be good politics for the Liberals to do what Hellyer recommended, and this Pearson did on the 10th, following his own discussions in Washington. Moreover, he did so in precisely the way Hellyer had advised two weeks before. Canada would go nuclear now, he said, and then set about changing its NATO role sometime later.

Infantry battalions have two colours, a Queen's Colour based on the national flag, and a Regimental Colour on which battle honours are emblazoned. Shown here is the Regimental Colour of the 1st Battalion, Royal 22e Régiment.

398

B Company of 3rd Battalion, Royal 22e Régiment, the 4 CIBG antitank company, parades in Fort Anne, Germany in its newly issued M-113 armoured personnel carriers. SS-11 antitank guided missiles are seen on the carrier on the left. R22eR Museum

Royal Canadian Electrical and Mechanical Engineers helicopter mechanics refuel an 8th Hussars Recce Squadron helicopter during NATO manoeuvres in the autumn of 1965. 8CH Archives

For this to happen, however, order had to be brought to the Department of National Defence. As Associate Minister, Hellyer had seen first-hand how competition for money had pitted service against service, sometimes with devastating results. Exploiting its superior public relations skills (and the threat of air attack), the RCAF had sold the St-Laurent government on a CF-105 interceptor programme which, it became clear by early 1957, would use up the entire capital equipment budget for the next several years, leaving the Army and Navy with no money whatsoever to modernize their inventories. Although the cancellation of the *Arrow* in 1958 cost Diefenbaker's Conservatives politically, Hellyer knew that the right decision had been taken: the Liberals would have done the same thing had they won the 1957 election.

There was also tremendous (and costly) triplication of effort in the three separate service headquarters in Ottawa as well as in the field. Although a number of medical, dental, transport, and legal services had been integrated on a tri-service basis in the early 1950s, there were still three personnel systems, three supply branches (each with its own numerical coding for the same item), and three administrative organizations — all doing essentially the same job. There were also three 'general' staffs and myriads of policy, planning, and procurement committees. Yet despite the existence of these committees and the Chairman, Chiefs of Staff, whose job it was to coordinate such things, it could not be said with any honesty that there was any real agreement among the Army, Navy, and Air Force on even the most basic questions.

Members of the Queen's Own Rifles climb aboard *HMCS St. Croix* during an amphibious landing exercise on the British Columbia coast, November 1965. DND/E-82165

Indeed, if one probed deeply enough, it seemed that Canada did not have a single, identifiable defence policy — apart, of course, from its general declarations of support for the Western Alliance. Each of the services, for one thing, had very different views about what the next conflict would be like. As we have seen, by 1963 the Army had just about given up on the idea that the Third World War would be a replay of the Second, and in so doing it had dispensed with the idea of despatching a large field army to Europe to augment the brigade group stationed there. Instead, Army planners were thinking in terms of a 'come-as-you-are' conflict, lasting about a month, the object of which was to hold the Soviets back using conventional, non-nuclear methods, but which allowed for carefully controlled escalation through the nuclear spectrum if that became necessary. The Air Force, on the other hand, envisaged a very short war of three to five days duration culminating in an all-out nuclear exchange against cities in Russia, Western Europe, and North America. The Navy, meanwhile, was still concentrating on the anti-submarine warfare techniques necessary to allow it to escort convoys overseas — convoys carrying troops the Army no longer planned to use and which, the soldiers said, would have no place to land anyway. By the time the Navy arrived, all of Western Europe's ports would have been obliterated.

It was all so absurd and counterproductive, Hellyer thought; it was also, he believed, endemic — built so deeply into the existing management, command, and administrative apparatuses that a 'victory' by one service in obtaining funds inevitably meant defeat for the other two. Accordingly, the three service chiefs could not be expected to offer objective advice, but only that which furthered the separate and distinct interests of the Navy, Army, and Air Force. Why else would a copy of an Air Force submission on long-range patrol aircraft buried in the RCAF's central registry carry the marginal notation, "This is our chance to screw the navy"?

The solution, Hellyer concluded, entailed a fundamental restructuring of the Department of National Defence, one involving integration of the three separate headquarters and, in the longer term, unification of the three separate services into one Canadian defence force. Neither proposal was altogether new. More and more things had been done on an integrated, tri-service basis since the creation of a single Department of National Defence in 1922, which was itself a step in the process, and in August 1960 Lester Pearson had spoken of the benefits to be derived from having "one chief of staff whose authority would extend to the army, navy, and air force" — a kind of integration by *fiat.*

An infantry section dismounting from an M-113 armoured personnel carrier at the Royal Canadian School of Infantry in Camp Borden, summer 1967. CFC-67-099-9

Officer Cadets at the Royal Canadian Armoured Corps School prepare ammunition for loading into a *Centurion* tank during gunnery training at the Meaford Tank Range, summer 1967. DND/CF-67-1000-70

Major-General Gilles Turcot, commander of NATO's ACE Mobile Force, with officers of the Norwegian Army during a NATO exercise in northern Norway, June 1968.
DND/CF-67-1000-70

It was not only politicians who thought this way. Charles Foulkes, who retired as Chairman, Chiefs of Staff Committee, in 1960, had also called for the creation of "a single service, with one chief of staff, a combined administration, and a series of task forces to replace the [present] service field forces," while Major General W.H. Macklin, formerly Adjutant General under Guy Simonds, declared that

... the old conception of sea power, land power, or air power as independent entities having little or no connection with each other is completely invalid. None of these forms of military power is of any avail by itself; they are now totally interdependent. If we have not learned that lesson by now, if we wait for some future enemy to demonstrate it over again, we shall probably perish in the process....

A unified armed force will give us more defence for less money. World War II proved that there had to be singleness [sic] of command; Canada's forces are now governed by a cascade of committees; the Chairman, Chiefs of Staff job is a phony substitute for unity.

B Squadron, 8th Canadian Hussars in *Lynx* reconnaissance vehicles during an exercise with American troops in the Mojave desert in California, May 1970. DND/PCN-71-242

These thoughts parallelled Hellyer's precisely, and were expressed (in slightly different language) in the White Paper on defence he presented to the House of Commons in March 1964. Establish single administrative, supply and personnel services, cut down on the number of headquarters, and force sailors, soldiers and airmen to talk with (rather than at) each other about what was best for the country, he reasoned, and there should be additional millions available for capital expenditures to provide the modern equipment each required.

Although the Minister also spoke about defining new "global mobile" roles for integrated task forces, for the moment no great changes were contemplated for the Army's NATO brigade group other than giving it the armoured personnel carriers and self-propelled guns it needed to be effective. ('Bumping' the infantry into battle in the back of 3/4-ton trucks was no longer a funny, temporary expedient.) The training of two of the three brigade groups at home would be broadened, however, so that they would be prepared for everything from peacekeeping to fighting brushfire wars in the third world to high intensity conflict. They too would be mechanized. The other Canadian-based brigade — which was, in effect, the returned Korean special force — would be converted into an airborne/ air portable formation capable of rapid deployment (in new *Hercules* aircraft) to trouble spots anywhere in the world. It was to be trained primarily in low-intensity conflict, but one battalion was also earmarked for a new role in Norway, on NATO's northern flank, as part of Allied Command Europe's ACE Mobile Force. With the stroke of a pen, therefore, all of the winter warfare training the Army had been conducting since the late 1940s was validated, and exercises conducted North of 60° took on a new importance. When the first test deployment of the ACE Mobile battalion proved successful in 1966, consideration was given to committing a battalion to NATO's southeastern flank as well, but this was given up as impractical before any exercises were conducted.

A troop of Fort Garry Horse *Centurion* tanks, just prior to the disbandment of the Regular Regiment during the summer concentration at Camp Wainwright, Alberta, June 1970.
FGH Photo

403

Colonel J.G. Bourne, Colonel of the Regiment, inspects Black Watch soldiers for the last time prior to the disbandment of the two Regular Force battalions on 1 July 1970. He is accompanied by Lieutenant-Colonel G.S. Morrison, commanding officer of 1 RHC. RHC Photo

Men of the 2nd Battalion, Royal 22e Régiment during jungle training in Jamaica, 1970. R22eR Photo

The Governor-General, the Right Honourable Roland Mitchener, inspects an 8th Canadian Hussars guard of honour at the opening of Parliament in February 1971.
DND Photo

The Army was happy at the prospect of receiving new equipment, but there were concerns about how far (and fast) the government intended to move in implementing the dual programmes of integration and unification. The former, it was felt, could be lived with, in Ottawa and perhaps even in the field: after all, there had been joint and combined commands during the Second World War. Still, there was some concern that Army units might end up under the command of an airman or sailor who knew nothing about soldiering.

Unification was another thing altogether. Since the White Paper was purposely vague on the subject, it was difficult to know exactly what the Minister had in mind, but it was easy to concoct a worst-case scenario in which soldiers, sailors, and airmen would become somehow interchangeable, subject to posting from one element to another, jacks of all trades, masters of none. There was also a fear that, in the drive to break with the past and build a new commonality, age-old traditions like the regimental system would be done away with. In the spring of 1964 this was all conjecture, however, and perhaps — as some hoped — useless conjecture at that. As unification had been touched upon only briefly in the White Paper, it was possible that it was not a necessary and inevitable outcome of reorganization if integration succeeded in cutting overheads and other costs sufficiently, and if it brought efficient management to the Department.

Bill C-90, which would amend the National Defence Act and create an integrated Canadian Forces Headquarters under a single Chief of Defence Staff, was introduced into the House of Commons on 13 April 1964. "This will not only simplify procedures and permit the development of a more efficient fighting force," the Minister explained

but it will also greatly facilitate the implementation of a long range, coordinated defence policy as set out in the White Paper. In the absence of a unified defence staff the implementation of such a policy would be extremely difficult and, in my opinion, virtually impossible.

Although even such traditionalists as Lieutenant-General Guy Simonds agreed that "Integration on a tri-service basis of higher commands and staffs was a perfectly legitimate goal," the road to reform was bumpy from the start. In the House of Commons special committee hearings that followed, witness after witness challenged the Minister's plan, some warning that the creation of a single Chief of Defence Staff or 'generalissimo' was bound to exacerbate civil-military tensions, others noting that if the roles of the Army, Navy, and Air Force were so uncoordinated and unrelated despite the existence of a Chairman, Chiefs of Staff, it was not likely that this would be fixed by the simple expedient of creating an integrated headquarters. Still others wondered who was going to look after the Army (or Navy or Air Force) in the new headquarters — and who would have the expertise to do so.

The badge of Mobile Command, formed in June 1965.

General Jean Victor Allard, first Commander of Mobile Command and the first Army officer to be appointed Chief of the Defence Staff, 1966-1969.
DND/REC-68-145

Bill C-90 passed third reading on 7 July 1964, and went into effect on 1 August. Army Headquarters disappeared, and with it the offices of CGS, VCGS, Adjutant General, and Quartermaster General. Gone, too, was the Army's general staff, although its functions could be traced through a wispy network of solid and dotted lines connecting the new offices of Chief of Defence Staff, Vice Chief of Defence Staff, and Chief of Operational Readiness, and that of the Deputy Minister. As with all new bureaucratic structures, however, it would take some time for the new Canadian Forces Headquarters to shake itself out so that the responsibilities belonging to these branches were actually undertaken.

Apart from the inevitable confusion involved, this initial step in the integration process had very little impact on Army units and formations in Europe or Canada. True, there were new people to report to in Ottawa, but the Army's five old regional commands — Eastern, Quebec, Central, Prairie, and Western, which facilitated contact with the local Militia and easy organization of operations to assist local civil authorities — all continued to exist.

They were the next to disappear, however, as the Army command and control organization was supplanted by six task-related, functional commands organized, generally, on a tri-service basis (Maritime, Air Transport, Training, Air Defence, Materiel, and Mobile) and five regions to provide administrative support. Although some identifiably 'Army' jobs were allocated to Training and Materiel Commands, Mobile Command, with headquarters at St. Hubert, Quebec, and

having responsibility for the three brigade groups in Canada, the Militia, and the tactical air forces, was obviously the institutional successor to the Army. Only the NATO brigade, which reported directly to Ottawa, was outside its control.

Yet the first commander of Mobile Command, Lieutenant-General J.V. Allard, who had commanded a British division in Germany before serving as the initial Chief of Operational Readiness, had no idea of 'what was meant by Mobile Command' when he took up his appointment. Was it "a force to intervene in unknown theatres of operations? A force for internal stabilization? A force for the defence of the northern territories?" Worse still, he was none the wiser when he asked Ottawa for advice. "No one could or would answer my questions." Left to his own devices, Allard gave himself "the responsibility of being able to deploy an element capable of commanding a division without the static Headquarters being paralyzed at all because of it" — with Europe the focus for a high intensity conflict involving nuclear weapons.

As he himself has recalled, General Allard ventured far beyond the boundaries of the government's announced policy in setting himself this task, and he could only hope that the politicians would support his call for 37,000 operational men "not counting the administrative staffs at the bases and regional headquarters." He also wanted unequivocal support for an airborne regiment which would " 'fill the line' between the time our government acceded to a request for intervention from outside and the arrival of the main body of troops."

A Royal Canadian Regiment mortar crew in action, Petawawa, March 1971.
DND/ISC-71-18-5

A 106mm recoilless rifle detachment from 1 R22eR crosses a stream during II German Corps' Exercise *Gutes Omen*, southern Germany, September 1971. R22eR Photo

General J.A. Dextraze

General Jacques Dextraze began his service as a private in the reserve battalion of the Fusiliers Mont-Royal in 1939, and enlisted for active service in 1940. He was commissioned in 1942, and during the invasion of Normandy in 1944 he proved to be a highly competent company commander. Later in 1944 he was promoted Lieutenant-Colonel and given command of the Fusiliers Mont-Royal. After victory in Europe, he served briefly as commanding officer of the Hastings and Prince Edward Regiment, intended to be part of the Pacific Force. He was demobilized in 1945, and until 1950 worked as a manager in manufacturing. Because of his Second World War reputation, he was asked to rejoin the Army in 1950 to command the 2nd Battalion, Royal 22e Régiment in operations in Korea. On returning from Korea in 1952, he remained in the Regular Army. From 1957 to 1960 he was commandant of the School of Infantry. In 1962 he was promoted Brigadier to command Eastern Quebec Area, and in 1963 he was appointed Chief of Staff at UN Headquarters in the Congo. While serving in the Congo he led a daring operation to rescue threatened missionaries, and for his gallant leadership was made a Commander of the Order of the British Empire, to which an Oak Leaf Cluster was added, the only time such an award has ever been made. He commanded 2nd Brigade 1964-66, and served as Chief of Staff Operations and Training at Mobile Command 1966-67. In 1967 he was promoted Major-General on appointment as deputy commander of Mobile Command. As a Lieutenant-General, he served as Chief of Personnel in NDHQ 1970-72. On being appointed Chief of the Defence Staff in 1972 he was promoted to the rank of General. He became Chairman of Canadian National Railway on his retirement from the Canadian Forces in 1977.

General Dextraze, known to the troops as 'Jadex', has a well-deserved place among Canada's great soldiers. He was an exceptionally capable field commander in two wars, and he was a highly respected leader of men throughout his years of service. A 'soldier's soldier', he readily inspired confidence in those who served under him.

The Cross of Valour. In 1972 the government instituted distinctly Canadian awards for bravery. The Cross of Valour is the most senior, and is awarded only for acts of conspicuous courage in circumstances of extreme peril. To date, no serving member of the Army or Land Force has been awarded a CV, although one retired officer, Major René Jalbert, received the Cross in 1984. The CV now ranks ahead of the Victoria Cross in Canada.

The Star of Courage. Second in precedence in the Canadian awards for bravery. The first member of the Army to be awarded the SC was Warrant Officer Robert Clark of the Queen's Own Rifles. It was also awarded to Captain Alain Forand and Private Joseph Plouffe for rescuing Canadians who had been wounded by hostile fire during the Turk invasion of Cyprus in 1974.

The Medal of Bravery, awarded for acts of bravery in hazardous circumstances. It ranks immediately below the Star of Courage.

Insignia of a Commander of the Order of Military Merit. The Order of Military Merit was instituted in 1972 to recognize conspicuous merit and exceptional service by members of the Canadian Forces. The degree of Commander is usually awarded only to officers above the rank of Colonel, and the number is limited to six percent of total membership in the Order.

Officer of the Order of Military Merit. This degree is usually awarded only to officers between the ranks of Major to Colonel.

Member of the Order of Military Merit. This degree of the Order is awarded to all ranks up to Major.

The oldest of Canada's regiments, the 8th Canadian Hussars, celebrated the 125th Anniversary of the regiment's formation in ceremonies at Petawawa and Moncton in June 1973. 8CH Archives

Although everything had not been settled by 30 May 1966, just before Mobile Command's first birthday, Allard was confident enough to tell the Commons special defence committee that things had gone well. In little under twelve months, he noted, he and his staff had created a "mobile global force, capable of rapid deployment anywhere in the world to carry out peacekeeping or peace-restoring tasks or to wage a limited, conventional war." It remained only for the government to approve the plan for the proto-divisional headquarters, authorize the formation of an airborne regiment, and for the Department of National Defence to work out how the new Air Force-style base organization that was being contemplated could handle combat service support in the field *if*, as most signs now indicated, there were not going to be separate static and field logistics and other such units.

A lot had happened in the twenty-seven months between the introduction of the Liberal White Paper and General Allard's report to Parliament. Yet for the regulars, at least, the changes so far had not been too traumatic. The Canadian Army still existed, as did its regiments and corps, and a number of promises regarding the purchase of new equipment were being kept. New 105 mm and self-propelled 155 mm howitzers would be supplied to the artillery; the Armoured Corps' *Centurion* tanks were being retro-fitted with the superb British 105 mm gun; and although the all-Canadian *Bobcat* armoured personnel carrier had proved to be a costly failure, the infantry would soon be mechanized when they received their American M113 APCs.

The Militia, on the other hand, had not fared so well. On 5 December 1963 the government announced a cut-back in its strength from 51,000 to 32,000, and following a review by the Suttie Committee a large number of regiments were relegated to the supplementary order of battle: 4 Princess Louise Dragoon Guards, the Halifax Rifles, 12th Manitoba Dragoons,

14th Canadian Hussars, 19th Alberta Dragoons, the Victoria Rifles, the Royal Rifles, the Perth Regiment, Le Régiment de Joliette, the Winnipeg Grenadiers, the Irish Fusiliers (Vancouver Regiment), the South Saskatchewan Regiment, and the Yukon Regiment. In addition, there were some amalgamations: the Sherbrooke Regiment with the 7th/11th Hussars to form the Sherbrooke Hussars, for example, and the Highland Light Infantry with the Scots Fusiliers to form the Highland Fusiliers. Two units, the Essex and Kent Scottish and the North Saskatchewan Regiment, were reduced to one battalion, and all Militia armoured units were converted to the reconnaissance role.

There were also significant changes for the survivors. Those which fell behind in recruiting to their maximum strength of three hundred (including band) risked being reduced to a new category of 'minor unit', which would be commanded by a major instead of a lieutenant-colonel. Moreover, a number of rural units that depended upon scattered, outlying platoon and company armouries to realize their recruiting potential had these facilities closed. The Lorne Scots, for example, who paraded four hundred-strong when they received their Colours in October 1963, lost drill halls in Milton, Orangeville, and Port Credit, Ontario, and so lost touch with Dufferin County and the northern and eastern reaches of Peel and Halton. In a similar fashion, the Loyal Edmonton Regiment lost sub-units in Vegreville, Dawson Creek, and Fort Smith; the Grey and Simcoe Foresters vacated their drill halls in Durham, Collingwood, and Orillia; and the Hastings and Prince Edward Regiment those at Trenton, Norwood, Port Hope, and Millbrook. In Quebec, the old Montmagny facilities transferred to Les Fusiliers du St-Laurent were shut, while 1 Nova Scotia Highlanders gave up their drill halls at Truro, Antigonish, and River Herbert. In terms of recruitment, none would ever fully recover.

The Royal 22e Régiment on exercise in Camp Valcartier, 1974.
DND/REC-74-676

The Queen's Silver Jubilee Medal, awarded in 1977 to 7000 members of the Canadian Forces.

Leopard I tanks, newly acquired by the Royal Canadian Dragoons, on the firing point during NATO's 1977 Canadian Army Trophy tank gunnery competition. The Dragoons won the competition, the first time that Canadian tank gunners had done so since the competitive shoot was begun in 1962. DND/ILC-77-365

The Governor General's Foot Guards parade their new Colours at Rideau Hall following presentation by Governor General Jules Léger, July 1977. Photo: M.G. Murgoci

Pipe-Major Coghill of the Cameron Highlanders of Ottawa plays the Lament at the National Remembrance Day ceremony in Ottawa, 11 November 1977. Photo: M.G. Murgoci

But there was more. When he was Chief of Operational Readiness, General Allard had lamented how the survival/civil defence role had cost the reserves "a good portion of their operational capability," and at that time he made known his intention to bring them back to operational standards. Once settled in at St. Hubert, however, he began to see things in a different light:

In the original plan ... the utilization of the Reserve was included. The idea I was trying to implement came from a lengthy study based on several inquiries carried out in the reserve units. In case of conflict, could they be mobilized in time to intervene? Faced with the new, technical and administrative complexities, could ... entire units still be mobilized, as was done in World War II ... or was it better to aim at a new, complementary, regular/reserve role.... My answer to this last question was affirmative.

Instead of mobilizing formed units, Militia units would henceforth provide trained officers, technicians, specialists, and combat personnel, usually on an individual basis, 'to fill gaps' in the Regular Army establishment. This, in fact, began on an experimental basis early in 1965, when a small number of Militia officers and senior NCOs were sent to Europe to serve with 4th Canadian Infantry Brigade Group. They had a terrific time, learned much, and brought many field skills back to their home units.

But some damage had also been done. Although the Militia's fine old regiments still paraded as units on week nights and some weekends, it was soon understood that none of them would ever see active service as such; instead, bits and pieces would be posted here and there, as required. While this may have been efficient, one of those intangibles that had helped Militia recruiting in the past was lost. When combined with the disappearance of outlying armouries and

Insignia of a Companion of the Order of Canada, instituted on 1 July 1967.

The Canadian Centennial Medal. Some 3500 medals were awarded to members of the Canadian Army on 1 July 1967.

Members of the Hastings and Prince Edward Regiment carry out the essential poison ivy scrub-down after training in the field.
Photo by Captain C. Almey

ties to local communities, the first doubts about the US experience in Vietnam, the growing length of civilian hair-styles, and — in a few years — the last summer camp at which militiamen trained as members of their own, formed unit, the new policy made reserve service in Canada just that much more meaningless and unattractive. The Royal Hamilton Light Infantry, who paraded 246 strong in 1968, were down to 171 in 1971, and in 1973 sent a grand total of twenty-seven, all ranks, to camp!

Centennial year, 1967, was turned over to celebration. The Army, both Regular and Militia, in all its ceremonial splendour, was prominent in every corner of the country as cities, towns, and villages did their best to mark Canada's 100th birthday. Militia units and their bands were present as countless Centennial projects were dedicated and opened to the public — parks, marinas, recreation centres and the like; Colours were trooped on Dominion Day; rifle regiments (there were now only three) fired their *feux de joie*, and gunners boomed out their salutes — much like the first 1st of July.

But the biggest and grandest spectacle of 1967 was the Armed Forces tattoo, elements of which criss-crossed the country, playing all the major football stadiums and hockey arenas, and some of the smaller ones as well. Sell-out crowds were entranced by the scenes of soldiering in New France; they watched the naval gun run in amazement; and they tapped their feet happily to the pipes accompanying the Highland dancers from the Black Watch. The First World War vignette, so utterly realistic, was devastating in its impact. And the music was good, from the initial fanfares to the languorous lament. Little wonder that, as the cast marched off to the Maple Leaf, Vive le Canadien, Scotland the Brave, and Marche Vanier, tears of pride flowed openly.

Air defence gunners fire a *Blowpipe*
anti-aircraft missile. DND-REC-78-426

A 1 RCHA M-109 self-propelled gun moving to a firing position in
the Munsterlager range in northern Germany, autumn 1978. DND/ILC-78-209

A Royal Canadian Dragoons *Leopard C1* tank passes through
a German village during a NATO exercise in 1979. DND/ILC-79-192

A new family of wheeled light armoured vehicles was brought into service in Mobile Command in 1979. Here, a *Grizzly* wheeled
armoured personnel carrier is seen on patrol during a NATO exercise in northern Norway in early 1980. DND/IOC-80-104 (WO Vic Johnson)

UNIFICATION

There were also tears of regret and, for some, sorrow. Although the Centennial celebrations brought a brief respite from concrete changes, Defence Minister Hellyer had decided early in the year to push ahead with his plan to unify the three services. Debate in the House of Commons was bitter; discussion before the Commons defence committee was hotter still. Some argued that since navies, armies, and air forces had distinct and separate primary roles and functions, "best understood in each service," it was a mistake to force them together. "To do so," one commentator noted, "would degrade their capability." Others, particularly sailors but also including Guy Simonds, could not accept the disappearance of the Royal Canadian Navy, Canadian Army, and Royal Canadian Air Force — and the history and traditions that had served them so well — on both practical and emotional grounds. What pride could anyone have, they asked, in the nondescript green uniform chosen for the new single service? The CDS, VCDS, Chief of Personnel, and Comptroller General all retired early, protesting the speed at which unification was proceeding, and Admiral Landymore was dismissed. But the unification bill passed in April 1967, to come into effect on 1 February 1968. Thus, when the last sailors, soldiers, and airmen of the Centennial Tattoo marched out of the stadium, spectators knew they were witnessing the end of an era. Within a few months, all that had just been celebrated and glorified would be no more.

1 February 1968 was a cold, bleak day, even where there was sunshine. Across Canada, and at Canadian military establishments around the world, traditional flags and ensigns were hauled down, replaced by a new device featuring the Canadian Maple Leaf in the fly, and the new Canadian Forces coat of arms. Later, in most messes, toasts were drunk to the Royal Canadian Navy, Canadian Army, and Royal Canadian Air Force. Did anyone lift a glass to the 'Canadian Armed Forces' with enthusiasm? Most of those present at these ceremonies still wore their old service dress, so there was still some colour, but in Ottawa especially an effort was made to ensure that the new green uniform was in evidence. Wing Commanders were now Lieutenant-Colonels; Naval Lieutenants were now Captains (and Naval Captains, Colonels); and the rank of Warrant Officer replaced that of Staff Sergeant.

At least the regimental system had survived — and in time, regimental devices and badges would find their way back onto the Canadian Forces uniform — but soldiering in Canada had changed forever. With the introduction of centralized personnel policies and promotion lists, unit COs lost traditional influence and authority. At times, unified Base units seemed more interested in keeping their files in order and their stores tidy than in providing real service to field units. And, with the creation of new, unified, 'green' logistics and administration branches, among others, it was felt that the institutional closeness that had existed between the various Corps of the old Army had been seriously undermined.

Ironically, the great architect of unification was no longer at his desk in the temporary buildings housing CFHQ on 1 February 1968. Having accomplished his task, Paul Hellyer had moved on to the Department of Transport and the campaign to succeed Lester Pearson as Liberal leader and Prime Minister. Despite all that he had promised about procuring new equipment with the savings produced by his reforms, capital spending actually fell from about $250 million in 1963-1964 to $212 million in 1966-1967. The strength of the regular forces — land, sea, and air — had also fallen, from 121,000 in 1963 to 110,000 in 1967, and more cuts were in the offing.

The Cameron Highlanders of Ottawa practising watermanship, August 1980.
Photo: M.G. Murgoci

General Ramsey M. Withers,
Chief of the Defence Staff
1980-1983. DND/REP-82-186

Gunner D.P. Bezeau of 30 Field Regiment adjusts the fuse of a
105mm high explosive round under the supervision of
Bombardiers Bachynsky and Guy, and of Sergeant Cummings,
Petawawa, February 1981. Photo: M.G. Murgoci

Private Bruce Applin, 1 PPCLI, guards the entrance during a
fighting in built-up areas exercise. DND/IM-81-300

THE TRUDEAU YEARS

In the event, it soon mattered little what Paul Hellyer had promised. On 6 April, three months after unification, Pierre Elliott Trudeau won Liberal leadership race and then, riding a wave of 'Trudeaumania,' obtained a clear majority in the general election held in June. Although two Ottawa veterans, Mitchell Sharp and Léo Cadieux, were named Ministers of External Affairs and National Defence, from the outset it was clear that the Prime Minister himself would play a major role in making foreign and defence policy, and that he would personally supervise the fundamental review of Canada's place in the world that he had promised during the election campaign.

That did not bode well for the military. Those who knew the Prime Minister well were aware that he did not look at the world in the old, bi-polar way: that he did not, for example, consider the Soviet Union as an inevitable ideological foe despite its invasion of Czechoslovakia in the spring of 1968. Nor, it was clear, did he have much regard for NATO and the theory of the collective trip-wire. As far back as 1963 he had denounced Lester Pearson's decision to acquire nuclear weapons as an unnecessary step since what Canada did was irrelevant: the defence of the West lay with the Americans, he said, and it was up to them — and the Soviets — alone to determine whether deterrence succeeded or failed and, consequently, whether there would be peace or war. Finally, he had also been heard to remark how this or that senior officer, though clearly able, had wasted his potential because he had remained in the Forces.

Although a new NATO role was accepted in 1968 — the Canadian Air/Sea Transportable (CAST) Brigade, which would be sent to Norway or Denmark in the event of conflict — it became clear, as the government's defence and foreign policy review progressed, that the permanent stationing of troops on Europe's Central Front could no longer be taken for granted. Canada's defence partners had had ample time to recover from the Second World War, the Prime Minister explained, and they should now be able to contribute more for their own defence. Moreover, once it was recognized (as Trudeau had) "that our fate would be determined by the United States' strategic arsenal, and not by our own efforts," a senior policy adviser pointed out, "then the Canadian Forces became little more than diplomatic baggage that had to be carried around but for that reason had to be kept as light as possible."

Weapons Technician by Catherine de Wolfe. CWM 81056

Troops of the Canadian Airborne Regiment during Exercise Réponse Spéciale at Earlton, Ontario, February 1982.
DND/ISC-82-410

A section of the Princess Patricia's Canadian Light Infantry practice an assault from a *Grizzly* armoured personnel carrier.
DND/IXC-81-299

The drama unfolded, scene by scene. On 29 May 1968 the Prime Minister committed the government to

... take a hard look, in consultation with our Allies, at our military role in NATO and determine whether our present military commitment is still appropriate to the present situation in Europe.

On 19 July he told his Cabinet that no one should make a public statement "which could be interpreted as supporting a continuing commitment to NATO by Canada." On 30 September, in company with the Minister of National Defence, he broached the subject of withdrawing Canadian troops with the Prime Minister of France. On 7 November he told an official from External Affairs that Canada should "perhaps ... be worried much more about civil war in North America" than "the European threat." Then, at a high-level meeting on 9 December he posed the following questions:

Will the US sacrifice Europe and NATO before blowing up the world?.... What is the point of having large convention forces if they are going to lose the conventional battle anyway.... Is NATO the best way to secure peace at the moment.... When are we going to arrive at a plan to achieve peace by not getting stronger militarily.... In what way is NATO of value to Canada?

With good reason, a sense of foreboding spread though Canadian Forces and Mobile Command Headquarters. The brigade group in Europe had been the cutting edge of the Army for more than a decade. It was the principal reason for most of the Army's heavier equipment, and for its size. The training that took place in Europe, just a few miles from the 'enemy' and in concert with British, American, and German allies, was the most realistic available to Canadian soldiers, keeping them on their toes and up-to-date, and making possible the Fort Garry Horse's brilliant performance in Exercise *Treble Chance*. If, however, the Army came home, what would it do? Purely domestic training, it was clear, could not make it battle-worthy, ready to be sent to the front-line as a crisis developed. Did the answer lie in the precedent of the dismal decades of the 1920s and 1930s? Would the Army shrink in size to the point that it was little more than a heavily-armed constabulary? Did the future belong entirely to peacekeeping — which, some thought, was hardly soldiering at all, no matter how commendable it might be?

With his ground well prepared when full Cabinet debate began at the end of March 1969, the Prime Minister declared his intention to "reduce and at the earliest possible time, end, the stationing of forces in Europe." The long-expected blow had fallen, but the Defence Minister, threatening resignation, fought a strong rear-guard action which, in the end, won the day. Rather than withdrawal, the government chose "a planned and phased reduction." That would see land and air forces remain in Europe for the foreseeable future, but in greatly reduced numbers. The overall commitment, it was decided after prolonged argument, would be halved to 5000 men, and the Army's share of the reduction included one complete infantry battalion, the *Honest John* batteries, combat service support units, and one company from each of the two remaining infantry battalions.

Members of the Canadian Airborne Regiment get set for a jump, 1984. DND/ISC-84-413

The new Mechanized Battle Group, as it would be called temporarily, was far too small and, maintained at only 58 percent of war footing, far too weak to hold a defensive position on the front line in the British Corps sector; and in time it was moved to Southern Germany, to Lahr and Baden, near the Rhine, where it would occupy old French barracks and, as the Central Army Group reserve, be allocated to support American or German forces in a counter-penetration role. Because of Léo Cadieux, the Army's place in Europe had been saved, but it was not the place it had once been. Allied commanders had always said that the Canadian troops were among the best in NATO. They still probably were. But their new role soon provided a ready excuse for postponing the purchase of new equipment.

The downgrading of Canada's NATO commitment was reflected (and, indeed, foretold) in the defence priorities announced by the Prime Minister on 3 April 1969: surveillance of our territory and coastline; the defence of North American in cooperation with United States forces; the fulfillment of such NATO commitments as may be agreed upon; and the performance of such international peacekeeping roles as we may from time to time assume. As one historian has noted, these not only turned Paul Hellyer's priorities 'upside down', but it could be argued that 'surveillance' was scarcely a 'hard' military role, and it certainly did not appear to offer much to the Army. Further personnel cuts were announced at the same time, reducing the regular forces to about 80,000-85,000, and the reserves from 23,000 to 19,000.

These included the cuts approved by Hellyer a year earlier. Between September 1968 and July 1970, The Canadian Guards, the Queen's Own Rifles, the Black Watch, and The Fort Garry Horse were all struck off the regular order of battle. Although their place was taken (to some extent) by the addition of third battalions to the RCR and PPCLI, by the creation of two French-language units — 12e Régiment blindé du Canada, and 5e Régiment d'artillerie légère du Canada — and, of course, by the formation of the Canadian Airborne Regiment, the fact that Canadian-based units were also maintained at considerably less than full war establishment meant that the result was a net loss.

Increasingly, it seemed that the armed forces were irrelevant to modern Canada. Apart from the fact that they were a source of disciplined manpower that could be used for any number of non-military tasks, their function was largely symbolic, and for that neither modern weapons nor large numbers were required. The debased place of the Canadian Forces could hardly have been made clearer than by the appointment of Donald Macdonald as Defence Minister in September 1970. An early advocate of a complete withdrawal from Europe, he set the Forces' first priority as guarding Canadian sovereignty and contributing to "the social and economic development of Canada" — tasks normally associated with the Departments of Regional and Industrial Expansion and Health and Welfare.

Her Royal Highness The Princess Alexandra, accompanied by Major John Hasek, talks to members of the Queen's Own Rifles during an exercise conducted as part of the regiment's 125th Anniversary festivities. Photo by Captain C. Almey

Senior officers scrambled to find relevance for the military in the new environment. General F. R. Sharp, then Chief of the Defence Staff, boasted in April 1970 that

... the Canadian Forces have contributed very significantly to the development and maintenance of a distinctive Canadian national identity....

The aim, over the long run, is to give absolute equality in a Canadian armed service that has uniquely Canadian manners, customs, and methods that have been developed by servicemen from both [English and French Canadian] cultures. It must not be a copy of the British, or of the American, or of the French — it must be our own — not because the British or the French or the Americans are not good ... but because, for national identity and sovereignty reasons we need uniquely Canadian Armed Forces [and] our own military professionalism.

Brigadier-General G.G. Bell, senior adviser to the CDS, was saying much the same thing two years later; however, he warned, "National defence activities should, where possible, enhance force effectiveness and must not degrade operational readiness."

He had good reasons for adding this last comment. For, in the fall of 1970, just as many soldiers were watching, in despair, what they thought was the beginning of the end of a fighting army, the citizens of Ottawa, Montreal, Quebec City and a number of smaller towns found themselves looking at bayonets in the streets.

White phosphorus smoke grenades explode forward of the firing point during Central Militia Area's *Cougar* gun camp at the Meaford Range, March 1985. Photo by Captain C. Almey

Soldiers of the Royal Canadian Regiment cross the Battle River in Camp Wainwright during Exercise Rendezvous 85. DND/RVC-85-10208A

Privates Davidson and Clazie of the 2nd Battalion,
Royal New Brunswick Regiment man a *Carl Gustaf* rocket launcher. CDQ Archives

Corporal Rick Ridsdill and Corporal Gus Theodorakidis
of the 48th Highlanders distribute blank ammunition prior
to a weekend exercise in CFB Borden. Photo by Captain C. Almey

A section of 1 PPCLI prepares to enter a building during a fighting
in built-up areas exercise, Germany, June 1985. DND/ILC-85-122

OPERATIONS ESSAY AND GINGER

Within Québec, the *Front de Libération du Québec* had, since 1963, added terrorism and violence to the political campaign for the province's independence from the rest of Canada. A minority on the radical fringe of Quebec's nationalist movement, the FLQ nevertheless grabbed a disproportionate share of media attention through its bombings of the Wolfe-Montcalm statue and several mail boxes — both regarded as symbols of Anglophone (and federal) domination — and the theft of rifles from the Fusiliers Mont-Royal armoury.

The attention such actions garnered was not matched by any real increase in support for the FLQ or, for that matter, for the idea of Quebec independence in general. Indeed, the maiming of an Armed Forces explosives expert who was trying to dismantle a bomb probably cost the FLQ more than it could ever have imagined in terms of public sympathy. Yet in October 1970 two FLQ cells in Montreal raised the stakes dramatically when they kidnapped British trade commissioner James Cross on the 5th and, when that failed to produce the desired results, Quebec labour minister and deputy premier Pierre Laporte five days later.

Within two days troops from 2 Combat Group at CFB Petawawa were in Ottawa, where they took over a number of security duties from the local police forces and the RCMP. The FLQ had planted bombs in the Ottawa area before, and now that it had turned to kidnapping the government felt it essential to provide a stronger force to protect VIPs and to guard vital points (like hydro-electric stations) and government buildings. Operation *Ginger*, as it was called, would eventually involve over 3000 service personnel, including soldiers from the 8th Canadian Hussars, 2 Royal Canadian Horse Artillery, 3 Royal Canadian Regiment, 1 Field Squadron, 2 Signals Squadron, and 1 Royal Canadian Regiment, and lasted from 12 October to 21 November 1970.

Cartier Square Drill Hall, in downtown Ottawa near the Rideau Canal, was headquarters for the operation which, more than once, involved sweeps and searches of the Quebec countryside following tips that Cross's kidnappers — or stores of weapons — were in the area. One such operation, codenamed *Underbrush*, involved a quick insertion into the bush near Luskville, a small community a few miles upstream from the capital, but turned up nothing.

During the October Crisis nearly the whole of the Canadian Army was deployed to Ottawa and Montreal in Operations *Essay* and *Ginger*. Shown here are 2 RCR M-113s on their way from Gagetown to Saint John to be loaded aboard ships bound for Montreal.

CDQ Archives

Ottawans were taken aback by the military presence in their midst and, perhaps, by the Prime Minister's easy dismissal of those who object to it as so many "bleeding hearts." Trucks, jeeps, and armoured personnel carriers could be seen everywhere in the city centre, helicopters flew overhead, and troops in combat gear and with weapons at the ready patrolled street corners. The country as a whole gasped when, on 15 October, the Quebec government asked for military assistance to "help the police protect the public and public buildings" and when, early the next morning, the government invoked the War Measures Act which, among other things, suspended a number of legal and civil rights across the country. Whether invoking the War Measures Act against the alleged 'apprehended insurrection' was the right thing to do has been debated ever since, the question usually turning on whether the government exaggerated the threat, but it was not for the military to question their orders.

Operation *Essay* began at 1307 hours on 15 October, when the Vice Chief of Defence Staff, Lieutenant-General M.R. Dare, ordered troops from 5e Groupement de Combat to move to assigned areas. Using helicopters, B Company of 2 R22eR was deployed to Montreal within the hour, while truck convoys from Valcartier were heading for Quebec City, the Saguenay, Trois-Rivières, and Sherbrooke, among other places. At Edmonton, the French-language 1er Commando Aéroporté of the Canadian Airborne Regiment was on its way by 1330 hours, while the next day 2 RCR from CFB Gagetown was also committed. Eventually, 5 RALC was stationed in Quebec City, 2 R22eR in Montreal West, 3 R22eR in central, eastern, and northern Montreal, with 12 RBC and 5 Escadron du Genie spread widely across the province. Airborne forces were retained for quick-reaction duties such as sweeps, raids, and mob control. As other units arrived they were deployed around various vulnerable points. 3 RCR, 1 RCR, 3 RCHA, and 1 Signals Regiment would be seen in Montreal, particulary at Dorval, while a squadron of the 8th Canadian Hussars from Gagetown went to Tadoussac to guard hydro lines there. Other units, including 2 PPCLI guarded VIPs, locks, other facilities along the St. Lawrence Seaway, and police stations — in shifts lasting eight to twelve hours. Air support was available on request.

'Van Doo' troops guard a helicopter at the entrance to the headquarters of the Quebec Provincial Police in Montreal, where counter-terrorist operations were coordinated in October 1970. R22eR Photo

The October Crisis of 1970 brought troops into the streets of Ottawa and Montreal to guard vital points and VIPs. In this photo the flags are at half-mast after the murder of the Hon. Pierre Laporte.
DND/PCN-70-465

All in all, 7500 troops were called out for service in Montreal. The military response could not prevent the murder of Laporte on 17 October, but his death probably solidified support against the FLQ and may have played a role in Premier Robert Bourassa's November election victory. Yet almost two months elapsed between Laporte's murder and the discovery of the house in which James Cross was held — through good, normal police work. Two companies from 3 R22^{e}R and one from 2 R22^{e}R sealed off the area and made contingency plans to assault the building, but after prolonged negotiations Cross was released on 3 December in return for granting the kidnappers safe passage to Cuba. After the units involved cleared up a few loose ends, Operation *Essay* came to an end a month later.

No matter how one views the political handling of the October crisis, the military operation was carried out with only the most minor hitches. Just a few shots were fired, mostly by accident; there was only one death — that of a soldier in Ottawa, again by accident; and while a very small number of civilians may have suffered a few bruises after taunting the odd soldier on duty, the troops acted professionally and with restraint: there were no bayonet charges, and no volleys of tear gas — nothing, in short, like the violence that had erupted in city streets and on college campuses in the United States just two years before. This was, perhaps, because so many of the troops involved most directly with the public were Francophone and had peacekeeping experience, because the FLQ did not enjoy wide support, and because only regular soldiers were used where there was any chance of interaction with the public.

Gunner Andrew Bateman and Bombardier Bill Atkinson of the 7th Toronto Regiment, RCA, practice gun recovery drills at CFB Borden, spring 1986. Photo by Captain C. Almey

Private Marc Villeneuve of the Algonquin Regiment stands sentry during the 1986 Militia concentration in CFB Borden.

Photo by Captain C. Almey

A Master-Corporal of the Essex and Kent Scottish helps a teammate across a rope bridge during the Central Militia Area infantry competition at CFB Borden in 1986. Photo by Captain C. Almey

Lieutenant-General James Fox, Commander of Mobile Command, talks to Corporal Jeffrey Pitblado of the Royal Regiment of Canada, CFB Borden, August 1986.

Photo by Captain C. Almey

Members of the 48th Highlanders practice rappelling down a cliff-face in the Militia Training Area at Meaford, Ontario, October 1986.

Photo by Captain C. Almey

DEFENCE IN THE 70's

In short, Operations *Essay* and *Ginger* were resounding successes from the military point of view, and when they were over servicemen believed that, because of them, the government must in future recognize the value and importance of its armed forces and treat them accordingly. But the armed forces' success in internal security operations did not alter Pierre Elliott Trudeau's view of the world, and did not result in any major increases in the defence budget. This was underscored in the 1971 White Paper *Defence in the 70s*. "It is in Canada's interest that war should be prevented," the pamphlet noted,

> ...*but if unavoidable that it should be halted before it can escalate into a broader conflict which could affect the security of Canada. The Government intends therefore to maintain within feasible limits [emphasis added] a general purpose combat capability of high professional standard within the Armed Forces, and to keep available the widest possible choice of options for responding to unforeseen international developments.*

However, the military would also be used for "to assist development in the civil sector, especially in the remote regions where disciplined task forces with wide experience in adapting to unusual or challenging circumstances are required." The Forces would also be tasked with "supporting the civil agencies in exercising pollution control in the North and off Canada's coasts and ... in providing relief and assistance in the event of natural disasters or other civil emergencies, including those resulting from oil spills or other forms of pollution."

Land forces would remain in Europe, but the intent was that they would be reconfigured to give them

> ... *the high degree of mobility needed for tactical reconnaissance missions in a Central Region reserve role. The Centurion medium tank will be retired, since this vehicle is not compatible with Canada-based forces and does not possess adequate mobility. In its place a light, tracked direct-fire support vehicle will be acquired as one of the main items of equipment. This vehicle, which is air portable, will be introduced later into combat groups in Canada. The result will be enhanced compatibility of Canadian and European based forces, and a lighter, more mobile land force capable of a wide range of missions....*

— none of which, it might be added, were of much relevance to the NATO context in Germany.

Indeed, the plan was never quite implemented, except that Regular Force armoured regiments in Canada were converted to 'light armour' when the *Centurion* was taken out of service. Instead, it was the commitment to NATO's Northern Flank, initially a battalion group to be followed up by a brigade group, that had the greatest prominence politically because training for possible operations in Norway required the Army to move into the Canadian north, where by definition it supported sovereignty.

Corporal Karl Valaitis of the Royal Regiment of Canada gives a teammate a 'head start' during the Central Militia Area infantry competition, 1986. Photo by Captain C. Almey

Militiamen, too, had greater prominence, but not in the ways they were used to. In 1971, 726 were attached to Permanent Force units in Canada, 149 were serving in Germany, and it was hoped that still more could be posted to units involved in peacekeeping operations, filling holes in a regular military establishment which, by 1975, had been cut to 78,000, of which 17,500 were in Mobile Command. Indeed, as the 1976 Report on National Defence proclaimed:

It is very seldom, nowadays, that the undertakings of Mobile Command's Reserves — the Militia — are the object of special attention. The stated mission of the reserves being to support the Regular Forces, the Militia now takes part in virtually all activities of Mobile Command to a point where it is increasingly difficult to identify Militia endeavours separately. Militia men and women, individually and collectively, have participated in all of the defence objectives in 1976.

That was wonderful, up-beat rhetoric, but in fact morale in the Land Forces, both Regular and Reserve, was low — despite the efforts of General J.A. Dextraze, CDS between 1972 and 1976, and Lieutenant-Generals S.C. Waters and J. Chouinard, who commanded Mobile Command during these years. All three did their best to persuade the country's soldiers that they still belonged to an Army, not some bureaucracy in uniform, but the troops' doubts about the government's commitment to NATO — and concern about their aging weapons systems and other equipment — were not easily overcome.

As things turned out, however, by 1976 the Trudeau government found that the general winding down of Canada's military contribution to NATO was a liability in terms of gaining access to European economic markets, and as a result steps were taken to give the Army the modern weapons it needed to remain a viable fighting force. Tube-launched, optically-tracked, wire guided (TOW) antitank missiles were procured to replace the old 106 mm recoilless rifle; British *Blowpipe* anti-aircraft missiles were to be obtained; and most important of all, the decision not to buy new main battle tanks to replace the *Centurion* was reversed, the nod going to the German *Leopard*, of which 128 would be purchased (at a cost of $210 million). In addition, orders would soon be placed for a new family of Canadian-built (but Swiss-designed) wheeled general purpose armoured vehicles "for infantry and armoured training in the Regular Force and the Militia" — the *Cougar*, mounting a 76 mm gun for direct-fire support, the machine-gun equipped *Grizzly*, and the *Husky* recovery vehicle — and for long-barrel 155 mm self-propelled howitzers.

Corporal K. Stravopoulos, Royal Regiment of Canada, during a house-clearing exercise, February 1987. Photo by Captain C. Almey

Sappers of 4 Canadian Engineer Regiment practice mine clearance. DND/ILC-87-716-16

Militia soldiers traverse an obstacle course. Photo by Captain C. Almey

An RCD armoured recovery vehicle crosses a temporary bridge over
the Lech River during the II German Corps fall exercise, 1987. DND/ILC-87-107-2

Members of the Royal Regiment
of Canada and 25 Medical
Company cooperate in a medical
evaluation exercise, January 1988.

Photo by Captain C. Almey

OPERATION GAMESCAN

The year 1976 also saw a major deployment of Army personnel to assist the civilian authorities in providing security as well as logistics, administrative, and medical support for the Olympic Games held that year in Montreal. Planning for Operation *Gamescan* had begun in 1973, and was heavily influenced by the tragedy that occurred at the Munich games the year before, when Palestinian terrorists seized and killed several members of the Israeli Olympic team.

The *Gamescan* force, which involved several thousand Reservists and Regulars, and was controlled by Mobile Command, was organized into a number of task forces. Task Force 1, found primarily from 5e Groupement de Combat at Valcartier but including 1 PPCLI and 1er Commando, Canadian Airborne Regiment, was assigned to the Olympic Stadium and Village and some of the smaller competition and training sites. It also deployed a small element from 12e RBC to guard the Quebec Hydro lines over the Saguenay River at Tadoussac. 5e RALC patrolled the American border to prevent terrorist infiltration. Task Force 2, provided by 2 Combat Group from CFB Petawawa, also guarded training and competition sites and, in addition, provided VIP, hotel, and baggage security. Task Force 3, primarily 2 Commando of the Airborne Regiment, was the strategic reserve, and was held at St. Jean. Task Force 4 provided security in Kingston, Toronto, and Ottawa. 2 RCR was allocated special tasks including protecting the Queen during her stay, guarding vital points in Montreal, and patrolling the Maine/New Brunswick border.

In some respects, *Gamescan* was a replay of *Essay* in that military checkpoints were established all around Montreal, but this time the soldiers were backing up the police and privately hired security personnel. And to make their presence less intrusive, most wore summer work dress and berets rather than combat dress and helmets. The Olympic Village was, however, primarily a military responsibility, and armed soldiers were continuously on patrol around its two-mile long perimeter.

Not everything was serious. Apparently esprit-de-corps within 2 R22eR

...dictated that the unit claim the Olympic Village for its own. The first day the troops began their protection duties, a Van Doo flag surreptitiously appeared high atop the Village's radio antenna. With every soldier privately smiling, the flag went unnoticed for four days. Then someone finally spotted it, and there was a brief flurry of activity as police reacted to the possibility of terrorists on the rooftops. The situation was quickly explained, and the police took the incident in good humour. However, the red, yellow, and blue pennant came down.

The Special Service Medal, approved in 1984 for award for service in exceptional circumstances in a clearly defined locality. It was first awarded with a bar inscribed 'Pakistan', for training Afghan refugees in mine clearance techniques, 1989-1990.

The Meritorious Service Cross, instituted in 1984 for award for the performance of military activity of such a rare high standard that it reflects great credit on the Canadian Forces. It was first awarded in 1985. Among the first recipients were Sergeant Larry Abbott, a Military Policeman, and Lieutenant-Colonel Donald Ethell, PPCLI.

1977 was a year of change for the Land Forces. The Canadian Airborne Regiment moved from Edmonton to Petawawa, where it became part of the newly created Special Service Force (which replaced the old 2 Combat Group and included, as well, 2 RCHA, 2 Service Battalion, 8th Canadian Hussars, 1 RCR, 2 Combat Engineer Regiment, and the tactical helicopters of 427 Squadron). In addition, the remaining two combat groups were re-designated Brigade Groups, and the CAST role was transferred to 5e Groupe-Brigade at Valcartier. 1 Brigade Group continued to fulfill Canada's commitment to the defence of North America, while the Special Service Force, a few cynics suggested, gave the country a specialized internal security force. (It would temporarily be given the CAST role in 1980, a move which reduced the Canadian commitment to Norway by about 1000 officers and men.)

Corporal Steve Monardo of 709 Communications Regiment repairs telephone lines during the 1988 Militia concentration in CFB Borden. Photo by Captain C. Almey

Cooks are an essential and often overlooked group in the success of Militia training. Here Lieutenant-Colonel Robert Hilliard of Toronto Militia District, a former commanding officer of 25 Service Battalion, finds himself very well fed. Photo by Captain C. Almey

In Europe, meanwhile, the training of 4 Canadian Mechanized Brigade Group was intensified as the new equipment procured the year before began to arrive at the 'sharp end'. The practice paid off. Despite only just obtaining *Leopards*, the Royal Canadian Dragoons were able to win the Canadian Army Trophy — NATO's tank gunnery competition — by outshooting opponents from Belgium, Britain, Germany, Holland, and the United States. And in 1979's *Constant Enforcer*, NATO's largest field exercise ever, 4 CMBG performed so effectively in night attacks that other Allied forces complained to the umpires that the Canadians "had to be cheating."

The renewed emphasis on combat readiness — and at headquarters on mobilization planning — did not reflect any substantive change in government policy, but rather a sense that somehow, after years of détente, East-West relations were deteriorating. The Soviet invasion of Afghanistan in 1979 further exacerbated tensions, and that year the Conservatives under Joe Clark won a general election with, among other things, campaign promises to increase the defence budget, enlarge the Regular Force by about 5000, and bring back distinctive uniforms for the land, sea, and air elements and a command structure which recognized the importance of the three separate environments.

Military Policeman, Private Steve Stecyk of 23 Military Police Platoon, checks a vehicle convoy during the 1988 Militia concentration. Photo by Captain C. Almey

The Conservative government did not survive long enough to implement these changes, and the Trudeau government which replaced it was more interested in national energy programmes, fighting the recession (and the Quebec referendum), and constitutional patriation than defence, although it did approve testing of the American cruise missile over Canadian territory. Indeed, in the fall of 1983 the Prime Minister began his lonely, and very individual, peace initiative. Yet despite a general lack of interest in military matters on the part of the government, defence spending was to rise 3 percent per year in real terms, and planning and training for combat was authorized on a scale rarely permitted during the 1970s.

In Exercise *Rendezvous* 81 held at CFB Gagetown in the summer of 1981, soldiers trained at the division level in the field for the first time since 1956. Militia personnel were intimately involved as part of a new 'total force' concept designed to allow augmentation of the Regular Force for a longer conventional war, which once again seemed a possibility. Widely regarded as a 'tonic' for the Army — that noun, but *never* capitalized, increasingly replaced 'land element' and 'land forces' even in official documents — and the brainchild of Mobile Command's Lieutenant-General C.H. Belzile, the *Rendezvous*-type exercise would become a biennial feature of Army life, the 1983 version (which involved the move of about 8000 troops and 2500 vehicles) taking place at Wainwright, Alberta, so that 1 Canadian Brigade Group could take part.

Members of the Royal Regiment of Canada prepare for a parade, autumn 1988. Photo by M.G. Murgoci

Bombardier Cara Camplejohn of 11 Field Regiment, RCA checks the lay of a 105mm gun, Petawawa, 1988. Photo by Captain C. Almey

THE MULRONEY YEARS

When Brian Mulroney's Conservatives won the election of September 1984 they did so having promised to do even more for the military. Within a few years, navy and air force blue, light tan, and white would join 'CF Green' as authorized uniform colours, considerable money was made available for new equipment, and it seemed that the Armed Forces would again be expanded to allow them to better fulfill the country's commitments abroad. In addition, the Reserves were to play an increasingly important role in Canada's 'total force', and because of Human Rights legislation there were now very few military occupations from which women could be excluded.

For the Army, it was planned that the NATO brigade would be strengthened by the addition of a squadron to its armoured regiment, a battery to 4 RCHA, an extra company to each of the two infantry battalions, and the creation of two air defence batteries. Moreover, as early as 1985 there was talk that Canada's ultimate commitment to the defence of Western Europe might again climb to a full division. That would give a sense of reality to the notional expansion plans contained in Mobile Command's 'Corps 86' concept for restructuring the Army to ensure that it contained all those small but essential units necessary to field a division and to provide whatever 'corps troops' were required. So far as equipment was concerned, orders were placed for improved TOW antitank missiles, a new family of 5.56 mm small arms based on the US Colt M16A2 rifle, and low-level air defence guns and missiles.

Soldiers at the Royal Canadian Regiment Battle School train with the new C-9 light machine gun. DND/ISC-88-1281

The pace of training also intensified. *Rendezvous* 85 was the largest exercise to be held in Canada since the Korean War. Almost 14,000 troops took part over a six-week period, allowing commanders and their staffs to practise all phases of war (advance, attack, defence, and withdrawal) at the divisional level and to test the ability of usually static combat service support units to fulfill their role under simulated battle conditions. This was an area where weaknesses had been found in earlier Rendezvous exercises, and it was one where considerable improvement was required if a self-contained Canadian division was, indeed, to take the field again. In fact, the move to the exercise area was almost test enough: 10,000 troops, 4000 vehicles, and 41,000 tonnes of equipment and supplies were carried to Alberta by rail, road, and air.

The first Defence White Paper in sixteen years was tabled in June 1987. In it, the government displayed a sourness about world affairs, détente, and the failure of arms control which confirmed previous statements about the importance of strengthening NATO's conventional capabilities

...to improve deterrence, reduce the likelihood of war, and raise the nuclear threshold. If our conventional forces are to deter, they must be able to defend. If they are to defend, they must be able to fight. To do that, we must maintain their readiness and provide for their sustainment.

Exercise *Trillium Thunder*, a hub-to-hub shoot
by 26 guns of the Royal Canadian Horse Artillery, 7th Toronto Regiment,
11 Field Regiment and 56 Field Regiment at Meaford, October 1988. Photo by Captain C. Almey

The Toronto Scottish Regiment and the Black Watch parade at Queen's Park, Toronto, on the occasion of a visit by the Queen Mother, the Colonel-in-Chief of both units, July 1989.
Toronto Scottish Museum

At the same time, the White Paper recognized that

...much of the equipment of most elements of the Canadian Forces is in an advanced state of obsolescence or is already obsolete. Modernization programs have not kept pace.... The land forces have severe equipment shortages and too few combat-ready soldiers, and the Militia is too small,' ill-equipped and insufficiently trained to make up the difference.

At home, therefore, it was proposed to

...create additional brigades, mainly from the Reserves, to improve the land force's capability to undertake operations in defence of Canada. There will also be a minimally-trained guard force created to protect vital military locations.

In Europe, following the less-than-successful 1986 Exercise *Brave Lion* (in which 5000 personnel from 5e Brigade were air- and sea-lifted to Norway to test the CAST concept) it was decided to consolidate the Army's NATO commitment in the Central Region in Germany. Instead of moving to the north in time of crisis, the former CAST brigade would join 4 CMBG in a reactivated 1 Canadian Division. Equipment for the Canada-based brigade would be pre-positioned in Germany, and new tanks would be purchased. Deciding that it would be too costly to meet this new commitment entirely with Regular Force personnel, the White Paper noted that "a unit responding to an emergency could be manned by any mix of Regulars and Reserves," and consequently undertook to increase the strength of the Reserve to 90,000 (four times the current establishment) and to open dedicated Militia training centres. In the specific case of 1 Canadian Division, it was assumed that one-third of its strength (i.e. that which was not provided by 4 CMBG or 5e Brigade) would be drawn from Regular or Reserve units across the country as "individual operational taskings." (That Militiamen could find the time to do the training that would be required of them was assumed — perhaps a little hastily and optimistically.)

A reconnaissance patrol of the Queen's York Rangers prepares for an exercise, summer 1990. Photo by Captain C. Almey

When all was said and done, for one brief, shining moment it looked very much as if the Army of the mid-1950s had been reborn. This White Paper was not just another example of tinkering with a throw-away force for a 'come-as-you-are' war, but instead sought to lay the foundations for national mobilization in an extended conflict in which sustaining and reinforcing the regiments and battalions at the front were taken for granted.

Time ran out on these initiatives even before they were all introduced. The national debt was rising at an alarming rate, and because of that the April 1989 budget cancelled or put on hold many of the programmes announced in the 1987 White Paper — including the Navy's nuclear submarines and the Army's new tanks.

The world itself had also changed. Mikhail Gorbachev's twin programmes of *glasnost* and *perestroika*, intended to correct the USSR's glaring domestic economic and political problems, were accompanied by an amazingly 'hands-off' attitude to similar reform demands in Eastern Europe. Communist governments were soon toppling throughout the former Soviet empire; the Berlin Wall, since 1961 the symbol of the Iron Curtain, came tumbling down; and the two Germany's were reunited with breathtaking speed. And, following a decision taken in 1990, the Warsaw Pact military alliance, NATO's old enemy, was dismantled on 1 April 1991. Soviet troops began to withdraw from Poland, Hungary, Czechoslovakia, and eastern Germany even before then.

Soldiers of the Essex and Kent Scottish man a machine gun during a summer exercise. CDQ Archives

Major-General J.K. Dangerfield formally assumed command of the newly recreated 1st Canadian Division in a ceremony in Lahr, Germany, December 1989. DND/LRC-89-939-18

"No one seriously believes that the current Soviet leadership has any intention of attacking Western Europe or North America," the 1989 DND Annual Report declared emphatically. As a result, Canada participated wholeheartedly in talks aimed at reducing the size of the Allied military establishment in Europe. Just how far the cuts would go, and how fast they would come, was anybody's guess, but for the first time since 1951 it was not unreasonable to suggest that perhaps everybody could go home — and soon. In the Canadian case, a greatly reduced Regular Army was likely to result.

General A.J.G.D. de Chastelain

General John de Chastelain was commissioned in the Princess Patricia's Canadian Light Infantry in 1960 on graduation from Royal Military College. In his early years of service he held a variety of appointments, including aide-de-camp to the Chief of General Staff, company commander with 1 PPCLI in Germany, Canada and Cyprus, and Brigade Major of 1 Combat Group 1968-70. In 1970 he was promoted Lieutenant-Colonel and appointed commanding officer of 2 PPCLI in Winnipeg. After attending a bicultural program at Laval University, he served in the Militia District headquarters in Quebec City, and then, as a Colonel, commanded Canadian Forces Base Montreal. In 1976 he was named commander of the Canadian Contingent in Cyprus and Deputy Chief of Staff of UNFICYP. He was promoted Brigadier-General in 1977 on appointment as commandant of Royal Military College, and he served as commander of 4th Canadian Mechanized Brigade Group in Germany 1980-82. Following a year as Director-General Land Doctrine and Operations in NDHQ, he was promoted Major-General and became deputy commander of Mobile Command. In 1986 he was appointed Assistant Deputy Minister (Personnel) and promoted Lieutenant-General. He became Vice Chief of the Defence Staff in 1988. In 1989 he was promoted to the rank of General and appointed Chief of the Defence Staff.

Brigadier-General Armand Roy, Commander of 5e Brigade, (right) visits a Royal 22e Régiment bivouac during Operation *Salon*, August 1990. DND/ISC-90-744

OPERATION SALON

However, as the DND report for 1989 also noted, as the world became "less dangerous" it also became "less stable and more unpredictable." Canadians learned that in spades in 1990. On 1 March, Mohawks of the Kanesatake community near Oka set up barricades to protest the town's decision to expand a golf course on land they claimed belonged to them. The situation remained unsatisfactory, but stable in a strange sort of way, until 11 July, when one hundred officers from the Sûreté du Québec tried to dismantle the blockade, and during the struggle one police officer was shot and killed. The confrontation escalated; further blockades were established at Kanesatake and Kahnawake (near Montreal); and access to the Mercier Bridge across the St. Lawrence River was blocked. After a month of incidental violence, on 17 August the Quebec government asked the armed forces to replace the provincial police and, ten days later, to dismantle the barricades.

In this photograph which came to symbolize Operation *Salon*, Private Patrick Cloutier of the Royal 22e Régiment calmly stood his ground while being threatened by a Mohawk 'Warrior'. Canapress Photo Shaney Komulailen

A 'Van Doo' soldier stands guard in the rain at a checkpoint near a Mohawk barrier at Oka, Quebec, August 1990.
DND/ISC-90-465

Members of the Royal 22e Régiment prepared for action during Operation *Salon*, September 1990.
DND/ISC-90-598

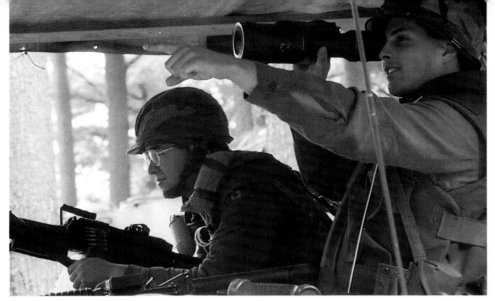

During Operation *Salon*, 5e Brigade troops carefully watched the activities of the so-called 'Warriors' using both thermal imaging and light intensification devices. DND/ISC-90-320

The professional restraint and unflinching discipline shown by soldiers in the face of continual provocation by the 'Warriors' gained great respect for the Army from the Canadian people. DND/ISC-90-592

Those at Kahnawake soon came down, although not without the odd moment of tension for 2 RCR, but at Oka a group of self-styled Warriors would not take down their barricades or give up their weapons — an arsenal which, it was thought, included heavy automatic weapons. From the beginning, the Chief of the Defence Staff, General John de Chastelain, made clear 5e Brigade was determined to carry out its task with a minimum of force, but it was also intent on making its presence felt. Once the armed forces were involved, the CDS explained, they had to win — as there was no one else to call upon. Television news each night presented vivid pictures of soldiers, some of them Militiamen, standing sometimes only a few inches from their Mohawk adversaries, staring at each other in unblinking concentration, and the young men of 2 R22eR gained considerable respect for their discipline and restraint. The odd time it seemed that things might break down, as both sides locked and loaded, but at long last, on 26 September, the Warriors left their refuge, creating some confusion in the process, it must be said, and the long affair was over with no other fatalities. One unpredicted result of Operation *Salon*, curiously enough, was that recruiting officers were soon besieged by young men wanting to join either the Regulars or Militia.

WAR IN THE GULF

Even before the Army was called to Oka, another event had taken place which brought Canada closer to war than at any time since Korea. On 2 August Iraq invaded and occupied Kuwait, and Canada, along with other member countries of the United Nations, backed up UN-imposed sanctions by sending three ships, one fighter squadron, and soldiers from the RCR and R22eR in Germany (as well as anti-aircraft gunners for the three ships) to the Persian Gulf. For the first time, women were prominent among those being sent to the potential war zone.

The war began on Thursday 17 January, and Canada was involved. But although the press was soon speculating about conscription, government spokesmen announced repeatedly that, apart from the two airfield defence companies, a few air defence gunners, and a field hospital — sent to meet a British request for assistance in treating both Allied wounded and enemy prisoners of war — the Canadian Army would take no direct part in the war. No one explained why this decision was taken, but those familiar with the Land Forces of 1991 needed no explanation. After years of neglect, underfunding, and reductions in strength, there was really no one available to send to Saudi Arabia — not if casualties were likely to be heavy.

Air defence gunners manning a 40mm gun aboard *HMCS Protecteur* in the Persian Gulf, autumn 1990.
DND Photo

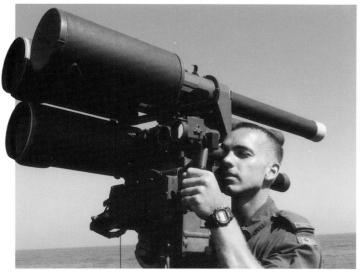

A gunner from 5e Régiment d'artillerie légère du Canada operates a *Javelin* air defence missile aboard a Canadian warship in the Persian Gulf, autumn 1990.
DND/ISC-90-2061

Royal Canadian Regiment soldiers guarding Canadian aircraft on the airfield at Qatar during the Persian Gulf crisis, autumn 1990. DND/IWC-90-409-37

A 'Van Doo' Master Corporal watches out over the desert surrounding the Canadian base at Qatar just prior to the outbreak of war. DND/IWC-90-520-15

Lieutenant-General Kent Foster, Commander of Mobile Command, inspects members of 4 Service Battalion during the war in the Persian Gulf, February 1991. DND/ISC-91-5337

As it turned out, following weeks of air operations, the land war was over almost as soon as it began. Enjoying complete air (and technological) superiority, American, British, French, Saudi, Kuwaiti, and Egyptian forces rolled over what was left of Iraq's southern field army in a matter of days. And Canadian sailors, airmen, and soldiers — including the field hospital — were all home by mid-April, with no loss of life.

But what were they returning to? Scarcely able to digest the pace of change in Europe, and bedevilled by domestic economic and constitutional problems, the government had not yet issued its post-Cold War White Paper on Defence.

And in the absence of direction, rumour abounded. Would the Army leave Europe by 1995? Would the *Leopard* be the last tank to see service in the Canadian Army? Was the Gulf War the kind of regional conflict likely to break out in the future? Was it best, therefore, for Canada to organize the kind of 'global mobile' Army able to fight low-to mid-intensity wars that Paul Hellyer had talked about nearly three decades earlier? Would this Army include a significantly higher proportion of Militiamen, as suggested by the Total Force concept, or was Total Force misguided and unrealistic in terms of producing large numbers of Reservists because it demanded too much of them? Time, of course, would tell.

The Gulf and Kuwait Service Medal, awarded to members of the Canadian Forces who served in the theatre of operations during the enforcement of United Nations sanctions and during Allied Coalition operations against Iraq. Those who served during the fighting (16 January — 3 March 1991) wear a silver bar on the ribbon.

CHAPTER 15

UNITED NATIONS PEACEKEEPING OPERATIONS

by
Norman Hillmer and Bill Rawling

Canada's peacekeeping tradition is indelibly linked to a diplomat and to a soldier — Lester Pearson and General E.L.M. Burns. In 1956 Pearson, then the Secretary of State for External Affairs in the government of Louis St. Laurent, engineered a United Nations Emergency Force (UNEF) to secure and supervise a cease-fire after British, French and Israeli troops mounted a direct military challenge to Egyptian President Nasser's takeover of the Suez Canal Company. General Burns, already in the Middle East as chief of staff of the United Nations Truce Supervision Organization (UNTSO), was a natural choice as commander of UNEF, the first large multinational force with serious peacekeeping responsibilities. Pearson was awarded the Nobel Peace Prize in 1957 for his innovative work in helping to extinguish the Suez fire, while black and white television images of the methodical, unsmiling, impartially severe Burns flickered back home from the trouble spots of the area.

Peacekeeping, Burns found, was a most unmilitary occupation. He expected to meet the hard problems of the Middle East as a soldier, at first approaching his UNEF responsibilities with the forcefulness and decisiveness of a man trained to take action. Not wanting the new force to be pushed to one side or ignored as UNTSO had been, he asked for a strong peacekeeping army, containing armour and fighting aircraft, capable of carrying out military operations. Instead he got something, he recalled in his memoirs, that was "much less potent...with defensive powers only, and limited defensive powers at that." Burns had been given the work not of a soldier or even a policeman but that of a diplomat — mediation, persuasion, and negotiation. Peacekeeping was a hard, monotonous mission without clearly defined victories.

Lieutenant-General E.L.M. Burns, Commander of the United Nations Emergency Force, November 1956 to December 1959. He is wearing a 'United Nations uniform' he designed.
DND/PL-106455

The United Nations Medal, with ribbon for service with the UN Truce Supervision Organization. Other than for UNEF, the same medal has been awarded for all UN peacekeeping missions, with a different ribbon for each operation. In most missions the medal is awarded for 90 days service

A Bedouin goat herder leads his flock past a patrol of the 8th Hussars Reconnaissance Squadron in the Sinai desert, autumn 1958. DND/ME-733

IN THEORY AND PRACTICE

Peacekeeping had not been envisaged by the founders of the United Nations. The charter states as a first principle that the UN seeks to "maintain international peace and security." It makes provision for a potentially powerful Military Staff Committee and calls upon member nations to keep military forces ready to combat aggression. Yet the international organization was never able to agree on such an arrangement, and its central body, the Security Council, was paralyzed from the start by Cold War tensions between the Soviet Union and the United States, each with a veto to prevent the taking of any measure it did not favour. Except in 1950, when the Council took advantage of a Soviet absence to move quickly against North Korea, it was impossible to get the United Nations behind concerted, substantial commitments to collective security. Thus a new concept, peacekeeping, lurched into view as a response to the world's many messy quarrels. Lester Pearson and others hoped that it would give time, a breathing space, so that real peace could be manufactured. All too often, however, peacekeeping became an end in itself.

Guard Post — Refuelling Stop, Sinai, 1975
by G.G. Jamieson. CWM 75084

Two types of UN peace forces evolved, both of which have been used frequently over the years. The first consists of individuals or small groups of observers; the second is composed of formed bodies of troops which are placed between two rivals. The earliest experiments in peacekeeping — UNTSO, for example — were limited efforts in observation and reporting. Then came UNEF, a major innovation because of its size and cost and because of its mandate to secure the armistice and maintain order, as well as monitor developments. This chapter will concentrate on major peacekeeping efforts such as UNEF, which many commentators argue are the only ones worthy of the name.

Peacekeeping rests on disinterestedness. The theory is that force cannot be used to impress, intimidate, or punish. Military personnel are inserted into a dispute not to fight but to watch impartially over the peace after a cease-fire is declared. They cannot strike out, except in self-defence or in carefully-defined circumstances. They have no powers of enforcement. They stand near or between nations or parties in conflict only with the consent of the protagonists, a consent which can be withdrawn at any time. In practice, as we shall see, some of these rules are broken, but peacekeepers always work under severe limitations.

A typical UN observation post in Cyprus. DND/ISC-84-336

**Patrol on Green Line,
Previous Site of
Heavy Bombing**
by W.S. Houston. CWM 72309

There is now — in 1991 — a substantial body of peacekeeping experience, and a long official list of UN peacekeeping operations:

1948-	**UNTSO** United Nations Truce Supervision Organization	1973-79	**UNEF II** Second United Nations Emergency Force
1949-	**UNMOGIP** United Nations Military Observer Group in India and Pakistan	1974-	**UNDOF** United Nations Disengagement Observer Force
1956-67	**UNEF I** First United Nations Emergency Force	1978-	**UNIFIL** United Nations Interim Force in Lebanon
1958	**UNOGIL** United Nations Observation Group in Lebanon	1988-90	**UNGOMAP** United Nations Good Offices Mission in Afghanistan and Pakistan
1960-64	**ONUC** United Nations Operation in the Congo	1988-	**UNIIMOG** United Nations Iran-Iraq Military Observer Group
1962-63	**UNTEA/UNSF** United Nations Temporary Executive Authority and United Nations Security Force in West New Guinea (West Irian)	1989-	**UNAVEM** United Nations Angola Verification Mission
1963-64	**UNYOM** United Nations Yemen Observation Mission	1989-90	**UNTAG** United Nations Transition Assistance Group in Namibia
1964-	**UNFICYP** United Nations Peacekeeping Force in Cyprus	1989-	**ONUCA** United Nations Observer Group in Central America
1965-66	**DOMREP** Representative of the Secretary-General in the Dominican Republic	1991-	**UNIKOM** United Nations Iraq/Kuwait Observer Mission
1965-66	**UNIPOM** United Nations India-Pakistan Observation Mission	1991-	**MINURSO** United Nations Mission for the Referendum in Western Sahara

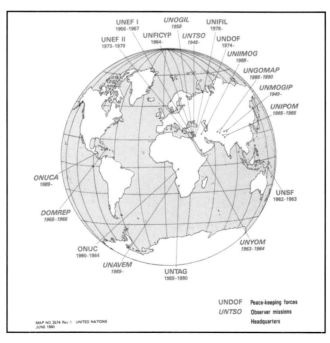

453

Canadian soldiers have brought great credit to the country by their performance in every UN peacekeeping operation in which Canada has been asked to participate. As of mid-1991, the Canadian Forces have taken part in 25 missions.
DND/IXC-88-322

Canadian officers serving with the International Commission for Supervision and Control in South Vietnam, July 1959.
DND/ZK-1722

The Canadian Armed Forces have participated in every one of these operations. Although the Air Force alone was sent to UNYOM in Yemen, the Army has been the workhorse of Canadian peacekeeping and has accounted for the vast majority of the over 80,000 men and women who have served as peacekeepers over the years in the Middle East, Africa, Latin America and Asia. The Korean 'Conflict' is frequently included in peacekeeping tallies, but it was clearly not that: it was a United Nations war, nothing less. Canada has also contributed to other peacekeeping efforts not sanctioned by the UN, notably the International Commissions for Supervision and Control (ICSCs) in Cambodia, Laos, and Vietnam, 1954-1973, and the International Commission of Control and Supervision (ICCS) in Vietnam, 1973. These international commissions were humiliating and dangerous affairs, characterized by internal squabbling and an unparalleled lack of co-operation from parties to the conflict. Canada was, furthermore, explicitly chosen to represent the Western point of view, and was therefore easily portrayed as a 'patsy' of the United States. That wounded policy-makers, who warmed to peacekeeping partly because it helped to draw out the distinctions between Canada and the U.S.

Officers serving with the International Commission for Supervision and Control oversee the transfer of North Vietnamese prisoners-of-war, May 1973.
DND/PCN-73-245

EARLY EXPERIMENTS

The UN established bodies of various shapes and sizes to sort out disputes that arose in the immediate aftermath of the Second World War. Two of these operations, one in the Middle East and the other in the Indian subcontinent, resulted from Great Britain's decision to begin divesting itself of its vast empire. These, we can see now, were the origins of UN peacekeeping.

In 1947 the British ceased to rule India. Predominantly Moslem Pakistan and mainly Hindu India emerged, with the northern State of Jammu and Kashmir a source of contention and soon armed conflict between the two. A United Nations Commission for India and Pakistan was set up in early 1948. It managed to bring both sides to the negotiating table, leading to a cease-fire, the Karachi Agreement, which became effective 1 January 1949. Some thirty-five observers of the United Nations Military Observer Group in India and Pakistan (UNMOGIP) were sent to the area to monitor the cease-fire line. Four Canadian Army reserve officers were among the original number.

A UN control headquarters was established in Srinagar on the Indian side of the cease-fire line but, in keeping with the organization's neutral status, this headquarters would only operate from May to November. For the other six months of the year it was located in Rawalpindi, Pakistan. Observers were distributed among a series of outposts on both sides of the line, when possible in strategic locations, and some were attached to the military headquarters of the opposing sides, where they could take note of violations of the cease-fire as well as engage in small exercises in persuasion. Though as observers only, they had no power to enforce the Karachi Agreement; they could and did intercede in arguments between the Pakistani and Indian military in an effort to defuse potentially explosive situations, trying to ensure, for example, that farmers by crossing the line did not spark renewed military operations. Investigations could be challenging in the mountainous country where, with roads limited to valleys and lower areas, it was often necessary to go by foot up winding paths for several days to reach the scene of a dispute. The first of four Canadian chief military observers who have participated in UNMOGIP over the years was Brigadier Henry H. Angle, a reserve officer in the Canadian Army, appointed in January 1950. He had served with the earlier Commission for India and Pakistan. On 17 July 1950, while the United Nations debated what to do about the recent invasion of South Korea, Brigadier Angle was killed in an airplane accident.

Brigadier H.H. Angle, first Chief Military Observer of the UN Military Observer Group in India and Pakistan, greets Pakistani officers in Kashmir, autumn 1949. UN Photo

In September 1965 the United Nations India-Pakistan Observer Mission was deployed to supervise a cease-fire along the India-Pakistan border. This photo depicts the environment in which the observers worked.

Photo by Lieutenant-General R. Gutknecht

The International Commission for Supervision and Control Medal, awarded for service with the Commission in Indochina between August 1954 and January 1973.

Major-General Bruce Macdonald, shown here with Nigerian officers, was commander of UNIPOM September 1965 to its disbandment in March 1966.

Photo by Lieutenant-General R. Gutknecht

The entrance to UNIPOM Headquarters in Lahore, Pakistan.
Photo by Lieutenant-General R. Gutknecht

The purpose of UNMOGIP was to encourage India and Pakistan to observe the terms of the Karachi Agreement until they could settle their differences peacefully. Encourage was the operative word. Relations between the two countries continued to be very difficult, and a few UN personnel could do relatively little. In 1965 war broke out along the Indian-Pakistani border, where clashes in the Rann of Kutch in April spread to Kashmir in August. The UN called repeatedly for a cease-fire and concocted the United Nations India-Pakistan Observation Mission (UNIPOM). That force's daunting mandate gave it responsibility for a thousand-mile section of the West Pakistan-India frontier, but the conditions for its own demise were agreed in advance: that is, when the withdrawal of all military personnel had taken place. The commander of UNIPOM was a Canadian experienced in peacekeeping, Major-General Bruce F. Macdonald. After reaching a peak strength of two hundred, over a hundred of whom were Canadian, UNIPOM was disbanded on 22 March 1966, having achieved its purpose.

UNMOGIP remained in place for Kashmir, and remains still. A 1972 article in the Montreal *Star* described a peacekeeping group of 54 men, including seventeen Canadians, frustrated by the endless haggling between India and Pakistan and powerless in the face of violations of the cease-fire by both sides. Eight of the Canadians were occupied in transporting supplies to the dozen outposts snaking along the demarcation line; the rest manned the outposts with soldiers from ten other countries. They seemed at least to be living relatively well, especially the eight, fresh from a summer on well-appointed houseboats on a Srinagar lake. Canada's commitment since 1979 has been limited to a single Hercules aircraft and crew available when needed.

The United Nations Truce Supervision Organization in the Middle East (UNTSO) has also become a permanent peacekeeping fixture. Like its counterpart in Kashmir, UNTSO was established to help prevent old conflicts from erupting into modern wars as Britain scurried away from empire.

Ceremony marking the restoration of the India-Pakistan border, and the successful end of the UNIPOM mission.
Photo by Lieutenant-General R. Gutknecht

Palestine was a British protectorate from 1919. It was predominately Arab, but massive immigration had swelled Jewish numbers to thirty percent of the population by 1939. The co-existence in a small area of two such fundamentally opposed groups ensured division and violence, and soon after the war London jettisoned Palestine, dumping the responsibility on the United Nations. The young international body attempted to partition Palestine into Arab and Jewish areas, but the Jewish population unilaterally declared independence as the state of Israel on 14 May 1948. The armed forces of Syria, Lebanon, Egypt, Iraq, and Trans-Jordan prepared military operations against the new nation. The war that followed was brief. Israel acquired more territory than the UN had originally allocated to the Jews, and created a refugee problem that still lingers on. Separate truces were eventually negotiated between Israel and Egypt, Jordan, Syria, and Lebanon. UNTSO was established in June to patrol demilitarized zones on Israel's borders with Egypt and Syria.

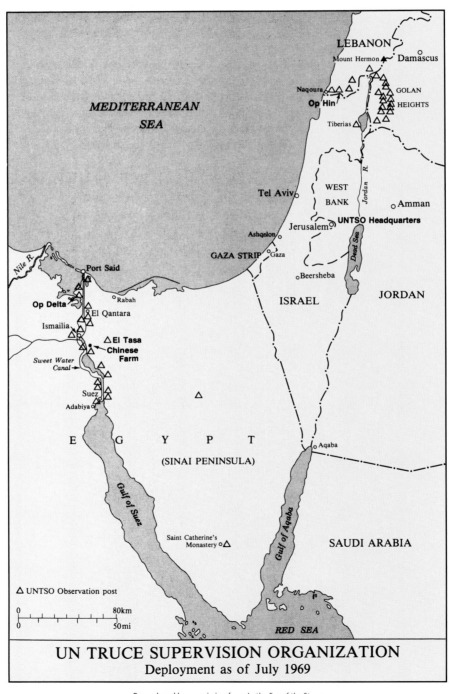

UN TRUCE SUPERVISION ORGANIZATION
Deployment as of July 1969

An observation post of the UN Truce Supervision Organization (UNTSO) on the Golan Heights between Syria and Israel. DND/ISC-84-273

UNTSO slightly predated UNMOGIP, but had no Canadian component until February 1954, when four Canadian Army officers arrived to take up observer duties. In September of that year, Major-General E.L.M. Burns became the force's chief of staff, on loan from the Canadian government. He had served in both great wars, commanding the Second Division in England and the 5th Armoured Division and I Corps in Italy during the Second World War. He retired in 1945 to become Deputy Minister of Veterans' Affairs, but was reinstated in the Army for continuous duty in July 1954 and immediately seconded to the Department of External Affairs for his UNTSO duties. His force, which numbered about six hundred at the time, included nine Canadian officers by 1956; the number increased to seventeen by the end of the decade and twenty in the 1960s. Tours of duty were normally one year.

Their task has sometimes been dangerous. Lieutenant-Colonels George A. Flint and Paul Bertrand were seriously wounded in July 1956 when an anti-personnel mine exploded during the search of a Jerusalem house. Two years later, not far from that site, Flint was shot and killed while holding a white flag on Mount Sinai in May 1958. That flag now resides with the Princess Patricia's Canadian Light Infantry, Flint's regiment. During the 1973 Arab-Israeli War, Captain H.S. Bloom of the Patricias was mistaken by Syrian troops for a downed Israeli pilot, or possibly a spy. He was fired on and was fortunate to sustain only a slight bayonet wound to his leg. Two weeks later Major W.R. MacNeil disarmed agitated Egyptian soldiers by dispensing cigarettes — they were his only weapons — beginning what he later believed "to be the first peace talks of the Yom Kippur War." In January 1984 Canadian members of UNTSO were temporarily restricted from participating in patrols after two colleagues from other countries were assassinated by Islamic Jihad, one of many factions fighting in the civil war in nearby Lebanon.

UNTSO was the beginning of a continuing and varied Canadian involvement in Middle East peacekeeping. Over the years, it has served as a resource from which the Canadian Army could draw experienced personnel for other missions when there was little time to select or to educate. To date some six hundred members of Canada's armed services have worked with the organization as observers or members of support staff.

UNITED NATIONS EMERGENCY FORCE

Canada's first contributions to the UN's attempts at conflict resolution had involved unarmed observers supervising truce arrangements. In 1956, as we have seen, the Suez Crisis led to the formation of a military organization, the United Nations Emergency Force, mandated to keep the peace. In early November, only a few weeks after war had broken out, the necessary agreements were in place for the UN contingent: a small army of thousands of men to be drawn from the infantry forces of Denmark, Norway, Brazil, India, Columbia and Finland.

But not from the Canadian infantry. The UNTSO group had by then been fulfilling a supervisory role in the region for eight years. It made good sense to transfer some of its observers, Canadians and others, to the new force so that organization could begin right away. General Burns himself slid easily over from UNTSO to become the commander of UNEF. Canada also offered an infantry battalion, the Queen's Own Rifles, at that time still a Regular Force regiment. Authorities in Cairo balked at this, however, pointing out that the name made it sound too much like a British unit, and the British, after all, had just quite unjustifiably attacked Egypt. Canadians, moreover, wore the same uniform as the British and flew the Red Ensign, a flag prominently displaying the Union Jack. After spirited negotiations, during which General Burns threatened to resign from the operation, Canada was allowed to contribute communications and logistics personnel: 56 Signal Squadron, 56 Transport Company, and 56 Infantry Workshop were all numbered for the year in which they were established. In addition, the Canadian Army formed 56 Armoured Reconnaissance Squadron, a composite unit

Members of the Royal Canadian Corps of Signals arrive in Egypt on the initial deployment of the UN Emergency Force, the first of the major UN peacekeeping operations, November 1956.
DND/ME-108

made up of men from Lord Strathcona's Horse and the Royal Canadian Dragoons, which undertook patrol duties from February 1957 to February 1958. The Reconnaissance Squadron of the 8th Hussars, and then other Canadian armoured units in turn took over for one-year tours until the last of them, a Squadron of the 8th Hussars, was withdrawn as an economy measure in February 1966.

Israelis return Egyptian prisoners-of-war under Canadian supervision, December 1956.
DND/ME-293

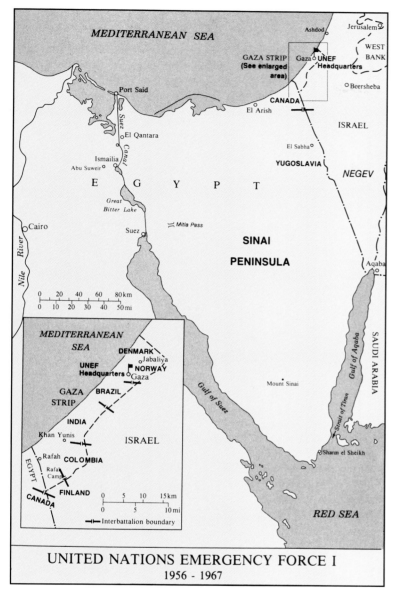

UNITED NATIONS EMERGENCY FORCE I
1956 - 1967

Reproduced by permission from *In the Eye of the Storm*

A Royal Canadian Ordnance Corps sergeant checks 'jerry cans' at Camp Rafah, in the Gaza Strip, 1956. DND/ME-317

UNEF was initially given the responsibility of watching the canal and overseeing withdrawals of the various forces to demarcation lines. The peacekeepers took up positions between the Egyptians and Anglo-French units in the canal zone and between the Egyptians and Israelis in the Sinai. They also followed the Israelis as they first pulled back from the canal and then from the Gaza strip. The latter became the site for UNEF headquarters.

The Canadian reconnaissance squadron's job was to patrol the international frontier, or IF. An early activity report by Lieutenant E.J. Wesson, a troop leader of the Royal Canadian Dragoons, is an illustration:

At approximately 1305 hours, I departed ST JOHN [an observation post] with a 2 jeep routine patrol SOUTH along the IF to CORNERBROOK. As I left NEW HAMBURG I swung WEST about 500 yds to observe from a high hill. I continued back along the IF towards CORNERBROOK about 10 minutes later....

When I reached OSHAWA, I observed boot prints along the IF, on top of the vehicle tracks made by my patrol earlier that morning. We followed the boot prints, and noted that violations of the IF had been made at three places, all within Grid Square 091034, about 200 yards away....

The boot prints led WEST, and we followed them to G[rid] R[reference] 0910 0345, where we found two hastily prepared observation/fire positions. There were many other tracks in the same area. I then observed four men heading NORTH NORTH WEST from this position at a distance of about 1000 yards. Their manner of movement and dress led me to believe they were [Arab] soldiers. I intended to pursue them for purposes of clarification when I observed four more men sitting on a rocky formation atop a hill, approximately 2000 yards distant. The first four were obviously heading in that direction, so I did not pursue them. I reported the incident, and shot bearings to determine the location of the rocky position atop the hill.... The tracks in the area are those of the first four men observed....

The United Nations Emergency Force Medal. Canadians were awarded a total of 9963 of these medals between November 1956 and June 1967.

Wesson had a more interesting day than most. By 1958 operations had settled into a routine of manning posts, carrying out patrols and, for the bulk of Canadian personnel, maintaining communications, repairing vehicles, and helping to administer the multi-national force. Temperatures in the desert frequently rose very high, and hot winds could turn the area into a large furnace. Land mines were a hazard for those whose duties required them to patrol demarkation lines, and Canada's first fatality with UNEF was Sapper R.H. Vézina of the Royal Canadian Engineers, who succumbed to a heart attack while attempting to give aid to an Egyptian wounded by a mine.

UNEF continued its patrols and observations into the 1960s with a smaller force, reduced from over seven thousand to about half that size. Tensions persisted in the region. Incursions of armed Arab guerrillas were mounted on Israel from Syrian territory. The Palestinian Liberation Organization was formed in 1964, and PLO raids on Israel from Jordan became commonplace. Israel itself pushed into areas that had been demilitarized. In November 1966 Egypt and Syria signed a defence treaty. Syria bombed Israel, and Israel retaliated. Another war, apparently, was in the offing.

Royal Canadian Dragoons *Ferret* scout cars at Outpost Hamilton in the Sinai desert, February 1957. RCD Archives

An 8th Canadian Hussar patrol meets a more traditional form of transport in the Sinai, 1964. DND/ME-64-076-4

It came quickly. On 16 May 1967 Egypt's Nasser demanded that UNEF withdraw, and there was no alternative but to do so, as fast as possible. Air Transport Command went to heroic lengths — two men received Queen's Commendations for bravery — to remove their Canadian colleagues to safety. The departure of Flight Lieutenant Michael Belcher's unit was carried out in such haste that he forgot to lower the flag. His commanding officer playfully reminded him of that once aboard one of the last *Caribous* to escape before the fighting started. Fifteen men were lost from the UNEF forces of other countries during the ensuing Six Day War.

There was great pessimism about the future of peacekeeping after Nasser's unceremonious dismissal of UNEF, and a great sense of betrayal after so much commitment and money had been dispensed. But UNEF had not failed. A relative peace had reigned on the Sinai for ten years, and the force surely deserved some of the credit for that. Canada had learned important lessons about the administration, logistics, and communications problems when small units from all over the world joined to form a single peacekeeping contingent. Though UNEF had been unable to prevent war, or even postpone conflict until a permanent settlement could be negotiated, its performance as a buffer force was a model for other peacekeeping attempts.

Corporal Furdyk of the Fort Garry Horse gives water to Bedouin children. Providing aid to the nomadic tribes in the desert was an important aspect of Canadian service in UNEF. FGH Archives

UNITED NATIONS IN THE CONGO

The UNEF pattern, indeed, had already been followed in the Congo, a Belgian colony until independence was declared in the summer of 1960. Less than a week after the transfer of power, Congolese soldiers mutinied against their white officers. Violence and panic and wild rumour ruled the streets, and Belgium flew in troops to guard nationals who had stayed on. Then, almost immediately, the wealthiest of the Congolese provinces, Katanga, declared a separate independence with the help of Belgian interests and foreign mercenaries. The United Nations, invited in by the Congo government, embarked on the most controversial operation of its peacekeeping career: controversial because of the huge annual costs of ONUC (Opération des Nations Unies au Congo); controversial because the Soviets accused the UN of a pro-West bias in its conduct of the operation; and controversial too because the UN was intervening in the internal affairs of an independent country, especially when it took military action against Katanga. Canadian peacekeeping expert Henry Wiseman recalls that ONUC "so divided the UN that its very existence was threatened."

CONGO (ZAIRE)
1960 - 1964

Reproduced by permission from *In the Eye of the Storm*

The UN requested Canadian assistance from the start — as it would turn out, they particularly needed personnel and equipment to maintain communications between forces spread over thousands of square kilometres. The Diefenbaker government in Ottawa, facing a difficult economic situation, was hesitant to send more than token aid, but pressure mounted from a media and public now very accustomed to peacekeeping. On 30 July 1960 Diefenbaker himself announced that a force of 500 soldiers, 200 signallers included, would be sent. Signallers from bases across Canada gathered at Barriefield, near Kingston, Ontario, to form 57 Signal Squadron, later redesignated 57 Signal Unit. They and their Army colleagues served in Leopoldville and in many small detachments spread over the length and breadth of the Congo in support of UN forces attempting to reestablish order. Some of the Canadian officers also filled key positions (Chief Signals Officer and Chief Operations Officer, to give two examples) at ONUC headquarters, and one of these, Lieutenant-Colonel J.A. Berthiaume, became the first Canadian since the Korean War to become an Officer of the Order of the British Empire. He was congratulated for his impressive organizational skills, but also for his bravery and for his "initiative, linguistic ability, and special aptitude for negotiating."

Lieutenant Terry Liston, R22eR, with machine-gunners of the Congolese Army, to which he was attached as a UN liaison officer.
DND photo

The linguistic skills of Berthiaume and others — their ability to speak both English and French — made Canadians a desirable commodity in a multinational force based in a former Belgian colony where French was commonplace. But this ability, and the fact that the Canadian uniform could be construed as its Belgian counterpart, served as a pretext for a number of serious incidents. In August 1960, in Leopoldville, the capital city, and again in Stanleyville, recently-arrived soldiers (Captain Jean Pariseau of the Princess Patricias among them) were detained, beaten and jailed by Congolese soldiers. There were protests from Ottawa, but the problem persisted in a less extreme form. Major I.D. Burch of the Ordnance Corps remembered several close calls. For example:

As the quartermaster, I was responsible for procuring material and equipping the Canadians for everything that they required. I was constantly out checking for spare parts and other items as required by the operational communications squadron. On two occasions, I was caught by a group of the Congolese Army who stopped me in my jeep. I was alone in this particular incident and they attempted to drag me from my vehicle. I did not speak French to them because I had been warned to be very careful because the Congolese Army thought anyone who spoke French was ipso facto a Belgian soldier and of course they hated the Belgians, so that it was very imprudent to speak French. I was speaking English to them saying I belonged to the United Nations and I was Canadian, but I don't think any of them understood and they continued to hit me and try to drag me from my vehicle. Fortunately, I was able to hook my foot under the brake pedal and kept holding on to the steering wheel. At the same time I kept the vehicle in first gear and gradually kept moving the vehicle forward. All of a sudden the group, and I would say there were 50 or 60 of them, parted and I was able to continue moving the jeep forward. I was in a quandary as to what exactly I should do as I didn't know whether they were going to shoot me in the back. I eased the vehicle forward and as soon as I felt that I was at a safe distance made a hasty retreat.

There was clearly a racial aspect in these difficulties as well.

Canadians serving with the UN in the Congo were periodically affected by the widespread instability in the new country. Here Captain Larry Marois, followed by Captain Jean Pariseau, PPCLI, enter the prison at Camp Ketele after being arrested by the Congolese on 27 August 1960. Photo courtesy of Dr. Jean Pariseau

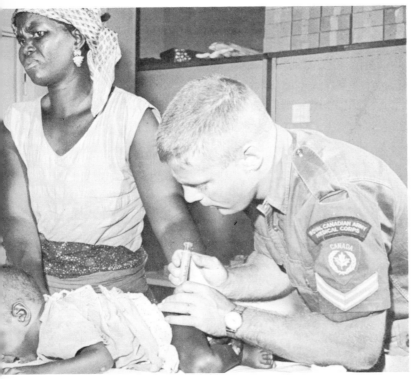

A Canadian Medical Corps corporal serving with 57 Signals Unit in Leopoldville gives a penicillin injection to a sick Congolese baby. DND Photo

The George Medal (reverse), instituted in 1940 to recognize acts of great bravery. Colonel Mayer and Sergeant J.A. Lessard received GMs for bravery during the rescue of missionaries in the Congo. Only 19 have been awarded to members of the Canadian Army.

Lieutenant-Colonel Paul Mayer of the Canadian Guards (right) speaking to Congolese troops immediately prior to a Canadian operation to rescue threatened missionaries. DND/UNC-64-009-15

Thus Canadian soldiers, whose ostensible role was to maintain communications, act as military police, and fill various staff positions, found themselves in a conflict that had no front line. They sometimes took great risks. Lieutenant J.F.T.A. Liston of the Royal 22e Régiment was made a member of the Order of the British Empire for saving a wounded Congolese from a minefield. Three others were recognized for their courage in evacuating missionaries in a daring operation in January 1964. Brigadier J.A. Dextraze, then the UN Chief of Staff in the Congo, was made a Commander of the Order of the British Empire for leading that operation; Lieutenant-Colonel Paul Mayer and Sergeant J.A. Léonce Lessard received the George Medal for their bravery in extracting the priests and nuns from very dangerous circumstances. Lessard did so while holding off fifteen or more of the enemy singlehandedly.

Thirty-four countries participated in the ONUC peacekeeping mission, whose strength peaked at over twenty-thousand personnel. The operation cost four hundred million dollars by the time troops were withdrawn in 1964. Two thousand Canadians served in the Congo during the four years. Two, Staff Sergeant J.P.C. Marquis of the Royal Canadian Ordnance Corps and Sergeant R.H. Moore of the Royal Canadian Corps of Signals, died of disease.

UNITED NATIONS FORCE IN CYPRUS

Just a few months before ONUC came to an end, and while it still had troops with UNEF, Canada made a further peacekeeping commitment, this time to the Mediterranean island of Cyprus. During 1964-1965, with the new effort in Cyprus, 2600 military personnel would be serving in various locales, the largest number in Canadian peacekeeping history. The original Cyprus mandate was only for three months, but the commitment continued, however, long after most of the other involvements of the mid-1960s were ended. It persists to this day.

A British crown colony which had received its independence in 1960, the island of Cyprus had a majority Greek population and a substantial Turkish minority of about twenty percent. The rivalry between the groups was intense, and each side had strong associations with and loyalty to its mother country. Greek Cypriots had long fought for a union (*enosis*) with Greece. The Turks wished a partitioning of the island into separate Greek and Turkish areas. The president

of Cyprus from 1960, Greek Orthodox Archbishop Makarios III, had championed *enosis*, but both it and partition were explicitly precluded as part of the Anglo-Greek-Turkish deal that had brought independence. Neither Greek nor Turkish Cypriots were satisfied with that arrangement, however, and they continued to wage their frequently violent campaigns with the support of their respective mother governments. By 1964 the problem was acute.

All this had serious international repercussions. Greece and Turkey were members of the North Atlantic Treaty Organization (NATO), and the Soviet Union was close enough to the area to cause real concern. NATO countries considered their own peacekeeping arrangement for the island, but Makarios insisted that the Security Council be involved, while the Turks called for a UN presence and the Soviet Union objected to NATO 'interference'. On 4 March 1964 the Security Council unanimously approved the creation of the United Nations Force in Cyprus (UNFICYP), with a very considerable target strength of six to seven thousand men.

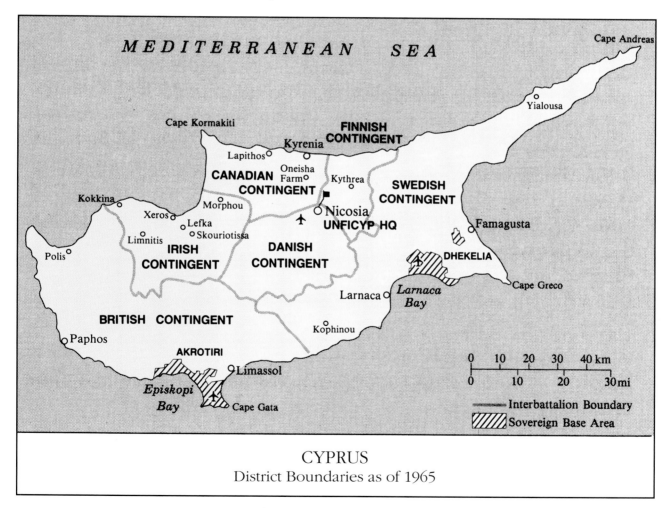

CYPRUS
District Boundaries as of 1965

Reproduced by permission from *In the Eye of the Storm*

Canadian Guardsmen man a rooftop observation post on the Green Line in Nicosia, autumn 1964. DND/CYP-64-097-10

Padre Bill Isaac visiting a Queen's Own Rifles OP in the Kyrenia mountains in northern Cyprus, May 1967. DND/CYP-67-167

Troops of the Royal 22e Régiment in a hastily erected camp on the outskirts of Nicosia, just after their arrival in Cyprus, March 1964. R22eR Museum

The deployment of troops was fast and ordered, one of the most efficient in UN history. Canadians of the Royal 22e Régiment and the Reconnaissance Squadron of the Royal Canadian Dragoons were on the ground and ready to begin operations in early April. At the end of that month a Canadian, Brigadier A. James Tedlie, assumed command of the Nicosia Zone, one of the most sensitive areas of contention between the two warring groups. Hearing that he ought to be ready for immediate action upon landing, Tedlie prepared for the worst as he flew toward Nicosia. He asked that his pistol be loaded (he had forgotten how) and made every effort to appear combat-ready, only to be met at the airport by a group of well-dressed Canadian and UN dignitaries. From the Canadian units and others from Austria, Denmark, Finland, Ireland, Sweden, and the United Kingdom, the United Nations created a peacekeeping force of about 6500 troops, headed by a general of the Indian Army. Commanding the Canadian contingent of eleven hundred was Colonel E.A.C. Amy.

In addition to static observation posts manned by infantry platoons, an armoured reconnaissance squadron was employed on mobile patrols throughout Kyrenia District to give protection to isolated Turk-Cypriot villages. Here, Lieutenant P.R. Bova of the Fort Garry Horse Recce Squadron is shown on patrol in a *Ferret* scout car, February 1967. DND

It was delicate work. No distinct line separated Greek from Turkish Cypriots. Disputes could erupt in any of many areas where the two groups lived in proximity, and disputes in the charged atmosphere of the time always had the potential of becoming much worse. Yet the UN had very little room for manoeuvre, very little real authority. Consequently, according to Major-General J.A. MacInnis, Canadian soldiers pushed the rules beyond their limits to keep the peace.

In these early days, the belligerent forces on both sides were for the most part bands of armed civilians under elected or self-appointed leaders, working within a loose and informal command structure. Situations therefore arose locally, and could generally be settled locally. Both sides could be impressed by a bold display of scout cars, armoured trucks, blue flags, and talk of 'the power and authority of the United Nations'. And this technique was used to dismantle provocative emplacements, to occupy and hold disputed ground, and to extract agreements. Use of force in this way, however, was clearly intimidation, and was, therefore, an unauthorized extension of UN powers.

In peacekeeping, beginnings are crucial, and the Canadians quickly and firmly established their presence. On one occasion in the first month, C Company of the Royal 22e Régiment fell under crossfire from Greeks and Turks in the mountains dominating the only road between the capital, Nicosia, and Kyrenia, a port on the northern coast. The commander, Major Patrick Tremblay, ordered his .30-calibre ma-

chine gun to fire in the general direction of the troublemakers, leading them to stop and reconsider. At about the same time, Sergeant-Major Georges Ouellet won the British Empire Medal for a quite extraordinary display of bravery and diplomacy. This citation accompanied his medal:

As a member of the Canadian Contingent, United Nations Force in Cyprus, Warrant Officer 2 Ouellet served as reconnaissance patrol leader with the 1st Battalion, Royal 22e Regiment. On 10 April 1964, when Turkish-Cypriots in the Kyrenia Pass area advanced toward the Greek-Cypriot positions in the area of Kato Khikomo they attacked with direct small-arms fire. Twelve unarmed Greek-Cypriot farmers scattered in the open fields on the Onisha cooperative farm. It was at this time that W.O.2 Ouellet arrived in the area with his patrol. He deployed his men and with complete disregard for his own safety, personally went to the rescue of the twelve farmers. During the next twenty minutes, under constant direct small-arms fire, he moved from one to the other, and safely brought them for protection into a farm building. Leaving two of his men with them, he then approached the Turkish-Cypriot positions, arranged for a temporary cease-fire and succeeded in evacuating the farmers to safety in a nearby Greek-Cypriot village. By his quick thinking and at the risk of his own life, he saved the lives of twelve Greek-Cypriots, gained the respect and admiration of his men and of the Greek- and Turkish-Cypriots, enhanced the prestige of the Canadian peacekeeping force and paved the way for an eventual stabilization of the cease-fire line in the area.

In the months that followed, the Canadians became firmly established on what came to be called the 'Green Line' separating Turkish from Greek enclaves in Nicosia. Infantry took up positions in deserted homes, stores, factories, and apartment buildings, making it very difficult for either side to engage in any but the smallest and most ineffective operations. Turkish and Greek Cypriots could still attempt to gain an advantage by occupying a building with good observation over the enemy or by blocking a road to isolate a small area and force its people to evacuate. In September 1964, in one of the largest of such incidents, the Turks cut off the road from Nicosia to Kyrenia. Negotiations reopened it, but Canadians and members of other contingents now had to be positioned on permanent escort duty to ensure safety for travellers. The Canadians' area of responsibility was shifted from Nicosia to the Kyrenia District in September 1965.

The UN forces could not prevent small bands from carrying out a guerrilla war of sporadic fighting and small, vengeance-motivated skirmishes. Makarios now represented the status quo as agreed in 1960, and he was opposed by Turkish and Greek Cypriot extremists determined to have their way. Turkey strongly supported the push of their compatriots in Cyprus for more rights and status, while Greece built up an illegal force on Cyprus which by 1967 numbered about ten thousand. That year a bloodless coup brought to Greece a right-wing junta and Greek Cypriot terrorists, expecting its full support, launched an attack against the village of Kophinou, killing thirty Turkish Cypriots. Turkey, never blameless in the escalation of violence, loaded troopships in preparation for an invasion of the island, but cooler international heads prevailed. As it happened, the UN might have prevented the killings. Canadian troops (the Fort Garry Horse Reconnaissance Squadron) had arrived in the village to reinforce the British garrison before the Greeks did, but the British UN district commander would not allow them to position themselves between the two factions. For the remainder of that tour, it was extremely difficult to convince Canadian soldiers that they had a genuine peacekeeping role to carry out.

During the Turkish invasion of Cyprus in late July 1974, troops of the 1st Commando, Canadian Airborne Regiment periodically came under hostile fire; 17 soldiers were wounded and two were killed later. This photo shows men of the Airborne Regiment observing the shelling of Nicosia Airport on 22 July. The Canadians took over the defence of the airfield the following day. DND/CYP-74-89A

When the armoured reconnaissance squadron was withdrawn in 1969, mobile patrolling was taken over by the infantry battalion. Here 2 RCR soldiers watch over a sector of Kyrenia District, autumn 1973. DND/PCN-73-681

By the early 1970s, the United Nations' chronic funding problems had contributed to a reduction of the force to 3650 personnel, including about 580 Canadians. Colonel C.E. Beattie, the senior Canadian in Cyprus and Deputy Chief of Staff of the overall UN effort at the time, reminded his troops that the essence of their task was "people problems", helping Cypriots to go about their life and work safely. If peacekeepers were bored, if nothing seemed to happen, that was a mark of success. And every so often, as Beattie well knew, something would happen, and it would be necessary to intervene decisively. In January 1972, for example, a Greek national guardsman began to harangue a Turk on the other side of the Green Line. A member of the Royal 22e Régiment, manning a UN outpost within view of both, watched the exchange, as the Turk shot and killed his adversary. The Canadian quickly contacted his headquarters and kept watch as a band of guardsmen gathered, bent on avenging their comrade's death. Canadian troops arrived and positioned themselves between the groups. According to Lieutenant-Colonel J.H. Allan, "No one wanted to attack the UN troops, so that incident ended right there. If there had been no one there to get in between there is no telling where the killing would have stopped."

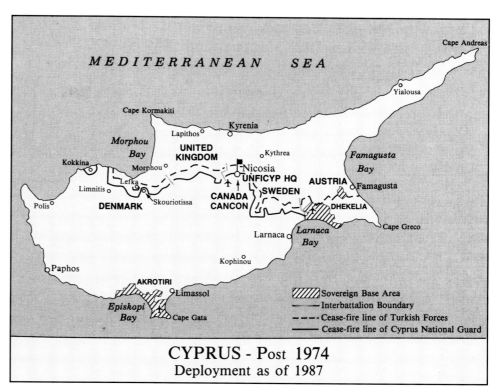

CYPRUS - Post 1974
Deployment as of 1987

Reproduced by permission from *In the Eye of the Storm*

A fragile cease-fire between the Turks and Greek Cypriots was negotiated by the UN on 23 July 1974 , but it was regularly violated. The Turks took additional ground in renewed fighting in mid-August before agreeing to a permanent cease-fire on 16 August. Here an Airborne Regiment Master Corporal is seen in negotiations with a Turkish officer.

DND/CYP-74-154

In 1974 Makarios was overthrown by Greek Cypriot forces, and Turkey (it said) invaded Cyprus with six thousand troops to right the wrong. The invasion was perhaps the worst single crisis Canadian peacekeepers have ever had to face, and they played a very important part in 'confronting' the Turks, especially at Nicosia airport. Instrumental in organizing and leading that operation was Lieutenant-Colonel Donald Manuel of the Canadian Airborne Regiment, who received an Order of Military Merit. Two of his soldiers, Private Joseph Plouffe and Captain Alain Forand, received the Star of Courage, Canada's second highest award for bravery. On 23 July 1974, a Canadian patrol conducting a group of combatants out of a UN-controlled area came under fire. Several soldiers were killed or wounded and the Canadian officer leading the escort party was wounded. Private Plouffe, a member of the escort party, went at once to the aid of the fallen officer, sustaining a bullet wound in the face moments later. Despite the injury, he continued to render first aid. Plouffe and the others were at the bottom of a creek bed, exposed to continuing machine-gun fire. Captain Forand now appeared on the scene. In the words of the citation for his Star of Courage, he "arranged for covering fire and, with complete disregard for his own safety, he crawled forward over the exposed ground, to aid the two casualties. Single-handedly, he managed to drag the wounded officer some distance up onto the bank of the creek where the others helped carry him out of the danger area." Forand then directed the rescue of Plouffe.

Two Canadians died in the aftermath of the Turkish invasion, after a cease-fire agreement had been reached. Private Gilbert Perron was shot by a sniper while investigating allegations that Turkish soldiers were laying wire in contravention of the cease-fire; Trooper Claude Berger was killed on his way to feed abandoned livestock. A total of seventeen Canadians were wounded during the invasion; nine were decorated for bravery.

Thereafter, the island was effectively partitioned into a Turkish area, representing about forty per cent of Cyprus' northern land mass, and a southern Greek area, with a UN monitored buffer zone between them. In 1975 the Turkish Cypriots unilaterally declared their independence. The paramilitary and guerrilla bands of the 1960s gave way to Turkish and Turkish Cypriot security forces on one side, and troops of the Greek Cypriot National Guard, with Greek officers in commanding positions, on the other.

Canadian troops had returned to their Nicosia area of responsibility in 1968. With a firm line now separating the two factions, rules of engagement changed. UN troops were allowed to use force to ensure that neither side established itself in the buffer zone. For example, in August 1986, when Turkish Cypriot soldiers took over some vacant buildings within the zone, members of the 3rd Battalion, Royal Canadian Regiment, carried out a lightning re-occupation at dawn. No casualties were registered on either side.

A 1 RCR patrol drives along the 'Green Line' in the old sector of Nicosia, where opposing forces are often separated only by the width of a narrow street.
DND/ISC-84-358 by WO Vic Johnson

A 2 PPCLI sergeant leads a foot patrol in a deserted building along the 'Green Line' in Nicosia, 1988.

A 5e Régiment d'artillerie légère du Canada guard checks a Cypriot civilian at the entrance to the main Canadian camp in Nicosia. DND/BAB-87-813-1

Canada currently maintains a contingent of just under six hundred in Cyprus, or about a quarter of the total eight-country strength of UNFICYP. Some thirty thousand Canadians have served there to date, and all Canadian regular regiments have contributed over the years. A 1989 estimate gave an overall figure of $3 billion spent on the operation, of which Canada had contributed around $400 million. Major-General Clive Milner, a former Commanding Officer of the Royal Canadian Dragoons, became Force Commander on 10 April 1989, the first Canadian commander of a UN peace mission since General Macdonald. Milner had served with UNICYP as a rookie lieutenant twenty-five years earlier. He looked back on that experience with matter-of-fact pride. "Some herdsman would allow his goats to go into no-man's-land," he recalled,

Shots would be fired. My troops would drive between the two firing sides, trusting that they would stop at the sight of the UN flag and the blue berets of the soldiers. Then we would get out, talk through interpreters to both sides, get them to back off 100 m, and eventually calm the whole thing down.

Patricia soldiers keep watch over their sector of the Buffer Zone from one of the 'country' OPs outside the built-up area of Nicosia. DND/IXC-88-308

It is easy enough to denigrate UNICYP. The problems of Cyprus remain deep and profound. There has been no peace treaty, no real peace-making process, and it may be that the forces' reassuring existence has in fact institutionalized the conflict, postponing efforts at finding a real solution. Yet it is also likely that UNICYP has prevented and is preventing civil war and international conflict. Andrew Boyd, an historian of the UN Security Council, asks that we consider the alternatives. "Can it be seriously contended that it would be better to leave the Cypriots to kill each other until the neighbour countries are dragged into a wider war?" "How many lives," adds General Milner, "have been saved by the UN presence?"

UNITED NATIONS EMERGENCY FORCE II

A 1970s renewal of UNEF peacekeeping efforts in the Middle East brought further need for Canadian contribution. In the 1967 Six Day War, Israel had captured ground on the Golan Heights, the West Bank of the Jordan River, the Gaza Strip, and the Sinai Peninsula. UNTSO set up posts in the Golan and along the canal to observe a cease-fire that was no more than a lull between campaigns. On 6 October 1973, Egyptian forces crossed the Suez Canal and assaulted Israeli positions in the Sinai. Soon after, Syrian armoured forces attacked through the Golan. Though for several days the Israeli Defence Forces were in jeopardy, they managed to recover, launch counterattacks and, on the Suez front, encircle the Egyptian Third Army. Then, under UN, American and Russian pressure, the belligerents agreed to an armistice. Israeli forces pulled back to the east side of the canal, which they had crossed a few days earlier in their enveloping manoeuvre.

The Second United Nations Emergency Force (UNEF II) was created on 25 October 1973, and for the first time in peacekeeping history, an operation had broad moral and financial backing from the UN membership. The first contingents were provided from Swedish, Finnish and Austrian forces from UNICYP; their experience proved useful in these first days of UNEF II's deployment. The Canadians began to arrive soon after. The airlift required to get the first troops to the Middle East was the biggest peacetime operation Air Transport Command had organized to that time, requiring most of the command's turbo-prop *Hercules* transport aircraft and nearly half of its Boeing 707 fleet.

The International Commission of Control and Supervision Medal, awarded for service in Vietnam between January and July 1973.

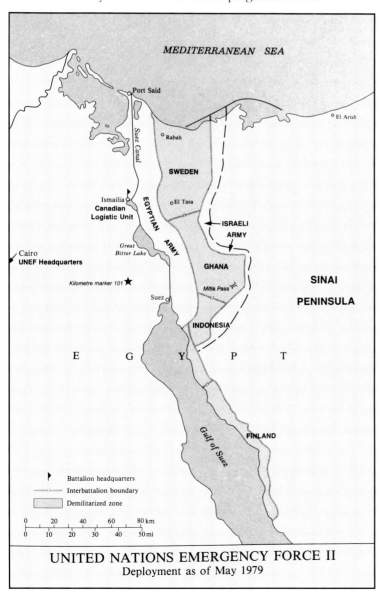

UNITED NATIONS EMERGENCY FORCE II
Deployment as of May 1979

Reproduced by permission from *In the Eye of the Storm*

Guard at the Canadian Contingent headquarters in Ismailia, Egypt, 1974. DND/ME-74-20

The Canadian contingent's main role was to supply and maintain the peacekeeping force. After a month a supply company, a maintenance company, a military police detachment, a movement control unit, and an air transport unit were all in place. The two main land-element units involved were 73 Service Battalion and 73 Signals Squadron, their numerical designations again being determined by the year in which they were formed. Personnel, including women in a UN peacekeeping operation for the first time, rotated through on six-month tours. Poland, Sweden, Finland, Austria, Indonesia, Peru, Panama, and Ireland also contributed to UNEF II. Canada's contribution was the largest, representing almost a quarter of the 4200-member force.

Private D.F. Dewolf of 1 Service Battalion watches as supplies for UNEF II are off-loaded in Alexandria harbour, November 1973. DND/ME-73-185

Canada shouldered the main burden of logistics. Poland, at Russian insistence, had initially been expected to share the work: a Warsaw Pact member counterbalancing Canada's NATO commitment. But the Israelis refused to allow the Poles through their lines with food and water because Poland had never recognized the State of Israel. One logistics officer, Captain Anthony McCormack, received what sometimes seems to have been the usual peacekeeping notice: while on language training, he was given two days to report to Canadian Forces Base Kingston. Once in Egypt, one of his many duties was to ensure that Muslim troops did not receive any pork products with their rations. McCormack's 73 Service Battalion was responsible for supplying the UN contingents, maintaining all western-bloc vehicles and equipment and, perhaps of greatest importance to the troops, sorting and delivering mail.

While there was little direction from UN headquarters on the important policy questions, there was no shortage of edicts on the way supplies were to be procured. A bemused Major Bill Aikman described the supply process in all its bureaucratic splendour:

The Supply Company handles requests very differently than in Canada. There is no handy list of NATO stock numbers to refer to, and even though two of the national contingents have a Canadian supply NCO at their locations, the language barriers can cause difficulties. When confusion arises, supply staff either ask the requesting unit to bring in the required part for comparison or have the requesting soldier identify the part by its picture in a parts catalogue. When a transaction is completed, no handy computer records the changes. The supply company uses a manual file-card system discarded years ago in Canada.

Ordering new material involves an incredibly complex system. For example, if UNEF needs more brooms, the supply company sends its request to UNEF Headquarters in a modern building complex in downtown Ismailia. There, the order is processed and sent on to UN Headquarters in New York. The United Nations gives all its member nations a chance to bid on its contracts, and therefore the broom contract is put out to world tender. After an appropriate time to allow bids to be submitted, the UN awards the contract.

The brooms are then manufactured in a country that could well be on the opposite side of the globe from UNEF in the Sinai. They are shipped to one of the UN's central storage depots in New York or Pisa, Italy, and from there to Port Said at the northern end of the Suez Canal. At Port Said, the shipment faces a one to three month wait as documents are processed through Egyptian customs.

When finally cleared, the brooms are shipped to the UNEF supply depot at Ismailia. Six to eight months after the order was first submitted, the brooms are ready for issue to units. By this time, the person who made up the order will almost certainly have been rotated back to Canada.

It is not surprising that the Maintenance Company's main problem was a shortage of spare parts.

Major Ted Selwyn mans a UNEF II observation post in the Sinai near Ismailia, May 1975. DND/PCN-75-1234

Organizing the communications element was somewhat easier. The bulk of personnel and equipment could come from 1 Canadian Signal Regiment. They set up a telephone network within their own camp, established a short-wave link with Canada (which UNEF I had lacked), and by the end of the year had deposited over sixty signallers with the UN battalions overseeing truce arrangements. Making the system work was nevertheless a challenge, as made clear in the log of Major Don Banks of Kingston. On 16 November 1973 he reported, using standard military abbreviations:

Comm plan now complete. However, no paper aval for duplicating machine.... Outage of approx 3 hrs during the night — maybe due to eqpt problems. TELEX link to Canada should be in tomorrow. Telephones at SHAMS CAMP finally in. [Message Centre] moved four times!!!!

The next day the situation had not substantially improved.

TELEX... still not in, trouble with contractors — no lines available within city. (What a bloody way to work). Moved into new HQ bldg today. Civies left the old HQ like rats deserting a sinking ship. As usual all accn was taken before we got there. Began phone installation — radio det being set up, require security guard and concertina around area. Space very limited, this place is as bad as the last one.

Banks' frustration mounted as he discovered that all requests for equipment or spare parts had to go through New York. He recorded on 21 February 1974:

Msg received from NY querying specifications of our switchboard request sent on 30 Nov 73. It is quite obvious that comms eqpt requests don't have the inside track in the race for priority. Still awaiting answers on our requests for generators which are urgently required. Latest hastener sent 5 Feb 74.

A Canadian soldier, one of many hastily transferred from UNEF II to UNDOF, talks to an Austrian signaller on the Golan Heights, autumn 1975. DND/MEC-76-11

At the outset of UNEF II operations, the lack of an agreement by the opposing sides on final demarcation lines complicated the investigation of breaches of the cease-fire. Negotiations, which included participation by Lieutenant-Colonel William Porter of the 12e Régiment blindé du Canada, led by 24 January 1974 to a detailed plan for the disposition of Egyptian and Israeli forces, which included the establishment of a buffer zone by early February. In March, the United Nations deployed to the zone four peacekeeping battalions made up of contingents from Sweden, Ghana, Indonesia, and Finland. Questions of war dead occupied the UN soldiers in the months that followed. Further agreements opened the Suez Canal in 1975 and the next year moved the buffer zone further east — into Israeli-occupied territory.

On 9 August 1974 members of UN organizations in the Middle East were reminded that peacekeepers regularly place themselves in harm's way. That day a Buffalo aircraft of 116 Air Transport Unit was on a routine flight from Ismailia to Damascus, by way of Beirut, when it crashed near the Syrian-Lebanese border. It had been shot down by Syrian troops firing surface-to-air missiles; somehow they had mistaken the slow-moving aircraft (which was admittedly ahead of schedule) for an Israeli plane. All nine Canadians aboard were killed, the worst single day in the history of the country's peacekeeping efforts.

In March 1979, Egypt and Israel signed a treaty calling for a neutral force to monitor the new Israeli-Egyptian border. UNEF II briefly carried on, but the organization's mandate, due to expire on 24 July, was not renewed. For the first time in the history of the United Nations, a peacekeeping force was terminated because peace had broken out.

A Canadian Engineer repairs a water line in the somewhat decrepit Canadian base camp in Ismailia, 1975. DND/ME-75-054

UNITED NATIONS DISENGAGEMENT OBSERVER FORCE

The UN was making progress in negotiating an end to the other half of the Yom Kippur War, where Israel, in counterattacking Syria's forces, had occupied more of that country's territory. However, on 31 May 1974, Israel agreed to withdraw from the ground it had captured the year before, retaining possession only of Syrian lands taken in 1967. To supervise Israel's withdrawal and inspect the resulting buffer zone, the UN formed the United Nations Disengagement Observer Force (UNDOF), comprising over twelve hundred personnel. UNTSO supplied experience and expertise, while UNEF II donated an infantry battalion from each of its Austrian and Peruvian contingents as well as Canadian and Polish logistics units, all under the command of a Peruvian. Land mines were a hazard to UNDOF units, and Syria restricted UN activities. Israel for its part continued to apply its policy of forbidding troops from nations that had not recognized Israeli sovereignty to move within areas it controlled. The Canadians, therefore, again carried the logistic load, providing transport service within Israel, as well as maintaining Western-pattern vehicles and equipment (including air conditioners, electric and electronic items, radios and generators), doling out rations to all the contingents, and keeping communications links between those contingents and UNDOF headquarters.

UN DISENGAGEMENT OBSERVER FORCE
Deployment as of October 1985

Reproduced by permission from *In the Eye of the Storm*

The gateway to 'Camp Roofless', the abandoned French Foreign Legion outpost that became home to Canadians serving with the UN Disengagement Observer Force on the Golan Heights, 1974. DND/ISC-74-1037A

One of the landmarks of UNDOF is Camp Ziouani, nicknamed Camp 'Roofless.' It had been a French Foreign Legion outpost in the 1920s and was little more than a ruin when Canadian and Peruvian soldiers set up shop there. This obstacle could be overcome, but nature and climate could not. According to Brigadier-General Douglas Yuill's description,

The Golan is an arid area where poisonous snakes, centipedes and spiders are common, and where living conditions are less than attractive no matter what accommodation is available. Summer temperatures in the 40 degree plus Celsius range are common, winds are often very high and the fall and winter rains often turn to snow which is wet, heavy and sometimes very deep. Few winters pass without some snow and two to three feet at one time has been known with the usual consequence of a plethora of vehicle accidents, collapsed buildings, including the Canlog mess hall on one occasion and severe flooding....

Canadians had often before faced the prospect of a long and apparently futile engagement with an observer or peacekeeping force. By 1985, however, Canadian troop morale in UNDOF was sinking with every passing month. According to Yuill, the fault lay with higher command which instituted a person-for-person rotation scheme, instead of sending personnel over in groups, and failed to implement effective screening or preparation for "the cultural, climactic and professional challenge of service in the Middle East." Ottawa requested that the Deputy Force Commander/Chief of Staff position in UNDOF headquarters be given to a Canadian, who would be able to make changes where they counted. As Yuill remembered it, the results of this innovation were striking:

Better selection and screening, quarterly rotations of half the Contingent at a time, pre-tour training, and significant improvements in Camp Ziouani itself were all put in train.... By the summer of 1987, the contingent was once again an effective unit with high morale, a strong work ethic, and great pride in serving in one of the most operational theatres open to Canadians.

A Canadian supply technician coordinates ration resupply for the UNDOF contingents with a Polish soldier. DND/ISC-84-309

UNITED NATIONS INTERIM FORCE IN LEBANON

For a few months in 1978 Canada was contributing to four peacekeeping or observer operations in the Middle East. UNTSO, UNEF II and UNDOF had yet to complete their missions, and a fourth mission was added, the United Nations Interim Force in Lebanon (UNIFIL).

UNIFIL's origins will sound all too familiar. In 1969, Egyptian mediation ended fighting between members of the Palestine Liberation Organization and regular forces of the Lebanese Army. The secret Cairo Agreement allowed the PLO to launch raids against Israel from Lebanese territory, but the treaty did not remain unknown for long. Israeli forces soon began to despatch retaliatory operations against their northern neighbour in order to force its government to repudiate the agreement. On 14 March 1978 Israel launched a limited invasion of Lebanon. The United Nations, having the experience of devising five different organizations to deal with Arab-Israeli confrontations in the previous thirty years, reacted the very day of the Israeli invasion. UNIFIL was given the task of organizing disengagement, once again requiring Israel to pull out of conquered territory, and creating a buffer zone in the hopes of keeping the two sides apart.

Camp Pearson, home of Canadian signallers assigned to UNIFIL headquarters on the Mediterranean coast at Naqoura, Lebanon, 1978. DND/ISC-78-307

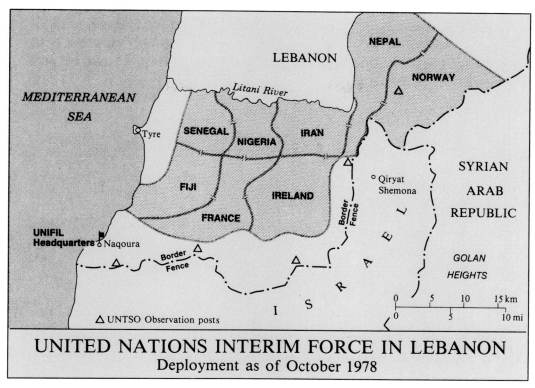

UNITED NATIONS INTERIM FORCE IN LEBANON
Deployment as of October 1978

Reproduced by permission from *In the Eye of the Storm*

Eight countries sent infantry forces to UNIFIL. These units were despatched according to the local religious and political make-up; for example, Iran was assigned a region inhabited by members of the Shia Muslim sect, while Irish and French forces took over areas dominated by Christians. The UN force employed Canadians in their now traditional role of signallers, the first signal group being drawn from the nearby UNEF II. Since communicators were still heavily involved in UNEF II, the government only promised a six month commitment to Lebanon.

By June 120 Canadians had worked or were working with UNIFIL. Their communications specialty brought them into contact and sometimes confrontation with paramilitary forces and militias. In correspondence with the Canadian War Museum's Fred Gaffen, Lieutenant B.W. Drummond, of the Royal Canadian Signal Corps, related one of his experiences.

The UNTSO officers were happy to have Canadian troops in the area as we were armed while they were not. Warrant Officer 'Turk' Deschamps and I would make tours of the radio detachments at the various contingents. We became quite familiar with passing through check-points. Generally, the first thing a militiaman or PLO type would do at a check-point was open the jeep door and push a rifle in at us. This procedure was, of course, intended to be intimidating. We counteracted by having my sub-machine gun, loaded and cocked, cradled casually in my lap....

There were fortunately no Canadian fatalities in UNIFIL.

It looked for a time as if the force would at least succeed in stabilizing southern Lebanon so that economic life could return to normal. But the cycle of violence between Israel and the PLO continued. In October 1978, having set up the necessary communications networks, and faced with the prospect of never-ending conflict, the Canadian government decided not to renew its commitment. Peacekeepers have long found that it takes two sides to make peace, but only one to make war. When Israel launched another major offensive in 1982, UNIFIL could do no more than stand aside. It was then the only peacekeeping operation that lacked Canadian participation.

PEACEKEEPING IN THE 1980s AND 1990s

Almost ten years passed before Canadian land forces contributed to another a new peacekeeping operation. During that time, contingents were maintained with UNFICYP, UNTSO, and UNDOF. In 1988 Canada's total contribution would rise to over 1400 personnel as land forces became involved in two more missions, UNGOMAP and UNIIMOG. In that year too, the Nobel Prize Committee awarded its Prize for Peace to military peacekeeping forces around the world. Corporal Jeff Docksey of Lord Strathcona's Horse was part of the honour guard for UN Secretary-General Javier Perez de Cuellar, who accepted the prize. Like the award to Lester Pearson over three decades earlier, it was a good moment for peacekeeping.

The United Nations Good Offices Mission in Afghanistan and Pakistan (UNGOMAP) was established to monitor the withdrawal of Soviet troops from Afghanistan. Canada sent five officers in the late summer of 1988, led by Lieutenant-Colonel Dave Leslie of the Royal Canadian Regiment. Later, military engineers were despatched to teach Afghan refugees how to clear mines. The first dozen of these, from eight bases and units in the regular force and reserves, moved out in March 1989 to join American, French, Italian, Norwegian, and Turkish engineer teaching teams. Only Canada, which had allowed women to enter the military engineering trades, could supply personnel to teach Afghan women how to recognize the signs of hidden mines and booby traps and avoid setting them off — in Afghan culture women can only speak to men of their immediate family. According to Captain Karen

The UN Secretary-General congratulates peacekeepers on the award of the Nobel Peace Prize for 1988. Corporal Jeff Docksey of Lord Strathcona's Horse (second from right) represented the Canadian Forces at the presentation ceremony in Oslo. UN Photo

Durnfurd, "The reason I wanted to be an engineer was to go into the field. But this is even better than being in a field regiment. This is the real world — with real mines and real people who need us." Three more engineer contingents would rotate through by the time the mission ended in July 1990.

Major R.G. Elms (centre right) and other members of the UN Good Offices Mission in Afghanistan and Pakistan confer with a Soviet liaison officer at Hayratan, on the Afghan-Soviet border, early 1989.

The second of 1988's new commitments was the United Nations Iran/Iraq Military Observer Group (UNIIMOG). After years of destruction and a million casualties, Iran and Iraq agreed to a cease-fire in the summer of 1988. To ensure that disagreements over demarcation lines or individuals seeking revenge did not touch off another general war, UNIIMOG was created out of about twenty-five national contingents. Canada's share consisted of some fifteen observers and five hundred signallers. Members of 88 Signal Squadron, carrying rifles, carried out their mission until November 1988, when they were brought home. The observers remained until Canada became involved in the United Nations action against Iraq after its invasion of Kuwait in the summer of 1990. Canada's part in the victorious UN coalition warfare against Iraq in early 1991 made many doubt that Canada could ever again act as an impartial peacekeeper. But when the UN set up a peacekeeping force, the United Nations Iraq/Kuwait Observer Mission (UNIKOM), Canada was again prominent among the participants. Three hundred Canadian military engineers were engaged in mineclearing duties by April 1991.

UNGOMAP's mission in Afghanistan — to oversee the withdrawal of Soviet troops — came to a successful end on 15 February 1989 when the last Russian vehicle crossed the bridge into the Soviet Union.

After the Soviet withdrawal from Afghanistan, the UN asked Canada to provide instructors to teach the Afghan people how to cope with the many thousands of mines littering the countryside. DND/IOC-89-13-47

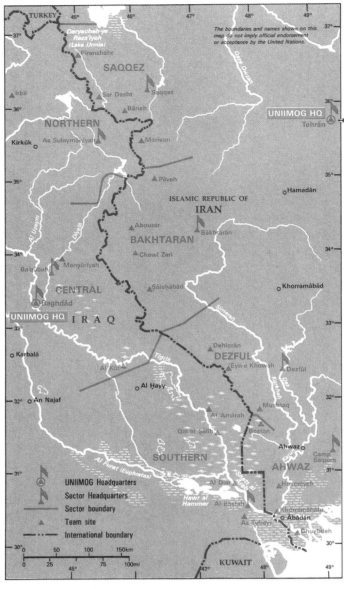

United Nations map

Men of 88 Signals Squadron muster in Baghdad prior to deployment to positions on the Iran-Iraq frontier, August 1988. DND/ISC-88-970-9

The year 1990 proved to be one of the busiest in Canada's peacekeeping history. Though only 1215 people participated, they staffed ten different missions. In addition to commitments in the Middle East and Cyprus, the Canadian Forces Attaché in Korea became a member of the United Nations Military Armistice Commission in that country, a Canadian contingent joined the United Nations Transition Assistance Group (UNTAG) in Namibia, and another group was sent to the Grupo de Observadores de los Naciones Unidos en Centroamerica (ONUCA).

Canada sent 89 Canadian Logistics Unit to deal with supply, transportation and maintenance for UNTAG. These responsibilities were shared with a Polish contingent, as was another task, the provision of police services north of Grootfontein, along the border with Angola, an area of 136,000 square kilometres.

Canada contributed about ninety observers and No. 89 Light Observation Helicopter Unit to ONUCA, for a total of 173 personnel. ONUCA demonstrated that, when both sides wish it, peacekeeping can be relatively straightforward. There were even instances of Sandinista forces providing transportation for Contra troops to the verification centres where they were to turn in their weapons. In June 1990 Captain J.M. Ghyslain Bergeron and Master Corporal J.L. Masson, both of CFB Bagotville, saved the Nicaraguan pilot of a crashed helicopter with the help of a Sandinista officer and a Contra rebel, who had just handed over his weapon. The incident could serve, or so it might be hoped, as a symbol of the end of civil war in Nicaragua. The UN asked Canada in the summer of 1990 to withdraw its helicopters and most of its personnel from ONUCA, but to leave thirty people behind to act as a resource should the peace process spread to El Salvador and Guatemala.

UNITED
NATIONS
TRANSITION
ASSISTANCE
GROUP
NAMIBIA

There will be more Canadian peacekeepers. Peacekeeping is a source of legitimacy for the government and the Armed Forces alike: supporting Canada's diplomacy and internationalist aims; operating within the scope of the country's military capacity; costing relatively little (only 0.4 percent of the total DND budget, 1949-1980); broadening the horizons of officers and men; creating and maintaining a truly Canadian expertise; providing experience in planning, logistics, signals and so on, although not in combat; winning popularity (usually) for the government and the Department of National Defence, because it is difficult to argue with a fight for peace; and giving the forces a responsibility which is removed from alliances and major weapons.

Members of 89 Canadian Logistics Unit check the Contingent's rifles after arriving in Namibia for service with the UN Transition Assistance Group, 1989. DND/IEC-89-003-54

For the Canadian Army (and Canadian Land Force after unification), peacekeeping has never been easy. No permanent high command or headquarters coordinates peacekeeping activities or gathers intelligence on potential areas of conflict. Thus contingent commanders and their staffs almost always find themselves thrust into situations for which they have not been prepared or properly briefed. They must adapt quickly or not at all. UNIIMOG's Chief of Staff was Canadian Colonel John Annand, and his early adventures were symptomatic of the ad hoc nature of peacekeeping operations even after four decades of experience. In Ottawa on a Monday, he made his way to United Nations' Headquarters on Tuesday, moved on to Frankfurt on Wednesday, and arrived in Tehran on Thursday — without any terms of reference. He sent regular situation reports to UN headquarters but "I never got anything back so I didn't have a clue what was happening over there."

Lack of a permanent peacekeeping force, or planning body, has repercussions for logistics and administration as well. Armies, like government departments, corporations, and other similar organizations, have standard procedures to ease the burden of staffs who ensure people are fed and vehicles can run. The same reports or indents are filed the same way and sent to the same people each time a similar situation presents itself. But in peacekeeping operations such procedures can quickly break down; first of all, because local conditions can be wildly at variance with what staffs have become used to in Canada or Germany; secondly, because UN forces must be put together very quickly from a wide variety of national contingents with standard operating procedures of their own. Therefore, those posted to administrative or logistical duties with a peacekeeping force must combine flexibility with patience.

Peacekeeping is seldom popular with the forces on the ground. Interviews done in Cyprus during the early 1970s indicated frustration, boredom, cynicism. There was not much to like about peacekeeping, one soldier complained. "It's just outpost work, which is kind of monotonous." Said another, "I suppose if you're standing in six feet of snow back in Canada, life seems pretty good in Cyprus. Personally, I can't stand it." And a third opinion: "All the Cypriots want out of the UN is the money. If they thought we were going to leave, someone would shoot off a gun just to keep us from going." No one, added the interviewer, hoped for peace more than the Canadians.

Major Shaun Tolson discusses deployment of ONUCA observers in Nicaragua with an Irish colleague, autumn 1990. DND/IXC-90-093

UNITED NATIONS OBSERVER GROUP IN CENTRAL AMERICA (ONUCA)

United Nations map

The UN is aware that low morale can be a problem. According to Brigadier-General Blake Baile, at one time commander of the Canadian contingent in UNEF II, "The United Nations encourages its soldiers in the Middle East to tour the surrounding countries, and travel is made easier through the possession of a UN identification card. This allows UN personnel to travel freely in Egypt, Israel, Syria and parts of Lebanon, which no one else has been able to do for over 30 years." Two-week leaves gave many the opportunity to visit Europe and, under a special Canadian plan, meet with spouses flown over to Germany. The UN also allowed its peacekeepers to use the organizations's vehicles, greatly increasing a soldier's freedom when not on duty.

Canadians continue to serve in UNTSO, UNDOF, UNICYP, and elsewhere on the peacekeeping front. Peacekeeping at the international level, like law enforcement within a city, is frequently met with ambiguity or failure. The Middle East remains a tinder-box. Kashmir threatens to spark yet another war between India and Pakistan. UNEF I ended in an ignominious retreat by peacekeeping troops (as well as a war between Israel and its Arab neighbours), and observers in Vietnam were given nothing to observe — except the failure of their mission. But there have been occasions — in Central America, Namibia, Afghanistan, in the Sinai — when international military forces have played an important role in encouraging the transition from war. Even in Cyprus, where there is little hope for a solution, peacekeeping troops serve as a safety valve for the frustrations of the protagonists. It is not peace ratified by treaty, nor is it necessarily a permanent peace, but it is a peace nonetheless.

Canadian and Spanish observers talk to a Honduran officer during an ONUCA patrol in Honduras, 1990. DND/IXC-90-085

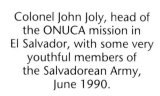

Colonel John Joly, head of the ONUCA mission in El Salvador, with some very youthful members of the Salvadorean Army, June 1990.

BADGES OF THE CANADIAN EXPEDITIONARY FORCE
1914-1918

Royal Canadian Artillery

Royal Canadian Engineers

Royal Canadian Corps of Signals

Machine Gun Corps

Canadian Army Service Corps

Canadian Medical Corps

Canadian Dental Corps

Canadian Veterinary Corps

Canadian Ordnance Corps

Canadian Chaplain Service

Canadian Army Pay Corps

Corps of Military Staff Clerks

CANADIAN CAVALRY BRIGADE

Royal Canadian Dragoons

Lord Strathcona's Horse

Fort Garry Horse

Royal Canadian Horse Artillery

1st CANADIAN DIVISION

1st Brigade

1st Battalion

2nd Battalion

3rd Battalion

4th Battalion

2nd Brigade

5th Battalion

7th Battalion

8th Battalion

10th Battalion

3rd Brigade

13th Battalion

14th Battalion

15th Battalion

16th Battalion

2nd CANADIAN DIVISION

4th Brigade

18th Battalion

19th Battalion

20th Battalion

21st Battalion

5th Brigade

22nd Battalion

24th Battalion

25th Battalion

26th Battalion

6th Brigade

27th Battalion

28th Battalion

29th Battalion

31st Battalion

3rd CANADIAN DIVISION

7th Brigade

Royal Canadian Regiment

Princess Patricia's
Canadian Light Infantry

42nd Battalion

49th Battalion

8th Brigade

1st CMR

2nd CMR

4th CMR

5th CMR

9th Brigade

43rd Battalion

52nd Battalion

58th Battalion

116th Battalion

4th CANADIAN DIVISION

10th Brigade

44th Battalion

46th Battalion

47th Battalion

50th Battalion

11th Brigade

54th Battalion

75th Battalion

87th Battalion

102nd Battalion

12th Brigade

38th Battalion

72nd Battalion

78th Battalion

85th Battalion

BADGES OF THE CANADIAN ARMY OVERSEAS
1939-1945

Royal Canadian Artillery

Royal Canadian Engineers

Royal Canadian Corps
of Signals

Royal Canadian Army
Service Corps

Royal Canadian Army
Medical Corps

Royal Canadian Dental
Corps

Royal Canadian
Ordnance Corps

Royal Canadian Electrical
& Mechanical Engineers

Royal Canadian Army
Pay Corps

Canadian Provost Corps

Canadian Postal Corps

Canadian Chaplain Corps

Canadian Intelligence
Corps

Canadian Women's Army
Corps

1st CANADIAN INFANTRY DIVISION

4th Princess Louise
Dragoon Guards

The Saskatoon Light
Infantry

1st Infantry Brigade

The Royal Canadian
Regiment

The Hastings and Prince
Edward Regiment

48th Highlanders of
Canada

2nd Infantry Brigade

Princess Patricia's
Canadian Light Infantry

The Seaforth Highlanders
of Canada

The Loyal Edmonton
Regiment

3rd Infantry Brigade

Royal 22e Régiment

The Carleton and York
Regiment

The West Nova Scotia
Regiment

2nd CANADIAN INFANTRY DIVISION

14th Canadian Hussars

The Toronto Scottish
Regiment

4th Infantry Brigade

The Royal Regiment
of Canada

The Royal Hamilton
Light Infantry

The Essex Scottish
Regiment

5th Infantry Brigade

The Black Watch (Royal
Highland Regiment)
of Canada

Le Régiment de
Maisonneuve

The Calgary Highlanders

6th Infantry Brigade

Les Fusiliers Mont-Royal

The Queen's Own Cameron
Highlanders of Canada

The South Saskatchewan
Regiment

3rd CANADIAN INFANTRY DIVISION

17th Duke of York's Royal
Canadian Hussars

The Cameron Highlanders
of Ottawa

7th Infantry Brigade

The Royal Winnipeg Rifles

The Regina Rifle
Regimentt

1st Battalion,
The Canadian Scottish
Regiment

8th Infantry Brigade

The Queen's Own Rifles
of Canada

Le Régiment de la
Chaudière

The North Shore
(New Brunswick)
Regiment

9th Infantry Brigade

The Highland Light
Infantry of Canada

The Stormont, Dundas
and Glengarry
Highlanders

The North Nova Scotia
Highlanders

4th CANADIAN ARMOURED DIVISION

The South Alberta
Regiment

4th Armoured Brigade

The Governor General's
Foot Guards

The Canadian Grenadier
Guards

The British Columbia
Regiment

10th Infantry Brigade

The New Brunswick
Rangers

The Lincoln and Welland
Regiment

The Algonquin Regiment

The Argyll and
Sutherland Highlanders
of Canada

The Lake Superior
Regiment

5th CANADIAN ARMOURED DIVISION

The Governor General's
Horse Guards

5th Armoured Brigade

Lord Strathcona's Horse
(Royal Canadians)

8th Princess Louise's
(New Brunswick) Hussars

The British Columbia
Dragoons

11th Infantry Brigade

The Princess Louise
Fusiliers

The Perth Regiment

The Cape Breton
Highlanders

The Irish Regiment of
Canada

The Westminster
Regiment (Motor)

1st CANADIAN ARMOURED BRIGADE

The Ontario Regiment

Three Rivers Regiment

The Calgary Regiment

2nd CANADIAN ARMOURED BRIGADE

1st Hussars

The Fort Garry Horse

The Sherbrooke Fusiliers Regiment

OTHER FORMATIONS

The Royal Canadian Dragoons

12th Manitoba Dragoons

1st Canadian Parachute Battalion

Royal Newfoundland Regiment

CANADIAN ARMY ORGANIZATION

The organization and strength of formations and units of the Canadian Army have been altered many times over the years as equipment and roles have changed. This chart is thus intended only to show relative size and composition, and to indicate command relationships.

Rank of Commander	Organization
GENERAL	**ARMY** Two or more Corps; compositon not fixed. *Example:* Second World War – First Canadian Army (165 thousand Canadians)
LIEUTENANT-GENERAL	**CORPS** Two or more Divisions, plus what are known as 'Corps Troops' – additional artillery and engineer regiments and logistic support units; composition not fixed. *Examples:* * First World War – The Canadian Corps (100 thousand men) * Second World War (Northwest Europe) – II Canadian Corps
MAJOR-GENERAL	**DIVISION** Usually three brigades, four artillery regiments, one engineer regiment, and supporting logistics and service units; composition can, however, vary. Strength: approximately 20 thousand. *Examples:* * First and Second World Wars, Post War – 1st Canadian Division * Second World War – 5th Canadian Armoured Division (15 thousand men)
BRIGADIER-GENERAL OR BRIGADIER	**BRIGADE** **Infantry Brigade** First World War – 4 infantry battalions (4500 men) Second World War – 3 battalions plus support arms and service units Post War – 3 battalions, one armoured regiment (N.B.: A Brigade Group adds an artillery and an engineer regiment and service support units) Strength: 3500 to 5500 men **Cavalry Brigade** First World War – 3 cavalry regiments, one horse artillery regiment, machine gun squadron **Armoured Brigade** Second World War – 3 armoured (tank) regiments

	BATTALION / REGIMENT	
LIEUTENANT-COLONEL	**Infantry Battalion**	3 or 4 rifle companies, support weapons platoons (mortar, machine gun, anti-armour, pioneer), administrative / logistics company
		Strength: variable, 700 – 950 men
		Example: Princess Patricia's Canadian Light Infantry
	Cavalry Regiment	(First World War) – 3 cavalry squadrons, machine gun troop
		Strength: approximately 450 – 500 men
		Example: The Fort Garry Horse
	Armoured Regiment	3 tank squadrons, headquarters (i.e., logistics) squadron, reconnaissance troop
		Strength: approximately 500 – 650 men
		Examples: The Three Rivers Regiment, The 1st Hussars
	Artillery Regiment	usually 3 batteries of guns (total 18 – 24 guns)
		Strength: approximately 800 – 1000 men
	COMPANY / SQUADRON / BATTERY	
MAJOR	**Rifle Company**	3 or 4 infantry platoons
		Strength: 150 – 180 men
	Cavalry Squadron	usually 4 cavalry troops
		Strength: 140 men
	Armoured Squadron	3 or 4 tank troops
		Strength: 110 – 125 men; 15 to 19 tanks
	Artillery Battery	6 to 8 guns, usually organized in two troops
	PLATOON / TROOP	
LIEUTENANT	**Infantry Platoon**	3 sections, each of 10 men
		Strength: up to 40 men
	Cavalry Troop	4 sections, each usually of 8 men and horses
		Strength: usually 34 men and horses
	Tank Troop	4 tanks
		Strength: usually 16 men

SELECTED BIBLIOGRAPHY

The history of the Canadian Army and its components has been extensively covered in a wide variety of excellent books. For those who would like greater detail of events described only briefly in this book, the authors have compiled this short list of recommended reading. A more comprehensive list of works on the Canadian Army can be found in Owen A. Cooke's, *The Canadian Military Experience 1867-1983: A Bibliography*, Ottawa: Directorate of History, 1984.

Official Histories

Nicholson, G.W.L. *The Canadians in Italy*. Ottawa: The Queen's Printer, 1957.

Nicholson, G.W.L. *The Canadian Expeditionary Force 1914-1919*. Ottawa: The Queen's Printer, 1962.

Stacey, C.P. *Six Years of War*. Ottawa: The Queen's Printer, 1955.

Stacey, C.P. *The Victory Campaign*. Ottawa: The Queen's Printer, 1960.

Wood, H.F. *Strange Battleground: The Operations in Korea and Their Effects on the Defence Policy of Canada*.
 Ottawa: The Queen's Printer, 1966.

General Works

Morton, Desmond. *A Military History of Canada*. Edmonton: Hurtig Publishers, revised 1990

Stanley, George F.G. *Canada's Soldiers 1604 - 1954: The Military History of an Unmilitary People*. Toronto: Macmillan, 1954.

Early History

Harris, Stephen. *Canadian Brass: The Making of a Professional Army 1860-1939*. Toronto: University of Toronto Press, 1988.

Morton, Desmond. *The Last War Drum: The North West Campaign of 1885*. Toronto: Hakkert, 1972.

Schull, Joseph. *Rebellion: The Rising in French Canada*. Toronto: Macmillan, 1971.

Stanley, G.F.G. *The War of 1812: Land Operations*. Toronto: Macmillan, 1983.

Boer War

Dancocks, Daniel. *Legacy of Valour: The Canadians at Passchendaele*. Edmonton: Hurtig, 1986.

Dancocks, Daniel. *Spearhead to Victory*. Edmonton: Hurtig, 1987.

Miller, Carman. *Painting the Map Red: Canada and the South African War 1899-1902*. McGill-Queen's / Canadian War
 Museum, (forthcoming 1992).

Swettenham, John. *To Seize the Victory: The Canadian Corps in World War I*. Toronto: McGraw-Hill Ryerson, 1965.

The Second World War

Cedarberg, Fred. *The Long Road Home: The Autobiography of a Canadian Soldier in Italy in World War II*.
 Toronto: General Publishing, 1984.

Dancocks, Daniel. *The D-Day Dodgers: The Canadians in Italy, 1943-1945*. Toronto: McClelland and Stewart, 1991.

Mowat, Farley. *The Regiment*. Toronto: McClelland and Stewart, 1955.

Robertson, Terrence. *The Shame and the Glory: Dieppe*. Toronto: McClelland and Stewart, 1962.

Roy, Reginald H. *1944: The Canadians in Normandy*. Toronto: Macmillan, 1984.

Villa, Brian Loring. *Unauthorized Action: Mountbatten and the Dieppe Raid*. Toronto: Oxford University Press, 1989.

Vincent, Carl. *No Reason Why: The Canadian Hong Kong Tragedy — An Examination*. Stittsville, Ontario: Canada's Wings, 1981.

Whitaker, W. Denis, and Shelagh Whitaker. *Tug of War: The Canadian Victory that Opened Antwerp*. Toronto: Stoddart, 1984.

Whitaker, W. Denis, and Shelagh Whitaker. *Rhineland: The Battle to End the War*. Toronto: Stoddart, 1989.

Williams, Jeffrey. *The Long Left Flank: The Hard-Fought Way to the Reich 1944-45*. Toronto: Stoddart, 1988.

Peacekeeping

Gaffen, Fred. *In the Eye of the Storm: A History of Canadian Peacekeeping*. Toronto: Deneau and Wayne, 1987.

Regimental Histories

Greenhous, Brereton. *Dragoon: The Centennial History of the Royal Canadian Dragoons, 1883-1983*. Ottawa: Guild of the
 Royal Canadian Dragoons, 1983.